Psychology and Society

Psychology and Society

Readings for General Psychology

Marvin Karlins

John Wiley and Sons, Inc., New York · London · Sydney · Toronto

To the other Crungalow

Preface

How do we arouse a student's interest in psychology? In one sense the task is simple; psychology, after all, deals with man's most fascinating subject matter—himself. The trick lies in the presentation of the subject matter. Each text selection must be meaningful to the reader and must stimulate his interest for the topic under consideration. This must be done for each major area of psychology without sacrificing a competent, accurate presentation of the discipline.

To the vast majority of students registering for their first course in the area, psychology is the study of man: an inquiry into the human condition. They expect to read about man; they *want* to read about man. But introductory psychology texts are usually a potpourri of scientific studies—many of which are too esoteric or seemingly irrelevant to arouse much interest. A book of readings is needed that is relevant to the field of psychology *and* the student of psychology: a volume that can bring to the student a sense of the excitement, expansiveness, and energy that is "psychology" today. I hope this volume accomplishes this purpose. My intention is reflected in the Contents. The titles stimulate reader interest and indicate the diversity of intriguing research topics currently under psychological investigation.

In attempting to compile a meaningful and representative set of basic readings I have included only the selections that, in addition to being relevant to the readership, meet the criteria of *recency* and *significance*.

Recency. With the exception of an article by Freud, all text selections have been published in the past two decades (90 percent of them have been published since 1960). In a rapidly advancing field like psychology—where today's discovery is tomorrow's footnote and the most exciting work is progressing along new research frontiers—knowledge of current scientific activity is imperative. Discussion of "classic studies" is reserved for editorial comment designed to place contemporary investigations in their proper historical perspective.

Significance. I have selected competent studies that are important pieces of scholarship—research efforts that make a contribution to the forward thrust of scientific psychology.

Finally, I have taken four precautions to make this book more useful and meaningful to the student and teacher alike.

1. The majority of the articles are based on research with human subjects; however, some studies using lower organisms provide insights into the behavior of man and, for this reason, are also included.

2. I have arranged the text selections into categories that correspond with those utilized by most of the major introductory psychology textbooks. Thus, sections of this book can be conveniently assigned as supplementary readings in courses that employ a standard text; or they can be assigned as primary readings in a class that depends exclusively on a collected volume of research to adequately portray the broad range of psychological activities.

3. *Editorial comment introduces each article and each section in the book.*

4. Today's student is caught up in a quest to improve the human condition and to guide mankind toward a meaningful destiny. In my introductory psychology class this effort is reflected in the question that students ask most often: "What can psychology do to aid man?" This question is being asked—and answered—by today's psychologists. There is no generation gap here. Never before have students been so concerned with psychology in the service of man; and, also, never have psychologists devoted as much attention to this topic (for instance, the theme of the 1969 American Psychological Association convention was "Psychology and the Problems of Society"). Because of the common interest and concern of both students and psychologists in psychology and human affairs I devoted one section to an examination of this topic. This emphasis distinguishes the present volume from many other general readings books in psychology—although, hopefully, this will not be the case in the future.

Marvin Karlins

Contents

Psychology
and
Society

Introduction:
The Science of
Psychology

Can you guess what the following inquiries have in common?

1. What happens when you electrically stimulate the brain of man?
2. Why do people ignore the pleas of a stranger in trouble?
3. What mechanisms are involved in learning and memory?
4. Can psychology be used for improving the human condition?
5. What type of person is creative?
6. Does sensory deprivation affect an individual's behavior?
7. Why do college students commit suicide?
8. Is ESP fact or fiction?
9. Are *Playboy* centerfolds effective therapeutic devices?
10. What psychological effects are produced by drugs?

All ten questions were asked by psychologists in the course of their research—*research described in this volume.* They are but a few examples of the many fascinating queries made by the psychologist in his quest to understand the behavior of organisms.

Now consider this list:

Division of general psychology
Division of the teaching of psychology
Division of experimental psychology
Division of evaluation and measurement
Division of physiological and comparative psychology

Division of developmental psychology
Division of personality and social psychology
The society for the psychological study of social issues
Division of psychology and the arts
Division of clinical psychology
Division of consulting psychology
Division of industrial psychology
Division of educational psychology
Division of school psychology
Division of counseling psychology
Division of psychologists in public service
Division of military psychology
Division on maturity and old age
The society of engineering psychologists
Division of psychological aspects of disability
Division of consumer psychology
Division of philosophical psychology
Division for the experimental analysis of behavior
Division of the history of psychology
Division of community psychology
Division of psychopharmacology
Division of psychotherapy
Division of psychological hypnosis
Division of state psychological association affairs

Each of the 29 categories above represents a division of the American Psychological Association (the professional organization of psychologists in the United States). The categories, when taken together, should give the reader a feeling for the scope of psychology today and, possibly better than any other way, emphasize that psychology is a lot more than a man reading Freud or studying rats.

People are often surprised to discover just how many different types of questions the psychologist does ask; how extensive and wide ranging his research efforts and interests have become. Little wonder! In the past two decades the scope of psychology has broadened to a point where it borders on all the social, biological, and physical sciences. It seems fair to say that the boundaries of today's psychology are the limits of the psychologist's imagination.

This growth of scientific psychology has not gone unnoticed. The steady expansion of psychological frontiers has been paralleled by the steady expansion of public interest in psychological findings. Witness, for example, the phenomenal success of the mass circulation magazine *Psychology Today*. Americans have good reason to be absorbed with psychology—never before has it played such a large role in their everyday lives and never again will it play such a small one. There are several reasons for this state of affairs, including: (1) accelerating research advances in psychology leading to new understandings and applications in the realm of human behavior; (2) an expectation on the part of government and governed alike that psychology has the right and obligation to take an active role in human affairs; (3) the increasing readiness of psychologists to accept such a role and utilize psychological findings in the service of man; and (4) the condition of man himself—never before has the individual needed the help of psychology so desperately (and never before has psychology been so willing and able to deliver that aid).

To give the reader an idea of how pervasive the influence of psychology has become in our everyday lives, consider the statement of Professor H. J. Eysenck.

> . . . in one way or another almost everyone has come up against the mixed blessings which applied psychology bestows on humanity. Decisions regarding the child's future education are being made on the basis of intelligence tests applied at the tender age of eleven or twelve; indeed, the whole modern system of education is based on psychological discoveries and theories which are relatively recent. The soldier's allocation to a particular arm or trade inside the service, as well as his advancement to officer status, is determined in part by psychological tests; our new rulers, the upper ranks of the Civil Service, are being selected by "new type" selection methods; vocational guidance and occupational selection are affecting the everyday working lives of many thousands. The extremely numerous nervous breakdowns which appear to characterize modern society are being diagnosed and treated by what purport to be psychological methods. Attitudes are being measured by Gallup and other polls, and the results of such surveys, some of them carried out by Government agencies on a fact-finding basis, help to lay the foundations for legislation and policy-making. Radio programs and many commercial products take into account survey figures regarding "audience reactions." Psychologists investigate optimum working conditions, spacing of rest pauses, systems of incentives, the spreading of rumors, causes of industrial unrest, and large numbers of other friction points in the political and social organism. Even old age is not safe from their scrutiny; the intellectual and emotional development of old people is being studied more and more intensely, and action based on the results.

Add to Dr. Eysenck's list psychologists' involvement in advertising, social service programs, counseling, personality assessment, and public relations and one begins to sense just how important the behavioral scientist is.

How important will psychology be in the future? Some individuals go so far as to claim "the psychology of today will be the society of tomorrow." Currently, at least, such a view is an exaggeration. One thing is certain, however: as psychology edges ever closer to its goal of understanding, predicting and controlling behavior it will have more and more to say about the destiny of mankind and the everyday activity of each human being. On completing this text the reader should be in a better position to judge just how far psychology has progressed toward such a goal.

An example of linear perspective—important in our perception of depth.
(TIM KANTOR | RAPHO GUILLUMETTE)

Section I
Perception

One philosopher put it this way: "All a man knows is what he perceives." A poet might say it a little differently:

A person's conceptions
grow from his perceptions

Philosopher or bard, the message is the same: A man's senses are his doorway to the world—the mechanisms by which he sees, hears, touches, tastes, and smells his way through life. It seems appropriate, then, that we begin our examination of psychology at the point where man begins to examine his world—with his perceptions.

When we examine the perceptual process we confront a topic that has fascinated generations of psychologists. Indeed, it is fair to say that the study of perception is intimately bound up with the history and progress of psychology as a science. Consider, for example, the work of Wilhelm Wundt. Prolific writer, solemn scholar, part philosopher, and part physiologist, Wundt was a learned German intellectual in the grand nineteenth century German tradition. Wundt was also psychology's founding father, a distinction achieved when he created the world's first psychology laboratory in 1879 (the year normally designated as the birthdate of our field). And what did Wundt study in this new laboratory? Perception.* So did his students—individuals like E. B. Titchener who would eventually carry on Wundt's pioneer work in America.

---

* Edwin Boring, in his definitive *History of Experimental Psychology* (1957), points out that half of the experimental researches conducted during the first 20 years at Wundt's laboratory dealt with matters of sensation and perception.

Almost a century has passed since Wundt first opened his laboratory at Leipzig, but time has not eroded psychological interest in the perceptual process. Many of today's psychologists (particularly Gestalt psychologists) study perception with an intensity reminiscent of Wundt's Promethean efforts. This long-term study of perception has provided the behavioral scientist with a better understanding of the perceptual process, an understanding that deepens as research continues. Yet, the contemporary investigator recognizes that much remains to be learned about how we perceive our world. Challenged by the mysteries that still confront him, he utilizes his scientific skills to seek new insights into the physiological and psychological components of perception.

We have spoken briefly of the psychologists' concern with perception but have failed to define what the term perception means. When we speak of perception we are referring to the process by which an individual acquires information from his environment. Forgus (1966) defines perception as "the process of information extraction." Both definitions focus on the organism's reception of specified stimulus inputs (for example, lights, sounds, and smells) from his surroundings. The types of information that the organism extracts from his environment will determine, in part, how effectively he is able to cope with that environment. Conceived in such a fashion, it becomes readily apparent that man's perceptual abilities play a vital role in his struggle to survive. Such is the importance of perception and, certainly, one major reason for studying it!

There are many examples of exciting perception articles appearing in recent scientific journals. Four of these are presented on the following pages. The authors of the first article, Albert Hastorf and Hadley Cantril, utilize students' perceptions of a Princeton-Dartmouth football game to remind us that our perceptions are influenced by our psychological needs, and that what we see is often what we *want* to see. (And sometimes what we want to see is a far cry from what is!) The second selection, by Martin Katz, Irene Waskow, and James Olsson, describes the impact of the powerful hallucinogen, LSD-25, on human perception. The impact of "mind expanding" drugs on human perceptions is a fascinating but little understood topic in modern psychology. The Katz, Waskow, and Olsson research is one step toward a better understanding.

What happens when a person is placed in an environment where his sensory experiences are restricted? Such a condition—called sensory deprivation—is described in a third article on perception by George Curtis and Marvin Zuckerman. In their study the authors report that a 21-year-old student manifested a psychopathological reaction when placed in a restricted perceptual environment. The message of the investigation is clear: man's need for sensory stimulation is strong indeed.

Moving from sensory deprivation to sensory speculation, an article by

R. A. McConnell rounds out the selections on perception. In his paper McConnell discusses one of the most controversial topics in contemporary science, extrasensory perception (ESP), and asks why psychologists are not interested in studying it. He also reviews some of the work done with ESP and comments on the nature of scientific inquiry.*

REFERENCES
Boring, E. G. *A history of experimental psychology* (2nd ed.). New York: Appleton-Century-Crofts, 1957.
Forgus, R. H. *Perception*. New York: McGraw-Hill, 1966.

* A more complete introduction to each reading selection precedes its placement in the text.

Introduction to
Hastorf and Cantril Article

If you are a sports fan then you know of the rivalry between the Princeton and Dartmouth football teams; if you are not, imagine the competitive spirit between opposing political candidates in a no-holds-barred election race and you will get an idea of the atmosphere surrounding a Princeton-Dartmouth encounter. Back in 1951 the atmosphere surrounding one of these "games" was more charged than usual—if that is humanly possible. Both teams were playing their final contest, Princeton was unbeaten, and its all-American candidate, Dick Kazmaier, was closing out his college gridiron career. Before the contest was completed Kazmaier was forced out with a broken nose, a Dartmouth player was carried off the field with a broken leg, and the referees were weary from calling penalties and keeping players from each other's throats.

In the weeks following the game Princeton and Dartmouth students busied themselves accusing each other's team of foul, dirty play. In the midst of such conflicting accusations Hastorf and Cantril showed some students from both universities actual films of the disputed game. Although both groups of men saw the same stimulus (film) one would not have thought so judging from their perceptions of the cinematic material. Faced with the same "objective" evidence Princeton students "saw" a Princeton version of the film ("look at those nasty Dartmouth players!") and Dartmouth students "saw" a Dartmouth version ("look at those nasty Princeton players!").

The differences indicate that a person's perceptions of the world are based, in part, on his particular needs and life history. The influence of various personality and social factors on a person's perceptions have been extensively studied in psychology, particularly by the "New Look" school of perception interested in the relationship between personal needs and perceptions (e.g., Bruner & Goodman, 1947; Bruner & Postman, 1948) and by social psychologists interested in the impact of group expectations on members' perceptions (e.g., Koslin, Haarlow, Karlins, & Pargament, 1968; Lambert, Libman, & Poser, 1960; Harvey, 1953). Recent studies also indicate that a person's cultural background can influence his perceptions (Allport & Pettigrew, 1957; Segall, Campbell, & Herskovits, 1966).

The contemporary psychologist is very interested in understanding the role that "personal" and "social" factors play in an individual's perceptions. After all, these factors influence what a person perceives and these perceptions, in turn, influence how the person behaves. The behavioral scientist who is able to understand the myriad factors affecting human perception will achieve a more meaningful understanding of human behavior.

REFERENCES

Allport, G., & Pettigrew, T. Cultural influence on the perception of movement: the trapezoidal illusion among Zulus. *Journal of Abnormal and Social Psychology*, 1957, **55**, 104–113.

Bruner, J., & Goodman, C. Value and need as organizing factors in perception. *Journal of Abnormal and Social Psychology*, 1947, **42**, 33–44.

Bruner, J., & Postman, L. An approach to social perception. In W. Dennis (Ed.), *Current trends in social psychology*. Pittsburgh: Univ. of Pittsburgh Press, 1948.

Harvey, O. An experimental approach to the study of status relations in informal groups. *American Sociological Review*, 1953, **18**, 357–367.

Koslin, B., Haarlow, R., Karlins, M., & Pargament, R. Predicting group status from members' cognitions. *Sociometry*, 1968, **31**, 64–75.

Lambert, W., Libman, E., & Poser, E. The effect of increased salience of a membership group on pain tolerance. *Journal of Personality*, 1960, **28**, 350–357.

Segall, M., Campbell, D., & Herskovits, M. *The influence of culture on visual perception*. New York: Bobbs-Merrill, 1966.

1

They Saw a Game:
A Case Study

Albert H. Hastorf and Hadley Cantril

On a brisk Saturday afternoon, November 23, 1951, the Dartmouth football team played Princeton in Princeton's Palmer Stadium. It was the last game of the season for both teams and of rather special significance because the Princeton team had won all its games so far and one of its players, Kazmaier, was receiving All-American mention and had just appeared as the cover man on *Time* magazine, and was playing his last game.

A few minutes after the opening kick-off, it became apparent that the game was going to be a rough one. The referees were kept busy blowing their whistles and penalizing both sides. In the second quarter, Princeton's star left the game with a broken nose. In the third quarter, a Dartmouth player was taken off the field with a broken leg. Tempers flared both during and after the game. The official statistics of the game, which Princeton won, showed that Dartmouth was penalized 70 yards, Princeton 25, not counting more than a few plays in which both sides were penalized.

Needless to say, accusations soon began to fly. The game immediately became a matter of concern to players, students, coaches, and the administrative officials of the two institutions, as well as to alumni and the general public who had not seen the game but had become sensitive to the problem of big-time football through the recent exposures of subsidized players, commercialism, etc. Discussion of the game continued for several weeks.

One of the contributing factors to the extended discussion of the game was the extensive space given to it by both campus and metropolitan newspapers. An indication of the fervor with which the discussions were carried on is shown by a few excerpts from the campus dailies.

SOURCE. *Journal of Abnormal and Social Psychology,* 1954, **49,** 129–134. Copyright 1954, by the American Psychological Association, and reproduced by permission.

For example, on November 27 (four days after the game), the *Daily Princetonian* (Princeton's student newspaper) said:

> This observer has never seen quite such a disgusting exhibition of so-called "sport." Both teams were guilty but the blame must be laid primarily on Dartmouth's doorstep. Princeton, obviously the better team, had no reason to rough up Dartmouth. Looking at the situation rationally, we don't see why the Indians should make a deliberate attempt to cripple Dick Kazmaier or any other Princeton player. The Dartmouth psychology, however, is not rational itself.

The November 30th edition of the *Princeton Alumni Weekly* said:

> But certain memories of what occurred will not be easily erased. Into the record books will go in indelible fashion the fact that the last game of Dick Kazmaier's career was cut short by more than half when he was forced out with a broken nose and a mild concussion, sustained from a tackle that came well after he had thrown a pass.
>
> This second-period development was followed by a third quarter outbreak of roughness that was climaxed when a Dartmouth player deliberately kicked Brad Glass in the ribs while the latter was on his back. Throughout the often unpleasant afternoon, there was undeniable evidence that the losers' tactics were the result of an actual style of play, and reports on other games they have played this season substantiate this.

Dartmouth students were "seeing" an entirely different version of the game through the editorial eyes of the *Dartmouth* (Dartmouth's undergraduate newspaper). For example, on November 27 the *Dartmouth* said:

> However, the Dartmouth-Princeton game set the stage for the other type of dirty football. A type which may be termed as an unjustifiable accusation.
>
> Dick Kazmaier was injured early in the game. Kazmaier was the star, an All-American. Other stars have been injured before, but Kazmaier had been built to represent a Princeton idol. When an idol is hurt there is only one recourse—the tag of dirty football. So what did the Tiger Coach Charley Caldwell do? He announced to the world that the Big Green had been out to extinguish the Princeton star. His purpose was achieved.
>
> After this incident, Caldwell instilled the old see-what-they-did-go-get-them attitude into his players. His talk got results. Gene Howard and Jim Miller were both injured. Both had dropped back to pass, had passed, and were standing unprotected in the backfield. Result: one bad leg and one leg broken.
>
> The game was rough and did get a bit out of hand in the third

quarter. Yet most of the roughing penalties were called against Princeton while Dartmouth received more of the illegal-use-of-the-hands variety.

On November 28 the *Dartmouth* said:

> Dick Kazmaier of Princeton admittedly is an unusually able football player. Many Dartmouth men traveled to Princeton, not expecting to win—only hoping to see an All-American in action. Dick Kazmaier was hurt in the second period, and played only a token part in the remainder of the game. For this, spectators were sorry.
> But there were no such feelings for Dick Kazmaier's health. Medical authorities have confirmed that as a relatively unprotected passing and running star in a contact sport, he is quite liable to injury. Also, his particular injuries—a broken nose and slight concussion—were no more serious than is experienced almost any day in any football practice, where there is no more serious stake than playing the following Saturday. Up to the Princeton game, Dartmouth players suffered about 10 known nose fractures and face injuries, not to mention several slight concussions.
> Did Princeton players feel so badly about losing their star? They shouldn't have. During the past undefeated campaign they stopped several individual stars by a concentrated effort, including such mainstays as Frank Hauff of Navy, Glenn Adams of Pennsylvania and Rocco Calvo of Cornell.
> In other words, the same brand of football condemned by the *Prince*—that of stopping the big man—is practiced quite successfully by the Tigers.

Basically, then, there was disagreement as to what had happened during the "game." Hence we took the opportunity presented by the occasion to make a "real life" study of a perceptual problem.[1]

PROCEDURE

Two steps were involved in gathering data. The first consisted of answers to a questionnaire designed to get reactions to the game and to learn something of the climate of opinion in each institution. This questionnaire was administered a week after the game to both Dartmouth and Princeton undergraduates who were taking introductory and intermediate psychology courses.

The second step consisted of showing the same motion picture of the game to a sample of undergraduates in each school and having them check

[1] We are not concerned here with the problem of guilt or responsibility for infractions, and nothing here implies any judgment as to who was to blame.

on another questionnaire, as they watched the film, any infraction of the rules they saw and whether these infractions were "mild" or "flagrant." [2] At Dartmouth, members of two fraternities were asked to view the film on December 7; at Princeton, members of two undergraduate clubs saw the film early in January.

The answers to both questionnaires were carefully coded and transferred to punch cards. [3]

RESULTS

Table 1 shows the questions which received different replies from the two student populations on the first questionnaire.

Questions asking if the students had friends on the team, if they had ever played football themselves, if they felt they knew the rules of the game well, etc. showed no differences in either school and no relation to answers given to other questions. This is not surprising since the students in both schools come from essentially the same type of educational, economic, and ethnic background.

Summarizing the data of Tables 1 and 2, we find a marked contrast between the two student groups.

Nearly all *Princeton* students judged the game as "rough and dirty"— not one of them thought it "clean and fair." And almost nine-tenths of them thought the other side started the rough play. By and large they felt that the charges they understood were being made were true; most of them felt the charges were made in order to avoid similar situations in the future.

When Princeton students looked at the movie of the game, they saw the Dartmouth team make over twice as many infractions as their own team made. And they saw the Dartmouth team make over twice as many infractions as were seen by Dartmouth students. When Princeton students judged these infractions as "flagrant" or "mild," the ratio was about two "flagrant" to one "mild" on the Dartmouth team, and about one "flagrant" to three "mild" on the Princeton team.

As for the *Dartmouth* students, while the plurality of answers fell in the "rough and dirty" category, over one-tenth thought the game was "clean and fair" and over a third introduced their own category of "rough and fair" to describe the action. Although a third of the Dartmouth students

[2] The film shown was kindly loaned for the purpose of the experiment by the Dartmouth College Athletic Council. It should be pointed out that a movie of a football game follows the ball, is thus selective, and omits a good deal of the total action on the field. Also, of course, in viewing only a film of a game, the possibilities of participation as spectator are greatly limited.

[3] We gratefully acknowledge the assistance of Virginia Zerega, Office of Public Opinion Research, and J. L. McCandless, Princeton University, and E. S. Horton, Dartmouth College, in the gathering and collation of the data.

TABLE 1
Data from First Questionnaire

Question	Dartmouth Students (N = 163) %	Princeton Students (N = 161) %
1. Did you happen to see the actual game between Dartmouth and Princeton in Palmer Stadium this year?		
Yes	33	71
No	67	29
2. Have you seen a movie of the game or seen it on television?		
Yes, movie	33	2
Yes, television	0	1
No, neither	67	97
3. (Asked of those who answered "yes" to either or both of above questions.) From your observations of what went on at the game, do you believe the game was clean and fairly played, or that it was unnecessarily rough and dirty?		
Clean and fair	6	0
Rough and dirty	24	69
Rough and fair[a]	25	2
No answer	45	29
4. (Asked of those who answered "no" on both of the first questions.) From what you have heard and read about the game, do you feel it was clean and fairly played, or that it was unnecessarily rough and dirty?		
Clean and fair	7	0
Rough and dirty	18	24
Rough and fair[a]	14	1
Don't know	6	4
No answer	55	71
(Combined answers to questions 3 and 4 above)		
Clean and fair	13	0
Rough and dirty	42	93
Rough and fair[a]	39	3
Don't know	6	4
5. From what you saw in the game or the movies, or from what you have read, which team do you feel started the rough play?		
Dartmouth started it	36	86
Princeton started it	2	0
Both started it	53	11
Neither	6	1
No answer	3	2
6. What is your understanding of the charges being made?[b]		
Dartmouth tried to get Kazmaier	71	47
Dartmouth intentionally dirty	52	44
Dartmouth unnecessarily rough	8	35

[a]This answer was not included on the checklist but was written in by the percentage of students indicated.
[b]Replies do not add to 100% since more than one charge could be given.

TABLE 1 (cont.)

Question	Dartmouth Students ($N = 163$) %	Princeton Students ($N = 161$) %
7. Do you feel there is any truth to these charges?		
Yes	10	55
No	57	4
Partly	29	35
Don't know	4	6
8. Why do you think the charges were made?		
Injury to Princeton star	70	23
To prevent repetition	2	46
No answer	28	31

felt that Dartmouth was to blame for starting the rough play, the majority of Dartmouth students thought both sides were to blame. By and large, Dartmouth men felt that the charges they understood were being made were not true, and most of them thought the reason for the charges was Princeton's concern for its football star.

When Dartmouth students looked at the movie of the game they saw both teams make about the same number of infractions. And they saw their own team make only half the number of infractions the Princeton students saw them make. The ratio of "flagrant" to "mild" infractions was about one to one when Dartmouth students judged the Dartmouth team, and about one "flagrant" to two "mild" when Dartmouth students judged infractions made by the Princeton team.

It should be noted that Dartmouth and Princeton students were thinking of different charges in judging their validity and in assigning reasons as to why the charges were made. It should also be noted that whether or not students were spectators of the game in the stadium made little difference in their responses.

TABLE 2

Data from Second Questionnaire Checked while Seeing Film

Group	N	Total Number of Infractions Checked Against			
		Dartmouth Team		Princeton Team	
		Mean	SD	Mean	SD
Dartmouth students	48	4.3[a]	2.7	4.4	2.8
Princeton students	49	9.8[a]	5.7	4.2	3.5

[a]Significant at the .01 level.

INTERPRETATION: THE NATURE OF A SOCIAL EVENT [4]

It seems clear that the "game" actually was many different games and that each version of the events that transpired was just as "real" to a particular person as other versions were to other people. A consideration of the experiential phenomena that constitute a "football game" for the spectator may help us both to account for the results obtained and illustrate something of the nature of any social event.

Like any other complex social occurrence, a "football game" consists of a whole host of happenings. Many different events are occurring simultaneously. Furthermore, each happening is a link in a chain of happenings, so that one follows another in sequence. The "football game," as well as other complex social situations, consists of a whole matrix of events. In the game situation, this matrix of events consists of the actions of all the players, together with the behavior of the referees and linesmen, the action on the sidelines, in the grandstands, over the loud-speaker, etc.

Of crucial importance is the fact that an "occurrence" on the football field or in any other social situation does not become an experiential "event" unless and until some significance is given to it: an "occurrence" becomes an *"event"* only when the happening has significance. And a happening generally has significance only if it reactivates learned significances already registered in what we have called a person's assumptive form-world (1).

Hence the particular occurrences that different people experienced in the football game were a limited series of events from the total matrix of events *potentially* available to them. People experienced those occurrences that reactivated significances they brought to the occasion; they failed to experience those occurrences which did not reactivate past significances. We do not need to introduce "attention" as an "intervening third" (to paraphrase James on memory) to account for the selectivity of the experiential process.

In this particular study, one of the most interesting examples of this phenomenon was a telegram sent to an officer of Dartmouth College by a member of a Dartmouth alumni group in the Midwest. He had viewed the film which had been shipped to his alumni group from Princeton after its use with Princeton students, who saw, as we noted, an average of over nine infractions by Dartmouth players during the game. The alumnus, who couldn't see the infractions he had heard publicized, wired:

> Preview of Princeton movies indicates considerable cutting of important part please wire explanation and possibly air mail missing part before showing scheduled for January 25 we have splicing equipment.

[4] The interpretation of the nature of a social event sketched here is in part based on discussions with Adelbert Ames, Jr., and is being elaborated in more detail elsewhere.

The "same" sensory impingements emanating from the football field, transmitted through the visual mechanism to the brain, also obviously gave rise to different experiences in different people. The significances assumed by different happenings for different people depend in large part on the purposes people bring to the occasion and the assumptions they have of the purposes and probable behavior of other people involved. This was amusingly pointed out by the New York *Herald Tribune's* sports columnist, Red Smith, in describing a prize fight between Chico Vejar and Carmine Fiore in his column of December 21, 1951. Among other things, he wrote:

> You see, Steve Ellis is the proprietor of Chico Vejar, who is a highly desirable tract of Stamford, Conn., welterweight. Steve is also a radio announcer. Ordinarily there is no conflict between Ellis the Brain and Ellis the Voice because Steve is an uncommonly substantial lump of meat who can support both halves of a split personality and give away weight on each end without missing it.
>
> This time, though, the two Ellises met head-on, with a sickening, rending crash. Steve the Manager sat at ringside in the guise of Steve the Announcer broadcasting a dispassionate, unbiased, objective report of Chico's adventures in the ring. . . .
>
> Clear as mountain water, his words came through, winning big for Chico. Winning? Hell, Steve was slaughtering poor Fiore.
>
> Watching and listening, you could see what a valiant effort the reporter was making to remain cool and detached. At the same time you had an illustration of the old, established truth that when anybody with a preference watches a fight, he sees only what he prefers to see.
>
> That is always so. That is why, after any fight that doesn't end in a clean knockout, there always are at least a few hoots when the decision is announced. A guy from, say, Billy Graham's neighborhood goes to see Billy fight and he watches Graham all the time. He sees all the punches Billy throws, and hardly any of the punches Billy catches. So it was with Steve.
>
> "Fiore feints with a left," he would say, honestly believing that Fiore hadn't caught Chico full on the chops. "Fiore's knees buckle," he said, "and Chico backs away." Steve didn't see the hook that had driven Chico back. . . .

In brief, the data here indicate that there is no such "thing" as a "game" existing "out there" in its own right which people merely "observe." The "game" "exists" for a person and is experienced by him only in so far as certain happenings have significances in terms of his purpose. Out of all the occurrences going on in the environment, a person selects those that have some significance for him from his own egocentric position in the total matrix.

Obviously in the case of a football game, the value of the experience of watching the game is enhanced if the purpose of "your" team is accomplished, that is, if the happening of the desired consequence is experienced—i.e., if your team wins. But the value attribute of the experience can, of course, be spoiled if the desire to win crowds out behavior we value and have come to call sportsmanlike.

The sharing of significances provides the links except for which a "social" event would not be experienced and would not exist for anyone.

A "football game" would be impossible except for the rules of the game which we bring to the situation and which enable us to share with others the significances of various happenings. These rules make possible a certain repeatability of events such as first downs, touchdowns, etc. If a person is unfamiliar with the rules of the game, the behavior he sees lacks repeatability and consistent significance and hence "doesn't make sense."

And only because there is the possibility of repetition is there the possibility that a happening has a significance. For example, the balls used in games are designed to give a high degree of repeatability. While a football is about the only ball used in games which is not a sphere, the shape of the modern football has apparently evolved in order to achieve a higher degree of accuracy and speed in forward passing than would be obtained with a spherical ball, thus increasing the repeatability of an important phase of the game.

The rules of a football game, like laws, rituals, customs, and mores, are registered and preserved forms of sequential significances enabling people to share the significances of occurrences. The sharing of sequential significances which have value for us provides the links that operationally make social events possible. They are analogous to the forces of attraction that hold parts of an atom together, keeping each part from following its individual, independent course.

From this point of view it is inaccurate and misleading to say that different people have different "attitudes" concerning the same "thing." For the "thing" simply is *not* the same for different people whether the "thing" is a football game, a presidential candidate, Communism, or spinach. We do not simply "react to" a happening or to some impingement from the environment in a determined way (except in behavior that has become reflexive or habitual). We behave according to what we bring to the occasion, and what each of us brings to the occasion is more or less unique. And except for these significances which we bring to the occasion, the happenings around us would be meaningless occurrences, would be "inconsequential."

From the transactional view, an attitude is not a predisposition to react in a certain way to an occurrence or stimulus "out there" that exists in its own right with certain fixed characteristics which we "color" according to our predisposition (2). That is, a subject does not simply "react to" an "object." An attitude would rather seem to be a complex of registered significances reactivated by some stimulus which assumes its own particular significance for us in terms of our purposes. That is, the object as experienced would not exist for us except for the reactivated aspects of the form-world which provide particular significance to the hieroglyphics of sensory impingements.

REFERENCES

1. Cantril, H. *The "why" of man's experience.* New York: Macmillan, 1950.
2. Kilpatrick, F. P. (Ed.) *Human behavior from the transactional point of view.* Hanover, N. H.: Institute for Associated Research, 1952.

Introduction to the
Katz, Waskow, and Olsson Article

Since the psychological effects of LSD were first accidently experienced less than 25 years ago much has been said, but little substantiated, concerning this most powerful "mind expanding" substance. Part of the reason for this state of affairs is the current legal status of the drug, which makes it unavailable for general research. In the absence of extensive scientific work with LSD, much of what we "know" concerning this hallucinogen originates with observations from scientifically untrained individuals reporting incidents from their own "trips" (conducted under uncontrolled conditions). Such information is interesting but often suspect since there is frequently no way of ascertaining (1) the psychological state of the person *before* he took LSD; (2) his expectations concerning what would happen; (3) the setting in which the drug was taken; and (4) the type and strength of psychedelic agent ingested. All these factors are known to influence the "psychedelic experience" and, as the authors below emphasize: "The influence of these diverse factors and the failure to adequately control them in much of this [LSD] research have led to the current confusion concerning the effects produced by LSD."

One of the important attributes of the following paper by Katz, Waskow, and Olsson is the effort to characterize the psychological state produced by LSD under *controlled* scientific conditions. Their work adds to our understanding of the "psychedelic experience," particularly the relationship between LSD and emotional behavior.*

* For the student who wants additional readings on LSD, an excellent bibliography is provided by Charles Tart in his book *States of altered consciousness* (New York: Wiley, 1969), pp. 480–483.

2

Characterizing the Psychological State Produced by LSD

Martin M. Katz, Irene E. Waskow,
and James Olsson

Two studies, involving 69 male inmates of an experimental penal institution, investigated the psychological states produced by LSD as compared with amphetamine and placebo controls. A number of scales on a newly developed subjective drug-effects questionnaire significantly differentiated the groups. This instrument was further used to identify 3 qualitatively different subjective states produced by LSD (moderately euphoric, dysphoric, and ambivalent). New techniques for exploring the perceptual and vocal components of emotional change were also applied. These techniques further elucidated the quality and possible origin of the psychological states produced by LSD. The results (which indicate the presence of highly intense but contradictory emotions) were interpreted in the light of a current theory of emotion and Bartlett's concept of "effort after meaning."

There has been a great deal of interest over the years in LSD and a very large volume of research on its psychological effects. The literature ranges from clinical descriptions of the psychological states produced (e.g., DeShon, Rinkel, & Solomon, 1952; Hoch, Cattell, & Pennes, 1952; Savage, 1952) through more systematic and objective studies of the effects of LSD on such aspects of functioning as cognition (Aronson, Watermann, & Klee, 1962; Levine, Abramson, Kaufman, & Markham, 1955; Silverstein & Klee, 1958), perception (Aronson, Silverstein, & Klee, 1959; Krus, Wapner, Free-

SOURCE. *Journal of Abnormal Psychology,* 1968, **73,** 1–14. Copyright 1968, by the American Psychological Association, and reproduced by permission. Based on a paper presented at the Symposium, "The Use of Psychotomimetic Agents as Treatments in Psychiatry, Including Relevant Basic Research on the Effects of Such Drugs in Man," at the Meetings of the Collegium Internationale Neuropsychopharmacologicum, Washington, D. C., March 28–31, 1966. The research was carried out at the Patuxent Institution, Jessup, Maryland.

man, & Casey, 1963; Leibert, Wapner, & Werner, 1957), and psychomotor performance (Abramson, Jarvik, & Hirsch, 1955; Kornetsky, 1960; Krus & Wapner, 1962; Landis & Clausen, 1954). Several researchers have also begun to look more systematically at the nature of the subjective experience itself (Abramson, Jarvik, Kaufman, Kornetsky, Levine, & Wagner, 1955; Linton & Langs, 1962).

Despite this volume of research, however, the total experience produced by LSD still eludes complete comprehension. Descriptions of the state have ranged from that of Hofman and the earlier investigators (e.g., Rinkel, DeShon, Hyde, & Solomon, 1952; Stoll, 1947) in which the toxic psychotic or schizophrenic-like qualities of the experience were emphasized to the more recent reports of mystical or transcendental states (Savage, Terrill, & Jackson, 1962). The range of states described is partly a function of dosage, but a great deal of influence has also been attributed to the role of non-drug factors in determining the quality of the experience (Cole & Katz, 1964; DiMascio & Rinkel, 1963; Hyde, 1958; Unger, 1963). The personality of the S, his preparation or set prior to the experiment, as well as the setting in which the drug is given, are all presumed to play a role in shaping an S's LSD experience. Thus, the problems of determining the actual effects of the drug itself and of unraveling the bases for these very unusual states are further complicated. The influence of these diverse factors and the failure to adequately control them in much of this research have led to the current confusion concerning the effects produced by LSD.

The first step in attempting to understand the nature of the experience should be the objective delineation of the psychological components, with special emphasis on the effects of the drug on the emotions. The available research literature does not indicate that the psychological states which are produced have been as carefully and unemotionally described or analyzed as they could be, or that the appropriate methods for their study have generally been applied. For example, the drug was usually not tested in a situation in which suggestion and previous knowledge of effects were controlled, and, although contrasted frequently with a placebo, its specificity has generally not been examined by comparing its effects with that of other similarly acting drugs, for example, drugs which also elevate mood. Further, the attempt to understand how a drug is capable of producing mystical states and profound alterations in consciousness appears to require an experimental approach which provides the conditions under which the early stages and the development of such states could be studied.

The present studies were designed to investigate, with the use of appropriate and adequate controls, the development and components of LSD-produced psychological states. A major problem was that of selecting and developing techniques for measuring these states.

If a drug results in unusual emotional, perceptual, and cognitive effects —effects which are not familiar—then it is likely that traditional techniques will be limited in helping to understand or to delineate these effects. An early review of the use of standard psychological procedures in the study of LSD is instructive here (Katz, 1959); little new information was provided by the standard techniques despite the fact that it was clear to all observers in research of this type that the drug was producing some very strange effects. Except for the work at the University of Maryland Psychiatric Institute (Klee, 1963), little has been added to the information in this area in recent years. Further, the conventional approaches to quantifying the subjective aspects of drug effects, that is, the usual symptom questionnaire and mood scales, did not speak the language of these effects, except in those cases where special-purpose questionnaires were constructed for use in LSD studies (Abramson, Jarvik, Kaufman, Kornetsky, Levine, & Wagner, 1955; Linton & Langs, 1962).

The conventional methodological approach to the study of drug effects can, however, be broadened and improved. The present authors have tried to do this by taking advantage of the attempts of others to articulate the effects of LSD-type drugs, by trying to describe and document what they have observed themselves, and by applying new methods to the study of the perceptual and verbal behavioral components in order to provide a more complete picture of the psychological states which are produced.

METHOD

In order to accomplish the aims of the research, it was extremely important to control for the influence of nondrug factors and to provide a situation in which the development of the LSD state could be adequately studied. Because of the special difficulties in controlling for such factors in LSD research, it was necessary to develop an experimental situation in which: (a) Ss were not familiar with the effects of the drug; (b) the drug was one of several drugs administered to different Ss (drugs which have very different effects, e.g., stimulation, sedation, etc.) so that a given S could not predict which he would be receiving; (c) a comfortable "safe" setting was provided, but the preparation was neutral; (d) the administered drug dosages were modest, sufficient in size to permit the characteristic effects of the drug to appear, but not so overwhelming that it was not possible to apply a broad range of psychological methods to their study.

Subjects

The two studies to be described took place at the Patuxent Institution, a treatment center in Maryland for emotionally unstable criminal offenders. The Ss were paid volunteers of at least dull-normal intelligence (WAIS IQ range, 80–125; average IQ, 102) and of sixth-grade educational level or above. All were screened psychiatrically to eliminate potentially psychotic or severely disturbed individuals. The Ss were between the ages of 21 and 40 and were sampled from the more "normal" segment of the prison population. Although the sample was similar to those used in many basic studies of drug effects, generalizations from the results have to be qualified somewhat by the nature of the population. There is obviously no ideal population for delineating the psychological effects of drugs; the members of this particular group were selected because they did not evidence any severe psychiatric disturbance, and because of their lack of familiarity with the expected effects of LSD.

Design

In the first study, an S, once he was screened and had volunteered to participate, was randomly assigned to one of four treatments: 50 λ of LSD, 15 mg. of amphetamine, 50 mg. of chlorpromazine,[1] and placebo. The conditions were double blind, so that neither S nor the several observers knew initially which treatment had been administered to a particular S, although the observers knew which drugs were involved in the study. The second study was similar to the first, but the chlorpromazine condition was eliminated, and there were some revisions of methodology based on experience from the first study. In the first study, there were 11 Ss in each of the four treatment groups; in the second study, there were 12 Ss in each of the three treatment groups.

Procedure and Experimental Setting

Following screening, all potential Ss were interviewed by the project coordinator, a psychologist, who instructed them as to the nature of the study. During this interview, Ss had the choice of volunteering or not volunteering for the study. They were told that the purpose of the study was to investigate the physical and psychological effects of several drugs, that the drugs were not new, but that more information was desired about their specific effects. It was emphasized that the drugs were safe under the dosages administered, that a physician would be checking on their condition throughout the day, and that they would stay in the hospital for routine observation the night after the drug study.

It was explained that the effects of the various drugs would range from mild to moderately strong depending upon the drug and how each person

---

[1] The use of chlorpromazine is related to the method-development aims of the project, and these results will not be reported here.

reacted to the drug. Also, Ss were informed, "Some effects might be pleasant, others might be uncomfortable, and other effects might be quite different than you've had before." In the course of the interview, Ss were encouraged to ask questions about the study and to tell the coordinator what they had heard from previous study Ss. If an S, based on his knowledge of previous Ss' reactions, seemed to have specific expectations, these were discussed with him, and he was told again that several different drugs were being used and that a number of different reactions were possible. The instructions were intended to reduce the likelihood that S would enter the experiment with any strong specific expectations.

Each S was run on a separate day, and he was seen on that day by a psychiatrist, a psychologist, and the project coordinator. Before administration of the drug, the psychiatrist and psychologist administered the baseline physiological and psychological tests. The psychiatrist briefly reiterated the instructions previously given to S by the coordinator. All drugs were then administered orally. Amphetamine, chlorpromazine, and placebo were given in capsule form with water; in the case of LSD the drug was in the water and the capsules were placebo. An hour later, testing was resumed and was repeated at specified intervals throughout the day. Observational ratings were made of S's behavior by the coordinator, psychiatrist, and psychologist at specified times before and after drug administration.

It should be emphasized that, in the instructions given S, in the atmosphere of the room, and in the interactions of the staff with S, an attempt was made to create a pleasant, but neutral, atmosphere, in which specific expectations on S's part would be at a minimum. In order to avoid a strictly experimental, impersonal approach, the coordinator kept in frequent touch with S throughout the day and tried to maintain a friendly, supportive relationship. The staff seemed successful in creating an unthreatening milieu, in which an S felt free to report what he was experiencing. The majority of Ss did not seem to have strong specific expectations and apparently believed that several different reactions were possible. No S, either before or after participation in the study, indicated that he knew what drugs were being used.

Experimental Measures

In addition to the newly designed methods, several conventional procedures for measuring drug response were included in the study. The physiological measures used were standard for this type of experiment and included measures of blood pressure, body temperature, and pupillary changes. The results of these will not be reported here except to note that expected effects in these areas, particularly with regard to the characteristic pupillary changes associated with LSD, were clearly in evidence. A set of rating scales was used for recording observations of *S*'s mood and behavior. This observational rating instrument was based on the format of the Clyde Mood Scale (Clyde, 1963) and included adjectives to represent the various factors of that scale. In addition, several adjectives more specific to LSD effects (e.g., suspicious, mood inappropriate, mood fluctuating) were also included.

The new methods used for characterization of the psychological states produced by LSD will now be described.

Subjective Drug Effects Questionnaire (SDEQ)

This instrument was developed to meet some of the shortcomings of subjective questionnaires previously used in drug research. The work with LSD has made it especially clear that (*a*) questionnaires have to include many new items involving unusual effects; (*b*) in order to determine the specificity of a particular drug, it is necessary to ask about effects not necessarily expected with that agent; (*c*) it is necessary to control for suggestion in the wording and in the manner in which the items are presented. The questionnaire which was developed for this study was designed to cover most possible changes in the thinking, feeling, perceptual, and somatic areas which occur as a function of the effects of the major classes of drugs. In order to minimize the role of suggestion, the format of the questionnaire allowed an *S* to endorse a particular effect and/or its opposite, and the order of presentation of these opposing effects was random.

Scales which describe the various facets of subjective response have been developed through an empirical clustering procedure, using a modification of the B-coefficient method (Holzinger & Harman, 1941).[2] The clusters are based on an analysis of the relationships among items when each *S* was at his peak response (i.e., the time when he endorsed the largest total number of items on the questionnaire). In addition to the empirical scales, a number of scales were developed which are based on the hypothesized effects of various drugs, particularly LSD, derived from the authors' experience in pilot work and the experience of others. Examples of these are feelings of decreased control, ambivalence, and euphoria-dysphoria. The empirical and a priori scales are presented in Table 1.[3]

Picture Rating Technique

The second new method in the study is the Picture Rating Technique. This method has its antecedents in Bartlett's (1932) "method of description"

---

[2] The authors gratefully acknowledge the assistance and consultation of B. K. Radhakrishnan, Biometric Laboratory, George Washington University, in providing the modified computer program for this analysis.

[3] A more detailed description of the development of this technique is in preparation.

TABLE 1
Subjective Drug Effects Questionnaire (SDEQ)

I. Empirical Scales: Based on Cluster Analysis of Items

General Response Scales	Specific Scales

A. Cognitive and psychomotor
  1. Improved: thinking enhanced, speech and movements quickened, and time sense improved (12)[a]
  2. Impaired: thinking impaired, movements slowed, time sense altered (7)
	D. Feelings
	  7. Dizzy, excited, silly (5)
	  8. Dreamlike, floating (4)
	  9. Dreamy, giddy (5)
	  10. Upset, unhappy, asocial (5)
	  11. Sober, serious (3)
	  12. Peaceful, sociable (3)

B. Bodily and feeling
  3. Relaxed, happy, light, controlled (12)
  4. Jittery, tense, hard to talk, less controlled (11)
	E. Perceptual
	  13. Sensory and perceptual sharpness (6)
	  14. Detachment and unreal quality to perceptions (6)
	  15. Altered perception of self and others (3)

C. Control
  5. Fear of loss of control (7)
  6. Feelings of increased control and good functioning (5)
	F. Somatic
	  16. Weak, sick (6)
	  17. Sluggish, stuffy, feeling of pressure (7)
	  18. Sympathetic arousal and increased sensitivity (6)
	  19. Parasympathetic arousal (4)

II. A Priori Scales: Based on Hypothesized Effects of Drugs

20. Increased awareness (6)
21. Decreased awareness (6)
22. Increased control (3)
23. Decreased control (7)
24. Ambivalence (67)
25. Euphoria (34)
26. Dysphoria (47)

[a]Number of items is in parentheses.

and is based on the hypothesis that internal changes in emotional state should result in changes in the individual's perception of the people around him. It was designed to assess the extent to which changes in mood are reflected in an individual's perception of the mood of others. The pictures were drawn from a larger group provided by Campbell (Campbell & Burwen, 1956). Three alternative sets of 10 pictures were developed, balanced for age, sex, and the "likability" of the faces in the photographs. The S describes each of the series of photographs of people on a list of adjectives, selected to cover basic mood factors that have been identified in previous psychometric studies of subjective mood states (Clyde, 1963;

Nowlis & Nowlis, 1956). A scoring system was developed which permits the profiling of the individual's perceptions of others, for example, the extent to which others appear "friendly," "fearful," "sad," etc. Thus, the use of projective stimulus material was combined with a quantitative system for dealing with the dimensions of mood. Early studies, without drugs, indicated modest relationships between personality characteristics and the tendency to perceive in certain directions and between mood states as reported on the Clyde Mood Scale (Clyde, 1963) and perceived mood, for example, between felt "jitteriness" and perceived "jitteriness." These findings support the basic validity of the approach.

Verbal and Vocal Behavior Scales

A third set of results to be reported is derived from the application of a set of verbal and vocal behavior scales to the measurement of emotional change. In addition to using previously developed measures of verbal behavior (both temporal and content), a set of scales for rating changes in vocal qualities has been developed in the course of this research, based on the idea that changes in affect are reflected in changes in the quality of the voice. Verbal samples taken before and during the drug experience were rated on a number of semantic-differential-type scales. The vocal aspects of speech were isolated for these ratings by the use of a filtering technique developed by Soskin (Soskin & Kauffman, 1961) in which frequencies above a particular point are greatly attenuated; this method eliminates the intelligibility of speech while retaining many voice characteristics. Each sample was rated by two research assistants with MA-level training in psychology, and the scores used were the means of the ratings of these two raters. This method of rating vocal aspects of speech is discussed more fully in a paper by Waskow (1967).

RESULTS

In the results to be reported, two somewhat distinct approaches have been applied to the analysis of the effects of LSD. The first is designed to delineate the specific subjective effects of LSD, by contrasting them with those which occur simply as a function of taking a drug (the placebo condition), and with those which occur with an agent which is similar to LSD with regard to elevating mood (i.e., amphetamine). This type of analysis cannot, however, delineate the qualitatively different psychological states which may be experienced by different individuals given the same drug. In the second type of analytic approach, an attempt is therefore made to identify the patterns of subjective response which are produced. This is followed by an analysis of the correlates of these "states" in the behavioral, perceptual, and verbal behavior areas.

Analysis of Specific LSD Effects

For the first type of analysis, groups were compared on each scale of the SDEQ taken at approximately 1½–2 hr. postdrug, the time at which peak effects occurred for most Ss, and at 3½ hr. postdrug. This analysis is based on data from the first study. Differences between groups were analyzed by t tests except in cases of extreme heterogeneity of variance, where Fisher exact-probability tests were substituted.

The picture one derives from comparing LSD with placebo on the SDEQ, as in Table 2, is that of a drug which produces a diverse range of effects in the cognitive, somatic, perceptual, and feeling areas. These effects, rather than resulting in a consistent or rational pattern, instead produce a somewhat confusing mixture of positive and negative components. The Ss appear to feel relaxed and happy, but also jittery, tense, dizzy, excited, dreamlike, and giddy; to report their thinking impaired and their movements slowed, but their senses and perception sharpened; to perceive themselves as detached and their world unreal; to perceive others in an altered

TABLE 2

Comparing LSD to Amphetamine and Placebo on the SDEQ[a]

I. LSD > Placebo	
More Significant**	Less Significant*
2. Impaired cognitive and psychomotor functioning	3. Relaxed, happy, light, controlled
4. Jittery, tense, hard to talk, less controlled	5. Fear of loss of control
7. Dizzy, excited, silly	13. Sensory and perceptual sharpness
8. Dreamlike, floating	16. Weak, sick
9. Dreamy, giddy	21. Decreased awareness
14. Detachment and unreal quality to perceptions	23. Decreased control
15. Altered perception of self and others	24. Ambivalence[b]
18. Sympathetic arousal and increased sensitivity	25. Euphoria
26. Dysphoria	

II. LSD not Significantly Different from Amphetamine in Either Period[c]
1. Improved cognitive and psychomotor functioning
3. Relaxed, happy, light, controlled
6. Feelings of increased control and good functioning
13. Sensory and perceptual sharpness
20. Increased awareness

[a]Univariate analyses at 1½ hours and 3½ hours ($N = 33$, Study 1 only).

[b]Based on analysis of frequency with which it occurred throughout the day.

[c]LSD significantly exceeds amphetamine in at least one period on scales in I which are not included in II, with the exceptions of Euphoria, Dysphoria, Decreased Awareness, and Decreased Control.

*$p < .05$ in at least one postdrug period.

**$p < .01$ in at least one postdrug period.

way; to feel that they have less control of themselves and to fear the loss of further control. They report a number of feelings to be occurring at approximately the same time which would appear to the rational observer as opposed and contradictory.

It is clear from this analysis that, if one were to evaluate LSD only on variables which were expected to occur with a stimulating or mood-elevating agent, the drug would appear to be a euphoriant. In the broader framework provided by the SDEQ, it appears to induce both euphoric *and* dysphoric effects. The comparison with amphetamine indicates that LSD can appear as stimulating as amphetamine, yet, on those factors which are most associated with the energized, confident feeling of a good stimulant, for example, feelings of increased control and improved cognition and psychomotor performance, amphetamine actually exceeds LSD.

In viewing the LSD effects which have been separated out in this analysis, it is a little hard to believe that they could be occurring together in the same people. Prior research on LSD has indicated that the effects are wavelike or cyclical, so that over the course of 6–8 hr. the mood of Ss may show considerable fluctuation. This wavelike nature of the effects would in part explain the above findings which appear to be contradictory. However, although the authors' observations confirmed the presence of wavelike effects in many Ss, it was also clear in the pilot work that certain of the opposing effects, particularly as regards mood, were actually occurring in the same people at the same time. On the basis of these observations, a way of quantifying this phenomenon from subjective reports was developed. The measure is called *ambivalence:* the extent to which feelings and experiences which are opposed to each other occur simultaneously or almost simultaneously in Ss.[4] Having observed and then demonstrated that this phenomenon does occur more frequently under LSD than under placebo or amphetamine, the authors view it as a major characteristic of the LSD experience. Its centrality as a phenomenon will become clearer in the discussion of the other study results.

Although most LSD Ss experienced, to some degree, the specific effects which have been described, it was obvious, also, that Ss were not reacting uniformly with regard to their overall pattern of response to either LSD or amphetamine. The next question to be considered, then, was whether qualitatively different, but identifiable, subjective states were produced in different Ss at that point in time when most Ss were at their peak response. Also, in order to increase understanding of these psychological states and to define them more fully, correlates in other areas of functioning were analyzed. These included changes in observed behavior, in perception of others, and in speech.

[4] The S received a score of 1 on the ambivalence scale each time he endorsed two apparently contradictory items, for example, feeling relaxed and tense, head feeling heavy and light.

Identification of Subjective States

From inspection of the data in the first study, different patterns of effects among Ss were clearly discernible. In attempting to identify any general patterns which may be represented in the data, the three authors independently sorted Ss into groups based on the similarity of their profiles of subjective effects. The authors concentrated on the pattern of relationships which existed among five general response scales on the SDEQ (cutting across somatic, feeling, cognitive, and control factors) [5] and used the specific scales as a secondary source of data for clarifying or confirming the existence of a particular pattern. It was revealed that only one of the specific scales, a feeling scale, was given much weight in the pattern analysis. By focusing on the levels and the relationships among these six dimensions, it was possible to separate out three general patterns which occurred with LSD and two with amphetamine. The ease with which these groups could be distinguished is reflected in the fact that all three authors, although sorting cases independently, came close to an identical breakdown of Ss into the groups outlined here.

One group which stood out very clearly in the LSD condition was composed of Ss who scored quite high on the relaxed, happy, peaceful, and improved cognition scales, but had relatively low scores on jittery, tense, fear of loss of control, and impaired cognition. A group in the amphetamine condition reported a pattern similar to this LSD group, but with markedly lower scores on some of the negatively toned scales. Another, very small, group of LSD Ss had similarly high scores on the positively toned scales, but scored very high on the negatively toned scales as well. A third group (of both LSD and amphetamine Ss), although not quite as distinct as the others, had higher scores on the negatively toned scales than they did on the positively toned ones. Thus, three main patterns of response were found in the first study. The Ss in the second study were then categorized according to this breakdown with few problems. The placement of only one or two or these Ss was at all equivocal. All drug-state comparisons are based on a combination of Study 1 and Study 2 Ss.

The three states produced by LSD are, then, a *moderately euphoric state* in which the extent of the relaxed, happy, peaceful, and improved cognition scores exceeds the jittery, tense, fear of loss of control, and impaired cognition aspects. The reverse is true for the *dysphoric state*. It should be noted, however, that, despite the presence of strong dysphoric elements, for example, jittery, tense, fear of loss of control, there still exists a moderate level of the happy, relaxed feeling, just as the moderately euphoric state contains some jitteriness. Neither of these states is, there-

---

[5] These scales were comprised of more items than the specific scales and, as would be expected, provided more range and more discrimination among Ss.

fore, clearly euphoric or dysphoric—they only lean more strongly in these directions. On the other hand, the *ambivalent state,* of which there are four cases, is more euphoric *and* dysphoric than is either of the other two states. The ambivalent state also exceeds the other two states on almost all of the factors which delineate the specificity of the LSD reaction. In short, it appears to represent the most extreme and most emotional of the states produced, and the reaction closest to that which is usually reported as occurring under higher doses of LSD.

The pattern of the amphetamine *euphoric* Ss is similar to that of the moderately euphoric LSD group, but manifests less jitteriness and more feelings of control and better functioning, and seems clearly stimulated and euphoric. The small group of amphetamine *dysphorics* is presented only for purposes of comparison. Their dysphoria is again more consistent than that which is found in the more contradictory LSD dysphoric group. The placebo *neutral* group is composed of those Ss who did not receive an active drug and did not subsequently report any subjective changes.

The patterns for each state, with mean scores on all relevant scales, are presented in Table 3. The a priori scales, euphoria, dysphoria, and ambivalence, which are also included in the table, were examined after the identification of the patterns and clearly support the differentiation of the states. The total number of Ss included in the drug-state comparisons is 40.[6]

Behavioral, Perceptual, and Speech Correlates of Subjective States

How are these subjective states manifested in the individual's behavior, perceptions, and manner of communicating? The authors were aware that the names given these states were somewhat oversimplified and not entirely accurate as descriptions. Through a study of the correlates of the states, it was expected that the nature of these experiences would become clearer.

Each group in the following analysis will be compared with a placebo group which did not respond with any subjective changes. The description of the results will also emphasize comparisons among the LSD states and between the LSD and amphetamine euphoric states. The latter comparison is of special interest because it would appear from the analysis of the subjective effects that the two states are quite similar. Yet it was clear even in those data that this similarity was very probably a superficial one.

Table 4 presents the patterns of behavior of these groups on variables derived from the set of observational rating scales. Each variable is based

---

[6] The 2 LSD and 12 amphetamine Ss omitted from this analysis had such mild or indistinct reactions that they could not be categorized into drug states; there were, for example, no clearly dysphoric amphetamine Ss in Study 2. Placebo Ss who had even mild reactions were excluded from the drug-state comparisons, since the purpose of including a placebo group in the analysis was to provide a "neutral" control against which the characteristics of the emotional states could be contrasted.

TABLE 3
Subjective States Produced by LSD, Amphetamine, and Placebo: Patterns of Response on the SDEQ

Treat-ment	Subjective State	N	Mean Scores on Dimensions Used for Identifying Patterns						A Priori Scales		
			Im-proved Cogni-tion	Relaxed, Happy	Peace-ful, Sociable	Im-paired Cogni-tion	Jittery, Tense	Fear of Loss of Control	Eu-pho-ria	Dys-phoria	Ambiva-lence
LSD	Moderately euphoric	8	5.25	7.38	2.13	2.63	2.25	.88	41.51	11.89	3.34
	Dysphoric	9	2.33	5.44	.89	5.00	7.33	4.00	18.98	38.48	7.12
	Ambivalent	4	7.25	7.50	3.00	4.50	8.00	4.25	46.11	40.03	20.97
Amphet-amine	Stimulated or euphoric	8	9.00	10.13	2.63	2.63	1.00	.88	54.78	12.77	5.80
	Dysphoric	3	.67	.67	.67	2.67	5.33	2.00	4.92	26.59	.45
Placebo	Neutral	8	.13	.63	.00	.38	.38	.25	3.64	5.87	.00

on one or two adjectives, rated on 4-point scales. Scores used are means of the ratings of two observers, the psychologist and psychiatrist. The variables selected are those which can be rated reliably and are relevant to the subjective states delineated. The different states were compared (with the exception of amphetamine-dysphoria) on each of these scales by means of t tests or Fisher exact-probability tests. The conclusions which can be drawn from these comparisons are limited, of course, by the size of the groups, but several things are fairly clear.

TABLE 4
Subjective States Produced by LSD, Amphetamine, and Placebo: Patterns of Observed Behavior

Treat-ment	Subjective States	N	Clear Think-ing[a]	Happy[a]	Afraid, Appre-hensive[b]	Sus-picious[b]	Giggly[a]	Mood Fluc-tuating[a]	Mood Inappro-priate[a]
LSD	Moderately euphoric	8	45.00**	52.50*	33.75*	35.00	47.50**	41.25**	47.50**
	Dysphoric	9	37.22**	41.12	38.88**	38.88	42.44**	40.00**	38.88**
	Ambivalent	4	46.25	55.00*	33.75	32.50	52.50**	52.50**	52.50**
Amphet-amine	Stimulated or euphoric	8	50.62	45.00	31.25	27.50	23.75[c]	27.50*[c]	21.25[c]
	Dysphoric	3	53.33	33.33	38.33	33.33	23.33	30.00	30.00
Placebo	Neutral	8	53.10	35.00	25.00	27.50	22.50	21.25	21.25

[a]Observations made at approximately $2\frac{1}{4}$ hours postdrug.
[b]Observations made at approximately $1\frac{1}{4}$ hours postdrug.
[c]Significantly different from the LSD euphoric condition at $p < .01$.
*Significantly different from the placebo condition at $p < .05$.
**Significantly different from the placebo condition at $p < .01$.

The LSD groups are more like each other in some very distinctive aspects of manifest behavior than they are like any of the other conditions, despite their differences in subjective emotional tone. They are strikingly more giggly, and their moods are seen as more fluctuating and inappropriate than are any of the other states. They are also seen as cognitively less clear and generally more afraid and apprehensive. On observed happiness, however, only euphoric and ambivalent Ss significantly exceed the placebo group. Where there might have been some difficulty in distinguishing the LSD euphoric state from the amphetamine euphoric on the basis of subjective data, it is clear that they are very different groups from the standpoint of manifest behavior. The amphetamine group, except for the mood-fluctuating variable, is not overtly very distinguishable from the placebo neutral group. Some differences in the observable behavior of the three LSD states (e.g., greater fear and suspiciousness and less clear thinking and happiness of dysphoric Ss and greater mood fluctuation of ambivalent Ss), although not reaching significance, are consistent with the distinction of the three subjectively different states. In general, however, although the internal states of the LSD groups appear to be quite different, the manifest behavior of these groups is not as clearly distinguishable.

When one turns to the results of the perceptual and the verbal data, the problems in analysis become more complicated. The measures are still in an experimental stage, and the small number of Ss in each group and the extent of their variability on the predrug scores limit the types of analyses which can be carried out. Attempts were made to take into account any differences in initial levels in interpreting results.

Only a few of the predrug group means for the picture ratings were significantly different from each other. In order to partially control for these differences, change scores were used in the analysis of these results, and differences between pairs of states were evaluated by t tests on these change scores.

When the several LSD states are compared with the placebo neutral state . . . it can be noted that the euphoric group appears to move in the direction of perceiving others as more friendly and less hostile and suspicious. The pattern of change is similar for the dysphoric group, but the contrast between these factors, the friendly and hostile, is less marked. The most striking changes are noted in the ambivalent group, where Ss' tendency to move in the direction of perceiving more friendliness *and* more suspiciousness is quite pronounced. The extent of perceived suspiciousness is significantly greater ($p < .05$) than that for each of the other LSD groups, and the sheer amount of overall change is quite striking. The emotionality and the contradictoriness—that is, the perceiving of both positive (friendly) and negative (suspicious) elements—are consistent with the picture presented in the subjective data.

[In comparing] the two euphoric states . . . the amphetamine state, although having an increase in perceived friendliness in common with the LSD condition, appears to be quite distinct in its overall pattern. There is a significantly greater decrease in perceived fearfulness as compared with placebo ($p < .05$), and slight increases in perceived hostility and suspiciousness in contrast to the decreases noted with LSD (differences between amphetamine and LSD on hostility, $p < .05$). The tendency for amphetamine to result in the perception of more "aggressiveness" in the environment is something which was found in an overall comparison of the drugs in this study. The meaning of the results with the picture rating technique is not completely clear at this point, but these subjective states appear to result in relatively distinct patterns of perception (except for the LSD dysphoric) and contribute to an understanding of the various psychological states.

The speech of Ss experiencing distinctively different emotional states might also be expected to differ along a number of dimensions. The verbal samples elicited in this study have been subjected to several different types of measurement, but only three of the most relevant measures will be presented here. These are the temporal measures of amount of speech produced and rate of articulation and the vocal rating on a bipolar scale of happy-sad. . . . (Although all groups were also compared with placebo-neutral Ss, this group is not graphed, but will be mentioned where relevant.)

The happy-sad ratings are most relevant to the emotional states that were produced. The LSD ambivalent group was the only one to move in the direction of sounding happier on the drug, while the LSD dysphoric group sounded most sad (although differences were not significant—using t tests between pairs of drug states—with these small Ns). The amphetamine and LSD euphoric groups fell between the others, as did the placebo group, and did not differ from each other. These findings may make most sense if one thinks of the happy-sad ratings as reflecting, at least in part, the extreme stimulation and emotionality of the ambivalent group, rather than simply the usual concept of happy. Euphoric Ss, who were happy in a quieter, less excited way, were thus heard as similar to placebo Ss on this dimension.

The interpretation of the results on the temporal measures is more complicated. Although the emotional states are differentiated in the same general way on both of these measures in the postdrug period, they already differ markedly on these measures predrug. Thus, the differences one sees among the four states on these variables seem to be characteristic of Ss who experience these states—before as well as during the actual drug experience. LSD ambivalent Ss talk a great deal and very rapidly, while LSD dysphoric Ss speak little and slowly (differences between ambivalent and dysphoric in productivity and rate, $p < .01$, $p < .05$, respectively, as indicated by t tests in both periods). Euphoric Ss again fall between. Although the meaning and correlates of productivity and rate of speech have been found to differ in different experimental situations (Mahl & Schulze, 1962), they might be thought of as reflecting amount of arousal and excitation, what has been called an "outgoing emotionality."

The results suggest that productivity and rate, differing both before and during the drug, may reflect a more permanent attribute of Ss, while the happy-sad dimension may be more responsive to transient emotional states such as those brought about by drugs. Thus, ambivalent Ss in this study appear to be higher both in their general level of emotionality and in the increased arousal due to the drug.

DISCUSSION

As noted in the introduction, this study was designed so that it might be possible to observe the effects of LSD in their very early stages. An understanding of how the more complicated conceptual reactions occur should be facilitated by a clearer picture of the basic psychological effects on the organism. The new methods provided a fairly comprehensive picture of the components of the response and the several emotional states which were experienced by the Ss. These results will be integrated later in this section in an attempt to characterize the three states produced. The reported findings do not, however, completely document some unusual effects occurring in the early stages of the LSD reaction, which were observed in this study and which deserve comment. The nature of these unusual effects, which relate primarily to the quality of the emotional experience, contributes to an understanding of the complex psychological states which are produced.

The most striking effect was the tendency for very intense emotions to occur in some Ss without any apparent outside stimulus and, initially, without any cognitive component or counterpart; for example, "I feel like I'm angry—I feel very angry—but I know that I have no reason to be, yet I'm getting angrier by the minute"; "I feel like something funny has happened—everything seems funny, but I don't know why." These effects have relevance to certain theoretical notions current in the field concerning whether a complete emotion can exist, or be experienced, without an appropriate cognitive counterpart. Schachter and his associates have proposed, on the basis of their research (Schachter & Singer, 1962), that it is not likely that complete emotions exist in the absence of a conceptual component; when S is aware that the physiological arousal is due to a drug, he is not likely to have an "emotion." Zubin and Katz (1964), in reviewing further evidence on the problem, have tended to support this theory. Careful observation of human Ss under LSD makes one question whether this is, in fact, the case. Several Ss, experiencing the usual signs of physiological arousal associated with LSD, reported what appear to be very strong emotions, prior to attaching to them any label or conceptual component and despite the fact that they were aware of the source of the arousal.

Thus, highly intense emotions, sometimes competing ones, which are initially free of situational and cognitive factors appear to be produced by LSD. These mixed emotional states, which create possibly new but confusing experiences for S, provide the substrate for many other things to occur in the perceptual and the cognitive spheres. This aspect of the total experience is an important one and may have implications for explaining the more elaborate mystical and conceptual reactions reported elsewhere. An attempt to integrate this quality of the experience with the other major perceptual, cognitive, and sensory phenomena will be made at the end of this section. But first it is important to review how these intense and diverse emotions are subsequently defined by Ss. The emotional states which result are, as expected from previous research with LSD, not uniform among Ss. They were effectively differentiated by the new methods employed. In characterizing these three states, the findings obtained with the various methods will be integrated and the states differentiated from those produced by another somewhat similarly acting drug.

1. The *moderately euphoric* LSD state is characterized by feelings of elation, cognitive and psychomotor improvement, some feelings of jitteriness and tension, but little or no fear of loss of control. To observers, Ss in this state appear happy, giggly, and a little afraid with inappropriate and fluctuating mood. Their perceptions are characterized by a tendency to see others as more friendly and less hostile, angry, and suspicious. Their vocal behavior is not very different from that of placebo Ss. The elated state of euphoric LSD Ss appears to be qualitatively different from that of amphetamine euphoric Ss, who report feeling even more confident, relaxed, and happy, see more improvement in their cognitive and psychomotor performance, and report almost no jitteriness. LSD euphoric Ss, however, appear happier to observers than amphetamine Ss, probably due to the greater expression of emotion by LSD Ss as seen in their laughter and fluctuating and inappropriate mood.

2. The *dysphoric* LSD state is characterized by feelings of jitteriness and tension, a fear of loss of control, feelings of impaired cognition and psychomotor performance, and also some seemingly contradictory feelings of relaxation and happiness. Behaviorally, these Ss appear less cognitively clear and more afraid and suspicious than other LSD Ss. Although they manifest some of the same giggliness and fluctuation of mood as do other LSD Ss, they are seen as less happy. Their perceptions of others are similar to those of placebo Ss. Their voices sound sadder, and they talk less and more slowly than do any other Ss. Thus, the dominant mood of fear and depression appears to override any positive feelings experienced by these Ss.

3. *Ambivalent* Ss are without doubt experiencing the most intense and most striking of the LSD states. On both positive and negative features, they generally report the greatest response: most relaxed, happy and sociable,

but also most jittery, tense, and fearful of losing control. They are seen by observers as the happiest of *S*s and as the most extreme in their giggliness and fluctuating and inappropriate moods. In their perceptions they are again ambivalent, seeing both more friendliness and suspiciousness in others. Their own voices sound happier. Their extreme emotionality is also expressed by their speaking a great deal and very rapidly. The quality of the euphoria that they experience is, to an even greater extent than was true for LSD euphoric *S*s, strikingly different from that of amphetamine *S*s. While the latter appear highly stimulated, LSD ambivalent *S*s are much more than stimulated; their strong sense of well-being, coupled with feelings of decreased control, gives rise to a state of exhilaration or marked elation. In all ways, these *S*s appear most emotional, and, although their elation might be the most impressive element, they tend to experience and to express strong, opposing emotions and perceptions.

This characterization of the three states highlights the differences in the direction and intensity of the emotional experiences and in the nature of cognitive and perceptual phenomena experienced by LSD *S*s. Despite these individual differences in quality and pattern of reaction, it is clear, also, from the analysis, that most of the LSD *S*s experienced, to some degree, all of the basic phenomena which differentiated LSD from placebo and amphetamine. These relatively uniform effects (see Table 2) were produced in a controlled setting in which *S*s were unfamiliar with the effects of the drug and in which there was a careful and fairly successful attempt at controlling and neutralizing expectations. Given these conditions, the basic effects must be traced in major part to the drug itself. The appearance of the different patterns of response is, on the other hand, most probably related to nondrug factors.[7]

In turning to the question of how, at the height of an LSD experience, profound alterations of consciousness and elaborate conceptualizations may develop, it will be useful to review the basic phenomena shared by most LSD *S*s and to consider the implications of a psychological state in which the following occur:

1. Very strong but opposing emotions occurring approximately at the same time, emotions which may not have a cognitive counterpart.

2. A feeling of being out of control of one's emotions and thoughts.

3. A feeling of detachment from the real world.

4. A feeling of perceptual sharpness, but at the same time perceptions of the outer world as having an unreal quality.

5. The perception of the world and others as "friendly" but "suspicious."

---

[7] The relationship of personality variables to drug response will be dealt with in another paper.

This assemblage of competing emotions and perceptual counterparts and the general intensity of the reaction would appear to create a very bizarre experience for most individuals in our culture to undergo—and one which may not easily be assimilated or integrated into previous experience.

It raises the question much considered in the past in psychology of how human beings actually come to terms with new, strange, highly charged experiences. Frederick Bartlett's (1932) theory held that when human beings are confronted with experiences which are not comprehensible to them in terms of previous experience they are driven to find meaning—sometimes any meaning—and the more awesome the experience, the more quickly they will evolve some rational construction.

In such a context, it seems reasonable to expect that nondrug factors—setting, suggestion, previous experience, "personality"—would come into play and help to shape the final pattern of response. Although these nondrug factors are thus likely to contribute to the meaning which is finally attributed to the experience, the elements of the new experience seem to be largely due to the unusual effects of the drug itself.

One of the most dominant aspects of the experience, then, appears to be the contradictoriness and intensity of the basic somatic, emotional, and perceptual effects which occur in the early stages of the LSD reaction. This ambivalent emotional and perceptual state might very well provide the basis for similar paradoxical phenomena which have been reported to occur later at the conceptual level. Although this sequence of effects does not completely explain the bases for the profound and paradoxical states of consciousness which have been described so vividly in the literature, it may contribute to one's understanding of where and how these very unusual experiences begin.

REFERENCES

Abramson, H. A., Jarvik, M. E., & Hirsch, M. W. Lysergic acid diethylamide (LSD-25): VII. Effect upon two measures of motor performance. *Journal of Psychology,* 1955, **39,** 455–464.

Abramson, H. A., Jarvik, M. E., Kaufman, M. R., Kornetsky, C., Levine, A., & Wagner, M. Lysergic acid diethylamide (LSD-25): I. Physiological and perceptual responses. *Journal of Psychology,* 1955, **39,** 3–60.

Aronson, H., Silverstein, A. B., & Klee, G. D. The influence of lysergic acid diethylamide (LSD-25) on subjective time. *American Medical Association Archives of Neurology and Psychiatry,* 1959, **1,** 469–472.

Aronson, H., Watermann, C. E., & Klee, G. D. The effect of d-lysergic acid diethylamide (LSD-25) on learning and retention. *Journal of Clinical and Experimental Psychopathology,* 1962, **23,** 17–23.

Bartlett, F. C. *Rembering: A study in experimental and social psychology.* Cambridge: Cambridge University Press, 1932.

Campbell, D. T., & Burwen, L. S. Trait judgments from photographs as a projective device. *Journal of Clinical Psychology*, 1956, **12**, 215–221.

Clyde, D. J. *Manual for the Clyde Mood Scale*. Coral Gables: University of Miami, Biometric Laboratory, 1963.

Cole, J. O., & Katz, M. M. The psychotomimetic drugs. *Journal of the American Medical Association*, 1964, **187**, 758–761.

DeShon, H. J., Rinkel, M., & Solomon, H. C. Mental changes experimentally produced by LSD (d-lysergic acid diethylamide tartrate). *Psychiatric Quarterly*, 1952, **26**, 33–53.

DiMascio, A., & Rinkel, M. Personality and drugs, "specific" or "non-specific" influence on drug actions. In M. Rinkel (Ed.), *Specific and non-specific factors in psychopharmacology*. New York: Philosophical Library, 1963. Ch. 7.

Hoch, P. H., Cattell, J. P., & Pennes, H. H. Effects of mescaline and lysergic acid (d-LSD-25). *American Journal of Psychiatry*, 1952, **108**, 579–584.

Holzinger, I. J., & Harman, H. H. *Factor analysis*. Chicago: University of Chicago Press, 1941.

Hyde, R. W. Psychological and social determinants of drug action. In G. J. Sarwer-Foner (Ed.), *The dynamics of psychiatric drug therapy*. Springfield, Ill.: Charles C Thomas, 1958. Pp. 297–315.

Katz, M. M. The psychological effects of psychochemical compounds. Symposium IX: Toxic chemical warfare agents. United States Army Chemical Warfare Laboratories, Edgewood, Md., Special Publication No. 3, May 1959.

Klee, G. D. Lysergic acid diethylamide (LSD-25) and ego functions. *Archives of General Psychiatry*, 1963, **8**, 461–474.

Kornetsky, C. Alterations in psychomotor functions and individual differences in responses produced by psychoactive drugs. In L. Uhr & J. G. Miller (Eds.), *Drugs and behavior*. New York: Wiley, 1960. Ch. 18.

Krus, D. M., & Wapner, S. Effect of LSD on pace of performing a variety of tasks. *Perceptual and Motor Skills*, 1962, **14**, 255–259.

Krus, D. M., Wapner, S., Freeman, H., & Casey, T. M. Differential behavioral responsivity to LSD-25: Study in normal and schizophrenic adults. *Archives of General Psychiatry*, 1963, **8**, 557–563.

Landis, C., & Clausen, J. Certain effects of mescaline and lysergic acid on psychological functions. *Journal of Psychology*, 1954, **38**, 211–221.

Levine, A., Abramson, H. A., Kaufman, M. R., & Markham, S. Lysergic acid diethylamide (LSD-25): XVI. The effect on intellectual functioning as measured by the Wechsler-Bellevue Intelligence Scale. *Journal of Psychology*, 1955, **40**, 385–395.

Liebert, R. S., Wapner, S., & Werner, H. Studies in the effects of lysergic acid diethylamide: Visual perception of verticality in schizophrenic and normal adults. *American Medical Association Archives of Neurology and Psychiatry*, 1957, **77**, 193–201.

Linton, H. B., & Langs, R. J. Subjective reactions to lysergic acid diethylamide (LSD-25). *Archives of General Psychiatry*, 1962, **6**, 352–368.

Mahl, G. J., & Schulze, G. Psychological research in the extralinguistic area. Paper presented at the Interdisciplinary Work Conference on Paralanguage and Kinesis, Indiana University, 1962.

Nowlis, V., & Nowlis, H. H. The description and analysis of mood. *Annals of the New York Academy of Sciences,* 1956, **65,** 345–355.

Rinkel, M., DeShon, H. J., Hyde, R. W., & Solomon, H. C. Experimental schizophrenia-like symptoms. *American Journal of Psychiatry,* 1952, **108,** 572–578.

Savage, C. Lysergic acid diethylamide (LSD-25): A clinical-psychological study. *American Journal of Psychiatry,* 1952, **108,** 896–900.

Savage, C., Terrill, J., & Jackson, D. D. LSD, transcendence, and new beginning. *Journal of Nervous and Mental Disease,* 1962, **135,** 425–439.

Schachter, S., & Singer, J. E. Cognitive, social, and physiological determinants of emotional state. *Psychological Review,* 1962, **69,** 379–399.

Silverstein, A. B., & Klee, G. D. Effects of lysergic acid diethylamide (LSD-25) on intellectual functions. *American Medical Association Archives of Neurology and Psychiatry,* 1958, **80,** 477–480.

Soskin, W. F., & Kauffman, P. F. Judgment of emotion in word-free voice samples. *Journal of Communication,* 1961, **11,** 73–80.

Stoll, W. A. Lysergsäure-diäthylamid, ein phantastikum aus der mutterkorngruppe. [Lysergic acid diethylamide, a phantasticon of the ergot group.] *Schweizer Archiv fur Neurologie und Psychiatrie,* 1947, **60,** 1–45.

Unger, S. M. Mescaline, LSD, psilocybin, and personality change. *Psychiatry,* 1963, **26,** 111–125.

Waskow, I. E. Vocal measures and drug effects. In K. Salzinger & S. Salzinger (Eds.), *Research in verbal behavior and some neurophysiological implications.* New York: Academic Press, 1967. Pp. 393–400.

Zubin, J., & Katz, M. M. Psychopharmacology and personality. In P. Worchel & D. Byrne (Eds.), *Personality change.* New York: Wiley, 1964. Ch. 11.

Introduction to
Curtis and Zuckerman Article

Imagine yourself having volunteered for a psychology experiment and you discover that participation involves lying quietly in a darkened room for 24 hours under conditions of reduced sensory input (you cannot see, hear, or touch anything). The experimenter promises you $25 if you remain in the room for the full 24 hours. The question is: Do you think you could last the day and pocket the money?

Did you answer yes? Most students do. However, if you actually participated in such an experiment you might change your mind fast enough! The task is not as "easy" as it might appear.

The experimental setting just described is called a "sensory-deprivation" condition. Such a condition is said to exist when an organism is placed in an environment severely deficient in "normal" sensory stimuli (for example, light, sound). Placed in such impoverished surroundings the average individual is anything but quiescent. Instead of relaxing and enjoying the absence of sensory bombardment, the subject often becomes disorganized, uncomfortable, restless, susceptible to hallucinations and unable to maintain a high level of cognitive functioning. Some individuals become so disturbed by sensory deprivation that they refuse to remain in the experimental room altogether.

The study below represents one extreme reaction to sensory-deprivation confinement. Although rare in occurrence, such a response serves to remind us that too little stimulation can be as debilitating to man as too much.

3

A Psychopathological Reaction Precipitated by Sensory Deprivation

George C. Curtis and Marvin Zuckerman

A young male subject developed an acute psychotic reaction during an eight-hour sensory deprivation experiment. His delusions lasted several days, and severe anxiety and depression lasted several weeks. This is the third reported case of such a prolonged reaction.

Although the immediate effects of sensory deprivation on mental function may be profound, clinically significant after-effects are rare. Azima and associates (2, 3) reported that two out of 18 hospitalized psychiatric patients who were isolated with sensory restriction for two to six days developed paranoid psychoses. They eventually required electroconvulsive therapy. As Miller (10) points out, subjects whose defensive equilibrium is severely threatened usually terminate the experiment on their own initiative.

The present case appears to be the third one reported in which an extended reaction occurred, and the only one in which the subject was not a psychiatric patient prior to sensory deprivation.

CASE REPORT

The subject, a 21-year-old male student, was recruited through an advertisement in his school newspaper. He denied any history of major medical illness or of psychological treatment. He was to be paid $40 on completion of an eight-hour experimental and an eight-hour control day.

SOURCE. *The American Journal of Psychiatry*, 1968, **125**, 255–260. Copyright 1968, the American Psychiatric Association. This work was supported by Public Health Service grant MH-07926 from the National Institute of Mental Health.

Personality Tests

Personality tests were administered to the subject prior to the sensory deprivation experiment. His test profile on the Minnesota Multiphasic Personality Inventory (MMPI) may be coded 546'83729-. The three scales above 70 (2 standard deviations above the mean) were: Femininity (Mf), Psychopathic Deviate (Pd), and Paranoia (Pa). The next highest scale was Schizophrenia (Sc) with a standard score of 62. The score on the R factor of the MMPI, interpreted by some as repression, was elevated. High Dominance and low Dependency scores were obtained. The subject's MMPI pattern resembles those of other college students characterized by home conflicts, nonresponsiveness in interviews, social insecurity, restlessness, and insomnia (4). This kind of pattern is seen with great frequency in paranoid schizophrenics and other patients characterized by hostility, suspiciousness, evasiveness, defensiveness, and denial (8). The high Femininity score, combined with an elevated Psychopathic Deviate score, could indicate homosexual problems. However, an elevated Femininity score is not uncommon in male liberal arts students who are sexually normal.

On the Gough-Heilbrun Adjective Check List, the only scale with any significant elevation was Aggression. The subject scored low on scales purporting to measure Personal Adjustment and Affiliative, Nurturant, and Heterosexual needs.

The subject's scores on the Edwards Personal Preference Schedule, a test where subjects are required to choose between needs, showed marked elevations on needs for Achievement and Deference and low scores on Change and Abasement needs. The low score on need for change or variety is consistent with the relatively low score the subject obtained on Zuckerman's (15) Sensation Seeking Scale.

On the Eysenck Personality Inventory, the subject scored in the extreme introvert range and was low on the Neuroticism score.

The total pattern indicated poor adjustment, hostility, defensiveness, lack of insight, and insecurity in interpersonal relationships.

The Experiment

The subject was confined in a 7 by 7 foot black (interior), soundproof room. He was loosely strapped into a form cut out of a foam rubber mattress in the shape of the human body. The foam rubber form was set on top of another foam rubber mattress on a low hospital bed. Foam rubber head forms restricted head movements. The apparatus accomplished effective restriction of gross body and limb movement without creating major body discomforts. The subject wore gauntlet gloves which restricted tactile stimulation. Confinement began at 9 A.M. After an initial testing and base line autonomic measurement periods, the lights in the room were turned off and the door was closed, shutting out all sounds from outside the room. The subject's heart rate remained fairly low and stable throughout the morning, but breathing, skin conductance, and galvanic skin response (GSR) fluctuations showed a marked increase in arousal after the first hour of confinement.

The subject was unstrapped and sat up for lunch. Afterward he was again strapped into the form and the lights were turned off. His heart rate rose sharply, ranging from 100 to 111 beats per minute during the mid-afternoon and above 85 for the rest of the confinement period. Skin conductance continued to rise, and breathing rate remained high. Later his urinary 17-ketogenic steroid excretion for the entire eight-hour period proved to be the second highest obtained in the experiment.

At no time during the experiment did the subject complain or ask to be released, although he was aware he was being monitored. Afterward he said the money kept him from quitting. He seemed disturbed on being released from confinement but took the postisolation paper and pencil tests without comment. However, during the postisolation interview he was angry and almost incoherent at times. He accused the experimenter of putting drugs into his sandwiches, giving him a spinal anesthetic "that was central nervous system numbing," and of piping some kind of gas into the room. He threatened to expose the experimenter's "immoral, illegal" activities in the newspapers. Asked about the reason for his beliefs, he said that there was a marked change in his body sensations after lunch. During the morning he had felt relaxed and almost euphoric. His body felt light and actually seemed to rise. After a while he lost all awareness of his body and was only conscious of his head. He described this as a Zen exercise. In the afternoon he felt much warmer and assumed that heat was being generated through the electrodes. His hands felt numb and he felt he was losing his sense of touch and then his consciousness. This feeling led to his idea of being drugged and given a spinal anesthetic. He smelled a gas and could not breathe well. He thought he saw an instrument shaped like a periscope dispensing the gas. At one point he saw something that looked like the shape of a shoulder and felt the presence of someone in the room.

The experimenter's reassurances and explanations did not dissuade the subject from his delusions and hallucinations. The experimenter urged the subject to speak to the psychiatrist associated with the group. The subject said he might do so and left.

Psychiatric Consultation

Exactly one month after the experiment, the subject telephoned the psychiatrist for an appointment and was seen two days later.

He appeared tense, and fine tremors of his lips and hands were often visible. Although his eyes frequently filled with tears, he wept openly only once and only for a few moments. He said he had called because of uncontrollable waves of anxiety and depression which had begun about three days after the experiment. He had often felt depressed before the experiment but never cried and usually knew why he was depressed. Now he cried often, thought of suicide, and did not know why. He described a recent attack of depression "as though I was surrounded by it and couldn't tell where it was coming from." Sleep disturbance was difficult to evaluate since he was accustomed to getting up and working all night when unable to sleep. His account of the experiment correlated closely with what he had said at the time and with the experimenter's observations.

He blamed insufficient explanation for all of his reactions. He had not expected to be strapped down, and this made him feel vulnerable and angry. He had not understood what the recording electrodes and electrode paste were for and had expected them to burn him. Two days after the experiment he had noted some marks where the electrodes had been, and it crossed his mind that he had been burned. The delusions were no longer fixed beliefs but ideas which crossed his mind. By the second interview he felt embarrassed by the whole affair, "like I made a fool of myself, building up a lot of things in my mind. . . . One of the things wrong with me is that I tend to distrust people and their motives." Need for the money was the only reason he could give for not terminating the experiment.

He had used the following types of drugs sporadically: marihuana, hallucinogens, sedatives, and tranquilizers. He denied the regular use of any of these drugs and stated that the only drug intake near the time of the experiment had been a marihuana cigarette about a week beforehand and another one shortly afterward.

Current Life Situation

It was never possible to assemble a very thorough picture of the subject's emotional life. Questions which approached sensitive areas usually resulted in vague, flustered, and tangential responses. Once this happened, any attempt to pursue the point only made matters worse. On the other hand, a number of very vivid and revealing vignettes emerged spontaneously and unpredictably during the course of his very brief psychotherapy.

He said, "I seem to need loneliness. People are distractions, and there are very few of them whom I can respect." He lived alone. He had no telephone because phone calls angered and frightened him. He disliked going out and tried to schedule all essential appointments on a single day so he could get them over with all at once. He also disliked receiving mail.

In the first interview he recited the following lines (1) as especially expressive of his philosophy:

> I am the solitude that asks and promises nothing;
> That is how I shall set you free. There is no love;
> There are only the various envies, all of them sad.

He felt unable to manage close relationships because he could not strike a balance between "activity" and "passivity" (his words). To him, being active meant dominating the other person, making the decisions, and having one's ideas and mannerisms copied. Passivity meant the reverse. He always tended to find himself in one role or the other, and both upset him. He feared that he would be unable to maintain his isolation, sometimes admitting and sometimes denying that he needed people.

His one current human contact was a male friend of several years' standing. Early in their relationship they had engaged in homosexual activity. After a few months they had stopped this but remained friends, and the patient thought it was better that way. Recently they had been arguing, getting angry, and seeing each other less. "I guess we know too much about each other."

During his first year in undergraduate school he had been close with a girl for about six months. In retrospect, he felt that she had been interested in him only because he represented what she herself wanted to be—talented, hard working, and high in academic standing. In order to please her, he began to neglect studies in order to go places with her. His grades slipped. He became "all wrapped up in her," drove by her house every night, and began to have violent arguments with her. Then she lost interest in him. He felt it should not bother him that she slept with other people, but it did. He had begun in the active role and switched to the passive. He intended to avoid repeating this experience.

Subsequently he had slept with a number of girls, but only casually and for one or two nights. "Girls have only an 'image' interest in boys. I have trouble trusting people. I keep a wall up between me and others."

He considered only one thing in life as worthwhile—his work. Without it, life had no meaning for him. He had worked very hard to pay for his undergraduate training. His parents did not contribute and in fact took money from him during his schooling. In graduate school he had some help from fellowships but was still working to help meet expenses. For reasons which never became clear, he felt that his studies were not progressing well enough. He made vague references to a tendency to start on new ideas rather than pursuing any one idea to its end, and he talked constantly of needing to combat this by driving himself to more and more solitary work.

History, Background, and Dynamics

The subject's earliest memory was of being in his room and being scolded for something he had done. Through the window he could see his father and brother in the yard playing baseball. Being sent to his room or restricted to the house was a frequent method of punishment, usually used by his mother. He was often confined to the house for two or three weeks for what seemed to him to have been minor offenses. In elementary school he was repeatedly made to sit in the corner "in isolation" for mischievousness and inattention.

Another memory was typical of numerous experiences. His father would beat his mother. The children would scream, "Don't, Daddy," and curse him. Afterward the father would do something to try to win the children over to his side. Each parent repeatedly told the children that the other was no good. The subject would side with one and feel guilty about betraying the other. The friction between the parents seemed to be mainly over money and the father's paranoid jealousy. The subject saw his mother as dominant and his father as detached and afraid.

As a child he had been afraid of both parents. In rages, his father often beat him with fists and once threw a knife which stuck in his brother's shoulder. His mother beat him with broomsticks, burned him with hot irons, jabbed him with knives, and threatened to hang herself if he was disobedient. After these punishments the subject would often spend an entire afternoon in the back yard quietly dismembering insects. He expressed admiration for Adolf Hitler, disagreeing with Hitler's aims but approving his methods.

When the subject was in college, he nursed his father through a long terminal illness and felt a great deal of pity for him. After his father's death his relationship with his mother became more comfortable.

Psychotherapy

The subject was seen twice weekly without charge for a total of 11 interviews. He was late for most of them. No drugs were given.

By the third interview his depression and anxiety were greatly reduced, but he began to have severe epigastric cramping. This was not consistently related to eating, and was relieved by taking an antacid/analgesic (Alka-Seltzer). He denied any past history of similar symptoms. Within another week the cramps, along with the remaining anxiety and depression, were gone. Meanwhile his facial expression on seeing the therapist began to reflect a childlike pleasure. He seemed to enjoy his visits, although the openness of his communications remained very erratic. When he expressed confidence that his symptoms would not recur, the therapist raised the question of help with his long-term problems. He said he was not interested in this and agreed to reducing the visits to one per week for several weeks and stopping if he continued to feel well. He gave no sign of any feeling, one way or the other, but failed to appear for the next interview. A letter was sent to him, but he did not reply.

Five and one-half months later, he returned to ask for "some old-fashioned advice." He had felt well in the interim and was quite happy with the progress of his work. He was living with a girl but sleeping clandestinely with his friend's girl. He and his friend's girl had decided that they preferred each other to their regular lovers. He was nervous, guilty about double-crossing his friend, and afraid that his own girl would attempt suicide if he left her. He was having a recurrence of epigastric cramps and burning. Most upsetting of all, he had become impotent, though only with his friend's girl. The alternatives were discussed with him, and he agreed to call again if he needed more help. He stated that he had stayed away from his last appointment because he felt guilty about saying that he felt no further need for treatment.

DISCUSSION

The experimenter has tested several hundred subjects in sensory deprivation experiments. Affect-laden hallucinations and delusions are rare but have occurred occasionally (13, 14). These reactions are usually transitory, and subjects usually express doubts about their reality after emerging from sensory deprivation. A case of this type was also reported by Mendelson and associates (9). Their subject developed delusions and hallucinations in sensory deprivation which led him to doubt his sanity. However, by the next day he seemed to be functioning well in most areas, though some paranoid trends were still present.

The reaction of the present subject was the most extreme the experimenter has seen. Drug intake, reported or unreported, may possibly have contributed to the reaction, but it seems quite implausible to assign the main responsibility to drugs. The reaction was too closely related in time to the experiment, and the capacity of sensory deprivation to disorganize psychological defenses is too well known.

Miller (10) suggests that vulnerability to disruptive isolation experiences may be increased by special regressive pressures in the experimental setting such as the feeding, washing, and toileting employed by Azima and associates (2, 3) in the neurotic patients who become psychotic. Special inducements to regression were not part of the present experiment. The atmosphere of the experiment was simple and businesslike, and the period of isolation was short.

Another frequent approach has been that of comparing adjustment to sensory deprivation with estimates of personality traits. The results of these studies are inconsistent and difficult to interpret (5, 6, 11, 12).

The clinical case study of such persons who react in various ways is a neglected and potentially useful approach. To be meaningful, such studies should include, when possible, the person's current emotional situation, the pattern of key childhood relationships, dreams, and earliest memories. These types of data indicate fairly clearly that the present subject unconsciously reacted to the experiment as a repetition of traumatic childhood experiences which included confinement, beating, burning of his skin, rage, fear, loneliness, and isolation. The experimental features of loneliness and isolation seem to have been intimately related to character traits which served defensively against powerful love needs and also as internalizations of parental punishments, perpetuating them as subtly self-destructive or self-punishing behavior. Finally, his defensive and adaptive capabilities seem to have been operating near capacity before the experiment, leaving him little reserve for coping with extra demands.

Another crucial factor probably was his failure to terminate the experiment in the face of an overwhelming eruption of affect. This is curious and merits close attention. His realistic need for money and the proviso that he would not be paid if he quit were clearly important in this respect but probably acted in combination with something else. His tenacity in the experimental situation had the same quality of a hostile, submissive, and self-punishing quest for recognition and approval as his tenacity to loneliness and hard work in his everyday life. Thus the pay arrangements did not protect him against his own masochism. Greater alertness on the part of the therapist to this as well as to other aspects of the experimenter-subject relationship might have yielded other valuable information, despite the difficulty of the interviewing problems which this subject presented. The importance of transference reactions of subjects to experimenters in shaping responses to experiments has been stressed by Margolin (7).

The relationship with the therapist, including not being charged, probably provided just enough giving and relatively nonthreatening human contact to reduce the strain on his ego and permit reintegration of his defenses. He terminated this relationship before having to risk reactivation in the transference of more powerful longings and their attendant fears of passive submission.

There is insufficient published material to estimate the generalizability of the findings in this subject to others who have disruptive reactions to sensory deprivation.

REFERENCES

1. Auden, W. H.: "In Praise of Limestone," in Nones. New York: Random House, 1951.
2. Azima, H., and Cramer, F.: Effects of Partial Perceptual Isolation in Mentally Disturbed Individuals, Dis. Nerv. Syst. 17:117–122, 1956.
3. Azima, H., Lemieux, M., and Azima, F. J.: Isolement Sensoriel. Etude Psychopathologique et Psychoanalytique de la Regression et du Schema Corporel, Evolut. Psychiat. 2:259–282, 1962.
4. Drake, L. E., and Oetting, E. R.: An MMPI Codebook for Counselors. Minneapolis: University of Minnesota Press, 1959.
5. Goldberger, L., and Holt, R. R.: "Experimental Interference with Reality Contact," in Solomon, P., Kubzansky, P. E., Liederman, P. H., Mendelson, J. H., Trumbull, R., and Wexler, D., eds.: Sensory Deprivation. Cambridge, Mass.: Harvard University Press, 1961, pp. 130–142.
6. Holt, R. R., and Goldberger, L.: "Assessment of Individual Resistance to Sensory Alteration," in Flaherty, B. E., ed.: Psychophysiological Aspects of Space Flight. New York: Columbia University Press, 1961, pp. 248–262.
7. Margolin, S. G.: The Behavior of the Stomach During Psychoanalysis, Psychoanal. Quart. 20:349–369, 1951.
8. Marks, P. A., and Seeman, W.: Actuarial Description of Abnormal Personality. Baltimore: Williams & Williams Co., 1963.
9. Mendelson, J. H., Kubzansky, P. E., Liederman, P. H., Wexler, D., and Solomon, P.: "Physiological and Psychological Aspects of Sensory Deprivation—A Case Analysis," in Solomon, P., Kubzansky, P. E., Liederman, P. H., Mendelson, J. H., Trumbull, R., and Wexler, D., eds.: Sensory Deprivation. Cambridge, Mass.: Harvard University Press, 1961, pp. 91–113.
10. Miller, S.: Ego-Autonomy in Sensory Deprivation, Isolation and Stress, Int. J. Psychoanal. 43:1–20, 1962.
11. Rossi, A. M., and Solomon, P.: Effects of Sensory Deprivation on Introverts and Extroverts: A Failure to Find Reported Differences, J. Psychiat. Res. 4:115–125, 1966.
12. Tranel, N.: Effects of Perceptual Isolation on Introverts and Extroverts, J. Psychiat. Res. 185–192, 1962.
13. Zuckerman, M.: Perceptual Isolation as a Stress Situation, Arch. Gen. Psychiat. 11:255–276, 1964.
14. Zuckerman, M., and Cohen, N.: Sources of Reports of Visual and Auditory Sensations in Perceptual Isolation Experiments, Psychol. Bull. 62:1–20, 1964.
15. Zuckerman, M., Kolin, E. A., Price, L., and Zoob, I.: Development of a Sensation Seeking Scale, J. Consult. Psychol. 28:477–482, 1964.

Introduction to
McConnell Article

"Why don't psychologists study ESP?" This is the question or, more aptly, the challenge raised by Professor McConnell as he examines the current status of this controversial psychic phenomenon. McConnell's question turns out to be rhetorical—and his answer is not very flattering to the behavioral investigator. As philosophers of science have done before him, McConnell dwells on the "conservatism of science"—a certain stubborn unwillingness by the scientific community to accept new or divergent ideas. McConnell feels that psychologists' lack of interest in ESP is indicative of such a conservative stance. In challenging the credibility of the scientist and the incredibility of ESP McConnell raises some interesting questions. By reprinting his paper in this psychology text I hope to have answered one of them.

4

ESP and Credibility
in Science

R. A. McConnell

In discussing extrasensory perception (ESP) before psychology students, it is not uncommon to stress the credulity of the public. Perhaps, instead, we ought to examine the credibility of scientists—including those on both sides of the controversy.

In ESP research whom shall we trust? One can rather easily imagine experimental precautions to keep participating subjects from cheating. But how do we know whether the experimenter is deliberately deceiving us? And in a world where people believe all kinds of nonsense, how can we be sure that the experimenter is not deceiving himself?

Let us suppose that 10 experimenters independently get the same result. Can we accept it? Ten is not a large number. There are about 150,000 names in *American Men of Science*. We may reasonably assume that at least 10,000 of these hold beliefs about the nature of reality that the majority of scientists would regard as wholly without foundation. Thus, on a subject like ESP, where there are no recognized authorities, why should we accept the word of 10 experimenters—or, for that matter, a thousand? Are we not, all of us, creatures of our culture? Is there any way we can be sure that a scientist in any field is as rational as he pretends to be?

Questions concerning the credibility of scientists are rarely asked in our classrooms. I have wondered why. Perhaps it makes us uncomfortable to consider the possibility of incompetence, dishonesty, or mental illness among professional people. Whatever the reason, this is forbidden territory for study.

SOURCE. *American Psychologist*, 1969, **24**, 531–538. Copyright 1969, by the American Psychological Association, and reproduced by permission. An invited lecture to the introductory psychology classes at Carnegie-Mellon University, December 18 and 19, 1967.

Once in a long while, these embarrassing ideas do come to the surface. Someone, a little bolder or a little more eccentric than the rest of us, may write an article that slips by the editorial censor. When that happens, we have a chance to learn what people really think.

When I accepted this invitation to talk to you, I was told I could give you an advance reading assignment. I asked that you read an eight-page article on ESP by G. R. Price (1955) that appeared in *Science* together with several letters to the editor (Soal; Rhine; Meehl & Scriven; Bridgman; Price; Rhine, 1956) written in reply to Price. These papers are currently available as part of the Bobbs-Merrill reprint series that is widely used for teaching psychology, and they have thus acquired a quasi-official status as source documents to which the very young may be exposed.

I also suggested that you read an analysis of Price's article (McConnell, 1955) that appeared in the *Journal of Parapsychology* and that was not included in the Bobbs-Merrill series. I hope that most of you have had a chance to study these references, which I shall now discuss briefly.

Price, a chemist by profession, presented a well-supported argument showing that existing experimental evidence constitutes conclusive proof of ESP if one accepts the good faith and sanity of the experimenters. But he went on to say that all of the otherwise convincing evidence for ESP can be easily explained away if one assumes that experimenters, working in collaboration with their witnesses, have intentionally faked their results.

Perhaps the most interesting thing about this unsubstantiated suggestion of fraud is that it was published on the first page of the most influential scientific journal in the United States. I will not say whether Price intended what he wrote as a joke. That is a riddle that I leave to you to answer. The important question is not whether Price took himself seriously, but whether you and I ought to do so.

I believe, as apparently does Price, that all kinds of fraud, even by highly placed scientists, are possible and that it is conceivable that there might be collaboration between two scientists in perpetuating a scientific hoax. Nevertheless, I think that those who accept Price's argument fail to understand two important things about science as a social enterprise.

First, they fail to realize that the way to tell whether a number of scientists are collaborating in a hoax is to consider the intricate web of public and private motivation, belief, and retribution that determines the behavior of professional people in our culture. Price suggested that scientists, university teachers, medical doctors, and intellectually prominent persons who have assisted in the investigation of ESP may have engaged in conscious collusive fraud. Price answered the question of how one might get such people to become willing accomplices by saying: "In recruiting, I would appeal not to desire for fame or material gain but to the noblest motives, arguing that much good to humanity could result from a small deception designed to strengthen religious belief." An experienced lawyer or even a politician would laugh at this explanation of a supposed conspiracy among well-educated and fully engaged members of our society, but evidently quite a few scientists find it plausible.

Second, those scientists who take Price seriously do not understand scientific method. Price suggested that the way to establish the scientific truth of ESP is to carry out a fraudproof experiment. In his words: "What is needed is one completely convincing experiment." He described in specific detail how this might be done by using prominent scientists and stage magicians as witnesses, backed up by motion pictures of the entire proceedings, plus photomicrographs of welded seals, and so on. This is nonsense because it assumes that scientific proof is of the same nature as legal proof. On the contrary, the acceptance of a scientific principle does not, and never can, depend upon the honesty of individual scientists.

I wish I had time to pursue with you the subtle psychological question of the nature of scientific proof and of how the method of science deals with individual experimenter error as well as mass irrationality. Those of you who are especially interested may wish to read a book by T. S. Kuhn (1962) titled *The Structure of Scientific Revolutions*.[1] Here today, I can only say that in my opinion, wittily or unwittingly, Price's article is a hoax about hoaxes and about the nature of science.

If you were to ask: "What does it signify that Price successfully placed his article in our most important journal of science?" I would answer as follows: There is a facade of respectability and belief that covers all of the activities of society and makes it possible for men to work together and for society to exist. Most people—including those who are well educated—are unaware of this false front and lose their equilibrium when they are forced by circumstances to penetrate behind it. On the other hand, those of you who are intellectually alienated from our culture understand quite well that this pretense exists. I hope that some day you will also understand why it is necessary and that it is not the contrivance of a group of evil men but reflects what existential philosophers refer to as "the human condition."

This curtain of propriety and convention exists in science also, where it allows us to believe that all is well with our knowledge system. ESP or any other revolutionary discovery may seem to threaten science. From time to time, when such a challenge is offered, the stagehands nervously fumble, the curtain slips, and we see a little of the normally concealed machinery. We get a glimpse of underlying reality, a glimpse of the ignorance and fear that govern the inner affairs of the mind of man. Such was the case when *Science* published Price's critique of ESP. That is why his article is important.

---

[1] For a condensation of this book see McConnell (1968b).

EVIDENCE AND BELIEF

Then, what about ESP? If laboratory scientists lack sophistication about human nature and even about the methodology of science, how do we decide for ourselves whether ESP is real or imaginary, true or false?

Before we try to answer so difficult a question, let us go back to the beginning. I shall give you an operational definition of ESP that you may find a bit confusing. Then I shall describe a test for ESP that I hope will make the matter clear to you.

The definition goes this way: "Extrasensory perception is a response to an unknown event not presented to any known sense." I shall not try to explain it. Instead, let me describe the test.

I have brought with me a deck of ESP cards. These cards have five different kinds of symbols printed on them: a circle, a square, a plus, a star, and wavy lines. Altogether, there are 25 cards, 5 of each kind.

Suppose I shuffle these cards, hide them, and ask you to guess them. By the theory of chance probability, the number you would most often get right is five. Sometimes you would get four or six or seven. Only once in a long while would you get 15 right out of 25. In fact, if you got more than 10 right very often, you would begin to suspect that it was not just good luck. It might even be ESP.

Of course, you could not be sure. It might be luck—or it might be something else. If you look closely at the backs of these cards, sometimes you can see the symbol showing through. Perhaps in this way you recognized some of the cards when I shuffled them. Or again, every time I asked whether you were ready for your next guess, perhaps I gave you a hint without knowing it. Perhaps, unconsciously, I raised the tone of my voice just a little when I came to each star—because I think of stars as being "higher" than the other symbols, or for some other trivial reason.

You can see that there are many subtle ways for information to leak through by sight or by sound. No serious scientist would try to conduct an ESP experiment in this fashion. My only purpose in showing you these cards is to let you know how some of the early tests for ESP were done at Duke University 35 years ago. I regard these cards as a museum piece, although they are a lot of fun and can be used in preliminary testing.

The experiments that are carried out today are often so complex that one cannot evaluate them without advanced training in statistics, physics, and psychology. For this reason, and because the field is too large to describe in one lecture, I have prepared a list of reading materials. Some of these are intended to show the scope of the subject (Heywood, 1964; Langdon-Davies, 1961; McConnell, 1966; Murphy & Dale, 1961); others are experimental reports (Anderson & McConnell, 1961; McConnell & Forwald,

1967a, 1967b, 1968; McConnell, Snowdon, & Powell, 1955; Sinclair, 1962; Soal & Bateman, 1954).

You will notice that I have listed only my own journal articles. For this I offer my apology along with the following explanation. In any frontier field of science there are experimental hazards. If someone questions the soundness of what I recommend to you as evidence, I can probably do a better job of explaining if I have chosen research with which I am most familiar. I also want to convey the idea that there has been a large amount of work done in this field. If you study my papers and cannot find anything wrong with them, you ought to remember that there have been perhaps a hundred other investigators who have found substantial evidence for ESP under controlled experimental conditions.

ESP is a controversial idea in psychology. Nevertheless, the psychologists whom I know personally agree with me on many things. I am sure we agree on what constitutes good quality experimental laboratory research. We also agree that there is a sizable body of high-grade evidence for ESP in the literature.

In 1947 I visited Duke University in North Carolina where a man by the name of Rhine was doing experiments on ESP. I wanted to get acquainted with Rhine and with the people who were working under him. Even more important, I wanted to talk to those faculty members who rejected Rhine's work. I rented a dormitory room, and during four weeks I interviewed everyone I could, beginning with the President of the University and working down to assistant professors in various departments. I shall not have time to describe that adventure, but I will tell you what I was told by one professor of psychology in a private interview.

He said that he was familiar with the experimental literature of ESP and that, in his opinion, if it were anything else *but* ESP, one-tenth of the published evidence would already have established the phenomenon. He also explained that he would not accept ESP himself because, as he put it, he found "a world without ESP a more comfortable place in which to live."

That trip to Duke University was part of a larger investigation that made me decide to leave engineering electronics, in which I had acquired some experience, and to devote my life to the investigation of ESP and related effects.

That was 20 years ago. What has happened in this field since then? Among other things, there has been time to publish 20 more volumes of the *Journal of Parapsychology*. That comes to about 4000 pages of research. There have been several thousand additional pages in the *Journal of the American Society for Psychical Research* and in the English and Continental journals. You might think that the argument would be settled by now.

Only recently, a brilliant young psychologist, who is here on your campus, gave a lecture on ESP in which he said "I tend to believe the evidence is as good as it is for many of our other psychological phenomena." He also said that "Psychologists will not be interested in ESP until there is a repeatable experiment."

Where my psychologist friends and I disagree, is that I believe that the available evidence for ESP is sufficient to establish its reality beyond all reasonable doubt. My psychologist friends think that the evidence is not yet conclusive. I do not regard this difference of opinion as very important. I am happy to allow anyone the privilege of doubt.

How else does the position of professional psychologists whom I know differ from my own? Perhaps the main difference—the really important difference—lies in our interpretation of the history and methodology of science—in what today we call the philosophy of science.

For one thing, my friends seem to believe that the only good evidence for ESP must come from controlled experimentation in a laboratory. My own belief is that all available evidence must be weighed, taking into account its source and the conditions under which it was gathered.

Perhaps it will clarify the problem if I say that there are only two important kinds of scientific evidence in this world: our own evidence and someone else's. Since most of us are not in a position to gather evidence of ESP, my remarks apply especially to other people's evidence.

The first thing to remember is that, no matter how reputable the scientific journal, someone else's evidence is always suspect. And if the matter is important, we ought to be *aggressively* skeptical about it.

Whether we are listening to a tale of a ghost in a haunted house or reading the tightly edited *Journal of Experimental Psychology,* we have to concern ourselves with two questions: what is the content of the report and what are the competence and motivation of the observer?

What I am suggesting is that our attitude toward *all* supposedly scientific reports must be that of the psychologist in receiving an introspective account from a human subject in a laboratory experiment—for it must be remembered that, as far as the reader is concerned, a journal article by a distant scientist is in some ways even less dependable than what psychologists, often condescendingly, refer to as a "verbal report."

From a study of the history of science, I have come to two conclusions in this connection: (*a*) the evidence presented in scientific journals by professional scientists for all kinds of ordinary phenomena is not as good as commonly supposed, and (*b*) on a controversial subject where the professionals do not agree, the evidence of the layman may have considerable scientific value. As corollaries, I suggest that the textbooks of science are often wrong and that contrary popular opinion is sometimes right. Let us examine these ideas.

STOREHOUSES OF KNOWLEDGE?

Textbooks are the storehouses of man's knowledge. They are presumed to contain all of the things we know to be true. If you are becoming a scientist, you will spend at least 18 years studying from books. It would be not entirely unfair to call most of this training a "brainwashing" process. Nearly everything you learn as factual reality must be accepted upon the word of some recognized authority and not upon your own firsthand experience. It should be a matter of concern to you whether you have been told the truth for those 18 years. Just how bad are the textbooks we use? Let me take an example from the field of geology.

Did you know that until the year 1800 the highest scientific authorities thought that there was no such thing as a meteorite? After all, there are no stones in the sky; so stones cannot fall out of the sky. Only a superstitious person would believe in meteorites.

Many of you are familiar with the work of Lavoisier. He was the founder of modern chemistry. He discovered that burning is the combining of oxygen with other things, and he helped to show that the formula for water is H_2O. He was one of the great scientists of all time.

In 1772 Lavoisier signed a report to the French Academy of Science in which he said he had examined a stone that was believed to have fallen from the sky in a great blaze of light. Lavoisier said in his report that this was just an ordinary stone that had been struck by lightning and had melted partly into glass while lying on the ground.

Eventually, of course, the leaders of science decided that meteorites do come from outer space, and they revised the textbooks accordingly. But in doing so, they forgot to mention that there had ever been any argument about the matter. So here we are, living in the space age, without realizing how hard it is to discover the truth about even a simple thing like meteorites, which can be seen as meteors in the sky on any clear night, and which have been found upon the surface of the earth since the dawn of history.

Even worse, as students, we have no way of estimating how many arguments are still going on in science and how many mistakes—truly serious mistakes—there are in the textbooks from which we study. It is my guess that we can safely believe nearly all of what is said in the physics and chemistry books. But we ought to believe only half of the ideas in the biological sciences—although I am not sure which half. And we should accept as final very little in the social sciences, which try to explain why groups of people behave as they do.

Our subject today is extrasensory perception, which belongs in psychology, one of the biological sciences. ESP is something about which the "authorities" are in error. Most psychology textbooks omit the subject entirely as unworthy of serious attention. But these books are mistaken, because ESP is a real psychological phenomenon.

Of course, I am only giving you my individual opinion about ESP. I do not want you to base your belief upon what I tell you. When you have studied advanced psychology and statistics, and when you come to realize that your professors cannot be expected to teach you everything you wish to know, then I hope you will go to the scientific journals and study the experiments that have been done and decide for yourself.

MENTAL RADIO

I have already discussed the credibility of experts and the errors we find in science textbooks. I would like to turn next to the other half of my thesis, namely, that evidence from a layman may sometimes have scientific value.

Most of you are familiar with the name Upton Sinclair, who was a socialist reformer and a writer active in the first half of the twentieth century. He died in 1968 at the age of 90. In his time he wrote nearly 90 books. One of the best known of these, published in 1906, was called *The Jungle*. It told about the cruel and unsanitary conditions in the processing of beef in the Chicago stock yards. As a result of that book, laws were passed, and today the situation is much improved. In a very real sense, all of us are indebted to this man.

Sinclair discovered that his wife had an unusual amount of what was then known as "psychic ability." (That was before the beginning of the ESP controversy.) After three years of serious experimentation, he wrote a book about it: *Mental Radio* (1962, orig. publ. 1930).

In his experiments, Sinclair, or someone else, would draw a secret picture and ask Mrs. Sinclair to draw another picture to match it. Some of the pairs of pictures are presented in the following examples.[2] The one on the left is always the original picture, and the one on the right is what Mrs. Sinclair got by ESP.

Sometimes the pictures were made as far apart as 40 miles. At other times the target picture was held by Mrs. Sinclair in her hand—without looking, of course—while she concentrated before drawing her matching picture. The degree of success did not seem to depend upon distance.

Let us examine some of the pictures. In Example 1 we see an almost perfect ESP response. It is a knight's helmet. Notice that for every important line in the left-hand picture there is a corresponding line on the right.

Compare that with Example 2. Here, the response on the right is not quite the same as the target on the left, but the idea is the same.

The next slide is Example 3. Sinclair drew a football as a target. Mrs. Sinclair made the drawing on the right, but she thought it was "a baby calf with a belly band." Why did her ESP make this mistake? We cannot

2 Illustrations from *Mental Radio* by Upton Sinclair are reproduced by permission of the publisher, Charles C Thomas, Springfield, Illinois.

EXAMPLE 1   EXAMPLE 2

EXAMPLE 3   EXAMPLE 4

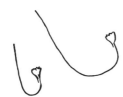

EXAMPLE 5   EXAMPLE 6

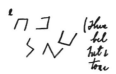

EXAMPLE 7   EXAMPLE 8

EXAMPLE 9   EXAMPLE 10

be sure, but we think it had something to do with the fact that in her childhood she had known a queer old man who raised calves as parlor pets and dressed them in embroidered belly bands.

Example 4 is another instance of the right shape with a wrong interpretation. Upton Sinclair drew a volcano, and Mrs. Sinclair drew what she called a black beetle. The beetle is upside down. If you turn the example over, you can more easily recognize its antennae and legs.

In Example 5 Sinclair drew a fish hook, which turned into two flowers.

Example 6 shows a fragmentary response. Sinclair drew a balloon. The response on the right is what his wife received by "mental radio." She was not sure what it was, so she wrote beside the picture: "Shines in sunlight, must be metal, a scythe hanging among vines or strings."

Example 7 on the left is a swastika. Mrs. Sinclair drew the response on the right. She did not know what it meant, but she wrote beside it, "These things somehow belong together, but won't get together." You can see some of her words which were accidentally included when the printer made the book. Here is the beginning of "These" and "belong" and "but won't" and "together."

Example 8 is a pair of drawings in which a stick man became a skull and crossbones.

Notice that in Example 9, Mrs. Sinclair left out some of the stars and added a moon instead.

In Example 10 Sinclair drew an umbrella. His wife responded with this curious picture, which she described in writing beside it as follows: "I feel that it is a snake crawling out of something—vivid feeling of snake, but it looks like a cat's tail." I might mention that she had a special fear of snakes, having grown up on a plantation in a Mississippi swamp.

The last example is the American flag and a response to it that could hardly be called a chance coincidence (Example 11).

You have seen a selection of 11 pictures out of a total of 290 trials made by Mrs. Sinclair. Perhaps 4 of the 11 would be called direct target hits. The rest are partial hits. Out of the 290 tries, 23% were rated by Upton Sinclair as hits, 53% were partial hits, and 24% were failures.

Of course, before you can be sure that these pictures were made by

EXAMPLE 11

ESP, many questions must be answered. Because Upton Sinclair and his wife were laymen, you will have to pay particular attention to their competence and motivation. On the other hand, one important feature of Sinclair's book is that you do not have to be a scientist to understand it. Even though you may not have studied statistics and psychology, you can read the book yourself and make up your mind as to its value on the basis of common sense. When you do, I think you will arrive at the same conclusion that many scientists have reached by entirely different kinds of experiments. I think you will decide that extrasensory perception is a reality regardless of the skepticism of the psychological profession.

A MATTER OF INTEREST

I have been told by my friends that psychologists will not be interested in ESP until someone discovers a repeatable experiment. Upton Sinclair repeated his experiments over a period of three years. In London, a mathematician by the name of Soal (Soal & Bateman, 1954) repeated certain card-guessing experiments again and again over a period of six years using two subjects and many different witnesses. What do psychologists mean by a repeatable experiment?

Evidently, they mean an experiment that is "repeatable by prescription." They want a standard experimental procedure that can be described on paper by which any qualified person—or at least some qualified persons—can guarantee to produce ESP upon demand. I must confess that we have not yet reached that stage in ESP research. And, until we do, I can sympathize with my skeptical friends. I can see why they, as busy individuals with other interests, are unwilling to reach a firm position about the reality of ESP.

What I cannot understand is why they say: "Psychologists will not be *interested* in ESP until there is a repeatable experiment."

It is a statement of fact that psychologists are *not* interested in ESP. Recently, I had occasion to examine a number of psychology textbooks. Only one of them mentioned ESP—that book, by Hilgard and Atkinson (1967). After reading the four pages which these authors devote to ESP, I have only two minor critical observations to offer.

The first is that the authors have given too much space to finding fault with unimportant papers. They go back 25 years to a journal article in which they accuse an ESP experimenter of over-analyzing his data. I am sure that comparable examples of weak statistical method could be found in any one of the quantitative journals of the APA—and we would not need to go back a generation in time to do it.

My second comment is that Hilgard and Atkinson may have tended to damage their own scholarly reputations by recommending as a "scholarly review" a book by C. E. M. Hansel (1966) titled *ESP: A Scientific Evaluation*. This book has been reviewed by S. S. Stevens of Harvard, who regards ESP as a Rabelaisian joke and who gave Hansel his unqualified approval. If you like amusing book reviews, I suggest that you read Stevens (1967). I regret that I do not have time here today to document for you the basis of my unfavorable opinion of Hansel's book.[3]

I have wandered over many facets of ESP. I shall now summarize what I think are the most important ideas. Since the scientific study of ESP was begun by the London Society for Psychical Research in 1882, there have been hundreds and perhaps thousands of experiments done with a care typical of the journals of the APA. Many psychologists of high repute admit that the evidence is as good as that for other phenomena that are accepted by their profession.

Surprising though it may seem, most of this research on ESP has been done by people who were not psychologists. From this fact and from the usual psychology textbook treatment of the subject as well as from private discussion, we know that psychologists are *not* interested in ESP. This raises a question—a very mysterious question that I invite you to try to answer: Why are psychologists not interested in ESP?[4]

REFERENCES

Anderson, M. L., & McConnell, R. A. Fantasy testing for ESP in a fourth and fifth grade class. *Journal of Psychology*, 1961, **52**, 491–503.

Clark, K. E., et al. The scientific and professional aims of psychology. *American Psychologist*, 1967, **22**, 49–76.

Hansel, C. E. M. *ESP: A scientific evaluation.* New York: Scribner's, 1966.

Heywood, R. *ESP: A personal memoir.* New York: Dutton, 1964.

Hilgard, E. R., & Atkinson, R. C. *Introduction to psychology.* New York: Harcourt, Brace & World, 1967.

Kuhn, T. S. *The structure of scientific revolutions* (Vol. II, No. 2, of the *International Encyclopedia of Unified Science*). Chicago: University of Chicago Press, 1962.

Langdon-Davies, J. *On the nature of man.* New York: New American Library Corporation, 1961.

Linder, R. Light one candle. *American Psychologist*, 1967, **22**, 804–805.

McConnell, R. A. Price in *Science. Journal of Parapsychology*, 1955, **19**, 258–261.

McConnell, R. A. ESP research at three levels of method. *Journal of Parapsychology*, 1966, **30**, 195–207.

McConnell, R. A. The ESP scholar. *Contemporary Psychology*, 1968, **13**, 41. (a)

McConnell, R. A. The structure of scientific revolutions: An epitome. *Journal of the American Society for Psychical Research*, 1968, **62**, 321–327. (b)

[3] This has since been done. See McConnell (1968a).

[4] Those who wish to answer this question might start their odyssey by visiting Clark et al. (1967) and Linder (1967).

McConnell, R. A., & Forwald, H. Psychokinetic placement: I. A re-examination of the Forwald-Durham experiment. *Journal of Parapsychology,* 1967, **31,** 51–69. (a)

McConnell, R. A., & Forwald, H. Psychokinetic placement: II. A factorial study of successful and unsuccessful series. *Journal of Parapsychology,* 1967, **31,** 198–213. (b)

McConnell, R. A., & Forwald, H. Psychokinetic placement: III. Cube-releasing devices. *Journal of Parapsychology,* 1968, **32,** 9–38.

McConnell, R. A., Snowdon, R. J., & Powell, K. F. Wishing with dice. *Journal of Experimental Psychology,* 1955, **50,** 269–275.

Murphy, G., & Dale, L. A. *Challenge of psychical research.* New York: Harper, 1961.

Price, G. R. Science and the supernatural. *Science,* 1955, **122,** 359–367.

Sinclair, U. *Mental radio.* Springfield, Ill.: Charles C Thomas, 1962.

Soal, S. G., & Bateman, F. *Modern experiments in telepathy.* London: Faber & Faber, 1954.

Soal, S. G.; Rhine, J. B.; Meehl, P. E., & Scriven, M.; Bridgman, P. W.; Price, G. R.; Rhine, J. B. (Letters to the editor in rejoinder to G. R. Price.) *Science,* 1956, **123,** 9–19.

Stevens, S. S. The market for miracles. *Contemporary Psychology,* 1967, **12,** 1–3.

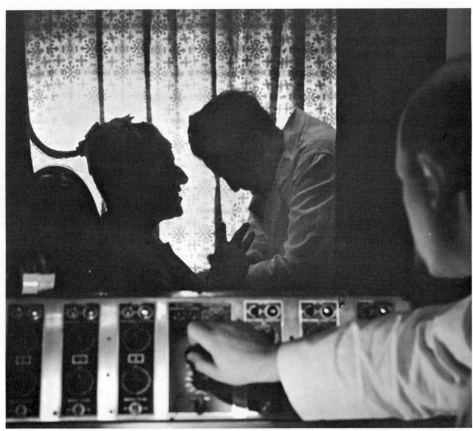

A man undergoing electrical stimulation of the brain. (JOHN LOENGARD LIFE MAGAZINE © TIME INC.)

Section II
Physiological Correlates
of Behavior

Consider the Scotland Yard inspector who knows a crime has been committed and is charged with the responsibility of ferreting out the guilty culprit from a roomful of suspects. The task confronting our Officer of the Peace is similar in many respects to that facing the physiological psychologist. The physiological psychologist knows that all behavior has a physiological basis—that physiological mechanisms underlie the actions of the organism. He is given the job of discovering which physiological event is responsible ("guilty") for a given unit of behavior. Put another way, the physiological psychologist tries to establish the physiological agent responsible for a behavioral act from a bodyful of suspects!

Uncovering the physiological mechanisms that underlie behavior is no easy task, but it is a fascinating one. In his work the physiological psychologist often finds himself rubbing shoulders with physiologists, medical doctors, biologists, pharmacologists, chemists, and zoologists. His range of problems is as wide as his circle of colleagues. To mention a few: drugs and memory; brain function and behavior; physiology of the senses; control of emotion, hunger, thirst, and sexual activity; behavioral correlates of bodily malfunction; and the biochemical basis of learning.

In the following section a few examples of contemporary physiological research are presented. In the first article Caggiula and Hoebel describe how rats exhibit sex and sex-related behaviors when electrically and chemically stimulated in the "copulatory reward site" of their brain. This is followed by Heath's study of electrical stimulation of the brain of man. A third selection by a team of investigators at the University of California centers on the attempt to identify, through research, what changes occur in the brain through experience. The findings from the investigation provide

71

us with important insights into the chemical and anatomical bases of learning. The final article in this section deals with the factors that influence eating behavior in man. The results of the research should be of interest (and practical application) to every person who has ever faced the terror of weight watching!

Introduction to
Caggiula and Hoebel Article

Suppose you wondered what would happen if you electrically stimulated the brain of a rat. To find out you would place an electrode deep inside the rodent's head and "turn on the juice" whenever the animal approached a designated spot on a large grid. How do you think the rat would respond? Would it stay clear of the area where the intercranial shock had been delivered (indicating the stimulation had been aversive) or would it approach the locale again (signifying the electric jolt had been rewarding)?

In the early 1950s James Olds answered that question and in so doing initiated an era of brain stimulation research that is still going strong today. What he found (in an experiment similar to the "hypothetical" example above) was that his experimental subjects seemed to "get a charge" out of the electricity (quite a shocking finding!). That is, they approached the area where they had received the electrical stimulation and centered their activities around that spot. To further clarify his rather unexpected findings Olds conducted a series of experiments (Olds, 1955, 1958) the results of which pointed to a series of "pleasure" and "pain" "centers" in the rat's brain.* When the rat was electrically stimulated in a "pleasure center" of its brain it performed acts that would reproduce such stimulation. Conversely, when the shock was administered to a "pain center" of the rat's brain it would take actions to avoid being stimulated further. In the years since Old's pioneer work the effects of brain stimulation found in rats have been observed in many other lower animals as well (Olds, 1969).

The most impressive aspect of brain stimulation is the fact that animals lower on the phylogenetic scale (such as monkeys, cats, rats) display rigid,

---

* Today some investigators choose to call these "centers" brain "areas" to emphasize they are not as localized as was once believed.

stimulus-bound behavior in the face of such stimulation. When one witnesses an animal under the influence of brain stimulation he cannot help but be awed by how the organism's behavior can be turned "on" and "off" at the experimenter's will. Another impressive aspect of brain stimulation is what it can get an animal to do or not to do. For example, brain stimulation has been used to stop an onrushing bull during a bullfight; make loving mother monkeys savagely attack their offspring; make male animals act like females; and cause rats to press a lever up to 7000 times an hour to get an intercranial electrical jolt!

As research has evolved, more and more behaviors of more and more animals under brain stimulation have been observed and reported. One of the most interesting and startling of these reports come from Anthony Caggiula and Bartley Hoebel. In their study the sexual behavior of male rats was controlled by electrical and chemical stimulation of the brain. When stimulated in their "copulatory reward site" male animals would do such things as copulate repeatedly with available females; perform a door-opening task to get to a receptive female; and even "self-stimulate" to the point of orgasm. Such is the power of brain stimulation when practiced on lower animals.

REFERENCES

Olds, J. Physiological mechanisms of reward. *Nebraska Symposium on Motivation,* 1955, **3,** 73–138.

Olds, J. Self-stimulation of the brain. *Science,* 1958, **127,** 315–324.

Olds, J. The central nervous system and the reinforcement of behavior. *American Psychologist,* 1969, **24,** 114–132.

5

"Copulation-Reward Site" in the Posterior Hypothalamus

Anthony Caggiula and Bartley Hoebel

Posterior hypothalamic self-stimulation of male rats, in which monopolar, platinum electrodes had been bilaterally implanted, increased after systemic injection of testosterone. Constant stimulation to the same site elicited immediate copulation with estrous female rats. During constant stimulation, males would press a bar to open a door for access to females. Even after ejaculation, males continued to open the door and to display sexual activity until stimulation terminated. Posterior hypothalamic stimulation is like normal sexual stimulation; it is rewarding, the reward varies with the amount of the sex hormone, and it elicits motivated copulation.

The reward of self-stimulation of the brain has been linked to normal appetitive behavior, particularly feeding. Self-stimulation of the lateral hypothalamus increases during food deprivation (1) and decreases after food intake (2). Stimulation of the same site elicits voracious feeding (1, 2). Even if a learned response is required to obtain food, the rat responds as soon as stimulation begins (3). Thus lateral hypothalamic stimulation not only elicits rewards that vary with food intake but it also motivates feeding.

On the basis of the discovery of a "feeding-reward site," we decided to look for a "copulation-reward site." Olds (4) found that in some areas of the brain self-stimulation decreased after castration and increased after testosterone replacement. Herberg (5) confirmed this for a specific site in the posterior hypothalamus where self-stimulation elicited ejaculation. If somewhere in this posterior region self-stimulation is related to mating, in the same

SOURCE. *Science*, September 9, 1966, **153**, 1284–1285. Copyright 1966, by the American Association for the Advancement of Science.

way that lateral hypothalamic self-stimulation is related to feeding, stimulation should motivate an animal to copulate. We have explored this possibility and now report the results.

The subjects were ten sexually experienced male Sherman rats with monopolar, platinum electrodes (0.023 cm outside diameter) bilaterally implanted in the posterior hypothalamus (6). The implants were made perpendicular to the skull, 4.5 mm anterior to the intra-aural line, 1.2 to 1.5 mm lateral to the midline, and 8.5 mm below the surface of the cortex.

Females for mating tests were brought into constant behavioral estrus by subcutaneous placement of two 26-gauge stainless steel tubes coated at the tips with estradiol (7).

The electrical stimulus was a train of 100 cy/sec, monophasic, negative, 0.1-millisecond square pulses passed through an isolation transformer to exclude direct current and produce a biphasic wave form. The intensities used were between 0.1 and 0.2 ma. All tests were conducted in a 46-cm, circular, opaque, chamber with a glass floor and an underview mirror. For self-stimulation, a lever was mounted on the chamber wall. Each time this lever was pressed it triggered a 0.5-second train of stimulation.

Because rats are most likely to be sexually active at night, dim red illumination was used for observation of behavior during the dark period of a reverse day-night cycle. Brain stimulation tests began a week after the implantation of electrodes. The male rat to be tested was allowed 30 minutes to become acclimated to the observation cage before a female rat was placed in the cage. The male then received continuous brain stimulation in 3-minute periods alternated with 3-minute periods when there was no stimulation. Mounts, intromissions, and ejaculations were recorded on an event recorder.

In these tests copulation became stimulus-bound, that is, the males copulated repeatedly when stimulation was on but seldom when it was off. At the end of one test session the male was resting far from the female while the stimulus was left off for 12 minutes; when the stimulus was again turned on, the male began copulating within 10 seconds (Fig. 1). Even after

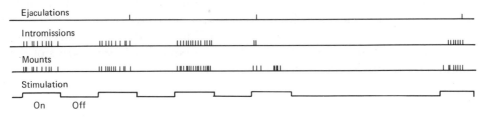

FIG. 1. Copulation during brain stimulation. Electrical stimulation in a posterior hypothalamic self-stimulation site elicits immediate sexual behavior which persists even after ejaculation. Each "on" period lasts 3 minutes.

	Mounts	Intromissions	Ejaculations
Stim. on	30 (13–61)	18 (7–44)	2 (1–4)
Stim. off	1 (0–5)	1 (0–3)	0 (0)

FIG. 2. Control of copulatory behavior by electrical stimulation of the posterior hypothalamus of male rats. Mean values are based on the last 30 minutes of one test session for each of ten rats. Sessions lasted 30 to 75 minutes. Range of individual scores are in parentheses.

ejaculating, the male remained sexually excited, often sniffing, nudging, and, in several instances, mounting the female until stimulation terminated (Fig. 1). The other rats behaved similarly (see Fig. 2).

Unlike copulation elicited from the anterior hypothalamus (8), the over-all frequency of copulation during stimulation was not unusually high. The striking fact is the extent to which stimulation controls copulatory behavior (Figs. 1 and 2). At the beginning of a test session the animals sometimes copulated whether stimulated or not, but after one or two stimulation periods they rarely copulated unless stimulated.

Stimulus-bound copulation was a persistent phenomenon. In one test session lasting 66 minutes (eleven 3-minute periods of stimulation), 115 mounts, 82 intromissions, and 6 ejaculations were recorded. During the eleven 3-minute periods, without stimulation there were only 5 mounts, 5 intromissions, and no ejaculations. Week after week the effect was reproducible in all ten animals. In one animal, stimulus-bound copulation occurred on each of 7 test days over a 4-month period.

Stimulation of the posterior hypothalamus induced copulation, not feeding. Four rats were tested with food, and then with both food and a female rat. Stimulation never elicited eating. If a male in the process of eating was stimulated, he stopped eating and mounted the female.

Males were highly motivated to mate during stimulation. This was demonstrated in two animals. A plexiglass partition with a closed door, separated the male and the female. The door opened when the male pressed a small bar protruding from the partition. If the male did not seek the female and did not copulate within 10 seconds, he was again confined to his side of the chamber. If he did enter the female's compartment and did copulate, he was allowed one intromission before he was returned to his side of the chamber. One rat had prior training in opening the door; the other was trained during stimulation. In both cases, the animals pressed the bar significantly more often when the stimulus was on than when it was off. The animal without prior training pressed the bar to open the door

29 times during nine stimulation periods, and only one time during alternate nonstimulation periods. He copulated within 10 seconds after 14 of the 29 bar presses. The fact that stimulation motivated animals to emit a learned response arbitrarily required by the experimenter shows that stimulus-bound copulation was neither mere indiscriminate activation nor rigid reflex. Stimulation elicited copulation with motivation characteristic of normal sexual behavior.

The same stimulation intensities which elicited copulation were also suitable for self-stimulation. Response rates in daily 10-minute sessions were 50 to 75 presses per minute.

Self-stimulation was sometimes accompanied by a penile discharge containing motile sperm. Five of the ten rats ejected seminal plugs. This usually occurred several seconds after deactivation of the self-stimulation lever. One of the rats exhibited ejaculation on ten different occasions. Penile erection was usually absent during self-stimulation, and neither pelvic thrusts nor the customary post-ejaculatory posture ever occurred in the absence of a female.

Self-stimulation varied positively with the androgen level. To date, two of the rats have been given daily injections of 50 μg of testosterone propionate in oil for 7 days. The self-stimulation rate during the 7 days of injection was compared with the 7-day base line immediately preceding the injections. Such comparison showed that self-stimulation increased 17 percent for one rat and 37 percent for the other rat. After 1 month of self-stimulation tests with no androgen injections (to reestablish the baseline rate) the test was repeated on the first animal. Self-stimulation again increased significantly—this time 23 percent. All increases were statistically significant ($P < .01$). This is similar to Herberg's result (5).

Histological examination of the brains revealed that the electrode tips had been in the medial forebrain bundle, just lateral to the fornix at the level of the premammillary nuclei in the posterior hypothalamus.

Thus, self-stimulation in the posterior hypothalamus is related to motivated sexual behavior. Electrical stimulation, like sexual stimulation, heightens sexual excitability to the point of copulation and orgasm and reinforces behavior leading to the stimulus. Therefore neural activity in the posterior hypothalamus may be normally involved in generating the excitement and reward of copulation.

REFERENCES AND NOTES
1. D. L. Margules and J. Olds, *Science* 135, 374 (1962).
2. B. G. Hoebel and P. Teitelbaum, *ibid.*, p. 375.
3. E. E. Coons, M. Levak, N. E. Miller, *ibid.* 150, 1320 (1965).

4. J. Olds, *J. Comp. Physiol. Psychol.* **51**, 320 (1958).
5. L. J. Herberg, *ibid.* **56**, 679 (1963).
6. B. G. Hoebel, *Electroencephalogr. Clin. Neurophysiol.* **16**, 399 (1964).
7. R. D. Lisk, private communication.
8. E. Vaughan and A. E. Fisher, *Science* **137**, 758 (1962).
9. Supported by NIH grant MH-08493.

Introduction to Heath Article

In the preceding article by Caggiula and Hoebel the impact of brain stimulation on animal behavior was described. By now you might be wondering if any brain stimulation research has been conducted with human subjects. The answer is yes—but not as often (e.g., Bishop, 1964; Delgado & Hamlin, 1960; Sem-Jacobson & Torkildsen, 1960).

The incidence of brain stimulation in man has, surprisingly, a relatively long history—being used for decades in medicine to treat pain and diagnose illness. But the use of brain stimulation to study behaviors and answer questions similar to those examined and asked by Olds and other physiological psychologists is a relatively new phenomenon. One of these newer researches is Heath's *Electrical Self-Stimulation of the Brain in Man*.

As you read the Heath article you might be struck by one major difference between human and rat behavior under the influence of brain stimulation. Unlike lower animals who display rigid, stimulus-bound behavior in the face of brain stimulation, man seems quite able to control his own actions while undergoing such treatment. Yet, just because man is less controlled by brain stimulation than the animals does not imply that such efforts with humans is a waste of time. Already brain stimulation has some value as a therapeutic device (as the Heath paper demonstrates) and it also helps us understand the complexities of human brain function.

REFERENCES
Bishop, M. Attempted control of operant behavior in man with intracranial self-stimulation. In R. Heath (ed.), *The role of pleasure in behavior*. New York: Hoeber, 1964.

Delgado, J., & Hamlin, H. In E. Ramey & D. O'Doherty (eds.), *Electrical studies on the unanesthetized brain*. New York: Hoeber, 1960.

Sem-Jacobson, C., & Torkildsen, A. In E. Ramey & D. O'Doherty (eds.), *Electrical studies on the unanesthetized brain*. New York: Hoeber, 1960.

6

Electrical Self-Stimulation of the Brain in Man

Robert G. Heath

At a symposium concerning depth electrode studies in animals and man in New Orleans in 1952, the Tulane investigators described (and illustrated with films of patients treated between 1950–1952) a pleasurable response with stimulation of specific regions of the brain (5). The pleasurable response to stimulation of some deep regions of the brain, first observed with electrical stimulation to the septal region, has proved a consistent finding in continuing studies (6, 7, 12). Since 1952 we have reported various aspects of the phenomenon including demonstration of relief of physical pain by stimulation to this pleasure-yielding area of the brain (11).

With the introduction of ingenious techniques for self-stimulation by Olds (14–17), the need to depend largely upon verbal reports of the subjective response was eliminated and it was possible to study apparent reward and aversive areas of the brain in animals. Subjective data, of course, were lacking in the animal studies.

During the last few years the Tulane researchers have incorporated and modified some animal intracranial self-stimulation (ICSS) methods for human investigation, permitting extension of the pleasurable phenomenon studies in man. An ICSS study recently published (3) was designed to explore human behavior under strict laboratory conditions of the type characteristically employed in animal studies. A study has also been described in

SOURCE. *The American Journal of Psychiatry*, 1963, **120**, 571–577. Copyright 1963, The American Psychiatric Association. Read at the 119th annual meeting of The American Psychiatric Association, St. Louis, Mo., May 6–10, 1963. At the time of presentation, a 16 mm. sound film was shown demonstrating the effects of stimulation by the transistorized portable self-stimulator to a number of specific regions of the brain in Patients No. B-7 and No. B-10. The two subjects were interviewed to obtain subjective descriptions of the effects of stimulation.

Supported by funds provided by the Louisiana State Department of Hospitals.

which a patient was equipped with a small portable self-stimulator with 3 buttons, permitting delivery of electrical stimuli of fixed parameters to any one of 3 brain sites (8). The primary motivation in these studies, as in all depth electrode studies in man at Tulane, was therapeutic (5).

Study of reward areas in the brain of man, including use of induced reward for therapeutic purposes, is extensive and complex. This presentation will focus on a description of the subjective responses of two patients treated by the self-stimulation technique. Their reports provide information concerning the reasons for repeated ICSS—information that is not available from animal studies.

MATERIAL AND METHODS

Two patients were used in the study. Patient No. B-7, age 28, with a diagnosis of narcolepsy and cataplexy, had failed to respond to conventional treatments. He had electrodes implanted by the method developed in our laboratory (1, 2) into 14 predetermined brain regions and fixed to remain in exact position for prolonged study. These small silver ball electrodes (most of those used in this study consisted of 3 leads each separated by 2 mm.) were placed into the right anterior and posterior septal region, left anterior and posterior septal region, right anterior hypothalamus, mid-line mesencephalic tegmentum, left anterior and posterior hippocampus, left anterior and posterior caudate nucleus and over the right frontal cortex, right and left mid-temporal cortex, and left anterior temporal cortex.

Patient No. B-10, age 25, a psychomotor epileptic with episodic brief periods of impulsive behavior uncontrolled with the usual treatments, had 51 leads implanted into 17 brain sites: left and right centromedian, left caudate nucleus, right ventricle, left and right hippocampus, mid-line mesencephalic tegmentum, left and right septal region, left amygdaloid nucleus, left paraolfactory area, and over the left and right temporal cortex, left and right occipital cortex, and left and right frontal cortex. Twenty-four leads were of stainless steel 0.003 inch in diameter coated with Teflon; 27 were the small silver ball type electrode.[1]

ICSS studies were not initiated until a minimal period of 6 months following operation, assuring elimination of any variables introduced by operative trauma, e.g., edema, anesthetic effects.

Stimuli were delivered from a specially constructed transistorized self-contained unit [2] which was worn on the patient's belt. The unit generated a pre-set train of bi-directional stimulus pulses each time that one of the

[1] Stainless steel array constructed of No. 316 stainless steel wire, 0.003 inch in diameter, with quad Teflon-coated leads and 6 contact points 2 mm. apart. Electrode designed and fabricated by Henry A. Schryver, 110 W. Packard St., Fort Wayne, Indiana.
[2] Technical Associates of New Orleans.

3 control buttons was depressed. Each button directed the pulse train to a different electrode pair permitting the operator a possible selection of cerebral sites. A mechanical counter was coupled to each button to record the total number of stimuli directed toward a given area. An internal timer limited each pulse train to 0.5 second for each depression, thereby prohibiting the operator from obtaining continuous stimuli merely by keeping the button depressed. An additional feature of the unit provided 3 separate level potentiometers to give wide-range control of stimuli for each electrode pair.

Circuit Details

To minimize the effects of dc polarization, a bi-directional pulse was chosen. . . . This pulse permitted restoration of the dc level to zero after each 1.0 millisecond stimulus and maintenance at zero during the entire dead time of 10 milliseconds.

A silicon unijunction timing circuit generated the basic 10 millisecond interval. The output from the unijunction transistor was gated off after 0.5 second operation by a diode gate driven from an R-G charging circuit. When the diode gate was open, the unijunction transistor generator drove two complementary one-shot multivibrators operated serially, permitting the falling edge of the first to trigger the second. The two multivibrators had equal periods of 0.5 millisecond. The multivibrator timing circuits saturated complementary output transistors which fed voltage to the load through isolating capacitors.

The stimuli were mono-polar; the indifference pole was a plate strapped to the subject's leg.

Studies conducted on the two patients differed somewhat because of therapeutic considerations. For studies with Patient No. B-7, the narcoleptic, the 3 buttons of the unit were attached to electrodes in the septal region, hippocampus, and mesencephalic tegmentum, and he was free to stimulate any of these sites as he chose. The patient wore the stimulator for a period of 17 weeks. Before he was equipped with the unit, baseline data concerning the time he spent sleeping during an arbitrary 6-hour period each day were charted by specified ward personnel. These data were later compared with sleeping time following attachment of the unit. This study was basically therapeutic (treatment results will be presented elsewhere) but from the experimental design we were able to obtain considerable subjective data regarding the effects of ICSS to several regions of the brain.

With Patient No. B-10, the psychomotor epileptic, a number of different experimental designs were employed to investigate the effects of ICSS. For illustrative purposes, the results of one study are presented herein as background for a description of the subjective responses. In the first part of the study a total of 17 different cerebral regions were stimulated. They were selected at random, the unit design permitting 3 sites to be hooked up at any one time. Each electrode was made available to the patient for stimulation for a minimal period of 2 hours. Various combinations of 3 sites were arranged. The purpose in making stimulation to different combinations of sites available was based on well-documented animal studies which indicate that rate of stimulation at a given site will vary somewhat depending upon the site stimulated beforehand. Data are presented in terms of the hourly stimulation to a given site as recorded with the automatic counter of the unit. Additionally, the same site of the brain was attached to different buttons to determine if the patient would relate a response to a given button. He reported, however, a consistent response to stimulation of a given electrode regardless of the button to which it was attached.

In the second part of the study the 3 sites of the brain which the subject had elected to stimulate most frequently during the first part of the study were compared over a 6-hour period.

RESULTS

Patient No. B-7

After randomly exploring the effects of stimulation with presses of each of the 3 buttons, Patient No. B-7 almost exclusively pressed the septal button. . . .

Stimulation to the mesencephalic tegmentum resulted in a prompt alerting, but was quite aversive. The patient, complaining of intense discomfort and looking fearful, requested that the stimulus not be repeated. To make certain that the region was not stimulated, he ingeniously modified a hair pin to fit under the button which directed a pulse train to the mesencephalic tegmentum so it could not be depressed.

Hippocampal stimulation was mildly rewarding.

Stimulation to the septal region was the most rewarding of the stimulations and, additionally, it alerted the patient, thereby combatting the narcolepsy. By virtue of his ability to control symptoms with the stimulator, he was employed part-time, while wearing the unit, as an entertainer in a night club.

The patient's narcolepsy was severe. He would move from an alert state into a deep sleep in the matter of a second. Recognizing that button pressing promptly awakened him, fellow patients and friends occasionally resorted to pushing the button if he fell asleep so rapidly that he was unable to stimulate himself.

The patient, in explaining why he pressed the septal button with such frequency, stated that the feeling was "good"; it was as if he were building up to a sexual orgasm. He reported that he was unable to achieve the orgastic end point, however, explaining that his frequent, sometimes frantic, pushing of the button was an attempt to reach the end point. This futile effort was frustrating at times and described by him on these occasions as a "nervous feeling."

Patient No. B-10

Studies conducted on the psychomotor epileptic patient were more varied and provided more information concerning subjective responses. The average number of button presses per hour for various regions of the brain is listed in Tables 1 and 2. Regions of the brain are listed in order of the frequency with which they were selectively stimulated by the subject. A summary of the principal subjective feelings is given.

The button most frequently pushed provided a stimulus to the centromedian thalamus. This stimulus did not, however, induce the most pleasurable response; in fact, it induced irritability. The subject reported that he was almost able to recall a memory during this stimulation, but he could not quite grasp it. The frequent self-stimulations were an endeavor to bring this elusive memory into clear focus.

The patient most consistently reported pleasurable feelings with stimulation to two electrodes in the septal region and one in the mesencephalic tegmentum. With the pleasurable response to septal stimuli, he frequently produced associations in the sexual area. Actual content varied considerably, but regardless of his baseline emotional state and the subject under discussion in the room, the stimulation was accompanied by the patient's introduction of a sexual subject, usually with a broad grin. When questioned about this, he would say, "I don't know why that came to mind—I just happened to think of it." The "happy feelings" with mesencephalic stimulation were not accompanied by sexual thoughts.

Patient No. B-10 also described as "good," but somewhat less in pleasurable-yielding quality, stimuli to two sites, the amygdaloid nucleus and the

TABLE 1
ICSS in Man
Reward (?) Sites

Region Stimulated	Average/ Hour	Subjective Response
L. Centromedian	488.8	Partial memory recall; anger and frustration
R. P. Septal	394.9	"Feel great"; sexual thoughts; elimination of "bad" thoughts
L. Caudate	373.0	Cool taste; "like it OK"
Mesenceph. Teg.	280.0	"Drunk feeling"; "happy button"; elimination of "bad" thoughts
A. Amygdala	257.9	Indifferent feeling; somewhat pleasant, but feeling not intense
P. Amygdala	224.0	Moderately rewarding; increase of current requested

TABLE 2
ICSS in Man
Aversive Sites

Region Stimulated	Average/Hour	Subjective Response
R. Hippocampus	1.77	Strongly aversive; "feel sick all over"
L. Paraolfactory	0.36	Moderately aversive
R. Parietal Cortex	0.50	
R. Frontal Cortex	0.00	
R. Occipital Cortex	0.00	No significant subjective response
R. Temporal Cortex	0.00	

caudate nucleus. Several other septal electrodes and one other electrode in the amygdaloid nucleus were stimulated a moderate number of times. His reports concerning these stimulations suggested a lesser magnitude of pleasurable response, but definitely not an unpleasant feeling.

Minimal positive response was obtained with stimulation of several other septal electrodes. The most aversive response ("sick feeling") was obtained with stimulation to one hippocampal electrode and one lead in the paraolfactory area. With stimulation of the latter lead, he complained of light flashes, apparently due to spread to the optic nerve, and of general discomfort.

No consistent changes, either significantly aversive or rewarding, were displayed with stimulation to any of 12 cortical leads dispersed widely over the cortical surface, including the frontal, temporal, occipital, and parietal lobes.

In the second part of the study the 3 electrodes which were stimulated most during the first phase of the study were attached to the 3 buttons. The sites of these electrodes were the centromedian thalamus, the septal region, and the mesencephalic tegmentum. Data indicated that the combination of sites available influenced the number of times that a given region of the brain was stimulated. . . . When coupled with the subjective reports, the data also suggested that the over-all state of the subject at a given moment was an influential determinant for selecting the region to be stimulated. For example, the centromedian thalamus was stimulated up to 1100 times per hour when in combination with relatively inactive sites of stimulation and only a maximum of 290 times per hour when in combination with two other highly rewarding areas, the septal region and the mesencephalic tegmentum.

The patient noted that the frustration and anger resulting from stimulation of the centromedian thalamus was alleviated with stimulation to the septal region and to the mesencephalic tegmentum. . . . The patient during the first two hours stimulated the centromedian thalamus most frequently.

This was associated with discomfort in his attempt to recapture a fleeting memory. He reported that stimulation of the other areas relieved this discomfort. There was little activity during the next two hours. Toward the end of the study, in the 5th and 6th hours, stimulation to septal and tegmental leads increased. During the 5th hour, the mesencephalic tegmentum was stimulated most frequently; during the 6th hour, the septal lead was stimulated most frequently. The patient evolved a pattern coupling the stimulus to the centromedian thalamus (which stirred his curiosity concerning the memory) with stimuli to the more pleasurable areas to lessen the feeling of frustration.[3]

DISCUSSION

Changes in parameters of stimuli to a given region of the brain, including current intensity, wave form, pulse width, and frequency, in many instances altered the patients' responses. This has similarly been reported with animal ICSS.

Information acquired from the patients' reporting of their reasons for button pressing indicates that all ICSS is not solely for pleasure. The highest rate of button pressing occurred with Patient No. B-7 when he was somewhat frustrated in his pleasurable pursuit and as he attempted to achieve an orgastic end point. In Patient No. B-10 the highest rate of button pressing also occurred with frustration, but of a different type, evolving with attempts to bring into focus a vague memory that ICSS had evoked. The subject's emotional state in this instance built into strong anger. It was interesting that the patient would button press to stimulate the region within the centromedian thalamus for a prolonged period, but at a slower rate when buttons providing more pleasurable septal and tegmental stimulation were also available. Depression of the septal button, with resultant pleasant feelings, alleviated the painful emergency state, according to the subject's report, and thereby provided him comfort to pursue his quest for the fleeting memory.

[3] When the paper was presented, it was here that the 16 mm. sound film was shown. Clinical effects of stimulation to a variety of deep regions of the brain, as summarized herein, were demonstrated.

In the last sequence of the film, Patient No. B-10, the psychomotor epileptic, was stimulated in the septal region during a period when he was exhibiting agitated, violent psychotic behavior. The stimulus was introduced without his knowledge. Almost instantly his behavioral state changed from one of disorganization, rage, and persecution to one of happiness and mild euphoria. He described the beginning of a sexual motive state. He was unable, when questioned directly, to explain the sudden shift in his feelings and thoughts. This sequence of film was presented to demonstrate a phenomenon which appears to be consistent and which has been repeated in a large number of patients in our laboratories. This phenomenon is the ability to obliterate immediately painful emergency emotional feelings in a human subject through introduction of a pleasurable state by physical or chemical techniques.

With septal stimulation in other patients, as well as the two subjects discussed here, a sexual motive state has frequently been induced in association with the pleasurable response. This sexual state has not developed in association with pleasurable feelings during stimulation to other regions. The consistent observation of a relation between sexual feelings and stimulation to the septal region has been described by MacLean in monkey experiments (13). These reports, in part, answer questions raised by Galambos regarding ICSS when he asked, "What motivates these animals to do such unheard-of-things? Is it some exquisite pleasure they receive, as several students of the problem staunchly contend, or the feeling of utter and complete well-being as others claim?" (4).

The ICSS techniques represent one of several methodologies that the Tulane researchers have used in man to investigate the pleasurable phenomenon associated with certain types of cerebral activity. These studies complement early subcortical electrical stimulation studies (5). The pleasurable response has also been induced in man with introduction of certain chemicals into specific deep brain regions (8–10). It is noteworthy that intense pleasurable responses induced with chemical stimulation of the brain occurred when a high amplitude spindling type of recording was set up in the septal region. . . .

The observation that introduction of a stimulus which induces pleasure immediately eliminates painful emergency states is quite consistent. If our psychodynamic formulations are correct, this basic observation may have widespread implication for the development of therapeutic methods to alter favorably disordered behavior.

SUMMARY

Studies are described of two human patients under treatment with ICSS. Their subjective reports in association with stimulation to reward areas of the brain are presented. The data indicate that patients will stimulate regions of the brain at a high frequency for reasons other than to obtain a pleasurable response. These data extend information obtained from ICSS in animals.

REFERENCES

1. Becker, H. C., et al.: In: Studies in Schizophrenia. Cambridge: Harvard Univ. Press, 1954, p. 565.
2. Becker, H. C., et al.: Electroenceph. Clin. Neurophysiol., 9, 533, 1957.
3. Bishop, M. P., et al.: Science, 140, 394, 1963.
4. Galambos, Robert: Fed. Proc., 20, 603, 1961.
5. Heath, R. G., et al.: Studies in Schizophrenia. Cambridge: Harvard Univ. Press, 1954, pp. 42, 46, 47, 50, 560.

6. Heath, R. G.: Psychosom. Med., **17**, 383, 1955.
7. Heath, R. G.: Confinia Neurol., **18**, 305, 1958.
8. Heath, R. G.: *In* Heath, R. G. (Ed.): Pleasure Integration and Behavior. New York: Hoeber. In press.
9. Heath, R. G., and deBalbian Verster, F.: Am. J. Psychiat., **117**, 980, 1961.
10. Heath, R. G., and Founds, W. L.: Electroenceph. Clin. Neurophysiol., **12**, 930, 1960.
11. Heath, R. G., *et al.: In:* Studies in Schizophrenia. Cambridge: Harvard Univ. Press, 1954, p. 555.
12. Heath, R. G., and Mickle, W. A.: *In* Ramey, R. R., and O'Doherty, D. S. (Eds.): Electrical Studies on the Unanesthetized Brain. New York: Hoeber, 1960.
13. MacLean, P. D., *et al.:* Trans. Am. Neurol. Ass., **84**, 105, 1959.
14. Olds, J.: Physiol. Rev., **42**, 554, 1962.
15. ———: Am. J. Physiol., **199**, 965, 1960.
16. Olds, J., and Milner, P.: J. Comp. Physiol. Psychol., **47**, 419, 1954.
17. Olds, J., and Olds, M. E.: *In* Heath, R. G. (Ed.): Pleasure Integration and Behavior. New York: Hoeber. In press.

Introduction to Bennett et al. Article

Do you ever wonder what is taking place in your brain while you are learning something? Do you suspect that the brain changes as it receives inputs from the outside world? Maybe you believe that the brain increases in size to accommodate new experiences. If so, will Person "A" who has experienced twice as much as Person "B" have a heavier brain? Or possibly you think that chemical changes in the "grey matter" occur when you experience something. If this is the case, will two individuals exposed to different experiences have a different brain chemistry? Certainly *something* has to be taking place in the brain when we learn a task or commit something to memory. The problem is discovering *what*.

"What" changes occur in the brain through experience is a topic that has fascinated philosophers and scientists for centuries. Some of their speculations, as you shall soon see, are not too different from the hypothetical questions that we proposed above. The Bennett et al. paper is important because it moves from the realm of speculation to the scientific arena of experimentally tested hypotheses. In the process the authors obtain some extremely provocative and interesting results which, if they hold up under repeated replications, provide us with important insights into the chemical and anatomical bases of learning.

7

Chemical and Anatomical Plasticity of Brain

Changes in brain through experience demanded by learning theories, are found in experiments with rats.

Edward L. Bennett, Marian C. Diamond, David Krech, and Mark R. Rosenzweig

Here it may be asked whether the organs [of the brain] increase by exercise? This may certainly happen in the brain as well as in the muscles; nay, it seems more than probable, because the blood is carried in greater abundance to the parts which are excited, and nutrition is performed by the blood. In order however, to be able to answer this question positively, we ought to observe the same persons when exercised and when not exercised; or at least observe many persons who are, and many others who are not, exercised during all periods of life. J. G. SPURZHEIM, 1815 (*1*).

I have shown that the brains of domestic rabbits are considerably reduced in bulk, in comparison with those of the wild rabbit or hare; and this may be attributed to their having been closely confined during many generations, so that they have exerted their intellect, instincts, senses and voluntary movements but little. CHARLES DARWIN, 1874 (*2*).

One might suppose that cerebral exercise, since it cannot produce new cells (neural cells do not multiply as do muscular cells) carries further than usual the development of protoplasmic expansions and neural collaterals, forcing the establishment of new and more extended intercortical connections. S. RAMÓN Y CAJAL, 1895 (*3*).

The question is not whether neural events change the status of the tissue in which they occur. The only question which may still be debated is: whether such changes as do undoubtedly occur have the permanence and those other properties which we must attribute to memory-traces. According to our present knowledge the primary effect which nerve impulses produce in ganglionic layers is chemical activity . . . WOLFGANG KÖHLER, 1938 (*4*).

Thus, the results of our original experiment and the replication strongly support these two general conclusions: (a) Manipulating the environment of animals during the 80 days after weaning can alter significantly the weight of the cerebral cortex, the total ChE [acetylcholinesterase] activity of the brain, and the cortical/subcortical distributions of the specific activity of ChE and of tissue weight. (b) Similar but much greater alterations in the brains of the animals can be accomplished by a program of genetic selection carried out over a few generations. M. R. ROSENZWEIG, D. KRECH, E. L. BENNETT, AND M. C. DIAMOND, 1962 (5).

As these quotations show, it has long been speculated that the use of the brain might lead to changes in its size, in the interconnections of its cells, and in its chemical composition. Speculation led to research, and in the last century measurements of the size and weight of brains of men were made in an effort to discover differences that might relate to the degree of intellectual attainment. The first results were encouraging, since men of distinction were usually found to have larger brains than those of inferior intellect. Gradually it was realized, however, that men of different stations in life often differed in health and nutrition as well as in intellect, and that the former factors might affect brain weight. There were also striking exceptions to the general relation—idiots with large brains and geniuses with small brains. The hypothesis of an intrinsic relation between brain size and cerebral exercise or ability was therefore generally abandoned. In its place there were suggestions of more subtle factors involving neural interconnections or chemical changes in the brain. The difficulty of working with such factors discouraged research, and the problem largely reverted to the speculative realm.

In spite of their speculative nature, physical or chemical residuals of experience in the brain continued to be incorporated in most physiological theories of learning. It was generally supposed that changes must occur in the brain in order to account for memory—the registration, the storage, and the retrieval of information. No other hypothesis seemed tenable. So certain were the theoreticians about this that they long ago gave names to these hypothesized changes—they called them "memory traces" or "brain engrams." But, unfortunately, the brain physiologists and anatomists were singularly unsuccessful in finding any solid evidence to justify the certainty of their colleagues. In time an alternative hypothesis was developed—the hypothesis that memory might be stored purely in the form of reverberating neural impulses. However, experiments in the late 1940's and early 1950's indicated that electrical shock could disrupt impulses and that low temperature could drastically reduce their number, but that in both of these cases memories formed before the treatment were still available afterwards. The reverberating impulse hypothesis of long-term memory was therefore abandoned, and the residual change hypothesis was revived. In fact most workers had never left it. Now it became even more important to find some evidence for physiological residuals of experience in the brain. Indeed, evidence for *brain plasticity* would seem to be propaedeutic and essential for the sound development of research on many major questions of brain-behavior relations.

We took up the search for responses of the brain to experience about 6 years ago in the context of a larger project dealing with relations of intelligent behavior in animals to brain chemistry. This project was started in 1953 by the two psychologists and the chemist of our group. It could not have begun nor continued without the interest and material support of Melvin Calvin, who has long espoused interdisciplinary research in chemistry and biological sciences. We have also benefited from the counsel of Everett Dempster on research involving genetic selection for brain chemicals. When we found evidence 4 years ago that experience could modify not only the chemistry but also the anatomy of the brain, a neuroanatomist joined the group in order to investigate both gross and microscopic anatomical changes in detail. What we have to report, therefore, is the result of several years of cooperative interdisciplinary effort on one research problem (*6*).

PREDICTION OF CHEMICAL CHANGE WITH TRAINING

Transmission of neural impulses across the synapses or junctions between neurons requires a chemical step. When the impulse reaches the end of a neuron, it causes the release of a chemical mediator which diffuses across the narrow synaptic gap and combines with receptor sites on the post-synaptic membrane. This alters the post-synaptic potential. If this potential reaches the threshold value, a nerve impulse is initiated. Acetylcholine was the first synaptic transmitter to be studied in the peripheral nervous system, and evidence for its role in the brain has been accumulating steadily. Once acetylcholine is liberated at a synapse, it is rapidly inactivated by the enzyme acetylcholinesterase, so that the synapse is restored to its resting state.

In earlier studies, we had found evidence that the ratio of cerebral acetylcholine concentration to acetylcholinesterase activity is positively related to problem-solving ability in rats (*7*); that is, the higher the ratio, the better the learning scores. We then hypothesized that differential experience would lead to quantitative changes in this synaptic transmitter system. Specifically, we predicted (*8*) that enhanced stimulation and training would increase the rate of liberation of acetylcholine, and that this in turn would lead to an increased rate of synthesis of acetylcholinesterase. We did not at the outset intend to look for changes in the size or weight of the brain, because the idea that "cerebral exercise" can increase the size of the brain had been pretty generally abandoned by the 20th century. Indeed, we had completed several experiments and published an article on effects of training on brain chemistry (8) before further examination of the data suggested that there are anatomical changes as well.

DESIGN OF BEHAVIORAL TREATMENTS

In designing an experimental approach to the problem, we followed the second proposal of Spurzheim by varying the amount of experience given to different groups of subjects. We incorporated several features in the design to reduce random variation among subjects and thus to increase the reliability of any results that we might obtain. All comparisons were made among animals alike in lineage, parentage, sex (male) and age, and differing systematically only in amount of experience. To test the generality of the effects, different lines of rats were employed in several of the experiments.

What type of experience might be important in producing measurable cerebral effects could not be foretold, so we combined both informal and formal training. The control animals are kept under colony conditions, housed three in a cage and exposed to ongoing activity in the room, but with no special treatment; this we term our Social Condition (SC). For enhanced experience, animals are given Environmental Complexity and Training (ECT). The ECT animals are housed in groups of 10 to 12 in large cages provided with "toys."

Every day they are placed for 30 minutes in a square field 90 cm on a side where the pattern of barriers is changed daily. In the home cage and in the open field, the rats play and explore as actively as kittens. After some weeks they are also given one or two trials a day in various standardized mazes for sugar pellet rewards. For the third condition—reduced experience —animals are caged singly in a dimly lit and quiet room where they cannot see or touch another animal (although they can hear and smell them); this is the Isolated Condition (IC). Animals in all three conditions have food and water available at all times, and all are weighed on the average of once in 2 weeks. In most of our experiments, animals are kept under the experimental conditions for 80 days and then are killed for analysis of the brain (9).

REMOVAL OF BRAIN SAMPLES AND CHEMICAL ANALYSIS

At the end of the behavioral phase of an experiment, the animals are delivered to the chemists under code numbers that do not reveal their group membership. The animals are killed by decapitation, members of a litter being taken in immediate succession but with randomized order for treatment within litters. In most experiments the brain is then removed and divided by gross dissection into the following five samples: (a) sample of visual cortex, (b) sample of somesthetic cortex, (c) remaining dorsal cortex, (d) ventral cortex and adjacent tissue including corpus callosum, hippocampus, and amygdala, and (e) the remaining brain or subcortex. The first four samples will be referred to collectively as "total cortex."

The visual and somesthetic samples are demarcated with a miniature plastic T-square, as Fig. 1 shows. In defining the regions from which the visual and somesthetic samples were selected, we were guided by earlier ablation and electrophysiological mapping studies of the rat cortex (*10*). Once these regions are circumscribed, they can be peeled cleanly from the underlying white matter, since in the rat brain there is a clear mechanical gradient between these two kinds of tissue. . . . The absence of folds in rat cortex also facilitates stripping off the cortex. As each sample is removed, it is weighed and then frozen on a block of dry ice. About 10 minutes elapse between decapitation and the weighing of the last sample for a rat. The samples are then stored at −20°C until they can be analyzed chemically.

Until the last few years we analyzed acetylcholinesterase activity by means of an automatic titrator or "*p*H-stat." Recently, we have speeded the analyses without sacrificing reliability by using a colorimetric method adapted from that of Ellman, Courtney, Andres, and Featherstone (*11*).

While reliability of chemical results *within* any experiment is high,

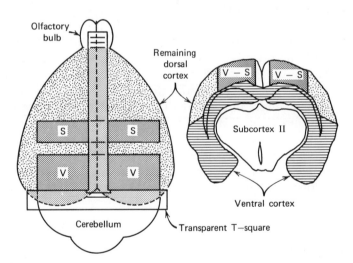

FIG. 1. To the left, the dorsal aspect of the rat brain, showing how samples of the visual cortex (*V*) and of the somesthetic cortex (*S*) are dissected, guided by a small transparent T-square. To the right, a transverse section of the rat brain. Total cortex is made up of four samples: the *V* and *S* sections—telescoped together in this diagram—plus the remaining dorsal cortex, plus the ventral cortex. The rest of the brain—labelled Subcortex II here—includes the olfactory bulbs and the cerebellum. [Reprinted with permission from *J. Comp. Physiol. Psychol.*]

there are some variations of absolute values from one experiment to another. We therefore found it prudent, when investigating the effects of new variables, to include our standard groups (ECT and IC) within each experiment. This has led to the replication of the main conditions in many successive experiments. While the replication is costly, the consistency of the results over many experiments provides great assurance about the existence of the effects which we will now describe.

EFFECTS OF EXPERIENCE ON WEIGHT OF BRAIN TISSUE

In seven successive experiments, we have used animals of the Berkeley S_1 line, putting them into the enriched and impoverished environments at weaning (about 25 days of age) and maintaining them there for about 80 days. Three of these experiments also included Social Control (SC) groups, as we will discuss later.

A highly consistent difference between the brains of littermates given enriched or restricted experience occurs in the weight of the cerebral cortex. The left column of data in Table 1 gives the mean weight of total cortex for each group in each of the seven experiments. It also gives the number of pairs in which the cortical weight of the ECT animal surpassed that of its IC littermate and the amount by which the ECT mean exceeded the IC mean, expressed as a percentage of the IC mean. As can be seen from Table 1, a highly consistent set of results was obtained in experiments performed over a 4-year period, sampling a number of different generations of the S_1 line, and with some experiments falling in each season of the year.

Several points should be noted with regard to this greater growth of cortex among the enriched-experience rats.

1. It does not reflect overall growth of the whole brain. As the right-hand column of Table 1 shows, outside of the cortex there is actually a slight decrease in weight of the brain of enriched-experience animals (1.2 percent, $p < .05$).

2. It does not reflect an increase in body weight. The enriched-experience animals end the experiment weighing about 7 percent *less* than their rather inactive isolated littermates. If we had calculated the results in terms of brain weight per unit of body weight rather than in terms of absolute brain weight, the relative difference between groups would have been much larger.

3. It does not occur equally throughout the cortex. Instead, as Table 2 shows, there is a pronounced regional distribution, the mean difference being greatest in the visual region (6.2 percent, $p < .001$) and least in the somesthetic region of the cortex (2.7 percent, $p < .05$).

TABLE 1

Brain Weights of Littermate S_1, Rats Exposed to Environmental
Complexity and Training (ECT) or Isolation Condition (IC)
from 25 to 105 Days of Age; Seven Replication Experiments

Experiment: Termination Date, N (Pairs)	Statistic	Weight (mg)	
		Total Cortex	Rest of Brain
May 1960, 11	ECT X	663	894
	IC X	626	896
	ECT > IC*	9/11	5/11
	% Diff.†	5.8	−0.1
Oct. 1960, 11	ECT X	682	971
	IC X	645	992
	ECT > IC*	9/11	5/11
	% Diff.†	5.8	−2.1
Dec. 1961, 11	ECT X	702	912
	IC X	672	922
	ECT > IC*	9/11	5/11
	% Diff.†	4.4	−1.1
Mar. 1962, 10	ECT X	705	916
	IC X	673	923
	ECT > IC*	9/10	5/10
	% Diff.†	4.8	−0.7
June 1962, 12	ECT X	740	977
	IC X	708	988
	ECT > IC*	10/12	5/12
	% Diff.†	4.5	−1.1
Dec. 1962, 12	ECT X	710	980
	IC X	688	982
	ECT > IC*	9/12	6/12
	% Diff.†	3.2	−0.2
July 1963, 10	ECT X	694	912
	IC X	667	942
	ECT > IC*	7/10	2/10
	% Diff.†	3.9	−3.2
1960–1963, 77	ECT X	700	939
	IC X	669	951
	ECT > IC*	62/77	33/77
	% Diff.†	4.6	−1.2
	p‡	<.001	<.05

*Number of littermate pairs in which the ECT value exceeds the IC value.
†Percentage by which the ECT mean exceeds the IC mean.
‡Probability values were determined by analyses of variance.

TABLE 2
Weights of Brain Regions from 77 Littermate Pairs of S_1 Rats in ECT and IC Conditions (Seven Experiments Combined)

| | Weight (mg) | | | | | | |
| | Cortex | | | | | | |
Statistic	Visual Sample	Somes-thetic Sample	Remain-ing Dorsal	Ventral	Total	Rest of Brain	Total Brain
ECT X	63.0	48.7	282	306	700	939	1639
IC X	59.3	47.4	268	294	669	951	1620
ECT > IC*	57/77	48/77	57/77	51/77	62/77	33/77	51/77
% Diff.†	6.2	2.7	5.2	4.0	4.6	−1.2	1.2
p‡	<.001	<.05	<.001	<.01	<.001	<.05	<.05

*Number of littermate pairs in which the ECT value exceeds the IC value.
†Percentage by which the ECT mean exceeds the IC mean.
‡Probability values were determined by analyses of variance.

4. It can be measured in other terms than wet weight of tissue, and completely comparable results are obtained. In two further experiments, we sectioned the brains for anatomical measurement instead of consuming them in chemical analysis (12). The depth of the cortex was measured from the pial surface down to the underlying white matter, using an optical micrometer. . . . Subcortical landmarks were used to locate comparable cortical regions to be measured in each animal. In the visual region, the cortex of enriched-experience rats was 6.2 percent thicker than that of their littermates ($p < .001$), while in the somesthetic region the difference was only 3.8 percent thicker ($p < .01$). The anatomists making these measurements did not, of course, know which experimental treatment any animal had received.

5. Finally, the increases in weight and depth of the cortex with experience do not mean that absolute weight of cortex can be used as a correlate of experience or ability. The absolute weight of the cortex is determined not only by experience but also by other factors such as heredity. For example, the Berkeley S_3 line [descendents of Tryon's maze-dull line (13)] has about one-tenth greater weight of cortical tissue than the S_1 line (descendents of Tryon's maze-brights). We have found the S_3 animals to be inferior to the S_1 animals in solving several standardized mazes (7, 14). Within each line, the enriched-experience animals develop significantly heavier cortices than their isolated littermates (15), but the ECT's of the S_1 line nevertheless have lighter cortices than the IC's of the S_3 line. It must be borne in mind that our experiments are all confined to the question, "How does experience transform the brain from what it would have been without that experience?"

EFFECTS OF EXPERIENCE ON ACETYLCHOLINESTERASE ACTIVITY

Activity of acetylcholinesterase (Table 3) was measured in the same seven experiments for which we have just considered the results on brain weight. Total activity of the enzyme was greater for the enriched-experience than for the isolated animals by 2.7 percent in total cortex ($p < .01$) and by 2.1 percent in the rest of the brain ($p < .001$). As was the case with tissue weight, the increase in total activity is greatest in the visual region of the cortex—3.6 percent—and least in the somesthetic region. Note that in each cortical region the relative increase in total acetylcholinesterase activity is less than the increase in tissue weight, as can be seen by comparing Tables 2 and 3. In the rest of the brain, however, the enzymatic activity goes up with enriched experience although weight decreases slightly. (These relations for both cortex and subcortex are shown in Fig. 2.) If enzymatic activity is measured *per unit of tissue weight*, as is often done, the enriched-experience rats have lower values than the restricted animals in the cerebral cortex but higher values in the rest of the brain. The possible significance of this peculiar pattern of changes will be discussed later.

Protein may provide a better base than wet weight of tissue for measuring enzymatic activity. Total protein was determined in experiments 4, 5, and 6 of Table 1 and was found to vary directly with tissue weight, as Fig. 2 shows; therefore the measures of enzymatic activity were quite comparable whichever base was used. If anything, we have found measures *per unit of protein* to be somewhat more stable, so that the statistical signifi-

TABLE 3

Total Acetylcholinesterase Activity of Brain Regions from S_1 Rats in ECT and IC Conditions (Seven Experiments Combined). Activity Is Expressed in Terms of Moles of Acetylcholine Hydrolyzed per Minute Under Our Standard Assay Conditions

	Activity (10^{-8} mole/min)						
	Cortex						
Statistic	Visual Sample	Somes-thetic Sample	Remain-ing Dorsal	Ventral	Total	Rest of Brain	Total Brain
ECT X	38.6	36.5	212	344	631	1825	2455
IC X	37.2	35.8	206	336	614	1787	2401
ECT > IC*	50/76	43/77	48/76	46/76	53/74	50/76	52/73
% Diff.†	3.6	1.8	3.2	2.6	2.7	2.1	2.2
p‡	<.01	N.S.§	<.01	<.10	<.01	<.001	<.001

*Number of littermate pairs in which the ECT value exceeds the IC value.
†Percentage by which the ECT mean exceeds the IC mean.
‡Probability values were determined by analyses of variance.
§N.S., not significant.

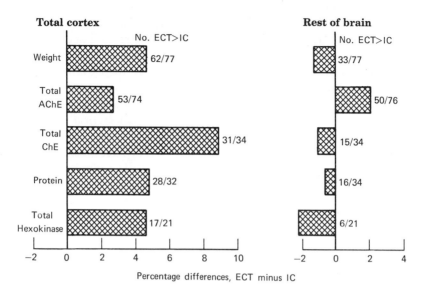

FIG. 2. Relative differences between enriched-experience (ECT) and restricted (IC) groups on several cerebral measures. Each difference is expressed as a percentage of the IC value. For each measure, the number of littermate pairs in which the ECT value exceeded the IC value is also given. In the cortex, the ECT-IC difference in acetylcholinesterase is less than that for tissue weight, the difference in cholinesterase is greater, and the differences in protein and hexokinase are almost identical to the weight difference. In the rest of the brain, only acetylcholinesterase is greater for the enriched-experience than for the restricted animals; all other measures show the ECT animals lower than the IC animals, and by roughly equal percentages. The figure is based entirely upon males of the Berkeley S_1 line.

cance of differences tended to be greater for this measure than for activity per unit of weight.

These differences in enzymatic activity are reliable, as is shown both by statistical analyses and by their consistency from replication to replication. The value for total acetylcholinesterase activity is greater for the ECT than for the IC groups in each of the seven experiments for total cortex (53 of 74 littermate pairs) and in six of the seven experiments for the rest of the brain (50 of 76 pairs). The chemists doing the analysis did not know to which group any animal belonged.

There still remain certain questions of validity: Is it certain that the changes we measure reliably are changes of acetylcholinesterase activity and that they occur in brain tissue rather than in the blood content of the brain? Certain possible interpretations that call the validity of our measures into question have been ruled out by further tests that we have made:

1. Acetylcholine can be split in the brain not only by the specific enzyme acetylcholinesterase, but also by a less specific enzyme, cholinesterase (16). Since our usual measure includes all enzymatic activity that hydrolyzes

acetylcholine, the effects so far reported might be due in whole or in part to changes in cholinesterase rather than acetylcholinesterase activity. In recent experiments with S_1 rats we have explicitly investigated this question. The results demonstrate that with our current methods, which employ acetylthiocholine as the substrate, at least 95 percent of the enzymatic activity measured in the rat brain is due to acetylcholinesterase and at least 90 percent of the changes reported here are due to acetylcholinesterase.

2. Our anatomical investigation has shown that the mean diameter of capillaries is greater in the cortices of enriched-experience animals than in those of their littermates (12). Since red blood cells contain acetylcholinesterase and blood serum contains cholinesterase, this raises the possibility that the increases in activities of the two enzymes in the cortex might only reflect increased blood content. We have investigated this possibility and have found that the activities per unit weight of these enzymes in blood are on the order of one-sixth of the values for cortical tissue. Thus, even if the entire increase in cortical weight were to be attributed to increased blood volume, the enzymes in the blood could not account for the observed changes.

ARE THE EFFECTS DUE TO VARIABLES OTHER THAN ENRICHED EXPERIENCE?

Let us now consider whether it is indeed enriched experience that is responsible for the changes in cerebral weight and acetylcholinesterase activity or whether other aspects of the behavioral conditions may bring about these effects. Three possible alternative explanations have been subjected to experimental tests:

1. Since the animals in the condition of environmental complexity and training receive more handling and are more active than the animals in isolation, can these components alone produce cerebral effects similar to those we have described?

2. May the differences between the groups be attributed chiefly to the isolation to which the restricted animals are subjected?

3. May the cerebral differences be due simply to alterations induced in the rate of early development by differential experience?

These questions will be taken up in turn in the next three sections.

POSSIBLE CEREBRAL EFFECTS OF HANDLING OR DIFFERENTIAL LOCOMOTION

Since handling has been shown to affect both physiological variables and later learning in the rat, we designed an experiment to look for possible cerebral effects of handling. Twenty-four animals were taken from their cages and handled daily, 12 for 30 days and 12 for 60 days, while littermates were never removed from their cages. This treatment started at weaning in order to provide a control for our previous studies. The results yielded no indication of cerebral changes with handling.

To control for differential locomotion, we ran two experiments in each of which some rats had free access to activity wheels while their littermates did not. No consistent differences were found between the active and inactive groups.

Recently, we ran another experiment in which rats of one group were handled daily and also had free access to activity wheels, while their littermates had neither of these forms of stimulation. Again, 80 days of this differential treatment did not produce significant cerebral differences between the groups. It is clear that neither differential handling, nor locomotion, nor the combination of both treatments can produce the cerebral changes we are considering.

IS ISOLATION STRESS THE CAUSE OF OUR EFFECTS?

Isolation has been reported to be stressful for rats, making them so aggressive that they cannot be handled with bare hands, producing caudal dermatitis, and making them much more susceptible to a toxic agent, isoprenaline (17). It is, therefore, possible that the differences we observed were due primarily to the deleterious effects of isolation stress on the restricted group. We doubt this interpretation for the following two reasons.

First, animals of our lines do not show the obvious signs of isolation stress described above. When isolated for 80 or even 160 days, they can still be picked up with bare hands for their occasional weighings, and they do not develop caudal dermatitis. The adrenals were weighed in some experiments, and those of the isolates were not enlarged. It may be that some strains are stressed severely by isolation while others are not.

Second, evidence comes from the last three of the seven experiments with S_1 rats; in these experiments we also included a colony or Social Control (SC) group in which animals were housed three to a cage. The results permit us to measure the effects of increasing or restricting experience, using the SC condition as a baseline (see Fig. 3). On every measure except weight of subcortex, the ECT group differed significantly from the SC group and differed further from them than did the IC group. Thus the bulk of the effects on cerebral weight and acetylcholinesterase activity is due to enriching rather than to restricting the experience of our colony animals (18). Similar findings for older animals will be reported in the next section.

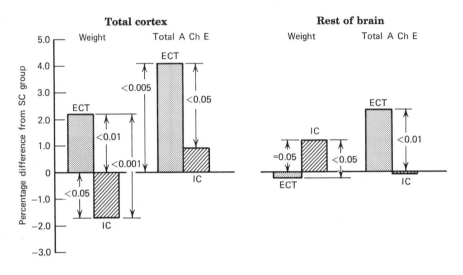

FIG. 3. Cerebral values of enriched-environment (ECT) and isolated (IC) groups, given in relation to the baseline of the standard colony (SC) group. In each case, the difference from the SC value is expressed as a percentage of the SC value. Where differences are significant, the p values are shown by the figures on the arrows. Thus, in weight of total cortex, the ECT animals were 2.2 percent heavier than the SC animals ($p < .01$), and the IC animals were 1.6 percent lighter than SC baseline ($p < .05$). The data were obtained in three experiments involving 34 sets of male triplets of the S_1 line. The rats were in the differential environments from the age of 25 days to the age of 105 days.

ARE CEREBRAL CHANGES CONFINED TO YOUNG ANIMALS?

The experiments described to this point have all been done with animals put into the differential environments at weaning, when they were about 25 days old, and maintained there until the age of about 105 days. During this period, colony animals show an increase of about 30 percent in total brain weight. To test the possibility that the complex environment and training simply accelerated the development of the normally rapidly growing young brain, we ran two successive experiments with older S_1 rats, employing 12 sets of male triplets in each experiment (*19*). One animal in each litter was assigned to the ECT condition, one to the SC condition, and one to the isolation condition. The animals were taken from the colony at about 105 days of age, the age at which the younger animals had been killed. At about 70 days rats are sexually mature, and during the 80-day period following 105 days of age, growth of total brain weight of rats in the colony is only about 6 percent—as contrasted with 30 percent in the preceding 80-day period.

The results for older animals, shown in Fig. 4, are seen to be rather similar to those for younger animals (Fig. 3). In Fig. 4, the ECT animals

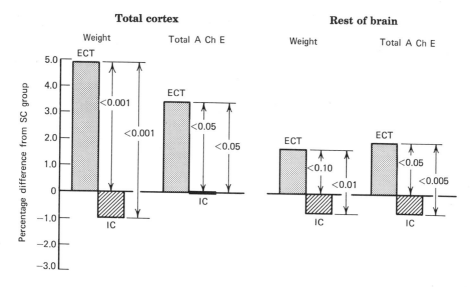

FIG. 4. Comparisons among brain values of littermate rats maintained in the ECT, SC, or IC conditions from 105 to 185 days of age. The same conventions are followed as in Fig. 5. Thus, in weight of total cortex, the ECT animals were 4.9 percent heavier than the SC group ($p < .001$) and the IC animals were 1.0 percent lighter than the SC animals (nonsignificant). The data were obtained in two experiments including 24 sets of male triplets of the S line.

surpass the colony controls significantly on every measure, while the IC animals do not differ significantly from the colony controls on any measure. The regional differentiation of effect among the adults, presented in Tables 4 and 5, is even sharper than that among the young animals (Tables 2 and 3). Among the adults the increases of total acetylcholinesterase approach more nearly the increases of cortical weight than was true among the young animals. At the subcortex, the adult ECT animals gain in tissue weight almost as much as they gain in total acetylcholinesterase activity, whereas the young ECT animals did not gain at all in subcortical weight.

We conclude that the adult brain shows increases in cortical weight and total acetylcholinesterase activity as readily as the young brain. The occurrence of such cerebral effects among adults supports the argument that these effects, rather than being consequences of accelerated early development, are residuals of experience.

EFFECTS ON OTHER CHEMICAL MEASURES

The pattern of change of acetylcholinesterase activity with experience differs from those of the four other chemicals that we have measured so far: cholinesterase, protein, hexokinase, and serotonin.

TABLE 4
Weights of Brain Regions from 24 Littermate Pairs of S_1 Rats in ECT and IC Conditions from 105 to 185 Days of Age (Two Experiments Combined)

| | Weight (mg) | | | | | | |
| | Cortex | | | | | | |
Statistic	Visual Sample	Somes- thetic Sample	Remain- ing Dorsal	Ventral	Total	Rest of Brain	Total Brain
ECT X	72.6	52.9	280	338	744	1019	1763
IC X	65.6	51.7	266	319	702	995	1697
ECT > IC*	20.5/24	12/24	17/24	18/24	22/24	17/24	17/24
% Diff.†	10.7	2.3	5.4	6.0	5.9	2.4	3.9
p‡	<.001	N.S.	<.005	<.001	<.001	<.01	<.001

*Number of littermate pairs in which the ECT value exceeds the IC value.
†Percentage by which the ECT mean exceeds the IC mean.
‡Probability values were determined by Duncan's new multiple range test, since the analysis of variance included the SC group.

Cholinesterase activity was determined in the last three experiments completed with S_1 rats, and the results are given in Table 6. Total cholinesterase activity in total cortex was 8.9 percent greater in the ECT than in the IC groups. As Fig. 3 (based on the same animals) indicates, cortical weight was greater by 3.9 percent and total acetylcholinesterase activity by 3.2 per-

TABLE 5
Total Acetylcholinesterase Activity of Brain Regions from S_1 Rats in ECT and IC Conditions from 105 to 185 Days of Age (Two Experiments Combined). Activity Is Expressed in Moles of Acetylcholine Hydrolyzed per Minute Under Our Standard Assay Conditions

| | Activity (10^{-8} mole/min) | | | | | | |
| | Cortex | | | | | | |
Statistic	Visual Sample	Somes- thetic Sample	Remain- ing Dorsal	Ventral	Total	Rest of Brain	Total Brain
ECT X	42.2	37.1	195	361	635	1828	2463
IC X	38.5	37.0	189	349	614	1779	2392
ECT > IC*	16/24	12/24	15/24	19/24	19/24	19/24	19/24
% Diff.†	9.6	0.3	2.9	3.4	3.4	2.8	3.0
p‡	<.001	N.S.	N.S.	N.S.	<.05	<.005	<.001

*Number of littermate pairs in which the ECT value exceeds the IC value.
†Percentage by which the ECT mean exceeds the IC mean.
‡Probability values were determined by Duncan's new multiple range test.

TABLE 6

Total Cholinesterase Activity of Brain Regions from 34 Sets of
Triplet S_1 Rats in ECT, SC, and IC Conditions from 25 to
105 Days of Age (Three Experiments Combined); Activity
Expressed in Moles of Butyrylthiocholine Hydrolyzed per
Minute Under Our Standard Assay Conditions

| | Activity (10^{-8} mole/min) | | | | | | |
| | Cortex | | | | | | |
Statistic	Visual Sample	Somesthetic Sample	Remaining Dorsal	Ventral	Total	Rest of Brain	Total Brain
ECT X	2.28	1.82	8.34	8.52	21.0	51.4	72.4
SC X	2.23	1.76	8.18	8.42	20.6	51.1	71.7
IC X	2.04	1.65	7.56	8.00	19.3	51.9	71.2
ECT > IC*	26/34	27/34	30/34	23/34	31/34	15/34	20/34
ECT > SC*	18/34	18/34	21/34	18/34	21/34	22/34	21/34
SC > IC*	24/34	23/34	25.5/34	24/34	28/34	13/34	19/34
% Diff., ECT-IC†	11.8	10.3	10.3	6.5	8.9	−1.0	1.7
% Diff., ECT-SC†	2.2	3.4	2.0	1.2	1.8	0.5	0.9
% Diff., SC-IC†	9.3	6.7	8.2	5.2	6.9	−1.5	0.8
p_{ECT-IC}‡	<.001	<.001	<.001	<.005	<.001	N.S.	=.05
p_{ECT-SC}‡	N.S.	<.10	N.S.	N.S.	=.10	N.S.	N.S.
p_{SC-IC}‡	<.01	<.005	<.001	<.05	<.001	N.S.	N.S.

*Number of cases in which the value of the littermate in the first condition exceeded that of the littermate in the second; for example, for the visual sample, the ECT value was greater than the IC value in 26 of the 34 littermate pairs.

†Percentage difference between means in the first and second conditions; for example, for the visual sample, the ECT mean exceeded the IC mean by 11.8 percent.

‡Probability values were determined by Duncan's multiple range test after analyses of variance.

cent. Thus, in terms of activity per unit of weight, cholinesterase increased in the cortex while acetylcholinesterase decreased. In the rest of the brain, however, cholinesterase activity remained essentially unchanged, while acetylcholinesterase activity rose significantly. The different patterns of change for tissue weight and total enzymatic activity are presented graphically in Fig. 2. With total cholinesterase activity, in contrast to the case for acetylcholinesterase activity, the major differences are found between the isolated and colony groups, rather than between the ECT and colony groups (see Table 6).

Certain other chemical measures show changes similar to those of tissue weight. We have already seen that this is true of protein. We have also measured hexokinase activity in experiment 4 of Table 1 and in one other experiment. This enzyme is important in the general metabolism of cells but it does not appear to have a different function in the nervous system from its function in other organs. Hexokinase activity per unit of weight did not alter with differential experience in either cortex or subcortex. A substance that has attracted a good deal of study recently with respect to brain activity is serotonin, which some investigators believe to be a central synaptic-transmitter agent. Gordon T. Pryor in our laboratories has assayed serotonin in S_1 littermates exposed to the ECT or IC conditions. While Pryor found the usual modifications of cortical weight and of acetylcholinesterase and cholinesterase activities, he was unable to find a significant difference between groups in the concentration of serotonin (see *20*).

In summary, when we compare the extreme experiential groups—ECT versus IC—the results show a clearly differentiated pattern among chemicals in the cortex. Acetylcholinesterase changes less with experience than does the weight of the tissue; cholinesterase changes more; and the others— protein, hexokinase, and serotonin—vary with tissue weight. The decrease in acetylcholinesterase activity per unit of cortical weight suggests that the growth of cortex with use involves especially elements low in acetylcholinesterase, such as glia, noncholinergic neurons, and blood vessels and blood volume. (Our finding of increased diameter of cortical blood vessels in ECT animals has already been cited.) The increase in cholinesterase activity per unit of cortical weight may be another indication of the growth of glia cells, since these are relatively high in cholinesterase activity. The lack of change in protein, hexokinase, and serotonin per unit of weight indicates that the additionally formed tissue is normal in its chemical endowment as far as these constituents are concerned.

GENERALITY OF EFFECTS OVER LINES

In addition to the S_1 animals, five other lines have been exposed to our standard ECT and IC conditions, and all lines have shown cerebral effects in the same directions but varying in magnitude (*5, 8*). The S_1 line was one of two lines showing relatively large effects, while the S_3 line was one of those showing relatively small effects. In order to determine the reliability of such genetic differences, we have performed three replications in each of which S_3 groups were run and analyzed simultaneously with S_1 groups. In all three cases, the S_1 animals showed larger effects on all measures than the S_3 animals (*15*). We conclude that while all lines show cerebral plasticity in response to environmental pressure, some lines are more readily modifiable than others.

BLINDNESS AND LIGHT DEPRIVATION

Further evidence of plasticity of the brain comes from experiments in which animals were blinded or totally deprived of light at about 25 days of age. The experiments continued for about 80 days. In two experiments (21) blinded animals, when compared with sighted littermates kept in the same enriched condition, showed a 5 percent loss in weight of the visual cortex and an 8 percent loss in the superior colliculi (midbrain visual reflex centers). Total acetylcholinesterase activity suprisingly increased by 4 percent in the visual cortex of the blinded rats and decreased by 21 percent in the superior colliculi. In three experiments we have found that deprivation of light in sighted animals produced anatomical and chemical effects similar in direction but generally smaller in magnitude than those following blinding (22). The results of these experiments suggest that modifying the amount of experience in one sensory modality can affect rather specifically the brain regions serving that modality. Further results suggest that impairment of one sensory channel leads to greater use of other modalities and thus to greater cerebral development ("compensation") in the corresponding brain areas. Specifically, if blinded or light-deprived animals are raised in a complex environment, the somesthetic area of the cortex shows increases in weight and total acetylcholinesterase activity, when compared with light-stimulated littermates raised in otherwise comparable environments. Results on this effect of blinding were published in 1963 (21). Since then, we have accumulated further confirmatory results on blinding, and Eleanor Saffran in our laboratories has found similar results in experiments with light deprivation.

SELECTIVE BREEDING

Darwin, as we have seen, offered evidence for brain plasticity through comparison of domestic and wild animals. It seems reasonable to suppose that the cumulative effects of generations of selection could produce large changes in the brain. In fact, a program of selection for cortical acetylcholinesterase carried out by T. H. Roderick in our laboratories has demonstrated relatively large changes in brain chemistry after six generations (23). Two foundation stocks (Castle and Dempster) were used for a simultaneous replication, and lines with both high and low acetylcholinesterase activity were selected from each stock. The Roderick Castle high and low lines differed by 34 percent ($p < .0005$) in acetylcholinesterase activity per unit of cortical weight, and the Roderick Dempster lines differed by 25 percent ($p < .0005$). These differences are several times larger than those that we have been able to produce by differential experience.

POSSIBLE FUNCTIONAL SIGNIFICANCE

We believe it essential now to extend our knowledge of cerebral changes with experience in order to determine what significance they may have for physiological theories of learning and memory. Further characterization of the effects is being pursued both chemically and anatomically. Ribonucleic acids, various brain lipids, the synaptic-transmitter acetylcholine, and other possible neural transmitters and their related enzymes will be assayed to determine whether their concentrations or activities are affected by differential experience. Anatomically, we are extending our measures to include ramification of neuronal processes, vascularization, skull volume and dimensions, the sizes of cell bodies and of nuclei of both glia and neurons, and the ratio of glial to neuronal number. We do not want to overlook the possible participation of glial cells in cerebral changes because of our preoccupation with neural cells.

It may seem premature to attempt to assess the possible functional significance of cerebral modifications already observed while we are still attempting to extend our knowledge of them, but neither we nor our readers can avoid making at least a preliminary assessment.

For purposes of discussion let us consider whether our findings are compatible with the hypothesis that long-term memory storage involves the formation of new synaptic connections among neurons. This was Ramón y Cajal's suggestion in the 1890's. It would appear from a number of considerations that the magnitude and nature of the observed effects are such as to accommodate a substantial increase in synaptic connections. Synaptic sites are known to be especially rich in acetylcholinesterase. An increase in number of functional synapses could, however, very well be many times greater than the concurrent increases in acetylcholinesterase activity and tissue weight. Thus, for example, Eayrs (24) reports that the number of interconnections per cortical neuron in the rat increases by about 400 percent between the ages of 15 and 36 days; meanwhile the cortex, according to data from our animals, is increasing in weight by only about 50 percent and in total acetylcholinesterase activity by only about 100 percent. These relations suggest the possibility that a 5-percent change in total acetylcholinesterase activity may reflect a 20-percent change in the number of synapses. A more direct test of this possibility may come from our attempts to measure neuronal ramifications.

Whatever the cerebral residuals of experience are, it is unlikely that they will involve large changes of either gross anatomy or chemistry. It is characteristic of the brain that its variability is extremely low. Weight of the brain varies less from individual to individual of a species than the weight of almost any other organ, and we have found the coefficients of variation for acetylcholinesterase activity to be almost as small as those for weight (25). Brain values can be modified by genetic selection, as we have seen, and drastic treatments such as thyroidectomy or prolonged undernourishment can alter the brain substantially. Short of such interfering factors, the enzymes and the weight of the brain are kept within tight limits. It can therefore be seen that even modifications that seem small in absolute terms may be large in terms of ordinary variability and may have functional consequences.

CONCLUSIONS

Our observations demonstrate that rats given enriched experience develop, in comparison to restricted littermates, greater weight and thickness of cortical tissue and an increase in total acetylcholinesterase activity of the cortex, the gain in weight being relatively larger than the increase in enzymatic activity. In the rest of the brain, acetylcholinesterase activity also increases, even though tissue weight decreases with enriched experience. These changes have been produced consistently in many replications; they have appeared in each line of rats tested to date, and they are found in adult as well as young animals. Control experiments have demonstrated that these changes cannot be attributed primarily to differential handling or locomotor activity, to isolation stress of restricted animals, or to altering the rate of development of the rapidly growing young brain. In a smaller number of experiments we have also found cholinesterase activity to change more than does tissue weight in the cortex but not in the rest of the brain. Protein, hexokinase activity, and serotonin follow closely the changes in weights of brain regions.

We wish to make clear that finding these changes in the brain consequent upon experience does not prove that they have anything to do with storage of memory. The demonstration of such changes merely helps to establish the fact that the brain is responsive to environmental pressure— a fact demanded by physiological theories of learning and memory. The best present conjecture, based both on the research reported here and on that of others, is that when the final story of the role of the brain in learning and memory is written, it will be written in terms of both chemistry and anatomy.

AN INVITATION

Because we believe that our findings demonstrate the feasibility of research on the effects of experience on the brain, and because we believe that such research offers many challenges and a wide field for investigation, we hope to see it taken up in other laboratories. To this purpose we offer qualified investigators animals from our special lines and complete information about our behavioral, biochemical, and anatomical procedures, either through written descriptions or by direct demonstration.

REFERENCES AND NOTES

1. J. G. Spurzheim, *The Physiognomical System of Drs. Gall and Spurzheim* (Baldwin, Cradock, and Joy, London, ed. 2, 1815), pp. 554–555.
2. C. Darwin, *The Descent of Man* (Rand, McNally, Chicago, ed. 2, 1874), p. 53.
3. S. Ramón y Cajal, *Les Nouvelles Idées sur la Structure du Système Nerveux chez l'Homme et chez les Vertébrés,* edition française revue et augmentée par l'auteur, L. Azoulay, trans. (Reinwald, Paris, 1895), p. 78.
4. W. Köhler, *The Place of Value in a World of Facts* (Liveright, New York, 1938), p. 239.
5. M. R. Rosenzweig, D. Krech, E. L. Bennett, M. C. Diamond, *J. Comp. Physiol. Psychol.* **55,** 429 (1962).
6. The collection and analysis of the data reported in this paper required the aid of chemists, anatomists, statisticians, and behavioral technicians. Among the chemists were Hiromi Morimoto, Marie Hebert, and Barbara Olton; among the anatomists, Fay Law and Helen Rhodes; among the statisticians, Carol Saslow, Bea Markowitz, and Peter Varkonyi; among the behavioral technicians, Frank Harris and Carol Poe. Roberta Robbins has been our secretary. The research has been supported by grants from the U. S. Public Health Service, the National Science Foundation, and the Surgeon General's Office. It has also been aided by the U. S. Atomic Energy Commission.
7. M. R. Rosenzweig, D. Krech, E. L. Bennett, *Psychol. Bull.* **57,** 476 (1960).
8. D. Krech, M. R. Rosenzweig, E. L. Bennett, *J. Comp. Physiol. Psychol.* **53,** 509 (1960).
9. The three conditions are described more fully in several of our reports: (*8*) and M. R. Rosenzweig, D. Krech, E. L. Bennett, in *Current Trends in Psychological Theory* (Univ. of Pittsburgh Press, Pittsburgh, 1961), p. 87.
10. I. Krechevsky, *J. Comp. Psychol.* **19,** 425 (1935); C. N. Woolsey and D. H. Le Messurier, *Federation Proc.* **7,** 137 (1948); J. P. Zubek, *J. Comp. Physiol. Psychol.* **44,** 339 (1951).
11. The automatic titrator method is described by M. R. Rosenzweig, D. Krech, E. L. Bennett, in a Ciba Foundation Symposium, *Neurological Basis of Behaviour* (Churchill, London, 1958), p. 337. The colorimetric method was adapted from G. L. Ellman, K. D. Courtney, V. N. Andres, Jr., R. M. Featherstone, *Biochem. Pharmacol.* **7,** 88 (1961).
12. M. C. Diamond, D. Krech, M. R. Rosenzweig, *J. Comp. Neurol.* **123,** 111 (1964).
13. R. C. Tryon, *Yearbook Natl. Soc. Stud. Educ.* **39,** part I, 111 (1940).
14. M. R. Rosenzweig, *Kansas Studies in Educ.* **14,** No. 3, 3 (1964).
15. M. R. Rosenzweig, E. L. Bennett, D. Krech, *Federation Proc.* **23,** 255 (1964), abstr.

16. In the past we and other investigators have called both enzymes "cholinesterase," but we are now employing the common terms recognized in the *Report of the Commission on Enzymes,* International Union of Biochemistry (Pergamon, New York, 1961).

17. T. Balazs, J. B. Murphy, H. C. Grice, *J. Pharm. Pharmacol.* 14, 750 (1962); A. Hatch, T. Balazs, G. S. Wiberg, H. C. Grice, *Science* 142, 507 (1963).

18. While the cerebral differences in weight and acetylcholinesterase activity occurred principally between the ECT and SC groups, these groups were almost identical in terminal body weights. The IC group, which was close to the SC group in cerebral measures, exceeded the SC group by about one-tenth in body weight.

19. M. R. Rosenzweig, E. L. Bennett, D. Krech, *J. Comp. Physiol. Psychol.* 57, 438 (1964).

20. G. T. Pryor, unpublished doctoral dissertation (Univ. of Calif., 1964); *Univ. of Calif. Radiation Lab. Rept. No. 1179* (1964).

21. D. Krech, M. R. Rosenzweig, E. L. Bennett, *Arch. Neurol.* 8, 403 (1963).

22. E. L. Bennett, M. R. Rosenzweig, D. Krech, *Federation Proc.* 23, 384 (1964), abstr.

23. T. H. Roderick, *Genetics* 45, 1123 (1960).

24. J. T. Eayrs, in *Structure and Function of the Cerebral Cortex,* D. B. Tower and J. P. Schadé, Eds. (Elsevier, Amsterdam, 1960), p. 43.

25. E. L. Bennett, M. R. Rosenzweig, D. Krech, H. Karlsson, N. Dye, A. Ohlander, *J. Neurochem.* 3, 144 (1958).

Introduction to Schachter Article

Think for a moment: Why do you eat? Did you reply: "Because I am hungry?" A reasonable response. But *why* were you hungry—because you had been without food for several hours? And *how* did you know you were hungry—because of contractions in your stomach? It turns out that the answers to such questions depend on what you weigh—whether you are overweight.

In an examination of the factors that influence eating behavior in man Stanley Schachter has brought together findings from his own and other investigations to suggest that obese people eat for different reasons than do persons of normal weight. Data from studies of hospital dieters, laboratory subjects, Jews fasting on Yom Kippur, students eating in campus dining halls, and flight crews indicate that individuals of normal weight eat in response to internal, physiological cues (e.g., stomach contractions), and obese persons eat in response to external, nonvisceral cues (e.g., smell, taste, the sight of food). This explains why a person of normal weight will pass up a bakery if he has just eaten a full meal (his viscera is satisfied) although an overweight individual, in the same circumstance, will respond to the external cues of the bakery and go inside.

What Schachter has to say should be of interest to every person who has ever faced the horrors of dieting! One of his statements is particularly enlightening:

These persistent findings that the obese are relatively insensitive to variations in the physiological correlates of food deprivation but highly sensitive to environmental, food-related cues is, perhaps, one key to understanding the notorious long-run ineffectiveness of virtually all attempts to treat obesity. The use of anorexigenic drugs such as amphet-amine or of bulk-producing, nonnutritive substances such as methyl cellulose is based on the premise that such agents dampen the intensity of the physiological symptoms of food deprivation. Probably they do, but these symptoms appear to have little to do with whether or not a fat person eats. Restricted, low-calorie diets should be effective just so long as the obese dieter is able to blind himself to food-relevant cues or so long as he exists in a world barren of such cues.

The Schachter work also serves to remind us that man is not simply the product of his physiology. To understand human behavior we must always consider the physiological correlates of behavior *and* the socio-environmental factors in a person's life. In the study reported below the eating behavior of normal-weight individuals was strongly regulated by the physiological correlates of food deprivation, and the same behavior in obese persons was primarily affected by factors external to the human body. The external environment around man and the internal environment within man—both are important in behavior determination.

8

Obesity and Eating

Internal and external cues differentially affect the eating behavior of obese and normal subjects.

Stanley Schachter

Current conceptions of hunger control mechanisms indicate that food deprivation leads to various peripheral physiological changes such as modification of blood constituents, increase in gastric motility, changes in body temperature, and the like. By means of some still debated mechanism, these changes are detected by a hypothalamic feeding center. Presumably some or all facets of this activated machinery lead the organism to search out and consume food. There appears to be no doubt that peripheral physiological changes and activation of the hypothalamic feeding center are inevitable consequences of food deprivation. On the basis of current knowledge, however, one may ask, when this biological machinery is activated, do we necessarily describe ourselves as hungry, and eat? For most of us raised on the notion that hunger is the most primitive of motives, wired into the animal and unmistakable in its cues, the question may seem farfetched, but there is increasing reason to suspect that there are major individual differences in the extent to which these physiological changes are associated with the desire to eat.

On the clinical level, the analyst Hilde Bruch (*1*) has observed that her obese patients literally do not know when they are physiologically hungry. To account for this observation she suggests that, during childhood, these patients were not taught to discriminate between hunger and such states as fear, anger, and anxiety. If this is so, these people may be labeling almost

SOURCE. *Science*, **150**, pp. 971–979, November 19, 1965. Copyright 1965, by the American for the Advancement of Science. This article is based on a speech delivered at a conference entitled "Biology and Behavior: Neurophysiology and Emotion," held at the Rockefeller University, New York, on December 10, 1965, under the sponsorship of the Russell Sage Foundation and the Rockefeller University.

any state of arousal "hunger," or, alternatively, labeling no internal state "hunger."

If Bruch's speculations are correct, it should be anticipated that the set of physiological symptoms which are considered characteristic of food deprivation are not labeled "hunger" by the obese. In other words the obese literally may not know when they are physiologically hungry. For at least one of the presumed physiological correlates of food deprivation, this does appear to be the case. In an absorbing study, Stunkard (2, 3) has related gastric motility to self-reports of hunger in 37 obese subjects and 37 subjects of normal size. A subject, who had eaten no breakfast, came to the laboratory at 9 A.M.; he swallowed a gastric balloon, and for 4 hours Stunkard continuously recorded gastric motility. Every 15 minutes the subject was asked if he was hungry. He answered "yes" or "no," and that is all there was to the study. We have, then, a record of the extent to which a subject's self-report of hunger corresponds to his gastric motility. The results show (a) that obese and normal subjects do not differ significantly in degree of gastric motility, and (b) that, when the stomach is not contracting, the reports of obese and normal subjects are quite similar, both groups reporting hunger roughly 38 percent of the time. When the stomach is contracting, however, the reports of the two groups differ markedly. For normal subjects, self-report of hunger coincides with gastric motility 71 percent of the time. For the obese, the percentage is only 47.6. Stunkard's work seems to indicate that obese and normal subjects do not refer to the same bodily state when they use the term *hunger*.

EFFECTS OF FOOD DEPRIVATION AND FEAR

If this inference is correct, we should anticipate that, if we were to directly manipulate gastric motility and the other symptoms that we associate with hunger, we would, for normal subjects, be directly manipulating feelings of hunger and eating behavior. For the obese there would be no correspondence between manipulated internal state and eating behavior. To test these expectations, Goldman, Gordon, and I (4) performed an experiment in which bodily state was manipulated by two means—(a) by the obvious technique of manipulating food deprivation, so that some subjects had empty stomachs and others had full stomachs before eating; (b) by manipulating fear, so that some subjects were badly frightened and others were quite calm immediately before eating. Carlson (5) has indicated that fear inhibits gastric motility; Cannon (6) also has demonstrated that fear inhibits motility, and has shown that it leads to the liberation, from the liver, of sugar into the blood. Hypoglycemia and gastric contractions are generally considered the chief peripheral physiological correlates of food deprivation.

Our experiment was conducted under the guise of a study of taste. A subject came to the laboratory in mid-afternoon or evening. He had been called the previous evening and asked not to eat the meal (lunch or dinner) preceding his appointment at the laboratory. The experiment was introduced as a study of "the interdependence of the basic human senses—of the way in which the stimulation of one sense affects another." Specifically, the subject was told that this study would be concerned with "the effects of tactile stimulation on the way things taste."

It was explained that all subjects had been asked not to eat a meal before coming to the laboratory because "in any scientific experiment it is necessary that the subjects be as similar as possible in all relevant ways. As you probably know from your own experience," the experimenter continued, "an important factor in determining how things taste is what you have recently eaten." The introduction over, the experimenter then proceeded as follows.

For the "full stomach" condition he said to the subject, "In order to guarantee that your recent taste experiences are similar to those of other subjects who have taken part in this experiment, we should now like you to eat exactly the same thing they did. Just help yourself to the roast beef sandwiches on the table. Eat as much as you want—till you're full."

For the "empty stomach" condition, the subjects, of course, were not fed.

Next, the subject was seated in front of five bowls of crackers and told, "We want you to taste five different kinds of crackers and tell us how they taste to you." The experimenter then gave the subject a long set of rating scales and said, "We want you to judge each cracker on the dimensions (salty, cheesy, garlicky, and so on) listed on this sheet. Taste as many or as few of the crackers of each type as you want in making your judgments; the important thing is that your ratings be as accurate as possible."

Before permitting the subject to eat, the experimenter continued with the next stage of the experiment—the manipulation of fear.

"As I mentioned," he said, "our primary interest in this experiment is the effect of tactile stimulation on taste. Electric stimulation is the means we use to excite your skin receptors. We use this method in order to carefully control the amount of stimulation you receive."

For the "low fear" condition the subject was told, "For the effects in which we are interested, we need to use only the lowest level of stimulation. At most you will feel a slight tingle. Probably you will feel nothing at all. We are only interested in the effect of very weak stimulation."

For the "high fear" condition the experimenter pointed to a large black console loaded with electrical junk and said, "That machine is the one we will be using. I am afraid that these shocks will be painful. For them to have any effect on your taste sensations, the voltage must be rather high. There will, of course, be no permanent damage. Do you have a heart condition?" A large electrode connected to the console was then attached to each of the subject's ankles, and the experimenter concluded, "The best way for us to test the effect of tactile stimulation is to have you rate the crackers now, before the electric shock, and then rate them again, after the shock, to see what changes in your ratings the shock has made."

The subject then proceeded to taste and rate crackers for 15 minutes, under the impression that this was a taste test; meanwhile we were simply counting the number of crackers he ate (7). We then had measures of the amounts eaten by subjects who initially had either empty or full stomachs and who were initially either frightened or calm. There were of course, two types of subjects: obese subjects (from 14 percent to 75 percent overweight) and normal subjects (from 8 percent underweight to 9 percent overweight).

To review expectations: If we were correct in thinking that the obese do not label as hunger the bodily states associated with food deprivation, then our several experimental manipulations should have had no effects on the amount eaten by obese subjects; on the other hand, the eating behavior of normal subjects should have directly paralleled the effects of the manipulations on bodily state.

It will be a surprise to no one to learn, from Fig. 1, that the normal subjects ate considerably fewer crackers when their stomachs were full than when their stomachs were empty. The results for obese subjects stand in fascinating contrast. They ate as much—in fact, slightly more—when their stomachs were full as when they were empty (interaction $P < .05$). Obviously the actual state of the stomach has nothing to do with the eating behavior of the obese.

In Fig. 2, pertaining to the effect of fear, we note an analogous picture. Fear markedly decreased the number of crackers the normal subjects ate but had no effect on the number eaten by the obese (interaction $P < .01$). Again, there was a small, though nonsignificant, reversal: the fearful obese ate slightly more than the calm obese.

It seems clear that the set of bodily symptoms the subject labels "hunger" differs for obese and normal subjects. Whether one measures gastric motility, as Stunkard did, or manipulates it, as I assume my co-workers and I have done, one finds, for normal subjects, a high degree of correspondence between the state of the gut and eating behavior and, for obese subjects, virtually no correspondence. While all of our manipulations have had a major effect on the amounts eaten by normal subjects, nothing that we have done has had a substantial effect on the amounts eaten by obese subjects.

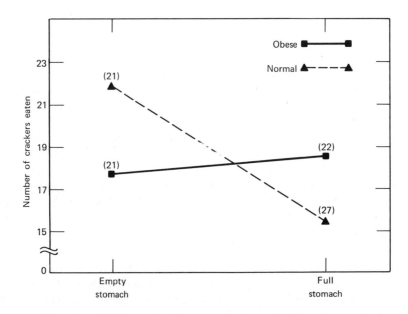

FIG. 1. Effects of preliminary eating on the amounts eaten during the experiment by normal and obese subjects. Numbers in parentheses are numbers of subjects.

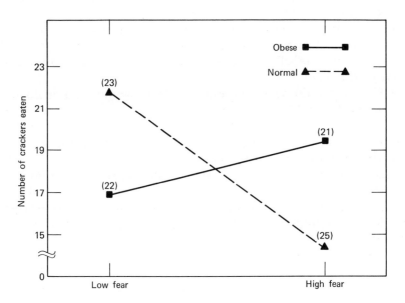

FIG. 2. Effects of fear on the amounts eaten by normal and obese subjects. Numbers in parentheses are numbers of subjects.

EFFECTS OF THE CIRCUMSTANCES OF EATING

With these facts in mind, let us turn to the work of Hashim and Van Itallie (*8*) of the Nutrition Clinic, St. Luke's Hospital, New York City. Their findings may be summarized as follows: virtually everything these workers do seems to have a major effect on the eating behavior of the obese and almost no effect on the eating behavior of the normal subject.

These researchers have prepared a bland liquid diet similar to commercial preparations such as vanilla-flavored Nutrament or Metrecal. The subjects are restricted to this monotonous diet for periods ranging from a week to several months. They can eat as much or as little of it as they want. Some of the subjects get a pitcher full and pour themselves a meal any time they wish. Other subjects are fed by a machine which delivers a mouthful every time the subject presses a button. With either feeding technique, the eating situation has the following characteristics: (a) The food itself is unappealing; (b) Eating is entirely self-determined: whether or not the subject eats, how much he eats, and when he eats are matters decided by him and no one else. Absolutely no pressure is brought to bear to limit his consumption; (c) The eating situation is devoid of any social or domestic trappings. It is basic eating; it will keep the subject alive, but it's not much fun.

To date, six grossly obese and five normal individuals have been subjects in these studies. In Fig. 3 the eating curves for a typical pair of subjects over a 21-day period are plotted. Both subjects were healthy people who lived in the hospital during the entire study. The obese subject was a 52-year-old woman, 5 feet 3 inches (1.6 meters) tall, who weighed 307 pounds (138 kilograms) on admission. The normal subject was a 30-year-old male, 5 feet 7 inches tall, who weighed 132 pounds.

The subject's estimated daily caloric intake before entering the hospital (as determined from a detailed interview) is plotted at the left in Fig. 3. Each subject, while in the hospital but before entering upon the experimental regime, was fed a general hospital diet. The obese subject was placed on a 2400-calorie diet for 7 days and a 1200-calorie diet for the next 8 days. As may be seen in Fig. 3, she ate everything on her tray throughout this 15-day period. The normal subject was placed on a 2400-calorie diet for 2 days, and he too ate everything.

With the beginning of the experiment proper, the difference in the eating behavior of the two subjects was dramatic and startling. The food consumption of the obese subject dropped precipitately the moment she entered upon the experimental regime, and it remained at an incredibly low level for the duration of the experiment. This effect is so dramatic that the weight of one obese subject who took part in the experiment for 8 months dropped from 410 to 190 pounds. On the other hand, the food consumption of the normal subject of Fig. 3 dropped slightly on the first 2

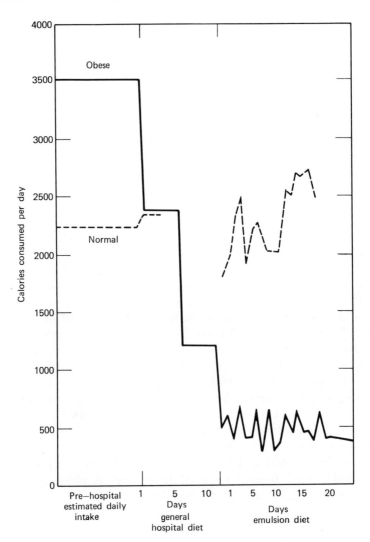

FIG. 3. The effects of an emulsion diet on the amounts eaten by an obese and a normal subject.

days, then returned to a fairly steady 2300 grams or so of food a day. The curves for these two subjects are typical. Each of the six obese subjects has manifested this marked and persistent decrease in food consumption during the experiment; each of the normal subjects has steadily consumed about his normal amount of food.

Before suggesting possible interpretations, I should note certain marked differences between these two groups of subjects. Most important, the obese subjects had come to the clinic for help in solving their weight problem and were, of course, motivated to lose weight. The normal subjects were simply volunteers. Doubtless this difference could account for the observed difference in eating behavior during the experiment, and until obese volunteers, unconcerned with their weight, are used as subjects in similar studies, we cannot be sure of the interpretation of this phenomenon. However, I think we should not, solely on grounds of methodological fastidiousness, dismiss these findings. It was concern with weight that brought these obese subjects to the clinic. Each of them, before entering the hospital and while in the hospital before being put on the experimental diet, was motivated to lose weight. Yet, despite this motivation, none of these subjects had been capable of restricting his diet at home, and each of them, when fed the general hospital diet, had eaten everything on his tray. Only when the food was dull and the act of eating was self-initiated and devoid of any ritual trappings did the obese subject, motivated or not, severely limit his consumption.

INTERNAL AND EXTERNAL CONTROL

On the one hand, then, our experiments indicate virtually no relationship between internal physiological state and the eating behavior of the obese subject; on the other hand, these case studies seem to indicate a close tie between the eating behavior of the obese and what might be called the circumstances of eating. When the food is dull and the eating situation is uninteresting, the obese subject eats virtually nothing. For the normal subject, the situation is just the reverse: his eating behavior seems directly linked to his physiological state but is relatively unaffected by the external circumstances or the ritual associated with eating.

Given this set of facts it seems clear that eating is triggered by different sets of stimuli in obese and normal subjects. Indeed, there is growing reason to suspect that the eating behavior of the obese is relatively unrelated to any internal state but is, in large part, under external control, being initiated and terminated by stimuli external to the organism. Let me give a few examples. A person whose eating behavior is under external control will stroll by a pastry shop, find the food in the window irresistible, and, even if he has recently eaten, go in and buy something. He will pass by a hamburger stand, smell the broiling meat, and, even though he has just eaten, buy a hamburger. Obviously such external factors—smell, sight, taste, other people's actions—to some extent affect anyone's eating. However, in normal individuals such external factors interact with internal state. They may affect what, where, and how much the normal individual eats, but they do so chiefly when he is in a state of physiological hunger. For the obese, I suggest, internal state is irrelevant and eating is determined largely by external factors.

This hypothesis obviously fits the data presented here, as well it should, since it is an *ad hoc* construction designed specifically to fit these data. Let us see, then, what independent support there is for the hypothesis, and where the hypothesis leads.

EFFECTS OF MANIPULATING TIME

Among the multitude of external food-relevant cues, one of the most intriguing is the passage of time. Everyone "knows" that 4 to 6 hours after eating his last meal he should eat his next one. Everyone "knows" that, within narrow limits, there are set times for eating regular meals. We should, then, expect that if we manipulate time we should be able to manipulate the eating behavior of the obese subjects. In order to do this, Gross and I (9) simply gimmicked two clocks so that one ran at half normal speed and the other, at twice normal speed. A subject arrives at 5:00 P.M., ostensibly to take part in an experiment on the relationship of base levels of autonomic reactivity to personality factors. He is ushered into a windowless room containing nothing but electronic equipment and a clock. Electrodes are put on his wrists, his watch is removed "so that it will not get gummed up with electrode jelly," and he is connected to a polygraph. All this takes 5 minutes, and at 5:05 he is left alone, with nothing to do for a true 30 minutes, while ostensibly we are getting a record of galvanic skin response and cardiac rate in a subject at rest. There are two experimental conditions. In one, the experimenter returns after a true 30 minutes and the clock reads 5:20. In the other, the clock reads 6:05, which is normal dinner time for most subjects. In both cases the experimenter is carrying a box of crackers and nibbling a cracker as he comes into the room; he puts the box down, invites the subject to help himself, removes the electrodes from the subject's wrists, and proceeds with personality testing for exactly 5 minutes. This done, he gives the subject a personality inventory which he is to complete and leaves him alone with the box of crackers for another true 10 minutes. There are two groups of subjects—normal and obese—and the only datum we collect is the weight of the box of crackers before and after the subject has had a chance at it.

If these ideas on internal and external controls of eating behavior are correct, normal subjects, whose eating behavior is presumably linked to internal state, should be relatively unaffected by the manipulation and should eat roughly the same number of crackers regardless of whether the clock reads 5:20 or 6:05. The obese, on the other hand, whose eating behavior is presumably under external control, should eat very few crackers when the clock reads 5:20 and a great many crackers when it reads 6:05.

The data of Fig. 4 do indeed indicate that the obese subjects eat almost twice as many crackers when they think the time is 6:05 as they do when they believe it to be 5:20. For normal subjects, the trend is just the reverse

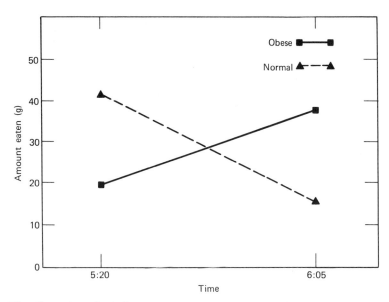

FIG. 4. The effects of manipulation of time on the amounts eaten by obese and normal subjects.

(interaction $P = .002$)—an unanticipated finding but one which seems embarrassingly simple to explain, as witness the several normal subjects who thought the time was 6:05 and politely refused the crackers, saying, "No thanks, I don't want to spoil my dinner." Obviously cognitive factors affected the eating behavior of both the normal and the obese subjects, but there was a vast difference. While the manipulation of the clock served to trigger or stimulate eating among the obese, it had the opposite effect on normal subjects, most of whom at this hour were, we presume, physiologically hungry, aware that they would eat dinner very shortly, and unwilling to spoil their dinner by filling up on crackers.

EFFECTS OF TASTE

In another study, Nisbett (*10*) examined the effects of taste on eating behavior. Nisbett reasoned that taste, like the sight or smell of food, is essentially an external stimulus to eating. Nisbett, in his experiment, also extended the range of weight deviation by including a group of underweight subjects as well as obese and normal subjects. His purpose in so doing was to examine the hypothesis that the relative potency of external versus internal controls is a dimension directly related to the degree of overweight. If the hypothesis was correct, he reasoned, the taste of food would have the greatest impact on the amounts eaten by obese subjects and the least impact on the amounts eaten by underweight subjects. To test this, Nisbett had his subjects eat as much as they wanted of one of two kinds of vanilla ice cream; one was a delicious and expensive product, the other an acrid concoction of cheap vanilla and quinine which he called "vanilla bitters." The effects of taste are presented in Fig. 5, in which the subjects' ratings of how good or bad the ice cream is are plotted against the amount eaten. As may be seen in Fig. 5, when the ice cream was rated "fairly good" or better, the obese subjects ate considerably more than the normal subjects did; these, in turn, ate more than the underweight subjects did. When the ice cream was rated "not very good" or worse, the ordering tended to reverse: the underweight subjects ate more than either the normal or the obese subjects. This experiment, then, indicates that the external, or at least nonvisceral, cue *taste* does have differential effects on the eating behavior of underweight, normal, and obese subjects.

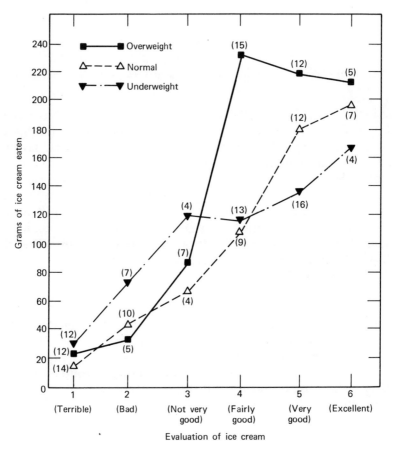

FIG. 5. The effects of food quality on the amounts eaten by obese, normal, and underweight subjects. Numbers in parentheses are numbers of subjects.

The indications, from Nisbett's experiment, that the degree of dependence on external cues relative to internal cues varies with deviation from normal weight are intriguing, for, if further work supports this hypothesis, we may have the beginnings of a plausible explanation of why the thin are thin and the fat are fat. We know from Carlson's work (5) that gastric contractions cease after a small amount of food has been introduced into the stomach. To the extent that such contractions are directly related to the hunger "experience"—to the extent that a person's eating is under internal control—he should "eat like a bird," eating only enough to stop the contractions. Eating beyond this point should be a function of external cues—the taste, sight, and smell of food. Individuals whose eating is externally controlled, then, should find it hard to stop eating. This hypothesis may account for the notorious "binge" eating of the obese (11) or the monumental meals described in loving detail by students (12) of the great, fat gastronomic magnificoes.

This rough attempt to explain why the obese are obese in itself raises intriguing questions. For example, does the external control of eating behavior inevitably lead to obesity? It is evident, I believe, that not only is such a linkage logically not inevitable but that the condition of external control of eating may in rare but specifiable circumstances lead to emaciation. A person whose eating is externally controlled should eat and grow fat when food-related cues are abundant and when he is fully aware of them. However, when such cues are lacking or when for some reason, such as withdrawal or depression, the individual is unaware of the cues, the person under external control would, one would expect, not eat, and, if the condition persisted, would grow "concentration-camp" thin. From study of the clinical literature one does get the impression that there is an odd but distinct relationship between obesity and extreme emaciation. For example, 11 of 21 subjects of case studies discussed by Bliss and Branch in *Anorexia Nervosa* (13) were, at some time in their lives, obese. In the case of eight of these 11 subjects, anorexia was preceded and accompanied by either marked withdrawal or intense depression. In contrast, intense attacks of anxiety or nervousness [states which our experiment (4) suggests would inhibit eating in normal individuals] seem to be associated with the development of anorexia among most of the ten subjects who were originally of normal size.

At this point, these speculations are simply idea-spinning—fun, but ephemeral. Let us return to the results of the studies described so far. These can be quickly summarized as follows:

1. Physiological correlates of food deprivation, such as gastric motility, are directly related to eating behavior and to the reported experience of hunger in normal subjects but unrelated in obese subjects (3, 4).

2. External or nonvisceral cues, such as smell, taste, the sight of other people eating, and the passage of time, affect eating behavior to a greater extent in obese subjects than in normal subjects (8–10).

OBESITY AND FASTING

Given these basic facts, their implications have ramifications in almost any area pertaining to food and eating, and some of our studies have been concerned with the implications of these experimental results for eating behavior in a variety of nonlaboratory settings. Thus, Goldman, Jaffa, and I (14) have studied fasting on Yom Kippur, the Jewish Day of Atonement, on which the orthodox Jew is supposed to go without food for 24 hours. Reasoning that, on this occasion, food-relevant external cues are particularly scarce, one would expect obese Jews to be more likely to fast than normal Jews. In a study of 296 religious Jewish college students (defined as Jewish college students who had been to a synagogue at least once during the preceding year on occasions other than a wedding or a bar mitzvah), this proves to be the case, for 83.3 percent of obese Jews fasted, as compared with 68.8 percent of normal Jews ($P < .05$).

Further, this external-internal control schema leads to the prediction that fat, fasting Jews who spend a great deal of time in the synagogue on Yom Kippur will suffer less from fasting than fat, fasting Jews who spend little time in the synagogue. There should be no such relationship for normal fasting Jews. Obviously, there will be far fewer food-related cues in the synagogue than on the street or at home. Therefore, for obese Jews, the likelihood that the impulse to eat will be triggered is greater outside of the synagogue than within it. For normal Jews, this distinction is of less importance. In or out of the synagogue, stomach pangs are stomach pangs. Again, the data support the expectation. When the number of hours in the synagogue is correlated with self-ratings of the unpleasantness of fasting, for obese subjects the correlation is $-.50$, whereas for normal subjects the correlation is only $-.18$. In a test of the difference between correlations, $P = .03$. Obviously, for the obese, the more time the individual spends in the synagogue, the less of an ordeal fasting is. For normals, the number of hours in the synagogue has little to do with the difficulty of the fast.

OBESITY AND CHOICE OF EATING PLACE

In another study (14) we examined the relationship of obesity to choice of eating places. From Nisbett's findings on taste, it seemed a plausible guess that the obese would be more drawn to good restaurants and more repelled by bad ones than normal subjects would be. At Columbia, students have the option of eating in the university dining halls or in any of the many restaurants that surround the campus. At Columbia, as probably at every similar institution in the United States, students have a low opinion of the institution's food. If a freshman elects to eat in a dormitory dining hall, he may, if he chooses, join a prepayment food plan at the beginning of the school year. Any time after 1 November he may, by paying a penalty of $15, cancel his food contract. If we accept prevailing campus opinion of the institution's food as being at all realistically based, we should anticipate that those for whom taste or food quality is most important will be the most likely to let their food contracts expire. Obese freshmen, then, should be more likely to drop out of the food plan than normal freshmen. Again, the data support the expectation: 86.5 percent of fat freshmen cancel their contracts as compared with 67.1 percent of normal freshmen ($P < .05$). Obesity does to some extent serve as a basis for predicting who will choose to eat institutional food.

OBESITY AND ADJUSTMENT TO NEW EATING SCHEDULES

In the final study in this series (14) we examined the relationship of obesity to the difficulty of adjusting to new eating schedules imposed by time-zone changes. This study involved an analysis of data collected by the medical department of Air France in a study of physiological effects of time-zone changes on 236 flight personnel assigned to the Paris–New York and Paris–Montreal flights. Most of these flights leave Paris around noon, French time; fly for approximately 8 hours; and land in North America sometime between 2:00 and 3:00 P.M. Eastern time. Flight-crew members eat lunch shortly after takeoff and, being occupied with landing preparations, are not served another meal during the flight. They land some 7 hours after their last meal, at a time that is later than the local lunch hour and earlier than the local dinner time.

Though this study was not directly concerned with eating behavior, the interviewers systematically noted all individuals who volunteered the information that they "suffered from the discordance between their physiological state and meal time in America" (15). One would anticipate that the fatter individuals, being sensitive to external cues (local meal hours) rather than internal ones, would adapt most readily to local eating schedules and be least likely to complain of the discrepancy between American meal times and physiological state.

Given the physical requirements involved in the selection of aircrews, there are, of course, relatively few really obese people in this sample. However, the results of Nisbett's experiment (10) indicate that the degree of reliance on external relative to internal cues may well be a dimension which varies with the degree of deviation from normal weight. It seems reasonable, then, to anticipate that, even within a restricted sample, there will be differences in response between the heavier and the lighter members of the sample. This is the case. In comparing the 101 flight personnel who are overweight (0.1 to 29 percent overweight) with the 135 who are not overweight (0 to 25 percent underweight), we find that 11.9 percent of the overweight complain as compared with 25.3 percent of the nonoverweight ($P < .01$). It does appear that the fatter were less troubled by the effects of time changes on eating than the thinner flyers (*16*).

These persistent findings that the obese are relatively insensitive to variations in the physiological correlates of food deprivation but highly sensitive to environmental, food-related cues is, perhaps, one key to understanding the notorious long-run ineffectiveness of virtually all attempts to treat obesity (*17*). The use of anorexigenic drugs such as amphetamine or of bulk-producing, nonnutritive substances such as methyl cellulose is based on the premise that such agents dampen the intensity of the physiological symptoms of food deprivation. Probably they do, but these symptoms appear to have little to do with whether or not a fat person eats. Restricted, low-calorie diets should be effective just so long as the obese dieter is able to blind himself to food-relevant cues or so long as he exists in a world barren of such cues. In the Hashim and Van Itallie study (*8*), the subjects did, in fact, live in such a world. Restricted to a Metrecal-like diet and to a small hospital ward, all the obese subjects lost impressive amounts of weight. However, on their return to normal living, to a man they returned to their original weights.

REFERENCES AND NOTES

1. H. Bruch, *Psychiat. Quart.* **35**, 458 (1961).
2. A. Stunkard, *Psychosomat. Med.* **21**, 281 (1959).
3. —— and C. Koch, *Arch. Genet. Psychiat.* **11**, 74 (1964).
4. S. Schachter, R. Goldman, A. Gordon, *J. Personality Soc. Psychol.,* in press.
5. A. J. Carlson, *Control of Hunger in Health and Disease* (Univ. of Chicago Press, Chicago, 1916).
6. W. B. Cannon, *Bodily Changes in Pain, Hunger, Fear and Rage* (Appleton, New York, 1915).
7. It is a common belief among researchers in the field of obesity that the sensitivity of their fat subjects makes it impossible to study their eating behavior experimentally—hence this roundabout way of measuring eating; the subjects in this study are taking a "taste test," not "eating."
8. S. A. Hashim and T. B. Van Itallie, *Ann. N. Y. Acad. Sci.* **131**, 654 (1965).
9. S. Schachter and L. Gross, *J. Personality Soc. Psychol.,* in press.
10. R. E. Nisbett, *ibid.,* in press.
11. A. Stunkard, *Amer. J. Psychiat.* **118**, 212 (1961).
12. L. Beebe, *The Big Spenders* (Doubleday, New York, 1966).
13. E. L. Bliss and C. H. Branch, *Anorexia Nervosa* (Hoeber, New York, 1960).
14. R. Goldman, M. Jaffa, S. Schachter, *J. Personality Soc. Psychol.,* in press.
15. J. Lavernhe and E. Lafontaine (Air France), personal communication.

16. Obviously, I do not mean to imply that the *only* explanation of the results of these three nonlaboratory studies lies in this formulation of the external-internal control of eating behavior. These studies were deliberately designed to test implications of this general schema in field settings. As with any field research, alternative explanations of the findings are legion, and, within the context of any specific study, impossible to rule out. Alternative formulations of this entire series of studies are considered in the original papers [see Schachter *et al.* (*4* and *9*), Nisbett (*10*), and Goldman *et al.* (*14*)].

17. A. Stunkard and M. McLaren-Hume, *Arch. Internal Med.* **103,** 79 (1959); A. R. Feinstein, *J. Chronic Diseases* **11,** 349 (1960).

18. Much of the research described in this article was supported by grants G23758 and GS732 from the National Science Foundation.

Snow geese will faithfully follow the stimulus object to which they were imprinted—even when that object is ethologist Konrad Lorenz! (NINA LEON | LIFE MAGAZINE © TIME INC.)

Section III
Learning and Memory

Man's capacity to learn and retain what he has learned makes him the most advanced form of life on this planet. Take these skills away from man and you take away his humanness. Generations of *homo sapiens* have exploited their learning and memory skills to conquer the most adverse environmental challenges on earth and even step foot into the heavens.

And yet learning and memory—the two skills that enable man to understand—are understood least! The complexities of the human brain are not easily accessible to scientific scrutiny! Far from discouraging the behavioral scientist, such complexities have stimulated an ever-growing volume of research aimed at comprehending how man acquires information and how he "stores it" in his head. Whether brain function is studied in lower animals or humans, surgically or verbally, with tests or drugs, the goal is always the same—to achieve an understanding of human cognitive processes and, through such comprehension, a better understanding of human behavior in general.

Three articles highlight our review of current research in learning and memory. Electrical stimulation of man's brain is again used, this time to study memory, in the first selection by Wilder Penfield. His findings that patients vividly recall experiences from their past when electrically stimulated on the surface of the cerebral cortex is very interesting.

An amusing and intriguing study of pigeons trained to perform human jobs in a drug company is provided by Thom Verhave in a second paper on learning and memory. The research indicates how, with a little creative imagination on the part of the investigator, lower animals can be taught to aid man by performing functions never dreamed of before the advent of modern psychology. The investigation also documents the value of studying animal behavior in psychology—not only does the study of pigeons lead to possible new applications of "pigeon power" to human ends, it also paves the way to new insights into the learning process.

In the final article in this section David Krech summarizes some of the recent research in learning and memory, and speculates about how findings from such research may someday be utilized in education to modify human mental processes.

Introduction to
Penfield Article

In two earlier articles (Caggiula & Hoebel; Heath) electrical stimulation of the brain was used to evoke behavioral responses in rats and men. If you recall in the Heath study one of the subjects attempted to bring to awareness an elusive memory by vigorously self-stimulating one section of his brain. In the following study electrical stimulation of the brain is again used, this time by the experimenter, to elicit the recall of memories in hospital patients.

William James once talked of the "stream of consciousness" when referring to one aspect of man's cognitive behavior. Penfield's description of his patients' cognitive behavior when electrically stimulated is in metaphorical harmony with James:

> There is an area of the surface of the human brain where local electrical stimulation can call back a sequence of past experience . . . It is as though a wire recorder, or a strip of cinematographic film with sound track, had been set in motion within the brain. The sights and sounds, and the thoughts, of a former day pass through the man's mind again.

Dr. Penfield went fishing in the human stream of consciousness for memories—his fishing pole a thin wire; his hook an electrode; his bait an electrical stimulus. And he was successful. When he stimulated the cerebral cortex of his patients they recalled memories from their past. What they recalled was not very significant (e.g., one patient heard his mother on the phone) but the memories were so vivid that they had difficulty believing the event was not actually taking place. Penfield's work is yet another example of how the study of neurophysiology provides us with insights into that most complex of behaviors, human thought.

9

The Interpretive Cortex

The stream of consciousness in the human
brain can be electrically reactivated.

Wilder Penfield

There is an area of the surface of the human brain where local electrical stimulation can call back a sequence of past experience. An epileptic
irritation in this area may do the same. It is as though a wire recorder, or
a strip of cinematographic film with sound track, had been set in motion
within the brain. The sights and sounds, and the thoughts, of a former day
pass through the man's mind again.

The purpose of this article is to describe, for readers from various disciplines of science, the area of the cerebral cortex from which this neuron
record of the past can be activated and to suggest what normal contribution
it may make to cerebral function.

The human brain is the master organ of the human race. It differs
from the brains of other mammals particularly in the greater extent of its
cerebral cortex. The gray matter, or cortex, that covers the two cerebral
hemispheres of the brain of man is so vast in nerve cell population that it
could never have been contained within the human skull if it were not
folded upon itself, and refolded, so as to form a very large number of fissures
and convolutions. . . . The fissures are so deep and so devious that by far
the greater portion of this ganglionic carpet (about 65 percent) is hidden in
them, below the surface (Fig. 1).

The portion that is labeled "interpretive" in Fig. 2 covers a part of
both temporal lobes. It is from these two homologous areas, and from nowhere else, that electrical stimulation has occasionally produced physical responses which may be divided into (a) experiential responses and (b) interpretive responses.

SOURCE. *Science*, June 26, 1959, **129**, 1719–1725.

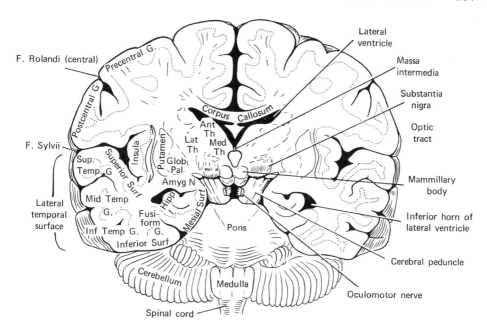

FIG. 1. The surfaces and convolutions of the temporal lobe are identified, and the relationship of one hemisphere to the other and the relationship of the hemispheres to the brain stem and cerebellum are shown.

EXPERIENTIAL RESPONSES

Occasionally during the course of a neurosurgical operation under local anesthesia, gentle electrical stimulation in this temporal area, right or left, has caused the conscious patient to be aware of some previous experience (1). The experience seems to be picked out at random from his own past. But it comes back to him in great detail. He is suddenly aware again of those things to which he paid attention in that distant interval of time. This recollection of an experiential sequence stops suddenly when the electrical current is switched off or when the electrode is removed from contact with the cortex. This phenomenon we have chosen to call an experiential response to stimulation.

Case Examples (2)

The patient S.Be. observed, when the electrode touched the temporal lobe (right superior temporal convolution), "There was a piano over there and someone playing. I could hear the song you know." When the cortex was stimulated again without warning, at approximately the same point, the patient had a different experience. He said: "Someone speaking to another,

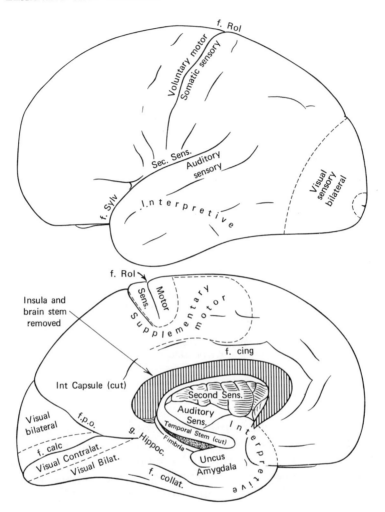

FIG. 2. The left cerebral hemisphere; the lateral surface is shown above and the mesial surface below. In the lower drawing the brain stem with the island of Reil has been removed to show the inner banks of the fissure of Sylvius and the superior surface of the temporal lobe. The interpretive cortex extends from the lateral to the superior surface of the temporal lobe. (Penfield and Roberts.)

and he mentioned a name but I could not understand it . . . It was like a dream." Again the point was restimulated without his knowledge. He said quietly: "Yes, 'Oh Marie, Oh Marie'! Someone is singing it." When the point was stimulated a fourth time he heard the same song again and said it was the "theme song of a radio program."

The electrode was then applied to a point 4 centimeters farther forward on the first temporal convolution. While the electrode was still in place, S.Be. said: "Something brings back a memory. I can see Seven-Up Bottling

Company—Harrison Bakery." He was evidently seeing two of Montreal's large illuminated advertisements.

The surgeon then warned him that he was about to apply the electrode again. Then, after a pause, the surgeon said "Now," but he did not stimulate. (The patient has no means of knowing when the electrode is applied, unless he is told, since the cortex itself is without sensation.) The patient replied promptly, "Nothing."

A woman (D.F.) (3) heard an orchestra playing an air while the electrode was held in place. The music stopped when the electrode was removed. It came again when the electrode was reapplied. On request, she hummed the tune, while the electrode was held in place, accompanying the orchestra. It was a popular song. Over and over again, restimulation at the same spot produced the same song. The music seemed always to begin at the same place and to progress at the normally expected tempo. All efforts to mislead her failed. She believed that a gramaphone was being turned on in the operating room on each occasion, and she asserted her belief stoutly in a conversation some days after the operation.

A boy (R.W.) heard his mother talking to someone on the telephone when an electrode was applied to his right temporal cortex. When the stimulus was repeated without warning, he heard his mother again in the same conversation. When the stimulus was repeated after a lapse of time, he said, "My mother is telling my brother he has got his coat on backwards. I can just hear them."

The surgeon then asked the boy whether he remembered this happening. "Oh yes," he said, "just before I came here." Asked again whether this seemed like a dream, he replied: "No, it is like I go into a daze."

J.T. cried out in astonishment when the electrode was applied to the temporal cortex: "Yes doctor, yes doctor. Now I hear people laughing—my friends in South Africa!"

When asked about this, he explained the reason for his surprise. He seemed to be laughing with his cousins, Bessie and Ann Wheliow, whom he had left behind on a farm in South Africa, although he knew he was now on the operating table in Montreal.

INTERPRETIVE RESPONSES

On the other hand, similar stimulation in this same general area may produce quite a different response. The patient discovers, on stimulation, that he has somehow changed his own interpretation of what he is seeing at the moment, or hearing or thinking. For example, he may exclaim that his present experience seems familiar, as though he had seen it or heard it or thought it before. He realizes that this must be a false interpretation. Or, on the contrary, these things may seem suddenly strange, absurd. Sights or sounds may seem distant and small, or they may come unexpectedly close and seem loud or large. He may feel suddenly afraid, as though his environment were threatening him, and he is possessed by a nameless dread or panic. Another patient may say he feels lonely or aloof, or as though he were observing himself at a distance.

Under normal circumstances anyone may make such interpretations of the present, and these interpretations serve him as guides to action or reaction. If the interpretations are accurate guides, they must be based upon previous comparable experience. It is conceivable, therefore, that the recall mechanism which is activated by the electrode during an experiential response and the mechanism activated in an interpretive response may be parts of a common inclusive mechanism of reflex recognition or interpretation.

No special function had been previously assigned by neurologists to the area in each temporal lobe that is marked "interpretive" in Fig. 2, though some clinicians have suggested it might have to do with the recall of music. The term *interpretive cortex,* therefore, is no more than slang to be employed for the purposes of discussion. The terms *motor cortex, sensory cortex,* and *speech cortex* began as slang phrases and have served such a purpose. But such phrases must not be understood to signify independence of action of separated units in the case of any of these areas. Localization of function in the cerebral cortex means no more than specialization of function as compared with other cortical regions, not separation from the integrated action of the brain.

Before considering the interpretive cortex further, we may turn briefly to the motor and sensory areas and the speech areas of the cortex. After considering the effects of electrical stimulation there, we should be better able to understand the results of stimulation in the temporal lobes.

SPECIALIZATION OF FUNCTION IN THE CORTEX

Evidence for some degree of localization within the brain was recognized early in the 19th century by Flourens. He concluded from experiment that functional subdivision of "the organ of the mind" was possible. The forebrain (*4*), he said [cerebral hemispheres and higher brain stem (Fig. 3)] had to do with thought and will power, while the cerebellum was involved in the coordination of movement.

In 1861, Paul Broca showed that a man with a relatively small area of destruction in a certain part of the left hemisphere alone might lose only the power of speech. It was soon realized that this was the speech area of man's dominant (left) hemisphere. In 1870, Fritsch and Hitzig applied an electric current to the exposed cortex of one hemisphere of a lightly anesthetized dog and caused the legs of the opposite side to move. Thus, an area of cortex called motor was discovered.

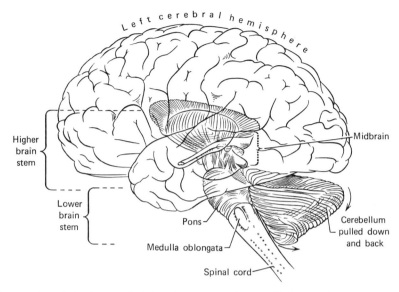

FIG. 3. Drawing of the left cerebral hemisphere, showing the higher brain stem, including the thalamus, within and the lower brain stem and spinal cord emerging below. The cerebellum is shown, attached to the lower brain stem. (Penfield and Roberts.)

After that, localization of function became a research target for many clinicians and experimentalists. It was soon evident that in the case of man, the precentral gyrus (Fig. 4) in each hemisphere was related to voluntary control of the contralateral limbs and that there was an analogous area of motor cortex in the frontal lobes of animals. It appeared also that other separate areas of cortex (Fig. 4) in each hemisphere were dedicated to sensation (one for visual sensation, others for auditory, olfactory, and discriminative somatic sensation, respectively).

It was demonstrated, too, that from the "motor cortex" there was an efferent bundle of nerve fibers (the pyramidal tract) that ran down through the lower brain stem and the spinal cord to be relayed on out to the muscles. Through this efferent pathway, voluntary control of these muscles was actually carried out. It was evident, too, that there were separate sensory tracts carrying nerve impulses in the other direction, from the principal organs of special sense (eye, ear, nose, and skin and muscle) into separate sensory areas of the cortex.

These areas, motor and sensory, have been called "projection areas." They play a role in the projection of nerve currents to the cortex from the periphery of the body, and from the cortex to the periphery. This makes possible (sensory) awareness of environment and provides the individual with a means of outward (motor) expression. The motor cortex has a specialized

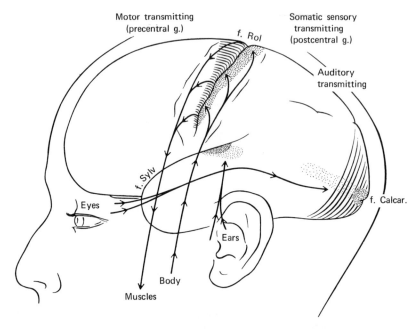

FIG. 4. Sensory and motor projection areas. The sensory areas are stippled, and the afferent pathways to them from eyes, ears, and body are indicated by entering arrows. The motor cortex is indicated by parallel lines, and the efferent corticospinal tract is indicated by emerging arrows. (Penfield and Roberts.)

use during voluntary action, and each of the several sensory areas has a specialized use, when the individual is seeing, hearing, smelling, or feeling.

TRAVELING POTENTIALS

The action of the living brain depends upon the movement, within it, of "transient electrical potentials traveling the fibers of the nervous system." This was Sherrington's phrase. Within the vast circuits of this master organ, potentials travel, here and there and yonder, like meteors that streak across the sky at night and line the firmament with trails of light. When the meteors pass, the paths of luminescence still glow a little while, then fade and are gone. The changing patterns of these paths of passing energy make possible the changing content of the mind. The patterns are never quite the same, and so it is with the content of the mind.

Specialized areas in the cortex are at times active and again relatively quiet. But, when a man is awake, there is always some central integration and coordination of the traveling potentials. There must be activity within the brain stem and some areas of the cortex. This is centrencephalic integration (5).

SENSORY, MOTOR, AND PSYCHICAL
RESPONSES TO CORTICAL STIMULATION

My purpose in writing this article is to discuss in simple words (free of technical terms) the meaning of the "psychical" responses which appear only on stimulation of the so-called interpretive cortex. But before considering these responses let us consider the motor and sensory activity of the cortex for a moment.

When the streams of electrical potentials that pass normally through the various areas of sensory cortex are examined electrically, they do not seem to differ from each other except in pattern and timing. The essential difference is to be found in the fact that the visual stream passes to the visual cortex and then to one subcortical target and the auditory stream passes through the auditory cortex and then on to another subcortical target.

When the surgeon stimulates the intact sensory cortex he must be sending a current along the next "piece of road" to a subcortical destination. This electrode (delivering, for example, 60 "waves" per second of 2-millisecond duration and 1-volt intensity) produces no more than elementary sight when applied to visual cortex. The patient reports colors, lights, and shadows that move and take on crude outlines. The same electrode, applied to auditory cortex, causes him to hear a ringing or hissing or thumping sound. When applied to postcentral gyrus it produces tingling or a false sense of movement.

Thus, sensation is produced by the passage inward of electrical potentials. And when the electrode is applied to the motor cortex, movement is produced by passage of potentials outward to the muscles. In each case positive response is produced by conduction in the direction of normal physiological flow—that is, by dromic conduction (6).

Responses to electrical stimulation that may be called "psychical," as distinguished from sensory or motor, have been elicited from certain areas of the human cortex (Fig. 5). But they have never been produced by stimulation in other areas. There are, of course, other large areas of cortex which are neither sensory nor motor in function. They seem to be employed in other neuron mechanisms that are also associated with psychical processes. But the function of these other areas cannot, it seems, be activated by so simple a stimulus as an electric current applied to the cortex.

DREAMY STATES OF EPILEPSY

"Epilepsy" may be defined, in Jackson's words, as "the name for occasional, sudden, excessive, rapid and local discharges of grey matter." Our aim in the operations under discussion was to remove the gray matter responsible for epileptic attacks if that gray matter could be spared. When the

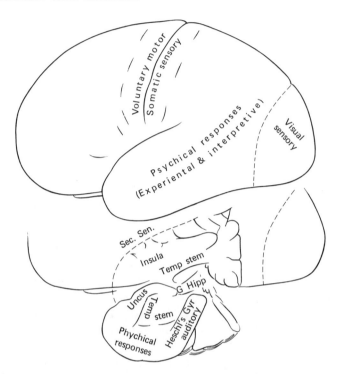

FIG. 5. The left cerebral hemisphere is shown with the temporal lobe cut across and turned down. The areas of cortex from which psychical responses have been elicited are indicated. (Penfield.)

stimulating electrode reproduced the psychical phenomenon that initiated the fit, it provided the guidance sought (7).

During the 19th century clinicians had recognized these phenomena as epileptic. They applied the term *intellectual aura* to such attacks. Jackson substituted the expression *dreamy states* (see *8*). These were, he said, "psychical states during the onset of certain epileptic seizures, states which are much more elaborate than crude sensations." And again, he wrote, "These are all voluminous mental states and yet of different kinds; no doubt they ought to be classified, but for my present purpose they may be considered together."

"The state," he said, "is often like that occasionally experienced by healthy people as a feeling of 'reminiscence.'" Or the patient has "dreamy feelings," "dreams mixing up with present thoughts," "double consciousness," a "feeling of being somewhere else," a feeling "as if I went back to all that occurred in my childhood," "silly thoughts."

Jackson never did classify these states, but he did something more important. He localized the area of cortex from which epileptic discharge would produce dreamy states. His localization was in the anterior and deep portions of the temporal lobes, the same area that is labeled "interpretive" cortex in Fig. 2.

Case Example

Brief reference may be made to a specific case. The patient had seizures, and stimulation produced responses which were first recognized as psychical.

In 1936, a girl of 16 (J.V.) was admitted to the Montreal Neurological Institute complaining of epileptic attacks, each of which was ushered in by the same hallucination. It was a little dream, she said, in which an experience from early childhood was reenacted, always the same train of events. She would then cry out with fear and run to her mother. Occasionally this was followed immediately by a major convulsive seizure.

At operation, under local anesthesia, we tried to set off the dream by a gentle electrical stimulus in the right temporal lobe. The attempt was successful. The dream was produced by the electrode. Stimulation at other points on the temporal cortex produced sudden fear without the dream. At still other points, stimulation caused her to say that she saw "someone coming toward me." At another point, stimulation caused her to say she heard the voices of her mother and her brothers (9).

This suggested a new order of cortical response to electrical stimulation. When the neighboring visual sensory area of the cortex is stimulated, any patient may report seeing stars of light or moving colors or black outlines but never "someone coming toward me." Stimulation of the auditory sensory cortex may cause any patient to report that he hears ringing, buzzing, blowing, or thumping sounds, perhaps, but never voices that speak. Stimulation in the areas of sensory cortex can call forth nothing more than the elements of visual or auditory or tactile sensation, never happenings that might have been previously experienced.

During the 23 years that have followed, although practically all areas of the cerebral cortex have been stimulated and studied in more than 1000 craniotomies, performed under local anesthesia, psychical responses of the experiential or interpretive variety have been produced only from the temporal cortex in the general areas that are marked "psychical responses" in Fig. 2 (10, 11).

CLASSIFICATION

It seems reasonable to subdivide psychical responses and psychical seizures (epileptic dreamy states) in the same way, classifying them as "interpretive" or "experiential." Interpretive psychical responses are those involving interpretations of the present experience, or emotions related to it; experiential psychical responses are reenactments of past experiences. Interpretive seizures are those accompanied by auras and illusions; experiential seizures are those accompanied by auras and hallucinations.

The interpretive responses and seizures may be divided into groups (11) of which the commonest are as follows: (a) recognition, the illusion that things seen and heard and thought are familiar (*déjà vu* phenomenon); (b) visual illusion, the illusion that things seen are changing—for example, coming nearer, growing larger (macropsia); (c) auditory illusion, the illusion that things heard are changing—for example, coming near, going away, changing tempo; (d) illusional emotion, the emotion of fear or, less often, loneliness, sorrow, or disgust.

Experiential phenomena (hallucinations) are an awareness of experiences from the past that come into the mind without complete loss of awareness of the present.

DISCUSSION

What, then, is the function of the interpretive cortex? This is a physiological question that follows the foregoing observations naturally.

An electrode, delivering, for example, 60 electrical pulses per second to the surface of the motor cortex, causes a man to make crude movements. When applied to the various sensory areas of the cortex, it causes him to have crude sensations of sight or sound or body feeling. This indicates only that these areas have something to do with the complicated mechanism of voluntary action or conscious sensation. It does not reveal what contribution the cortex may make, or in what way it may contribute to skill in making voluntary movement or qualify the incoming sensory streams.

In the case of the interpretive cortex, the observations are similar. We may say that the interpretive cortex has something to do with a mechanism that can reactivate the vivid record of the past. It has also something to do with a mechanism that can present to consciousness a reflex interpretation of the present. To conclude that here is the mechanism of memory would be an unjustified assumption. It would be too simple.

What a man remembers when he makes a voluntary effort is apt to be a generalization. If this were not so, he might be hopelessly lost in detail. On the other hand, the experiential responses described above are detailed reenactments of a single experience. Such experiences soon slip beyond the range of voluntary recall. A man may summon to mind a song at will. He hears it then in his mind, not all at once but advancing phrase by phrase. He may sing it or play it too, and one would call this memory.

But if a patient hears music in response to the electrode, he hears it in one particular strip of time. That time runs forward again at the original tempo, and he hears the orchestration, or he sees the player at a piano "over there." These are details he would have thought forgotten.

A vast amount of work remains to be done before the mechanism of memory, and how and where the recording takes place, are understood. This record is not laid down in the interpretive cortex, but it is kept in a part of the brain that is intimately connected with it.

Removal of large areas of interpretive cortex, even when carried out on both sides, may result in mild complaints of memory defect, but it does not abolish the capacity to remember recent events. On the other hand, surgical removals that result in bilateral interference with the underlying hippocampal zone do make the recording of recent events impossible, while distant memory is still preserved (12, 13).

The importance of the hippocampal area for memory was pointed out long ago in a forgotten publication by the Russian neurologist Bechterew (14). The year before publication Bechterew had demonstrated the case before the St. Petersburg Clinic for Nervous and Mental Diseases. The man on whom Bechterew reported had "extraordinary weakness of memory, falsifications of memory and great apathy." These defects were shown at autopsy to be secondary to lesions of the mesial surface of the cortex of both temporal lobes. The English neurologists Glees and Griffith (15) reported similar defects, a half century later, in a patient who had symmetrical lesions of the hippocampus and of hippocampal and fusiform gyri on both sides.

The way in which the interpretive cortex seems to be used may be suggested by an example: After years of absence you meet, by chance, a man whose very existence you had forgotten. On seeing him, you may be struck by a sudden sense of familiarity, even before you have time to "think." A signal seems to flash up in consciousness to tell you that you've seen that man before. You watch him as he smiles and moves and speaks. The sense of familiarity grows stronger. Then you remember him. You may even recall that his name was Jones. The sight and the sound of the man has given you an instant access, through some reflex, to the records of the past in which this man has played some part. The opening of this forgotten file was subconscious. It was not a voluntary act. You would have known him even against your will. Although Jones was a forgotten man a moment before, now you can summon the record in such detail that you remark at once the slowness of his gait or a new line about the mouth.

If Jones had been a source of danger to you, you might have felt fear as well as familiarity before you had time to consider the man. Thus, the signal of fear as well as the signal of familiarity may come to one as the result of subconscious comparison of present with similar past experience.

One more example may be given from common experience. A sudden increase in the size of objects seen and in sounds heard may mean the rapid approach of something that calls for instant avoidance action. These are signals that, because of previous experience, we sometimes act upon with little consideration.

SUMMARY

The interpretive cortex has in it a mechanism for instant reactivation of the detailed record of the past. It has a mechanism also for the production of interpretive signals. Such signals could only be significant if past records are scanned and relevant experiences are selected for comparison with present experience. This is a subconscious process. But it may well be that this scanning of past experience and selection from it also renders the relevant past available for conscious consideration as well. Thus, the individual may refer to the record as he employs other circuits of the brain.

Access to the record of the past seems to be as readily available from the temporal cortex of one side as from that of the other. Auditory illusions (or interpretations of the distance, loudness, or tempo of sounds) have been produced by stimulation of the temporal cortex of either side. The same is true of illusional emotions, such as fear and disgust.

But, on the contrary, visual illusions (interpretations of the distance, dimension, erectness, and tempo of things seen) are only produced by stimulation of the temporal cortex on the nondominant (normally, right) side of the brain. Illusions of recognition, such as familiarity or strangeness, were also elicited only from the nondominant side, except in one case.

CONCLUSION

"Consciousness," to quote William James (16), "is never quite the same in successive moments of time. It is a stream forever flowing, forever changing." The stream of changing states of mind that James described so well does flow through each man's waking hours until the time when he falls asleep to wake no more. But the stream, unlike a river, leaves a record in the living brain.

Transient electrical potentials move with it through the circuits of the nervous system, leaving a path that can be followed again. The pattern of this pathway, from neuron to neuron along each nerve-cell body and fiber and junction, is the recorded pattern of each man's past. That complicated record is held there in temporal sequence through the principle of durable facilitation of conduction and connection.

A steady stream of electrical pulses applied through an electrode to some point in the interpretive cortex causes a stream of excitation to flow from the cortex to the place where past experience is recorded. This stream of excitation acts as a key to the past. It can enter the pathway of recorded consciousness at any random point, from childhood on through adult life. But having entered, the experience moves forward without interference from other experiences. And when the electrode is withdrawn there is a likelihood, which lasts for seconds or minutes, that the stream of excitation will enter the pathway again at the same moment of past time, even if the electrode is reapplied at neighboring points (17).

Finally, an electric current applied to the surface of what may be called the interpretive cortex of a conscious man (a) may cause the stream of former consciousness to flow again or (b) may give him an interpretation of the present that is unexpected and involuntary. Therefore, it is concluded that, under normal circumstances, this area of cortex must make some functional contribution to reflex comparison of the present with related past experience. It contributes to reflex interpretation or perception of the present.

The combination and comparison of present experience with similar past experience must call for remarkable scanning of the past and classification of similarities. What contribution this area of the temporal cortex may make to the whole process is not clear. The term *interpretive cortex* will serve for identification until students of human physiology can shed more light on these fascinating findings.

REFERENCES AND NOTES

1. W. Penfield, *J. Mental Sci.* **101**, 451 (1955).
2. These patients, designated by the same initials, have been described in previous publications in much greater detail. An index of patients (designated by initials) may be found in any of my books.
3. This case is reported in detail in W. Penfield and H. Jasper, *Epilepsy and the Functional Anatomy of the Human Brain* (Little, Brown, Boston, 1954) [published in abridged form in Russian (translation by N. P. Graschenkov and G. Smirnov) by the Soviet Academy of Sciences, 1958].
4. The forebrain, or prosencephalon, properly includes the diencephalon and the telencephalon, or higher brain stem, and hemispheres. Flourens probably had cerebral hemispheres in mind as distinguished from cerebellum.
5. "Within the brain, a central transactional core has been identified between the strictly sensory or motor systems of classical neurology. This central reticular mechanism has been found capable of grading the activity of most other parts of the brain"—H. Magoun, *The Waking Brain* (Thomas, Springfield, Ill., 1958).
6. W. Penfield, *The Excitable Cortex in Conscious Man* (Thomas, Springfield, Ill., 1958).
7. It did more than this; it produced illusions or hallucinations that had never been experienced by the patient during a seizure.

8. J. Taylor, Ed., *Selected Writings of John Hughlings Jackson* (Hodder and Stoughton, London, 1931), vol. 1, *On Epilepsy and Epileptiform Convulsions.*

9. Twenty-one years later this young woman, who is the daughter of a physician, was present at a meeting of the National Academy of Sciences in New York while her case was discussed. She could still recall the operation and the nature of the "dreams" that had preceded her seizures [W. Penfield, *Proc. Natl. Acad. Sci. U. S.* **44,** 51 (1958)].

10. In a recent review of the series my associate, Dr. Phanor Perot, has found and summarized 35 out of 384 temporal lobe cases in which stimulation produced experiential responses. All such responses were elicited in the temporal cortex. In a study of 214 consecutive operations for temporal lobe epilepsy, my associate Sean Mullan found 70 cases in which interpretive illusion occurred in the minor seizures before operation, or in which an interpretive response was produced by stimulation during operation. In most cases it occurred both before and during operation.

11. S. Mullan and W. Penfield, *A.M.A. Arch. Neurol. Psychiat.* **81,** 269 (1959).

12. This area is marked "Hipp" and "Hipp., G" in Fig. 1 and "g. Hippoc." and "amygdala" in Fig. 2.

13. W. Penfield and B. Milner, *A.M.A. Arch. Neurol. Psychiat.* **79,** 475 (1958).

14. W. V. Bechterew, "Demonstration eines Gehirns mit Zerstörung der vorderen und inneren Theile der Hirnrinde beider Schläfenlappen," *Neurol. Zentralbl. Leipzig* **19,** 990 (1900). My attention was called to this case recently by Dr. Peter Gloor of Montreal.

15. P. Glees and H. B. Griffith, *Monatsschr. Psychiat. Neurol.* **123,** 193 (1952).

16. W. James, *The Principles of Psychology* (Holt, New York, 1910).

17. Thus, it is apparent that the beam of excitation that emanates from the interpretive cortex and seems to scan the record of the past is subject to the principles of transient facilitation already demonstrated for the anthropoid motor cortex [A. S. F. Grünbaum and C. Sherrington, *Proc. Roy. Soc. (London)* **72B,** 152 (1901); T. Graham Brown and C. S. Sherrington, *ibid.* **85B,** 250 (1912)]. Similarly subject to the principles of facilitation are the motor and the sensory cortex of man [W. Penfield and K. Welch, *J. Physiol. (London)* **109,** 358 (1949)]. The patient D.F. heard the same orchestra playing the same music in the operating room more than 20 times when the electrode was reapplied to the superior surface of the temporal lobe. Each time the music began in the verse of a popular song. It proceeded to the chorus, if the electrode was kept in place.

18. W. Penfield and L. Roberts, *Speech and Brain Mechanisms* (Princeton Univ. Press, Princeton, N. J., 1959).

19. G. Jelgersma, *Atlas anatomicum cerebri humani* (Scheltema and Holkema, Amsterdam).

Introduction to Verhave Article

The use of animals to supplement or replace human effort in various tasks is not new. Falcons help us hunt; horses aid in hauling and travel; dogs protect our homes and "see" for the blind. Animals can also be taught to perform acts that entertain us—like the trained elephants, lions, and chimps in the circus.

With the coming of operant conditioning procedures (methods to shape and control behavior developed by B. F. Skinner and his colleagues) animal training—both to aid and amuse man—has turned into an exacting scientific enterprise. The results of Skinner's methods are nothing short of sensational: at one point operant conditioning procedures were utilized to turn pigeons into guidance systems for World War II missiles (Skinner, 1960).

The article below by Thom Verhave is one excellent example of operant conditioning methods employed to teach an organism new tricks. The research indicates how, with a little creative imagination on the part of the investigator, lower animals can be taught to aid man by performing functions never dreamed of before the advent of modern psychology. The investigation also documents the value of studying animal behavior in psychology—not only does the study of pigeons lead to possible new applications of "pigeon power" to human ends, it also paves the way to new insights into the learning process. Would it surprise you to discover, for example, that operant conditioning procedures affect humans much the same way as they influence birds? By examining the behavior of lower organisms we are often able to reach deeper understandings about human behavior. One should not forget this when he asks "Why study animals in psychology?"

There is also a moral in the Verhave experiment: no matter how effectively you train an animal to perform human tasks, such efforts will go to waste if man is not ready to relinquish his labors to lower organisms. Man is a strange creature indeed! He thinks nothing of entrusting his life to a dog or horse but recoils at the thought of a pigeon sorting pills on an assembly line. It would seem that man and beast must both be trained before scientists like Verhave can aid humankind with their efforts.

REFERENCE

Skinner, B., Pigeons in a pelican. *American Psychologist,* 1960, **15,** 28–37.

10

The Pigeon as a
Quality-Control Inspector

Thom Verhave

Many of the operations involved in the quality-control inspection of commercial products consist of monotonous checking jobs performed by human operators. In addition to monotony, these (usually visual) inspection jobs have several other characteristics in common: (*a*) They require little if any manual skill or dexterity, (*b*) they require good visual acuity, (*c*) they require a capacity for color vision, and (*d*) they are extremely difficult to automate. There is, however, an organic device which has the following favorable properties: (*a*) an average life span of approximately 10–15 years (Levi, 1963), (*b*) an extreme flexibility in adjusting to its environment as well as an enormous learning ability (Ferster & Skinner, 1957; Smee, 1850), (*c*) a visual acuity as good as the human eye (Reese, 1964), (*d*) color vision (Reese, 1964). The price for one such device is only (approximately) $1.50; its name: *Columba livia domestica* or the pigeon.

Because of the characteristics listed above it is quite feasible to train pigeons to do all the visual checking operations involved in commercial manufacture. What follows is a brief account of an exploratory attempt to put the above suggestion into actual practice (Verhave, 1959). This paper is written partially in self-defense: Stories about the pill-inspecting pigeons have circulated for many years—many versions containing gross inaccuracies.

In July of 1955 I was employed as a "psychopharmacologist" at one of the larger pharmaceutical companies. The main purpose of the laboratory

SOURCE. *American Psychologist,* 1966, **21,** 109–115. Copyright 1966 by the American Psychological Association, and reproduced by permission. Opinions and conclusions contained in this article are those of the author. They are not to be construed as necessarily reflecting the views or the endorsement of either the pharmaceutical industry or any pigeon.

I am indebted to John E. Owen, my former collaborator, for a critical reading of this paper, which saved me from many errors due to faulty memory.

was to develop and evaluate techniques for the experimental analysis of the effects of drugs on the behavior of animals.

Sometime, probably early in 1958, I finally took the tour of the plant, which is mandatory for all new employees. During the all-day tour of the extensive research and manufacturing facilities, I ran into the (gelatin) drug-capsule facilities. The capsules are manufactured by several very large and extremely complex machines, which together have a maximum production capacity of approximately 20,000,000 capsules per day. All of the capsules, which are made in a large number of sizes, and colors, are visually inspected. This job was done by a contingent of about 70 women. After inspection the capsules go to other machines which fill them automatically with the appropriate pharmaceuticals. The capsules are inspected in batches. The number of caps in a batch depends on the volume or size of the capsule: the larger the capsule size the smaller the number in a batch to be inspected. All of the capsules in a particular batch are of the same shape, size, and color. A big reservoir with a funnel drops the capsules at a fixed rate on an endless moving belt. The inspector, or "capsule sorter" as she is called, is located in front of the moving belt which is illuminated from underneath. She "pattern scans" the capsules as they move by and picks up and throws out all "skags." A skag is a discard capsule because it is off-color, has a piece of gelatin sticking out, or has a dent in it. This also includes all double-cap capsules. When the capsule comes to the capsule sorter, it is already closed by putting two halves, a cap and a body, together. This step was already performed by the production machine. Sometimes, however, during transportation or in storage a second cap (the larger half of a capsule) is put on top of an already capped capsule (a cap and body may vibrate apart and a loose cap may then slide over the body of another already capped capsule). Such a "double-cap skag" produces problems later on in the filling machine. After inquiry, I was told that the double-cap skag is also one of the more difficult types to spot.

The sorters (all female) are paid off on a group-bonus schedule employing "error cost." After the inspection of a batch is completed, a supervisor (usually also female) scoops a ladleful of inspected capsules out of the barrel in which they were collected. The types of skag defects are categorized and the inspector can allow up to three or four of the more minor imperfections per sample before a batch is rejected. If she finds more than the allowed number of skags in the sample ladled from the batch, the inspector has to reinspect the entire batch of capsules. She is thus likely to reduce her bonus pay for the day since it depends partially on her own inspection output.

To come back to the main story: On seeing those women and their simple monotonous task, and knowing about Skinner's "Pigeons in a Pelican" (1960, 1965), I said to myself, "Hell, a pigeon can do that!" Sometime later, I mentioned my birdbrain idea to a friend and fellow scientist in the physiochemistry department who also supervised the electronics shop which supported the research division. He almost fell out of his chair and choked in a fit of laughter. However, after the joke had worn off, we talked more seriously about my odd notion, especially after I told him about Project ORCON (organic control—Skinner, 1960, 1965). Eventually the director of research and I talked about it. It so happened that I had come up with my suggestion at an opportune time. The company had recently spent a considerable sum of money on a machine constructed by an outside engineering firm designed to inspect automatically for double caps. It did not work. After some deliberation the director of research gave me the go-ahead to build a demonstration and tryout setup. With the able help and splendid cooperation of the instrument-shop people, under the direction of my friend of the physiochemistry department, a demonstration apparatus was built. The result of our labors is shown in Figures 1, 2, 3, and 4. Figure 1 provides a general overview of the entire apparatus except the endless belt-driving mechanism, a close-up of which is given in Figure 2. Figure 3 gives a top view of the "business end" of the pigeon's work space, and Figure 4 shows one of the birds in action.

FIG. 1. General overview of pill-inspection apparatus (except endless belt-driving mechanism).

While the apparatus was being designed and built, I had plenty of opportunity to consider varying aspects of the discrimination-training problems I would be faced with. The first decision to be made was which particular "skag" problem to tackle first. I obtained samples of various sized capsules of different colors. It was tempting to tackle the most troublesome problem first: the double-cap skag, especially those involving small capsules of colorless and transparent gelatin. On the actual inspection line these were the most difficult to spot. After playing around with different ways of presenting these capsules to a pigeon behind a modified pigeon key, a simple solution to the double-cap problem was discovered by accident. One of the minor problems to be solved was the lighting of the capsules presented behind the key. I discovered that by shining a narrow beam of light at the proper angle on a three-dimensional transparent curved surface, one obtains a focal point inside the object. (The tops and bottoms of all capsules are either round or oval.) In the case of a double-cap skag, one gets two clearly distinct focal points in slightly different positions. So, even in the case of

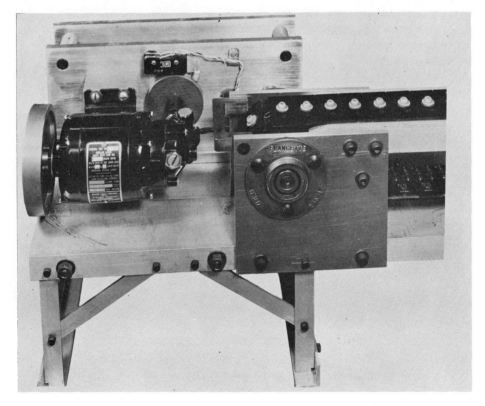

FIG. 2. Close-up of endless belt-driving mechanism of pill-inspection apparatus.

FIG. 3. Pill-inspection apparatus: top view of work space.

the transparent double-cap capsule, all a pigeon had to do was to discriminate between one versus two bright spots of light inside the curious objects behind his key: no problem! [1]

For the purpose of working out the details of the actual training and work procedure, however, I decided to take the simplest discrimination problem possible. I chose a simple color discrimination: white versus red capsules. Two naive birds were selected for inspection duty. For one bird the red capsules were arbitrarily defined as skags (S^Δ). For the other bird, the white capsules were given the same status.

As is clear from Figure 4, there were two pigeon keys. One key was actually a small transparent window, the other was opaque. The capsules could be brought into view behind the transparent key one by one at a maximum rate of about two per second. After a preliminary training phase, the birds were run as follows: A single peck on the weakly illuminated opaque

---

[1] The opaque, single-color double cap may still be a difficult discrimination problem, even for a pigeon.

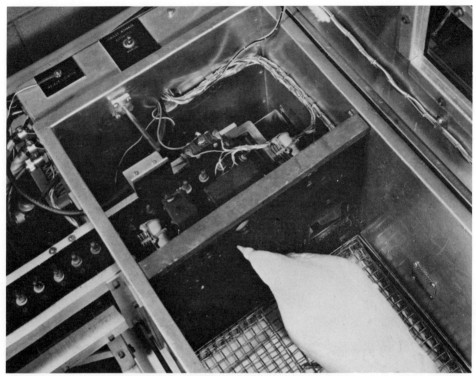

FIG. 4. Pill-inspection apparatus: pigeon at work.

key would (*a*) momentarily (.5 second) turn off the light behind the transparent key, and (*b*) weakly illuminate the window key to an extent insufficient to see much of the capsule in place behind it.

Next, a single peck on the now weakly lit window key would turn on a bright and narrow beam of light which clearly illuminated the capsule. The capsules were individually mounted in small and hollow bottlestops glued onto the metal plates of the endless belt (see Figures 2, 3, 4). If the bird now pecked three more times on the window key with the new illuminated capsule exposed to view, a brief tone would sound. Next came the moment of decision. If the capsule exposed to view was judged to be a skag, the bird was required to make two more pecks on the window key. This would (*a*) turn off the beam of light illuminating the capsule, (*b*) move up the next capsule, and (*c*) produce food by way of the automatic hopper on a fixed-percentage basis (usually 100%). However, if the capsule was considered to be acceptable, the bird indicated this by changing over to the opaque key. A peck on this key would also (*a*) turn off the beam of light behind the other key (window), and (*b*) move up the next capsule. It would not, however, produce reinforcement.

A bird, then, determined his own inspection rate. A peck on the opaque key would initiate an inspection cycle. However, reinforcement came only after making the appropriate number of pecks on the window key in case of a true skag only. Skags occurred rarely; they made up 10% of all the capsules on the belt. Wrong pecks, either false alarms or misses, did not get reinforced, and produced a blackout (Ferster, 1954) of 30 seconds. The results were very encouraging: Both birds inspected on a 99% correct basis within 1 week of daily discrimination training. The director of the pharmacology division, my immediate superior, who had watched the entire project with serious misgiving since its inception (he was sincerely afraid I was making a fool of myself), was delighted. In his immediate enthusiasm he called the director of research, who came over for a look. One week later the vice presidents as well as the president of the company had been given a demonstration. Everybody, including my immediate associates and co-workers, was greatly excited. The situation, as Skinner had previously discovered in a similar situation (Skinner, 1960), was a great source for jokes. There was talk about a new company subsidiary: "Inspection, Inc.!" (Company slogan: "It's for the birds!")

There were some sobering thoughts, however. One of them concerned the staggering problem of the logistics involved in getting pigeons to inspect as many as 20,000,000 separate objects each day. Although this problem did not seem insoluble to me, the details of the various possible approaches to a solution were never worked out.

After the company president had watched my feathered pupils perform, he congratulated me on my achievement. I was subsequently informed that serious consideration would be given to the further use and development of the method. I was also told that I could expect a visit from the chairman of the board and his brother, both elder statesmen of the company, who made all final policy decisions of importance. During their brief visit to the laboratory, one of them raised the question of possible adverse publicity. What about the Humane Society, and more important, suppose salesmen from other pharmaceutical houses would tell doctors not to buy any of our company's products: "Who would trust medicine inspected by pigeons?!" I suggested that the use of pigeons was incidental, and that, for example, one could use hawks just as well; after all, what is better than a hawk's eye? This suggestion produced a wan smile.

One other problem that was brought up raised the question of the pigeons coming in contact with what was being inspected. The competition could well choose to ignore the mechanical details of the situation and exploit the more distasteful but imaginary possibilities. Even though the birds would only see the capsules at a distance through a window, the first mental picture [2] is usually one of a pigeon "manually" (proboscically?) sorting cap-

---

[2] If a behaviorist may be excused for using such illegitimate terms . . .

sules, a thought no doubt repulsive to many people, especially to those who already have an aversion to birds as such.

After a brief stay, and a polite pat on the back, my distinguished visitors left.

Three weeks went by without any further word from HUM (Higher-Up-Management—Verhave, 1961). I concluded that probably meant that my pigeons were finished. I was right. Sometime later I was so informed. Through the grapevine I learned that the board of directors had voted 13 to 1 not to continue to explore the use of animals for quality-control inspection. The one "yes" vote presumably came from the director of research who initially had given me the green light for the preliminary demonstration.

There is one further amusing tale to the story: The company did try to patent my inspection method. The poor lawyer assigned to the case almost developed a nervous breakdown. It turned out to be "unpatentable" because, as the lawyers of the patent office put it (so succinctly), the method involved "a mental process" which is unpatentable in principle.[3] I tried to pin my lawyer friends down on what they meant by a "mental process." I suggested that the pigeon was merely an organic computer. However, I got nowhere. Lawyers apparently want no part of either physicalism or behaviorism.

So much as far as my own story is concerned. My efforts stimulated another exploratory attempt by my friend William Cumming, of Columbia University, who trained pigeons to inspect diodes. Brief descriptions of his work can be found in an article by Ferster and Ferster (1962), an anonymous (1959) article in *Factory,* and a recent article in *The Atlantic Monthly* by R. J. Herrnstein (1965).

One problem not yet touched on deserves some discussion. In the demonstration apparatus the capsules were coded as to whether they were acceptable or skags. In this way the automatic programing (relay) circuit could set up and enforce the appropriate discriminatory behavior of the birds. However, on an actual inspection line, this aspect of the training procedure could no longer be maintained. There would be no way of knowing which capsules are skags except by actual inspection. Consequently on a real inspection line there would be no way of knowing when to reward or not to reward the animal inspector! As a result, due to the lack of differential reward, the animal's discriminations would rapidly deteriorate.[4] There are two solutions. I discarded the first and most obvious one because it seemed mechanically cumbersome and not as interesting as the other solution.

[3] On this point, I may refer the reader to a recent article in *Science* by J. H. Munster, Jr., and Justin C. Smith (1965).

[4] Skinner, in his World War II project to train pigeons to home missiles, did not face this problem. His birds were meant to "extinguish" after a brief period of duty.

The first solution would involve the use of known skags. A certain percentage of the capsules inspected would consist of such labeled duds, and be used to check up on the discriminatory behavior of the birds. This is similar to the use of catch tests in human psychophysical experiments. This solution to the problem of guaranteeing that the animal inspector conforms to the values of his human employers makes it necessary to determine what minimum percentage of the objects inspected have to be planted skags in order to keep the inspecting behavior at an acceptable level of reliability.[5]

As a solution to the conformity-enforcement problem, however, this general solution is expensive and awkward. The on-line inspection equipment would need special machinery to insert in a random manner a fixed percentage of "stool-pigeon skags" and after inspection remove them again automatically for later reuse. The slightest observable difference between the "planted" objects and the other ones would lead to the development of a conditional discrimination (Lashley, 1938), and reintroduce the problem one set out to solve initially.

The second solution is simpler from a purely mechanical point of view. It also is of more theoretical or philosophical interest.

Briefly, it would involve the use of a minimum of two animals to simultaneously inspect each object. Initially, each animal would be trained to inspect capsules by using a training apparatus such as the one I had already constructed. In this apparatus all the capsules would be labeled as to whether they were skags or not and thus control the reward circuit.

After the desired discriminatory performance was well established the two birds would be removed to the on-line inspection situation. From then on the birds would only be rewarded if they *both* agreed on whether a particular object was a skag or not. Such an agreement-contingency setup would most likely be quite adequate to maintain the desired behavior. There is, of course, the possibility that both birds would indeed, once in a while, agree to treat a skag as an acceptable object. However, the probability of this happening for any particular object on a particular inspection trial is the product of the error frequencies (the probability of such an error) of each bird. If, therefore, each bird independently has an error frequency as high as 1 out of 100, the probability of both birds being wrong but still rewarded would be 1 out of 10,000! Hooking additional animals into the agreement-contingency circuit would make the possibility of the development of a "multiple folly" [6] very unlikely.

The solution is of some philosophical interest because it makes the pigeon observers act according to Charles Pierce's (1923, orig. publ. 1878) pragmatic theory of truth: "The opinion which is fated to be ultimately

[5] This question was investigated experimentally by Cumming.
[6] "folie a deux, trois, . . . n."

agreed to by all who investigate, is what is meant by the truth, and the object represented in this opinion is real [pp. 56–57]." It also appears to me that the agreement-contingency type of arrangement provides a basic paradigm for the experimental analysis of social behavior, a terra incognita so far hardly even explored by a systematic experimental investigation (Verhave, 1966).

In conclusion, let me point out that the idea of using trained animals for the dubious purposes of Homo sapiens is very old indeed. Since antiquity man has domesticated many animals. It seems an obvious development to apply our modern knowledge of behavior theory to the task of training some of our animal companions for the performance of various sophisticated tasks (Clarke, 1958; Herrnstein, 1965).

The obstacle in the way of such developments is not our ignorance of behavior, though it is still large, but mainly, it seems, the obstinate belief of man in his intellectual superiority over other creatures as well as a generalized fear of the imagined consequences of novel developments.

REFERENCES

Anonymous. This inspector is a bird. *Factory*, 1959 (Dec.), 219–221.

Clarke, A. C. Our dumb colleagues. *Harper's Magazine*, 1958, **216**, 32–33.

Ferster, C. B. Use of the blackout in the investigation of temporal discrimination in fixed-interval reinforcement. *Journal of Experimental Psychology*, 1954, **47**, 69–74.

Ferster, C. B., & Skinner, B. F. *Schedules of reinforcement.* New York: Appleton-Century-Crofts, 1957.

Ferster, Marilyn B., & Ferster, C. B. Animals as workers. *New Scientist*, 1962, **15**, 497–499.

Herrnstein, R. J. In defense of bird brains. *Atlantic Monthly*, 1965 (Sept.), **216**, 101–104.

Lashley, K. S. Conditional reactions in the rat. *Journal of Psychology*, 1938, **6**, 311–324.

Levi, W. M. *The pigeon.* (Rev. ed.) Sumter, S. C.: Levi Publishing Company, 1963.

Munster, J. H., Jr., & Smith, J. C. The care and feeding of intellectual property. *Science*, 1965, **148**, 739–743.

Peirce, C. How to make our ideas clear. (Orig. publ. 1878) In M. R. Cohen (Ed.), *Chance, love and logic.* New York: Harcourt, Brace, 1923.

Reese, E. P. *Experiments in operant behavior.* New York: Appleton-Century-Crofts, 1964.

Skinner, B. F. Pigeons in a pelican. *American Psychologist*, 1960, **15**, 28–37.

Skinner, B. F. Stimulus generalization in an operant: A historical note. In D. I. Mostofsky (Ed.), *Stimulus generalization.* Stanford: Stanford Univer. Press, 1965.

Smee, A. *Instinct and reason.* London: Reeve, Benham & Reeve, 1850.

Verhave, T. Recent developments in the experimental analysis of behavior. *Proceedings of the Eleventh Research Conference, American Meat Institute Foundation*, 1959, Mar., 113–116.

Verhave, T. Is the system approach of engineering psychology applicable to social organizations? *Psychological Record*, 1961, 11, 69–86.

Verhave, T. *The experimental analysis of behavior: Selected readings.* New York: Appleton-Century-Crofts, 1966, in press.

Introduction to
Krech Article

David Krech is one of our most colorful and outspoken psychologists as the title and contents of the following article will soon reveal. The tone and emphasis of the paper is set down at the very beginning: "Our psychology—especially when combined with educational practice and theory—must now be listed among the Powerful and, even perhaps, the Dangerous sciences. I refer specifically to the recent research developments in brain biochemistry and behavior—to some of which research I now turn."

After summarizing some of the recent psychophysiological research in learning and memory (including the Bennett et al. work appearing earlier in this volume), Krech speculates about how such findings may someday be utilized in education to modify human mental processes. He also points to the study of language as the best way to understand human behavior; he stresses the role of "species-specific" experiences in brain development; and he predicts that eventually ". . . the development of the mind of the child will come to rest in the knowledge and skills of the biochemist, and pharmacologist, and neurologist, and psychologist, and educator." To Krech, human learning and memory will someday be entrusted to ". . . a new expert abroad in the land—the psychoneurobiochemeducator. This multihybrid expert will have recourse . . . to protein memory consolidators, antimetabolite memory inhibitors, enzymatic learning stimulants, and many other potions and elixirs of the mind from our new psychoneurobiochemopharmacopia."

Now if the last quote left you somewhere between Isaac Asimov and Daniel Webster, don't despair. Approach the Krech paper with an open mind and a scrabble board and you will be ready for some interesting reading.

11

Psychoneurobiochemeducation

David Krech

I am a rat-brain psychologist with a weakness for speculation. Now time was when rat research was a fairly harmless activity, pursued by underpaid, dedicated, well-meaning characters. The world took little note and cared even less about our researches on how rats learned to thread their way through mazes. Oh, occasionally a misguided educator would take us seriously and try to fashion an educational psychology out of our rats-in-a-maze studies. But the classroom teachers—once removed from the school of education—would quickly see through such nonsense, and, forsaking all rats, would turn to the serious and difficult task of teaching children—unencumbered and unaided by our research and theory.

But time no longer is. Our psychology—especially when combined with educational practice and theory—must now be listed among the Powerful and, even perhaps, the Dangerous sciences. I refer specifically to the recent research developments in brain biochemistry and behavior—to some of which research I now turn.

The research I will discuss really concerns itself with the venerable mind-body problem beloved of philosophers and theologians. For brain biochemistry and behavior research seeks to find the *physical* basis for memory. In essence it asks the following question: In what corporal forms do we retain the remembrance of things past? What are the chemical or neurological or anatomical substrates of the evocative ghosts we call "memories"? Over the centuries of thought and decades of scientific research we have gained but very little on this question. Today, however, there is a feeling abroad that we are on the verge of great discoveries. Indeed, some researchers be-

SOURCE. *Phi Delta Kappan,* 1969, **50**, 370–375.

lieve that we already know, in the rough, the form the final answer will take to the question I have raised. And it is this: The physical basis of any memory, whatever else it may be, involves either the production of new proteins, the release of differentiated molecules of ribonucleic acids (RNA's) or the induction of higher enzymatic activity levels in the brain. In a word, for every separate memory in the mind we will eventually find a differ-entiated chemical in the brain—"chemical memory pellets," as it were.

What warrant do we have for such a prophecy? To begin with, we have reason to believe that the storage of memory in the brain is a many-splen-dored, multi-phased, actively changing affair. That is, any single memory is not merely "deposited" in a completed form in the brain. Rather, it goes through a complex developmental history in the brain in which it changes from a short-term into a long-term memory. And each stage in this con-solidation process seems to be dependent upon different although interre-lated chemical mechanisms. Let me indicate to you one set (of quite a num-ber which are now available) of speculative hypotheses concerning this de-velopmental transformation of memories.

First we can assume that immediately after every experience, a rela-tively short-lived reverberatory process is set up within the brain. This process continues for a time after the stimulus disappears and permits us to remember events which occurred moments or minutes ago. But this rever-beratory process fairly quickly decays and disappears—and as it does, so does the related memory. However, under certain conditions, the short-term reverbatory process, before it disappears completely from the scene, triggers off a second and quite different series of events in the brain. This second series of events involves the release of new RNA's or the production of new proteins and other macromolecules. And these chemical changes are rela-tively long-lasting and serve as the physical bases of our long-term memories.

Now it can be supposed that if we increased the robustness or the sur-vival time of the initial reverberatory process we might increase the prob-ability of converting the short-term memory into a long-term memory. There are several ways one could do that. Through the repetition of the same stimulus one could presumably prolong or continually reinstate the reverberatory process and thus, perhaps, make it more effective in inducing permanent chemical changes in the brain. The old-fashioned term for this procedure is "drill" or "practice," and drill and practice are indeed effective techniques for helping the conversion of short-term memories into long-term ones.

But James McGaugh, at the University of California at Irvine, got the bright idea that he could achieve much the same results chemically. His argument—very much simplified—went something like this: A drug which would increase neural and chemical activity within the brain might either increase the vigor of the reverberatory process, or the ease with which the long-term chemical processes would "take off," and thus facilitate the conversion of short-term memories into long-term ones. Apparently his idea was a sound one, for with the use of chemical compounds like strychnine and metrazol, which are central nervous system stimulants, McGaugh has been eminently successful in raising the intellectual level of hundreds of southern California mice.

In one of his experiments which is most pregnant with social implications and promises and forebodings for the future, McGaugh tested the maze-learning ability of two quite different strains of mice. One of the strains was, by heredity, particularly adept at maze learning; the other, particularly stupid at that task. Some animals from each strain were injected with different doses of metrazol after each daily learning trial to see whether there would be an improvement in their ability to retain what they had learned on that trial—and some were not. The findings pleased everyone—presumably even the mice. With the optimal dosage of metrazol, the chemically treated mice were 40 percent better in remembering their daily lessons than were their untreated brothers. Indeed, under metrazol treatment the hereditarily stupid mice were able to turn in better performances than their hereditarily superior but untreated colleagues. Here we have a "chemical memory pill" which not only improves memory and learning but can serve to make all mice equal whom God—or genetics—hath created unequal. May I suggest that some place in the back of your mind, you might begin to speculate on what it can mean—socially, educationally, politically—if and when we find drugs which will be similarly effective for human beings.

But let me continue with my story. What chemistry can give, it can also take away—as Agranoff and his now notorious goldfish at the University of Michigan have shown. Agranoff argued that if we could prevent the brain from manufacturing the chemicals involved in the long-term memory process, then we would create an animal which might have normal short-term memories, but would be incapable of establishing enduring memories. Agranoff trained his fish to swim from one side of an aquarium to another, whenever a signal light was turned on, in order to avoid an electric shock. Goldfish can learn this task within a 40-minute period, and once it is learned, they remember it over many days. Now Agranoff varied his experiments. Immediately before, and in some experiments immediately after, training, Agranoff injected puromycin or actinomycin-D (two antibiotics which prevent the formation of new proteins or nuclear RNA) into the brains of a new group of goldfish. His findings were most encouraging (to Agranoff, that is, not necessarily to the goldfish). The injected goldfish were not impaired in their *learning* of the shock-avoidance task since, presumably, the short-term reverberatory process which enables a fish to remember its lesson from one trial to another—a matter of a few seconds—does not involve the synthesis of new proteins or nuclear RNA. But when tested a day or two later the fish showed almost no retention for the task they had known so well the day before—indicating that the long-term process *is* dependent upon the synthesis of these compounds in the brain. Here, then, we find not only support for our general theory but we have a suggestion that there exist in antimetabolites whole families of chemical memory preventatives which seem not to interfere with the individual's immediate capacity to obey immediate orders, but which do prevent him from building up a permanent body of experiences, expectations, and skills. Conjure up, if you are of that mind, what evils such weapons can wreak in the hands of the Orwellian authorities of 1984—but I must hurry on to our next set of experiments.

A number of years ago, James McConnell at the University of Michigan threw all the brain researchers into a tizzy by reporting that he had succeeded in teaching planaria—a fairly primitive type of flatworm—to make a simple response to a light signal, that he then ground up his educated flatworms, fed the pieces to untrained fellow worms—and lo and behold, the uneducated flatworms wound up with the *memories* of the worms which they had just eaten, and, without any training, could perform the response of the late-lamented and digested "donor" worms!

But then all hell broke loose when other workers in other laboratories and in other countries reported that they could train a *rat*, make an extract from its brain, inject this extract into an untrained rat, and by so doing cause the recipient rat to acquire the memories of the now-dead donor rat. It is one thing to claim this for the primitive planaria, which, after all, do not have very much in the way of a structurally differentiated and organized brain. It is a very different thing to claim it for the rat, which *is* a serious mammal, with a highly developed brain, not too different in complexity, in differentiation, and in organization from our own.

The dust raised by these reports has not yet settled. Indeed, most scientists are definitely on the side of the nonbelievers—but the work goes on, and we cannot predict the final outcome of these experiments, many of which have given negative results. However, as a result of this work, a number of brain researchers have been moved, over the last two or three years, from the position of stiff-necked disbelief to the position of "well, maybe—I don't believe it, but well, maybe." And this is where *I* stand at the moment—fearless and foursquare proclaiming "well, maybe. . . ." Now, if it should come to pass that McConnell and his fellow believers are right, then we will indeed have made a huge jump forward. For we would then have a most effective behavioral assay method which should enable us to zero in on this marvelous brain-goulash which can transfer information from one brain to another, and isolate and identify in detail all the "memory" proteins, enzymes, RNA's, or other macromolecules. After that—the world of the mind is ours! But that day is not here yet. Let me leave these brave new world experimenters and go on with another question and another set of experiments.

Does the research I have reviewed mean that if and when we will have developed get-smart pills (*a la* McGaugh), or chemical erasures of wrong mental habits (*a la* Agranoff), or specific knowledge pills (*a la* McConnell), we will be able to do without Head Start programs, educational enrichment programs, school supervisors, educational research, and, indeed, without most of our educational paraphernalia? The answer to this question, gentlemen, is a most reassuring "NO." I might even say, *"Au contraire."* Precisely because of the advances in brain biochemistry, the significance of the educator will be greatly increased—*and just as greatly changed*. Let me tell you why I think so by describing to you the results of some of our own work in the Berkeley laboratories.

Some time ago we set ourselves the following problem: If the laying down of memories involves the synthesis of chemical products in the brain, then one should find that an animal which has lived a life replete with opportunities for learning and memorizing would end with a brain chemically and morphologically different from an animal which has lived out an intellectually impoverished life. For almost two decades, now, E. L. Bennett, Marion Diamond, M. R. Rosenzweig, and I, together with technical assistants, graduate students, and thousands of rats, have labored—and some of us have even sacrificed our lives—to find such evidence. Let me tell you some of what we found.

At weaning time we divide our experimental rats into two groups, half of the rats being placed in an "intellectually enriched" environment, the other half—their brothers—in the deprived environment. While both groups receive identical food and water, their psychological environments differ greatly. The animals in the first group live together in one large cage, are provided with many rat toys (tunnels to explore, ladders to climb, levers to press), and they are assigned to graduate students who are admonished to give these rats loving care and kindness, teach them to run mazes, and in general to provide them with the best and most expensive supervised higher education available to any young rat at the University of California. While these rats are thus being encouraged to store up many and varied memories, their brother rats, in the deprived group, live in isolated, barren cages, devoid of stimulation by either their environmental appurtenances, fellow rats, or graduate students. After about 80 days of this differential treatment, all the animals are sacrificed, their brains dissected out and various chemical and histological analyses performed. The results are convincing. The brain from a rat from the enriched environment—and presumably, therefore, with many more stored memories—has a heavier and thicker cortex, a better blood supply, larger brain cells, more glia cells, and increased activity of two brain enzymes, acetylcholinesterase and cholinesterase, than does the brain from an animal whose life has been less memorable.

We can draw several morals from these experiments. First, the growing animal's psychological environment is of crucial importance for the development of its brain. By manipulating the environment of the young, one can truly create a "lame brain"—with lighter cortex, shrunken brain cells, fewer glia cells. smaller blood vessels, and lower enzymatic activity levels—or one can create a more robust, a healthier, a more metabolically active brain. If it should turn out that what is true for the rat brain is also true for the human brain, and that by careful manipulation of this or that group's early environment we can develop among them bigger and better brains or smaller and meaner ones, the wondrous promises of a glorious future or the monstrous horrors of a Huxlian brave new world are fairly self-evident.

The second conclusion I draw from our experiments is this: Since the effect of any chemical upon an organ is, in part, a function of the beginning chemical status of that organ, and since—as we have just seen—the chemical and anatomical status of the individual's brain is determined by his educational experience, then the effectiveness of the biochemist's "get smart pill" will depend upon how the educator has prepared the brain in the first instance. Indeed, a review of all the data indicates that manipulating the educational and psychological environment is a more effective way of inducing long-lasting brain changes than direct administration of drugs. Educators probably change brain structure and chemistry to a greater degree than any biochemist in the business. Another way of saying this is: The educator *can potentiate or undo the work of the brain biochemist.*

But there is still more to report, and more lessons to draw. Consider the experimental problem we faced when we tried to create a psychologically enriched environment for our Berkeley rats. We did not really know how, so we threw everything into the environment, including, almost the kitchen sink, and called it "a psychologically enriched environment." The cages were kept in brightly lighted, sound-filled rooms; the rats were given playmates to relate to, games to manipulate, maze problems to solve, new areas to explore. They were fondled and tamed and chucked under the chin at the drop of a site-visitor. In other words, we provided our happy rats with almost every kind of stimulation we could think of—or afford. And it seems to have worked. But of course it is quite possible that in our "kitchen-sink design," many of the things we did were not at all necessary—indeed, some may have had an adverse effect. And so we undertook a series of experiments to discover which elements of our environment were effective and which were not. I shall not bore you with the details of the many experiments already run and the many more which are now being run in the Berkeley laboratory. Let me list, however, some of the tentative conclusions which one can already make:

First: Sheer exercise or physical activity alone is not at all effective in developing the brain. A physical training director seems not to be an adequate substitute for a teacher.

Second: Varied visual stimulation, or indeed any kind of visual stimulation, is neither necessary nor sufficient to develop the brain, as we were able to demonstrate by using rats blinded at weaning age.

Third: Handling, or taming, or petting is also without effect in developing the growing rat's brain. Love is Not Enough.

Fourth: The presence of a brother rat in our intellectually deprived rat's cage helps him not a whit. *Bruderschaft* is not enough.

Fifth: Teaching the rat to press levers for food—that and only that seems to help somewhat, but only minimally. Not every problem-set will do, either.

The only experience we have thus far found really effective is freedom to roam around in a large object-filled space. From a recent experiment in Diamond's laboratory there are some suggestions that if the young rat is given continuous and varied maze-problems to solve—that and little else— the rat will develop a number of the same brain changes (at least the morphological ones) which we had observed in our randomly "enriched" environment.

It is clear, then, that not *every* experience or variation in stimulation contributes equally to the development of the brain. But of even greater interest is the suggestion in the above data that the most effective way to develop the brain is through what I will call *species-specific enrichment experiences.* Here is what I mean: The ability of a rat to learn its way through tunnels and dark passages, to localize points in a three-dimensional space full of objects to be climbed upon, burrowed under, and crawled through is, we can assume, of particular survival value for the rat as he is now constituted. Presumably, through the selective evolutionary process, the rat has developed a brain which is peculiarly fitted to support and enhance these skills. The "effective rat brain," therefore, is one which is a good "space-brain"—not a lever-pressing brain or an arithmetic-reasoning brain. The effective stimulating environment, correspondingly, would be one which makes *spatial learning* demands on that brain—which "pushes" that particular kind of brain in that particular way. To generalize this hypothesis, I would suggest that *for each species there exists a set of species-specific experiences which are maximally enriching and which are maximally efficient in developing its brain.*

If there be any validity to my hypothesis, then the challenge to the human educator is clear. For the educator, too, you may have noticed, has been using the kitchen-sink approach when he seeks to design a psychologically or educationally enriched environment for the child. Some educators would bombard the child—practically from infancy on—with every kind of stimulus change imaginable. His crib is festooned with jumping beads and dangling colored bits and pieces of wood (all sold very expensively to his affluent parents); he is given squishy, squeaking, squawking toys to play with, to fondle, to be frightened by, to choke on. He is jounced and bounced and picked up and put down. And when he goes to school—he finds the same blooming, buzzing confusion. He is stimulated with play activities, with opportunities for social interaction, with rhythmic movements, with music, with visual displays, with contact sports, with tactual experiences, and with anything and everything which the school system can think of—or afford. But it may be that a "stimulating environment" and an "enriched environment" are not one and the same thing. It is not true that a brain is a brain is a brain. The rat is a rat and he hath a rat's brain; the child is a child and he hath a child's brain—and each, according to my hypothesis, requires its own educational nutrient. What, then, are the species-specific enrichments for the human child?

Of course I do not know the answer to this question, but let me share with you my present enthusiastic guess that in the language arts will you find part of the answer.

I can start with no better text than a quotation from my teacher, Edward Chace Tolman, who was a completely devoted rat psychologist. "Speech," he wrote, ". . . is in any really developed and characteristic sense, the sole prerogative of the human being. . . . It is speech which first and foremost distinguishes man from the great apes" (1932).[1] In my opinion, it is in the study of language, above anything else, that the psychologist will discover the psychology of man, and that the educator will discover how to educate man.

In the first place, and we must be clear about this, human language, with its complex and *abstract structure,* has *nothing* in common with animal communication. Language is probably the clearest instance of a pure species-specific behavior. This is true whether you study language as a neurologist, or as a psychologist. Let us look at some brain research first.

Recently Robinson, at the National Institute of Mental Health (1967), attempted to discover which areas of the monkey's brain controlled its vocalizations.[2] Now the monkey most certainly uses vocalization for communication, but principally for communications with emotional tone such as threat, fear, pain, and pleasure. In Robinson's study 15 unanesthetized animals, with brains exposed by surgery, were used. Some 5,880 different loci or spots in the brain were stimulated by electrodes to see whether such stimulation could bring forth vocalization. The loci explored included neocortical areas as well as areas in the limbic system, that older part of the mammalian brain which is most intimately involved with motivational and emotional responses.

Robinson's results were clear-cut: First, despite his exploration of several hundred different neocortical sites he was unable to raise a single sound from his animals by stimulating their *neocortex*. Second, stimulation of the limbic system brought forth regular, consistent, and identifiable vocalizations.

These results differ sharply from those found with the human brain. While there is some evidence that human cries and exclamations—uttered in moments of excitement—are also controlled by the limbic system, *speech and language clearly depend upon neocortical areas*—areas for which there simply are no analogues in the brain of any other animal. These areas are, of course, the well-known Broca and Wernicke areas in the left hemisphere of the human brain. It seems clear, as Robinson puts it, that "human speech did not develop 'out of' primate vocalization, but arose from *new tissue* [italics my own] which permitted it the necessary detachment from immediate, emotional situations." Man's brain, *and man's brain alone,* is a language-supporting brain.

Corresponding to the neurological picture is the psycholinguist's view of language. Almost every psycholinguist is impressed not only with the unique nature of language itself but with its unique mode of achievement by the child. Whatever value so-called reinforcement or stimulus-response theories of learning may have for describing acquisition of motor skills by people, maze-learning by rats, and bar-pressing by pigeons—these theories are assessed as completely trivial and utterly irrelevant when it comes to understanding that "stunning intellectual achievement" (McNeill, 1966),[3] the acquisition of language by the child. Indeed, in reading the psycho-linguist's work one is left with the impression that we will have to develop a species-specific learning theory for this species-specific behavior of language. I must confess that I agree with them. And if we ever achieve an understanding of language development, and if we learn how to push the *human* brain with this *human* experience, then will we indeed by on our way.

I know that other people have proposed other ways with which to enrich the child's education. Some plug for what are referred to as "cognitive" experience or "productive thinking" experiences, etc. Let me hasten to record that I quite agree with them. As a matter of fact, I am not at all certain that I am saying anything other than what my cognitive friends propose. For I hold with McNeill's judgment that ". . . the study of how language is acquired may provide insight into the very basis of mental life." And, I would go on, being human *means* having an effective mental, cognitive life.

It is for these and many, many other reasons that I would urge the educator to turn to the psycholinguist—as well as to Piaget and Crutchfield and Bruner—for his major guides in designing a rational educational enrichment program.

Whether my guess merits this enthusiasm or not will perhaps eventually be determined by research. But here is the challenge and here is the promise for the educator. Drop your kitchen-sink approach, and specify and define for us the species-specific psychologically enriching experiences for the child —and we will be off and running!

Where will we run? Let me speculate out loud. It is perfectly reasonable to suppose that we will be able to find specific biochemical boosters and biochemical inhibitors for different kinds of memories and imagery, or for different kinds of abilities, or for different kinds of personality or temperament traits. With such chemical agents in hand, and with appropriate educational and training procedures, we may use them as supplementary therapy for those failing in this or that trait and thus will we be able to rectify and heal some of the mentally retarded and the senile. Of course we may use these agents for evil—to create docile, intellectually limited, but efficient human beasts of burden without memories beyond the order of the day (remember Agranoff's fish?).

But above all, there will be great changes made in the first and foremost and continuing business of society: the education and training of the young. The development of the mind of the child will come to rest in the knowledge and skills of the biochemist, and pharmacologist, and neurologist, and psychologist, and educator. And there will be a new expert abroad in the land—the psychoneurobiochemeducator. This multi-hybrid expert will have recourse—as I have suggested elsewhere—to protein memory consolidators, antimetabolite memory inhibitors, enzymatic learning stimulants, and many other potions and elixirs of the mind from our new psychoneurobiochemopharmacopia.

There is a grievous problem here, however. Experts, whatever else they may be, are notorious order-takers. *Who* will direct our psychoneurobiochemeducator where to work his expertise, and *what* shall we tell him to do? Here we are talking about goals, values, and aims. Shall our expert raise or lower docility, aggressiveness, musical ability, engineering ability, artistic sensitivity, effective intellectual functioning? Shall different ethnic or racial or national or social groups receive different treatments? In past centuries, and even today, this differential group treatment is precisely what our relatively primitive but quite effective medical and educational experts have been ordered by us to carry out. And lo, they have done so! On one side of the town they have created enclaves of the sickly, the weak, the ignorant, the unskilled—in a word, the brutalized social vanquished. On the other side of the town they have created the social victors—the healthy, the strong, the knowledgeable, the skilled. Will we continue to do this in the future with our much more sophisticated and effective psychoneurobiochemeducators? Who, in other words, will control the brain controllers— and to what ends?

I have thought and worried about these questions, and I must confess to you that I cannot avoid a dread feeling of unease about the future.

At the same time I keep whistling the following tune in an attempt to cheer myself up: If there be any validity at all to my speculations this afternoon, they add up to this: The biochemist, neurologist, psychologist, and educator will eventually add to the intellectual stature of man. With this in mind, and clinging to a life-long faith in the virtues of knowledge and the intellect (for certainly, at this stage I can do no less), I find myself believing that man who by taking thought will have added cubits to his intellectual stature, will also acquire the added bit of wisdom and humaneness that will save us all. Let me stop on this note—before I scrutinize this faith and this hope too carefully.

NOTES AND REFERENCES

1. Edward Chace Tolman, *Purposive Behavior in Animals and Men*. New York: The Century Company, 1932.
2. B. W. Robinson, "Vocalization Evoked from Forebrain in *Macaca Mulatta*," *Physiology and Behavior*, 1967, No. 2, pp. 345–54.
3. D. McNeill, "The Creation of Language," *Discovery*, 1966, No. 27, pp. 34–38.

Psychologists are finding out some exciting new things about how and when children learn best. (LYNN MCLAREN | RAPHO GUILLUMETTE)

Section IV
Growth and Development

"As the trunk grows, so the tree is bent." This old adage expresses succinctly the reason why psychologists must study the growth and development of the organism if they ever hope to understand his behavior. The more the scientist learns about the early years of a child's life the more proficient he becomes in comprehending human behavior during *all* stages of life. We are in some measure what we were—and the psychologist who investigates early life experiences finds a fertile area for scientific insights into the mysteries of human conduct.

The greatest of all psychological thinkers, Sigmund Freud, was quick to recognize and emphasize the role of early childhood experiences in personality development. To Freud an individual's personality was basically determined for life by the youthful age of six! Therefore, he looked to childhood experiences in his quest to explain adult behavioral aberrations. In his clinical practice Freud would often "take the patient back to his childhood" to uncover the underlying cause of his condition—a cause usually centered around the patient's interpersonal relations or sexual development in youth. Such was the importance of growth and development to Freud in his conception of human behavior.

Recently the study of human growth and development has enjoyed a renaissance of sorts—a period of scientific breakthroughs spearheaded by such able thinkers as Swiss psychologist Jean Piaget and Harvard University's Jerome Bruner. Today we are closer to understanding the way in which cognitive development takes place in the child and the importance of infant activity in the first two years of life for healthy mental growth. At the same time studies by psychologists working with animals (e.g., Harlow) point to possible conditions that should be present in a young infant's life if proper, healthy development is to take place.

In the papers that follow some of the "scientific breakthroughs" referred to above are presented or discussed. In the first paper A. S. Neill, founder of the Summerhill school in England, presents his educational system which, supposedly, can make children grow up happy and free. This is followed by Sava's article, which focuses on the new discoveries concerning intellectual growth in childhood and discusses the implications of these discoveries for American education. The importance of early education is stressed— education designed to take advantage of, and stimulate, the intellectual growth of the young child. The third article by Harry Harlow records the sexual inadequacies of monkeys who, in early life, were raised apart from other monkeys. Like the Sava article before it, the Harlow document points to the importance of early experiences in the growing and developing organism for behavior in later life.

Introduction to
Neill Article

There is no doubt that a child's education influences his personality development and the way in which he interacts with his environment. It has been suggested, for example, that if our educational system taught children to think in a creative manner, we would produce graduates better able to cope with today's complex and changing world (Schroder, Karlins, & Phares, 1971). Many people view school as a second major force (parents are the first) in transmitting to the child the expectations and regulations of his society. As Americans, we are education conscious and education goers. In such an atmosphere—where education is so important and where most of us attend school for such long periods of time—it seems eminently worthwhile to examine various educational systems and philosophies and see how they affect the growth and development of the child.

One educational approach that has been gaining increasing attention and popularity of late is proposed by A. S. Neill the English founder and director of the Summerhill school. For Neill, education is part of the child-rearing process—a part that will greatly affect the growth and development of the individual. Neill's educational philosophy and practice are intertwined in his school where the importance of each individual student is emphasized and freedom is stressed in the teaching and learning process.

We can gain great insight into the philosophy of Summerhill and Neill's beliefs concerning the education and upbringing of children by examining his writings below. As you shall see, Neill believes in the innate goodness of the child. Give the child the freedom to develop on his own, claims Neill, and he will grow into a happy, healthy, self-actualized individual. Neill emphasizes the importance of happiness in life and, in a key phrase that gives great insight into the Summerhill philosophy, he claims: "I would rather see a school produce a happy street cleaner than a neurotic scholar."

After reading the paper below you might respond as many of my students have: "Gee, it sounds great—but what happens to the children once they leave Summerhill and must return to a society where Summerhill freedom does not exist? Will they be prepared to live and function in such a world?" One answer to this question comes from a follow-up study of Summerhill graduates (Bernstein, 1968). In his investigation, Bernstein interviewed 50 Summerhill graduates to see how they were getting along after leaving Neill's school. Although his study can be challenged on methodological grounds (his sampling and interviewing techniques) Bernstein, nonetheless, does provide us with a composite picture of the Summerhillian graduate ". . . working, raising responsive children, enjoying life." Bernstein's findings also suggest that a Summerhill education is most beneficial when it is not too long (e.g., four years of attendance seems better than ten or more) and that self-confident, outgoing children gain more from the Summerhill environment than shy, withdrawn individuals.*

REFERENCE

Bernstein, E. What does a Summerhill old school tie look like? *Psychology Today,* 1968, **2**, 37–41+.

Schroder, H., Karlins, M., & Phares, J. *Education for freedom.* Unpublished manuscript, 1971.

* For the interested student, two recent books on Summerhill have just been published: (1) Neill, A. S. *The last man alive.* New York: Hart, 1969; (2) Walmsley, J. *Neill and Summerhill: a man and his work* (a pictorial study). Baltimore: Penguin, 1969.

12

Summerhill
(Excerpts from the Introduction)

A. S. Neill

This is a story of a modern school—Summerhill.

Summerhill was founded in the year 1921. The school is situated within the village of Leiston, in Suffolk, England, and is about one hundred miles from London.

Just a word about Summerhill pupils. Some children come to Summerhill at the age of five years, and others as late as fifteen. The children generally remain at the school until they are sixteen years old. We generally have about twenty-five boys and twenty girls.

The children are divided into three age groups: The youngest range from five to seven, the intermediates form eight to ten, and the oldest from eleven to fifteen.

Generally we have a fairly large sprinkling of children from foreign countries. At the present time (1960) we have five Scandinavians, one Hollander, one German and one American.

The children are housed by age groups with a house mother for each group. The intermediates sleep in a stone building, the seniors sleep in huts. Only one or two older pupils have rooms for themselves. The boys live two or three or four to a room, and so do the girls. The pupils do not have to stand room inspection and no one picks up after them. They are left free. No one tells them what to wear: they put on any kind of costume they want to at any time.

Newspapers call it a *Go-as-you-please School* and imply that it is a gathering of wild primitives who know no law and have no manners.

It seems necessary, therefore, for me to write the story of Summerhill as honestly as I can. That I write with a bias is natural; yet I shall try to

SOURCE. *Summerhill: A radical approach to child rearing.* New York: Hart Publishing Co., 1950.

show the demerits of Summerhill as well as its merits. Its merits will be the merits of healthy, free children whose lives are unspoiled by fear and hate.

Obviously, a school that makes active children sit at desks studying mostly useless subjects is a bad school. It is a good school only for those who believe in *such* a school, for those uncreative citizens who want docile, uncreative children who will fit into a civilization whose standard of success is money.

Summerhill began as an experimental school. It is no longer such; it is now a demonstration school, for it demonstrates that freedom works.

When my first wife and I began the school, we had one main idea: *to make the school fit the child*—instead of making the child fit the school.

I had taught in ordinary schools for many years. I knew the other way well. I knew it was all wrong. It was wrong because it was based on an adult conception of what a child should be and of how a child should learn. The other way dated from the days when psychology was still an unknown science.

Well, we set out to make a school in which we should allow children freedom to be themselves. In order to do this, we had to renounce all discipline, all direction, all suggestion, all moral training, all religious instruction. We have been called brave, but it did not require courage. All it required was what we had—a complete belief in the child as a good, not an evil, being. For almost forty years, this belief in the goodness of the child has never wavered; it rather has become a final faith.

My view is that a child is innately wise and realistic. If left to himself without adult suggestion of any kind, he will develop as far as he is capable of developing. Logically, Summerhill is a place in which people who have the innate ability and wish to be scholars will be scholars; while those who are only fit to sweep the streets will sweep the streets. But we have not produced a street cleaner so far. Nor do I write this snobbishly, for I would rather see a school produce a happy street cleaner than a neurotic scholar.

What is Summerhill like? Well, for one thing, lessons are optional. Children can go to them or stay away from them—for years if they want to. There *is* a timetable—but only for the teachers.

The children have classes usually according to their age, but sometimes according to their interests. We have no new methods of teaching, because we do not consider that teaching in itself matters very much. Whether a school has or has not a special method for teaching long division is of no significance, for long division is of no importance except to those who *want* to learn it. And the child who *wants* to learn long division *will* learn it no matter how it is taught.

·   ·   ·   ·

Summerhill is possibly the happiest school in the world. We have no truants and seldom a case of homesickness. We very rarely have fights—

quarrels, of course, but seldom have I seen a stand-up fight like the ones we used to have as boys. I seldom hear a child cry, because children when free have much less hate to express than children who are downtrodden. Hate breeds hate, and love breeds love. Love means approving of children, and that is essential in any school. You can't be on the side of children if you punish them and storm at them. Summerhill is a school in which the child knows that he is approved of.

.   .   .   .

In Summerhill, everyone has equal rights. No one is allowed to walk on my grand piano, and I am not allowed to borrow a boy's cycle without his permission. At a General School Meeting, the vote of a child of six counts for as much as my vote does.

But, says the knowing one, in practice of course the voices of the grown-ups count. Doesn't the child of six wait to see how you vote before he raises his hand? I wish he sometimes would, for too many of my proposals are beaten. Free children are not easily influenced; the absence of fear accounts for this phenomenon. Indeed, the absence of fear is the finest thing that can happen to a child.

Our children do not fear our staff. One of the school rules is that after ten o'clock at night there shall be quietness on the upper corridor. One night, about eleven, a pillow fight was going on, and I left my desk, where I was writing, to protest against the row. As I got upstairs, there was a scurrying of feet and the corridor was empty and quiet. Suddenly I heard a disappointed voice say, "Humph, it's only Neill," and the fun began again at once. When I explained that I was trying to write a book downstairs, they showed concern and at once agreed to chuck the noise. Their scurrying came from the suspicion that their bedtime officer (one of their own age) was on their track.

I emphasize the importance of this absence of fear of adults. A child of nine will come and tell me he has broken a window with a ball. He tells me, because he isn't afraid of arousing wrath or moral indignation. He may have to pay for the window, but he doesn't have to fear being lectured or being punished.

.   .   .   .

The most frequent remark that visitors make is that they cannot tell who is staff and who is pupil. It is true: the feeling of unity is that strong when children are approved of. There is no deference to a teacher as a teacher. Staff and pupils have the same food and have to obey the same community laws. The children would resent any special privileges given to the staff.

When I used to give the staff a talk on psychology every week, there was a muttering that it wasn't fair. I changed the plan and made the talks open to everyone over twelve. Every Tuesday night, my room is filled with eager youngsters who not only listen but give their opinions freely. Among the subjects the children have asked me to talk about have been these: The Inferiority Complex, The Psychology of Stealing, The Psychology of the Gangster, The Psychology of Humor, Why Did Man Become a Moralist?, Masturbation, Crowd Psychology. It is obvious that such children will go out into life with a broad clear knowledge of themselves and others.

The most frequent question asked by Summerhill visitors is, "Won't the child turn round and blame the school for not making him learn arithmetic or music?" The answer is that young Freddy Beethoven and young Tommy Einstein will refuse to be kept away from their respective spheres.

The function of the child is to live his own life—not the life that his anxious parents think he should live, nor a life according to the purpose of the educator who thinks he knows what is best. All this interference and guidance on the part of adults only produces a generation of robots.

You cannot *make* children learn music or anything else without to some degree converting them into will-less adults. You fashion them into accepters of the *status quo*—a good thing for a society that needs obedient sitters at dreary desks, standers in shops, mechanical catchers of the 8:30 suburban train—a society, in short, that is carried on the shabby shoulders of the scared little man—the scared-to-death conformist.

Introduction to
Sava Article

Sometimes the study of human growth and development leads to changes in our cultural institutions and practices. Changes occur when experimental findings tell us something about childhood behavior that we did not realize before—something that requires us to modify our institutions and practices to adjust to such insights. Nowhere is there a clearer example of the relationship between scientific discovery and institutional change than in the recent revelations concerning childhood intelligence.

Until a few decades ago a child's early years were thought of as relatively unimportant to his intellectual growth. Little wonder. Most of the time the child ate and slept—and when he was not snacking and snoozing he was engaged in seemingly inconsequential play. It is now believed that much of the child's intellectual growth is accomplished in these early years of life, and even such actions as "inconsequential play" serve to teach the child about the world and to develop his cognitive potential. Just as Freud earlier recognized the importance of childhood in determining the course of human personality, researchers now understand ". . . that the years from birth to six may well be the most important to a child's intellectual growth, as well as to his social and emotional development" (Sava, 1968).

In his article below Samuel Sava discusses the implications of these recent findings in growth and development for American education. The importance of early education is stressed—education designed to take advantage of, and to stimulate, the intellectual growth of the young child. The author is basically saying: "Look, now that we have learned of the young child's intellective needs and growth let us shape our educational institutions to satisfy his needs and aid his growth."

Sava's message to the school administrator, based on the recent research findings in human growth and development, is sobering and straightforward: "The evidence is indisputable that we are wasting enormous amounts of human ability through our failure to teach children when they are most capable of learning and eager to do it. We should realize that a massive investment in early childhood education today may be our best buy for a more intelligent citizenry tomorrow."

13

When Learning Comes Easy

Samuel G. Sava

At least since Charles Darwin began keeping records of his children's words and actions in an effort to relate them to his theory of evolution, investigators have been trying to trace the labyrinths of human mental development. A century of inquiry has raised as many questions as it has answered, partly because children—unlike mice—cannot be reared by the hundreds under laboratory conditions that enable scientists to regulate each of the factors that influence growth and development. Although the process of analyzing mental development is difficult and erratic, the information we already have indicates that we may be making some monumental mistakes in our efforts to develop human potential.

Consider the arrangement of our educational system. Generally speaking, the older a youngster is, the more time and effort we devote to his education. During the 1966–67 academic year, American taxpayers spent an average of $455 to instruct each public grammar school student, $680 on each high school student, and $1,518 on each college student. While the average elementary-school teacher had twenty-six pupils in her class, the high-school teacher had twenty, and the college professor, only twelve.

To a degree, this pattern of expenditure, rising with age, reflects equipment and personnel costs that cannot be reduced. While college-level instruction in science, for instance, may require analytical balances, electron microscopes, centrifuges, and a professor with a Ph.D., an imaginative teacher with a B.S. can introduce first-graders to some elementary scientific concepts with such humble materials as salt and pepper, a drinking glass, and a candle. But this pattern probably also reflects a feeling that the lower levels of education are neither as complex nor important as initiating col-

SOURCE. *Saturday Review,* November 16, 1968. Copyright 1968 Saturday Review, Inc.

lege sophomores into the mysteries of vector analysis, the Brownian movement, and the reasons for the decline of the Hapsburg Empire.

In fact, research on the learning process suggests that early childhood education may be both more important and more demanding than any instruction that follows. The United States, like every other "advanced" nation, may have its spending priorities upside down. It may be that we would make much better use of our educational resources if, instead of beginning the formal educational process at the age of six, we started it at two or three, and if instead of spending an average of $2,000 or more to instruct each twenty-year-old, we devoted that amount to each three-year-old. Perhaps, in other words, we could have a better system of education if we took the present one and stood it on its head.

But the entire history of early childhood education and the folklore that has grown up around it stand in the way of any such revolution. Formal preschool education is nearly 200 years old, dating from the *crèches* and *salles d'asile* established in France in the late 1700s to protect children from the influences of the streets. For the next century and-a-half, early childhood education continued to be conceived in social-welfare terms, as a way of shielding children from harmful influences, of enabling patriotic mothers to work in war plants, and even as a way of protecting property.

Dr. Maria Montessori, for example, inaugurated her experiments in child development not at the invitation of an education-minded group, but at the earnest solicitation of some Italian slum-landlords whose tenements were being vandalized by the unsupervised progeny of working mothers. All the landlords hoped was that Dr. Montessori would keep the children occupied and out of mischief; that she taught them to read, write, and figure was quite incidental.

Since the mid-1950s, however, research into human development has begun to suggest that the almost exclusive emphasis on social and emotional development of most contemporary pre-school education is misplaced, and that the years from birth to six may well be the most important to a child's *intellectual* growth, as well as to his social and emotional development. Programs such as Head Start and the current agitation in some states for universal free kindergarten may signify a growing awareness among public policy-makers of the importance of early childhood education.

However, neither Head Start nor kindergarten starts early enough. Last January, Dr. John Fischer, president of Columbia Teachers College, summarized the case for early childhood education in the annual report to President Johnson from the National Advisory Council on the Education of Disadvantaged Children:

> There is substantial evidence that the level of intellectual capability young people will achieve at seventeen is already half-determined by the age of four, and that another 30 per cent is predictable at seven years.

This is no ground for believing that a child's academic fate is sealed by his seventh birthday, but it means that a community that seriously wants to improve its children's opportunities will start them to school early. *In terms of sheer economy, it can be shown that the earlier the investment in systematic intellectual development is begun, the greater will be the rate of return.*

Though this statement focuses on the importance of early childhood education to culturally deprived children, the remarks about the early predictability of intellectual capacity hold true for *all* youngsters.

But one of the major obstacles to any national program is bound up in the words "systematic intellectual development." This harmless-sounding phrase conceals a battle that has been raging among child development specialists since the late 1850s, when German immigrants to this country brought with them Friedrich Frobel's *kindergarten:* should early childhood education amuse children, or should it teach them?

We know now that the two go hand-in-hand, and that children find learning fun, provided the process is properly handled. Until recently, however, the answer usually given was "amuse." Kindergarten, nursery schools, and other forms of preschool education, it was felt, should provide a worthwhile social experience by giving children a chance to mix with their peers, and the whole thing ought to be fun—but "pushing" children to learn anything of an intellectual nature might warp their psyches and turn them into sober academic drudges, cheated of the unplanned joy that is childhood's basic right.

This view, in turn, was supported by the belief that intellectual capacity is fixed at birth; if heredity determines a child's IQ once and for all, this line of reasoning concluded, there's no point in trying to change the unchangeable with early learning.

Especially in the last decade, though, new studies as well as more careful analysis of older data began to contradict the doctrine of fixed intelligence. In many cases, psychologists concentrated on studying identical twins because, having the same genetic legacy, the twins should therefore have the same fixed IQs.

But they didn't. The IQs of identical twins raised apart from each other (as in the case of orphans sent to different foster homes) varied much more than did the IQs of twins raised together. Researchers found that the IQ of a child measured at brief intervals often fluctuated substantially between tests, and frequently showed little relation to his IQ as an adult. In a number of studies, infants raised in single-family homes consistently scored better on IQ and other developmental tests than did infants raised in orphanages.

Clearly, what went on *outside* the child's head influenced (either stimulated or frustrated) what was going on *inside*. These studies seemed to show that intellectual potential was *not* fixed at birth, and that environment—the circumstances of the home, the education of the natural or foster parents, the influences to which the growing child is exposed—could make a difference in intellectual development. And the clear implication was that, if we could learn to encourage more of the intellectual potential that humans are born with, we could rear new generations much more intelligent than ever before.

This was a dramatic possibility; it meant not simply that each generation would *know* more than its parents (this is ultimately true of every new generation), but that it would have the intellectual capacity to derive more personal and social value from the information it had. It meant, in short, the difference between a father's knowing the world is round, and a son's decision to sail for the Americas that *ought* to be beyond the horizon.

The success of any effort to develop this potential, however, required a carefully elaborated theory of human development, a kind of map of what goes on in a human's mind at different stages. And though the cartographers of the brain will undoubtedly be re-drawing boundaries and arguing about frontiers for decades to come, a provocative theory has been developed in our time by the Swiss psychologist Jean Piaget. Like Darwin, he began by keeping a daily journal of his children's sayings and actions; unlike Darwin, however, Piaget did not try to relate his observations to a previously developed theory about the evolution of higher forms from lower, but refined a new theory from the evidence he collected.

Piaget writes of *assimilation* and *accommodation,* operations by which a child's mind reacts to its environment and is itself altered as it tries to make sense of that environment—as it develops new "muscles" to cope with the information entering through its eyes, ears, and other senses. Provided that this information is not too much for the child's intellectual "muscles" to deal with, the interrelated processes of assimilation and accommodation not only produce an act of learning, but actually *generate a positive appetite* for more learning. Infants not only enjoy stimulation, but *crave* it; the more they have seen and heard, according to Piaget, the more they want to see and hear.

Basic to Piaget's conception of assimilation and accommodation is the notion of the "proper discrepancy" between what the child already knows and the demands that new information makes upon him to learn. Put in metaphorical terms, the mind might be considered at any point to be ready to set out on a journey, to step forward from where it is—to learn something qualitatively new. According to Piaget, the *length* of that journey is crucial to success or failure in the learning process: a child's mind at a given moment might be capable of taking one step forward; if a stimulus—a sight, a sound, a problem of putting small boxes into larger ones—requires precisely one step (the "proper discrepancy"), the child enjoys both the challenge and the experience of learning. But should the challenge from a stimulus require *two* steps when the child's mind is capable of only one ("discrepancies too great to be accommodated"), he is likely to become frustrated or upset, and draw back from trying to learn any more.

Dr. J. McVicker Hunt, author of *Intelligence and Experience*—a difficult book, but perhaps the best survey of the new approaches to developmental theory, as well as the most stimulating presentation of the possibilities that the new "cognitive" approach to early childhood holds out—calls this matter of finding the proper discrepancy, "the problem of the match"— finding the proper "fit" between a new learning problem and an established schema, or learning-pattern the child has already developed. How do we know when a youngster is ready to make his next, great mental leap forward? How do we know when he is ready to perform his first mental push-up, having grown tired of less demanding intellectual exercises?

The answer is that we don't know. That is what makes sound, early education such a demanding process—much more demanding for the three-year-old's teacher than an exposition of systems-analysis, for example, is for the graduate student's full-fledged professor. We are still at the trial and error stage in solving the "problem of the match," but the game, as Dr. Hunt points out, is well worth the candle.

The major question, however, is not whether we can advance our present knowledge of the "match," but whether we will have the wit and the determination to put what we already know to work. More than being a "challenge," as Dr. Hunt says, developing early childhood programs is very nearly a social imperative, for the speculations and research of developmental specialists have two broad implications for education.

The first is that there is an ideal time for a human to acquire any new skill, be it learning to read or rumba, and that if we do not find this ideal time, a youngster will not only never learn the skill as *readily* at a later age, but may never learn it as *well*.

This is not to say that, having once missed the educational boat, a child can never again clamber aboard. It is to point out, as Dr. Benjamin Bloom did in his classic study, *Stability and Change in Human Characteristics,* that "As time goes on . . . more and more powerful changes are required to produce a given amount of change in a child's intelligence (if it can be produced at all), and the emotional cost it exacts is increasingly severe."

A second implication follows from the concept of the "match." If the discrepancy between what the child knows and what the environment offers him is just large enough, according to Piaget, the result is pleasure; if the discrepancy is too large, the result is distress. A logical corollary to these two statements would seem to be that if there is no discrepancy at all—if the environment offers a youngster no possibility for learning—the results is likely to be boredom.

This possibility may help explain the puzzling phenomenon that, as a number of school systems have discovered, dropouts frequently include brighter students than those who remained in class. Lacking the social and family pressures which help keep bored, middle-class students in school, highly intelligent but highly bored lower-class students elect to seek more interesting activities in the streets. And boredom may also help account for the learning "losses" reported among Head Start children after they began regular classes; they found no discrepancy, no distance, between what they already knew and what first grade offered to teach them.

If preschool programs are to work, then, we will have to revise the educational system upwards from the bottom, building the work of the primary grades upon that of early childhood education. As matters stand now, we are working backwards; rather than trying to discern what three- or four-year-olds are capable of learning, we look ahead to what they will learn in kindergarten and first grade, and water down preschool curricular content to make sure that it remains "easier" than the lessons to come. What we must do now, in essence, is lift the whole house a few feet so that we can slip the proper foundation under it—and then remodel the upstairs.

Drastic as this working from the bottom up may sound, it can be partly achieved by using some educational techniques we already have.

Nongraded classes, for example, permit a precocious five-year-old to take some classes with six-, seven-, and eight-year-olds, and the rest with youngsters his own age. The key to excellent instruction at any level is tailoring it to each student's ability, so that his academic work neither frustrates him with too much difficulty, nor bores him with repetition. Team-teaching, computer-assisted instruction, and flexible scheduling based on time elements are other ways of making each youngster's curriculum more individual, and ways of approaching the "problem of the match." It is time we applied to the education of three-year-olds what we have learned from teaching nine-year-olds.

Further, we can make widespread use of teacher-aides, recognizing that many a mother short on academic credentials but long on patience and interest can, with modest training and supervision, provide the personal attention that excellent preschool education requires.

Regardless of any short-cuts we might manage through better use of techniques and technology, however, early childhood education will be expensive. Finding the proper "match" between a child's present abilities and a new learning unit is a highly individual process. But if the cognitive psychologists are right, sound early childhood education—for all its initial cost—could produce undreamed-of economies, in terms of educational results. For one, it could give us highly motivated adolescents who want to learn for the pleasure of it, and who can exercise as they mature a greater independence in fashioning their own curricula.

A sound early childhood program could make available to youngsters from culturally deprived homes alternative environments in which to develop appropriate learning and growth skills and future goals. Further, a preschool classroom is the ideal place to diagnose and correct in three-year-olds physical, emotional, and mental disorders that impair learning and may never be overcome at later ages. After studying causes of reading failure, for instance, Katrina de Hirsch and her associates concluded that many "intelligent but educationally disabled children . . . would not have required help had their difficulties been recognized at early ages. Early identification would have obviated the need for later remedial measures."

The evidence is indisputable that we are wasting enormous amounts of human ability through our failure to teach children when they are most capable of learning and eager to do it. We should realize that a massive investment in early childhood education today may be our best buy for a more intelligent citizenry tomorrow.

Introduction to Harlow Article

The research of Harry Harlow (presented below) takes on added significance if we consider it in conjunction with the work by Bennett et al., and Sava reported earlier in this volume. These two articles are similar to the Harlow study in that they point to the importance of early experiences in the growing and developing organism for later behavior: Bennett, et al. in detailing what happens when rats are brought up in sensory rich or sensory impoverished environments; Sava in claiming that the first six years of human life are most important for intellectual growth; and, finally, Harlow in demonstrating the long lasting effect of early social deprivation on subsequent behavior in monkeys. It seems that what happens during the first few years of an organism's growth and development greatly affects not only his early behavior but his behavior in later life as well.

In his delightful, witty prose Harlow records the hapless, hopeless sexual behavior of monkeys who, in early life, were raised apart from other monkeys. But let not the enjoyable reading detour you from the gravity of the message: there is a tragic lesson to be learned about the importance of early social relationships for normal behavior in mature monkeys. And, if the Harlow findings with macaques are applicable to human behavior (as some studies of children in orphanages suggest), then the plight of the child deprived of normal parent and peer relations in youth should be all too apparent.

14

The Heterosexual Affectional System in Monkeys

Harry F. Harlow

The inspiration for this address came from observational data obtained from seven guinea pigs—two males and three females in a colony and two females brought in temporarily. Observations were provided by my ten-year-old daughter Pamela. These observations were made with love and endearment, and the behavior observed was endearment and love. Furthermore, these observations were made at a level of objectivity difficult for an adult to attain in this field.

Male and female guinea pigs are very fond of each other. They stare blissfully into the limpid pink or ruby or midnight-blue pools of each other's eyes. They nuzzle and they cuddle and the end production is not characterized by rush or rape. After all, one does not have to hurry if there is no hurry to be had. This, Pamela has witnessed several times. A caged, virgin adult female was brought by a friend for mating. Twirp, Pamela's large, black, gentle male, was put into the cage with the new female. He purred, nuzzled her, brushed up against her, smelled and licked her, and gradually conquered the frightened animal. A half-hour later they were snuggled up next to each other, peaceful and content, and they lived in bliss for several weeks until another friend brought in her female and Twirp repeated his patient, gentle approach. Twirp has convinced me that some male guinea pigs, at least, are endowed with an innate sense of decency, and I am happy to say that this is the way most male monkeys behave. I presume that there are some men who have as deep a depth of dignity as guinea pigs.

SOURCE. *American Psychologist*, 1962, **17**, 1–9. Copyright 1962 by the American Psychological Association, and reproduced by permission. This research was supported by funds received from the Graduate School of the University of Wisconsin, from the Ford Foundation, and from Grant M-4528, National Institutes of Health.

The guest stands, unfortunately, ended peaceful coexistence in the colony. For many months the five adult guinea pigs had lived amiably in one large cage, with Twirp in command and the second male playing second fiddle. While Twirp was host to the visiting females, White Patch commanded the permanent harem. When Twirp was reintroduced to the colony cage, it took but ten seconds to discover that he would not be tolerated. White Patch bared his teeth and lunged at Twirp, and to save the males, a new cage was acquired.

This led to various divisions of the females and led Pamela to discover particular male guinea pigs like particular female guinea pigs, and they squeal piteously when separated, even when the female is so bulging with babies that she can offer the male nothing in terms of drive reduction. Particular female guinea pigs like particular male guinea pigs. Tastes seem fairly stable, for even after weeks of peaceful residence with the unfavored male, the female will still attempt to get to her favorite male, and after weeks of quiet residence with unfavored females, the male will still try to get to his favorite female.

The females, like the males, defend their rights. In the happy one-cage days two females were separated from the group to care for their litters. White Thrush, in an advanced stage of pregnancy, lived alone with the males. When Chirp was returned to the colony cage after three weeks of maternal chores, both males approached enthusiastically, making friendly gestures. But Hell hath no fury like a female guinea pig spurned, and White Thrush would not tolerate infidelity. She hissed at Chirp, and lunged, and as Chirp fled from the cage, White Thursh pursued, teeth bared. The males also pursued, clucking and purring in anticipation. The males won, and White Thrush sulked the rest of the day. Guinea pigs apparently have a well-developed heterosexual affectional system.

Sex behavior in the guinea pig has been intensively investigated, and there are exhaustive studies on what has been called the sex drive, but I know of no previous mention of or allusion to the guinea pig's heterosexual affectional system. No doubt this stems from the paradigm which has been established for research in this area.

In a typical experiment a male guinea pig and a female guinea pig in estrus are taken from their individual cages, dropped into a barren chamber, and observed for 15 minutes. In such a situation there is a high probability that something is going to happen and that it will happen rapidly and repeatedly. The thing that happens will be reliable and valid, and all that one needs to do to score it is to count. It is my suggestion that from this time onward it be known as the "flesh count." Sometimes I wonder how men and women would behave if they were dropped naked into a barren chamber with full realization that they had only fifteen minutes to take advantage of the opportunities offered them. No doubt there would be individual differences, but we would obtain little information on the human heterosexual affectional system from such an experiment.

Sex is not an adventitious act. It is not here today and gone tomorrow. It starts with the cradle, and as a part of the human tragedy it wanes before the grave. We have traced and are tracing the development of the heterosexual affectional system in monkeys.

We believe that the heterosexual affectional system in the rhesus monkey, like all the other affectional systems, goes through a series of developmental stages—an infantile heterosexual stage, a preadolescent stage, and an adolescent and mature heterosexual stage. Although these stages are in considerable part overlapping and cannot be sharply differentiated in time, we would think of the infantile stage as lasting throughout the first year and being characterized by inadequate and often inappropriate sexual play and posturing. The preadolescent stage, beginning in the second year and ending in the third year in the female and the fourth year in the male, is characterized by adequate and appropriate sexual play and posturing, but incompleteness. The adolescent and adult stage is characterized by behaviors which are similar in form but give rise to productive outcomes which are also reproductive.

Since in this paper sex is an unavoidable issue, we present illustrations of normal adult macaque monkey sex behavior. Sexual invitation may be initiated by the female, as in Figure 1, by a present pattern with buttocks oriented toward the male, tail elevated, and the female looking backward with a fear-grimace (not threat) pattern involving flattened ears and lip smacking. As you can see, this pattern need not involve rape nor even rush

FIG. 1. Initial response to female sexual-present posture. The male subsequently accepted the invitation.

FIG. 2. Initial response to male sexual-present posture. The female (No. 48) subsequently approached and groomed the male.

on the part of the male. The male may also solicit, as in the case of the animal in the foreground of Figure 2; this animal has assumed a posture soliciting either grooming or more intimate favors. These patterns seldom elicit violent, uncontrolled, reflex behaviors. Normal male and female overt sex behavior is shown in Figure 3, the male having assumed the complex sex posture involving ankle clasp, dorsoventral mounting, and clasp of the female's buttocks. The partner demonstrates the complete female sexual

FIG. 3. Normal male and female sexual positioning.

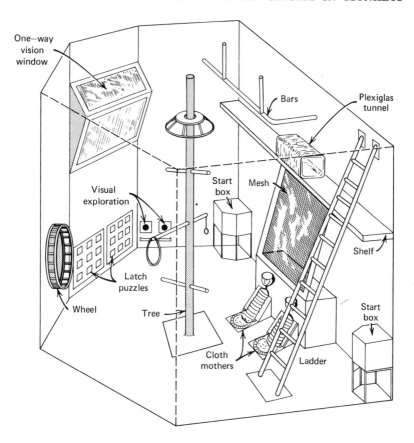

FIG. 4. Playroom test situation.

pattern of elevating the buttocks, lowering the head, and looking backward. There have been millions of rhesus monkeys for millions of years, and there will be more in the future.

We have traced the development of the infantile heterosexual stage during the first year of life in two test situations using observational techniques. One is our playroom, illustrated in Figure 4, which consists of a room 8 ft. high with 36 feet of floor space. In this room are a platform, ladder, revolving wheel, and flying rings to encourage the infants' adaptation to a three-dimensional world, and there is an assortment of puzzles and toys for quieter activities. Two groups of four infants each, half of each group male and half female, have been observed in the playroom daily over many months. The second apparatus is shown in Figure 5. This is the playpen situation, and it consists of four large living cages and adjoining pens. Each living cage houses a mother and infant, and a three-inch by five-inch opening in the wall between cage and playpen units enables the infants to leave the home cage at any time but restrains the mothers. The playpen units are separated by wire-mesh panels which are removed one or two hours a day to allow the infants to interact in pairs during the first 180 days and both in pairs and in groups of four during the next half-year of life. Again, we are referring to data gathered from two playpen setups, each housing four infants and their real or surrogate mothers. Insofar as the infantile heterosexual stage is concerned, it makes little or no difference from which situation we take our data.

The outstanding finding in both the playroom and playpen is that male and female infants show differences in sex behavior from the second month of life onward. The males show earlier and more frequent sex behavior than do females, and there are differences in the patterns displayed by the sexes. The males almost never assume the female sex-posture patterns, even in the earliest months. The females, on the other hand, sometimes display the male pattern of sex posturing, but this is infrequent after ten months of age. Predominantly, females show the female pattern and exceptional instances are to other females, not males. Frequency of sex behavior for both males and females increases progressively with age. There is no latency period—except when the monkeys are very tired.

The early infantile sexual behaviors are fragmentary, transient, and involve little more than passivity by the female and disoriented grasping and thrusting by the male. Thus, the male may thrust at the companion's head in a completely disoriented manner or laterally across the midline of

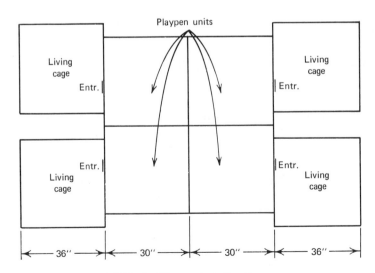

FIG. 5. Playpen test situation.

FIG. 6. Immature male and female sexual posturing, playroom observation.

the body, as in Figure 6. However, it is our opinion that these behaviors are more polymorphous than perverse.

Thus, as soon as the sexual responses can be observed and measured, male and female sexual behaviors differ in form. Furthermore, there are many other behaviors which differ between males and females as soon as they can be observed and measured. Figure 7 shows the development of threat responses by males and females in the playroom, and these differences are not only statistically significant, but they also have face validity. Analysis of this behavior shows that males threaten other males and females but that females are innately blessed with better manners; in particular, little girl monkeys do not threaten little boy monkeys.

The withdrawal pattern—retreat when confronted by another monkey —is graphed for the playroom in Figure 8, and the significance is obvious. Females evince a much higher incidence of passive responses, which are characterized by immobility with buttocks oriented toward the male and head averted, and a similar pattern, rigidity, in which the body is stiffened and fixed.

In all probability the withdrawal and passivity behavior of the female and the forceful behavior of the male gradually lead to the development of normal sex behaviors. The tendency for the female to orient away from the male and for the male to clasp and tussle at the female's buttocks predisposes the consorts to assume the proper positions. The development of the dorsally oriented male sex-behavior pattern as observed in the playroom situation is shown in Figure 9 and may be described as a composite yearning and learning curve.

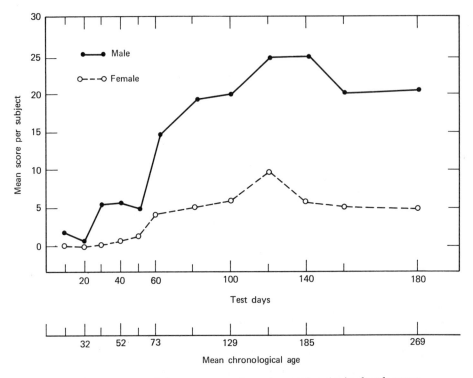

FIG. 7. Frequency of threat responses by males and females in the playroom.

Infant male and female monkeys show clear-cut differences in behavior of far greater social significance than neonatal and infantile sex responses. Grooming patterns, which are basic to macaque socialization, show late maturation, but as is seen in Figure 10, when they appear, they sharply differentiate the two sexes. Caressing is both a property and prerogative of the females. Basic to normal macaque socialization is the infant-infant or peer-peer affectional system, and this arises out of and is dependent upon the play patterns which we have described elsewhere and only mention here. As is shown in the solid lines of Figure 11, play behavior in the play-room is typically initiated by males, seldom by females. However, let us not belittle the female, for they also serve who only stand and wait. Contact play is far more frequent among the males than the females and is almost invariably initiated by the males. Playpen data graphed in Figure 12 show that real rough-and-tumble play is strictly for the boys.

I am convinced that these data have almost total generality to man. Several months ago I was present at a school picnic attended by 25 second-graders and their parents. While the parents sat and the girls stood around or skipped about hand in hand, 13 boys tackled and wrestled, chased and

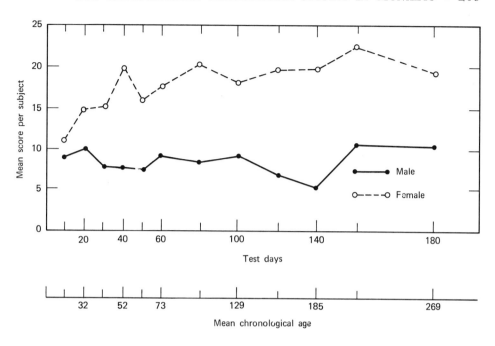

FIG. 8. Frequency of withdrawal responses by males and females in the playroom.

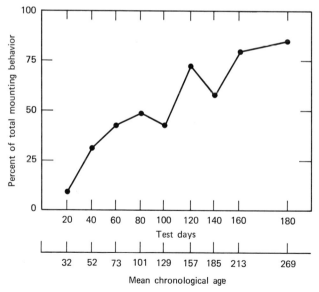

FIG. 9. Percentage of all male mounts (immature and mature) in the playroom that shows dorsal orientation (mature pattern).

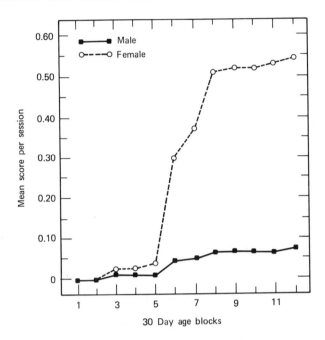

FIG. 10. Frequency of grooming responses made by males and females in the playroom.

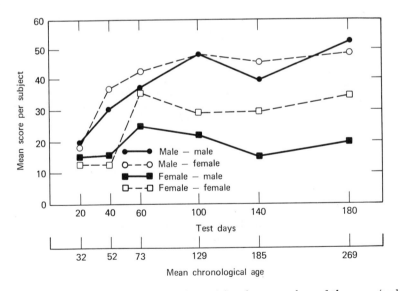

FIG. 11. Frequency of play-initiations by males and females to monkeys of the same (male-male, female-female) and other sex (male-female, female-male). Observations are from the playroom.

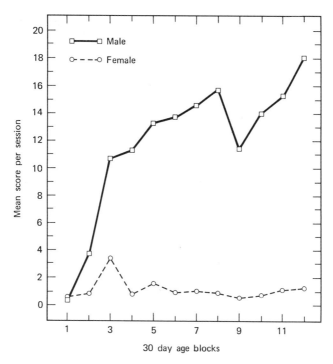

FIG. 12. Frequency of occurrence of "rough-and-tumble" play for two males and two females in the playroom through the first year of life.

retreated. No little girl chased any little boy, but some little boys chased some little girls. Human beings have been here for two million years, and they'll probably be here two million more.

These secondary sex-behavior differences probably exist throughout the primate order, and, moreover, they are innately determined biological differences regardless of any cultural overlap. Because of their nature they tend automatically to produce sexual segregation during middle and later childhood, but fortunately this separation is neither complete nor permanent. Behavioral differences may very well make it easy through cultural means to impose a sexual latency period in the human being from childhood to puberty. We emphasize the fact that the latency period is not a biological stage in which primary sex behavior is suppressed, but a cultural stage built upon secondary behavioral differences.

We believe that our data offer convincing evidence that sex behaviors differ in large part because of genetic factors. However, we claim no originality for the discovery of intersex behavioral differences. In 1759 Laurence Sterne in his book *Tristram Shandy* described male and female differences at the most critical period in Tristram Shandy's development; indeed, it would not be possible to conceive of a more critical period.

"*Pray, my dear,* quoth my mother, *have you not forgot to wind up the clock?* —— *Good G——!* cried my father, making an exclamation, but taking care to moderate his voice at the same time—— *Did ever woman, since the creation of the world, interrupt a man with such a silly question?*" [1]

Men and women have differed in the past and they will differ in the future.

It is possible that the listener has been dismayed by the frequent reference to sex and the relatively infrequent reference to affection. Out of these infantile behavior patterns, both sexual and nonsexual, develop the affectional bonds and the social ordering that appear to be important or even essential to the full development of the heterosexual affectional system of macaques. Traumatic affectional errors, both transient and prolonged, may have devastating effects upon subsequent social and sexual behaviors.

For some years we have been attempting to establish experimental neuroses in infant monkeys by having them live on unfriendly and inconsistent mother surrogates. One preparation was a rejecting mother that on schedule or demand separated her baby when a wire frame embedded in her spun-nylon covering was displaced violently upward and backward. The baby was disturbed, but as soon as the frame was returned to its resting position, the baby returned to cling to its surrogate mother as tightly as ever. Next we developed an air-blast mother with a series of nozzles down the entire center of her body which released compressed air under high pressure—an extremely noxious stimulus to monkeys. The blasted baby never even left the mother, but in its moments of agony and duress, clung more and more tightly to the unworthy mother. Where else can a baby get protection? Apparently our infant had never read Neal Miller's theory that avoidance gradients are precipitous and approach gradients gradual and tenuous, for love conquered all.

We next devised a shaking mother, which on schedule or demand shook her infant with unconscionable violence until its teeth chattered. The infant endured its tribulations by clinging more and more tightly. At the present time we believe we may be on the threshold of success through Jay Mowbray's creation of the porcupine mother, which extrudes brass spikes all over its ventral surface. Preliminary studies on two infants suggest that they are emotionally disturbed. Whether or not we eventually succeed, the fact remains that babies are reluctant to develop experimental neuroses, and at one time we even wondered if this were possible.

During the time that we were producing these evil mothers, we observed the monkeys which we had separated from their mothers at birth

---

[1] Sterne, Laurence. *The life and opinions of Tristram Shandy, Gentleman.* J. A. Work (Ed.), New York: The Odyssey Press, 1940, p. 5.

and raised under various mothered and nonmothered conditions. The first 47 baby monkeys were raised during the first year of life in wire cages so arranged that the infants could see and hear and call to other infants but not contact them. Now they are five to seven years old and sexually mature. As month after month and year after year have passed, these monkeys have appeared to be less and less normal. We have seen them sitting in their cages strangely mute, staring fixedly into space, relatively indifferent to people and other monkeys. Some clutch their heads in both hands and rock back and forth—the autistic behavior pattern that we have seen in babies raised on wire surrogates. Others, when approached or even left alone, go into violent frenzies of rage, grasping and tearing at their legs with such fury that they sometimes require medical care.

Eventually we realized that we had a laboratory full of neurotic monkeys. We had failed to produce neurotic monkeys by thoughtful planning and creative research, but we had succeeded in producing neurotic monkeys through misadventure. To err is human.

Because of housing pressures some of these monkeys and many of our surrogate-raised monkeys lived in pairs for several years while growing to sexual maturity, but we have seldom seen normal sex behavior, and we certainly have not had the validating criterion of newborn baby monkeys. Instead, these monkeys treat each other like brother and sister, proving that two can live in complete propinquity with perfect propriety as long as no one cares.

Their reason for being, as we saw it, was to produce babies for our researches, and so at this point we deliberately initiated a breeding program which was frighteningly unsuccessful. When the older, wire-cage-raised males were paired with the females at the peak of estrus, the introduction led only to fighting, so violent and vicious that separation was essential to survival. In no case was there any indication of normal sex behavior. Frequently the females were the aggressors; even the normal praying mantis waits until the sex act is completed.

Pairing such cloth-surrogate-raised monkeys as were sexually mature gave little better end results. Violent aggression was not the rule, and there was attempted sex behavior, but it was unreproductive since both the male and female behaviors were of the infantile type we have already described.

At this point we took the 17 oldest of our cage-raised animals, females showing consistent estrous cycles and males obviously mature, and engaged in an intensive re-education program, pairing the females with our most experienced, patient, and gentle males, and the males with our most eager, amiable, and successful breeding females. When the laboratory-bred females were smaller than the sophisticated males, the girls would back away and sit down facing the males, looking appealingly at these would-be consorts. Their hearts were in the right place, but nothing else was. When the females were larger than the males, we can only hope that they misunderstood the males' intentions, for after a brief period of courtship, they would attack and maul the ill-fated male. Females show no respect for a male they can dominate.

The training program for the males was equally unsatisfactory. They approached the females with a blind enthusiasm, but it was a misdirected enthusiasm. Frequently the males would grasp the females by the side of the body and thrust laterally, leaving them working at cross purposes with reality. Even the most persistent attempts by these females to set the boys straight came to naught. Finally, these females either stared at the males with complete contempt or attacked them in utter frustration. It became obvious that they, like their human counterpart, prefer maturer men. We realized then that we had established, not a program of breeding, but a program of brooding.

We had in fact been warned. Our first seven laboratory-born babies were raised in individual cages while being trained on a learning test battery. William Mason planned to test their social behaviors subsequently, and great care had been taken to keep the babies socially isolated and to prevent any physical contacts. Neonatal baby monkeys require 24-hour-a-day care, and infant monkeys need ministrations beyond a 40-hour week. We had assigned the evening care to Kathy, a maternal bit of fluff who had worked for several years as a monkey tester while studying to become an elementary school teacher.

Checking on his wards one night near 10 P.M., Mason found Kathy sitting on the floor surrounded by seven baby monkeys, all eight of the primates playing happily together. Before the horrified scientist could express his outrage, Kathy had risen to her full height of five feet two. Already anticipating the carping criticisms which he was formulating, she shook her finger in his face and spoke with conviction: "Dr. Mason, I'm an education student and I know that it is improper and immoral to blight the social development of little children. I am right and you are wrong!"

Although we were angry with Kathy, we did think there was a certain humor in the situation and we did not worry about our monkeys. We simply transferred Kathy to an office job. Alas, she could not have been more right and we could not have been more wrong! We have already described the social-sexual life of these 7 monkeys and the next 40 to come.

Two years later we had more than theoretical reasons to be disturbed because Mason tested a group of these isolation-raised monkeys, then between 2.5 and 3.5 years of age, and found evidence of severe social abnormalities, which might be described as a sociopathic syndrome. He matched the laboratory-raised monkeys on the basis of weight and dentition patterns with monkeys that had been born and raised in the wild for the first 12 to 18 months, then captured and subjected to various kinds of housing and caging treatments for the next year or two. In the test situations the laboratory-raised monkeys, as compared with feral monkeys, showed infantile sexual behavior, absence of grooming, exaggerated aggression, and absence of affectional interaction as measured by cooperation.

We are now quite certain that this sociopathic syndrome does not stem from the fact that the baby monkeys were raised in the laboratory but from *how* they were raised in the laboratory. Our infants raised in the laboratory by real monkey mothers and permitted opportunity for the development of normal infant-infant affection demonstrate normal male and female sexual behavior when they enter the second year of life. Furthermore, our play-room and playpen studies show that infant monkeys raised on cloth mothers but given the opportunity to form normal infant-infant affectional patterns, also develop normal sexual responses.

In a desperate attempt to assist a group of 18 three- to four-year-old cloth-surrogate-raised monkeys, half of them males and half females, we engaged in a group-psychotherapy program, placing these animals for two months on the monkey island in the Madison Zoo, as shown in Figure 13. Their summer vacation on the enchanted island was not without avail, and social grooming responses rapidly developed and were frequent in occurrence. After a few days of misunderstanding, patterns of social ordering developed, and a number of males and females developed friendship patterns. Unfortunately, sexual behavior was infrequent, and the behavior that was observed was completely inadequate—at least from our point of view. In desperation we finally introduced our most experienced, most

FIG. 13. Group of cloth-surrogate-raised monkeys on the monkey island in the Madison Zoo.

patient, and most kindly breeding male, Smiley (the male in Figures 1 and 2), and he rapidly established himself as king of the island and prepared to take full advantage of the wealth of opportunity which surrounded him. Fortunately, the traumatic experiences he encountered with unreceptive females have left no apparent permanent emotional scars, and now that he has been returned to our laboratory breeding colony, he is again making an important contribution to our research program. If normal sexual behavior occurred, no member of our observational team ever saw it, and had a female become pregnant, we would have believed in parthenogenesis.

But let us return to the monkeys that we left on the island and the older ones that we left in their cages. A year has passed, and the frustrations that both we and our monkeys experienced are in some small part nothing but a memory. We constructed larger and more comfortable breeding cages, and we designed a very large experimental breeding room 8 feet by 8 feet by 8 feet in size with appropriate platforms and a six-foot tree. Apparently we designed successful seraglios for I can report that not all love's labors have

FIG. 14. Typical behavior of unmothered mother toward her infant. Mother is looking upward while crushing her baby against the cage floor.

been lost. It does appear that the males are completely expendable unless they can be used in a program of artificial insemination. Certainly we can find no evidence that there is a destiny that shapes their ends unless some Skinnerite can help us with the shaping process. We have, however, had better success with some of the females, particularly the females raised on cloth surrogates.

Even so, one of the wire-cage-raised females is a mother and another is pregnant. Three cloth-surrogate females are mothers and four or five are expectant. We give all the credit to three breeding males. One, Smiley, does not take "no" for an answer. Smiley has a way with females. Patient, gentle, and persuasive, he has overcome more than one planned program of passive resistance. One female did not become pregnant until the fifth successive month of training. Month after month she has changed, and now she is mad about the boy. Male No. 342 behaves very much like Smiley. Even when females threaten him, he does not harm them. Given time, he has been able to overcome more than one reluctant dragon, and he is a master of the power of positive suggestion.

Breeding male No. 496 has helped us greatly, particularly with the younger, cloth-surrogate-raised females. His approach differs from that of Smiley and No. 342. His technique transcends seduction, and in contract bridge terms it may be described as an approach-forcing system.

Combining our human and male-monkey talents, we are winning the good fight and imparting to naive and even resistant female monkeys the priceless gift of motherhood. Possibly it is a Pyrrhic victory. As every scientist knows, the solution of one scientific problem inevitably leads to another, and this is our fate (Figure 14). Month after month female monkeys that never knew a real mother, themselves become mothers—helpless, hopeless, heartless mothers devoid, or almost devoid, of any maternal feeling.

Through projective tests the psychologist learns about the human personality.
(VAN BUCHER)

Section V
Personality

The contemporary psychologist is concerned with predicting, controlling, and understanding the behavior of organisms. How does he do it? That is no simple question! Actually, there are many ways in which the psychologist attempts to unravel the mysteries of behavior. The approach that he chooses often determines the "area" or "field" of psychology in which he works. For example, if the scientist investigates the physiological mechanisms of the organism that underlie behavior he is called, appropriately, a physiological psychologist; if he concentrates on the psychopathological conditions found in man he is labeled a clinical psychologist. The findings from all the subfields of psychology, when taken together, provide us with a richer, more complete understanding of the behavioral process. Each specialized field of psychology is like a piece of a puzzle—a unit of information that, when placed together with other units of information, will provide us with an overall picture of the behaving organism. It is the *personality* area of psychology that will concern us in this section of the text.

What is "personality"? Psychologists Richard Lazarus and Edward Opton, Jr. describe it effectively.

> . . . the whole integrated pattern of behavior which distinguishes one man from another as uniquely as fingerprints and as distinctively as photographs. . . . Personality consists not of incidental, emotionally neutral features such as the whorls of fingerprints, but of the most important things we can say about a person, the things that will make us love him or hate him or feel indifferent to his fate: personality includes what a man wants, what he will do to get it, and how he copes with his inability to get everything he needs and desires. Personality also deals

213

with how a man is shaped by, and how he shapes, the social milieu in which he lives (Lazarus & Opton, 1967).

The personality psychologist studies the uniqueness of each person and the differences between persons. In doing so he deals with such concepts as "intelligence," "need for achievement," "authoritarianism," "creativity," "anxiety," and "self-concept" among others. Some of the world's best known psychologists have been recognized for their contributions to the understanding of human personality—men like Sigmund Freud, Carl Jung, Erich Fromm, Carl Rogers, and many more.

In the articles that follow three personality characteristics—intelligence, need for achievement, and creativity—are examined in detail. The first paper is Otto Klineberg's article on Negro-white differences in intelligence —an issue currently under much discussion. In the selection on creativity Donald MacKinnon tries to shed some light on the creative process by studying individuals of established creative caliber. His report, detailing an intensive, in-depth investigation of world-renown architects (who served as subjects in a three-day experiment at the University of California) gives us a rare glimpse into the behavior of truly gifted men. Finally, in the paper on "achievement motivation" David McClelland focuses on the relationship between need for achievement and economic growth—specifically, how the businessman with high achievement motivation behaves.

REFERENCE
Lazarus, R., and Opton, E. (Eds.). *Personality*. Baltimore: Penguin, 1967.

Introduction to
Klineberg Article

In the winter 1969 issue of *Harvard Educational Review* Arthur R. Jensen published an article that led to heated debate and embitterments inside and outside the academic community, between and among blacks and whites, and throughout the behavioral sciences. In his work Jensen argued that intelligence was primarily a function of genetic inheritance rather than environmental influences and that whites were intellectually superior to blacks. The study of black-white differences in intelligence is not new—such research has been going on for decades. What makes the Jensen investigation different is its findings and philosophy: the vast majority of today's behavioral investigators do not support the claim of differences in intelligence between blacks and whites when environmental influences have been similar for both groups, and behavioral investigators generally do not agree with Jensen about the overriding role of genetic versus environmental factors in determining intelligence.

The well-known scholar Otto Klineberg propounds the view held by most contemporary scientists when he insists that ". . . since innate psychological differences between ethnic groups have never been satisfactorily demonstrated, we have no right to act as if they had been. The science of psychology can offer no support to those who see in the accident of inherited skin color or other physical characteristics any excuse for denying to individuals the right to full participation in American democracy." His reasons for such a belief are expressed in his paper below.

15

Negro-White Differences in Intelligence Test Performance:

A new look at an old program

Otto Klineberg

I have written this article at the suggestion of the Society for the Psychological Study of Social Issues (SPSSI), Division 9 of the American Psychological Association. It is based in part on some of my own earlier publications and in part on a chapter which I have prepared for a forthcoming book; it represents an attempt to bring up to date a psychological analysis of an old problem. The substantial number of recent publications in this field, some of which have attracted considerable popular attention; the many "letters to the editor"; the unfortunate tendency, all too frequent, to stray from an interpretation of the data to an attack on the ethnic origins or the alleged political positions of the persons involved; the accusation of a "conspiracy"; and finally, the practical implications which have been drawn for public policy—all of these developments have made a factual reappraisal desirable. I had hoped that this might be done by another psychologist, one less closely identified with a definite stand on one side of this issue. As the next best thing, I have tried to look, as honestly as my own biases would permit, at the evidence which has accumulated on both sides. It goes without saying that I am writing as an individual, and that neither the Council nor the membership of SPSSI should be held responsible for what follows.

THE ISSUE

I shall restrict my discussion of Negro-white differences to that aspect of the issue on which we, as psychologists, may claim to speak with pro-

SOURCE. *American Psychologist*, 1963, **18**, 198–203. Copyright 1963 by the American Psychological Association, and reproduced by permission.

fessional competence, namely, the interpretation of the results obtained from the application of mental tests. There are other aspects of at least equal importance; whether, for example, there is any acceptable indication of biological superiority or inferiority; whether one can argue from the nature of a culture to the genetic factors responsible, etc. On these and related questions the anthropologists are better qualified than we are to express a judgment. I leave these matters, therefore, with the single reminder that the American Anthropological Association has taken the position that there is no scientifically acceptable basis for a genetic hierarchy among ethnic groups.

As far as mental tests are concerned, the issue is *not* one of whether *on the average* Negro children obtain lower test scores than whites. Of that there can be no doubt. My own earlier survey (Klineberg, 1944), in which I was greatly aided by Kenneth B. Clark, was based on 27 studies, and led me to the conclusion that an IQ of 86 represented the approximate Negro median. Shuey (1958), after a much more thorough and complete survey, obtained substantially similar results; on verbal group tests alone, she located no fewer than 72 studies, based upon tests of 36,000 colored children, and her estimate of the average IQ is 85. (I might add parenthetically that in my own earlier survey I found median IQs for children of Italian, Portuguese, and Mexican parentage at or below those of American Negroes, and those of American Indians definitely below.) Shuey's estimate is therefore very close to mine.

The addition of so many further studies has, however, supplied very little new insight. One is reminded of the *Literary Digest* poll in connection with the Roosevelt-Landon electoral contest in 1936; on the basis of more than 2,000,000 ballots, it was predicted that Landon would win an overwhelming victory. As is well known, there was a systematic bias in the sample. The addition of another 100 studies of Negro children would not strengthen Shuey's (1958) conclusion that there are "some native differences between Negroes and whites as determined by intelligence tests" (p. 318), if some systematic error entered into the test results.

As far back as 1933, Garrett and Schneck in their book on *Psychological Tests* reminded us that "the examiner must always remember that comparisons are permissible only when environmental differences are absent, or at least negligible" (p. 24). This appears to be the crucial issue. What comparisons of Negroes and whites have been made under such conditions?

THE ARGUMENT FOR "SOME NATIVE DIFFERENCES"

There are three major studies cited by Shuey and others as demonstrating that differences persist even when environmental factors have been "equated." (I have put this word in quotation marks for reasons which will appear later.) One of these is by Myrtle Bruce (1940), who matched Negroes and whites in a rural community in southern Virginia on the Sims Socio-economic scale, and still found a difference, with a resulting mean IQ on the Binet of 86 for the whites and 77 for the Negroes. Those who have used Bruce's results have not always gone on to note her careful qualifications.

> Although the white and Negro samples equated for social status still show statistical differences in IQ on each of the three intelligence tests, this fact cannot be considered proof of the superiority of the white group, since the equation of the two groups *is not entirely valid* (p. 20, italics supplied).

Even a quick look at her graph on page 20 shows more whites at the upper levels and more Negroes at the lower. Bruce herself "is inclined to believe that there is an innate difference between the particular white and Negro groups studied" (p. 97). She does not, however, extend this conclusion to the ethnic groups in general; she speaks, for example, of the skewness of the Negro IQ distribution as something which "prevents this study from being used as evidence for the superiority of the white race to the Negro race" (p. 97).

Suppose, however, that the two groups had really been "equated" for their scores on a satisfactory socioeconomic scale. Can this possibly be regarded as taking care of all the relevant environmental variables? This appears to be the assumption underlying the study by McGurk (1951) in New Jersey and Pennsylvania. Negro and white high school seniors were matched for socioeconomic level, and still there was a difference, the Negroes overlapping the white means by 29%. This would be an important finding (as would also the demonstration that there was about as much difference between the two groups on test items identified as "cultural" and "noncul-tural," respectively) if socioeconomic level were all that mattered. Can any-one really believe that? Do motivation, self-confidence, opportunity for wider experience, and other related factors count for nothing?

In a recent critical review, Dreger and Miller (1960) insist that it is not enough to equate ethnic groups in terms of social class and economic variables; that there is a caste as well as a class difference; that even those Negroes whose economic status is higher than that of most white persons will still in most cases be prevented from living the same kind of life in all respects; these writers insist that many other factors may also be important. Incidentally, they emphasize that they "are not taking sides at this point in the hereditary-environment controversy . . ." (p. 367). They show their impartiality in a striking and (to me) slightly painful manner by stating that "Shuey does the same rationalizing from an hereditarian standpoint that Klineberg did in his earlier 'review' from an environmental standpoint" (p. 364). To return to McGurk, it is impossible to accept the contention that all relevant environmental factors have been considered, just because socioeconomic status has been controlled.

The third study which has figured prominently on this side of the argument is by Tanser (1939). This was conducted in Kent County, Ontario, Canada, where the Negroes have lived since before the Civil War; Tanser writes that they are on a level with the whites in regard to "every political and social advantage." On the Pintner-Paterson tests, the mean white IQ was 109.6, the Negro, 91; on the Pintner nonlanguage test, the means were 111 and 95; on the National Intelligence Test the respective figures were 104 and 89. On this last test, 20% of the Negroes reached or exceeded the white median; 29% of the Negroes and 56% of the whites reached or surpassed the *National* test norms. (Tanser's study is unfortunately not available to me in Paris; I have quoted these figures from Shuey.)

If Tanser is right with regard to "every political and social advantage," these results must be taken seriously. A comment by Anastasi (1958) is, however, pertinent.

> Nevertheless significant differences were found in the socio-economic level of the two groups. Moreover, it is reported that the white children attended school more regularly than the Negro, a difference often associated with social class differences. Thus within the entire sample of white children tested, school attendance averaged 93.38%; within the Negro sample, it averaged 84.77% (pp. 556–557).

I have only one comment to add. I was born in Canada, and lived there the first 25 years of my life. I would have said that Negroes were reasonably well off there, but emphatically not that they lived under conditions of complete equality, or that the social environment was free of prejudice. I would have thought that Canada was in this respect similar to the northeastern United States, with Negroes occupying about the same relative position. As a matter of fact Chant and Freedman (1934) report a correlation of .98 between scale values assigned to the same list of ethnic groups, including Negroes, by Canadian as by American students. I do not know Kent County, Ontario, and I cannot take it for granted that the same attitudes would be found there. I cannot help wondering, however, whether this particular Canadian community can be so exceptional. I would like to see a replication of this study, with full attention to social and sociological variables, and to patterns of personal development and interpersonal relations. In the meantime, Tanser's results cannot be dismissed, but they appear to me to be outweighed by the evidence on the other side.

THE ARGUMENT AGAINST NATIVE DIFFERENCES

The evidence against the assumption of native differences in intelligence test performance between Negroes and whites still seems to me to be very convincing. The relevant studies, most of which are already well known and will therefore be presented in brief outline, include the following.

Among infants during the first year of life the earlier finding by McGraw (1931) was that southern Negro babies showed inferiority on the Hetzer-Wolf tests. McGraw concludes:

> It is significant that with even the very young subjects, *when environmental factors are minimized* [italics supplied], the same type and approximately the same degree of superiority is evidenced on the part of the white subjects as that found among older groups.

In New Haven, however, where Negro mothers obtained more adequate nourishment and where the general economic level of the families had improved, Pasamanick (1946) found no Negro inferiority or retardation. A follow-up of 40 cases at a mean age of about two years still showed no retardation (Knobloch & Pasamanick, 1953; Pasamanick & Knobloch, 1955). Using different tests, Gilliland (1951) also reports no significant differences between Negro and white infants in Chicago.

For preschool children, Anastasi and d'Angelo (1952), found no significant differences on Goodenough Draw-a-Man IQ between samples of Negroes and whites attending Day Care Centers in New York City. Dreger and Miller (1960) comment:

> With due recognition of the limitations of the Goodenough as a test of intelligence, we may yet regard Anastasi and d'Angelo's results as a challenge to nativist theories of intellectual differences between the races (p. 366).

It is as the children get older that differences in test performance appear. Surely this is to be expected on the basis of the cumulative effect of an inferior environment. Such an effect has been demonstrated in the case of white children as well. To mention only one example out of many, Sherman and Key (1932) found a striking decrement with age among white children living in the "hollows" of the Blue Ridge Mountains; there was a Pintner-Cunningham IQ of 84 at ages 6–8; 70 at 8–10; and 53 at 10–12. This is a much more dramatic drop than any with which I am familiar in the case of Negro children; it shows what *can* happen when a poor environment persists over a long period.

Conversely, when the environment improves, test scores go up. In the case of Negro children they do not usually go up all the way to meet the white norms, but this is to be expected if the discriminatory treatment persists, and even *for a time* if discrimination were to be completely eliminated. The atmosphere in the home, the conversation around the dinner table, the use of leisure time, the books read and discussed—these and other factors contributing to "intelligence" cannot be expected to change over night or even possibly in one generation. With this in mind, the changes that have been reported in Negro IQs become all the more impressive.

When my students and I indicated (Klineberg, 1935) that test scores of southern Negro children improved in proportion to their length of residence in New York City, we were perfectly aware that they still did not reach the white norms, and we pointed that out. Could anyone have expected them to do so under Harlem living conditions, and in the Harlem schools as they were at that time? Could anyone possibly suggest that in New York or in Philadelphia, where Lee (1951) obtained similar results, there is *no* discrimination against Negroes? There was improvement, however, because there was *less* discrimination than where they came from.

In some cases, the improvement has even been dramatic. Shuey (1958, p. 87) points out that in my review of Negro intelligence testing (Klineberg, 1944) I gave special prominence to a study by W. W. Clark in Los Angeles (1923). This I did because of the striking finding that the Negro children attending 5 elementary schools obtained an average National Intelligence Test IQ of 104.7 as compared with an IQ of 106 for all the children in 15 schools. Shuey indicates that she wrote to Clark asking for further details, and was informed by him that "the *National* norms available in 1922 were probably *about 5 per cent too high*" (p. 87, italics supplied). Surely 5% does not change the results greatly. Besides, in that case the results for the comparison group of 15 schools would also have to be reduced by a similar proportion.

I also wrote to Clark for further information, and he indicated that the obtained IQs were too high, but that he could not determine by how much. The fact remains that if they were too high for the Negroes, they were also too high for the rest of the Los Angeles school population. Clark's original article indicates that there was *no significant difference* shown in the intelligence level of the Negro children and the 15 schools in general, nor were there significant differences in reading comprehension, arithmetic ability, spelling, as well as educational accomplishment in general. He writes: "The average accomplishment and range of accomplishment for Negro children is practically the same as for the total population of the fifteen schools."

Shuey reports further that research conducted in Los Angeles Public Schools in 1928 (unpublished) revealed a median IQ for Negro children of 95. If that is the case, it is difficult to understand Clark's finding of "no significant difference." Even if we accept this estimate, however, the fact remains that in the relatively friendly climate of Los Angeles, Negro IQs have shown a tremendous leap upwards. Compare even this lower estimate of 95 with the 76 reported by Bruce for rural Virginia. Could "selective migration" account for this large difference? Shuey writes:

> If we were correct in assuming an IQ difference of about 9 points between northern and southern Negro children, then about half to two-thirds of this difference may reasonably be attributed to environmental factors and the remainder to selective migration (p. 314).

Here the difference is 19 points, and "half to two-thirds" would suggest that Shuey would accept an improvement of 10 to 12 points in IQ as attributable to the superior environment. I am putting this figure *at its most conservative,* since I have found no acceptable evidence for this kind of selective migration, but even then the environmental rise is clear, and it is considerable.

The desegregation of elementary schools, particularly in the border states and cities where the process has more than a "token" character, gives us another opportunity to see what an improved educational environment may accomplish. This situation has been studied in Washington, D. C., although the measures used were tests of achievement rather than of intelligence. Stallings (1960) writes:

> The Washington study showed that during the five years following integration, marked progress has been made in academic achievement . . . a gain was made in the median score for every [school] subject tested at every grade level where the tests were given.

With regard to Louisville, Kentucky, Omer Carmichael, Superintendent of Public Schools, reported (1959) as follows:

> When we tested, we looked at the results the year before desegregation and then looked at them after the second year of desegregation and found that the Negro in all grades had improved—and by an amount that was statistically significant.

This does not mean that average differences between Negroes and whites have disappeared; it does mean that they have been reduced. Nor has this occurred as the result of "pulling down" the white level. Carmichael reports that there "was a slight improvement for the whites; a substantial improvement for the Negroes." For the difference to disappear completely, much more has to happen. (Even among whites, the difference in the IQ of occupational classes is substantial.) Until that "more" has happened, we have no right to assume that Negroes are, on the average, innately inferior.

AVERAGES AND INDIVIDUALS

In many of the recent analyses of ethnic differences, including the extensive one by Shuey, a great deal of emphasis has been placed on the extent of overlapping. Her own estimate is that the median overlap among school children was between 10 and 20%. (In McGurk's study it was 29%, and presumably in Clark's it was close to 50%.) As every psychology student (but unfortunately not every layman) knows, this refers to the percentage of the "inferior" group who reach or exceed the mean of the "superior." As Anastasi (1958) points out:

> If 30 per cent of the Negroes reach or exceed the white median, the percentage who reach or exceed the lowest score of the white group will be approximately 99. Under these conditions, therefore, the ranges will overlap almost completely (p. 549).

Clearly, then, statements to the effect that there was "only 20% overlap" obscure the degree of similarity in the total distributions.

This fact comes out strikingly when one looks more closely at Bruce's findings on the Kuhlmann-Anderson scale. For the total population examined (521 whites and 432 Negroes), the range in IQ was 52 to 129 for the former and 39 to 130 for the latter. When equated on the Sims scale, the range was 51 to 115 for the whites, and 41 to 130 for the Negroes. On the Binet, the two ranges were 51 to 125, and 51 to 130; on the Grace Arthur scale, 46 to 140, and 51 to 120, respectively. On three out of these four comparisons, one or more Negroes obtained higher scores than *any* of the whites; on two out of the four, one or more whites obtained scores as low as, or lower than, those of *any* Negro.

Let us suppose for the purpose of this argument (a supposition for which I perceive no acceptable evidence) that there is a difference in averages due to genetic factors. What about the individuals who "overlap"? I learned my statistics from a good teacher, a former psychologist at Columbia University, who kept reminding us not to forget the *range* when we compared two distributions. We were both students of that wise man, R. S. Woodworth, for whom the essence of psychology, as I understood him, was the behavior and characteristics of the *individual*. In one of his texts (1929) he defined psychology as the scientific study of the activities of the individual.

It is perhaps beyond the scope of this paper to consider the practical implications of psychological research on Negro-white differences and similarities, but I hope I may be permitted one observation. Lines of demarcation between groups of people, in employment, in education, in opportunities for development, based on alleged differences in averages which are essentially abstractions, do violence to the facts of individual capacities and potentialities. At the most, group differences are obscure and uncertain; we are faced with the living reality of individual human beings who have a right to the opportunity to show what they can do when they are given an equal chance. Perhaps I am allowing my own value system to influence me to look at the whole range of individual variations and not just at averages. I should have thought, however, that concern with the individual represented one value on which all psychologists might find themselves in agreement.

CONCLUSION

I can only conclude that there is no scientifically acceptable evidence for the view that ethnic groups differ in innate abilities. *This is not the same as saying that there are no ethnic differences in such abilities.* In the first place, I do not feel that mental tests can by themselves alone be used to prove this negative proposition. Perhaps in the future new techniques will be developed, better than our present tests, less subject to possible variations in interpretation, more conclusive in their results. I doubt that this would really change the picture, but the possibility must be kept open. Secondly, it is exceedingly difficult ever to prove the absence of something, because one can never be certain that all the relevant factors have been taken into account. We can, however, say to those who have claimed to find evidence for ethnic differences in innate mentality: You have not proved your case. You have not been able to demonstrate that such differences exist.

We can go a little farther than that. We can point to the improvement in achievement when conditions of life improve. We can emphasize the tremendous variations within each ethnic group, much greater than the differences between groups even under discrepant environmental stimulation. We can insist that since innate psychological differences between ethnic groups have never been satisfactorily demonstrated, we have no right to act as if they had been. The science of psychology can offer no support to those who see in the accident of inherited skin color or other physical characteristics any excuse for denying to individuals the right to full participation in American democracy.

REFERENCES

Anastasi, Anne. *Differential psychology.* (3rd ed.) New York: Macmillan, 1958.

Anastasi, Anne, & d'Angelo, R. Y. A comparison of Negro and white preschool children in language development and Goodenough Draw-a-Man IQ. *J. genet. Psychol.,* 1952, **81,** 147–165.

Bruce, M. Factors affecting intelligence test performance of whites and Negroes in the rural South. *Arch. Psychol., N. Y.,* 1940, No. 252.

Carmichael, O. Television Program of Sept. 13, 1959. Report, Dec. 15, 1959, Southern Regional Council, Atlanta.

Chant, S. N. F., & Freedman, S. S. A quantitative comparison of the nationality preferences of two groups. *J. soc. Psychol.,* 1934, **5,** 116–120.

Clark, W. W. Los Angeles Negro children. *Educ. Res. Bull., Los Angeles,* 1923, 3(2), 1–2.

Dreger, R. M., & Miller, K. S. Comparative psychological studies of Negroes and whites in the United States. *Psychol. Bull.,* 1960, **57,** 361–402.

Garrett, H. E., & Schneck, M. R. *Psychological tests, methods and results.* New York: Harper's, 1933.

Gilliland, A. R. Socioeconomic status and race as factors in infant intelligence test scores. *Child Developm.,* 1951, **22,** 271–273.

Klineberg, O. *Negro intelligence and selective migration.* New York: Columbia Univer. Press, 1935.

Klineberg, O. (Ed.) *Characteristics of the American Negro.* New York: Harper, 1944.

Knobloch, H., & Pasamanick, B. Further observations on the behavioral development of Negro children. *J. genet. Psychol.,* 1953, **83,** 137–157.

Lee, E. S. Negro intelligence and selective migration: A Philadelphia test of Klineberg's hypothesis. *Amer. sociol. Rev.,* 1951, **61,** 227–233.

McGraw, M. B. A comparative study of a group of southern white and Negro infants. *Genet. Psychol. Monogr.,* 1931, **10,** 1–105.

McGurk, F. C. J. *Comparison of the performance of Negro and white high school seniors on cultural and non-cultural psychological test questions.* Washington, D. C.: Catholic Univer. America Press, 1951.

Pasamanick, B. A comparative study of the educational development of Negro infants. *J. genet. Psychol.,* 1946, **69,** 3–44.

Pasamanick, B., & Knobloch, H. Early language behavior in Negro children and the testing of intelligence. *J. abnorm. soc. Psychol.,* 1955, **50,** 401–402.

Sherman, M., & Key, C. B. The intelligence of isolated mountain children. *Child Developm.,* 1932, **3,** 279–290.

Shuey, A. M. *The testing of Negro intelligence.* Lynchburg, Va.: J. P. Bell, 1958.

Stallings, F. H. Atlanta and Washington: Racial differences in academic achievement. Report No. L-16, Feb. 26, 1960, Southern Regional Council, Atlanta.

Tanser, H. A. *The settlement of Negroes in Kent County, Ontario, and a study of the mental capacity of their descendants.* Chatham, Ont.: Shepherd, 1939.

Woodworth, R. S. *Psychology.* (Rev. ed.) New York: Holt, 1929.

Introduction to MacKinnon Article

For almost a century psychologists have sought to understand how man solves complex problems. An early approach to the study of problem solving was through intelligence assessment. Recently, however, many psychologists and educators have come to feel that intelligence may not be the only important variable in problem-solving behavior. This has led to a second approach to viewing such activity—through creativity.

Although the experimental investigation of creativity (Dearborn, 1898) is almost as old as scientific psychology itself, intensive research efforts aimed at comprehending the creative process have been primarily a product of the past two decades. This intensification of interest came about once creativity was staked out as a characteristic of human cognitive functioning separate from intellective functioning (e.g., Wallach & Kogan, 1965).

Today those who study creativity face the same problem as investigators who examine intelligence—the subject matter is highly resistant to scientific scrutiny! Why does the creative process seem so invulnerable to scientific understanding? Part of the problem lies with the complexity of the topic. As Robert MacCleod once said: "Once we have reached the point of being certain how to construct a theory of creativity, we shall also be certain how to construct a poem." Such difficulties have not, however, detoured the psychologist in his quest to strip away the mysteries surrounding the creative process. If anything, the challenge has made him redouble his efforts.

Currently there are almost as many different approaches to the study of creativity as there are investigators in the area! Although it is still too early to tell which of these approaches will be most fruitful—one research strategy, studying creative individuals to gain insight into the creative process, seems particularly promising. Most of the important efforts in this direction have been undertaken at the Institute of Personality Assessment and Research located at the University of California (Berkeley). A summary of some of that research is presented by MacKinnon below. I suspect that you will be impressed by the scope, design, and outcome of the research. I was. You will also get a rare look into the behavior of highly gifted, world-renowned architects.*

REFERENCES

Dearborn, G. A study of imagination. *American Journal of Psychology*, 1898, **9,** 183–190.

Wallach, M., & Kogan, N. *Modes of thinking in young children.* New York: Holt, 1965.

* For the interested reader, two other highly readable works are available on the Berkeley studies: (1) Barron, F. The psychology of creativity, in: *New directions in psychology II.* New York: Holt, 1965; (2) Barron, F. *Creativity and personal freedom.* Princeton: Van Nostrand, 1968 (see ch. 19).

16

The Nature and Nurture
of Creative Talent

Donald W. MacKinnon

Let me say first how deeply appreciative I am of the honor of having been chosen the Walter Van Dyke Bingham Lecturer for 1962. It has for me especial meaning to be provided this opportunity to honor the memory of a man I respected so much and whose work was such a pioneering contribution to that field of psychology to which I have given most of my energies as a psychologist. I am grateful, too, for this opportunity to express to Mrs. Bingham the gratitude of all psychologists for her generosity in establishing this series of annual lectures on the discovery and development of exceptional abilities and capacities. Our literature has been greatly enriched by the lectures which she has made possible.

I should like also to congratulate Yale University for having been chosen this year as the institution to be honored for its contributions to the study of talent, and to thank all those who have made such pleasant arrangements for this occasion.

There is a story, first told I believe by Mark Twain which, had Dr. Bingham known it, would have been, I am sure, one of his favorites. It is about a man who sought the greatest general who had ever lived. Upon inquiring as to where this individual might be found, he was told that the person he sought had died and gone to Heaven. At the Pearly Gates he informed St. Peter of the purpose of his quest, whereupon St. Peter pointed to a soul nearby. "But that," protested the inquirer, "isn't the greatest of all generals. I knew that person when he lived on earth, and he was only a

SOURCE. *American Psychologist*, 1962, **17,** 484–495. Copyright 1962 by the American Psychological Association, and reproduced by permission. The Walter Van Dyke Bingham Lecture given at Yale University, New Haven, Connecticut, April 11, 1962.

cobbler." "I know that," replied St. Peter, "but if he had been a general he would have been the greatest of them all."

Dr. Bingham spent his life worrying about cobblers who might have been generals and indeed about all those who fail to become what they are capable of becoming because neither they nor others recognize their potentialities and nourish their realization. Dr. Bingham was one of the first to insist that it is not enough to recognize creative talent after it has come to expression. He reminded us that it is our task as psychologists and as educators either through our insights or through the use of validated predictors to discover talent when it is still potential and to provide that kind of social climate and intellectual environment which will facilitate its development and expression.

Whatever light I shall be able to shed on the nature and nurture of creative talent comes in the main from findings of researches carried on during the last six years in the Institute of Personality Assessment and Research on the Berkeley campus of the University of California, and supported in large part by the Carnegie Corporation of New York.

In undertaking such a study one of our first tasks was to decide what we would consider creativity to be. This was necessary, first, because creativity has been so variously described and defined, and second, because only when we had come to agreement as to how we would conceive creativity would we be in a position to know what kinds of persons we would want to study.

We came easily to agreement that true creativeness fulfills at least three conditions. It involves a response or an idea that is novel or at the very least statistically infrequent. But novelty or originality of thought or action, while a necessary aspect of creativity, is not sufficient. If a response is to lay claim to being a part of the creative process, it must to some extent be adaptive to, or of, reality. It must serve to solve a problem, fit a situation, or accomplish some recognizable goal. And, thirdly, true creativeness involves a sustaining of the original insight, an evaluation and elaboration of it, a developing of it to the full.

Creativity, from this point of view, is a process extended in time and characterized by originality, adaptiveness, and realization. It may be brief, as in a musical improvisation, or it may involve a considerable span of years as was required for Darwin's creation of the theory of evolution.

The acceptance of such a conception of creativity had two important consequences for our researches. It meant that we would not seek to study creativity while it was still potential but only after it had been realized and had found expression in clearly identifiable creative products—buildings designed by architects, mathematical proofs developed by mathematicians, and the published writings of poets and novelists. Our conception of creativity forced us further to reject as indicators or criteria of creativeness the performance of individuals on so-called tests of creativity. While tests of this sort, that require that the subject think, for example, of unusual uses for common objects and the consequences of unusual events, may indeed measure the infrequency or originality of a subject's ideas in response to specific test items, they fail to reveal the extent to which the subject faced with real life problems is likely to come up with solutions that are novel and adaptive and which he will be motivated to apply in all of their ramifications.

Having thus determined that we would limit our researches to the study of persons who had already demonstrated a high level of creative work, we were still confronted with the problem of deciding from which fields of creative endeavor we would seek to recruit our subjects.

The fields which we finally sampled were those of creative writing, architecture, mathematics, industrial research, physical science, and engineering.

If one considers these activities in relation to the distinction often made between artistic and scientific creativity, it may be noted that we have sampled both of these domains as well as overlapping domains of creative striving which require that the practitioner be at one and the same time both artist and scientist.

Artistic creativity, represented in our studies by the work of poets, novelists, and essayists, results in products that are clearly expressions of the creator's inner states, his needs, perceptions, motivations, and the like. In this type of creativity, the creator externalizes something of himself into the public field.

In scientific creativity, the creative product is unrelated to the creator as a person, who in his creative work acts largely as a mediator between externally defined needs and goals. In this kind of creativeness, the creator, represented in our studies by industrial researchers, physical scientists, and engineers, simply operates on some aspect of his environment in such a manner as to produce a novel and appropriate product, but he adds little of himself or of his style as a person to the resultant.

Domains of creative striving in which the practitioner must be both artist and scientist were represented in our researches by mathematicians and architects. Mathematicians contribute to science, yet in a very real sense their important creative efforts are as much as anything else personal cosmologies in which they express themselves as does the artist in his creations. So, too, in architecture, creative products are both an expression of the architect and thus a very personal product, and at the same time an impersonal meeting of the demands of an external problem.

If in reporting the findings of our researches I draw most heavily upon data obtained from our study of architects (MacKinnon, 1962), it is for two reasons. First, it is the study for which, in collaboration with Wallace B.

Hall, I have assumed primary responsibility. Second, it is in architects, of all our samples, that we can expect to find what is most generally characteristic of creative persons. Architecture, as a field of creative endeavor, requires that the successful practitioner be both artist and scientist—artist in that his designs must fulfill the demands of "Delight," and scientist in that they must meet the demands of "Firmnesse" and "Commodity," to use the words of Sir Henry Wotton (1624). But surely, one can hardly think that the requirements of effective architecture are limited to these three demands. The successful and effective architect must, with the skill of a juggler, combine, reconcile, and exercise the diverse skills of businessman, lawyer, artist, engineer, and advertising man, as well as those of author and journalist, psychiatrist, educator, and psychologist. In what other profession can one expect better to observe the multifarious expressions of creativity?

It should be clear that any attempt to discover the distinguishing traits of creative persons can succeed only in so far as some group of qualified experts can agree upon who are the more and who are the less creative workers in a given field of endeavor. In our study of architects we began by asking a panel of experts—five professors of architecture, each working independently—to nominate the 40 most creative architects in the United States. All told they supplied us with 86 names instead of the 40 they would have mentioned had there been perfect agreement among them. While 13 of the 86 architects were nominated by all five panel members, and 9 nominated by four, 11 by three, and 13 by two, 40 were individual nominations each proposed by a single panel member.

The agreement among experts is not perfect, yet far greater than one might have expected. Later we asked 11 editors of the major American architectural journals, *Architectural Forum, Architectural Record,* the *Journal of the American Institute of Architects,* and *Progressive Architecture,* to rate the creativity of the 64 of the nominated architects whom we invited to participate in the study. Still later we asked the 40 nominated creative architects who actually accepted our invitation to be studied to rate the creativity of the invited 64 architects, themselves included. Since the editors' ratings of the creativity of the architects correlated +.88 with the architects' own ratings, it is clear that under certain conditions and for certain groups it is possible to obtain remarkable agreement about the relative creativeness of individual members of a profession and thus meet the first requirement for an effective study of creative persons.

A second requirement for the successful establishment of the traits of creative individuals is their willingness to make themselves available for study. Our hope was to win the cooperation of each person whom we invited to participate in the research, but as I have already indicated in the case of the architects, to obtain 40 acceptances, 64 invitations had to be sent out.

The invitation to this group, as to all the creative groups which we have studied, was to come to Berkeley for a weekend of intensive study in the Institute of Personality Assessment and Research. There, in groups of ten, they have been studied by the variety of means which constitute the assessment method—by problem solving experiments; by tests designed to discover what a person does not know or is unable or unwilling to reveal about himself; by tests and questionnaires that permit a person to manifest various aspects of his personality and to express his attitudes, interests, and values; by searching interviews that cover the life history and reveal the present structure of the person; and by specially contrived social situations of a stressful character which call for the subject's best behavior in a socially defined role.

The response of creative persons to the invitation to reveal themselves under such trying circumstances has varied considerably. At the one extreme there have been those who replied in anger at what they perceived to be the audacity of psychologists in presuming to study so ineffable and mysterious a thing as the creative process and so sensitive a being as a creative person. At the other extreme were those who replied courteously and warmheartedly, welcoming the invitation to be studied, and manifesting even an eagerness to contribute to a better understanding of the creative person and the creative process.

Here we were face to face with a problem that plagues us in all our researches: Are those who are willing to be assessed different in important ways from those who refuse? With respect to psychological traits and characteristics we can never know. But with respect to differences in creativeness, if any, between the 40 who accepted and the 24 who declined our invitation, we know that the two groups are indistinguishable. When the nominating panel's ratings of creativity were converted to standard scores and the means for the 24 versus the 40 were compared, they were found to be identical. When the editors' ratings were similarly converted to standard scores, the mean for the nonassessed group was slightly higher (51.9) than for the assessed sample (48.7), but the difference is not statistically significant.

Certainly we cannot claim to have assessed the 40 most creative architects in the country, or the most creative of any of the groups we have studied; but it is clear that we have studied a highly creative group of architects indistinguishable in their creativity from the group of 24 who declined to be studied, and so with the other groups too.

A third requirement for the successful determination of the traits of highly creative persons in any field of endeavor is that the profession be widely sampled beyond those nominated as most creative, for the distinguishing characteristics of the restricted sample might well have nothing to do with their creativeness. Instead they might be traits characterizing all members of the profession whether creative or not, distinguishing the professional group as a whole but in no sense limited or peculiar to its highly creative members. In the case of the architects, to use them once again as an example, two additional samples were recruited for study, both of which matched the highly creative sample (whom I shall now call Architects I) with respect to age and geographic location of practice. The first supplementary sample (Architects II) had had at least two years of work experience and association with one of the originally nominated creative architects. The second additional sample (Architects III) was composed of architects who had never worked with any of the nominated creatives.

By selecting three samples in this manner, we hoped to tap a range of talent sufficiently wide to be fairly representative of the profession as a whole; and we appear to have succeeded. The mean rating of creativity for each of the three groups—the ratings having been made on a nine-point scale by six groups of architects and experts on architecture—was for Architects I, 5.46; for Architects II, 4.25; and for Architects III, 3.54, the differences in mean ratings between each group being statistically highly significant.

So much for method and research design. I turn now to a discussion of the nature of creative talent as it has been revealed to us in our researches.

Persons who are highly creative are inclined to have a good opinion of themselves, as evidenced by the large number of favorable adjectives which they use in self-description and by the relatively high scores they earn on a scale which measures basic acceptance of the self. Indeed, there is here a paradox, for in addition to their favorable self-perceptions the very basic self-acceptance of the more creative persons often permits them to speak more frankly and thus more critically and in unusual ways about themselves. It is clear, too, that the self-images of the more creative differ from the self-images of the less creative. For example, Architects I, in contrast to Architects II and III, more often describe themselves as inventive, determined, independent, individualistic, enthusiastic, and industrious. In striking contrast Architects II and III more often than Architects I describe themselves as responsible, sincere, reliable, dependable, clear thinking, tolerant, and understanding. In short, were creative architects more often stress their inventiveness, independence, and individuality, their enthusiasm, determination, and industry, less creative members of the profession are impressed by their virtue and good character and by their rationality and sympathetic concern for others.

The discrepancies between their descriptions of themselves as they are and as they would ideally be are remarkably alike for all architects regardless of their level of creativeness. All three groups reveal themselves as desiring more personal attractiveness, self-confidence, maturity, and intellectual competence, a higher level of energy, and better social relations. As for differences, however, Architects I would ideally be more sensitive, while both Architects II and III wish for opposites if not incompatibles; they would ideally be more original but at the same time more self-controlled and disciplined.

As for the relation between intelligence and creativity, save for the mathematicians where there is a low positive correlation between intelligence and the level of creativeness, we have found within our creative samples essentially zero relationship between the two variables, and this is not due to a narrow restriction in range of intelligence. Among creative architects who have a mean score of 113 on the Terman Concept Mastery Test (1956), individual scores range widely from 39 to 179, yet scores on this measure of intelligence correlate −.08 with rated creativity. Over the whole range of intelligence and creativity there is, of course, a positive relationship between the two variables. No feeble-minded subjects have shown up in any of our creative groups. It is clear, however, that above a certain required minimum level of intelligence which varies from field to field and in some instances may be surprisingly low, being more intelligent does not guarantee a corresponding increase in creativeness. It just is not true that the more intelligent person is necessarily the more creative one.

In view of the often asserted close association of genius with insanity it is also of some interest to inquire into the psychological health of our creative subjects. To this end we can look at their profiles on the Minnesota Multiphasic Personality Inventory (MMPI) (Hathaway & McKinley, 1945), a test originally developed to measure tendencies toward the major psychiatric disturbances that man is heir to: depression, hysteria, paranoia, schizophrenia, and the like. On the eight scales which measure the strength of these dispositions in the person, our creative subjects earn scores which, on the average, are some 5 to 10 points above the general population's average score of 50. It must be noted, however, that elevated scores of this degree on these scales do not have the same meaning for the personality functioning of persons who, like our subjects, are getting along well in their personal lives and professional careers, that they have for hospitalized patients. The manner in which creative subjects describe themselves on this test as well as in the life history psychiatric interview is less suggestive of psychopathology than it is of good intellect, complexity and richness of personality, general lack of defensiveness, and candor in self-description—in other words, an openness to experience and especially to experience of one's inner life. It must also be noted, however, that in the self-reports and in the MMPI profiles of many of our creative subjects, one can find rather clear evidence of psychopathology, but also evidence of adequate control mechanisms, as the success with which they live their productive and creative lives testifies.

However, the most striking aspect of the MMPI profiles of all our male creative groups is an extremely high peak on the *Mf* (femininity) scale.

This tendency for creative males to score relatively high on femininity is also demonstrated on the Fe (femininity) scale of the California Psychological Inventory (CPI) (Gough, 1957) and on the masculinity-femininity scale of the Strong Vocational Interest Blank (Strong, 1959). Scores on the latter scale (where high score indicates more masculinity) correlate −.49 with rated creativity.

The evidence is clear: The more creative a person is the more he reveals an openness to his own feelings and emotions, a sensitive intellect and understanding self-awareness, and wide-ranging interests including many which in the American culture are thought of as feminine. In the realm of sexual identification and interests, our creative subjects appear to give more expression to the feminine side of their nature than do less creative persons. In the language of the Swiss psychologist, Carl G. Jung (1956), creative persons are not so completely identified with their masculine *persona* roles as to blind themselves to or to deny expression to the more feminine traits of the *anima*. For some, to be sure, the balance between masculine and feminine traits, interests, and identification, is a precarious one, and for several of our subjects it would appear that their presently achieved reconciliation of these opposites of their nature has been barely effected and only after considerable psychic stress and turmoil.

The perceptiveness of the creative and his openness to richness and complexity of experience is strikingly revealed on the Barron-Welsh Art Scale of the Welsh Figure Preference Test (Welsh, 1959), which presents to the subject a set of 62 abstract line drawings which range from simple and symmetrical figures to complex and asymmetrical ones. In the original study (Barron & Welsh, 1952) which standardized this scale, some 80 painters from New York, San Francisco, New Orleans, Chicago, and Minneapolis showed a marked preference for the complex and asymmetrical, or, as they often referred to them, the vital and dynamic figures. A contrasting sample of nonartists revealed a marked preference for the simple and symmetrical drawings.

All creative groups we have studied have shown a clear preference for the complex and asymmetrical, and in general the more creative a person is the stronger is this preference. Similarly, in our several samples, scores on an Institute scale which measures the preference for perceptual complexity are significantly correlated with creativity. In the sample of architects the correlation is +.48.

Presented with a large selection of one-inch squares of varicolored posterboard and asked to construct within a 30-minute period a pleasing, completely filled-in 8″ × 10″ mosaic (Hall, 1958), some subjects select the fewest colors possible (one used only one color, all white) while others seek to make order out of the largest possible number, using all of the 22 available colors. And, again citing results from the architects, there is a significant though low positive correlation of +.38 between the number of colors a subject chooses and his creativity as rated by the experts.

If one considers for a moment the meaning of these preferences on the art scale, on the mosaic test, and on the scale that measures preference for perceptual complexity, it is clear that creative persons are especially disposed to admit complexity and even disorder into their perceptions without being made anxious by the resulting chaos. It is not so much that they like disorder per se, but that they prefer the richness of the disordered to the stark barrenness of the simple. They appear to be challenged by disordered multiplicity which arouses in them a strong need which in them is serviced by a superior capacity to achieve the most difficult and far-reaching ordering of the richness they are willing to experience.

The creative person's openness to experience is further revealed on the Myers-Briggs Type Indicator (Myers, 1958), a test based largely upon Carl G. Jung's (1923) theory of psychological functions and types.

Employing the language of the test, though in doing so I oversimplify both it and the theory upon which it is based, one might say that whenever a person uses his mind for any purpose, he performs either an act of perception (he becomes aware of something) or an act of judgment (he comes to a conclusion about something). And most persons tend to show a rather consistent preference for and greater pleasure in one or the other of these, preferring either to perceive or to judge, though every one both perceives and judges.

An habitual preference for the judging attitude may lead to some prejudging and at the very least to the living of a life that is orderly, controlled, and carefully planned. A preference for the perceptive attitude results in a life that is more open to experience both from within and from without, and characterized by flexibility and spontaneity. A judging type places more emphasis upon the control and regulation of experience, while a perceptive type is inclined to be more open and receptive to all experience.

The majority of our creative writers, mathematicians, and architects are perceptive types. Only among research scientists do we find the majority to be judging types, and even in this group it is interesting to note that there is a positive correlation (+.25) between a scientist's preference for perception and his rated creativity as a scientific researcher. For architects, preference for perception correlates +.41 with rated creativity.

The second preference measured by the Type Indicator is for one of two types of perception: sense perception or sensation, which is a direct becoming aware of things by way of the senses versus intuitive perception or intuition, which is an indirect perception of the deeper meanings and possibilities inherent in things and situations. Again, everyone senses and intuits, but preliminary norms for the test suggest that in the United States three out of four persons show a preference for sense perception, concentrating upon immediate sensory experience and centering their attention upon existing facts. The one out of every four who shows a preference for intuitive perception, on the other hand, looks expectantly for a bridge or link between that which is given and present and that which is not yet thought of, focusing habitually upon possibilities.

One would expect creative persons not to be bound to the stimulus and the object but to be ever alert to the as-yet-not-realized. And that is precisely the way they show themselves to be on the Type Indicator. In contrast to an estimated 25% of the general population who are intuitive, 90% of the creative writers, 92% of the mathematicians, 93% of the research scientists, and 100% of the architects are intuitive as measured by this test.

In judging or evaluating experience, according to the underlying Jungian theory of the test, one makes use of thought or of feeling; thinking being a logical process aimed at an impersonal fact-weighing analysis, while feeling is a process of appreciation and evaluation of things that gives them a personal and subjective value. A preference for thinking or for feeling appears to be less related to one's creativity as such than to the type of materials or concepts with which one deals. Of our creative groups, writers prefer feeling, mathematicians, research scientists, and engineers prefer thinking, while architects split fifty-fifty in their preference for one or the other of the two functions.

The final preference in Jungian typology and on the test is the well-known one between introversion and extraversion. Approximately two-thirds of all our creative groups score as introverts, though there is no evidence that introverts as such are more creative than extraverts.

Turning to preferences among interests and values, one would expect the highly creative to be rather different from less creative people, and there is clear evidence that they are.

On the Strong Vocational Interest Blank, which measures the similarity of a person's expressed interests with the known interests of individuals successful in a number of occupations and professions, all of our creative subjects have shown, with only slight variation from group to group, interests similar to those of the psychologist, author-journalist, lawyer, architect, artist, and musician, and interests unlike those of the purchasing agent, office man, banker, farmer, carpenter, veterinarian, and interestingly enough, too, policeman and mortician. Leaving aside any consideration of the specific interests thus revealed we may focus our attention on the inferences that may be drawn from this pattern of scores which suggest that creative persons are relatively uninterested in small details, or in facts for their own sake, and more concerned with their meanings and implications, possessed of considerable cognitive flexibility, verbally skillful, interested in communicating with others and accurate in so doing, intellectually curious, and relatively disinterested in policing either their own impulses and images or those of others.

On the Allport-Vernon-Lindzey Study of Values (1951), a test designed to measure in the individual the relative strength of the six values of men as these values have been conceptualized and described by the German psychologist and educator, Eduard Spranger (1928), namely, the theoretical, economic, esthetic, social, political, and religious values, all of our creative groups have as their highest values the theoretical and the esthetic.

For creative research scientists the theoretical value is the highest, closely followed by the esthetic. For creative architects the highest value is the esthetic, with the theoretical value almost as high. For creative mathematicians, the two values are both high and approximately equally strong.

If, as the authors of the test believe, there is some incompatibility and conflict between the theoretical value with its cognitive and rational concern with truth and the esthetic value with its emotional concern with form and beauty, it would appear that the creative person has the capacity to tolerate the tension that strong opposing values create in him, and in his creative striving he effects some reconciliation of them. For the truly creative person it is not sufficient that problems be solved, there is the further demand that the solutions be elegant. He seeks both truth and beauty.

A summary description of the creative person—especially of the creative architect—as he reveals himself in his profile on the California Psychological Inventory (Gough, 1957) reads as follows:

> He is dominant (Do scale); possessed of those qualities and attributes which underlie and lead to the achievement of social status (Cs); poised, spontaneous, and self-confident in personal and social interaction (Sp); though not of an especially sociable or participative temperament (low Sy); intelligent, outspoken, sharp-witted, demanding, aggressive, and self-centered; persuasive and verbally fluent, self-confident and self-assured (Sa); and relatively uninhibited in expressing his worries and complaints (low Wb).
>
> He is relatively free from conventional restraints and inhibitions (low So and Sc), not preoccupied with the impression which he makes on others and thus perhaps capable of great independence and autonomy (low Gi), and relatively ready to recognize and admit self-views that are unusual and unconventional (low Cm).
>
> He is strongly motivated to achieve in situations in which independence in thought and action are called for (Ai). But, unlike his less creative colleagues, he is less inclined to strive for achievement in settings where conforming behavior is expected or required (Ac). In effi-

ciency and steadiness of intellectual effort (Ie), however, he does not differ from his fellow workers.

Finally, he is definitely more psychologically minded (Py), more flexible (Fx), and possessed of more femininity of interests (Fe) than architects in general.

There is one last finding that I wish to present, one that was foreshadowed by a discovery of Dr. Bingham in one of his attempts to study creativity. The subject of his study was Amy Lowell, a close friend of his and Mrs. Bingham's, with whom he discussed at length the birth and growth of her poems, seeking insight into the creative processes of her mind. He also administered to her a word association test and "found that she gave a higher proportion of unique responses than those of any one outside a mental institution" (Bingham, Millicent Todd, 1953, p. 11). We, too, administered a word association test to our subjects and found the unusualness of mental associations one of the best predictors of creativity, and especially so when associations given by no more than 1% to 10% of the population, using the Minnesota norms (Russell & Jenkins, 1954), are weighted more heavily than those given by less than 1% of the population. Among architects, for example, this weighted score is for Architects I, 204; Architects II, 128; and Architects III, 114; while for the total sample this measure of unusualness of mental associations correlates +.50 with rated creativity.

And Dr. Bingham, like us, found that there are certain hazards in attempting to study a creative poet. His searchings were rewarded by a poem Amy Lowell later wrote which was first entitled "To the Impudent Psychologist" and published posthumously with the title "To a Gentleman who wanted to see the first drafts of my poems in the interest of psychological research into the workings of the creative mind." We, I must confess, were treated somewhat less kindly by one of our poets who, after assessment, published an article entitled "My Head Gets Tooken Apart" (Rexroth, 1959).

Having described the overall design of our studies, and having presented a selection of our findings which reveal at least some aspects of the nature of creative talent, I turn now, but with considerably less confidence, to the question as to how we can early identify and best encourage the development of creative potential. Our findings concerning the characteristics of highly creative persons are by now reasonably well established, but their implications for the nurture of creative talent are far from clear.

It is one thing to discover the distinguishing characteristics of mature, creative, productive individuals. It is quite another matter to conclude that the traits of creative persons observed several years after school and college characterized these same individuals when they were students. Nor can we be certain that finding these same traits in youngsters today will identify those with creative potential. Only empirical, longitudinal research, which we do not yet have, can settle such issues. Considering, however, the nature of the traits which discriminate creative adults from their noncreative peers, I would venture to guess that most students with creative potential have personality structures congruent with, though possibly less sharply delineated than, those of mature creatives.

Our problem is further complicated by the fact that though our creative subjects have told us about their experiences at home, in school, and in college, and about the forces and persons and situations which, as they see it, nurtured their creativeness, these are, after all, self-reports subject to the misperceptions and self-deceptions of all self-reports. Even if we were to assume that their testimony is essentially accurate we would still have no assurance that the conditions in the home, in school, and society, the qualities of interpersonal relations between instructor and student, and the aspects of the teaching-learning process which would appear to have contributed to creative development a generation ago would facilitate rather than inhibit creativity if these same factors were created in today's quite different world and far different educational climate.

In reporting upon events and situations in the life histories of our subjects which appear to have fostered their creative potential and independent spirit, I shall again restrict myself to architects. One finds in their histories a number of circumstances which, in the early years, could well have provided an opportunity as well as the necessity for developing the secure sense of personal autonomy and zestful commitment to their profession which so markedly characterize them.

What appears most often to have characterized the parents of these future creative architects was an extraordinary respect for the child and confidence in his ability to do what was appropriate. Thus they did not hesitate to grant him rather unusual freedom in exploring his universe and in making decisions for himself—and this early as well as late. The expectation of the parent that the child would act independently but reasonably and responsibly appears to have contributed immensely to the latter's sense of personal autonomy which was to develop to such a marked degree.

The obverse side of this was that there was often a lack of intense closeness with one or both of the parents. Most often this appeared in relation to the father rather than to the mother, but often it characterized the relationship with both parents. There were not strong emotional ties of either a positive or a negative sort between parent and child, but neither was there the type of relationship that fosters overdependency nor the type that results in severe rejection. Thus, if there was a certain distance in the relationship between child and parent, it had a liberating effect so far as the child was concerned. If he lacked something of emotional closeness which some children experience with their parents, he was also spared that type of psychological exploitation that is so frequently seen in the life histories of clinical patients.

Closely related to this factor of some distance between parent and child were ambiguities in identification with the parents. In place of the more usual clear identification with one parent, there was a tendency for the architects to have identified either with both parents or with neither. It was not that the child's early milieu was a deprived one so far as models for identification and the promotion of ego ideals were concerned. It was rather that the larger familial sphere presented the child with a plentiful supply of diverse and effective models—in addition to the mother and father, grandfathers, uncles, and others who occupied prominent and responsible positions within their community—with whom important identifications could be made. Whatever the emotional interaction between father and son, whether distant, harmonious, or turbulent, the father presented a model of effective and resourceful behavior in an exceptionally demanding career. What is perhaps more significant, though, is the high incidence of distinctly autonomous mothers among families of the creative architects, who led active lives with interests and sometimes careers of their own apart from their husbands'.

Still other factors which would appear to have contributed to the development of the marked personal autonomy of our subjects were the types of discipline and religious training which they received, which suggest that within the family there existed clear standards of conduct and ideas as to what was right and wrong but at the same time an expectation if not requirement of active exploration and internalization of a framework of personal conduct. Discipline was almost always consistent and predictable. In most cases there were rules, family standards, and parental injunctions which were known explicitly by the children and seldom infringed. In nearly half the cases, corporal punishment was not employed and in only a few instances was the punishment harsh or cruel.

As for religious practices, the families of the creative architects showed considerable diversity, but what was most widely emphasized was the development of personal ethical codes rather than formal religious practices. For one-third of the families formal religion was important for one parent or for both, but in two-thirds of the families formal religion was either unimportant or practiced only perfunctorily. For the majority of the families, in which emphasis was placed upon the development of one's own ethical code, it is of interest to inquire into the values that were most stressed. They were most often values related to integrity (e.g., forthrightness, honesty, respect for others), quality (e.g., pride, diligence, joy in work, development of talent), intellectual and cultural endeavor, success and ambition, and being respectable and doing the right thing.

The families of the more creative architects tended to move more frequently, whether within a single community, or from community to community, or even from country to country. This, combined with the fact that the more creative architects as youngsters were given very much more freedom to roam and to explore widely, provided for them an enrichment of experience both cultural and personal which their less creative peers did not have.

But the frequent moving appears also to have resulted frequently in some estrangement of the family from its immediate neighborhood. And it is of interest that in almost every case in which the architect reported that his family differed in its behavior and values from those in the neighborhood, the family was different in showing greater cultural, artistic, and intellectual interests and pursuits.

To what extent this sort of cultural dislocation contributed to the frequently reported experiences of aloneness, shyness, isolation, and solitariness during childhood and adolescence, with little or no dating during adolescence, or to what extent these experiences stemmed from a natural introversion of interests and unusual sensitivity, we cannot say. They were doubtless mutually reinforcing factors in stimulating the young architect's awareness of his own inner life and his growing interest in his artistic skills and his ideational, imaginal, and symbolic processes.

Almost without exception, the creative architects manifested very early considerable interest and skill in drawing and painting. And also, with almost no exception, one or both of the parents were of artistic temperament and considerable skill. Often it was the mother who in the architect's early years fostered his artistic potentialities by her example as well as by her instruction. It is especially interesting to note, however, that while the visual and artistic abilities and interests of the child were encouraged and rewarded, these interests and abilities were, by and large, allowed to develop at their own speed, and this pace varied considerably among the architects. There was not an anxious concern on the part of the parents about the skills and abilities of the child. What is perhaps most significant was the wide-spread definite lack of strong pressures from the parents toward a particular career. And this was true both for pressures away from architecture as well as for pressures toward architecture by parents who were themselves architects.

The several aspects of the life history which I have described were first noted by Kenneth Craik in the protocols for the highly creative Architects I. Subsequently, in reading the protocols for Architects II and III as well as Architects I, a credit of one point for the presence of each of the factors was assigned and the total for each person taken as a score. The correlation of these life history scores with rated creativity of the architects is +.36, significant beyond the .005 level of confidence.

And now I turn finally to a consideration of the implications of the nature of creative talent for the nurturing of it in school and college through the processes of education.

Our findings concerning the relations of intelligence to creativity suggest that we may have overestimated in our educational system the role of intelligence in creative achievement. If our expectation is that a child of a given intelligence will not respond creatively to a task which confronts him, and especially if we make this expectation known to the child, the probability that he will respond creatively is very much reduced. And later on, such a child, now grown older, may find doors closed to him so that he is definitely excluded from certain domains of learning. There is increasing reason to believe that in selecting students for special training of their talent we may have overweighted the role of intelligence either by setting the cutting point for selection on the intellective dimension too high or by assuming that regardless of other factors the student with the higher IQ is the more promising one and should consequently be chosen. Our data suggest, rather, that if a person has the minimum of intelligence required for masterly of a field of knowledge, whether he performs creatively or banally in that field will be crucially determined by nonintellective factors. We would do well then to pay more attention in the future than we have in the past to the nurturing of those nonintellective traits which in our studies have been shown to be intimately associated with creative talent.

There is the openness of the creative person to experience both from within and from without which suggests that whether we be parent or teacher we should use caution in setting limits upon what those whom we are nurturing experience and express.

Discipline and self-control are necessary. They must be learned if one is ever to be truly creative, but it is important that they not be overlearned. Furthermore, there is a time and place for their learning, and having been learned they should be used flexibly, not rigidly or compulsively.

If we consider this specifically with reference to the attitudes of perceiving and judging, everyone must judge as well as perceive. It is not a matter of using one to the exclusion of the other, but a question of how each is used and which is preferred. The danger for one's creative potential is not the judging or evaluating of one's experience but that one prejudges, thus excluding from perception large areas of experience. The danger in all parental instruction, as in all academic instruction, is that new ideas and new possibilities of action are criticized too soon and too often. Training in criticism is obviously important and so widely recognized that I need not plead its case. Rather I would urge that, if we wish to nurture creative potential, an equal emphasis be placed on perceptiveness, discussing with our students as well as with our children, at least upon occasion, the most fantastic of ideas and possibilities. It is the duty of parents to communicate and of professors to profess what they judge to be true, but it is no less their duty by example to encourage in their children and in their students an openness to all ideas and especially to those which most challenge and threaten their own judgments.

The creative person, as we have seen, is not only open to experience, but intuitive about it. We can train students to be accurate in their perceptions, and this, too, is a characteristic of the creative. But can we train them to be intuitive, and if so how?

I would suggest that rote learning, learning of facts for their own sake, repeated drill of material, too much emphasis upon facts unrelated to other facts, and excessive concern with memorizing, can all strengthen and reinforce sense perception. On the other hand, emphasis upon the transfer of training from one subject to another, the searching for common principles in terms of which facts from quite different domains of knowledge can be related, the stressing of analogies, and similes, and metaphors, a seeking for symbolic equivalents of experience in the widest possible number of sensory and imaginal modalities, exercises in imaginative play, training in retreating from the facts in order to see them in larger perspective and in relation to more aspects of the larger context thus achieved—these and still other emphases in learning would, I believe, strengthen the disposition to intuitive perception as well as intuitive thinking.

If the widest possible relationships among facts are to be established, if the structure of knowledge (Bruner, 1960) is to be grasped, it is necessary that the student have a large body of facts which he has learned as well as a large array of reasoning skills which he has mastered. You will see, then, that what I am proposing is not that in teaching one disdain acute and accurate sense perception, but that one use it to build upon, leading the student always to an intuitive understanding of that which he experiences.

The independence of thought and action which our subjects reveal in the assessment setting appears to have long characterized them. It was already manifest in high school, though, according to their reports, tending to increase in college and thereafter.

In college our creative architects earned about a B average. In work and courses which caught their interest they could turn in an A performance, but in courses that failed to strike their imagination, they were quite willing to do no work at all. In general, their attitude in college appears to have been one of profound skepticism. They were unwilling to accept anything on the mere say-so of their instructors. Nothing was to be accepted on faith or because it had behind it the voice of authority. Such matters might be accepted, but only after the student on his own had demonstrated their validity to himself. In a sense, they were rebellious, but they did not run counter to the standards out of sheer rebelliousness. Rather, they were spirited in their disagreement and one gets the impression that they learned most from those who were not easy with them. But clearly many of them were not easy to take. One of the most rebellious, but, as it turned out, one of the most creative, was advised by the Dean of his School to quit because he had no talent; and another, having been failed in his design dissertation which attacked the stylism of the faculty, took his degree in the art department.

These and other data should remind all of us who teach that creative students will not always be to our liking. This will be due not only to their independence in situations in which nonconformity may be seriously disruptive of the work of others, but because, as we have seen, more than most they will be experiencing large quantities of tension produced in them by the richness of their experience and strong opposites of their nature. In struggling to reconcile these opposites and in striving to achieve creative solutions to the difficult problems which they have set themselves they will often show that psychic turbulence which is so characteristic of the creative person. If, however, we can only recognize the sources of their disturbance, which often enough will result in behavior disturbing to us, we may be in a better position to support and encourage them in their creative striving.

REFERENCES

Allport, G. W., Vernon, P. E., & Lindzey, G. *Study of values: Manual of directions.* (Rev. ed.) Boston: Houghton Mifflin, 1951.

Barron, F., & Welsh, G. S. Artistic perception as a possible factor in personality style: Its measurement by a figure preference test. *J. Psychol.,* 1952, **33,** 199–203.

Bingham, Millicent Todd. Beyond psychology. In, *Homo sapiens auduboniensis: A tribute to Walter Van Dyke Bingham.* New York: National Audubon Society, 1953. Pp. 5–29.

Bruner, J. S. *The process of education.* Cambridge, Mass.: Harvard Univer. Press, 1960.

Gough, H. G. *California Psychological Inventory manual.* Palo Alto, Calif.: Consulting Psychologists Press, 1957.

Hall, W. B. The development of a technique for assessing aesthetic predispositions and its application to a sample of professional research scientists. Paper read at Western Psychological Association, Monterey, California, April 1958.

Hathaway, S. R., & McKinley, J. C. *Minnesota Multiphasic Personality Inventory.* New York: Psychological Corporation, 1945.

Jung, C. G. *Psychological types.* New York: Harcourt, Brace, 1923.

Jung, C. G. *Two essays on analytical psychology.* New York: Meridian, 1956.

MacKinnon, D. W. The personality correlates of creativity: A study of American architects. In G. S. Nielsen (Ed.), *Proceedings of the XIV International Congress of Applied Psychology, Copenhagen 1961.* Vol. 2. Copenhagen: Munksgaard, 1962. Pp. 11–39.

Myers, Isabel B. *Some findings with regard to type and manual for Myers-Briggs Type Indicator, Form E.* Swarthmore, Pa.: Author, 1958.

Rexroth, K. My head gets tooken apart. In, *Bird in the bush: Obvious essays.* New York: New Directions Paperbook, 1959. Pp. 65–74.

Russell, W. A., & Jenkins, J. J. The complete Minnesota norms for responses to 100 words from the Kent-Rosanoff Word Association Test. Technical Report No. 11, 1954, University of Minnesota, Contract N8 onr-66216, Office of Naval Research.

Spranger, E. *Types of men.* (Trans. by Paul J. W. Pigors) Halle (Saale), Germany: Max Niemeyer, 1928.

Strong, E. K., Jr. *Manual for Strong Vocational Interest Blanks for Men and Women, Revised Blanks (Form M and W).* Palo Alto, Calif.: Consulting Psychologists Press, 1959.

Terman, L. M. *Concept Mastery Test, Form T manual.* New York: Psychological Corporation, 1956.

Welsh, G. S. *Welsh Figure Preference Test: Preliminary manual.* Palo Alto, Calif.: Consulting Psychologists Press, 1959.

Wotton, Henry. *The elements of architecture.* London: John Bill, 1624.

Introduction to
McClelland Article

Try to picture in your mind the type of people you think might be successful in business. Can you describe what they would be like and how they would behave? Now consider the following description—does it fit your image of what a successful businessman would be like?

> [Such people] ". . . work harder at laboratory tasks, learn faster, do somewhat better school work in high school even with IQ partialled out, and seem to do their best work when it counts for their record and not when other special incentives are introduced such as pressure from the outside to do well, money prizes, or time off from work. They are more resistant to social pressure, choose experts over friends as work partners, and tend to be more active in college or community activities, like risky occupations, perform better under long odds, and choose moderate risks over either safe or speculative ones. Finally they come from families in which there has been stress on early self reliance and mastery . . . [such] a person . . . wants to do well at what he undertakes, . . . is energetic, non-conforming, and tends to be predisposed toward innovations, toward working at tasks which are not safe and traditional but involve some element of risk—perhaps because only then can he feel enough subjective satisfaction from succeeding."

Such a description actually represents a composite profile of individuals who possess what Harvard psychologist David McClelland calls a "high need for achievement." * Like intelligence, creativity, authoritarianism, and extraversion, the need for achievement is a personality characteristic; and

* The quote is found on p. 521 of Atkinson's *Motives in fantasy action and society* (Princeton: Van Nostrand, 1958).

like other personality characteristics it varies among individuals. Some persons have a high need for achievement; others not so high; still others a very low need for achievement. Where do such individual differences in need for achievement originate? They begin in early childhood experiences at home. It seems that a person's level of "achievement motivation" is the result of his upbringing—the achievement motive is transmitted from parent to child in the family setting.

Primarily through the work of McClelland and two other psychologists (Henry Murray and John Atkinson) a test has been developed to measure an individual's need for achievement. The instrument is the Thematic Apperception Test (TAT), a series of pictures that the testee writes stories about.

For two decades McClelland has studied the role of achievement motivation in human behavior and the impact of high need achieving behavior on society and its institutions (e.g., Atkinson, 1958; McClelland, 1961). In the article below McClelland focuses on the relationship between need for achievement and economic growth—specifically, how the businessman with high achievement motivation behaves.

REFERENCES

Atkinson, J. (Ed.) *Motives in fantasy, action and society*. Princeton: Van Nostrand, 1958.

McClelland, J. *The achieving society*. New York: Van Nostrand, 1961.

17

Business Drive
and National Achievement

Achievement motivation leads to success in business. The author
suggests that the same is true for a country, or the world as a whole.

David C. McClelland

- What accounts for the rise in civilization? Not external resources
(i.e., markets, minerals, trade routes, or factories), but the entrepreneurial
spirit which exploits those resources—a spirit found most often among businessmen.
- Who is ultimately responsible for the pace of economic growth in
poor countries today? Not the economic planners or the politicians, but the
executives whose drive (or lack of it) will determine whether the goals of
the planners are fulfilled.
- Why is Russia developing so rapidly that—if it continues its present
rate of growth—it will catch up economically with the most advanced country in the world, the United States, in 25 or 30 years? Not, as the U.S.S.R.
claims, because of the superiority of its Communist system, but because—by
hook or by crook—it has managed to develop a stronger spirit of entre-
preneurship among executives than we have today in the U.S.
- How can foreign aid be most efficiently used to help poor countries
develop rapidly? Not by simply handing money over to their politicians or
budget makers, but by using it in ways that will select, encourage, and develop those of their business executives who have a vigorous entrepreneurial
spirit or a strong drive for achievement. In other words: *invest in a man,
not just in a plan.*

What may be astonishing about some of these remarks is that they come
from a college professor, and not from the National Association of Manufacturers. They are not the defensive drum rattlings of an embattled capitalist,

SOURCE. *Harvard Business Review,* July–August 1962, 99–112. Copyright 1962 by the President and Fellows of Harvard College; all rights reserved.

What is your own achievement motivation? Before you read further, we suggest that you take
this test, which is explained in detail later in the article. Look at this picture for ten or fifteen
seconds. Now write a brief but imaginative story suggested by the picture and by the following
questions: (1) What is happening? Who is the man? (2) What has led to this situation? That is,
what has happened in the past? (3) What is the man thinking? What is wanted? By whom?
(4) What will happen? What will be done? Now go ahead with your reading. [Later] . . . you
can get an indication of your own achievement motivation by determining which of the illustrative stories your story most resembles.

but are my conclusions, based on nearly 15 years of research, as a strictly
academic psychologist, into the human motive that appears to be largely
responsible for economic growth—research which has recently been summarized in my book, entitled *The Achieving Society*.[1]

Since I am an egghead from way back, nothing surprises me more than
finding myself rescuing the businessman from the academic trash heap, dust-
ing him off, and trying to give him the intellectual respectability that he
has had a hard time maintaining for the last 50 years or so. For the fact is
that the businessman has taken a beating, not just from the Marxists, who
pictured him as a greedy capitalist, and the social critics, who held him responsible for the Great Depression of the 1930's, but even from himself,
deep in his heart.

One of the queerest ironies of history, as John Kenneth Galbraith
points out in *The Affluent Society*,[2] is that in a sense Marx won his case
with his sworn enemies, the capitalists. Marx loudly asserted that they were

[1] Princeton, D. Van Nostrand Co., Inc., 1961.
[2] Boston, Houghton Mifflin Company, 1958.

selfish and interested only in profits. In the end many agreed. They accepted
the Marxist materialistic view of history. The modern businessman, says
Galbraith, "suspects that the moral crusade of reformers, do-gooders, liberal
politicians, and public servants, all their noble protestations notwithstanding, are based ultimately on self-interest. 'What,' he inquires, 'is their
gimmick' " [3]

If not only the Marxists, but Western economists, and even businessmen themselves, end up assuming that their main motive is self-interest and
a quest for profit, it is small wonder that they have had a hard time holding
their heads high in recent years.

But now the research I have done has come to the businessman's rescue
by showing that everyone has been wrong, that it is *not* profit per se that
makes the businessman tick but a strong desire for achievement, for doing a
good job. Profit is simply one measure among several of how well the job
has been done, but it is not necessarily the goal itself.

THE ACHIEVEMENT GOAL

But what exactly does the psychologist mean by the "desire for achievement"? How does he measure it in individuals or in nations? How does he
know that it is so important for economic growth? Is it more important for
businessmen to have this desire than it is for politicians, bishops, or generals? These are the kinds of questions which are answered at great length
and with as much scientific precision as possible in my book. Here we must
be content with the general outline of the argument, and develop it particularly as it applies to businessmen.

To begin with, psychologists try to find out what a man spends his
time thinking and day-dreaming about when he is not under pressure to
think about anything in particular. What do his thoughts turn to when he
is by himself or not engaged in a special job? Does he think about his
family and friends, about relaxing and watching TV, about getting his
superior off his back? Or does he spend his time thinking and planning how
he can "sell" a particular customer, cut production costs, or invent a better
steam trap or toothpaste tube?

If a man spends his time thinking about doing things better, the psychologist says he has a concern for achievement. In other words, he cares
about achievement or he would not spend so much time thinking about it.
If he spends his time thinking about family and friends, he has a concern
for affiliation; if he speculates about who is boss, he has a concern for power,
and so on. What differs in my approach from the one used by many psychologists is that my colleagues and I have not found it too helpful simply
to *ask* a person about his motives, interests, and attitudes. Often he himself

[3] Ibid., p. 71.

does not know very clearly what his basic concerns are—even more often he may be ashamed and cover some of them up. So what we do is to try and get a sample of his normal waking thoughts by asking him just to tell a few stories about some pictures.

Stories Within Stories

Let us take a look at some typical stories written by U. S. business executives. These men were asked to look briefly at a picture—in this case, a man at a worktable with a small family photograph at one side—and to spend about five minutes writing out a story suggested by the picture. Here is a very characteristic story:

> The engineer is at work on Saturday when it is quiet and he has taken time to do a little day-dreaming. He is the father of the two children in the picture—the husband of the woman shown. He has a happy home life and is dreaming about some pleasant outing they have had. He is also looking forward to a repeat of the incident which is now giving him pleasure to think about. He plans on the following day, Sunday, to use the afternoon to take his family for a short trip.

Obviously, no achievement-related thoughts have come to the author's mind as he thinks about the scene in the picture. Instead, it suggests spending time pleasantly with his family. His thoughts run along *affiliative* lines. He thinks readily about interpersonal relationships and having fun with other people. This, as a matter of fact, is the most characteristic reaction to this particular picture. But now consider another story:

> A successful industrial designer is at his "work bench" toying with a new idea. He is "talking it out" with his family in the picture. Someone in the family dropped a comment about a shortcoming in a household gadget, and the designer has just "seen" a commercial use of the idea. He has picked up ideas from his family before—he is "telling" his family what a good idea it is, and "confidentially" he is going to take them on a big vacation because "their" idea was so good. The idea will be successful, and family pride and mutual admiration will be strengthened.

The author of this story maintains a strong interest in the family and in affiliative relationships, but has added an achievement theme. The family actually has helped him innovate—get a new idea that will be successful and obviously help him get ahead. Stories which contain references to good new ideas, such as a new product, an invention, or a unique accomplishment of any sort, are scored as reflecting a concern for achievement in the person who writes them. In sum, this man's mind tends to run most easily along the lines of accomplishing something or other. Finally, consider a third story:

> The man is an engineer at a drafting board. The picture is of his family. He has a problem and is concentrating on it. It is merely an everyday occurrence—a problem which requires thought. How can he get that bridge to take the stress of possible high winds? He wants to arrive at a good solution of the problem by himself. He will discuss the problem with a few other engineers and make a decision which will be a correct one—he has the earmarks of competence.

The man who wrote this story—an assistant to a vice president, as a matter of fact—notices the family photograph, but that is all. His thoughts tend to focus on the problem that the engineer has to solve. In the scant five minutes allowed, he even thinks of a precise problem—how to build a bridge that will take the stress of possible high winds. He notes that the engineer wants to find a good solution by himself, that he goes and gets help from other experts and finally makes a correct decision. These all represent different aspects of a complete achievement sequence—defining the problem, wanting to solve it, thinking of means of solving it, thinking of difficulties that get in the way of solving it (either in one's self or in the environment), thinking of people who might help in solving it, and anticipating what would happen if one succeeded or failed.

Each of these different ideas about achievement gets a score of $+1$ in our scoring system so that the man in the last incident gets a score of $+4$ on the scale of concern or need for achievement (conventionally abbreviated to n Achievement). Similarly, the first man gets a score of -1 for his story since it is completely unrelated to achievement, and the second man a score of $+2$ because there are two ideas in it which are scorable as related to achievement.

Each man usually writes six such stories and gets a score for the whole test. The coding of the stories for "achievement imagery" is so objective that two expert scorers working independently rarely disagree. In fact, it has recently been programed for a high-speed computer that does the scoring rapidly, with complete objectivity, and fairly high accuracy. What the score for an individual represents is the frequency with which he tends to think spontaneously in achievement terms when that is not clearly expected of him (since the instructions for the test urge him to relax and to think freely and rapidly).

Thinking Makes It So

What are people good for who think like this all the time? It doesn't take much imagination to guess that they might make particularly good business executives. People who spend a lot of their time thinking about getting ahead, inventing new gadgets, defining problems that need to be solved, considering alternative means of solving them, and calling in experts for help should also be people who in real life *do* a lot of these things or at the very best are readier to do them when the occasion arises.

I recognize, of course, that this is an assumption that requires proof. But, as matters turned out, our research produced strong factual support. Look, for instance, at Exhibit 1. It shows that in three countries representing different levels and types of economic development managers or executives scored considerably higher on the average in achievement thinking than did professionals or specialists of comparable education and background. Take the two democratic countries shown there:

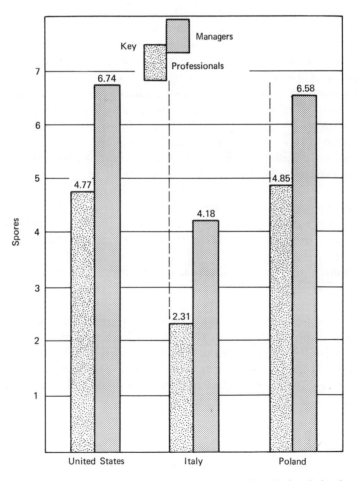

EXHIBIT 1. Average *n* achievement scores of managers and professionals in three countries.

• In the United States the comparison was between matched pairs of unit managers and specialists of the same position level, age, educational background, and length of service in the General Electric Company. The managers spent more of their time in the test writing about achievement than the specialists did.

• The same was true of middle-level executives from various companies in Italy when contrasted with students of law, medicine, and theology who were roughly of the same intelligence level and social background.

In other words it takes a concern for achievement to be a manager in a foreign country like Italy, for instance, just as it does in the United States. It is worth noting in passing, however, that the level of achievement thinking among Italian managers is significantly lower than it is among American managers—which, as will be shown later, quite probably has something to do with the lower level and rate of economic development in Italy.

What about a Communist country? The figures for Poland are interesting, because (1) the level of concern for achievement is about what it is in the United States, and (2) even in businesses owned and operated by the state, as in Poland, managers tend to have a higher concern for achievement than do other professionals.

Another even more striking result, not shown in Exhibit 1, is the fact that there is *no real difference* between the average n Achievement score of managers working for the U. S. government (9.3) and those in U. S. private business generally (8.90). Apparently, a manager working for the Bureau of Ships in the Department of the Navy spends as much time thinking about achievement as his counterpart in Ford or Sears, Roebuck; government service does not weaken his entrepreneurial spirit. Whether he is able to be as effective as he might be in private business is another matter, not touched on here.

Careful quantitative studies of the prevalence of achievement concern among various types of executives also yield results in line with what one one would expect. Thus, sales managers score higher than other types of managers do.

In general, more successful managers tend to score higher than do less successful managers (except in government service where promotion depends more on seniority). The picture is clear in small companies, where the president tends to score higher than his associates. In large companies, the picture is a little more complicated. Men in the lowest salary brackets (earning less than $20,000 a year) definitely have the lowest average n Achievement scores, while those in the next bracket up ($20,000 to $25,000 a year) have the highest average n Achievement level. Apparently an achievement concern helps one get out of the ranks of the lowest paid into a higher income bracket. But from there on, the trend fades. Men in the highest income brackets have a somewhat lower average concern for achievement, and apparently turn their thoughts to less achievement-oriented concerns. Possibly these men are doing well enough to relax a little.

BUSINESSMEN AND ACHIEVEMENT

Businessmen usually raise either one of two questions at this point:

1. "Where can I get this test for *n* Achievement? It sounds like a good way of picking young executives!"
2. "Why is this concern for achievement specific to being a success as a business manager? What about other types of achievement? Why isn't the entrepreneurial spirit necessary for success as an opera star, a preacher, a great teacher, or a great scientist?"

The answer to the first question, unfortunately, is simple: no practicable, marketable test for assessing achievement concern exists as yet. The method of measurement we have been using is too sensitive, too easily influenced by the social atmosphere surrounding the people who take the test, to give reliable individual results. Under carefully controlled conditions it works adequately to distinguish large groups of people like managers versus professionals, but it is not yet useful for individual selection. What we have here is a theoretical, scientific "breakthrough," not a practicable working device.

The second question is harder to answer but it takes us further in the direction of understanding exactly what kind of a person it is who spends a lot of his time thinking about achievement. To begin with, the facts are clear: many important types of professionals (doctors, lawyers, priests, or research scientists) fail to score on the average as high as business executives, yet clearly their work is in every sense as much of an achievement as the businessman's. How come?

Let us consider a particular case for a moment—that of the research scientist. Certainly his work represents an important achievement, for he is the one who often makes the breakthrough on which new technological and economic advances depend. Shouldn't he be thinking about defining a problem, doing a good job of solving it, getting help from experts, etc.?

Yet, when we tested a number of such scientists—including several outstanding Nobel prize winners—we found, somewhat to our surprise, that they were not unusually high in *n* Achievement but rather tended to be average. Then it occurred to us that having a very high concern for achievement might make a person unsuitable for being a research scientist. Why? Simply because in research a man must often work for what may become very long periods of time without any knowledge of how well he is doing. He may not even know if he is on the right track for as much as five or ten years. But a man with a high need for achievement likes to know quickly whether he is accomplishing anything and quite possibly would become frustrated by the lack of feedback in basic science as to whether he is getting anywhere. He would then more likely move into an area such as management where results are more tangible. On the other hand, the research scientist obviously needs *some* achievement concern, or he is not likely to want to engage in his occupation at all.

Characteristics of Achievers

Considerations like these focus attention on what there is about the job of being a business entrepreneur or executive that should make such a job peculiarly appropriate for a man with a high concern for achievement. Or, to put it the other way around, a person with high *n* Achievement has certain characteristics which enable him to work best in certain types of situations that are to his liking. An entrepreneurial job simply provides him with more opportunities for making use of his talents than do other jobs. Through careful empirical research we know a great deal by now about the man with high *n* Achievement, and his characteristics do seem to fit him unusually well for being a business executive. Specifically:

1. *To begin with, he likes situations in which he takes personal responsibility for finding solutions to problems.* The reason is obvious. Otherwise, he could get little personal achievement satisfaction from the successful outcome. No gambler, he does not relish situations where the outcome depends not on his abilities and efforts but on chance or other factors beyond his control. For example:

> Some business school students in one study played a game in which they had to choose between two options, in each of which they had only one chance in three of succeeding. For one option they rolled a die and if it came up, say, a 1 or a 3 (out of six possibilities), they won. For the other option they had to work on a difficult business problem which they knew only one out of three people had been able to solve in the time allotted.
>
> Under these conditions, the men with high *n* Achievement regularly chose to work on the business problem, even though they knew the odds of success were statistically the same as for rolling the dice.

To men strong in achievement concern, the idea of winning by chance simply does not produce the same achievement satisfaction as winning by their own personal efforts. Obviously, such a concern for taking personal responsibility is useful in a business executive. He may not be faced very often with the alternative of rolling dice to determine the outcome of a decision, but there are many other ways open to avoid personal responsibility, such as passing the buck, or trying to get someone else (or a committee) to take the responsibility for getting something done.

The famed self-confidence of a good executive (which actually is related to high achievement motivation) is also involved here. He thinks it can be done if *he* takes responsibility, and very often he is right because he has spent so much time thinking about how to do it that he does it better.

2. *Another characteristic of a man with a strong achievement concern is his tendency to set moderate achievement goals and to take "calculated risks."* Again his strategy is well suited to his needs, for only by taking on moderately difficult tasks is he likely to get the achievement satisfaction he wants. If he takes on an easy or routine problem, he will succeed but get very little satisfaction out of his success. If he takes on an extremely difficult problem, he is unlikely to get any satisfaction because he will not succeed. In between these two extremes, he stands the best chance of maximizing his sense of personal achievement.

The point can be made with the children's game of ring toss, some variant of which we have tried out at all ages to see how a person with high *n* Achievement approaches it. To illustrate:

> The child is told that he scores when he succeeds in throwing a ring over a peg on the floor, but that he can stand anywhere he pleases. Obviously, if he stands next to the peg, he can score a ringer every time; but if he stands a long distance away, he will hardly ever get a ringer.
>
> The curious fact is that the children with high concern for achievement quite consistently stand at moderate distances from the peg where they are most apt to get achievement satisfaction (or, to be more precise, where the decreasing probability-of-success curve crosses the increasing satisfaction-from-success curve). The ones with low *n* Achievement, on the other hand, distribute their choices of where to stand quite randomly over the entire distance. In other words, people with high *n* Achievement prefer a situation where there is a challenge, where there is some real risk of not succeeding, but no so great a risk that they might no overcome it by their own efforts.

Again, such a characteristic would seem to suit men unusually well for the role of business entrepreneur. The businessman is always in a position of taking calculated risks, of deciding how difficult a given decision will be to carry out. If he is too safe and conservative, and refuses to innovate, to invest enough in research or product development or advertising, he is likely to lose out to a more aggressive competitor. On the other hand, if he invests too much or overextends himself, he is also likely to lose out. Clearly, then, the business executive should be a man with a high concern for achievement who is used to setting moderate goals for himself and calculating carefully how much he can do successfully.

Therefore, we waste our time feeling sorry for the entrepreneur whose constant complaints are that he is overworking, that he has more problems than he knows how to deal with, that he is doomed to ulcers because of overwork, and so on. The bald truth is that if he has high *n* Achievement, he loves all those challenges he complains about. In fact, a careful study might well show that he creates most of them for himself. He may talk about quitting business and living on his investments, but if he did, he might then *really* get ulcers. The state of mind of being a little overextended is precisely the one he seeks, since overcoming difficulties gives him achievement satisfaction. His real problem is that of keeping the difficulties from getting *too* big for him, which explains in part why he talks so much about them because it is a nagging problem for him to keep them at a level he can handle.

3. *The man who has a strong concern for achievement also wants concrete feedback as to how well he is doing.* Otherwise how could he get any satisfaction out of what he had done? And business is almost unique in the amount of feedback it provides in the form of sales, cost, production, and profit figures. It is really no accident that the symbol of the businessman in popular cartoons is a wall chart with a line on it going up or down. The businessman sooner or later knows how well he is doing; salesmen will often know their success from day to day. Furthermore, there is a concreteness in the knowledge of results which is missing from the kind of feedback professionals get.

Take, for example, the teacher as a representative professional. His job is to transmit certain attitudes and certain kinds of information to his students. He does get some degree of feedback as to how well he has done his job, but results are fairly imprecise and hardly concrete. His students, colleagues, and even his college's administration may indicate that they like his teaching, but he still has no real evidence that his students have *learned* anything from him. Many of his students do well on examinations, but he knows from past experience that they will forget most of that in a year or two. If he has high *n* Achievement and is really concerned about whether he has done his job well, he must be satisfied with sketchy, occasional evidence that his former pupils did absorb some of his ideas and attitudes. More likely, however, he is not a person with high *n* Achievement and is quite satisfied with the affection and recognition that he gets for his work which gratify other needs that he has.

The case of the true entrepreneur is different. Suppose he is a book publisher. He gets a manuscript and together with his editors decides that it is worth publication. At time of issuance, everyone is satisfied that he is launching a worthwhile product. But then something devastatingly concrete happens—something far more definite than ever happens to a teacher— namely, those monthly sales figures.

Obviously not everyone likes to work in situations where the feedback is so concrete. It can prove him right, but it also can prove him wrong. Oddly enough, the person with high n Achievement has a compelling interest to know whether he was right or wrong. He thrives and is happier in this type of situation than he is in the professional situation.

Two further examples from our research may make the point clearer. Boys with high n Achievement tend to be good with their hands, to like working in a shop or with mechanical or electrical gadgets. What characterizes such play again is the concrete feedback it provides as to how well a person is doing. If he wires up an electric circuit and then throws the switch, the light either goes on or it does not. Knowledge of results is direct, immediate, and concrete. Boys with high n Achievement like this kind of situation, and while some may go on to become engineers, others often go into business where they can continue getting this kind of concrete feedback.

What Money Means

In business, this feedback comes in the form of money, in costs and profits that are regularly reported. It is from this simple fact that the confusion between the so-called profit motive and the achievement motive has arisen in the minds of both Marxist and classical economists. For, in the typical case, a concern for profit in a capitalist economy does *not* mean that the businessman is primarily interested in money for its own sake. Rather, this concern is merely the *symptom* of a strong achievement concern, since profitability in a capitalist economy provides the best and simplest measure of success. It provides the same sort of concrete knowledge of achievement that a person with high n Achievement seeks all the time. Research findings clearly support this analysis. If you simply offer a person with high n Achievement a larger money reward for doing a certain task, he doesn't do any better than he did without the prize. In fact, he tends to do a little worse because the money makes him nervous. Not so the person with low n Achievement; he works harder when he has a chance of taking some money away from a situation. The money in and of itself means more to him than it does to the person with high n Achievement.

Of course, it follows that concrete measures of achievement other than money could be devised by other types of economic systems to satisfy the entrepreneurial spirit. Something like this has apparently happened in Communist states like Poland and Russia, where plant managers work under a fairly rigid quota system which demands that they make their quotas—or else! In the free enterprise system a businessman must make his profit—or else. The psychological effects, so far as the achievement motive is concerned, are apparently pretty much the same. In both systems the manager gets feedback in concrete terms as to how well he is doing. If he has high n Achievement, he is more likely to live and survive under such a challenge.

While these three characteristics of people with a strong concern for achievement—the desire for personal responsibility, the tendency to set moderate achievement goals, and the need for concrete feedback of results— are the most important, there are some other minor characteristics possessed by these people which tend to suit them for an entrepreneurial job. They like to travel, they are willing to give up one bird in the hand to get two in the bush, and they prefer experts to friends as working partners. But to discuss any of these in detail would take us far afield.

ACHIEVING NATIONS

If the theory underlying the experiments with determining n Achievement in individuals is correct, then what is true for groups of individuals might well prove true for nations. Does a high achievement concern herald a nation's rise? Let's take a look at the facts.

Naturally, tests of individual businessmen in particular countries would not prove very much about the influence of achievement concern on the nation's success. However, we figured that by coding popular literature of past and present, we could get a rough estimate of the strength of the concern for achievement in a given country at a given time period. So we took samples from various time periods of a wide variety of the most popular imaginative literature we could find—poems, songs, plays—and scored them for n Achievement just as we had scored the simple stories written by individuals.

When we plotted the number of achievement ideas per hundred lines sampled in a given time period against economic indexes for the same time period, we got two curves that showed a very interesting relationship to each other. Normally, we found, a high level of concern for achievement is followed some 50 years or so later by a rapid rate of economic growth and prosperity. Such was certainly the case in ancient Greece and in Spain in the late Middle Ages. Furthermore, in both cases a decline in achievement concern was followed very soon after by a decline in economic welfare. The relationship between the two curves is shown most dramatically in Exhibit 2, which plots the data for the 300-year time span from Tudor times to the Industrial Revolution in England:

There were two waves of economic growth in this time period, one smaller one around 1600 and a much larger one around 1800 at the beginning of the Industrial Revolution. Each wave was preceded by a

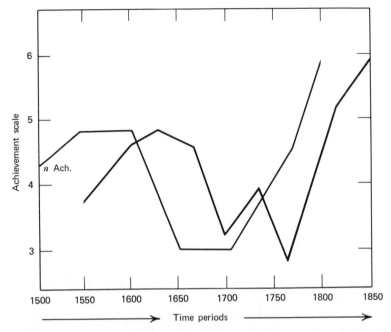

EXHIBIT 2. How achievement thinking expressed in English literature predicts the rate of industrial growth 50 years later. NOTE: Achievement thinking (*n*. Ach.) = Mean number of achievement images per 100 lines. Rate of industrial growth = Rate of gain in coal imports at London, as deviations from average trend (standard deviation units).

wave of concern for achievement reflected in popular literature, a smaller one prior to the growth spurt around 1600 and a larger one prior to the Industrial Revolution.

What clearer evidence could one ask for? What people are concerned about determines what they do, and what they do determines the outcome of history!

Present Confirms Past

In modern nations, too, the picture is very much the same. Children's stories used in public school textbooks proved to be the most standardized form of popular literature that we could get from a large number of different countries. As a matter of fact, the simple imaginative stories that every country uses to teach its children to read are very similar in format to the stories produced by individuals when we test them as described earlier, particularly if one concentrates as we did on second-, third-, and fourth-grade readers, where normally political influences are quite unimportant. The stories could be coded quite easily by the standard n Achievement scoring system.

Growth rates had to be estimated from the only figures available that could be trusted on such a wide variety of countries—namely, the figures showing electric power consumption—but there is ample evidence to show that electricity consumed is probably the best single available index of gross national income in modern times.

The n scores, when compared with the subsequent rates of economic growth for various countries, confirm the findings of the historical studies to a surprising extent. The higher the n Achievement level in the children's readers around 1925, the more rapid the subsequent rate of economic growth. (For 22 countries, the correlation was actually a substantial .53.) Furthermore, the higher the n Achievement level in a country's children's readers around 1950, the more rapid its rate of growth between 1952–1958. In fact, of 20 countries above average in n Achievement in 1950, 13 (or 65%) showed a rapid rate of economic growth in 1952–1958. Whereas, of 19 low in n Achievement, only 5 (or 26%) achieved a rapid rate of growth.

Prediction Possibilities

How meaningful are these findings, especially when one realizes the crudity of the data? In a certain sense, the cruder one admits the data to be, the more remarkable the findings appear. After all, the data suggests that one could have got a pretty good line on the economic future of various countries by studying its stories for children in 1925—regardless of a major depression, a World War, and a host of other political and economic factors.

Is it possible that we have stumbled on a way of predicting the future course of history? And from such an almost laughable source—stories for children—rather than the serious pronouncements of statesmen, generals, and economists? How is it possible?

The best interpretation of such findings would appear to run something as follows. The stories tell us what is on the minds of significant elites in the country, what these influential persons tend to think about most naturally, when they are "off guard," so to speak, and not under any particular pressure to think one thing or another. In this sense, the stories are exactly analogous to the ones written for us by individuals. If you ask a man whether he is interested in achievement, the chances are that he will tell you that of course he is. Similarly, if you were to ask a country's leaders whether they wanted their nation to forge ahead, they would find it un-patriotic to say no. But, regardless of what such leaders say in public, the stories in the children's readers of many nations will show whether their peoples' thoughts turn naturally to achievement or to matters other than achievement.

Here is an illustration. Take a simple story theme like one in which some children are building a boat. Such themes are frequently borrowed by one culture from another and appear in several different readers, but the way they are embroidered may be quite different and quite revealing. For example:

• In Country A, an *achievement*-oriented country, the emphasis is on making the boat, on constructing something that will work, and not sink or tip over in a strong wind.
• In Country B, the emphasis may be on *affiliation,* on the fun that the children have in playing together to sail their boat. Here little may be said about the details of constructing a seaworthy craft and much about the personal interaction of the children.
• In Country C, the story may center on *power,* and describe how the children were organized to produce the boat. One boy might set himself up as a leader, coordinating the work of the other children and telling them what to do.

Apparently, what comes most readily to the minds of these authors—whether concepts of achievement, affiliation, or power—reflects sufficiently well what is on the minds of key people in the country. And not only will these concepts seem natural and pleasing to the readers of these stories but will determine what they spend their time doing in the years to come. Thus, if the stories stress achievement, it means that an entrepreneurial spirit is abroad in the land. It indicates that many key people are thinking in achievement terms even when they do not need to.

In a nation, a strong achievement orientation affects particularly the business or economic sector of the population. And if the entrepreneurial types are strongly motivated to do well, they apparently succeed in getting the economy moving at a faster rate. So the children's stories are a symptom of the quality or "drive" of the entrepreneurial sector of an economy.

Rising and Falling Nations
With this in mind it is interesting to look at scores for particular countries—if only to make a better guess as to where to invest one's money! A generation ago, the North European countries, particularly Sweden and England, were very high in *n* Achievement, but both have fallen in the 1950's to well below average. Is it just a coincidence that one hears reports of stagnation or "maturity" in both economies? Are England's present difficulties the fault of outside circumstances, or do these difficulties stem from the fact that its citizens have lost their achievement drive? For some reason, the Central European countries—France, Germany, and Russia—

were all low in achievement concern in 1925, but by the 1950's all had increased sharply.

The case of Russia is particularly critical for us. How does the United States stand in achievement motivation as compared to the U.S.S.R.? According to a historical study, achievement concern in the United States increased regularly from 1800 to around 1890 but has decreased more or less regularly since, although there is a possibility that the decline has leveled off in the past 30 years. We are still above average and, in fact, were at approximately the same level as Russia in 1950, although we were probably on the way down while they were certainly on the way up.

From the point of view of this analysis, the argument as to whether a socialist or a free enterprise system is the better way of stimulating an economy has been based on a false premise all along. Americans claimed that the success of their economy resulted, naturally, from the free enterprise system. Then, when the Soviet Union scored successes in outer space and in other fields, the Russians immediately claimed these great economic and technological achievements stemmed from the superiority of their system.

Both contentions may well be wrong. Economic success and technological development depend on achievement motivation, and the rapid rate of Russian economic growth is due to an increase in her achievement concern just as ours was a generation or so earlier. There are other issues involved in comparing the two social systems, of course, but so far as this particular issue is concerned it has been misunderstood by both sides.

Need for Acceptance

There is one final question that must be answered before we move on. Is it possible that achievement motivation will be aroused in *any* nation which comes in contact with modern technology and sees vividly the opportunity for a better life? Can't achievement motivation be "borrowed" or assimilated from one nation to another? Are there not good illustrations of countries in which need for achievement has risen as they see more and more clearly the possibilities of growing and developing into modern, economically advanced nations? Are we just describing the "revolution of rising expectations" in fancy psychological jargon?

Opportunity is part of the story, of course. It does arouse people to act, but it arouses precisely those who have some need for achievement *already*. The soil must be ready for the seeds, if they are to grow. After all, many countries have been in touch with Western technology for generations—for example, the Islamic nations around the Mediterranean; yet they have been very slow to respond to the possibilities of a better life clearly presented to them all this time.

Consider, for example, a nation like Nigeria, which provides a good illustration of how opportunity and motivation must interact. Nigeria is essentially a federation of three regions, each of which is dominated by a different cultural group. Only one of these groups—the Yoruba—is known to be very high in need for achievement. In fact, long before the Yoruba had much contact with the West, this tribe was noted for its skill and interest in trade and native financial transactions. An indication of the validity of the achievement theory is shown by the fact that the Yoruba tribe, when exposed to new opportunities, produced a much stronger and more successful economic response than did the other tribes—as would be predicted. The regional bank operated by the Yoruba is in a much sounder position, for example, than the other two regional banks in Nigeria.

Opportunity challenges those who are achievement-oriented. Like two other groups high in n Achievement, American Jews and American Catholics between the ages of 35 and 45 (President Kennedy, for instance), the Yoruba reacted vigorously to develop economic opportunities as they became available. Exposure to economic and technological opportunities did not produce as vigorous a response from groups lower in n Achievement in Nigeria any more than a similar exposure has done through the years to similar low n Achievement groups in the United States.

WHAT CAN WE DO?

Is it inevitable that the achievement concern shown by U. S. citizens should continue to decline? Must we fade out in time as all other civilizations have in the past? Not if we understand what is happening and take steps to change it. Not if we move decisively and quickly to influence the sources of achievement concern in individuals and in our nation.

What are those sources? Clearly, not race or climate—those traditional external explanations of the superior energies of some nations. For Russia's n Achievement level has increased decisively since 1925, while Sweden's and England's have dropped. Certainly there have been no equally decisive changes in the gene pools or the climates of those nations in that time period.

In fact, external factors are usually unimportant, though occasionally they may play a role, as they have in helping to create generally high levels of n Achievement in immigrant countries like the United States, Canada, and Australia. Such nations tended to attract immigrants higher in n Achievement, because:

1. They drew their population initially from countries that were higher in achievement concern than those from which the Latin American countries drew.

2. They provided a haven for many persecuted religious minorities whose achievement concern was very strong.

3. They did not provide as many opportunities for getting rich quick as did Mexico and Peru, for example, with their plentiful supplies of gold and silver.

In short, countries like the United States were lucky. The barrier to migration was so formidable that primarily those with high n Achievement climbed it.

Historians have sometimes claimed that it was the great frontier in the United States that provided the challenge and stimulus to development. Nonsense. Great frontiers have existed and still exist in many South American countries without eliciting a similar response. It was the achievement-oriented immigrants to America who regarded the frontier as a challenge to be overcome. It was not the frontier that made them achievement-oriented. Opportunities, like new frontiers, always exist, but it takes a certain kind of person to see them and believe he can exploit them.

While our distance from Europe, our tolerance for religious minorities, our good fortune in drawing immigrants initially from countries high in n Achievement tended to ensure that we got more citizens with high achievement motivation, our later restrictive immigration policies have drastically reduced our chances of continuing to receive such people. These policies continue to give preference to immigrants from the North European countries, whose achievement drive has dropped significantly, and to restrict immigration from other countries where the n Achievement has been rising sharply. It would be a tragic irony of history if in an endeavor to protect ourselves, we managed to shut off the supply of that entrepreneurial spirit that made our country great!

Sources of Achievement

Where does strong achievement motivation come from? Values, beliefs, ideology—these are the really important sources of a strong concern for achievement in a country. Studies of the family have shown, for instance, that for a boy three factors are important in producing high n Achievement —parents' high standards of achievement, warmth and encouragement, and a father who is not dominating and authoritarian. Here is a typical study that reveals this fact:

A group of boys were blindfolded and asked to stack irregularly shaped blocks on top of each other with their left hands, at home in front of their parents. Separately, the mothers and fathers were asked how high they thought their sons could stack the blocks. Both parents of a boy with high n Achievement estimated that their boys should do better; they expected more of him than did the parents of a boy with low n Achievement. They also encouraged him more and gave him more affection and reward while he was actually doing the task. Finally, the fathers of boys with high n Achievement directed the behavior of their sons much less when they were actually stacking the blocks; that is, they told them less often to move their hands this way or that, to try harder, to stop jiggling the table, and so forth, than did the fathers of boys with low n Achievement.

Other studies have shown that fathers must be respected by their sons; but after the boy is capable of achieving something for himself, his father must stop directing every step he takes if the boy is to develop a strong concern for achievement.

In a sense, however, these family studies only push the question further back. Where did the parents get their standards? Why do some emphasize achievement and affectionately reward self-reliance? Because, very simply, they themselves believe in achievement for their family or for their political, social, or religious group. For one reason or another they are caught up in some great wave of achievement ideology.

One of the paradoxes of history is that often the achievement concern was not itself initially directed toward business or economics. For instance, the two great waves of achievement concern in the history of England shown in Exhibit 2 were each associated with waves of Protestant reform or revival, whose explicit aims were not secular but strictly religious. The Methodists, for example, in the second wave of the English Protestant revival, stressed religious perfection in this life; yet even John Wesley recognized with some puzzlement that devout Methodists tended to get rich, a fact which he considered a handicap in attaining religious perfection.

But now we can understand what happened. The strong concern for Christian perfection in this world tended to produce an achievement orientation in Methodist parents and their sons that turned the boys toward business because, as we have shown above, an achievement concern is most easily satisfied in business. In our day, it is the secular religious of nationalism and communism that have placed the highest emphasis on achievement and tended to create higher levels of n Achievement in underdeveloped and Communist countries. Communism lays the same claims to superiority as a means of salvation that Christianity once did. However wrong we may feel it to be, we must recognize that it tends to create a strong atmosphere of achievement that has important consequences for economic growth.

THE ACHIEVEMENT CHALLENGE

If we are to compete successfully with Russia in the economic sphere, we must develop an achievement ideology at least as strong as hers. If we are to help poor countries develop rapidly and become self-reliant, we must recognize that the first order of priority lies in fostering the entrepreneurial spirit in those countries, not in simply providing them with material capital or in meeting their physical needs.

Oddly enough, a businessman knows this about his own company. He knows that in the final analysis it is the spirit in the company that counts most—the entrepreneurial drive of the executives, the feeling of all that they are working together to achieve a common goal; it is not "hardware" that counts in the long run—the size and slickness of the plant, or the money in the bank. These assets will melt away like snow in a hot sun without the proper achievement orientation in the company. Knowing this, the wise executive acts accordingly. He is concerned to keep the achievement orientation of the company alive by talking about its aims, by setting moderate but realizable goals for himself and his associates, by assigning personal responsibility, by making sure that people know how well they are doing, by selecting executives with high n Achievement or by developing it in those who need it.

What is true for a business is also true for a country, but this is not widely recognized. And we must realize that it is important to foster the achieving spirit not only at home but abroad if we are to be effective as a nation. American foreign policy is currently based on two main strategies: (a) the provision of political freedom and (b) material aid. Both are excellent goals, but they are not enough. How long would a company last if its chief goals were freedom from interference by others and freedom from want? It needs positive, specific goals such as a more effective marketing program, or a strict cost reduction program; something dynamic is necessary to keep a company—and a country—alive and growing.

Over and over again we have failed to learn the lesson that political freedom without a strong drive for progress is empty and impossible to maintain for long. China was politically free under Chiang Kai-shek, but it lacked the dynamic of a really self-sacrificing achievement effort until it was taken over by the Communists. Unless we learn our lesson and find ways of stimulating that drive for achievement under freedom in poor countries, the Communists will go on providing it all around the world. We can go on building dikes to maintain freedom and impoverishing ourselves to feed and arm the people behind those dikes, but only if we develop the entrepreneurial spirit in those countries will we have a sound foreign policy. Only then can they look after their own dikes and become economically self-sufficient.

Compare India and China, for example. Despite newspaper reports to the contrary, economic experts assure us that China is developing much more rapidly economically today than is India. Why? Is it because the West has given less material help to India than the Communist world has to

China? Probably not. Is it because there is less political freedom in India than in China? Certainly not. Yet if the keystones of our foreign aid policy are the ensuring of political freedom and the granting of economic aid, these measures are clearly not doing very well as far as developing India is concerned. Russia has apparently exported something more important to China—namely, an achievement dynamic that has galvanized the whole country. There is absolutely no evidence that this dynamic needs to be associated with regimentation and lack of personal freedom as it is in China, for the United States had this dynamic once, still has quite a lot of it, and could export it more effectively—if we really tried.

Hard to Export

Actually, we have been hampered in exporting our achievement dynamic, not only by a misguided emphasis on material as opposed to motivational factors, but also by a laudable desire to avoid appearing superior. When Americans travel and discover how poor people are in many countries and how inferior their political institutions appear to be to ours, they often either withdraw in horror into their own American enclaves and become "ugly Americans" or they remember their college anthropology and become cultural relativists, deciding that after all there is some good in all ways of life and we must not impose ours on other people. Neither of these reatcions is very intelligent. For the fact is that all poor countries are going to modernize and want to modernize. They refuse to remain quaint, impoverished specimens for the anthropologist to study.

How can we help provide such countries with an achievement dynamic without seeming to impose it on them? One simple way is to sell them on *their own country* and *its* possibilities, not on *ours*. It may sound absurd to say that our job is to help sell the Tanganyikans on Tanganyika or the Mexicans on Mexico, but the fact is that in many of these countries most of the people have never even heard of the nation of which they are citizens, and know little or nothing about the possibilities for a better life that they may have at home.

In other words, our job really is to do what Americans have been so good at doing—creating wants, selling a people on their future, making them believe in their own achievement.

Our other difficulty is organizational. Somewhere along the line we decided that federal funds for foreign aid must be spent by federal employees, usually in the form of grants or loans to be doled out by federal employees in other countries. This is a natural enough policy, because foreign relations are sensitive matters, but there is nothing inevitable about it. In fact, there is considerable evidence that aid channeled through non-official or private agencies is much more welcome in many countries and also less expensive.

Private organizations in the U. S. have had a long record of useful service abroad. Why should their resources not be increased by federal grants so that they can do their job even more effectively and on a larger scale? Why do new federal agencies have to be created all the time to try to hire people away from such groups when they are already organized to do a good job? Why must the Peace Corps compete for scarce specialists, whom it is currently having trouble recruiting? Why couldn't it make grants to organizations which already have such specialists on their staffs and instruct them to expand their efforts abroad?

Often such organizations can do a better job because they are not official representatives of Uncle Sam. They would certainly be more welcome in countries like Mexico, which will not accept Peace Corps volunteers because as U. S. employees they have political significance. What if some of these organizations are religious, when we believe in the separation of church and state? This is true, of course, but *all* Russians sent abroad are "religious" Communists. Can we really object to helping a few Christians go abroad, particularly if they are not official representatives of our government?

CONCLUSION

Our biggest challenge is to find some way to harness the enormous potential of American business to help develop poor countries. Why should creeping federalism continue to spawn new agencies for providing economic assistance to foreign countries when such agencies already exist under private ownership in the United States? For example, if Brazil needs a new electric power system somewhere, why should our government not help by working out a contract, complete with all the necessary credits or loans, with one of our own light and power companies? Aid, in other words, would be on a company-to-company basis rather than on a government-to-government basis. In the long run, it would probably prove to be cheaper and more efficient. More important, the achievement orientation of our business executives could make itself felt in various ways in the newly developing companies abroad.

This idea has many complexities which need to be worked out—some of which are dealt with in *The Achieving Society*—but basically it is designed to harness some of the enormous reserves of achievement ideology and skill in American business to the gargantuan task of developing poor countries. Money is not enough. Drive and enthusiasm are needed. Ways of locating and exporting these resources must be found.

If there is one thing that all this research has taught me, it is that men can shape their own destiny, that external difficulties and pressures are not nearly so important in shaping history as some people have argued. It is how people respond to those challenges that matters, and how they respond depends on how strong their concern for achievement is. So the question of what happens to our civilization or to our business community depends quite literally on how much time tens of thousands or even millions of us spend thinking about achievement, about setting moderate achievable goals, taking calculated risks, assuming personal responsibility, and finding out how well we have done our job. The answer is up to us.

The individual in a group setting is a prime target for social psychological study.
(JERRY FRANK | D.P.I.)

Section VI
Social Psychology

There has always been a friendly rivalry between sociologists and psychologists concerning the relative importance of their respective fields. Given this sense of friendly competition you can imagine the frenzied activity in both disciplines when the first two books devoted to social psychology appeared in the same year (1908)—one written by sociologist Edward Ross, the other by psychologist William McDougall. Both authors brought to their texts the traditions of their own fields; and to this day such differential emphases have been preserved in social psychology courses that are taught from a sociological perspective in sociology departments and a psychological perspective in psychology departments.

Actually, the differences between sociological and psychological approaches to social psychology occur primarily in the types of problems chosen for study and emphasis. The definition of the topic is basically the same for both disciplines: *the scientific study of the interaction between man and his environment.* Note the word "interaction" in the definition. It is important. When we speak of studying the *interaction* between man and his environment we are concentrating on the *interplay* of two forces—the person and his social world—in behavior determination. These forces cannot be studied in isolation; they do not work that way. Further, one factor cannot be ignored at the expense of the other—both are important in effecting human actions. As the eminent social psychologist Kurt Lewin once observed, behavior is a function of the person *and* his environment. The social psychologist, by studying both these factors in combination, is in a much better position to arrive at an understanding of complex human behavior.

In his work the social psychologist studies a wide variety of topics. Some of the more popular of these include attitudes and attitude change, socialization, interpersonal relations and social influence, conformity and deviation, group structure and processes, social factors in cognitive functioning, leadership and organizational behavior, and social aspects of aggression, stress, and conflict.

The breadth of social psychologists' interests should become more apparent when you read through the five articles in this section. The first, by Lambert, Libman, and Poser, documents the power of groups in regulating the actions of their individual members. Findings from the study suggest that even a person's capacity to endure pain seems open to group influence.

Social reinforcement is the focus of study in a second selection by Calvin. In his experiment the author explains how a small group of coeds were able to control the dressing habits of a whole college through the use of verbal "rewards" and "punishments."

In the Karlins, Coffman, and Walters investigation the changing stereotypes of various national and ethnic groups are seen through the eyes of three generations of Princeton University undergraduates. Particularly noteworthy are the changes in the way the students characterize Negroes, Jews, and Americans over forty years of American history.

"Territoriality"—the manner in which humans and lower animals regulate the distance between themselves and other members of their own and other species—is the fascinating topic of Robert Sommers paper. In this work the author describes what happens when a person's "personal space" is invaded. The results are often amusing, sometimes startling.

A final, sobering article for this section is Professor Milgram's "Study of Obedience." It is an almost terrifying report of what people will do to other people when "under orders." It is doubtful that any of us can find much solace or pride in the Milgram findings.

Introduction to
Lambert, Libman, and Poser Article

Group control over individual behavior is a well-documented phenomenon in psychological research. Even something as basic as a person's own perceptions can be influenced by group affiliations—as we saw in the Hastorf and Cantril football study earlier in this volume.

Some of the best and most important work on group influence was conducted by social scientists in the 1950s. The power of groups in regulating members' behavior was documented in many different settings, including military academies (Dornbusch, 1955), industrial shops (Roy, 1952), doctors' offices (Coleman, Katz, & Menzel, 1957), and neighborhoods (Festinger, Schachter, & Back, 1950; Whyte, 1954). Yet, to appreciate the power of groups over an individual's actions you need not rely on published findings—simply recall the number of times *your* behavior has been regulated by groups to which you belonged or wanted to belong.

Studies from the sixties continue to illustrate the pervasive influence of groups in regulating human behavior (e.g., Alexander, 1964; Nahemow & Bennett, 1967). One such investigation is reported below. The findings from the study suggest that even a person's capacity to endure pain seems open to group influence!

REFERENCES

Alexander, C. Consensus and mutual attraction in natural cliques: A study of adolescent drinkers. *American Journal of Sociology*, 1964, **69**, 395–403.

Coleman, J., Katz, E., & Menzel, H. The diffusion of an innovation among physicians. *Sociometry*, 1957, **20**, 253–270.

Dornbusch, S. The military academy as an assimilating institution. *Social Forces,* 1955, **33,** 316–321.

Festinger, L., Schachter, S., & Back, K. *Social pressures in informal groups: a study of human factors in housing.* New York: Harper & Row, 1950.

Nahemow, L., & Bennett, R. Conformity, persuasibility and counternormative persuasion. *Sociometry,* 1967, **30,** 14–25.

Roy, D. Quota restriction and goldbricking in a machine shop. *American Journal of Sociology,* 1952, **57,** 427–442.

Whyte, W. The web of word of mouth. *Fortune,* November, 1954.

18

The Effect of Increased Salience
of a Membership Group
on Pain Tolerance

Wallace E. Lambert, Eva Libman, and Ernest G. Poser

Membership in a group requires a certain amount of behavioral conformity to the rules, either explicit or implicit, which have been established by all members of that group. The concept of "group" itself signifies that there is some distinctive pattern of behaviors which characterizes members of a particular group and differentiates them from others. The fact that people are always members of more than one group indicates that their patterns of behavior should vary as they take on particular roles in one group and temporarily shed the roles of another. While this generalization is verified in the every day experiences of most human beings, few experimental demonstrations are available of behavioral variations attributable to changes in one's roles or his feelings of identification with certain groups. Newcomb (1950, p. 275 ff.) has discussed the significance of this phenomenon and Charters and Newcomb (1958) have demonstrated how social attitudes vary when individuals' awareness of being members of religious groups is experimentally modified. In their research plan, some Ss were made aware that they were expressing attitudes as Catholics (or Jews, or Protestants, depending on their actual religious affiliation) while other Ss gave their attitudes as they assumed the role of university students. Those Catholic Ss whose religious affiliation was made salient manifested a pattern of attitudes much more similar to the orthodox Catholic position than did control Ss for whom religious affiliation was not made salient. The results for Jews and Protestants were less clear, suggesting that the two roles required of Catholic students (as Catholics and as students) are comparatively more dissimilar, at least in terms of the attitudes given consideration in the study.

SOURCE. *Journal of Personality,* 1960, **28,** 350–357.

The purpose of the present studies was to extend our understanding of the effect of group membership by paying attention to aspects of behavior other than social attitudes. We attempted to vary experimentally the salience of religious-group membership and to observe changes in Ss' responses to pain. Responses to pain have been related to religious affiliation by Chapman (1944) and Zborowski (1952). Chapman showed that samples of Jewish Ss exhibited both lower pain perception and pain-tolerance thresholds than non-Jewish Ss with North European ethnic backgrounds. Zborowski found that Jewish Americans tended to exaggerate their reactions and sensitivity to pain more than Americans of other religious or ethnic backgrounds. Social psychologists have become interested in the matter of pain tolerance since Moede (see Murphy & Murphy, 1931) demonstrated that thresholds for intolerable pain were increased when onlookers were present or when competition existed between Ss.

In the two studies presented here, Ss' pain-tolerance thresholds were measured, first, when they were asked to assume the role of university students volunteering to assist in a scientific investigation, and then, after certain information was given them, as potential contributors to their own religious group's comparative standing in ability to tolerate pain. Between the two measurements for pain tolerance, Ss were told that members of their religious groups had been found, on the average, to have a lower (in Experiment II, either lower or higher) pain-tolerance threshold when compared to other religious groups and that the objective of the experiment was to test the reliability of the evidence. We predicted that this procedure would prompt the experimental Ss to compete against the hypothetical "other groups," as though we were manipulating an ethnocentric prestige motive, somewhat analogous to rivalry in Moede's study.

EXPERIMENT I

Method

The sample consisted of 40 Jewish and 40 Protestant Ss, all women students ranging in age from 18 to 23 years. Ss were selected from the McGill University library and other parts of the campus in the following manner: each individual was approached by E (E.L.) and asked if she would be willing to participate in a short research project. Attention was paid to physical characteristics in order to estimate the religion of each S. At the time of testing, religious affiliation was verified and only the data from Jewish and Protestant Ss are considered here. Ss were alternately placed in experimental and control groups.

The instrument used for testing pain tolerance consisted of a clinical sphygmomanometer with sharp, hard rubber projections sewn into the

THE EFFECT OF INCREASED SALIENCE ON PAIN TOLERANCE · 281

pressure cuff. The cuff was adjusted with the hard rubber projections resting against the medial surface of the S's upper arm, and the pressure was gradually increased at the rate of approximately 10 mm. Hg per sec. A pressure reading was taken at the moment when S first felt pain (this measure is not considered here) and then when the S pronounced the pain intolerable, the index of pain-tolerance level, measured as mm. of Hg on a standard sphygmomanometer gauge. Pressure was then released. This method has high reliability and correlates well with the usual methods for producing superficial pain (see Clark & Bindra, 1956). After the pain-tolerance level had been determined each S was told that she would be given a retest approximately five minutes later "for purposes of establishing reliability." During this period of time, the experimental Ss were told in a casual manner (usually they asked about the purpose of the study at this time) that there was experimental evidence that Jews (Protestants) have a lower pain-tolerance level (take less pain) than non-Jews (other groups), and that the object of the experiment was to test the reliability of the evidence. Control Ss simply waited for five minutes between their first and second measures of pain tolerance.

Results and Discussion

From Table 1, it is clear that Jewish experimental Ss significantly increased their pain-tolerance scores on retest while Jewish control Ss showed an insignificant decrease. No difference was found between Protestant experimental and control Ss: both groups showed hardly any change in pain-tolerance scores on retest. We conclude that the Jewish Ss were clearly influenced by the interpolated statement which alluded to Jewish "inferiority" with regard to withstanding pain. The fact that an equivalent provoking statement had no apparent effect on Protestants can be interpreted

TABLE 1

Pain-Tolerance Scores for Jewish and Protestant Ss, Experiment I

	Jewish				Protestant			
	Experimental ($N = 20$)		Control ($N = 20$)		Experimental ($N = 20$)		Control ($N = 20$)	
	Test 1	Test 2	Test 1	Test 2	Test 1	Test 2	Test 1	Test 2
Mean[a]	86	103	83	77	115	114	92	90
Mean Differences	+17		−6		−1		−2	
t	2.78[b]		n.s.		n.s.		n.s.	

[a]Units are in mm. Hg; the higher the score the greater the pain tolerance.
[b]$p < .01$, 2-tailed test for correlated data.

as meaning that Protestantism does not function as a reference group in the same sense that Judaism does. It may well be, however, that the reference to own-group inferiority in comparison to non-Jews was more provocative for Jews in the sense that they very likely compared themselves with Christians and thought about the issue of Jewish-Christian prejudice. Protestants, on the other hand, were directed to compare their group's performance with other groups and they need not have interpreted this in terms of a Protestant-Jewish issue nor made any other comparison which would be emotionally involving. Following this reasoning, we predicted that an explicit comparison of Jews and Christians would be more equally provocative for members of both religious groups and that Christians receiving this information would display an increased pain-tolerance threshold.

The change in the pain-tolerance threshold for the Jewish Ss indicates that they were motivated to reduce the discrepancy between their group's purported pain sensitivity and that of non-Jews, but it is not clear whether they were interested in (a) surpassing non-Jews (thereby making their own group distinctive) or (b) merely closing the gap (thereby making their own group indistinguishable from non-Jews). If Jewish Ss were told that their religious group reportedly could tolerate more pain than Christians, we could then determine the nature of their motivation: if motivated to surpass the Christians, their pain-tolerance thresholds should still increase, but if they reduced their pain-tolerance thresholds we could conclude that they were oriented to close the gap. The second experiment was carried out to investigate these extensions of the findings reported above.

EXPERIMENT II

Method

The Ss were 160 women undergraduate students of McGill University; 80 were Jewish and 80 were Protestant. The same general procedure used in Experiment I was repeated with several modifications. A different sphygmomanometer and different (but supposedly identical) hard rubber projections were used in the second study. Two Es, one recognizably Jewish and the other recognizably not Jewish, were both present at each testing, either one applying the pressure cuff and giving the interpolated information, the other recording the results which were read out to her in code.[1]

---

[1] We are especially grateful to Sandra Freedman and Janet Barclay for their assistance as Es for this part of the study. As will be seen by comparing Tables 1 and 2, the means of the pain tolerance measures are markedly higher in the second study. We are unable to account fully for these differences. A different apparatus and different E's were used; furthermore, in the second study measurements were always taken with one E as an onlooker while the other conducted the study. Whatever the reason(s), the measures were higher in the second study, and in three or four cases Ss were dropped because their pain perception thresholds were so high that the Es felt that there would be too little opportunity for change to be recorded after the experimental treatment.

Between the first and second measures of pain tolerance, 30 Jewish Ss were told that it had been reported in the literature that Jews as a group take less pain than Christians, and 30 were told that Jews take more pain than Christians. Two groups of 30 Christian Ss were given the same information—for one group that Christians take less pain than Jews and for the other that Christians take more pain than Jews. Two control groups (one Jewish and one Christian) of 20 Ss each were given no information between their two tests.

Results and Discussion

The results are presented in Table 2. There is a clear replication of the findings of the first experiment in that the Jewish Ss reliably increased their tolerance threshold upon being informed that Jews as a group take less pain than Christians. The Jewish control Ss, who were given no interpolated information, show an insignificant decrease in their threshold, a finding that supports the conclusion that the change in threshold for the Jewish experimental Ss is not due to taking the test twice nor to the unreliability of the measure. When Jewish Ss are informed that Jews typically take more pain than Christians they tend to "hold the line" rather than reducing their thresholds ("closing the gap") or increasing their thresholds ("extending the differences"). Although this group does increase its mean tolerance threshold (from 163 to 172 units) this is not a reliable change. When the difference scores (subtracting the first from the second tolerance scores) for this group are compared with the difference scores for the Jewish control Ss, again there is no reliable increase for that group, $t = 1.29$ with 48 df.

The Christian Ss also are clearly affected by the interpolated information. There are significant increases in tolerance thresholds when they are informed that Christians typically take less pain or take more pain than

TABLE 2

Pain-Tolerance Scores for Jewish and Protestant Ss, Experiment II

Condition	Jewish						Christian					
	Take Less		Take More		Control		Take Less		Take More		Control	
Test	1	2	1	2	1	2	1	2	1	2	1	2
Mean[a]	160	179	163	172	139	133	187	202	158	180	156	150
Mean Difference	+19		+ 9		− 6		+15		+22		− 6	
N	30		30		20		30		30		20	
t	2.74[b]		1.21		.68		2.34		2.76		.88	
p	.02		n.s.		n.s.		.03		.01		n.s.	

[a]Units are in mm. Hg; the higher the score the greater the pain tolerance.
[b]Two-tailed tests of significance for correlated data are used throughout.

Jews. We have evidence here that Christianity (which more clearly calls to mind the Christian-Jewish comparison) is a more effective reference group than Protestantism as used in the first experiment. We also have evidence that the Christian Ss are motivated to extend the difference between Christians and Jews on pain tolerance in that they increase their threshold when informed that their religious group typically takes more pain than Jews.

In summary, the over-all findings suggest that Ss do change their patterns of behavior in meaningful ways when they alternately refer themselves to different membership groups, in this case first as university students contributing to a scientific investigation and then as members of a particular religious group. Samples of Jewish Ss appear to be interested in both reducing any differences between their religious group and Christians with respect to ability to withstand pain as well as maintaining any superiority they may have in this regard (although the latter point is not clear from our data). Christian Ss (but not "Protestants") appear ready to eliminate any inferiority their group may have in regard to pain tolerance when compared to Jews and to extend the difference between groups when they are led to believe their group is superior in withstanding pain.

Others working with pain sensitivity have reported differences attributable to religious affiliation (e.g., Chapman, 1944). We were able to compare our Jewish and Christian Ss on their pain-tolerance thresholds (first test) since no experimental treatment was given to any S until after the first measure of pain tolerance. For the Ss in Experiment I, the mean threshold for Jews was not reliably different from that of the Protestants, $t = 1.63$, $df = 78$, corrected for heterogeneous variances. For Ss in Experiment II, the Jewish mean was again not reliably different from that of Protestants, $t = 1.08$, $df = 158$. We therefore offer no evidence for differences in pain sensitivity attributable to religious affiliation for Jewish and Protestant women. In both studies, however, we do find significantly less variance of pain-tolerance scores for Jewish in contrast to Christians Ss, in Experiment I, $F = 3.15$ ($p = .01$) and Experiment II, $F = 1.56$ ($p < .05$). One explanation for this reliable finding comes from Zborowski's (1952) interpretation of the social and cultural significance of pain. He finds that Jewish patients typically search for the symptomatic meaning of pain and communicate their concern about their health and their family's welfare to family members and associates. Zborowski feels that this reaction pattern is acquired "by the individual members of the society from the earliest childhood along with other cultural attitudes and values which are learned from parents . . ." (p. 28). He argues that each culture develops an ideal pattern of attitudes and reactions to pain which are passed on during socialization. Our findings of more homogeneous reactions to pain among Jews would suggest that something like an ideal pattern of reactions to pain is either more standardized and/or more effectively communicated among Jews than Christians.

SUMMARY

Jewish and Protestant female Ss were tested for their tolerance of pain first when they were asked as students to participate in a scientific study and then, after their religious membership group was made salient to them by having them believe that scientific evidence indicated that their religious group characteristically is less able to withstand pain than others. The Jewish, but not the Protestant, Ss showed a reliable increase in their mean pain-tolerance threshold after this information was given them.

In a second experiment subgroups of Jewish and Protestant Ss were told either that their religious group typically takes less or more pain than other religious groups but in this case an explicit comparison was made between Jews and Christians. Both Jewish and "Christian" Ss increased their pain tolerance when told their groups were typically inferior in regard to this variable. The Christian Ss who were informed that their group was superior in pain tolerance further increased their tolerance while Jewish Ss, similarly treated, showed no reliable change in their tolerance levels. The findings are conceptualized in terms of a theory of membership groups.

No evidence was found for differences in normal pain-tolerance thresholds attributable to religious differences, although Jewish Ss showed reliably less variability of pain-tolerance scores than did Protestant Ss in both studies.

REFERENCES

Chapman, W. P. Measurements of pain sensitivity in normal control subjects and in psychoneurotic patients. *Psychosom. med.,* 1944, **6**, 252–257.

Charters, W. W., & Newcomb, T. M. Some attitudinal effects of experimentally increased salience of a membership group. In Maccoby, Eleanor E., Newcomb, T. M., & Hartley, E. L. (Eds.), *Readings in social psychology.* New York: Holt & Co., 1958.

Clark, J. W., Bindra, D. Individual differences in pain thresholds. *Canad. J. Psychol.,* 1956, **10**, 69–76.

Newcomb, T. M. *Social psychology.* New York: Dryden Press, 1950.

Murphy, G., & Murphy, L. B. *Experimental social psychology.* New York: Harper, 1931.

Zborowski, M. Cultural components in response to pain. *J. Soc. Issues,* 1952, **8**, 16–30.

Introduction to Calvin Article

"The concept of 'honor among thieves' seems alien to many people. Why should a captured criminal refuse to inform on his buddies, even in cases where their negligence led to his arrest? Understood in a group context, such behavior is eminently reasonable. . . . The person is rewarded for conforming to the standards of the group and punished for deviating from them. But to what group does the criminal belong? Certainly his allegiance is not to 'establishment' groups. To the lawbreaker the mores of the criminal group become his mores; he behaves in accordance with the reward and punishment sanctions imposed by this group. And one of the most sacrosanct dictates of the criminal code is never to 'squeal to the cops.' The 'stoolie'—the man who 'rats' on other criminals—is punished by his peers. The man who keeps his mouth shut is rewarded for his behavior. Is it any wonder the criminal refuses to cooperate with authorities? Such behavior is respected in the criminal culture, the culture of prime importance to the lawbreaker.

"All groups attempt to regulate members' behavior by application of rewards and punishments. Sometimes the 'systems of reinforcement' are highly structured, formal, and clearly understood, as in the case of the military. Other times they are more flexible, informal, and open to interpretation, as in the academic profession" (Karlins & Abelson, 1970).

The study by Calvin below provides us with insight into the dynamics of reinforcement in regulating human behavior and the methods by which groups can utilize such reinforcement in controlling an individual's actions.

REFERENCE
Karlins, M., & Abelson, H. *Persuasion*. New York: Springer, 1970.

19

Social Reinforcement

Allen D. Calvin

A. INTRODUCTION

1. Subjects

As one of the outside reading assignments in my introductory class, all of the students read Skinner's *Walden Two* (2). In last year's spring semester class, as in previous classes, the book provoked a spirited discussion of social reinforcement. Several of the students suggested that we attempt to actually demonstrate the effect of social reinforcement in our college environment. The following is a report of the results of this undertaking.

B. METHOD

1. Subjects

The *S*s were the approximately 550 members of the student body at Hollins College, except for the 24 members of my introductory class who served as the *E*s. Hollins is a liberal arts girls' school whose student body is composed primarily of upper-middle and lower-upper class Protestant whites.

2. Procedure

Almost all of the girls eat lunch in the dining hall which is open from 11:30 A.M. until 1:15 P.M. The lunch period was divided into two shifts,

SOURCE. *The Journal of Social Psychology,* 1962, **56,** 15–19. The author is indebted to Dr. R. Lowell Wine of the Hollins College Department of Statistics for his discussion of the statistical analysis in the present experiment.

and two girls from my introductory class served as Es on each shift. This gave us a total of four Es each day. The girls who served as Es on a particular day were selected at random from volunteers from the class as a whole. Since extra credit was given for acting as an E, there were always plenty of volunteers, and an attempt was made to let everyone serve as an E approximately the same number of times. The E's task was to count the number of students wearing the color clothes that we were interested in on a particular day. Each E made her judgments independently.

If any S asked what the Es were recording, they were told that it was a survey to see how many people ate lunch at various times of the lunch hour. No one questioned this explanation.

On Thursday, April 10, 1958, the Es tabulated the number of students at lunch who wore blue clothes. Only large outer garments such as dresses, sweaters, skirts, coats, and the like counted. After lunch on this date, all the members of the class had been instructed to reward any students seen wearing blue clothes at any time with such expressions as, "My that is a nice looking sweater," "That coat certainly is attractive," etc.

The Es checked the lunch periods for blue clothes every Tuesday and Thursday for the remainder of the month of April and again on May 13. After April 22, they stopped the reinforcing of blue clothes. Beginning April 22 in addition to counting the number of Ss wearing blue clothes the Es also determined the number of Ss wearing red, and they continued to count the number of Ss wearing red every Tuesday and Thursday through May 13. After lunch on April 24 the class began to reinforce red and continued to do so through May 13.

C. RESULTS

There was quite often a slight difference between the Es in their judgment of the number of Ss wearing the designated color, and when this occurred, their observations were averaged, and the average score was used for that period.

Let us look at the results for blue first. On the initial check the day before social reinforcement was begun 25 per cent of the Ss wore blue. Five days later after reinforcement the percentage had risen to 37 per cent. The average percentage wearing blue on succeeding check days during the reinforcement period was 38 per cent. The next check day covered a period in which blue was not reinforced, and the reinforcement of red had not begun—the percentage of blue dropped to 27 per cent. Five days later another check was made. During this five-day period blue was not reinforced but red was, and the percentage wearing blue rose, reaching 35 per cent. The final check was made two weeks later after a period of non-reinforcement of blue but with reinforcement of red. At this time the percentage wearing blue had returned to 38 per cent.

A Chi-square between the first day prior to reinforcement (25 per cent wearing blue) and the first day after reinforcement (37 per cent wearing blue) was computed and a Chi-square of 17.03 was obtained. The Chi-square between the first day prior to reinforcement (25 per cent wearing blue) and the weighted mean of all the reinforcement check days (38 per cent wearing blue) was 17.64. The Chi-square between the first day prior to reinforcement (25 per cent wearing blue) and the weighted mean of all the post-reinforcement check days (34 per cent wearing blue) was 9.11. The Chi-square between the first day prior to reinforcement (25 per cent wearing blue) and the weighted mean of all the other check days combined (36 per cent wearing blue) was 12.46. A Chi-square of 6.64 is significant at the .01 level.[1]

A comparison of the last reinforcement check day (38 per cent wearing blue) with the first post-reinforcement check day (27 per cent wearing blue) yielded a Chi-square of 12.95. A comparison of the last reinforcement check day (38 per cent wearing blue) with the weighted mean of the other two post-reinforcement check days (37 per cent) gave a Chi-square of .21.

Now let us look at the results for red. For this color there were two check days prior to reinforcement. The percentage wearing red on the first check day was 13 per cent, and on the next check day 11 per cent. After five days of reinforcement, the percentage wearing red rose to 22 per cent. During the next four check days, all with red reinforced, the average percentage wearing red was 18 per cent.

The Chi-square between the weighted mean of the two check days prior to reinforcement (12 per cent wearing red) and the first day after reinforcement (22 per cent wearing red) was 14.34. The Chi-square between the weighted mean of the two check days prior to reinforcement (12 per cent wearing red) and the weighted mean of all the reinforcement check days (19 per cent wearing red) was 8.86. As mentioned previously, a Chi-square of 6.64 is significant at the .01 level.

[1] One of the assumptions for Chi-square is independence which we do not have in the present experiment, and the Chi-square test for correlated proportions cannot be applied here. However, Edwards points out (1, p. 91) that when a correlation is positive, failure to take into account the correlation in a Chi-square analysis increases the likelihood that we will fail to reject the null hypothesis, i.e., the Chi-square becomes overly conservative. Thus, making the reasonable assumption that our correlation is positive, we are most likely underestimating the actual level of significance in the Chi-square analyses in the present experiment. Since all but one of our differences were of such a large magnitude that the Chi-square we obtained were all greater than that required for significance at the 1 per cent level, this probable "over conservatism" would not likely alter the analyses presented here. The one exception is in the case of the Chi-square between reinforcement and post-reinforcement for blue where red too was being reinforced, and in this case with a Chi-square of .21 it seems highly unlikely that we have committed a Type II error, although such a possibility cannot be eliminated with certainty.

D. DISCUSSION

The fact that marked increases occurred with two different colors after social reinforcement increased the general prestige of reinforcement theory tremendously in the eyes of the students. However, it was necessary to point out that we could not unequivocally attribute the increase of the wearing of the reinforced color to the social reinforcement since we had only a one-group design. What was needed for a definitive experiment was another college population with the same characteristics as Hollins which would have been treated in the same manner except for the social reinforcement. In spite of this limitation, the present findings are certainly encouraging for the hypothesis that social reinforcement can markedly influence behavior of the kind studied in the present investigation. It would be desirable for some psychologists in a setting more conducive to a multi-group design, for example, in a military or prison situation, to follow up and extend the present findings.

The behavior of the Ss during the post-reinforcement period is interesting. The initial drop in the percentage of Ss wearing blue followed by a return to the percentage of blue worn during the reinforcement period might be due to the fact that we were reinforcing red during the post-reinforcement rise for blue; thus, a person previously reinforced for blue—when reinforced for red—may have been "reminded" of previous blue reinforcements. Particularly, if the reinforcements came from the same individuals for both red and blue, considerable response generalization could reasonably be expected. This hypothesis, of course, must be verified experimentally before much confidence can be placed in it.

Some of the Es suggested that we try some social punishment, i.e., tell the Ss that they looked bad whenever we saw them wearing blue. However, the possible consequences of such an approach were too disquieting to allow us to carry out the proposal. Again it is hoped that some psychologist in a setting better suited for such an attempt will try it, as such data would certainly be highly valuable for behavior theory. In this regard, it is interesting to note that a large number of the Es reported that as they continued to go about reinforcing Ss, they became very "popular." Shades of Dale Carnegie! Perhaps "How to Win Friends and Influence People" boils down to making oneself a secondary reinforcer. One can't help but wonder what would have happened to our Es "popularity" if we had tried social punishment. . . .

E. SUMMARY

An attempt was made to use social reinforcement to alter the color of the clothes worn by female college students. Twenty-four Hollins College students served as *E*s while the rest of the approximately 550 students served as *S*s. Marked changes occurred in the expected direction after social reinforcement. Because of the limitation of a one-group design, the results cannot be considered as definitive, but they certainly are encouraging for the hypothesis that behavior of the nature studied in the present investigation can be changed by social reinforcement.

REFERENCES
1. Edwards, A. L. Experimental Design in Psychological Research. New York: Rinehart, 1950.
2. Skinner, B. F. Walden Two. New York: MacMillan, 1948.

Introduction to
Karlins, Coffman, and Walters Article

In many instances we make judgments about individuals based on their group affiliations. For example, how many times have you heard someone say something like: "That guy must be hip—he's a member of Phi Mu Sigma" or "Jane Jones has to be liberal, she's a Bennington girl!" It is well known that American culture is saturated with images and caricatures of various groups. These "pictures in our heads," which Walter Lippman first identified as stereotypes, have come to be regarded as highly significant factors in intergroup and interpersonal relations. Most of us, at one time or another, have predicted a person's behavior by knowing his group membership. Further, such judgments are not limited to a few groups; they seem to encompass groups of all sizes and complexity, from a neighborhood clique to national and ethnic groups.

The stereotyping of national and ethnic groups has been particularly noticeable in our culture. We characterize Germans as being "scientifically minded" and refer to the Irish as "quick tempered." But have Germans and Irish always been characterized this way by Americans? And has the tendency for Americans to stereotype such groups been consistent over the years? The study below tries to answer these questions. Looking at the stereotyping behavior in three generations of Princeton University undergraduates, the investigators produce some interesting findings indicating that: (1) contrary to the expectations of some social scientists, the tendency to stereotype national and ethnic groups is as prevalent today as in the 1930s; (2) the content of stereotypes characterizing the various national and ethnic groups have changed markedly in three generations of college students. Particularly noteworthy are the changes in stereotype content for Negroes, Jews, and Americans.

20

On the Fading
of Social Stereotypes:

Studies in three generations of college students

Marvin Karlins, Thomas L. Coffman, and Gary Walters

The social stereotypes of Princeton undergraduates in 1967 were compared with those in two earlier studies. In contrast to the "fading effect" observed by Gilbert in 1951, current stereotypes of 10 national and ethnic groups were found to be highly uniform, a phenomenon reported by Katz and Braly in 1933. However, several important differences in the 1967 sample were observed: Students protested the unreasonableness of ethnic generalizations; major changes occurred in stereotype content; uniformity of stereotypes was positively correlated with favorableness of traits assigned; and the autostereotype of Americans fell from first to fifth place in favorableness. Distinctions are made among personal, social, contemporary, and traditional stereotypes, and the relationship of stereotyping to prejudice and ethnocentrism is discussed.

It is well known that American culture is saturated with images and caricatures of various ethnic groups. These "pictures in our heads" which Lippmann (1922) called stereotypes have come to be regarded as highly significant factors in intergroup and interpersonal relations. Stereotypes are generalized impressions of groups, acquired by individuals from a number of sources, including sometimes direct experience with members of the stereotyped groups. For the most part, however, stereotypes appear to be learned by word of mouth or from books and films. These media create a vast cultural matrix in which images can develop and persist irrespective of the reality they are supposed to represent:

SOURCE. *Journal of Personality and Social Psychology*, 1969, **13,** 1–16. Copyright 1969 by the American Psychological Association, and reproduced by permission. The authors acknowledge a grant from Princeton University to support the research. They gratefully acknowledge the aid of G. M. Gilbert and D. Katz for their suggestions in the initial stages of the research and S. Klineberg and P. Warr for reading and aiding in the preparation of the manuscript.

Apparently there are latent in fiction, in folklore, and in the educational system, certain images of peoples, images of centuries standing perhaps. Within these images there may be "kernels of truth"; or there may be a dried hulk of what might have been truth decades ago [Buchanan & Cantril, 1953, p. 96].

In their pioneer investigation of verbal stereotypes, Katz and Braly (1933) inspected the five key traits used by 100 Princeton undergraduates to describe 10 different racial and national groups. The results showed an impressively high degree of agreement in verbal characterizations and yielded a distinctive set of popular labels—many of them highly derogatory— for each of the 10 groups. Uniformity in stereotyping Negroes, Germans, and Jews was so high that certain traits were ascribed to those groups by more than 75% of the subjects. Since most students had no contact with members of the stereotyped groups, it was obvious that they had simply absorbed the prevalent images of their day and culture.

Nearly 20 years later, Centers (1951) presented the original Princeton norms to students at the University of California at Los Angeles and found that each of the trait lists was correctly identified by a large majority of students, ranging from 75% who recognized the 1933 characterizations of Japanese, Chinese, and Turks, to 95% who recognized the 1933 descriptions of English and Jews. Countless other investigations confirm that this fairly standardized set of ethnic images is widely recognized by Americans, and sometimes forms the basis of deep prejudices concerning the groups in question.

Around the same time as Centers' demonstration, however, Gilbert (1951) repeated Katz and Braly's experiment at Princeton, with the discovery that uniformity in verbal stereotyping was considerably reduced. For example, in 1951 the social stereotype of Negroes (defined as 50% of the "key" traits assigned) was comprised of 12 different terms, whereas only 5 adjectives sufficed in 1933. In general, moreover, the stereotyping in 1951 appeared to be more realistic and reasonable than before. Especially noteworthy were the spontaneous comments of students in 1951, expressing great irritation at being asked to make such generalizations—and about people they scarcely knew. This kind of resistance was not encountered by Katz and Braly. It was suggested by Gilbert that the differences could be attributed to three factors. First, the entertainment and communications media were curtailing and discouraging traditional patterns of stereotyping in American culture. Second, students in 1951 were displaying more interest in social science than ever before, so that on the whole they would probably be more sophisticated about making ethnic generalizations. The third factor was the changing composition of the Princeton undergraduate population. In 1951 there was no longer the preponderance of well-to-do, "privileged" students that had once dominated the Princeton scene. As Gilbert noted, the 1951 population "represented much more of a cross-section of American youth," as a result of the G.I. Bill and the spread of higher education generally. "This intergroup contact is not only a broadening influence, but minimizes the superior in-group complexion of the population tested [Gilbert, 1951, p. 253].

Limited evidence such as this has led to a cautious optimism that traditional stereotypes may be disappearing or declining in influence. Gilbert's findings are frequently cited as an example of improvement in the perception of ethnic groups and a sign that stereotyping itself may be waning in younger, more broadly educated generations (e.g., Allport, 1954; Bettleheim & Janowitz, 1964; Secord & Backman, 1964). We were curious about whether these trends could be confirmed in a new Princeton population, whether the apparent fading of social stereotypes has continued; especially since the three relevant factors noted by Gilbert are, if anything, more evident today.

Most of the data currently available do indicate an overall decline in ethnic prejudice among young Americans over the last two decades, with a corresponding decline in derogatory stereotyping. Bettleheim and Janowitz (1964) have found this to be true in their review of the evidence on anti-Negro and anti-Semitic attitudes. But little has been done in the way of systematic follow-up studies:

> Despite the proliferation of national attitude surveys, no comprehensive and systematic body of trend data has been collected over these years. Investigations have been episodic and specialized. . . . there has been . . . little emphasis on the repeated use of standardized questions over time to chart contemporary social history. Social scientists engaged in survey research have not assumed the responsibility for writing current social history by means of systematic trend reporting [Bettleheim & Janowitz, 1964, p. 4].

Thus, while we could only sample a very restricted population, there seemed to be a definite need for examining changes in stereotyping behavior in greater detail than is usual in survey research.

We therefore repeated the Katz and Braly (1933) study in the spring of 1967 with yet a third generation of Princeton students—most of whom were born about the time of the Gilbert investigation. In addition, we obtained estimates of the "favorableness" of terms in the checklist, in somewhat the same way that Katz and Braly obtained ratings of the desirability of traits in their second study (Katz & Braly, 1935). With this information we hoped to deal with some issues pertaining to the evaluative component of stereotyping and to clarify the relationship between uniformity and favorableness of social stereotypes. Finally, it was decided to compare the stereotypes of two subsets of the Princeton population: those who had graduated from public high schools versus those who had attended private secondary schools. In this comparison we attempted to isolate the "superior ingroup" from the broader "cross-section of American youth" referred to by Gilbert, and thus to test the implication that the former would stereotype more severely than the latter.

Briefly then, the object of the present paper was to examine five aspects of stereotyping by Princeton students over a 35-year period: (a) changes in stereotype content; (b) changes in stereotype uniformity; (c) changes in the favorableness of stereotypes; (d) the relationship between uniformity and favorableness of stereotypes; and (e) differences between social stereotypes of high school versus "prep" school graduates in the current population.[1]

In the study to be described we shall be examining *contemporary social* stereotypes. For purposes of discussion the initial Katz and Braly results will be designated as *traditional* or classical stereotypes. How these norms have changed over the years will be a major focus of attention.

METHOD

Subjects

Responses were scored from 150 subjects chosen as follows: Two hundred and fifty freshmen and sophomores enrolled in introductory psychology

[1] Before examining the data, it will be helpful to note two important distinctions which are frequently neglected in studies of sterotypes. Hopefully, this step will prevent some confusion over the matter of "reduction of stereotyping." (a) *Personal versus social stereotypes:* As a first precaution, it is essential to resist careless analogies between social stereotypes and personal views. If a stereotype is operationally defined as the collection of traits assigned to the members of a category, we may refer to a single individual's assignments as his *personal stereotype* and to the consensual assignments of a given population of judges as a *social stereotype* (Secord & Backman, 1964). Hence, social stereotypes, as determined in these and most other studies are essentially *social norms* for describing recognized groups of persons. From our data we shall be able to observe if there has been a diminished consensus in verbal stereotyping and if major changes have occurred in the content of prevailing stereotypes. But these norms cannot reveal the details or the functions of *Personal* stereotypes and attitudes. We cannot, for example, use comparisons between social stereotypes measured in 1933 and 1967 as a basis for conclusions about the rigidity, intensity, clarity, or complexity of personal stereotyping. (b) *Traditional versus contemporary stereotypes:* A second distinction will be made in order to acknowledge the possibility of shifting patterns in social stereotyping. The familiar and infamous "traditional" stereotypes, to be sure, deserve special consideration—because of their durability and because of the ancient prejudices they help to sustain. So, it is instructive to set these traditional images as standards against which to compare contemporary judgments. At the same time, we should like to avoid treating a particular set of generalizations as though it were *the* stereotype of a given group. Saenger and Flowerman (1954), for instance, showed that tolerant persons do not accept traditional stereotypes of Italians and Jews, and thereupon state as a general rule that "reduction of hostility is always accompanied by a reduction of stereotypy [p. 235]." But just as traditions give way to new social practices, so can traditional images be replaced by new, contemporary stereotypes. While Saenger and Flowerman's unprejudiced judges, in comparison with their more prejudiced neighbors, were relatively unwilling to endorse the usual negative characterizations of Italians and Jews, they were *more* prone to endorse positive generalizations, thus producing social stereotypes of a newly positive kind. The absence of a traditional pattern of stereotyping may not indicate a decline of stereotyping itself, but perhaps the formation of a revised social consensus. The two notions must be kept distinct.

courses were sent letters requesting their participation. The criteria of class and course made our sample comparable to those of two previous studies in representing the Princeton undergraduate population (note that none of these samples represents the student body as a whole). One-half of the prospective subjects had graduated from public high schools and the other half from private high schools. (Secondary schools considered as private were "parochial," "day," or "prep" as officially listed in *The Handbook of Private Schools*, 1965.)

Approximately 200 students actually participated. On the basis of anonymous questionnaires at the end we eliminated foreign subjects, Negro subjects, and those who indicated familiarity with the Katz and Braly study. Of the remainder, data for 90 public school graduates and 60 private school graduates were retained. This 90:60 ratio is important because it represents the proportion of public to private school graduates at Princeton today (60% to 40%). In comparison, when Gilbert administered this test in 1951 the ratio was 45% public to 55% private. Before 1940, fewer than 25% of the Princeton student body came from public high schools.

Procedure

The same procedure employed by Katz and Braly (1933) and Gilbert (1951) was followed in this study. Each subject received a 12-page booklet. Page 1 contained an alphabetical list of 84 adjectives or trait names. Page 2 began with the following instructions:

> Read through the list of words on page 1 and select those which seem to you typical of the *Germans*. Write as many of these words in the following space as you think are necessary to characterize these people adequately. If you do not find appropriate words on page 1 for all of the typical German characteristics, you may add those which you think necessary for an adequate description. When you finish your list go on to the next page.

On pages 3–11, the subjects were asked to repeat this procedure in turn for Italians, Negroes, Irish, English, Jews, Americans, Chinese, Japanese, and Turks. The last page instructed the subject to go back over his 10 lists of words and mark with an x the *five words in each list* which seemed to him the most typical of the groups in question.

Once this had been completed, we asked the subjects to rate the favorableness of the adjectives on the list. This section was *not* included in the Katz and Braly (1933) and Gilbert (1951) studies. The instructions read as follows:

> Look again at the adjectives on the next page. Decide for each one whether it is favorable, unfavorable, or neutral, as normally used to describe people.

Indicate the degree of favorableness of each adjective as follows:

1. If the adjective is *favorable*, write a plus (+) beside it. If it is *very favorable*, write two pluses (++) beside it.

2. If the adjective is neutral, write a zero (0) beside it.

3. If the adjective is *unfavorable*, write a minus (−) beside it. If it is *very unfavorable*, write two minuses (− −) beside it.

There may be several usages or criteria to consider in determining the degree of favorableness implied by a given adjective. We want only a global or "average" rating, so give us your immediate *first impressions*, and don't spend too much time on any single one.

RESULTS AND DISCUSSION

Comparison of Stereotype Content

Table 1 presents lists of the adjectives or traits most frequently assigned by the students to the 10 groups in question. These traits represent the 5 "key" traits which were selected or checked by each subject as being the most characteristic of each group. For the purpose of comparison we have included in the table (*a*) the 12 traits most frequently selected in 1933; (*b*) the additional traits reported by Gilbert for 1951 (marked with an *a*); and (*c*) the new traits needed in 1967 to account for the 10 most frequently selected traits today (marked with a *b*). The 1951 percentages for some of the 1933 traits were not reported by Gilbert, and the previous percentages of "new" traits are indeterminant. These unknown values are indicated by blanks in the table. Since they represent only small percentages in each case, our overall picture of stereotype persistence and change will be relatively complete. In reviewing these findings, the reader may wish to keep in mind the suggestion of Gilbert and others that younger generations are less "stereotype-ridden" than were students in the past. Evidence confirming or disconfirming this notion is perhaps the real crux of the present study.

Americans

The subjects' characterization of themselves in 1967 is decidedly less flattering than before. The terms "intelligent," "industrious," and "alert" have steadily declined in frequency and by far the majority now describe themselves as "materialistic." The 67% recorded for this trait is greater than that for any other adjective used to characterize any other group today. "Ambitious" received 42% of the choices, followed by "pleasure loving" (28%) and then "industrious" (23%) and "intelligent" (20%). The low frequencies of remaining adjectives make the present characterization of Americans one of the sharpest images in the study. Katz and Braly's observation in 1933 that "the description is not greatly at variance with the

TABLE 1

Comparison of Stereotype Trait Frequencies

Trait	% checking trait			Trait	% checking trait		
	1933	1951	1967		1933	1951	1967
Americans				Germans			
Industrious	48	30	23	Scientifically minded	78	62	47
Intelligent	47	32	20	Industrious	65	50	59
Materalistic	33	37	67	Stolid	44	10	9
Ambitious	33	21	42	Intelligent	32	32	19
Progressive	27	5	17	Methodical	31	20	21
Pleasure loving	26	27	28	Extremely nationalistic	24	50	43
Alert	23	7	7	Progressive	16	3	13
Efficient	21	9	15	Efficient	16	—	46
Aggressive	20	8	15	Jovial	15	—	5
Straightforward	19	—	9	Musical	13	—	4
Practical	19	—	12	Persistent	11	—	4
Sportsmanlike	19	—	9	Practical	11	—	9
Individualistic[a]	—	26	15	Aggressive[a]	—	27	30
Conventional[b]	—	—	17	Arrogant[a]	—	23	18
Scientifically minded[b]	—	—	15	Ambitious[b]	—	—	15
Ostentatious[b]	—	—	15	Irish			
Chinese				Pugnacious	45	24	13
				Quick tempered	39	35	43
Superstitious	34	18	8	Witty	38	16	7
Sly	29	4	6	Honest	32	11	17
Conservative	29	14	15	Very religious	29	30	27
Tradition loving	26	26	32	Industrious	21	8	8
Loyal to family ties	22	35	50	Extremely nationalistic	21	20	41
Industrious	18	18	23	Superstitious	18	—	11
Meditative	19	—	21	Quarrelsome	14	—	5
Reserved	17	18	15	Imaginative	13	—	3
Very religious	15	—	6	Aggressive	13	—	5
Ignorant	15	—	7	Stubborn	13	—	23
Deceitful	14	—	5	Tradition loving[b]	—	—	25
Quiet	13	19	23	Loyal to family ties[b]	—	—	23
Courteous[b]	—	—	20	Argumentative[b]	—	—	20
Extremely nationalistic[b]	—	—	19	Boastful[b]	—	—	17
Humorless[b]	—	—	17	Italians			
Artistic[b]	—	—	15	Artistic	53	28	30
English				Impulsive	44	19	28
				Passionate	37	25	44
Sportsmanlike	53	21	22	Quick tempered	35	15	28
Intelligent	46	29	23	Musical	32	22	9
Conventional	34	25	19	Imaginative	30	20	7
Tradition loving	31	42	21	Very religious	21	33	25
Conservative	30	22	53	Talkative	21	23	23
Reserved	29	39	40	Revengeful	17	—	0
Sophisticated	27	37	47	Physically dirty	13	—	4
Courteous	21	17	17	Lazy	12	—	0
Honest	20	11	17	Unreliable	11	—	3
Industrious	18	—	17	Pleasure loving[a]	—	28	33
Extremely nationalistic	18	—	7	Loyal to family ties[b]	—	—	26
Humorless	17	—	11	Sensual[b]	—	—	23
Practical[b]	—	—	25	Argumentative[b]	—	—	19

TABLE 1—(Continued)

Trait	% checking trait			Trait	% checking trait		
	1933	1951	1967		1933	1951	1967
Japanese				**Negroes**			
				Superstitious	84	41	13
				Lazy	75	31	26
Intelligent	45	11	20	Happy-go-lucky	38	17	27
Industrious	43	12	57	Ignorant	38	24	11
Progressive	24	2	17	Musical	26	33	47
Shrewd	22	13	7	Ostentatious	26	11	25
Sly	20	21	3	Very religious	24	17	8
Quiet	19	—	14	Stupid	22	10	4
Imitative	17	24	22	Physically dirty	17	—	3
Alert	16	—	11	Naive	14	—	4
Suave	16	—	0	Slovenly	13	—	5
Neat	16	—	7	Unreliable	12	—	6
Treacherous	13	17	1	Pleasure loving[a]	—	19	26
Aggressive	13	—	19	Sensitive[b]	—	—	17
Extremely nationalistic[a]	—	18	21	Gregarious[b]	—	—	17
Ambitious[b]	—	—	33	Talkative[b]	—	—	14
Efficient[b]	—	—	27	Imitative[b]	—	—	13
Loyal to family ties[b]	—	—	23	**Turks**			
Courteous[b]	—	—	22				
				Cruel	47	12	9
Jews				Very religious	26	6	7
				Treacherous	21	3	13
				Sensual	20	4	9
Shrewd	79	47	30	Ignorant	15	7	13
Mercenary	49	28	15	Physically dirty	15	7	14
Industrious	48	29	33	Deceitful	13	—	7
Grasping	34	17	17	Sly	12	7	7
Intelligent	29	37	37	Quarrelsome	12	—	9
Ambitious	21	28	48	Revengeful	12	—	6
Sly	20	14	7	Conservative	12	—	11
Loyal to family ties	15	19	19	Superstitious	11	—	5
Persistent	13	—	9	Aggressive[b]	—	—	17
Talkative	13	—	3	Quick tempered[b]	—	—	13
Aggressive	12	—	23	Impulsive[b]	—	—	12
Very religious	12	—	7	Conventional[b]	—	—	10
Materialistic[b]	—	—	46	Pleasure loving[b]	—	—	11
Practical[b]	—	—	19	Slovenly[b]	—	—	10

[a]Indicates the additional traits reported by Gilbert (1951).
[b]Indicates the new traits needed in 1967 to account for the 10 most frequently selected traits today.

stereotypes held by non-Americans [p. 206]" is also applicable to the 1967 results. Interestingly enough, the only important term which shows equal salience in all three studies is "pleasure loving," which captured slightly over one-fourth of the votes each time.

Chinese

Since 1933, the cruel and condescending characterization of the Chinese has given way to a markedly positive, as well as a more definite, stereotype. "Loyal to family ties" (50%) and "tradition loving" (32%) have replaced "superstitious" and "sly" as central traits. "Industrious," "quiet," "meditative," and "courteous" each are selected by at least one-fifth of the students. It is remarkable that such an image should be prevalent in the midst of our cold war with Communist China and her highly publicized domestic upheaval. Only the appearance of "extremely nationalistic" (19%) hints at a recognition of these events in the stereotype.

While the positive image is certainly more encouraging than that of the "sly heathen," and could be more relevant to Nationalist China alone, Gilbert noted that even in 1951, the current attributes (emerging then) were "perhaps a generation behind the times as indications of national character [p. 250]." The present stereotype of the Chinese is a good example of the tenuous and selective nature of the relationship between stereotype and "reality."

English

Although definite variations in emphasis exist, the same traits used in 1933 and 1951 to characterize the English are also used today; the traits "sportsmanlike," "intelligent," and "conventional" have diminished in frequency, only to be replaced by "conservative" (53%), "sophisticated" (47%), "reserved" (40%), and "practical" (25%). Gilbert suggested that this particular stereotype is more firmly based in realities of national character than most. But it seems ironic that in spite of broad social reforms, dissolution of Empire, a liberal welfare-state government, and the influence of the Beatles and Carnaby Street on college youth, the picture of a staid and proper Englishman should remain so immutable.

Germans

The characterization of the Germans today appears to be a composite of the 1933 and 1951 stereotypes. As in both previous studies, "industrious" (59%) and "scientifically minded" (47%) are still the two most common traits selected, although the image of the methodical scientist has been modified to that of an efficient technician over the last 25 years. "Scientifically minded" has declined from its former salience (78% of the subjects in 1933) and "stolid" has been replaced by "efficient" (46%) in the top three attributes.

The concept of "aggressive, arrogant nationalism" which emerged following World War II has not disappeared, but it is now tempered by less negative terms such as "ambitious" (15%) and "progressive" (13%). Overall, the German image did not change nearly so much in these three studies as did that of the Japanese, who were still rather poorly regarded in 1951 (cf. Seago, 1947).

Irish

Gilbert in 1951 noted a definite fading of the "fighting Irish" stereotype. The 1967 data indicate that the image has merely taken on a slightly different form. While "pugnacious" has declined to 13%, the Irish are now described as "quick tempered" (43%), "stubborn" (23%) "argumentative" (20%), and "boastful" (17%). There also appears to be a second cluster of equal importance emphasizing perceived group loyalties of the Irish: "extremely nationalistic" (41%), "tradition loving" (25%), "loyal to family ties" (23%), and "very religious" (27%). The present image seems more strongly influenced by the proud independence of the Irish Republic, and less a caricature (e.g., the decline of "witty" as a trait) of early Irish immigrants to this country.

Italians

The "fading image" of the artistic and hot-tempered Italian, noted by Gilbert and cited by Allport (1954) as evidence for the weakening of stereotypes, appears now to have been merely transitory to the emergence of a more gigololike relative to his formerly aesthetic cousin. The artistic cluster —"artistic," "musical," "imaginative"—is now represented only "artistic" (reduced from 53% to 30%). But the temperamental cluster—"passionate" (44%), "impulsive" (28%), and "quick tempered" (28%)—remains, and is supplemented by "pleasure loving" (33%) and "sensual" (26%).

It is probable that highly successful movies over the years have served to buttress this side of the Italian stereotype (recent examples: *Marriage Italian Style* and *Divorce Italian Style*), though we would note that one-fourth of our subjects also checked "loyal to family ties" and/or "very religious." As Gilbert pointed out, the very religious trait is consistently applied to the predominantly Catholic nationalities. About one-fourth of the students in each study have used this term for both Irish and Italians.

Japanese

The change in Japanese stereotype content from 1933 to 1951 to 1967 provides a clear case of a stereotype responding to the currents of history and changing events. In 1933, the Japanese were recognized for their emerging industrialized society: "intelligent" (45%), "industrious" (43%), "progressive" (24%). Then, the hostilities of World War II and the destruction of the wartime industrial machine were followed by a characterization in 1951 principally noteworthy for its vague negativity. The first-ranking adjective—at a mere 24%—was the rather obtuse "imitative." Then followed "sly" (21%), "extremely nationalistic" (18%), and "treacherous" (17%). Furthermore, the terms "intelligent" and "industrious" practically disappeared, in contrast to their persistence in the German stereotype following the war.

Nevertheless, the stigma produced by war was apparently short-lived. The Japanese are now described as "industrious" (57%), "ambitious" (33%), "efficient" (27%), and "intelligent" (20%). It is interesting to note the recurrence of this cluster in traits in association with rapid technological development in the countries concerned (Germany, America, Japan in 1933).

Jews

The greatly improved image of the Jews is one of the outstanding long-term trends in this series. Perhaps more significant is the extent to which the core of the Jewish stereotype matches that of the American characterization—with both images clearly dominated by the terms "ambitious" and "materialistic." We may at last be observing the decline of the cultural phenomenon noted by Allport (which he attributed to Robert K. Merton):

> Why do so many people admire Abraham Lincoln? . . .
>
> Why do so many people dislike the Jews? They may tell you it is because they are (he was) thrifty, hardworking, eager for knowledge, ambitious, devoted to the rights of the average man, and eminently successful in climbing the ladder of opportunity.
>
> Of course, the terms used may be less laudatory in the case of the Jews: one may say they are tight-fisted, overambitious, pushing, and radical. But the fact remains that, essentially, the personality qualities admired in Abraham Lincoln are deplored in Jews. [Allport, 1954, p. 189].

Manifestly there are remnants of the noxious Shylock traits, "mercenary" (15%) and "grasping" (17%), but those are clearly superseded by "intelligent" (37%) and "industrious" (33%), with only the more neutral "shrewd" (30%) being selected by more than one-fourth of the students. At least in respect to the terms used most today, the image of Jews is a very complimentary one.

Negroes

The most dramatic and consistent trend over the 25-year period has been the more favorable characterization of the Negro. In 1933, "superstitious" and "lazy" accounted for one-third of all responses. The number of students checking "superstitious" has dropped from a near-unanimous 84% to 13%, which is the largest difference found in the present study (71%). And the 49% decrease in "lazy" (from 75% to 26%) runs a strong second. Moreover, only a mere handful of students today refer to the Negro as "ignorant" (11%) or "stupid" (4%), compared to 38% and 22%, respectively, in 1933.

The "new view" of the Negro focuses on the term "musical" (47%) and includes "pleasure loving" (26%), "ostentatious" (25%), and "happy-go-lucky" (27%).[2] This image would appear to be a more innocuous modern counterpart of the minstrel figure, probably reflecting the success of Negroes in the popular entertainment world supported by teen-age and collegiate audiences.

Certainly the Civil Rights movement of the past decade has strongly influenced the present generation of college students, and the appearance of "sensitive" (17%) in the top six traits might well indicate a projection of some of our subjects' own heightened awareness into the decidedly neutralized stereotype. In addition, there are traces of assimilation in that "pleasure loving" is assigned with equal frequencies to Negroes and to Americans, and the "Negro" trait "ostentatious" is now assigned by 15% of the respondents to "Americans."

Turks

The greatest enigma in these three related studies is the persistence with which the subjects have harshly characterized the Turks. Except for the definite derogatory nature of the traits, the subjects show very little agreement as to what constitutes a clear-cut image of the Turks. One subject in this study claimed that although he was not familiar with the Turks, he had nevertheless received from hearsay and mass media the image of a "cloak and dagger" type people. As a matter of fact, 28 subjects, or a little more than one-sixth of the total sample, either refused to list any traits for the Turks or did so with the qualification that their lists were based on hearsay

[2] By comparison, University of Oklahoma males in 1954 selected from the Katz and Braly list "musical" (66%), "pleasure loving" (48%), "lazy" (41%), "happying-go-lucky" (41%), and "superstitious" (34%) (Sommer & Killian, 1954).

and not firsthand experience. The reaction of the 1967 subjects to the Turks then was quite similar to that found by Gilbert in 1951. The subjects today appear not only more hesitant to stereotype the Turks, but also to a degree more hesitant to stereotype in severe terms. For example, the trait "cruel" was listed by 47% of the subjects in 1933 and by only 9% of the subjects in 1967. More harmless traits such as "aggressive," "quick tempered," and "impulsive" are emerging. In general, however, the "Terrible Turk" has not been able to shake his seemingly incorrigible image.

Comparisons of Stereotype Uniformity

As a measure of stereotype uniformity (consistency), Katz and Braly and Gilbert computed the smallest number of traits required to include one-half of all possible designations for a basis of easy comparison we have done the same. Since there are 150 subjects in this study who chose five traits for each group, our uniformity scores represent the smallest number of traits required to total 375 selections per ethnic group. These scores indicate the extent to which subjects agree in the traits they assign to a given group: the smaller the number of traits, the more definite or uniform is the social stereotype.

Table 2 contains the uniformity scores for the three studies. It will be noted that between 1933 and 1951 there was a decrease in uniformity of stereotype (an increase in the number of traits) for every group.

TABLE 2

Comparisons of Stereotype Uniformity: Least Number of Traits Needed to Account for One-Half of the Total Selections for Each Group

Ethic Group	1933	1951	1967
Americans	8.8	13.6	9.6
Chinese	12.0	14.5	10.8
English	7.0	9.2	8.0
Germans	5.0	6.3	6.3
Irish	8.5	17.5	10.3
Italians	6.9	11.3	8.6
Japanese	10.9	26.0	9.4
Jews	5.5	10.6	7.7
Negroes	4.6	12.0	12.3
Turks	15.9	32.0	25.6
M	8.5	15.3	10.9
ρ			
1951	.781**		
1967	.794**	.781**	

*$p < .05$.
**$p < .01$.

Our subjects displayed the same reluctance to proceed with the task that Gilbert found in 1951. The following subject's comments illustrate this fact:

> I must make it clear that I think it ludicrous to attempt to classify various ethnic groups. Perhaps my answers are a factor of the stereotypes that arise from individual interactions I have had with various members of these groups.
>
> I don't believe that any people can accurately be depicted as having, in total, certain characteristics. I have, however, attempted to relate my impression of the members of each of whom I have met. I would point out that in several stances, the number of such members is rather low.

The reservations expressed by many of our subjects when instructed to stereotype lends support to Gilbert's conclusion that college students have become more "sophisticated" and "objective" about making generalizations of other groups. Table 2, however, ironically indicates an unexpected change: stereotype uniformity has *increased* for every group except the Negroes. We had expected the same low uniformity (high scores) that Gilbert obtained in 1951, but the 1967 characterizations have in fact assumed very nearly the same high levels of consensus found by Katz and Braly. By the Wilcoxon matched-pairs signed-ranked T test (Siegel, 1956) each of the shifts between studies is significant, but the difference in scores between 1933 and 1967 is the least impressive in degree.

It should also be noted that the *relative* uniformity of stereotypes of the 10 groups has not radically changed over the 35-year period, as evidenced by significant rank-order correlations between sets of uniformity scores in Table 2. Successive student samples remain in close agreement among themselves concerning the images of Germans and Jews, and their impressions of Chinese and Turks still show the least uniformity of opinion, even though the precise composition of all those images has altered considerably over the years.

Favorableness of Traits Assigned

The ratings of favorableness-unfavorableness give us a reasonably objective estimation of the value of the Katz and Braly adjectives as used by college students today in describing people. The subjects' plus and minus ratings yielded a 5-point scale on which any adjective rated by all the subjects as *very favorable* $(++)$ would have a value of 2, and any adjectives unanimously rated as *very unfavorable* $(--)$ would have a value of -2. The observed mean values and standard deviations are reported in Table 3. "Brilliant" is the most favorable adjective with a mean value of 1.70. "Cruel" is the most unfavorable adjective with a value of -1.80.

TABLE 3

Favorableness of Terms in the Katz and Braly Checklist

Adjective	M	SD	Adjective	M	SD
Brilliant	1.70	.680	Extremely nationalistic	.10	.892
Intelligent	1.61	.627	Conservative	− .06	.632
Honest	1.56	.611	Talkative	− .13	.775
Alert	1.44	.576	Impulsive	− .22	.750
Imaginative	1.39	.531	Ponderous	− .23	.654
Artistic	1.34	.669	Conventional	− .30	.614
Industrious	1.32	.598	Materialistic	− .45	.772
Kind	1.29	.564	Radical	− .45	.783
Faithful	1.23	.697	Argumentative	− .50	.728
Sportsmanlike	1.19	.638	Frivolous	− .53	.717
Efficient	1.18	.523	Suggestible	− .55	.726
Courteous	1.18	.561	Sly	− .58	.855
Generous	1.17	.707	Stubborn	− .58	.705
Ambitious	1.06	.727	Imitative	− .63	.715
Witty	1.01	.601	Naive	− .66	.637
Individualistic	1.01	.712	Pugnacious	− .73	.680
Sensitive	.99	.750	Suspicious	− .75	.722
Progressive	.99	.534	Evasive	− .83	.616
Straight-forward	.96	.525	Loud	− .83	.624
Jovial	.92	.583	Superstitious	− .84	.761
Musical	.90	.618	Mercenary	− .88	.845
Neat	.86	.481	Ostentatious	− .89	.625
Persistent	.85	.638	Quick tempered	− .90	.664
Practical	.82	.523	Humorless	− .92	.718
Scientifically minded	.81	.699	Grasping	− .97	.790
Sophisticated	.74	.705	Boastful	−1.11	.567
Meditative	.59	.619	Quarrelsome	−1.11	.616
Loyal to family ties	.57	.643	Lazy	−1.12	.595
Pleasure loving	.46	.754	Gluttonous	−1.13	.580
Suave	.45	.706	Slovenly	−1.25	.651
Happy-go-lucky	.45	.816	Revengeful	−1.28	.640
Passionate	.41	.652	Arrogant	−1.30	.712
Sensual	.39	.728	Ignorant	−1.37	.676
Stolid	.32	.754	Physically dirty	−1.45	.666
Gregarious	.30	.834	Conceited	−1.50	.625
Tradition loving	.25	.703	Stupid	−1.59	.602
Methodical	.24	.670	Cowardly	−1.63	.590
Very religious	.23	.814	Unreliable	−1.64	.553
Quiet	.20	.548	Treacherous	−1.65	.577
Aggressive	.18	.984	Rude	−1.67	.538
Shrewd	.18	.847	Deceitful	−1.73	.568
Reserved	.12	.551	Cruel	−1.77	.624

Note: Ratings on a 5-point scale from −2 to +2.

TABLE 4

Mean Favorableness of Traits Comprising Each Stereotype

Ethnic Group	1933	1951	1967
Americans	.99	.86	.49
Chinese	−.12	.25	.46
English	.63	.59	.51
Germans	.89	.57	.77
Irish	.14	.00	−.13
Italians	.48	.44	.27
Japanese	.66	− .14	.84
Jews	.24	.45	.66
Negroes	−.70	− .37	.07
Turks	−.98	−1.03	−.62
M	.22	.16	.33
ρ			
1951	.770**		
1967	.745*	.515	

*$p < .05$.
**$p < .01$.

We used these values to derive a score of favorableness from the *traits comprising the uniformity scores* of each stereotype.[3] Each trait's frequency was multiplied by its favorableness value and the sum of the values divided by the total frequency. The results are shown in Table 4.

These scores are presented with three notes of caution: (*a*) The ratings of a word out of context may not accurately reflect its connotation in a given stereotype (Saenger & Flowerman, 1954). (*b*) Inevitable shifts in evaluation reduce the accuracy of today's ratings for the interpretation of some terms as used in earlier studies. For instance, it is doubtful that the adjectives "conservative" and "conventional" would have received from 1933 and 1951 subjects the same negative values they are now assigned. As a check on this factor, we have compared the ordering of 1933 stereotypes based on 1967 values of terms with Katz and Braly's (1935) orderings based on their desirability ratings. The rank-order correlation is .88. (*c*) Since Gilbert in most cases did not provide frequencies for all of the traits comprising the 1951 uniformity scores, our estimations of favorableness for the 1951 stereotypes are derived from fewer than 50% of the responses and are less reliable than the others.

Despite these limitations, the ratings are especially useful for present and future investigations, and they provide us with an overall index of the

[3] As Vinacke (1956) has pointed out, averaging all the terms assigned would probably give a slightly different value, corresponding more closely to the underlying attitudes. But we were concerned specifically with the value of the social stereotype as operationally defined herein.

direction and intensity of stereotype composition. The figures in Table 4 summarize our impressions of the major evaluative trends: the precipitous decline and rise in the Japanese image, faintly echoed in that of the Germans; marked improvement in the characterizations of Jews and Chinese; neutralization of the Negro stereotype; and the students' increasingly critical self-evaluation. Even the perennial sameness of the stereotyped Englishman shows up as the most stable value score in the table. In addition, we note that the Italian image by losing its artistic flavor has declined in favorableness.

The rank-order correlations of favorableness scores, like those of the uniformity scores, demonstrate considerable present-day agreement with previous stereotypes in the relative positions of the groups in question. For example, the Germans have maintained high esteem, the Irish stay fairly neutral, and the Turks anchor the negative end of every list.

By these calculations (viz., shifts between studies were not statistically significant), it does not appear that social stereotypes in general have become more positive or more negative in composition. There is, however, a predominantly positive trend if the images of Americans are excepted. In addition, several other features of these data on favorableness of trait assignments are relevant to our understanding of the relationship between social stereotypes and ethnic prejudice.

First, every stereotype in these studies is comprised of both positive and negative terms. The consensus is never purely favorable or unfavorable, although the degree of *evaluative differentiation* within the stereotype varies widely from one image to another. The overall "neutral" images of Irish (in 1933, 1951, and 1967), of Japanese (in 1951), and of Negroes (in 1967) actually contain combinations of terms loaded in both directions. This multiformity of evaluation deserves further attention in both personal and social stereotypes.

Second, positive values consistently outweigh negative values: only 8 of the 30 characterizations are decidedly unfavorable in overall composition. In a strictly quantitative sense, without evidence that these assignments undervalue the actual distributions of "good" and "bad" qualities of groups, the stereotyping on the whole must be viewed as complimentary (even though Germans, for example, might consider it inaccurate and uncomplimentary to be regarded collectively as "scientifically minded").

Finally, there is the obvious fact that some characterizations are unduly harsh while others are too good to be true. In particular, the autostereotype (self-stereotype) of Americans both in 1933 and in 1951 includes a greater weight of desirable traits than does any other image in the same study. This classic tendency to favor Europeans ("like us") over non-Europeans ("not like us") is also strong. Is it not the case that the *relative* evaluations show the true ethnocentrism of stereotyping? Again the 1967 data contradict expectations. Today's students have assigned more favorable traits to Japanese, Germans, Jews, and English than to themselves as Americans.

Vinacke's (1956) examination of autostereotypes suggests that the Americans may have rated self-traits (e.g., materialism, ambitiousness) more highly than would non-Americans, and thus were more generous with themselves on this count than others might have been. If so, then the comparatively low status of the national group is all the more remarkable. Other, more subtle ethnocentric devices may have been operative. By using independent ratings of group preference, Child and Doob (1943) and Vinacke (1956) have found that preferred groups are generally assigned approved self-traits and nonpreferred groups receive more disapproved non-self-traits. Similarly, perhaps, our subjects tended to favor Germans and Japanese alike by stressing those qualities which are perennially valued by and in Americans themselves: ambitiousness, industriousness, efficiency, intelligence. However, "preference" does not constitute grounds for defining the reference group essential to ethnocentrism as generally understood, and none of the more obvious possibilities (nationality, skin color, language, political alignment) seems to underlie the evaluative component of these stereotypes. From yet another perspective, there is an American-centered frame of reference involved in regarding the English, say, as reserved, and the Italian as impulsive. But again, these are not the kinds of bias by which ethnocentric prejudice is identified.

According to the 1967 results, therefore, the conclusion may be drawn that social stereotypes do not always favor their own group. The character of stereotyping may follow an ethnocentric pattern or may not, depending upon the perceivers, but ethnocentrism is evidently not inherent in the stereotyping itself.

Uniformity and Favorableness of Stereotyping

Does the *uniformity* of stereotyping give any indication of prejudice or of the attitudes among respondents? Katz and Braly (1933, 1935, 1947) observed in summarizing their own findings that the degree of agreement in stereotyping a particular group was not related to the degree of prejudice exhibited toward that group. For example, Negroes and Turks were the targets of greatest antagonism, according to various measures, at that time and received the most unfriendly trait assignments. But the images of those groups were, respectively, the highest and the lowest in uniformity. Using another approach to the question, Edwards (1940a) took samples of subjects having opposing attitudes to the same stimulus group (Communists) and found that the social stereotypes of friendly subjects differed from those of hostile subjects in content, but were equivalent in uniformity. In a third kind of analysis, Vinacke (1956) examined a large number of trait assignments over several stimulus groups, finding that the frequency of endorsement of a stereotype trait ("uniformity" of single traits) was not related to the term's favorableness or unfavorableness. Other factors, such as familiarity or contact with the stereotyped group, have been considered as possible mediating variables (Murphy, Murphy, & Newcomb, 1937; Schoenfeld, 1942; Triandis & Vassiliou, 1967; Vinacke, 1956), but still no consistent pattern has emerged to link uniformity of stereotyping to an evaluative component.

Stereotype uniformity nevertheless continues to be widely thought of as undesirable. Doubtless a central reason is the large number of investigations concerned with ethnic prejudice, investigations which define stereotyping operationally as the endorsement of traditional negative images. Studies using this approach nearly always show stereotyping to be related to hostility, and they find a reduction of stereotyping (reduction of uniformity) to be associated with the decline of hostility (e.g., Bettleheim & Janowitz, 1964; Saenger & Flowerman, 1954). But these specialized studies focus on derogatory images to begin with, and seldom record the appearance of new images, so they do not provide satisfactory evidence for an invariant connection between stereotype uniformity and unfriendly attitudes. There is no direct support for designating stereotypes as a whole, for instance, as "the language of prejudice" (Ehrlich & Rinehart, 1965.

We examined this issue further by computing rank-order correlations between uniformity scores and favorableness scores in each study. The results were as follows: for 1933, $\rho = .164$ (ns); for 1951, $\rho = .677$ ($p < .05$); for 1967, $\rho = .770$ ($p < .01$). Even if we entertain slight reservations about the accuracy of 1951 values, it is plain that greater stereotype uniformity in the later studies is associated with the *more favorable* images (Germans, Jews, English), whereas low uniformity occurs for the less favorable stereotypes (Turks, Negroes, Irish). Overall, the verbal norms in 1967 more nearly approach a vocabulary for friendly attitudes—a "language of tolerance," so to speak. The results here again rule out an inherent relationship between uniformity and hostility in social stereotypes.

Although we do not have an independent assessment of attitude in this case, the results seem consistent with Edwards' (1940b) finding that friendly observers develop standardized images just as do unfriendly observers. To the extent that it is attitudes (rather than, say, stimulus factors) which count in producing stereotype uniformity, it is not the direction of attitude which matters, but the *homogeneity* of attitudes among the respondents. As in Edwards' study, less agreement will occur in a population where attitudes toward the stimulus group(s) are widely disparate (the pros and the antis combined).

By the same token, we might expect that *contact* with members of a group would lead to uniformity of stereotypes if the subjective experiences of the observers, whether favorable or unfavorable, were *similar* experiences. The favorableness or unfavorableness of first-hand experiences would affect the content of the images though not the uniformity. Triandis and Vassiliou's (1967) findings about contact and reciprocal stereotyping by Greek and American subjects are consistent with such an interpretation.

Comparisons of Stereotypes of Public School and Private School Graduates
As mentioned earlier, Gilbert (1951) felt that the 1933 stereotypes may have been influenced by the allegedly greater ethnocentrism of privately educated students who formerly made up a large majority of the Princeton population. Comparisons of the stereotypes held by subjects from private versus public high schools in the 1967 sample indicates, however, that such a distinction is inappropriate for today's students. The uniformity scores and the favorableness scores were virtually identical for the two groups of subjects, giving no evidence of real differences between them in stereotyping behavior (Tables 5 and 6). On the contrary, the trait assignments by the respective subgroups of students were so much alike that they may be taken as evidence of the reliability of the Katz and Braly technique in tapping verbal norms, and of the generality of those norms within the population sampled (Table 7). Even in the case of the Turks, for whom responses were thinly scattered among a large number of different terms, there is remark-

TABLE 5

Comparison of Stereotype Uniformity for Private Versus
Public High School Graduates in 1967 Sample:
Least Number of Traits Required

Group	Total Sample ($N = 150$)	Private School ($N = 60$)	Public School ($N = 90$)
Americans	9.6	9.9	9.4
Chinese	10.8	11.5	10.2
English	8.0	7.0	8.4
Germans	6.3	6.2	6.4
Irish	10.3	10.6	10.1
Italians	8.6	9.1	8.3
Japanese	9.4	9.9	9.0
Jews	7.7	7.6	7.8
Negroes	12.3	12.6	12.1
Turks	25.6	21.5	28.5
M	10.9	10.6	11.0

$\rho = .96$

TABLE 6

Comparison of Favorableness of Traits Checked by Private Versus
Public High School Graduates in 1967

Group	Total Sample ($N = 150$)	Private School ($N = 60$)	Public School ($N = 90$)
Americans	.49	.44	.52
Chinese	.46	.41	.50
English	.51	.52	.50
Germans	.77	.77	.77
Irish	−.13	−.05	−.19
Italians	.27	.30	.24
Japanese	.84	.84	.84
Jews	.66	.63	.68
Negroes	.07	.00	.12
Turks	−.62	−.63	−.62
M	.33	.32	.34

$\rho = .98$

able similarity in the frequencies of traits assigned by the two subsets of students.

These findings may be a result of a liberalization of attitudes in independent schools in recent years, or, more broadly, the homogenization of student culture through travel, television, movies, and so forth. But the "ethnocentrism gap" which may formerly have existed between independent and public school students does not show up in the 1967 stereotypes.

TABLE 7

Chi-Square Comparisons of the Frequencies of 10 Traits Assigned by
Private Versus Public High School Graduates in 1967

Group	χ^2	p
Americans	3.0	.98
Chinese	4.3	.90
English	6.4	.70
Germans	3.7	.95
Irish	10.7	.30
Italians	10.1	.40
Japanese	8.9	.50
Jews	14.0	.20
Negroes	5.1	.90
Turks	10.4	.40

SUMMARY AND IMPLICATIONS

Most of the trends noted by Gilbert in 1951 are confirmed by the 1967 results. Younger generations show more careful thinking about ethnic generalizations than their counterparts of the 1930s. Now, as in 1951,

> Some students regard it as almost an insult to their intelligence to be required to make such generalizations, while others do so with considerable reservations. . . . those [generalizations] they do make tend to be based more on cultural and historical realities and less on fictitious caricatures or the prejudices of their parents [Gilbert, 1951, p. 252].

These trends have continued to the present, and a comparison between responses by the two subsets of 1967 students indicates that the findings are reliable.

At the same time, the apparent "fading" of social stereotypes in 1951 is not upheld as a genuine overall trend. Where traditional assignments have declined in frequency they have, in the long run, been replaced by others, resulting in restored stereotype uniformity. Only the Turks do not now obtain high frequencies for a few major traits.

A feature of these data which is still impressive is the extent to which "new" stereotypes resemble previous ones. Paradoxically enough, the changes which have occurred stand out because so much has remained the same. Uniformity and favorableness scores correlate significantly across the three generations of students. The collections of traits selected to characterize specific groups are very much alike from one generation to the next, though the relative popularities of those traits have been thoroughly rearranged. A great deal of change consists of a shift of emphasis in the already existing picture.

How were these results affected by the use of the 1933 checklist? An alternative approach in repeating Katz and Braly's investigation would have been to construct, by pretesting (as they did), an up-to-date list of traits. Although the subjects were directed to add terms as they wished, the constraints of a provided list are fairly strong (Ehrlich & Rinehart, 1965), and, typically, few subjects in these studies departed from the list. We suspect that a comprehensive list for today would have to include several terms not found in the 1933 version, terms which might have been widely subscribed to by our subjects. Even the 1933 results might have looked slightly different if the checklist included such standard terms as temperamental (Italians), militaristic (Germans), clannish (Jews), poor (Chinese, Negroes), and so on. As far as present findings are concerned, it should be borne in mind that the results probably over-estimate somewhat the presence of traditional stereotype content in the views of later Princeton students. As for uniformity, since the sole criterion for inclusion of a trait is its popularity, any replacement of terms in the composite images would only have increased the uniformity scores; so, if anything, the more recent uniformity scores are under-estimations.

For comparative purposes, of course, the list afforded the key element of control. The original procedure having been repeated in this detail, we can be certain that the differences found in this series of investigations are due only to subject factors, and are not a result of modifications in the task. Such an approach has enabled us to lay major stress on certain issues concerning the phenomenon of stereotyping itself.

The character of the new stereotypes is consistent with the more liberal attitudes found in most college communities today, where, as Triandis and Vassiliou (1967) have pointed out, "it is no longer appropriate to be prejudiced toward other groups [p. 238]." Since this liberalization of views was to be expected, the more outstanding aspect of the recent stereotypes is their uniformity. According to most of the standard interpretations of stereotyping, the students' protestations and their apparent lack of ethnocentrism should not have been accompanied by such highly standardized impressions of the groups in question. One explanation is that the students have reported hearsay generalizations that mean nothing at all to them personally (as a few of them were anxious to insist). Eysenck and Crowne (1948), on discovering that was true of many of their respondents, proposed "application of the principle that stereotyped views may be merely the last resort of a subject driven into a neurotic choice situation ('I don't know the answer—I must be given an answer') [p. 11]." Yet it is no more helpful to dismiss the responses as spurious than it is to regard all ethnic generalizations as pregnant with hostility. For one thing, the wholesale shifts of emphasis indicate some concerted opinion of a definite kind, rather than an empty parroting of familiar terms. For another, the case of the Turks provides a specific example wherein disaffection with the traditional view was *not* offset by emergence of a revised image. When they really had no reasonable basis for responding, nearly 20% of the subjects refused to cooperate entirely. The implication is that in contrast, their generalizations about the other nine groups met at least minimum criteria for acceptability, and thus had some degree of meaning for the respondents. But how much "meaning" and how significant is that?

Many of the knotty issues of interpretation can, we think, be unraveled in the following way. There are critical differences between personal attitudes and personal stereotypes (which may or may not entail strong affect or conviction), as well as between personal stereotypes and social stereotypes (which probably do not adequately represent any single respondent's view). Much of the confusion about stereotypes comes about from a failure to respect these boundaries. Until the correspondences and the links between the three sets of phenomena are better established, more caution needs to be exercised in making inferences from one to the other. The importance of recognizing these distinctions is demonstrated by Bettleheim and Janowitz's (1964) studies in depth of prejudice in 150 war veterans. Data based on long interviews showed no significant relationship between the particular sets of generalizations (personal stereotypes) made about Negroes or Jews, and the degree of hostility displayed toward the group (personal attitudes) by demands for restrictions. However, those persons who were more outspoken and intense in their feelings against a group employed the negative generalizations much more frequently throughout the course of the interview. Certainly it is true, as other investigations have shown, that the content of stereotypes will often correspond to attitudes in a general way. That would seem to be the case for the Princeton students. But the findings of Bettleheim and Janowitz stress the necessity of looking separately at stereotyping and attitude variables. These authors advise that "even the most tolerant person is not entirely free of occasionally stereotyped thinking in problems of interethnic relations [p. 300]." Our results suggest this as well by showing that the students possess stereotypes even though they may not often make use of them or feel that their judgments are affected by them.

REFERENCES

Allport, G. W. *The nature of prejudice.* New York: Addison-Wesley, 1954. (Republished: New York, Anchor Books, 1958.)

Bettleheim, B., & Janowitz, M. *Social change and prejudice.* New York: Free Press of Glencoe, 1964.

Buchanan, W., & Cantril, H. *How nations see each other.* Urbana: University of Illinois Press, 1953.

Centers, R. An effective classroom demonstration of stereotypes. *Journal of Social Psychology,* 1951, **34**, 41–46.

Child, I. L., & Doob, L. W. Factors determining national stereotypes. *Journal of Social Psychology,* 1943, **17**, 203–219.

Edwards, A. L. Four dimensions in political stereotypes. *Journal of Abnormal and Social Psychology,* 1940, **35**, 566–572.

Edwards, A. L. Studies of stereotypes: I. The directionality and uniformity or responses to stereotypes. *Journal of Social Psychology,* 1940, **12**, 357–366.

Ehrlich, H. J., & Rinehart, J. W. A brief report on the methodology of stereotype research. *Social Forces,* 1965, **43**, 564–575.

Eysenck, H. J., & Crowne, S. National stereotypes: An experimental and methodological study. *International Journal of Opinion and Attitude Research,* 1948, **2**, 1–14.

Gilbert, G. M. Stereotype persistence and change among college students. *Journal of Abnormal and Social Psychology,* 1951, **46**, 245–254.

The handbook of private schools. Boston: Sargent, 1965.

Katz, D., & Braly, K. W. Racial stereotypes of one hundred college students. *Journal of Abnormal and Social Psychology,* 1933, **28**, 280–290.

Katz, D., & Braly, K. W. Racial prejudice and racial stereotypes. *Journal of Abnormal and Social Psychology,* 1935, **30,** 175–193.

Katz, D., & Braly, K. W. Racial stereotypes and racial prejudice. In T. M. Newcomb & E. L. Hartley (Eds.), *Readings in social psychology.* New York: Holt, 1947.

Lippmann, W. *Public opinion.* New York: Harcourt, Brace, 1922.

Murphy, G., Murphy, L. B., & Newcomb, T. M. *Experimental social psychology.* New York: Harper, 1937.

Saenger, G., & Flowerman, S. Stereotypes and prejudicial attitudes. *Human Relations,* 1954, **7,** 217–238.

Schoenfeld, N. An experimental study of some problems relating to stereotypes. *Archives of Psychology,* 1942, No. 270.

Seago, D. W. Stereotypes: Before Pearl Harbor and after. *Journal of Psychology,* 1947, **23,** 55–63.

Secord, P. F., & Backman, C. W. *Social Psychology.* New York: McGraw-Hill, 1964.

Siegel, S. *Non-parametric statistics for the behavioral sciences.* New York: McGraw-Hill, 1956.

Sommer, R., & Killian, L. M. Areas of value difference: I. A. method for investigation. *Journal of Social Psychology,* 1954, **39,** 227–235.

Triandis, H. C., & Vassiliou, V. Frequency of contact and stereotyping. *Journal of Personality and Social Psychology,* 1967, **7,** 316–328.

Vinacke, W. E. Explorations in the dynamic processes of stereotyping. *Journal of Social Psychology,* 1956, **43,** 105–132.

Introduction to
Sommer Article

The next time you board a bus or enter an airport terminal note the way people have distributed themselves in the available seats. If it is not very crowded you will observe a consistency in the way individuals maintain spatial distance between themselves and their neighbors. One general rule that seems to hold is that strangers will never take adjoining seats if other empty seats are available. Thus, when strangers board a bus containing, for example, ten double seats you can be relatively certain that none will be filled (two passengers sitting abreast) until *each* double seat has been occupied by one person first.

There seems to be definite consistencies in the ways humans govern the space around them—that is, the manner in which they regulate the distance between themselves and other persons. The term for such spatial regulation is "territoriality"—and the "territorial imperative" is practiced by humans and lower animals alike. The underlying principle of territoriality is that many species of life desire and attempt to maintain a specified amount of space for themselves.

At this point you might be wondering what importance the concept of territoriality has for psychology. It helps to explain a lot of otherwise seemingly unrelated behaviors in and between many animal species (including man). Far more important than this, however, is the realization (based on recent research) that the study of territoriality leads us to new discoveries and insights basic to the very survival of life! From the investigation of the "territorial imperative" has come the understanding that territoriality serves to insure survival of the species and that prolonged violation of the "territorial imperative" (e.g., overcrowding) leads to behavior pathology in the affected organisms and sometimes death. The implications of such experimental findings for man, living as he does in teeming, densely populated cities, should be obvious.

Recently a rash of books have appeared on the topic of territoriality. Some are "popularized" presentations like Ardrey's *African Genesis* (1961) and *The Territorial Imperative* (1966) or Morris' *The Naked Ape* (1967) or *The Human Zoo* (1969).* Others are more scientifically oriented (but no less interesting) like Sommer's *Personal Space* (1969) or Hall's *The Silent Language* (1959) and *The Hidden Dimension* (1966). Several important scientific articles on the subject also are available (e.g., Wynne-Edwards, 1964).

I have chosen a chapter from Robert Sommer's *Personal Space* to introduce you to the topic of territoriality. In this engrossing segment of his highly readable book Sommer examines what happens when an individual's "personal space" is violated. Did you know, for example, that there are cultural differences in the way people regulate the personal space around them? Were you cognizant of the fact that audiences waiting to see an "earthy" movie will line up twice as densely as patrons of a family picture? Did you realize that a person can be driven from his seat if, in a relatively empty room, he is confronted by an individual who takes a chair right next to his own? Such information, and more, is distributed throughout the Sommer selection.

REFERENCES

Ardrey, R. *African genesis.* London: Colins, 1961.
Ardrey, R. *The territorial imperative.* New York: Atheneum, 1966.
Baumgold, J. A guide to the hidden meanings of New York parties. *New York,* April 28, 1969, 24–32.
Hall, E. *The silent language.* New York: Doubleday, 1959.
Hall, E. *The hidden dimension.* New York: Doubleday, 1966.
Morris, D. *The naked ape.* New York: McGraw-Hill, 1967.
Morris, D. *The human zoo.* New York: McGraw-Hill, 1969.
Sommer, R. *Personal space: The behavioral basis of design.* New York: Prentice-Hall, 1969.

* The concept of territoriality is well portrayed in the "turf wars" between Jets and Sharks in *West Side Story*; and the concept is even used to explain the "hidden meanings in New York Parties" (Baumgold, 1969)!

21

Spatial Invasion

Robert Sommer

Dear Abby: I have a pet peeve that sounds so petty and stupid that I'm almost ashamed to mention it. It is people who come and sit down beside me on the piano bench while I'm playing. I don't know why this bothers me so much, but it does. Now you know, Abby, you can't tell someone to get up and go sit somewhere else without hurting their feelings. But it would be a big relief to me if I could get them to move in a nice inoffensive way . . .

Lost Chord

Dear Lost: People want to sit beside you while you're playing because they are fascinated. Change your attitude and regard their presence as a compliment, and it might be easier to bear. P.S. You might also change your piano bench for a piano stool. (ABIGAIL VAN BUREN, *San Francisco Chronicle,* May 25, 1965.)

The best way to learn the location of invisible boundaries is to keep walking until somebody complains. Personal space refers to an area with invisible boundaries surrounding a person's body into which intruders may not come. Like the porcupines in Schopenhauer's fable, people like to be close enough to obtain warmth and comradeship but far enough away to avoid pricking one another. Personal space is not necessarily spherical in shape, nor does it extend equally in all directions. (People are able to tolerate closer presence of a stranger at their sides than directly in front.) It has been likened to a snail shell, a soap bubble, an aura, and "breathing room." There are major differences between cultures in the distances that

SOURCE. *Personal Space: The Behavioral Basis of Design.* Copyright 1969. Reprinted by permission of Prentice-Hall, Inc., Englewood Cliffs, New Jersey.

people maintain—Englishmen keep further apart than Frenchmen or South Americans. Reports from Hong Kong where three million people are crowded into 12 square miles indicate that the population has adapted to the crowding reasonably well. The Hong Kong Housing Authority, now in its tenth year of operation, builds and manages low-cost apartments for families that provide approximately 35 square feet per person for living-sleeping accommodations. When the construction supervisor of one Hong Kong project was asked what the effects of doubling the amount of floor area would be upon the living patterns, he replied, "With 60 square feet per person, the tenants would sublet!" [1]

Although some people claim to see a characteristic aura around human bodies and are able to describe its color, luminosity, and dimensions, most observers cannot confirm these reports and must evolve a concept of personal space from interpersonal transactions. There is a considerable similarity between personal space and *individual distance,* or the characteristic spacing of species members. Individual distance exists only when two or more members of the same species are present and is greatly affected by population density and territorial behavior. Individual distance and personal space interact to affect the distribution of persons. The violation of individual distance is the violation of society's expectations; the invasion of personal space is an intrustion into a person's self-boundaries. Individual distance may be outside the area of personal space—conversation between two chairs across the room exceeds the boundaries of personal space, or individual distance may be less than the boundaries of personal space—sitting next to someone on a piano bench is within the expected distance but also within the bounds of personal space and may cause discomfort to the player. If there is only one individual present, there is infinite individual distance, which is why it is useful to maintain a concept of personal space, which has also been described as a *portable territory,* since the individual carries it with him wherever he goes although it disappears under certain conditions, such as crowding.

There is a formula of obscure origin that a man in a crowd requires at least two square feet. This is an absolute minimum and applies, according to one authority, to a thin man in a subway. A fat man would require twice as much space or more. Journalist Herbert Jacobs became interested in spatial behavior when he was a reporter covering political rallies. Jacobs found that estimates of crowd size varied with the observer's politics. Some estimates by police and politicians were shown to be twenty times larger than the crowd size derived from head count or aerial photographs. Jacobs found a fertile field for his research on the Berkeley campus where outdoor rallies are frequent throughout the year. He concluded that people in dense crowds

[1] American Institute of Planners Newsletter, January 1967, p. 2.

have six to eight square fee each, while in loose crowds, with people moving in and out, there is an average of ten square feet per person, Jacobs' formula is that crowd size equals length × width of the crowd divided by the appropriate correction factor depending upon whether the crowd is dense or loose. On the Berkeley campus this produced estimates reasonably close to those obtained from aerial photographs.[2]

Hospital patients complain not only that their personal space and their very bodies are continually violated by nurses, interns, and physicians who do not bother to introduce themselves or explain their activities, but that their territories are violated by well-meaning visitors who will ignore "No Visitors" signs. Frequently patients are too sick or too sensitive to repel intruders. Once surgery is finished or the medical treatment has been instituted, the patient is left to his own devices to find peace and privacy. John Lear, the science editor of the *Saturday Review*, noticed an interesting hospital game he called, "Never Close the Door," when he was a surgery patient. Although his physician wanted him protected against outside noises and distractions, the door opened at intervals, people peered in, sometimes entered, but no one ever closed the door. When Lear protested, he was met by hostile looks and indignant remarks such as, "I'm only trying to do my job, Mister." It was never clear to Lear why the job—whatever it was— required the intruder to leave the door ajar afterwards.[3]

Spatial invasions are not uncommon during police interrogations. One police textbook recommends that the interrogator should sit close to the suspect, with no table or desk between them, since "an obstruction of any sort affords the subject a certain degree of relief and confidence not otherwise obtainable."[4] At the beginning of the session, the officer's chair may be two or three feet away, "but after the interrogation is under way the interrogator should move his chair in closer so that ultimately one of the subject's knees is just about in between the interrogator's two knees."[5]

Lovers pressed together close their eyes when they kiss. On intimate occasions the lights are typically dim to reduce not only the distracting external cues but also to permit two people to remain close together. Personal space is a culturally acquired daylight phenomenon. Strangers are affected differently than friends by a loss of personal space. During rush hour, subway riders lower their eyes and sometimes "freeze" or become rigid as a form of minimizing unwanted social intercourse. Boy-meets-girl on a crowded rush hour train would be a logical plot for an American

[2] Jacobs, "How Big Was the Crowd?" Talk given at California Journalism Conference, Sacramento, February 24–25, 1967.

[3] John Lear, "What's Wrong with American Hospitals?" *Saturday Review* (February 4, 1967), pp. 59–60.

[4] F. E. Inbau and J. E. Reid, *Criminal Interrogation and Confessions* (Toronto: Burns and MacEachern, 1963).

[5] Inbau and Reid, *op. cit.*

theater based largely in New York City, but it is rarely used. The idea of meeting someone under conditions where privacy, dignity, and individuality are so reduced is difficult to accept.

A driver can make another exceedingly nervous by tailgating. Highway authorities recommend a "space cushion" of at least one car length for every ten miles per hour of speed. You can buy a bumper sticker or a lapel button with the message "If you can read this, you're too close." A perceptive suburban theater owner noticed the way crowds arranged themselves in his lobby for different pictures. His lobby was designed to hold approximately 200 customers who would wait behind a roped area for the theater to clear.

> When we play a [family picture like] *Mary Poppins, Born Free,* or *The Cardinal,* we can line up only about 100 to 125 people. These patrons stand about a foot apart and don't touch the person next to them. But when we play a [sex comedy like] *Tom Jones* or *Irma la Douce,* we can get 300 to 350 in the same space. These people stand so close to each other you'd think they were all going to the same home at the end of the show! [6]

Animal studies indicate that individual distance is learned during the early years. At some stage early in his life the individual learns how far he must stay from species members. When he is deprived of contact with his own kind, as in isolation studies, he cannot learn proper spacing, which sets him up as a failure in subsequent social intercourse—he comes too close and evokes threat displays or stays too far away to be considered a member of the group. Newborn of many species can be induced to follow novel stimuli in place of their parents. If a newly hatched chicken is separated from his mother and shown a flashing light instead, on subsequent occasions he will follow the flashing light rather than his mother. The distance he remains behind the object is a function of its size; young chicks will remain further behind a large object than a small one.[7]

Probably the most feasible method for exploring individual distance and personal space with their invisible boundaries is to approach people and observe their reactions. Individual distance is not an absolute figure but varies with the relationship between the individuals, the distance at which others in the situation are placed, and the bodily orientations of the individuals one to another. The most systematic work along these lines has been undertaken by the anthropologist Ray Birdwhistell who records a person's response with zoom lenses and is able to detect even minute eye

[6] Bob Ellison, "If the Movie Is Comic, Sex Is OK, in Suburbia," *Chicago Sun Times,* Jan. 15, 1967, Section 3, p. 4.

[7] Peter H. Klopfer and J. P. Hailman, *An Introduction to Animal Behavior* (Englewood Cliffs, N. J.: Prentice-Hall, Inc., 1967).

movements and hand tremors as the invader approaches the emotionally egotistic zone around the victim.[8]

One of the earliest attempts to invade personal space on a systematic basis was undertaken by Williams, who wanted to learn how different people would react to excessive closeness. Classifying students as introverts or extraverts on the basis of their scores on a personality test, he placed each individual in an experimental room and then walked toward the person, telling him to speak out as soon as he (Williams) came too close. Afterward he used the reverse condition, starting at a point very close and moving away until the person reported that he was too far away for comfortable conversation. His results showed that introverts kept people at a greater conversational distance than extroverts.[9]

The same conclusion was reached by Leipold, who studied the distance at which introverted and extroverted college students placed themselves in relation to an interviewer in either a stress or a non-stress situation. When the student entered the experimental room, he was given either the stress, praise, or neutral instructions. The stress instructions were, "We feel that your course grade is quite poor and that you have not tried your best. Please take a seat in the next room and Mr. Leipold will be in shortly to discuss this with you." The neutral control instructions read, "Mr. Leipold is interested in your feelings about the introductory course. Would you please take a seat in the next room." After the student had entered and seated himself, Mr. Leipold came in, recorded the student's seating position, and conducted the interview. The results showed that students given praise sat closest to Leipold's chair, followed by those in the neutral condition, with students given the stress instructions maintaining the most distance from Leipold's chair behind the desk. It was also found that introverted and anxious individuals sat further away from him than did extroverted students with a lower anxiety level.[10]

Glen McBride has done some excellent work on the spatial behaviors of fowl, not only in captivity but in their feral state on islands off the Australian coast. He has recently turned his attention to human spatial behavior using the galvanic skin response (GSR) as an index of emotionality. The GSR picks up changes in skin conductivity that relate to stress and emotional behavior. The same principle underlies what is popularly known as the lie detector test. McBride placed college students in a chair from which they were approached by both male and female experimenters as well as by paper figures and nonhuman objects. It was found that GSR was greatest (skin resistance was least) when a person was approached

[8] R. L. Birdwhistell, *Introduction to Kinetics* (Washington: Foreign Service Institute, 1952).

[9] John L. Williams, "Personal Space and its Relation to Extroversion-Introversion" (Master's thesis, University of Alberta, 1963).

[10] William E. Leipold, "Psychological Distance in a Dyadic Interview" (Ph.D. thesis, University of North Dakota, 1963).

frontally, whereas a side approach yielded a greater response than a rear approach. The students reacted more strongly to the approach of someone of the opposite sex than to someone of the same sex. Being touched by an object produced less of a GSR than being touched by a person.[11]

A similar procedure without the GSR apparatus was used by Argyle and Dean, who invited their subjects to participate in a perceptual experiment in which they were to "stand as close as comfortable to see well" to a book, a plaster head, and a cut-out life-size photograph of the senior author with his eyes closed and another photograph with his eyes open. Among other results, it was found that the subjects placed themselves closer to the eyes-closed photograph than the eyes-open photograph.[12] Horowitz, Duff, and Stratton used a similar procedure with schizophrenic and non-schizophrenic mental patients. Each individual was instructed to walk over to a person, or in another condition a hatrack, and the distance between the goal and his stopping place was measured. It was found that most people came closer to the hatrack than they did to another person. Each tended to have a characteristic individual distance that was relatively stable from one situation to another, but was shorter for inanimate objects than for people. Schizophrenics generally kept greater distance between themselves and others than did nonpatients.[13] The last finding is based on average distance values, which could be somewhat inflated by a few schizophrenics who maintain a large individual distance. Another study showed that some schizophrenic patients sat "too close" and made other people nervous by doing this. However, it was more often the case that schizophrenics maintained excessive physical distance to reduce the prospects of unwanted social intercourse.[14]

In order to explore personal space using the invasion technique, but to avoid the usual connotations surrounding forced close proximity to strangers, my own method was to undertake the invasion in a place where the usual sanctions of the outside world did not apply. Deliberate invasions of personal space seem more feasible and appropriate inside a mental hospital than outside. Afterward, it became apparent that this method could be adapted for use in other settings such as the library in which Nancy Russo spent many hours sitting too close to other girls.

The first study took place at a 1500-bed mental institution situated in parklike surroundings in northern California. Most wards were unlocked, and patients spent considerable time out of doors. In wooded areas it was common to see patients seated under the trees, one to a bench or knoll.

[11] Glen McBride, M. G. King, and J. W. James, "Social Proximity Effects on GSR in Adult Humans," *Journal of Psychology*, LXI (1965), 153–57.

[12] Michael Argyle and Janet Dean, "Eye Contact, Distance, and Affiliation," *Sociometry*, XXVIII (1965), 289–304.

[13] Mardi J. Horowitz, D. F. Duff, and L. O. Stratton, "Body-Buffer Zone," *Archives of General Psychiatry*, XI (1964), 651–56.

[14] Robert Sommer, "Studies in Personal Space," *Sociometry*, XXII (1959), 247–60.

The wards within the buildings were relatively empty during the day because of the number of patients outside as well as those who worked in hospital industry. This made it possible for patients to isolate themselves from others by finding a deserted area on the grounds or remaining in an almost empty building. At the outset I spent considerable time observing how patients isolated themselves from one another. One man typically sat at the base of a fire escape so he was protected by the bushes on one side and the railing on the other. Others would lie on benches in remote areas and feign sleep if approached. On the wards a patient might sit in a corner and place magazines or his coat on adjacent seats to protect the space. The use of belongings to indicate possession is very common in bus stations, cafeterias, waiting rooms, but the mental patient is limited in using this method since he lacks possessions. Were he to own a magazine or book, which is unlikely, and left it on an empty chair, it would quickly vanish.

Prospective victims had to meet three criteria—male, sitting alone, and not engaged in any definite activity such as reading or playing cards. When a patient fitting these criteria was located, I walked over and sat beside him without saying a word. If the patient moved his chair or slid further down the bench, I moved a like distance to keep the space between us to about six inches. In all sessions I jiggled my key ring a few times to assert my dominance, the key being a mark of status in a mental hospital. It can be noted that these sessions not only invaded the patient's personal space but also the nurse's territory. It bothered the nurses to see a high status person (jacket, white shirt, tie, and the title "Doctor") entering their wards and sitting among the patients. The dayroom was the patients' territory vis-à-vis the nurses, but it was the nurses' territory vis-à-vis the medical staff. Control subjects were selected from other patients who were seated some distance away but whose actions could be observed.

Within two minutes, all of the control subjects remained but one-third of the invasion victims had been driven away. Within nine minutes, fully half of the victims had departed compared with only 8 per cent of the controls (see Fig. 1). Flight was a gross reaction to the intrusion; there were many more subtle indications of the patient's discomfort. The typical sequence was for the victim to face away immediately, pull in his shoulders, and place his elbows at his sides. Facing away was an almost universal reaction among the victims, often coupled with hands placed against the chin as a buffer. Records obtained during the notetaking sessions illustrate this defensive pattern.

Example A

    10:00. Seat myself next to a patient, about sixty years of age; he is smoking and possibly watching TV.

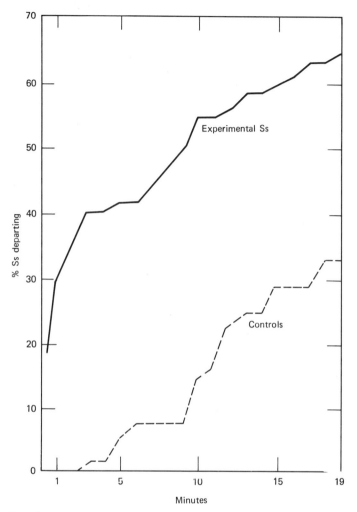

FIG. 1. Cumulative percentage of patients departing at each one-minute interval.

10:04. Patient rubs his face briefly with the back of his hand.

10:05. Patient breathes heavily, still smoking, and puts his ashes into a tin can. He looks at his watch occasionally.

10:06. He puts out his cigarette, rubs his face with the back of his hand. Still watching TV.

10:12. Patient glances at his watch, flexes his fingers.

10:13. Patient rises, walks over and sits at a seat several chairs over. Observation ended.

Example B

8:46. Seat myself next to a 60-year-old man who looks up as I enter the room. As I sit down, he begins talking to himself, snuffs out his cigarette, rises, and walks across the room. He asks a patient on the other side of the room, "You want me to sit here?" He starts arranging the chairs against the opposite wall and finally sits down.

Ethologist Ewan Grant has made a detailed analysis of the patient's micro behaviors drawing much inspiration from the work of Tinbergen [15] as well as his own previous studies with colonies of monkeys and rats. Among a group of confined mental patients he determined a relatively straightforward dominance hierarchy based on aggression-flight encounters between individuals. Aggressive acts included threat gestures ("a direct look plus a sharp movement of the head towards the other person"), frowns, and hand-raising. Flight behaviors included retreat, bodily evasions, closed eyes, withdrawing the chin into the chest, hunching, and crouching. These defensive behaviors occurred when a dominant individual sat too close to a subordinate. This could be preceded by some overt sign of tension such as rocking, leg swinging, or tapping. Grant describes one such encounter: "A lower ranking member of the group is sitting in a chair; a dominant approaches and sits near her. The first patient begins to rock and then frequently, on one of the forward movements, she gets up and moves away." [16]

In seventeen British old folks homes Lipman found that most of the patients had favorite chairs that they considered "theirs." Their title to these chairs was supported by the behavior of both patients and staff. A newly admitted inmate had great difficulty in finding a chair that was not owned by anyone. Typically he occupied one seat and then another until he found one that was "unowned." When he sat in someone else's chair, he was told to move away in no uncertain terms.[17] Accidental invasions were an accepted fact of life in these old folks homes. It is possible to view them as a hazing or initiation ceremony for new residents to teach them the informal institutional rules and understandings. Such situations illustrate the importance of knowing not only how people mark out and personalize spaces, but how they respond to intrusions.

We come now to the sessions Nancy Russo conducted in the study hall of a college library, a large high-ceilinged room with book-lined walls. Because this is a study area, students typically try to space themselves as far as possible from one another. Systematic observations over a two-year period

---

[15] N. Tinbergen, *Social Behaviour in Animals* (London: Methuen & Co. Ltd., 1953).
[16] Grant, *op. cit.*
[17] Alan Lipman, "Building Design and Social Interaction," *The Architects Journal*, CXLVII (1968), 23–30.

disclosed that the first occupants of the room generally sat one to a table at end chairs. Her victims were all females sitting alone with at least one book in front of them and empty chairs on either side and across. In other words, the prospective victim was sitting in an area surrounded by empty chairs, which indicated something about her preference for solitude as well as making an invasion relatively easy. The second female to meet these criteria in each session and who was visible to Mrs. Russo served as a control. Each control subject was observed from a distance and no invasion was attempted. There were five different approaches used in the invasions—sometimes Mrs. Russo would sit alongside the subject, other times directly across from her, and so forth. All of these were violations of the typical seating norms in the library, which required a newcomer to sit at a considerable distance from those already seated unless the room was crowded.

Occupying the adjacent chair and moving it closer to the victim, produced the quickest departures, and there was a slight but also significant difference between the other invasion locations and the control condition. There were wide individual differences in the ways the victims reacted—there is no single reaction to someone's sitting too close; there are defensive gestures, shifts in posture, and attempts to move away. If these fail or are ignored by the invader, or he shifts position too, the victim eventually takes to flight. Crook measured spacing of birds in three ways: *arrival distance* or how far from settled birds a newcomer will land, *settled distance* or the resultant distance after adjustments have occurred, and the *distance after departure* or how far apart birds remain after intermediate birds have left.[18] The methods employed in the mental hospital and portions of the library study when the invader shifted his position if the victim moved, maintained the *arrival distance* and did not permit the victim to achieve a comfortable *settled distance*. It is noteworthy that the preponderance of flight reactions occurred under these conditions. There was a dearth of direct verbal responses to the invasions. Only two of the 69 mental patients and one of the 80 students asked the invader to move over. This provides support for Edward Hall's view that "we treat space somewhat as we treat sex. It is there, but we don't talk about it." [19]

Architecture students on the Berkeley campus now undertake behavioral studies as part of their training. One team noted the reactions of students on outdoor benches when an experimenter joined them on the same bench. The occupant shifted position more frequently in a specified time-frame and left the bench earlier than control subjects who were alone. A second team was interested in individual distance on ten-foot benches.

---

[18] J. H. Crook, "The Basis of Flock Organization in Birds," in *Current Problems in Animal Behavior*, eds. W. H. Thorpe and O. L. Zangwill (London: Cambridge University Press, 1961).

[19] Edward T. Hall, *The Silent Language* (Garden City, New York: Doubleday & Company, Inc., 1959).

When the experimenter seated himself one foot from the end of the bench, three-quarters of the next occupants sat six to eight feet away, and almost half placed books or coats as barriers between themselves and the experimenter. Another two students studied eyeblink and shifts in body position as related to whether a stranger sat facing someone or sat facing away. Observations were made by a second experimenter using binoculars from a distance. A male stranger directly facing a female markedly increased her eyeblink rate as well as body movements but had no discernible effect on male subjects.[20]

The different ways in which victims react to invasions may also be due to variations in the perception of the expected distance or in the ability to concentrate. It has been demonstrated that the individual distance between birds is reduced when one bird's attention is riveted to some activity.[21] The invasions can also be looked at as nonverbal communication with the victims receiving messages ranging from "This girl considers me a nonperson" to "This girl is making a sexual advance." The fact that regressed and "burnt out" patients can be moved from their places by sheer propinquity is of theoretical and practical importance. In view of the difficulty that nurses and others have in obtaining any response at all from these patients, it is noteworthy that an emotion sufficient to generate flight can be produced simply by sitting alongside them. More recently we have been experimenting with visual invasions, or attempts to dislodge someone from his place by staring directly at him. In the library at least, the evil eye seems less effective than a spatial invasion since the victims are able to lose themselves in their books. If they could not escape eye contact so easily, this method might be more effective. Mrs. Russo was sensitive to her own feelings during these sessions and described how she "lost her cool" when a victim looked directly toward her. Eye contact produced a sudden realization that "this is a human being," which subsided when the victim turned away. Civil rights demonstrators attempt to preserve their human dignity by maintaining eye contact with their adversaries.

There are other sorts of invasions—auditory assaults in which strangers press personal narratives on hapless seatmates on airplanes and buses, and olfactory invasions long celebrated in television commercials. Another interesting situation is the two-person invasion. On the basis of animal work, particularly on chickens crowded in coops, it was discovered that when a subordinate encounters a dominant at very close quarters where flight is difficult or impossible, the subordinate is likely to freeze in his tracks until the dominant departs or at least looks away. Two faculty members sitting on

[20] These were term projects in Architecture 140 taught by Professor Richard Seaton. They are available on microfilm from the Dept. of Architecture, University of California, Berkeley 94704.

[21] Crook, *op. cit.*

either side of a student or two physicians on either side of a patient's bed would probably produce this type of freezing. The victim would be unlikely to move until he had some sign that the dominants had their attention elsewhere.

The library studies made clear that an important consideration in defining a spatial invasion is whether the parties involved perceive one another as persons. A nonperson cannot invade someone's personal space any more than a tree or chair can. It is common under certain conditions for one person to react to another as an object or part of the background. Examples would be the hospital nurses who discuss a patient's condition at his bedside, seemingly oblivious to his presence, the Negro maid in the white home who serves dinner while the husband and wife discuss the race question, and the janitor who enters an office without knocking to empty the wastebaskets while the occupant is making an important phone call. Many subway riders who have adjusted to crowding through psychological withdrawal prefer to treat other riders as nonpersons and keenly resent situations, such as a stop so abrupt that the person alongside pushes into them *and then apologizes,* when the other rider becomes a person. There are also riders who dislike the lonely alienated condition of subway travel and look forward to emergency situations in which people become real. When a lost child is looking for his mother, a person has been hurt, or a car is stalled down the tracks, strangers are allowed to talk to one another.

It is paradoxical but perhaps not illogical that the best way to study invasions of privacy is to stage them deliberately.

Introduction to Milgram Article

Obedience—we see it in the child obeying the dictates of his parents; in the willingness of the student to do the biddings of his teacher; in the actions of the athlete carrying out his coach's instructions. We also see obedience carried to its perverse extreme in reviewing the Nazi atrocities committed during World War II. It took the terrible shock of the concentration camps to awaken psychologists to the urgency of studying and understanding the phenomenon of obedience.

In 1963 Stanley Milgram, then at Yale University, performed one of the most controversial and important experiments in the study of obedience (Milgram, 1963; Baumrind, 1964; Milgram, 1964). The findings of the investigation, reported below, should cause us all to pause and think hard about human nature in general and man's ability to obediently carry out atrocities in particular. It is doubtful that any of us can find much solace or pride in the Milgram findings.*

REFERENCES

Baumrind, D. Some thoughts on ethics of research: After reading Milgram's "Behavioral study of obedience." *American Psychologist,* 1964, **19,** 421–423.

Milgram, S. Behavioral study of obedience. *Journal of Abnormal and Social Psychology,* 1963, **67,** 371–378.

Milgram, S. Group pressure and action against a person. *Journal of Abnormal and Social Psychology,* 1964, **69,** 137–143.

Milgram, S. Issues in the study of obedience: A reply to Baumrind. *American Psychologist,* 1964, **19,** 848–852.

Milgram, S. Liberating effects of group pressure. *Journal of Personality and Social Psychology,* 1965, **1,** 127–134.

* The Milgram work has been effectively portrayed in the film "Obedience," available from the New York University film library. More recent research on obedience is also available (Milgram, 1964, 1965).

22

Behavioral Study of Obedience

Stanley Milgram

This article describes a procedure for the study of destructive obedience in the laboratory. It consists of ordering a naive S to administer increasingly more severe punishment to a victim in the context of a learning experiment. Punishment is administered by means of a shock generator with 30 graded switches ranging from Slight Shock to Danger: Severe Shock. The victim is a confederate of the E. The primary dependent variable is the maximum shock the S is willing to administer before he refuses to continue further. 26 Ss obeyed the experimental commands fully, and administered the highest shock on the generator. 14 Ss broke off the experiment at some point after the victim protested and refused to provide further answers. The procedure created extreme levels of nervous tension in some Ss. Profuse sweating, trembling, and stuttering were typical expressions of this emotional disturbance. One unexpected sign of tension—yet to be explained—was the regular occurrence of nervous laughter, which in some Ss developed into uncontrollable seizures. The variety of interesting behavioral dynamics observed in the experiment, the reality of the situation for the S, and the possibility of parametric variation within the framework of the procedure, point to the fruitfulness of further study.

Obedience is as basic an element in the structure of social life as one can point to. Some system of authority is a requirement of all communal living, and it is only the man dwelling in isolation who is not forced to respond, through defiance or submission, to the commands of others. Obedi-

SOURCE. *Journal of Abnormal and Social Psychology,* 1963, **67,** 371–378. Copyright 1963 by the American Psychological Association, and reproduced by permission. This research was supported by a grant (NSF G-17916) from the National Science Foundation. Exploratory studies conducted in 1960 were supported by a grant from the Higgins Fund at Yale University. The research assistance of Alan C. Elms and Jon Wayland is gratefully acknowledged.

ence, as a determinant of behavior, is of particular relevance to our time. It has been reliably established that from 1933–45 millions of innocent persons were systematically slaughtered on command. Gas chambers were built, death camps were guarded, daily quotas of corpses were produced with the same efficiency as the manufacture of appliances. These inhumane policies may have originated in the mind of a single person, but they could only be carried out on a massive scale if a very large number of persons obeyed orders.

Obedience is the psychological mechanism that links individual action to political purpose. It is the dispositional cement that binds men to systems of authority. Facts of recent history and observation in daily life suggest that for many persons obedience may be a deeply ingrained behavior tendency, indeed, a prepotent impulse overriding training in ethics, sympathy, and moral conduct. C. P. Snow (1961) points to its importance when he writes:

> When you think of the long and gloomy history of man, you will find more hideous crimes have been committed in the name of obedience than have ever been committed in the name of rebellion. If you doubt that, read William Shirer's "Rise and Fall of the Third Reich." The German Officer Corps were brought up in the most rigorous code of obedience . . . in the name of obedience they were party to, and assisted in, the most wicked large scale actions in the history of the world [p. 24].

While the particular form of obedience dealt with in the present study has its antecedents in these episodes, it must not be thought all obedience entails acts of aggression against others. Obedience serves numerous productive functions. Indeed, the very life of society is predicated on its existence. Obedience may be ennobling and educative and refer to acts of charity and kindness, as well as to destruction.

General Procedure

A procedure was devised which seems useful as a tool for studying obedience (Milgram, 1961). It consists of ordering a naive subject to administer electric shock to a victim. A simulated shock generator is used, with 30 clearly marked voltage levels that range from 15 to 450 volts. The instrument bears verbal designations that range from Slight Shock to Danger: Severe Shock. The responses of the victim, who is a trained confederate of the experimenter, are standardized. The orders to administer shocks are given to the naive subject in the context of a "learning experiment" ostensibly set up to study the effects of punishment on memory. As the experiment proceeds the naive subject is commanded to administer increasingly more intense shocks to the victim, even to the point of reaching the level marked Danger: Severe Shock. Internal resistances become stronger, and at a certain point the subject refuses to go on with the experiment. Behavior prior to this rupture is considered "obedience," in that the subject complies with the commands of the experimenter. The point of rupture is the act of disobedience. A quantitative value is assigned to the subject's performance based on the maximum intensity shock he is willing to administer before he refuses to participate further. Thus for any particular subject and for any particular experimental condition the degree of obedience may be specified with a numerical value. The crux of the study is to systematically vary the factors believed to alter the degree of obedience to the experimental commands.

The technique allows important variables to be manipulated at several points in the experiment. One may vary aspects of the source of command, content and form of command, instrumentalities for its execution, target object, general social setting, etc. The problem, therefore, is not one of designing increasingly more numerous experimental conditions, but of selecting those that best illuminate the *process* of obedience from the sociopsychological standpoint.

Related Studies

The inquiry bears an important relation to philosophic analyses of obedience and authority (Arendt, 1958; Friedrich, 1958; Weber, 1947), an early experimental study of obedience by Frank (1944), studies in "authoritarianism" (Adorno, Frankel-Brunswik, Levinson, & Sanford, 1950; Rokeach, 1961), and a recent series of analytic and empirical studies in social power (Cartwright, 1959). It owes much to the long concern with *suggestion in social psychology*, both in its normal forms (e.g., Binet, 1900) and in its clinical manifestations (Charcot, 1881). But it derives, in the first instance, from direct observation of a social fact; the individual who is commanded by a legitimate authority ordinarily obeys. Obedience comes easily and often. It is a ubiquitous and indispensable feature of social life.

METHOD

Subjects

The subjects were 40 males between the ages of 20 and 50, drawn from New Haven and the surrounding communities. Subjects were obtained by a newspaper advertisement and direct mail solicitation. Those who responded to the appeal believed they were to participate in a study of memory and learning at Yale University. A wide range of occupations is represented in the sample. Typical subjects were postal clerks, high school teachers, salesmen, engineers, and laborers. Subjects ranged in educational level from one who had not finished elementary school, to those who had doctorate

TABLE 1

Distribution of Age and Occupational Types in the Experiment

Occupations	20–29 Years n	30–39 Years n	40–50 Years n	Percentage of Total (Occupa-tions)
Workers, skilled and unskilled	4	5	6	37.5
Sales, business, and white-collar	3	6	7	40.0
Professional	1	5	3	22.5
Percentage of total (Age)	20	40	40	

Note: Total $N = 40$.

and other professional degrees. They were paid $4.50 for their participation in the experiment. However, subjects were told that payment was simply for coming to the laboratory, and that the money was theirs no matter what happened after they arrived. Table 1 shows the proportion of age and occupational types assigned to the experimental condition.

Personnel and Locale

The experiment was conducted on the grounds of Yale University in the elegant interaction laboratory. (This detail is relevant to the perceived legitimacy of the experiment. In further variations, the experiment was dissociated from the university, with consequences for performance.) The role of experimenter was played by a 31-year-old high school teacher of biology. His manner was impassive, and his appearance somewhat stern throughout the experiment. He was dressed in a gray technician's coat. The victim was played by a 47-year-old accountant, trained for the role; he was of Irish-American stock, whom most observers found mild-mannered and likeable.

Procedure

One naive subject and one victim (an accomplice) performed in each experiment. A pretext had to be devised that would justify the administration of electric shock by the naive subject. This was effectively accomplished by the cover story. After a general introduction on the presumed relation between punishment and learning, subjects were told:

> But actually, we know *very little* about the effect of punishment on learning, because almost no truly scientific studies have been made of it in human beings.

For instance, we don't know how *much* punishment is best for learning—and we don't know how much difference it makes as to who is giving the punishment, whether an adult learns best from a younger or an older person than himself—or many things of that sort.

So in this study we are bringing together a number of adults of different occupations and ages. And we're asking some of them to be teachers and some of them to be learners.

We want to find out just what effect different people have on each other as teachers and learners, and also what effect *punishment* will have on learning in this situation.

Therefore, I'm going to ask one of you to be the teacher here tonight and the other one to be the learner.

Does either of you have a preference?

Subjects then drew slips of paper from a hat to determine who would be the teacher and who would be the learner in the experiment. The drawing was rigged so that the naive subject was always the teacher and the accomplice always the learner. (Both slips contained the word "Teacher.") Immediately after the drawing, the teacher and learner were taken to an adjacent room and the learner was strapped into an "electric chair" apparatus.

The experimenter explained that the straps were to prevent excessive movement while the learner was being shocked. The effect was to make it impossible for him to escape from the situation. An electrode was attached to the learner's wrist, and electrode paste was applied "to avoid blisters and burns." Subjects were told that the electrode was attached to the shock generator in the adjoining room.

In order to improve credibility the experimenter declared, in response to a question by the learner: "Although the shocks can be extremely painful, they cause no permanent tissue damage."

Learning Task

The lesson administered by the subject was a paired-associate learning task. The subject read a series of word pairs to the learner, and then read the first word of the pair along with four terms. The learner was to indicate which of the four terms had originally been paired with the first word. He communicated his answer by pressing one of four switches in front of him, which in turn lit up one of four numbered quadrants in an answer-box located atop the shock generator.

Shock Generator

The instrument panel consists of 30 lever switches set in a horizontal line. Each switch is clearly labeled with a voltage designation that ranges from 15 to 450 volts. There is a 15-volt increment from one switch to the next going from left to right. In addition, the following verbal designations are clearly indicated for groups of four switches going from left to right: Slight Shock, Moderate Shock, Strong Shock, Very Strong Shock, Intense Shock, Extreme Intensity Shock, Danger: Severe Shock. (Two switches after this last designation are simply marked XXX.)

Upon depressing a switch: a pilot light corresponding to each switch is illuminated in bright red; an electric buzzing is heard; an electric blue light, labeled "voltage energizer," flashes; the dial on the voltage meter swings to the right; various relay clicks are sounded.

The upper left-hand corner of the generator is labeled Shock Generator, Type ZLB, Dyson Instrument Company, Waltham, Mass. Output 15 Volts–450 Volts.

Details of the instrument were carefully handled to insure an appearance of authenticity. The panel was engraved by precision industrial engravers, and all components were of high quality. No subject in the experiment suspected that the instrument was merely a simulated shock generator.[1]

Sample Shock

Each naive subject is given a sample shock on the shock generator, prior to beginning his run as teacher. This shock is always 45 volts, and is applied by pressing the third switch of the generator. The shock is applied to the wrist of the naive subject, and has its source in a 45-volt battery wired into the generator. This further convinces the subject of the authenticity of the generator.

Shock Instructions

The subject is told to administer a shock to the learner each time he gives a wrong response. Moreover—and this is the key command—the subject is instructed to "move one level higher on the shock generator each time the learner flashes a wrong answer." He is also instructed to announce the voltage level before administering a shock. This serves to continually remind subjects of the increasing intensity of shocks administered to the learner.

[1] A related technique, making use of a shock generator, was reported by Buss (1961) for the study of aggression in the laboratory. Despite the considerable similarity of technical detail in the experimental procedures, both investigators proceeded in ignorance of the other's work. Milgram provided plans and photographs of his shock generator, experimental procedure, and first results in a report to the National Science Foundation in January 1961. This report received only limited circulation. Buss reported his procedure 6 months later, but to a wider audience. Subsequently, technical information and reports were exchanged. The present article was first received in the Editor's office on December 27, 1961; it was resubmitted with deletions on July 27, 1962.

Preliminary and Regular Run

Pretests revealed that the procedure of reading words and administering shocks requires some practice before it can be handled smoothly. Therefore, immediately preceding the regular run, the teacher is given a preliminary series of 10 words to read to the learner. There are 3 neutral words in the practice series (i.e., words that the learner answers correctly), so that shocks are administered for 7 of the words, with the maximum shock at 105 volts (moderate shock). Almost all subjects master the procedure by the time the preliminary run is over.

Subjects are then presented with a second list, and are told that the procedure is the same as for the first list; the experimenter adds, however:

> When you get to the bottom of the list, repeat it over again, and continue giving shocks, until the learner has learned all the pairs correctly.

The experimenter instructs the subject to,

> start from 15 volts and increase the shock level one step each time the learner gives a wrong answer.

Feedback from the Victim

In all conditions the learner gives a predetermined set of responses to the word pair test, based on a schedule of approximately three wrong answers to one correct answer. In the present experimental condition no vocal response or other sign of protest is heard from the learner until Shock Level 300 is reached. When the 300-volt shock is administered, the learner pounds on the wall of the room in which he is bound to the electric chair. The pounding can be heard by the subject. From this point on, the learner's answers no longer appear on the four-way panel.

At this juncture, subjects ordinarily turn to the experimenter for guidance. The experimenter instructs the subject to treat the absence of a response as a wrong answer, and to shock the subject according to the usual schedule. He advises the subjects to allow 5–10 seconds before considering no response as a wrong answer, and to increase the shock level one step each time the learner fails to respond correctly. The learner's pounding is repeated after the 315-volt shock is administered; afterwards he is not heard from, nor do his answers reappear on the four-way signal box.

Experimenter Feedback

At various points in the experiment the subject may turn to the experimenter for advice on whether he should continue to administer shocks.

Or he may indicate that he does not wish to go on. It was important to standardize the experimenter's responses to these inquiries and reactions.

If the subject indicated his unwillingness to go on, the experimenter responded with a sequence of "prods," using as many as necessary to bring the subject into line.

Prod 1: Please contine. *or* Please go on.
Prod 2: The experiment requires that you continue.
Prod 3: It is absolutely essential that you continue.
Prod 4: You have no other choice, you *must* go on.

The prods were always made in sequence: Only if Prod 1 had been unsuccessful, could Prod 2 be used. If the subject refused to obey the experimenter after Prod 4, the experiment was terminated. The experimenter's tone of voice was at all times firm, but not impolite. The sequence was begun anew on each occasion that the subject balked or showed reluctance to follow orders.

Special prods. If the subject asked if the learner was liable to suffer permanent physical injury, the experimenter said:

Although the shocks may be painful, there is no permanent tissue damage, so please go on. [Followed by Prods 2, 3, and 4 if necessary.]

If the subject said that the learner did not want to go on, the experimenter replied:

Whether the learner likes it or not, you must go on until he has learned all the word pairs correctly. So please go on. [Followed by Prods 2, 3, and 4 if necessary.]

Dependent Measures

The primary dependent measure for any subject is the maximum shock he administers before he refuses to go any further. In principle this may vary from 0 (for a subject who refuses to administer even the first shock) to 30 (for a subject who administers the highest shock on the generator). A subject who breaks off the experiment at any point prior to administering the thirtieth shock level is termed a *defiant* subject. One who complies with experimental commands fully, and proceeds to administer all shock levels commanded, is termed an *obedient* subject.

Further Records

With few exceptions, experimental sessions were recorded on magnetic tape. Occasional photographs were taken through one-way mirrors. Notes were kept on any unusual behavior occurring during the course of the experiments. On occasion, additional observers were directed to write objective descriptions of the subjects' behavior. The latency and duration of shocks were measured by accurate timing devices.

Interview and Dehoax

Following the experiment, subjects were interviewed; open-ended questions, projective measures, and attitude scales were employed. After the interview, procedures were undertaken to assure that the subject would leave the laboratory in a state of well being. A friendly reconciliation was arranged between the subject and the victim, and an effort was made to reduce any tensions that arose as a result of the experiment.

RESULTS

Preliminary Notions

Before giving an account of the experimental results, it is instructive to consider how persons predict others will perform when commanded to administer powerful shocks to another person. Fourteen Yale seniors, all psychology majors, were provided with a detailed description of the experimental situation. They were asked to reflect carefully on it, and to predict the behavior of 100 hypothetical subjects. More specifically, they were instructed to plot the distribution of obedience of "100 Americans of diverse occupations, and ranging in age from 20 to 50 years," who were placed in the experimental situation.

There was considerable agreement among the respondents on the expected behavior of hypothetical subjects. All respondents predicted that only an insignificant minority would go through to the end of the shock series. (The estimates ranged from 0 to 3%; i.e., the most "pessimistic" member of the class predicted that of 100 persons, 3 would continue through to the most potent shock available on the shock generator—450 volts.) The class mean was 1.2%. The question was also posed informally to colleagues of the author, and the most general feeling was that few if any subjects would go beyond the designation of Very Strong Shock.

Result of Experiment I

Subjects Accept Situation

With few exceptions subjects were convinced of the reality of the experimental situation, that they were administering shocks to another person, and the most potent shocks were extremely painful. In the post-experimental interview subjects were asked: "How painful to the learner were the last few shocks that you administered to him?" Subjects were instructed to indicate their answers on a printed 14-point scale ranging from "Not at all painful" to "Extremely painful." The modal response was 14 (Extremely painful) with the mean at 13.42.

Signs of Extreme Tension

Many subjects showed signs of nervousness in the experimental situation, and especially upon administering the more powerful shocks. In a large number of cases the degree of tension reached extremes that are rarely seen in sociopsychological laboratory studies. Subjects were observed to sweat, tremble, stutter, bite their lips, groan, and dig their fingernails into their flesh. These were characteristic rather than exceptional responses to the experiment.

One sign of tension was the regular occurrence of nervous laughing fits. Fourteen of the 40 subjects showed definite signs of nervous laughter and smiling. The laughter seemed entirely out of place, even bizarre. Full-blown, uncontrollable seizures were observed for 3 subjects. On one occasion we observed a seizure so violently convulsive that it was necessary to call a halt to the experiment. The subject, a 46-year-old encyclopedia salesman, was seriously embarrassed by his untoward and uncontrollable behavior. In the post-experimental interviews subjects took pains to point out that they were not sadistic types, and that the laughter did not mean they enjoyed shocking the victim.

Distribution of Scores

It had been conjectured that persons would not, in general, agree to administer shocks beyond the level designated as Very Strong Shock. The distribution of maximum shocks for this experiment is shown in Table 2. The obtained distribution of scores deviates radically from the prediction.

Upon command of the experimenter, each of the 40 subjects went beyond the expected breakoff point. No subject stopped prior to administering Shock Level 20. (At this level—300 volts—the victim kicks on the wall and no longer provides answers to the teacher's multiple-choice questions.)

Of the 40 subjects, 5 refused to obey the experimental commands beyond the 300-volt level. Four more subjects administered one further shock, and then refused to go on. Two broke off at the 330-volt level, and 1 each at 345, 360, and 375 volts. Thus a total of 14 subjects defied the experimenter. It is instructive to reprint their remarks at the point of defiance, as transcribed from the tape recordings:

TABLE 2
Distribution of Breakoff Points

Verbal Designation and Voltage Indication	Number of Subjects for Whom this Was Maximum Shock	Verbal Designation and Voltage Indication	Number of Subjects for Whom this Was Maximum Shock
Slight shock		Intense shock	
15	0	255	0
30	0	270	0
45	0	285	0
60	0	300	5
Moderate shock		Extreme intensity shock	
75	0	315	4
90	0	330	2
105	0	345	1
120	0	360	1
Strong shock		Danger: severe shock	
135	0	375	1
150	0	390	0
165	0	405	0
180	0	420	0
Very strong shock		XXX	
195	0	435	0
210	0	450	26
225	0		
240	0		

[0124] I think he's trying to communicate, he's knocking. . . . Well it's not fair to shock the guy . . . these are terrific volts. I don't think this is very humane. . . . Oh, I can't go on with this; no, this isn't right. It's a hell of an experiment. The guy is suffering in there. No, I don't want to go on. This is crazy. [Subject refused to administer more shocks.]

[0123] He's banging in there. I'm gonna chicken out. I'd like to continue, but I can't do that to a man. . . . I'm sorry I can't do that to a man. I'll hurt his heart. You take your check. . . . No really, I couldn't do it.

These subjects were frequently in a highly agitated and even angered state. Sometimes, verbal protest was at a minimum, and the subject simply got up from his chair in front of the shock generator, and indicated that he wished to leave the laboratory.

Of the 40 subjects, 26 obeyed the orders of the experimenter to the end, proceeding to punish the victim until they reached the most potent shock available on the shock generator. At that point, the experimenter called a halt to the session. (The maximum shock is labeled 450 volts, and is two steps beyond the designation: Danger: Severe Shock.) Although obedient subjects continued to administer shocks, they often did so under extreme stress. Some expressed reluctance to administer shocks beyond the 300-volt level, and displayed fears similar to those who defied the experimenter; yet they obeyed.

After the maximum shocks had been delivered, and the experimenter called a halt to the proceedings, many obedient subjects heaved sighs of relief, mopped their brows, rubbed their fingers over their eyes, or nervously fumbled cigarettes. Some shook their heads, apparently in regret. Some subjects had remained calm throughout the experiment, and displayed only minimal signs of tension from beginning to end.

DISCUSSION

The experiment yielded two findings that were surprising. The first finding concerns the sheer strength of obedient tendencies manifested in this situation. Subjects have learned from childhood that it is a fundamental breach of moral conduct to hurt another person against his will. Yet, 26 subjects abandon this tenet in following the instructions of an authority who has no special powers to enforce his commands. To disobey would bring no material loss to the subject; no punishment would ensue. It is clear from the remarks and outward behavior of many participants that in punishing the victim they are often acting against their own values. Subjects often expressed deep disapproval of shocking a man in the face of his objections, and others denounced it as stupid and senseless. Yet the majority complied with the experimental commands. This outcome was surprising from two perspectives: first, from the standpoint of predictions made in the questionnaire described earlier. (Here, however, it is possible that the remoteness of the respondents from the actual situation, and the difficulty of conveying to them the concrete details of the experiment, could account for the serious underestimation of obedience.)

But the results were also unexpected to persons who observed the experiment in progress, through one-way mirrors. Observers often uttered expressions of disbelief upon seeing a subject administer more powerful shocks to the victim. These persons had a full acquaintance with the details of the situation, and yet systematically underestimated the amount of obedience that subjects would display.

The second unanticipated effect was the extraordinary tension generated by the procedures. One might suppose that a subject would simply break off or continue as his conscience dictated. Yet, this is very far from what happened. There were striking reactions of tension and emotional strain. One observer related:

I observed a mature and initially poised businessman enter the laboratory smiling and confident. Within 20 minutes he was reduced to a twitching, stuttering wreck, who was rapidly approaching a point of nervous collapse. He constantly pulled on his earlobe, and twisted his hands. At one point he pushed his fist into his forehead and muttered: "Oh God, let's stop it." And yet he continued to respond to every word of the experimenter, and obeyed to the end.

Any understanding of the phenomenon of obedience must rest on an analysis of the particular conditions in which it occurs. The following features of the experiment go some distance in explaining the high amount of obedience observed in the situation.

1. The experiment is sponsored by and takes place on the grounds of an institution of unimpeachable reputation, Yale University. It may be reasonably presumed that the personnel are competent and reputable. The importance of this background authority is now being studied by conducting a series of experiments outside of New Haven, and without any visible ties to the university.

2. The experiment is, on the face of it, designed to attain a worthy purpose—advancement of knowledge about learning and memory. Obedience occurs not as an end in itself, but as an instrumental element in a situation that the subject construes as significant, and meaningful. He may not be able to see its full significance, but he may properly assume that the experimenter does.

3. The subject perceives that the victim has voluntarily submitted to the authority system of the experimenter. He is not (at first) an unwilling captive impressed for involuntary service. He has taken the trouble to come to the laboratory presumably to aid the experimental research. That he later becomes an involuntary subject does not alter the fact that, initially, he consented to participate without qualification. Thus he has in some degree incurred an obligation toward the experimenter.

4. The subject, too, has entered the experiment voluntarily, and perceives himself under obligation to aid the experimenter. He has made a commitment, and to disrupt the experiment is a repudiation of this initial promise of aid.

5. Certain features of the procedure strengthen the subject's sense of obligation to the experimenter. For one, he has been paid for coming to the laboratory. In part this is canceled out by the experimenter's statement that:

Of course, as in all experiments, the money is yours simply for coming to the laboratory. From this point on, no matter what happens, the money is yours.[2]

[2] Forty-three subjects, undergraduates at Yale University, were run in the experiment without payment. The results are very similar to those obtained with paid subjects.

6. From the subject's standpoint, the fact that he is the teacher and the other man the learner is purely a chance of consequence (it is determined by drawing lots) and he, the subject, ran the same risk as the other man in being assigned the role of learner. Since the assignment of positions in the experiment was achieved by fair means, the learner is deprived of any basis of complaint on this count. (A similar situation obtains in Army units, in which—in the absence of volunteers—a particularly dangerous mission may be assigned by drawing lots, and the unlucky soldier is expected to bear his misfortune with sportsmanship.)

7. There is, at best, ambiguity with regard to the prerogatives of a psychologist and the corresponding rights of his subject. There is a vagueness of expectation concerning what a psychologist may require of his subject, and when he is overstepping acceptable limits. Moreover, the experiment occurs in a closed setting, and thus provides no opportunity for the subject to remove these ambiguities by discussion with others. There are few standards that seem directly applicable to the situation, which is a novel one for most subjects.

8. The subjects are assured that the shocks administered to the subject are "painful but not dangerous." Thus they assume that the discomfort caused the victim is momentary, while the scientific gains resulting from the experiment are enduring.

9. Through Shock Level 20 the victim continues to provide answers on the signal box. The subject may construe this as a sign that the victim is still willing to "play the game." It is only after Shock Level 20 that the victim repudiates the rules completely, refusing to answer further.

These features help to explain the high amount of obedience obtained in this experiment. Many of the arguments raised need not remain matters of speculation, but can be reduced to testable propositions to be confirmed or disproved by further experiments.[3]

The following features of the experiment concern the nature of the conflict which the subject faces.

10. The subject is placed in a position in which he must respond to the competing demands of two persons: the experimenter and the victim. The conflict must be resolved by meeting the demands of one or the other; satisfaction of the victim and the experimenter are mutually exclusive. Moreover, the resolution must take the form of a highly visible action, that of continuing to shock the victim or breaking off the experiment. Thus the subject is forced into a public conflict that does not permit any completely satisfactory solution.

11. While the demands of the experimenter carry the weight of scientific authority, the demands of the victim spring from his personal experi-

---

[3] A series of recently completed experiments employing the obedience paradigm is reported in Milgram (1964).

ence of pain and suffering. The two claims need not be regarded as equally pressing and legitimate. The experimenter seeks an abstract scientific datum; the victim cries out for relief from physical suffering caused by the subject's actions.

12. The experiment gives the subject little time for reflection. The conflict comes on rapidly. It is only minutes after the subject has been seated before the shock generator that the victim begins his protests. Moreover, the subject perceives that he has gone through but two-thirds of the shock levels at the time the subject's first protests are heard. Thus he understands that the conflict will have a persistent aspect to it, and may well become more intense as increasingly more powerful shocks are required. The rapidity with which the conflict descends on the subject, and his realization that it is predictably recurrent may well be sources of tension to him.

13. At a more general level, the conflict stems from the opposition of two deeply ingrained behavior dispositions: first, the disposition not to harm other people, and second, the tendency to obey those whom we perceive to be legitimate authorities.

REFERENCES

Adorno, T., Frenkel-Brunswik, Else, Levinson, D. J., & Sanford, R. N. *The authoritarian personality.* New York: Harper, 1950.

Arendt, H. What was authority? In C. J. Friedrich (Ed.), *Authority.* Cambridge: Harvard Univer. Press, 1958, Pp. 81–112.

Binet, A. *La suggestibilité.* Paris: Schleicher, 1900.

Buss, A. H. *The psychology of aggression.* New York: Wiley, 1961.

Cartwright, S. (Ed.) *Studies in social power.* Ann Arbor: University of Michigan Institute for Social Research, 1959.

Charcot, J. M. *Oeuvres complètes.* Paris: Bureaux du Progrès Médical, 1881.

Frank, J. D. Experimental studies of personal pressure and resistance. *J. gen. Psychol.,* 1944, 30, 23–64.

Friedrich, C. J. (Ed.) *Authority.* Cambridge: Harvard Univer. Press, 1958.

Milgram, S. Dynamics of obedience. Washington: National Science Foundation, 25 January 1961. (Mimeo)

Milgram, S. Some conditions of obedience and disobedience to authority. *Hum., Relat.,* 1964, in press.

Rokeach, M. Authority, authoritarianism, and conformity. In I. A. Berg & B. M. Bass (Eds.), *Conformity and deviation.* New York: Harper, 1961. Pp. 230–257.

Snow, C. P. Either-or. *Progressive,* 1961 (Feb.), 24.

Weber, M. *The theory of social and economic organization.* Oxford: Oxford Univer. Press, 1947.

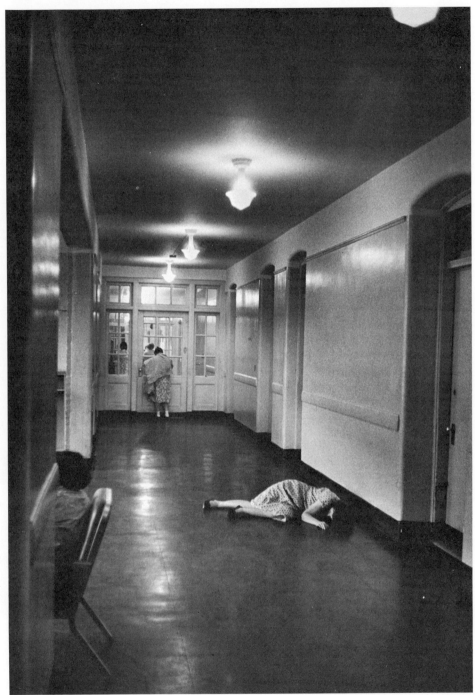

The tragedy of mental illness. Psychologists are working to avert it.
(KEN HEYMAN)

Section VII
Psychopathology

In introductory psychology one topic consistently holds the most fascina-tion for the majority of undergraduates: psychopathology or, as George Kisker (1964) calls it, the "disorganized personality." What causes this stu-dent interest in the examination of mental aberrations is open to specula-tion—possibly it is the Freudian mystique or the desire to understand a condition that seems so prevalent in contemporary society. Maybe it is even the wish by each student to diagnose his own mental condition by psycho-logical standards.

The undergraduate is not alone in his fascination with psychopathology. Clinical psychology—the branch of our discipline that deals with mental disorders—has one of the largest memberships in the American Psychological Association and, year after year, the competition for admission into graduate school clinical programs is the fiercest for any area of psychology.

What exactly is the role of the clinical psychologist with regard to psychopathology? Basically, he is devoted to the establishment and main-tenance of sound mental health in the community; promoting the ". . . wel-fare of the individual human being through diagnostic assessment, psycho-therapy, consultation or research. Clinical psychologists carry on some or all of these functions in federal, state, or private hospitals, community clinics, social agencies, industry, military and in private practice. (Singer, 1968)"

The student is probably most familiar with the clinical psychologist in his therapeutic role. What the student might not realize is that there are many forms of therapy utilized in working with patients—with some thera-pists combining two or three different types with one patient.

Probably the most well known (certainly the most publicized) type of therapy is psychoanalysis, the method of treating mental disorders developed by Freud. Yet, psychoanalysis is no longer the most widely practiced form of therapy—in fact it has recently been reported that fewer than one-half of one percent of Americans seeking professional help for psychological problems are treated by qualified psychoanalysts. Today, other forms of therapy are gaining popular support among clinical psychologists and psychiatrists—particularly the "nondirective" and "behavior modification" approaches.

The contemporary clinical psychologist, more than ever before, is expected to know a great deal of information from many scientific disciplines to more effectively diagnose, treat, and cure mental disorders. He is expected to understand the organic basis of various mental aberrations; the role of various therapeutic procedures in treating such aberrations; and the various symptoms that signal (and sometimes identify) psychological problems.

During the past decade we have witnessed great advances in the understanding and control of mental disorders. As our knowledge of the psychological and physiological factors underlying psychopathological conditions increases, we can expect even greater insights in the years to come.

The reading selections for this section begin, appropriately, with an article by the master himself: Sigmund Freud. In this particular paper the greatest of all psychological thinkers explores a possible relationship between two types of behavior familiar to us all—obsessive acts and religious practices. This piece is followed by two articles on the popular new "behavior modification" (or reinforcement) therapy. Both papers are case studies describing the use of behavior modification therapy to treat, in one instance, a compulsive horse-race gambler and, in the other, a college student with sexual problems.

In a third reading selection Dr. Szasz challenges the entire conception of psychopathology with his provocative argument. His thesis that ". . . mental illness is a myth, whose function is to disguise and thus render more palatable the bitter pill of moral conflicts in human relations . . ." will probably find many sympathetic listeners in today's younger generation.

The final article in this section deals with student suicides at the University of California. It is hoped that by studying this tragic problem we shall eventually be in a better position to overcome it.

REFERENCES

Kisker, G. *The disorganized personality*. New York: McGraw-Hill, 1964.

Singer, J. Clinical psychology. In: J. Woodruff (Ed.) Psychology: Training and vocational opportunities. Unpublished manuscript, 1968. (Printed in Section X of this volume.)

Introduction to
Freud Article

No book of introductory psychology readings would be complete without a contribution from Sigmund Freud, one of the truly great intellectual forces of this (or any other) century. No other psychologist has ever left such an impressive legacy of insights into human behavior nor numbered as many benefactors who labor in the shadows of his discoveries.

To describe the breadth and depth of Freud's impact on modern psychology, to indicate how his thinking has shaped the very foundation and form of our discipline—is a truly monumental undertaking. It might be easier to describe what Einstein contributed to modern physics or what biology would be like without Charles Darwin!

Like all great thinkers, Freud's postulates about behavior have been so widely accepted and worked into the very fabric of scientific thought that many people act as if they were "always there"—sort of "scientific givens" without a source. For this reason we sometimes tend to forget that some "obvious universal truths" today were Freudian hypotheses just a half century ago (not so obviously true to the chagrined Victorians of Freud's time!).

It is because Freud was such an innovative thinker in his day that he became so important. By assaulting the rationality of man in an era committed to human reason and by understanding and emphasizing sexual factors in behavior determination at a time when it was highly unpopular to do so, Freud was able to overturn some of the popular misconceptions of his age and bring us to a new understanding of human behavior. It is because Freud's insights continue to be relevant for comprehending man's actions that he remains important today.

In the selection below, Freud examines (with his usual clarity and insight) a possible connection between two types of behavior familiar to all of us: Obsessive acts and religious practices. In his writings Freud had much to say on the topic of religion and most of it was not exactly calculated to endear him to the clergy! Whether Freud's views on religion are correct is still open to speculation and scientific investigation—and the student might want to keep this in mind when reading the material below.*

REFERENCES
Freud, S. Analysis of a phobia in a five-year-old boy (1st ed., 1909). In *The Complete Psychological Works of Sigmund Freud*. Vol. X. London: Hogarth Press, 1962.

Hall, C. *A primer of Freudian psychology*. New York: New American Library, 1954.

* For the student who wants some additional readings relevant to Freud and his work, a good, brief introduction to Freud is provided by Calvin Hall's paperback *Primer of Freudian Psychology* (1954). An excellent case study in psychoanalysis is Freud's own *Analysis of a Phobia in a Five-Year-Old Boy* (1909).

23

Obsessive Actions and Religious Practices

Sigmund Freud

I am certainly not the first person to have been struck by the resemblance between what are called obsessive actions in sufferers from nervous affections and the observances by means of which believers give expression to their piety. The term "ceremonial," which has been applied to some of these obsessive actions, is evidence of this. The resemblance, however, seems to me to be more than a superficial one, so that an insight into the origin of neurotic ceremonial may embolden us to draw inferences by analogy about the psychological processes of religious life.

People who carry out obsessive actions or ceremonials belong to the same class as those who suffer from obsessive thinking, obsessive ideas, obsessive impulses and the like. Taken together, these form a particular clinical entity, to which the name of "obsessional neurosis" ["*Zwangsneurose*"] it customarily applied.[1] But one should not attempt to deduce the character of the illness from its name; for, strictly speaking, other kinds of morbid mental phenomena have an equal claim to possessing what are spoken of as "obsessional" characteristics. In place of a definition we must for the time being be content with obtaining a detailed knowledge of these states, since we have not yet been able to arrive at a criterion of obsessional neuroses; it probably lies very deep, although we seem to sense its presence everywhere in the manifestations of the illness.

Neurotic ceremonials consist in making small adjustments to particular

SOURCE. Chapter II of Volume II of *The Collected Papers of Sigmund Freud*, edited by Ernest Jones, M.D., Basic Books, Inc., Publishers, New York, 1959.

[1] See Löwenfeld (1904). [According to that author (ibid., 8) the term *"Zwangsvorstellung"* ("obsessional idea" or simply "obsession") was introduced by Krafft-Ebing in 1867. The concept (and the term) "obsessional neurosis" originated (on the same authority, ibid., 296 and 487) from Freud himself. His first published use of it was in his first paper on anxiety neurosis (1895*b*).]

everyday actions, small additions or restrictions or arrangements, which have always to be carried out in the same, or in a methodically varied, manner. These activities give the impression of being mere formalities, and they seem quite meaningless to us. Nor do they appear otherwise to the patient himself; yet he is incapable of giving them up, for any deviation from the ceremonial is visited by intolerable anxiety, which obliges him at once to make his omission good. Just as trivial as the ceremonial actions themselves are the occasions and activities which are embellished, encumbered and in any case prolonged by the ceremonial—for instance, dressing and undressing, going to bed or satisfying bodily needs. The performance of a ceremonial can be described by replacing it, as it were, by a series of unwritten laws. For instance, to take the case of the bed ceremonial: the chair must stand in a particular place beside the bed; the clothes must lie upon it folded in a particular order; the blanket must be tucked in at the bottom and the sheet smoothed out; the pillows must be arranged in such and such a manner, and the subject's own body must lie in a precisely defined position. Only after all this may he go to sleep. Thus in slight cases the ceremonial seems to be no more than an exaggeration of an orderly procedure that is customary and justifiable; but the special conscientiousness with which it is carried out and the anxiety which follows upon its neglect stamp the ceremonial as a "sacred act." Any interruption of it is for the most part badly tolerated, and the presence of other people during its performance is almost always ruled out.

Any activities whatever may become obsessive actions in the wider sense of the term if they are elaborated by small additions or given a rhythmic character by means of pauses and repetitions. We shall not expect to find a sharp distinction between "ceremonials" and "obsessive actions." As a rule obsessive actions have grown out of ceremonials. Besides these two, prohibitions and hindrances (abulias) make up the content of the disorder; these, in fact, only continue the work of the obsessive actions, inasmuch as some things are completely forbidden to the patient and others only allowed subject to his following a prescribed ceremonial.

It is remarkable that both compulsions and prohibitions (having to do something and having *not* to do something) apply in the first instance only to the subject's solitary activities and for a long time leave his social behaviour unaffected. Sufferers from this illness are consequently able to treat their affliction as a private matter and keep it concealed for many years. And, indeed, many more people suffer from these forms of obsessional neurosis than doctors hear of. For many sufferers, too, concealment is made easier from the fact that they are quite well able to fulfil their social duties during a part of the day, once they have devoted a number of hours to their secret doings, hidden from view like Mélusine.[2]

---

2 [A beautiful woman in mediaeval legend, who led a secret existence as a water-nymph.]

It is easy to see where the resemblances lie between neurotic ceremonials and the sacred acts of religious ritual: in the qualms of conscience brought on by their neglect, in their complete isolation from all other actions (shown in the prohibition against interruption) and in the conscientiousness with which they are carried out in every detail. But the differences are equally obvious, and a few of them are so glaring that they make the comparison a sacrilege: the greater individual variability of [neurotic] ceremonial actions in contrast to the stereotyped character of rituals (prayer, turning to the East, etc.), their private nature as opposed to the public and communal character of religious observances, above all, however, the fact that, while the minutiae of religious ceremonial are full of significance and have a symbolic meaning, those of neurotics seem foolish and senseless. In this respect an obsessional neurosis presents a travesty, half comic and half tragic, of a private religion. But it is precisely this sharpest difference between neurotic and religious ceremonial which disappears when, with the help of the psycho-analytic technique of investigation, one penetrates to the true meaning of obsessive actions.[3] In the course of such an investigation the appearance which obsessive actions afford of being foolish and senseless is completely effaced, and the reason for their having that appearance is explained. It is found that the obsessive actions are perfectly significant in every detail, that they serve important interests of the personality and that they give expression to experiences that are still operative and to thoughts that are cathected with affect. They do this in two ways, either by direct or by symbolic representation; and they are consequently to be interpreted either historically or symbolically.

I must give a few examples to illustrate my point. Those who are familiar with the findings of psycho-analytic investigation into the psychoneurosis will not be surprised to learn that what is being represented in obsessive actions or in ceremonials is derived from the most intimate, and for the most part from the sexual, experiences of the patient.

(a) A girl whom I was able to observe was under a compulsion to rinse round her wash-basin several times after washing. The significance of this ceremonial action lay in the proverbial saying: "Don't throw away dirty water till you have clean." Her action was intended to give a warning to her sister, of whom she was very fond, and to restrain her from getting divorced from her unsatisfactory husband until she had established a relationship with a better man.

(b) A woman who was living apart from her husband was subject to a compulsion, whenever she ate anything, to leave what was the best of it behind; for example, she would only take the outside of a piece of roast meat.

[3] See the collection of my shorter papers on the theory of the neuroses published in 1906 [Standard Ed., 3].

This renunciation was explained by the date of its origin. It appeared on the day after she had refused marital relations with her husband—that is to say, after she had given up what was the best.

(*c*) The same patient could only sit on one particular chair and could only get up from it with difficulty. In regard to certain details of her married life, the chair symbolized her husband, to whom she remained faithful. She found an explanation of her compulsion in this sentence: "It is so hard to part from anything (a husband, a chair) upon which one has once settled."

(*d*) Over a period of time she used to repeat an especially noticeable and senseless obsessive action. She would run out of her room into another room in the middle of which there was a table. She would straighten the table-cloth on it in a particular manner and ring for the housemaid. The latter had to come up to the table, and the patient would then dismiss her on some indifferent errand. In the attempts to explain this compulsion, it occurred to her that at one place on the table-cloth there was a stain, and that she always arranged the cloth in such a way that the housemaid was bound to see the stain. The whole scene proved to be a reproduction of an experience in her married life which had later on given her thoughts a problem to solve. On the wedding-night her husband had met with a not unusual mishap. He found himself impotent, and "many times in the course of the night he came hurrying from his room into hers" to try once more whether he could succeed. In the morning he said he would feel ashamed in front of the hotel housemaid who made the beds, and he took a bottle of red ink and poured its contents over the sheet; but he did it so clumsily that the red stain came in a place that was very unsuitable for his purpose. With her obsessive action, therefore, she was representing the wedding-night. "Bed and board" [4] between them make up marriage.

(*e*) Another compulsion which she started—of writing down the number of every bank-note before parting with it—had also to be interpreted historically. At a time when she was still intending to leave her husband if she could find another more trustworthy man, she allowed herself to receive advances from a man whom she met at a watering-place, but she was in doubt as to whether his intentions were serious. One day, being short of small change, she asked him to change a five-kronen [5] piece for her. He did so, pocketed the large coin and declared with a gallant air that he would never part with it, since it had passed through her hands. At their later meetings she was frequently tempted to challenge him to show her the five-kronen piece, as though she wanted to convince herself that she could believe in his intentions. But she refrained, for the good reason that it is impossible to distinguish between coins of the same value. Thus her doubt remained un-

---

[4] [In German *"Tisch und Bett"* ("table and bed"). Cf. a paper on fairy tales in dreams (1913*d*), *Standard Ed.*, **12**, 282, footnote 3.]

[5] [Equivalent at that time to four shillings or a dollar.]

resolved; and it left her with the compulsion to write down the number of each bank-note, by which it *can* be distinguished from all others of the same value.[6]

These few examples, selected from the great number I have met with, are merely intended to illustrate my assertion that in obsessive actions everything has its meaning and can be interpreted. The same is true of ceremonials in the strict sense, only that the evidence for this would require a more circumstantial presentation. I am quite aware of how far our explanations of obsessive actions are apparently taking us from the sphere of religious thought.

It is one of the conditions of the illness that the person who is obeying a compulsion carries it out without understanding its meaning—or at any rate its chief meaning. It is only thanks to the efforts of psycho-analytic treatment that he becomes conscious of the meaning of his obsessive action and, with it, of the motives that are impelling him to it. We express this important fact by saying that the obsessive action serves to express *unconscious* motives and ideas. In this, we seem to find a further departure from religious practices; but we must remember that as a rule the ordinary pious individual, too, performs a ceremonial without concerning himself with its significance, although priests and scientific investigators may be familiar with the—mostly symbolic—meaning of the ritual. In all believers, however, the motives which impel them to religious practices are unknown to them or are represented in consciousness by others which are advanced in their place.

Analysis of obsessive actions has already given us some sort of an insight into their causes and into the chain of motives which bring them into effect. We may say that the sufferer from compulsions and prohibitions behaves as if he were dominated by a sense of guilt, of which, however, he knows nothing, so that we must call it an unconscious sense of guilt, in spite of the apparent contradiction in terms.[7] This sense of guilt has its source in certain early mental events, but it is constantly being revived by renewed temptations which arise whenever there is a contemporary provocation. Moreover, it occasions a lurking sense of expectant anxiety, an expectation of misfortune, which is linked, through the idea of punishment, with the internal perception of the temptation. When the ceremonial is first being constructed, the patient is still conscious that he must do this or that lest some ill should befall, and as a rule the nature of the ill that is to be expected

[6] [Freud discussed this case again at considerable length in Lecture XVII of his *Introductory Lectures* (1916–17).]

[7] [The German word used here for "sense of guilt" is *"Schuldbewusstsein,"* literally "consciousness of guilt." This seems to be the earliest explicit appearance of the "unconscious sense of guilt" which was to play such an important part in Freud's later writings—e.g. at the beginning of the last chapter of *The Ego and the Id* (1923*b*). The way had been prepared for the notion, however, very much earlier, in Section II of the first paper on "The Neuro-Psychoses of Defence" (1894*a*).]

is still known to his consciousness. But what is already hidden from him is the connection—which is always demonstrable—between the occasion on which this expectant anxiety arises and the danger which it conjures up. Thus a ceremonial starts as an *action for defence* or *insurance, a protective measure.*

The sense of guilt of obsessional neurotics finds its counterpart in the protestations of pious people that they know that at heart they are miserable sinners; and the pious observances (such as prayers, invocations, etc.,) with which such people preface every daily act, and in especial every unusual undertaking, seem to have the value of defensive or protective measures.

A deeper insight into the mechanism of obsessional neurosis is gained if we take into account the primary fact which lies at the bottom of it. This is always *the repression of an instinctual impulse* [8] (a component of the sexual instinct) which was present in the subject's constitution and which was allowed to find expression for a while during his childhood but later succumbed to suppression. In the course of the repression of this instinct a special *conscientiousness* is created which is directed against the instinct's aims; but this psychical reaction-formation feels insecure and constantly threatened by the instinct which is lurking in the unconscious. The influence of the repressed instinct is felt as a temptation, and during the process of repression itself anxiety is generated, which gains control over the future in the form of *expectant* anxiety. The process of repression which leads to obsessional neurosis must be considered as one which is only partly successful and which increasingly threatens to fail. It may thus be compared to an unending conflict; fresh psychical efforts are continually required to counterbalance the forward pressure of the instinct.[9] Thus the ceremonial and obsessive actions arise partly as a defence against the temptation and partly as a protection against the ill which is expected. Against the temptation the protective measures seem soon to become inadequate; then the prohibitions come into play, with the purpose of keeping at a distance situations that give rise to temptation. Prohibitions take the place of obsessive actions, it will be seen, just as a phobia is designed to avert a hysterical attack. Again, a ceremonial represents the sum of the conditions subject to which something that is not yet absolutely forbidden is permitted, just as the Church's marriage ceremony signifies for the believer a sanctioning of sexual enjoyment which would otherwise be sinful. A further characteristic of obsessional neurosis, as of all similar affections, is that its manifestations (its symptoms, including the obsessive actions) fulfil the condition of being a compromise between the warring forces of the mind. They thus always reproduce something of the

8 [*"Triebregung."* This appears to be Freud's first published use of what was to be one of his most used terms.]

9 [This passage foreshadows the concept of "anticathexis," which is developed at length in Section IV of the paper on "The Unconscious" (1915e), *Standard Ed.,* **14,** 180 ff.]

pleasure which they are designed to prevent; they serve the repressed instinct no less than the agencies which are repressing it. As the illness progresses, indeed, actions which were originally mostly concerned with maintaining the defence come to approximate more and more to the proscribed actions through which the instinct was able to find expression in childhood.

Some features of this state of affairs may be seen in the sphere of religious life as well. The formation of a religion, too, seems to be based on the suppression, the renunciation, of certain instinctual impulses. These impulses, however, are not, as in the neurosis, exclusively components of the sexual instinct; they are self-seeking, socially harmful instincts, though, even so, they are usually not without a sexual component. A sense of guilt following upon continual temptation and an expectant anxiety in the form of fear of divine punishment have, after all, been familiar to us in the field of religion longer than in that of neurosis. Perhaps because of the admixture of sexual components, perhaps because of some general characteristics of the instincts, the suppression of instinct proves to be an inadequate and interminable process in religious life also. Indeed, complete backslidings into sin are more common among pious people than among neurotics and these give rise to a new form of religious activity, namely acts of penance, which have their counterpart in obsessional neurosis.

We have noted as a curious and derogatory characteristic of obsessional neurosis that its ceremonials are concerned with the small actions of daily life and are expressed in foolish regulations and restrictions in connection with them. We cannot understand this remarkable feature of the clinical picture until we have realized that the mechanism of psychical *displacement,* which was first discovered by me in the construction of dreams,[10] dominates the mental processes of obsessional neurosis. It is already clear from the few examples of obsessive actions given above that their symbolism and the detail of their execution are brought about by a displacement from the actual, important thing on to a small one which takes its place—for instance, from a husband on to a chair.[11] It is this tendency to displacement which progressively changes the clinical picture and eventually succeeds in turning what is apparently the most trivial matter into something of the utmost importance and urgency. It cannot be denied that in the religious field as well there is a similar tendency to a displacement of psychical values, and in the same direction, so that the petty ceremonials of religious practice gradually become the essential thing and push aside the underlying thoughts. That is why religions are subject to reforms which work retroactively and aim at a re-establishment of the original balance of values.

[10] See *The Interpretation of Dreams* (1900a), Chapter VI, Section B [*Standard Ed.,* 4, 305 ff.].

[11] [Freud had already described this mechanism in his book on jokes (1905c), near the end of Section 11 of Chapter II. He often recurred to the point—for instance, in the "Rat Man" analysis (1909d), *Standard Ed.,* 10, 241, and in the metapsychological paper on repression (1915d), ibid., 14, 157.]

The character of compromise which obsessive actions possess in their capacity as neurotic symptoms is the character least easily detected in corresponding religious observances. Yet here, too, one is reminded of this feature of neuroses when one remembers how commonly all the acts which religion forbids—the expressions of the instincts it has suppressed—are committed precisely in the name of, and ostensibly for the sake of, religion.

In view of these similarities and analogies one might venture to regard obsessional neurosis as a pathological counterpart of the formation of a religion, and to describe that neurosis as an individual religiosity and religion as a universal obsessional neurosis. The most essential similarity would reside in the underlying renunciation of the activation of instincts that are constitutionally present; and the chief difference would lie in the nature of those instincts, which in the neurosis are exclusively sexual in their origin, while in religion they spring from egoistic sources.

A progressive renunciation of constitutional instincts, whose activation might afford the ego primary pleasure, appears to be one of the foundations of the development of human civilization.[12] Some part of this instinctual repression is effected by its religions, in that they require the individual to sacrifice his instinctual pleasure to the Deity: "Vengeance is mine, saith the Lord." In the development of the ancient religions one seems to discern that many things which mankind had renounced as "iniquities" had been surrendered to the Deity and were still permitted in his name, so that the handing over to him of bad and socially harmful instincts was the means by which man freed himself from their domination. For this reason, it is surely no accident that all the attributes of man, along with the misdeeds that follow from them, were to an unlimited amount ascribed to the ancient gods. Nor is it a contradiction of this that nevertheless man was not permitted to justify his own iniquities by appealing to divine example.

VIENNA, *February* 1907

[12] [This idea was expanded by Freud in the paper on sexual ethics written about a year later (1908).

Introduction to
Goorney and Davison Articles

There are many types of therapy that a clinical psychologist or psychiatrist may utilize in treating various psychopathological conditions. Psychoanalysis is one form of therapy; the so called "nondirective" or "client-centered" therapy is a second type. One relatively new form of therapy that is becoming increasingly popular for treating a wide range of behavior disorders is "behavior modification" or "reinforcement therapy."

What is reinforcement therapy? It is a scientific procedure for systematically changing behavior through the application of rewards and/or punishments. Defined in such a manner, free of scientific jargon, you might think there is nothing new in such a method and that you have been utilizing it for quite some time! In one way you would be correct: The man who purchases flowers for his wife or spanks his child is practicing a *rudimentary* form of reinforcement therapy ("rudimentary" in comparison to the more sophisticated, effective therapy practiced by professionals). On the other hand, you would be incorrect in assuming that reinforcement therapy is "old hat." The novelty of the approach is the use of psychological learning principles in the clinical setting. Not everybody is familiar with these principles or how to employ them—yet, it is these scientific procedures that determine the ultimate success or failure of the therapy. The psychologist understands these procedures and utilizes them in creating an *effective* reinforcement therapy capable of modifying behavior; the layman, unacquainted with these procedures, cannot expect to do likewise.

Although the major thrust of reinforcement therapy is a product of the last ten years, the impetus for the movement came in the earlier decades of this century. One classic and influential study was performed in 1920 by John Watson, father of psychological behaviorism and advocate of human behavior control. Watson was convinced that such control was feasible and, not one to hide his convictions, once boasted: "Give me a dozen healthy infants, well formed, and my own specified world to bring them up in and I'll guarantee to take any one at random and train him to become any type of specialist I might select—doctor, lawyer, merchant-chief, and yes, even beggar-man and thief, regardless of his talents, penchants, tendencies, abilities, vocations, and race of his ancestors." Unlike many of his contemporaries who speculated on such matters but went no further, Watson set out to substantiate his claims in the laboratory. His proof was gathered at the expense of Albert, a normal, healthy infant. Albert was basically stolid and unemotional. He cried infrequently, did not scare easily and—except when confronted with loud sounds—showed no signs of fear. When, at nine months of age, he was suddenly presented with objects he had never seen before—including a white rat, rabbit, dog, monkey, cotton, and wool—he approached them without apprehension.

At this juncture Watson set out to prove his point: that he could control Albert's behavior at will and, specifically, make him afraid of the white rat he had approached earlier. The animal was reintroduced into Albert's playroom as before but now each time the child reached for the animal, a loud gong was struck nearby. In a very short time Albert would cry and scurry away whenever he saw the rat—even when the gong did *not* sound. Further, the child showed fear of other objects that looked like a rat, e.g., the white rabbit he had earlier approached. By a few pairings of a negative reinforcer (loud sound) with an initially attractive plaything Watson was effectively able to condition little Albert's emotional behavior and make him fear a whole class of objects similar to, and including, a white rat.

Another early experiment, by Paul Fuller in 1949, attempted to use reinforcement therapy to teach a "vegetative human organism" a simple response. As reported in the *American Journal of Psychology,* this investigator worked with an institutionalized 18-year-old patient who could neither walk nor talk. Day after day he lay flat on his back, unable to turn over, unable even to chew his food. According to hospital personnel, the patient had never learned to perform the simplest of tasks. Fuller set out to see if the young man could learn to raise his right arm to receive food. First, the patient was deprived of food for fifteen hours; then, whenever he raised his right arm, he was syringe-fed a sugar-milk solution. After a few sessions the patient was raising his right hand regularly to receive food reward. When the food was taken away, the hand-raising response "extinguished" (i.e., gradually disappeared in the absence of reinforcement).

The Watson and Fuller experiments share one important characteristic: the application of reinforcement to change behavior. Reinforcement therapy works by increasing or decreasing the likelihood of a specified behavioral response through systematic reward and punishment. Little Albert received negative reinforcement, and it is assumed that such punishment should eventually lead to the cessation of the reinforced behavior. In the case of the bed-ridden patient, the reinforcement is positive and it is expected that rewarded behavior will be maintained (often increasing in frequency). The process by which reinforcement becomes associated with certain behaviors is called conditioning. The therapist utilizes his knowledge of conditioning principles to make his efforts more effective.

But enough of explanations. You are probably asking: "So what? So you can use reinforcement to teach an infant or an imbecile a simple trick. What about complex adult behavior? Is reinforcement therapy successful in treating the intricate problems of the mature mind?" The next two reading selections (by A. Goorney and G. Davison) should show that the answer is yes. Dr. Goorney used reinforcement therapy to treat a highly complex adult behavior: compulsive gambling; Dr. Davison utilized the same form of therapy to treat a college student with sexual problems.

In considering the impressive results obtained by Goorney and Davison utilizing reinforcement therapy one is tempted to view it as a panacea—man's new cure-all for the multiple problems created in this technological, rapidly changing world. A word of caution, however: in a field as young as the science of reinforcement therapy research conclusions are open to modification and even disconfirmation as additional information is amassed. Psychologists know little of the long-term effectiveness of reinforcement therapy and under which conditions it can be successfully administered. More time is needed to accurately assess the promise and versatility of reinforcement therapy in changing behavior.*

REFERENCES

Fuller, P. Operant conditioning of a vegetative human organism. *American Journal of Psychology,* 1949, **62,** 587–590.

Watson, J., & Rayner, R. Conditioned emotional reactions. *Journal of Experimental Psychology,* 1920, **3,** 1–14.

* Sections of the preceding discussion were taken from Andrews, L., and Karlins, M. *Requiem for democracy?* (New York: Holt, 1971). Another example of reinforcement therapy is provided in an article by Hamblin, et al. in Section IX of this text.

24

Treatment of a Compulsive Horse Race Gambler by Aversion Therapy

A. B. Goorney

INTRODUCTION

References to compulsive gambling are found in the psychiatric literature as early as 1914 (von Hattingberg) and 1920 (Simmel). These and subsequent literature on the psychodynamics and treatment by analytical methods were summarized by Harris in 1964. In the past year references have been made to the treatment by aversion therapy of isolated cases of horse race gamblers and of a "one-armed bandit" gambler (Barker and Miller, 1966b, Seager *et al.*, 1966, Barker and Miller, 1966a). A further case of a compulsive horse race gambler treated by aversion therapy seems worth presenting, in view of the sparse literature on treatment of the condition by this method, and also because in this case, the therapy was immediately followed by remission of a long-standing marital disharmony which is believed to have been one major precipitating cause of the gambling.

CASE HISTORY

A thirty-seven-year-old man was referred as a result of his wife's complaints of debts incurred by reckless gambling. He gave a thirteen-year history of compulsive gambling restricted to horse racing; this occurred in bouts lasting three to six months, with at least one bout a year. He invariably lost, often heavily, but was unable to stop until either he ran out of money or his wife found out. The gambling had been started off by newspaper publicity of a forthcoming classical race or by receiving ready cash as expense repayments; there was also another factor, for the patient later admitted that

SOURCE. *British Journal of Psychiatry,* 1968, 114, 329–333.

at the time his relationship with his wife was particularly poor. The relationship had, he said, been unsatisfactory from the start of the marriage; he described his wife as "cold, undemonstrative, highly strung," "wearing the pants" and suggested that his gambling "might be an attempt to hurt her— can't stand up to her in any other way." Gambling, confined to horses, had started within a year of his marriage. There was no evidence of other compulsive phenomena, or any psychiatric abnormality.

His father and one brother were heavy gamblers and drinkers (causes unknown). A second brother was a non-gambler and a social drinker. His mother was described as quiet, shy and a cronic invalid. Childhood memories were of an unhappy, impecunious home. He described himself as a "nervous child," timid, puny and shy. After uneventful schooling and several menial jobs he joined the Royal Air Force at 17½, with which career he has remained satisfied. Sexual development and orientation were normal, but experience with females before marriage was limited because of shyness. There are two children of the marriage. He is teetotal, but smokes about thirty cigarettes a day.

Discussion of the gambling habit revealed that:

1. Selections were recorded from the racing page of his daily paper each morning at about 8.45. Buying the paper and making the selections evoked pleasurable emotions.

2. Selection was by a random choice of one of a small number (2–3) of top class jockeys and picking this jockey's mounts for the day.

3. Bets were placed with a bookmaker directly or by telephone.

4. Fantasies of horse selection, betting prices and envisaged profits were frequently imagined during the day, evoking pleasurable emotions.

5. Results were obtained at 4.30 P.M. from the radio news. This was anticipated with pleasure and the results evoked considerable emotion— pleasure if winning—misery if losing.

6. If the races were televised, they were avidly watched and again the results evoked the relative emotions.

7. He only occasionally visited racecourses and disliked being in close proximity to horses.

TREATMENT

Aversion therapy to all the individual components of the habit was by random faradic shocks of 1–2 seconds' duration and unpleasant intensity (35 volts) to the upper arms (right if writing, otherwise varied), from an apparatus based on the design described by McGuire and Vallance (1964). The sessions were conducted daily during the course of five activities:

I. 8.45 A.M. whilst selecting and recording from his newspaper.

II.
III. Between 10 A.M.–3.30 P.M. Three randomly timed sessions to imagina-
IV. tion of selected names, races, odds and winnings.

V. 4.30 P.M. To radio results.

VI. To televised races in which selections featured, when viewing was available. (In lieu of session IV.)

Each session was of about ten minutes' duration and comprised fifteen shocks, administered at random during sessions II, III and IV but specifically during the choosing and recording of the selection during session I, and during broadcast of selected names when listening to results or watching television (sessions V and VI).

In all, nine days of treatment were given over two weeks (45 sessions, 675 shocks).

ATTITUDE CHANGES DURING TREATMENT

On the fourth day of treatment the patient volunteered that he was having to force himself to open the paper and make his selections. He also revealed that he was having difficulty in evoking and maintaining thoughts of selections and anticipated profits during the aversion sessions directed at the imagery. He still thought about the selections between sessions and anticipated with pleasure the checking of results. By the seventh day thoughts of the selection were no longer occurring between sessions, and he had no desire to watch televised racing or to listen to the results.

Objective and subjective concomitants of anxiety were noted on the second day of treatment. The patient expressed the opinion that it was only the realization that he must obtain a cure that was keeping him going. Objective evidence of emotional stress was suppressed by the third day, but recurred briefly on the sixth day, with barely controlled anger towards the therapist, and again on the ninth day whilst listening to the radio results. He did not, however, refuse or request to terminate any session.

FOLLOW-UP

The first review was made one month after completion of therapy. The patient stated that he had stopped buying his morning newspaper, and had no desire to place a bet and no interest in horses. He also volunteered that his relationship with his wife had considerably improved both at the sexual and interpersonal levels. The wife independently confirmed these reports.

Regular reviews now extending beyond twelve months have revealed continued lack of interest in all aspects of gambling and maintained improvement in the marital situation.

DISCUSSION

Analysts have interpreted compulsive gambling as an outlet for repressed ano-sadistic impulses (Simmel), a form of masochism (von Hattingberg), (Burgler), satisfaction of the demands of a punitive superego (Menninger), an unresolved Oedipus conflict with fate the father projection (Freud). In terms of Learning Theory, on the other hand, compulsive gambling could be considered a maladaptive behaviour response acquired by learning. There are indications in the history of this case of psychopathological factors pertinent to analytical interpretations. There is also evidence of opportunity for the "learning" of gambling responses from childhood associations.

Where time is limited and a patient requests relief from a behaviour pattern which is causing unfortunate consequences, behaviour therapy techniques may provide the treatment of choice. Before choosing aversion for this case, however, consideration was given to treatment through:

I. Joint interviews directed at the marital problems, and
II. Systematic desensitization in imagination (Wolpe, 1958) to the gambling-provoking situations.

These alternatives did not appear promising. The evidence that gambling bouts were precipitated by the stimulus of classical races or ready money in the pocket suggested that the habit was an extensive behaviour response and not confined to the marital situation. Systematic desensitization appeared initially to offer advantages in that the marital situation could be simultaneously tackled as one of the hierarchies. There were, however, practical difficulties in establishing a valid hierarchy without seeming partisan and precipitating further complications. Having chosen aversion, it was considered advisable to ignore the marital problems until this treatment was completed for fear that the patient might associate aversion with his wife as punishment.

The importance of treating maladaptive behaviour "at all possible points in the sequence from initiation in internal feelings and imagery to its final expression in overt behaviour" has been stressed by Marks and Gelder (1967). Latency and duration of imagery have been used as a measure of the effectiveness of aversion therapy (Rachman, 1961; Marks and Gelder, 1967) and the direction of imagery for the same purpose (Solyom and Miller, 1965). Though sensory stimulation by films and sound have been utilized in the aversion treatment of compulsive gamblers (Barker and Miller, 1966b), aversion of imagery was not included in the techniques employed. The need to deal with the fantasy situation in the present case was made obvious by the patient's reporting frequent pleasurable daydreams of the outcome of his morning selections, and therefore during treatment approximately half of the aversion sessions were directed at the imagery. It was hoped that random timing of the sessions would reduce the tendency to fantasize between sessions. Additionally, the uncertainty of timing had been reported by previous patients (and was later reported by the present patient) as increasing the aversive properties of the therapeutic sessions.

It might be proposed that, as the patient displayed insight during initial interviews, this factor in itself could explain the resolution of the gambling habit. Insight had been present, however, for some considerable time at the level expressed by the patient, but had not reduced the frequency or extent of his gambling. Indeed, the way in which the insight was expressed might lead to the conjecture that it added to the strength of his gambling drive as the most suitable weapon he possessed to attack his wife.

It might also be proposed that the resolution of the marital disharmony had effected a cure by removing the stimulus for gambling, in which case the aversion was unnecessary. The resolution of marital difficulties must undoubtedly be playing a part in the maintenance of the patient's remission if the conjecture as to their part in the aetiology is correct. There is no evidence, however, that the improvement in the marital situation initiated the remission. Furthermore, the changed marital situation occurring immediately after completion of the aversion therapy in itself warrants consideration.

In view of the periodicity of the gambling habit, the remission might be considered spontaneous rather than a specific therapeutic effect related to the aversion. The absence of desire to gamble has now however been retained continuously for over twelve months, which is considerably longer than any between-bout remission previously experienced. Additionally, there is evidence that changes occurred in the patient's attitudes towards gambling during the course of the aversion therapy. These subjectively-noted changes indicating a progressive reluctance to indulge in the pleasures previously experienced are in accord with expectations if extinction of the gambling habit was taking place during therapy. They compare with attitude changes noted in the treatment of sexual deviants by aversive methods (Marks and Gelder, 1967). Furthermore the overall treatment time of nine days is similar to that reported by Barker and Miller for their horse gambler (1966b). It is thus suggested that the remission was in fact effected specifically by the aversion therapy.

Attitude changes subsequent to treatment by behaviour techniques have been noted previously. Where they have occurred following aversion therapy they have usually related to the behaviour problem under treatment, and are understandable in that light, e.g. improved heterosexual activity following aversion for transvestism and fetishism (Barker, 1965; Marks *et al.,* 1965; Marks and Gelder, 1967). In the latter two papers measurements by semantic differential techniques suggested that attitudes to concepts not immediately related to the fetish underwent minor shifts only. Marks and Gelder (1967), however, additionally noted improvement in interpersonal relationships following treatment. Kraft (1967) records the disappearance of homosexual and transvestite behaviour in a patient treated for a traffic phobia. Shafar and Jaffe (1965) record in one patient improvement in acrophobia following resolution of marital stress treated by psychotherapeutic exploration, and, later, reduction in anxieties related to work following treatment of car phobia by hypnotic desensitization. Measures of improvement in social and interpersonal adjustments following treatment of phobias by desensitization in imagination have been compared favourably with changes in similar parameters in matched patients treated by psychotherapy (Gelder *et al.,* 1967). In the present case a change is again recorded in a pattern of behaviour other than that immediately under treatment. An explanation of the improved marital state could be hypothesized as a show of warmth and approval by the wife following the patient's treatment, acting as the reinforcement for an operant-conditioning process of gambling avoidance, and resulting both in the maintenance of an improved marital relationship and in the continued remission of the gambling habit.

SUMMARY

A case of compulsive horse race gambling is reported in which treatment by aversion therapy has been followed by remission lasting over twelve months.

The necessity to treat all aspects of the behaviour pattern including the fantasy projection is noted.

Considerable improvement in long-standing marital disharmony occurred following treatment; the significance of this is discussed.

REFERENCES

1. Barker, J. C. (1965). "Behaviour therapy for transvestism: a comparison of pharmacological and electrical aversion techniques." *Brit. J. Psychiat.,* 111, 268–276.
2. Barker, J. C., and Miller, M. (1966a). "Aversion therapy for compulsive gambling." *Lancet, i,* 491.
3. ———, ——— (1966b). "Aversion therapy for compulsive gambling." *Brit. med. J., ii,* 115.

4. Bergler, E. (1957). *The Psychology of Gambling*. New York: Hill & Wang Inc.
5. Freud, S. (1928). "Dostoevsky and parricide." Collected Paper, V.
6. Gelder, M. G., Marks, I. M., and Wolff, H. H. (1967). "Desensitization and psychotherapy in the treatment of phobic states. A controlled inquiry." *Brit. J. Psychiat.*, 113, 53–73.
7. Harris, H. I. (1964). "Gambling addiction in an adolescent male." *Psychoanal. Quart.*, 33 (4), 513–525.
8. Von Hattingberg, H. (1914). "Analerotik, Angstlust und Eigensinn." *Int. Ztschr. f. Psychoan.*
9. Kraft, T. (1967). Unpublished paper to Behaviour Therapy Seminar. Middlesex Hospital. January 1967.
10. Marks, I. M., and Gelder, M. G. (1967). "Transvestism and fetishism: clinical and psychological changes during faradic aversion." *Brit. J. Psychiat.*, 113, 711–729.
11. ———, Rachman, S., and Gelder, M. G. (1965). "Methods for assessment of aversion treatment in fetishism with masochism." *Behav. Res. Ther.*, 3, 253–258.
12. McGuire, R. J., and Vallance, M. (1964). "Aversion therapy by electric shock, a simple technique." *Brit. med. J.*, i, 151–152.
13. Menninger, K. (1938). "Criminal behaviour as a form of masked self-destruction." *Bull. Menninger Clinic II.*
14. Rachman, S. (1961). "Sexual disorders and behaviour therapy." *Amer. J. Psychiat.*, 118, 235–240.
15. Seager, C. P., Pokorny, M. R., and Black, D. (1966). "Aversion therapy for compulsive gambling." *Lancet, i,* 546.
16. Shafar, S., and Jaffe, J. R. (1965). "Behaviour therapy in the treatment of psychoneurosis." *Brit. J. Psychiat.*, 111, 1199–1203.
17. Simmel, E. (1920). "On psychoanalysis of the gambler." Paper given at 6th International Congress of Psychoanalysis.
18. Solyom, L., and Miller, S. (1965). "A differential conditioning procedure as the initial phase of the behaviour therapy of homosexuality." *Behav. Res. Ther.*, 3, 147–160.
19. Wolpe, J. (1958). *Psychotherapy by Reciprocal Inhibition*. Stanford, California: Stanford University Press.

25

Elimination of a Sadistic Fantasy by a Client-Controlled Counterconditioning Technique

Gerald C. Davison

To the best of the author's knowledge, this is the 1st report of the elimination of a sadistic fantasy by conditioning methods, as well as the 1st to describe a client-controlled technique for counterconditioning sexual responses. The mainstay of the therapy entailed client-controlled masturbation sessions, in which strong sexual feelings were paired with pictures and images of females in nonsadistic contexts. This presumed positive counterconditioning was supplemented in the consulting room by imaginal aversive counterconditioning ("covert sensitization"), whereby an extremely disgusting scene was paired in imagination with a typical sadistic fantasy. Furthermore, therapeutic change seemed to be facilitated through the client's reconstruction of his problem in conditioning terms, rather than in terms of mental illness and putative unconscious processes.

The modification of deviant sexual behavior has been approached largely through the contiguous pairing of a primary aversive stimulus with a stimulus eliciting an undesirable response (the "symptom"), the goal being to endow the inappropriate stimulus with negative properties, or at least to eliminate the unwanted positive attributes. Many such cases have been reviewed by Bandura (in press), Feldman (1966), Grossberg (1964), Kalish (1965), Rachman (1961), and Ullmann and Krasner (1965). Therapy of fetishism, homosexuality, and transvestism has tended to follow this counterconditioning model (e.g., Blakemore, Thorpe, Barker, Conway, & Lavin, 1963; Davies & Morgenstern, 1960; Freund, 1960; Lavin, Thorpe, Barker, Blake-

SOURCE. *Journal of Abnormal Psychology*, 1968, **73**, 84–90. Copyright 1968 by the American Psychological Association, and reproduced by permission. This paper was written during a postdoctoral traineeship at the Veterans Administration Hospital, Palo Alto, California. For critical comments and helpful suggestions, the author thanks Walter Mischel, Arnold A. Lazarus, David Fisher, and Thomas J. D'Zurilla.

more, & Conway, 1961; Raymond, 1956; Thorpe, Schmidt, Brown, & Castell, 1964). In addition, several workers have introduced complementary procedures in attempts to endow suitable social stimuli with the positive attributes necessary to make less likely a reversion to the inappropriate goal-object. Thus, for example, Freund (1960) gave his male homosexuals not only aversion conditioning trials to pictures of men, but also exposures to pictures of nude women after injection of male hormones. Similar procedures have been employed by Thorpe, Schmidt, and Castell (1963) and Feldman and MacCulloch (1965).

Of particular relevance to the present study is the work of Thorpe et al. (1963). These writers report therapeutic benefit following presumably counterconditioning sessions during which efforts were made to pair female pictures with orgasm from masturbation. It was assumed that this intensely pleasurable sexual response counterconditioned the aversion to females which appeared to play a crucial role in the behavior of the homosexuals. These authors recognized the importance of a person's fantasy life to his overt behavioral adjustment, and they assumed that beneficial generalization would occur from pictorial to the real-life situation, similar to the assumptions made for systematic desensitization (Davison, in press; Wolpe, 1958). Although the therapeutic outcomes reported by Thorpe and his co-workers are equivocal in respect to actual sexual behavior, the procedures did have considerable effect on fantasies.

The possibility of extending this kind of work to an out-patient setting presented itself to the author during the course of his private practice. Various modifications of procedures used by Thorpe et al. (1963) were employed, apparently to good effect. In addition, other important issues became evident in the course of therapy, which required fewer than 5 consulting-room hours over a span of 10 wk., and it is for these heuristic reasons that the following is reported.

CASE STUDY

The client was a 21-yr.-old unmarried white male college senior majoring in history. The university counseling center had received an anxious letter from his parents, requesting help for their son in treating his introversion, procrastination, and "masochism." After working with the student for a few weeks on his tendency to wait until the last minute in his academic work, the psychologist at the center referred him to the author for help with his sexual difficulties.

Mr. M's statement of the problem was: "I'm a sadist." There followed a rather troubled account of a complete absence of "normal" sexual fantasies and activities since age 11. Masturbating about five times a week, the client's fantasies had been exclusively sadistic ones, specifically, inflicting tortures on women. He declared emphatically that he had never been sexually aroused by any other kind of image. Although generally uninterested in dating girls, he felt no aversion to them; on the contrary, he sometimes felt a "warm glow" when near them, but did not describe this at all in sexual terms. Because of his extreme concern over the content of his fantasies, however, he had dated very little and expressed no interest in the co-eds at the college. He recalled having kissed only two girls in his life, with no sexual arousal accompanying these fleeting episodes. He had never engaged in any homosexual activities or fantasies. Although expressing no guilt about his problem, he was very much worried about it inasmuch as he felt it impossible to ever contemplate marriage. This concern had recently been markedly increased upon reading an account of a Freudian interpretation of "sadomasochism." He was especially perturbed about the poor prognosis for this "illness."

Because his concern over the gravity and implications of his problem seemed at least as disruptive as the problem itself, the therapist spent most of the first session raising arguments against a disease interpretation of unusual behavior. Psychoanalytic notions were critically reviewed, and attention was directed especially to the untestability of many Freudian concepts (Levy, 1963). Instances in the therapist's own clinical work were cited to illustrate the liberating effects observed in many people when they interpret their maladaptive behavior as determined by "normal" psychological processes rather than by insidious disease processes (cf. Davison, 1966; Glasser, 1965; Maher, 1966; Mainord, 1962). Mr. M frequently expressed relief at these ideas, and the therapist, indeed, took full advantage of his prestigious position to reinforce these notions.

At the end of the session, the counterconditioning orientation which would be followed was explained (Davison, in press; Guthrie, 1935; Wolpe, 1958), as well as the specific activities which he was to engage in during the coming week. When assured of privacy in his dormitory room (primarily on the weekend), he was first to obtain an erection by whatever means possible— undoubtedly with a sadistic fantasy, as he indicated. He was then to begin to masturbate while looking at a picture of a sexy, nude woman (the "target" sexual stimulus); *Playboy* magazine was suggested to him as a good source. If he began losing the erection, he was to switch back to his sadistic fantasy until he could begin masturbating effectively again. Concentrating again on the *Playboy* picture, he was to continue masturbating, using the fantasy only to regain erection. As orgasm was approaching, he was at all costs to focus on the *Playboy* picture, even if sadistic fantasies began to intrude. It was impressed on him that gains would ensue only when sexual arousal was associated with the picture, and that he need not worry about indulging in sadistic fantasies at this point. The client appeared enthusiastic and hopeful as he left the office. (Table 1 summarizes the client-controlled

TABLE 1

"Target" and "Back-Up" Sexual Stimuli for
Client-Controlled Masturbation Sessions

Week	Target Stimulus	Back-up Stimulus
1	*Playboy*, real stimulus	Sadistic fantasy
2	Bathing-suit, real stimulus	*Playboy*, real stimulus
	Playboy, imaginal stimulus	Sadistic fantasy
3	Same as Week 2	Same as Week 2
4	Bathing-suit, real stimulus	*Playboy*, real stimulus
	Playboy, imaginal stimulus	None

masturbation assignments following this and succeeding consulting-room sessions.)

At the second session he reported success with the assignment: he had been able to masturbate effectively and enjoyably three times over the weekend to a particular picture from *Playboy* without once have to use a sadistic fantasy; however, it did take significantly longer to climax with the *Playboy* photograph than with the usual kind of sadistic fantasy. During the rest of the week, when he had not had enough privacy for real-life visual stimulation, he had "broken down" a few times and used his sadistic fantasies.

Much of this session was then spent in talking to him about some of social-sexual games which most males play in our culture, especially the "mental undressing" of attractive women. The purpose was to engage him in the kind of "stud" conversation which he had never experienced and which, it was felt, would help to change his orientation toward girls. The therapist reassured him that the first direct contacts with girls are sometimes disappointing; he had to admit, however, that his extreme sensitivity about the sadistic fantasies had severely limited his experience.

During the coming week he was, first of all, to ask out on a coffee date any girl whom he felt he *might* find attractive, even for a sadistic fantasy. He was also to spend some time between classes just looking at some of the co-eds and noting some of their more remarkable attributes. Finally, his masturbation sessions were to be structured as follows: The real-life pictorial stimuli were to be girls either in bathing suits or lingerie, used in the same way as the *Playboy* picture the preceding week; this latter stimulus was to be used as "back-up" stimulus, replacing the sadistic fantasies in the event that he was losing his erection. Attention was also to be directed to imaginal sexual stimuli, and when masturbating in this way he was to use the *Playboy* image, with a sadistic fantasy as back-up.

The third session lasted half an hour. He had procrastinated so long in asking for a date that the girls he contacted had already made other plans; the therapist expressed his disappointment quite openly and urged him even more strongly to follow through with this task. He had managed to spend some time looking at girls but did not note significant sexual arousal, except when a sadistic fantasy crept in occasionally. He had masturbated only once to real-life stimuli, using some bathing-suit pictures from a weekly national news magazine; this was successful, though it took longer even than when the *Playboy* material was used previously. When masturbating to imaginal sexual stimuli, he had relied almost exclusively on his sadistic fantasies rather than utilizing the *Playboy* picture in imagination as he had in real life 1 wk. earlier.

His reluctance to give up the sadistic fantasies prompted the use of the following procedure, the idea for which had been obtained from Lazarus (1958). With his eyes closed, he was instructed to imagine a typical sadistic scene, a pretty girl tied to stakes on the ground and struggling tearfully to extricate herself. While looking at the girl, he was told to imagine someone bringing a branding iron toward his eyes, ultimately searing his eyebrows. A second image was attempted when this proved abortive, namely, being kicked in the groin by a ferocious-looking karate expert. When he reported himself indifferent to this image as well, the therapist depicted to him a large bowl of "soup," composed of steaming urine with reeking fecal boli bobbing around on top. His grimaces, contortions, and groans indicated that an effective image had been found, and the following 5 min. were spent portraying his drinking from the bowl, with accompanying nausea, at all times while peering over the floating debris at the struggling girl. After opening his eyes at the end of the imaginal ordeal, he reported spontaneously that he felt quite nauseated, and some time was spent in casual conversation in order to dispel the mood.

His assignments for masturbation during the coming week entailed increasing the frequency of his real-life masturbatory exposures to bathing-suit pictures, along with concerted efforts to use the *Playboy* stimuli in imagination as he had in real life 2 wk. earlier, resorting to sadistic fantasies if necessary.

The fourth session lasted only 15 min. He had managed to arrange a date for the coming weekend and found himself almost looking forward to it. Again, he had masturbated several times to a real-life picture of a bathing beauty. In fantasy he had managed to use the *Playboy* girl exclusively two out of five times, with no noticeable diminution in enjoyment.

He was to continue using the bathing-suit pictures while masturbating to real-life stimuli, but to avoid sadistic fantasies altogether, the idea being that any frustration engendered by this deprivation would simply add to his general sexual arousal and thereby make it all the easier to use the *Playboy* stimuli in imagination.

The fifth session, also lasting only 15 min., opened with Mr. M animatedly praising the efficacy of the therapy. He had masturbated several times, mostly to real-life bathing-suit pictures, with no problems and, most importantly, had found himself *unable* to obtain an erection to a sadistic fantasy. In fact, he even had difficulty conjuring up an image. He had also spent considerable time with two girls, finding himself at one point having to resist an urge to hug one of them—a totally new experience for him. He enthusiastically spoke of how different he felt about "normal dating," and a 1-mo. period without interviews was decided upon to let him follow his new inclinations.

The sixth session, 1 mo. later, revealed that his sadistic fantasies had not reappeared, and that he had been masturbating effectively to both real-life and imaginal appropriate sexual stimuli. He had not, however, been dating, and some time was spent stressing the importance of seeking "normal" sexual outlets. He felt strongly, however that the sexual problem had been successfully handled and requested that his procrastination problem be taken up. Two sessions were subsequently devoted to following the same general strategy that had been adopted, with some success, by the college counselor, that is, arranging for various rewards to be made contingent upon certain academic task-performances. Mr. M did report doing "an enormous amount of work" during 1 wk.—out of fear of having to admit to the therapist that he had been loafing. Practical considerations, however, made it clear that this handling of the problem, even if it should prove effective, was not as realistic as his facing the reality that there was no "magic pill" to eliminate his procrastination. Therapy, therefore, was terminated, with no sadistic fantasies having occurred for over 1 mo., and with the problem of procrastination left more or less untouched.

A follow-up of 1 mo. was obtained by telephone. Mr. M reported that there was still no sign of sadistic fantasies and that, indeed, he was no longer even thinking about the issue. He had still not "gotten around" to asking any girl out on a date, and the therapist urged him in no uncertain terms to tackle this aspect of his procrastination problem with the vigor that he had shown in regard to his studies (where significant improvement had been made). Extensive and persistent questioning failed to evoke any reported aversion to girls as the basis of his reluctance to ask them out.

DISCUSSION

As with every case study, one must necessarily speculate, to a large extent, on the "active ingredients." Hypotheses are not readily strengthened from such data. As a demonstration of various strategies, however, the present report does seem to be of heuristic value.

1. The first significant event in therapy was the author's general re-action to the client's statement of the problem, "I'm a sadist." After Mr. M

had recounted the horror with which he had read about his mysterious "illness" in Freudian terms, the therapist countered with a logical attack that made the hour take on more the characteristics of a graduate seminar than a psychotherapy session, except perhaps for the warmth, support, and acceptance which were deliberately conveyed. A key factor in this initial phase was an attempt to change the client's general orientation to his problem. As this writer has usually found, the client had been regarding himself as "sick," qualitatively different from so-called "normals." Furthermore, the idea that much of his behavior was determined by forces working in devious ways in his "unconscious" was quite troubling, as was the poor prognosis. As reported in the case material, these issues were dealt with immediately, and significant relief was afforded the young man simply by reconstructing the problem for him in conditioning terms. It would, indeed, have been interesting and valuable to attempt some sort of assessment of improvement at this very point.

2. Inextricably intertwined with the foregoing was the outlining of a therapeutic strategy: his sadistic fantasies were to be attacked by procedures aimed at counterconditioning the maladaptive emotional reactions to specific kinds of stimuli. The client perceived the theoretical rationale as reasonable and was satisfied with the actual techniques which would be employed. Furthermore, being able to buttress the plan with both clinical and experimental data added to its credibility. It must be emphasized that whether the data cited, or the explanation offered, are valid is an irrelevant question in the present situation. The important point is that the client's enthusiastic participation was enlisted in a therapeutic regime which, by all counts, was to be highly unconventional.

3. A third conceivably relevant variable was the "older brother" type of relationship which the therapist established in talking with Mr. M about conventional sex. Clearly the client had missed this part of the average American male's upbringing and, as has been reported, much time was spent in deliberately provocative "locker-room talk," not as an end in itself, but rather as a means of exposing him to the kinds of heterosexual ideations which seemed to the author useful in promoting nonsadistic fantasies about girls.

4. It is likely that the two positive exposures to actual women contributed to therapeutic improvement. Mr. M, having been goaded into direct social contact with girls, was fortunately able to appreciate the enjoyment that can come from a satisfactory relationship with a woman, albeit on nonsexual terms. In addition, having felt a very strong urge to hug one of them, in a nonsadistic fashion, was reported by the client as a highly significant event and must surely have fostered some change in his concept of himself as a sexual misfit. Furthermore, aside from any alleged counterconditioning with respect to appropriate stimuli (see below), it is also sug-

gested that a favorable change in self-concept developed as he saw himself able to respond sexually to imaginal and pictorial stimuli that had previously left him unaroused.

5. It is assumed that the most important variable in therapy was the masturbation sessions which the client carried out privately. As discussed by Thorpe et al. (1963), it was felt that more appropriate social-sexual behavior would probably follow upon a change in sexual fantasies; in the present case a focus on the fantasies seemed all the more reasonable in view of the fact that *they formed the basis of the referral.* According to the client, it was his fantasy life which had retarded his sexual development, and it was this that he was most worried about. It was assumed that generalization to real-life girls would be effected in a fashion similar to the generalization which has been reported for Wolpe's technique of systematic desensitization (Davison, in press; Lang & Lazovik, 1963; Lang, Lazovik, & Reynolds, 1965; Lazarus, 1961; Paul, 1966; Paul & Shannon, 1966; Rachman, 1966; Schubot, 1966; Wolpin & Raines, 1966; Zeisset, 1966). Of course, whether Mr. M would actually begin dating regularly, or at all, would seem to depend importantly on factors other than those dealt with in this brief therapy, for example, the client's physical attractiveness, his conversational and sexual techniques, the availability of women attractive to him, and so forth. The generalization spoken of here, then, is best restricted to the thoughts and feelings which he had about women and about the prospects of relating to them nonsadistically; the case-study data contain ample verification for this.

The actual procedure followed was unique in that control of the pairing was vested entirely in the client, as is done in the use of differential relaxation with in vivo exposures to aversive stimuli (Davison, 1965; Wolpe & Lazarus, 1966). The sadistic fantasies were used initially to enable Mr. M to obtain and maintain an erection. During this arousal, he looked at culture-appropriate sexual stimuli (a nude *Playboy* photo) and masturbated. The assumption is made (and must obviously be investigated experimentally) that the pairing of masturbatory arousal with the *Playboy* picture served to replace neutral emotional responses to the picture with intensely pleasurable sexual responses. In succeeding sessions the content of the new sexual stimuli was changed to less openly provocative female pictures (bathing-suit photographs), with the already established *Playboy* picture used as back-up. Then the stimuli were made solely imaginal in similar fashion. Obviously, if this procedure worked for counterconditioning reasons, the client exhibited considerable control over the content of his fantasies, switching back and forth as he had been directed. This control of imagery is a central issue in desensitization research as well (Davison, in press).

6. Probably very instrumental in changing the content of his fantasies was the intensive "imaginal aversive counterconditioning" (or "covert sensitization," viz., Cautela, 1966; Lazarus, 1958) conducted by the therapist, in

which extreme feelings of disgust were generated by fantasy and then related to the sadistic image. One can fruitfully compare this technique with the "emotive imagery" procedure described by Lazarus and Abramovitz (1962), in which pleasant images were generated in fearful children and then related by the therapist to conditioned aversive stimuli. The procedure was resorted to in the present case because the client appeared unable to give up the sadistic fantasy solely on the basis of beginning to find the nonsadistic pictures and images effective in maintaining erection and leading to orgasm.

The assessment of therapeutic outcome poses some difficulty here, as indeed it does for any therapy. Explicitly rejected as criteria of "cure" are the client's "self-actualization," "mental health," "ego strength," or other vague notions. While the intention is not simply to beg the question, it does seem more appropriate for the present case report to restrict judgment to the problem as presented by the client, namely, the sadistic fantasies and the attendant worry and doubt about suitability for normal human intercourse.

The clinical data on change in fantasy are self-reports, supplemented by the therapist's inference of the client's credibility. The orderliness of response to therapy, along with the enthusiasm which accompanied the progress reports, serves to bolster the conclusion that Mr. M did, in fact, give up his sadistic fantasies of 10 years' standing in favor of the kinds of fantasies which he felt were a sine qua non for appropriate sociosexual behavior. Both preceding and accompanying these changes was the radical difference in outlook. Simply stated, Mr. M stopped worrying about himself as an "oddball," doomed to a solitary life, and did make some initial attempts to establish appropriate relationships with girls. That he has not yet done so (as of this writing) may, indeed, be due to a return of the original problem; however, this alternative seems less likely than that verbalized by the client, namely, that he has always had trouble doing what he knows he ought to do, and that, above all, being a so-called sexual deviate has ceased being an issue for him. Moreover, as mentioned above, variables other than the content of fantasies would seem to bear importantly on the matter of overt sexual behavior. Clearly, if usual dating habits were to be used as a criterion for outcome, the therapy must be considered a failure—although this would qualify many a young adult as "maladjusted" or "abnormal." Be that as it may, a relevant, well-established class of behaviors was modified, setting the stage for a social adjustment from which the client had initially seen himself utterly alienated.

Supplementary Follow-Up Data

A follow-up report was received by mail 16 mo. following termination. The client reported that, since the therapy had so readily eliminated the arousal from sadistic fantasies, and, most importantly, had altered his outlook for "normal" sexual behavior, he allowed himself, "premeditatedly," to return to the use of the sadistic fantasies 6 mo. after termination, ". . . resolving to enjoy my fantasies until June 1, and then to reform once more. This I did. On June 1 [1967], right on schedule, I bought an issue of *Playboy* and proceeded to give myself the treatment again. Once again, it worked like a charm. In two weeks, I was back in my reformed state, where I am now [August 1967]. I have no need for sadistic fantasies. . . . I have [also] been pursuing a vigorous (well, vigorous for *me*) program of dating. In this way, I have gotten to know a lot of girls of whose existence I was previously only peripherally aware. As you probably know, I was very shy with girls before; well, now I am not one-fifth as shy as I used to be. In fact, by my old standards, I have become a regular rake!"

A telephone call was made to obtain more specific information about his return to the sadistic fantasies. He reported that the return was "fairly immediate," with a concomitant withdrawal of interest in conventional sexual stimuli. His self-administered therapy in June 1967 followed the gradual pattern of the original therapy, although progress was much faster. The author advised him not to make any more "premeditated" returns, rather to consolidate his gains in dating and other conventional heterosexual activities and interests. The client indicated that this plan could and would be readily implemented.

Of the past 16 mo., then, the client has been free of the sadistic fantasies for 7 mo., the other 9 mo. involving what he terms a willful return to sexual stimulation while masturbating. Constant throughout this follow-up period has been the relief which he derived from finding himself able to respond sexually to conventional sexual stimuli. Additional gains are his dating activities, which, it will be recalled, were not in evidence while the writer was in direct contact with him.

Still aware of the limitations of these case-study data, it does seem noteworthy and possibly quite important that the client's self-initiated partial "relapse" took place in a step-wise fashion, that is, without a *gradual* reorientation to the sadistic fantasies: he reported himself almost immediately excited by them once he had made the decision to become so. This sudden shift raises questions as to whether "aversive counterconditioning" underlay the indifference to the fantasies which was effected during therapy. This surprising finding also underlines the probable importance of other-than-conditioning variables in the treatment.

REFERENCES

Bandura, A. *Principles of behavior modification.* New York: Holt, Rinehart & Winston, in press.

Blakemore, C. B., Thorpe, J. G., Barker, J. C., Conway, C. G., & Lavin, N. I. The application of faradic aversion conditioning in a case of transvestism. *Behaviour Research and Therapy*, 1963, **1**, 29–34.

Cautela, J. R. Treatment of compulsive behavior by covert sensitization. *The Psychological Record*, 1966, **16**, 33–41.

Davies, B., & Morgenstern, F. A case of cysticercosis, temporal lobe epilepsy, and transvestism. *Journal of Neurological and Neurosurgical Psychiatry*, 1960, **23**, 247–249.

Davison, G. C. Relative contributions of differential relaxation and graded exposure to in vivo desensitization of a neurotic fear. *Proceedings of the 73rd annual convention of the American Psychological Association*, 1965, 209–210.

Davison, G. C. Differential relaxation and cognitive restructuring in therapy with a "paranoid schizophrenic" or "paranoid state." *Proceedings of the 74th annual convention of the American Psychological Association*, 1966, **2**, 177–178.

Davison, G. C. Systematic desensitization as a counterconditioning process. *Journal of Abnormal Psychology*, 1968, in press.

Feldman, M. P. Aversion therapy for sexual deviations: A critical review. *Psychological Bulletin*, 1966, **65**, 65–79.

Feldman, M. P., & MacCulloch, M. J. The application of anticipatory avoidance learning to the treatment of homosexuality: I. Theory, technique and preliminary results. *Behaviour Research and Therapy*, 1965, **2**, 165–183.

Freund, K. Some problems in the treatment of homosexuality. In H. J. Eysenck (Ed.), *Behaviour therapy and the neurosis*. London: Pergamon, 1960. Pp. 312–326.

Glasser, W. *Reality therapy: A new approach to psychiatry*. New York: Harper & Row, 1965.

Grossberg, J. M. Behavior therapy: A review. *Psychological Bulletin*, 1964, **62**, 73–88.

Guthrie, E. R. *The psychology of learning*. New York: Harper, 1935.

Kalish, H. I. Behavior therapy. In B. B. Wolman (Ed.), *Handbook of clinical psychology*. New York: McGraw-Hill, 1965. Pp. 1230–1253.

Lang, P. J., & Lazovik, A. D. Experimental desensitization of a phobia. *Journal of Abnormal and Social Psychology*, 1963, **66**, 519–525.

Lang, P. J., Lazovik, A. D., & Reynolds, D. J. Desensitization, suggestibility, and pseudotherapy. *Journal of Abnormal Psychology*, 1965, **70**, 395–402.

Lavin N. I., Thorpe, J. G., Barker, J. C., Blakemore, C. B., & Conway, C. G. Behavior therapy in a case of transvestism. *Journal of Nervous and Mental Disease* 1961, **133**, 346–353.

Lazarus, A. A. New methods in psychotherapy: A case study. *South African Medical Journal*, 1958, **33**, 660–663.

Lazarus, A. A. Group therapy of phobic disorders by systematic desensitization. *Journal of Abnormal and Social Psychology*, 1961, **63**, 504–510.

Lazarus, A. A., & Abramovitz, A. The use of "emotive imagery" in the treatment of children's phobias. *Journal of Mental Science*, 1962, **108**, 191–195.

Levy, L. H. *Psychological interpretation*. New York: Holt, Rinehart & Winston, 1963.

Maher, B. A. *Principles of psychopathology: An experimental approach.* New York: McGraw-Hill, 1966.

Mainord, W. A. A therapy. *Research Bulletin,* Mental Health Research Institute, Ft. Steilacom, Washington, 1962, **5,** 85–92.

Paul, G. L. *Insight vs. desensitization in psychotherapy: An experiment in anxiety reduction.* Stanford: Stanford University Press, 1966.

Paul, G. L., & Shannon, D. T. Treatment of anxiety through systematic desensitization in therapy groups. *Journal of Abnormal Psychology,* 1966, **71,** 124–135.

Rachman, S. Sexual disorders and behaviour therapy. *American Journal of Psychiatry,* 1961, **118,** 235–240.

Rachman, S. Studies in desensitization—III: Speed of generalization. *Behaviour Research and Therapy,* 1966, **4,** 7–15.

Raymond, M. J. Case of fetishism treated by aversion therapy. *British Medical Journal,* 1956, **2,** 854–857.

Schubot, E. The influence of hypnotic and muscular relaxation in systematic desensitization of phobias. Unpublished doctoral dissertation, Stanford University, 1966.

Thorpe, J. G., Schmidt, E., Brown, P. T., & Castell, D. Aversion-relief therapy: A new method for general application. *Behaviour Research and Therapy,* 1964, **2,** 71–82.

Thorpe, J. G., Schmidt, E., & Castell, D. A comparison of positive and negative (aversive) conditioning in the treatment of homosexuality. *Behaviour Research and Therapy,* 1963, **1,** 357–362.

Ullmann, L., & Krasner, L. P. (Eds.) *Case studies in behavior modification.* New York: Holt, Rinehart & Winston, 1965.

Wolpe, J. *Psychotherapy by reciprocal inhibition.* Stanford: Stanford University Press, 1958.

Wolpe, J., & Lazarus, A. A. *Behavior therapy techniques.* New York: Pergamon, 1966.

Wolpin, M., & Raines, J. Visual imagery, expected roles and extinction as possible factors in reducing fear and avoidance behavior. *Behaviour Research and Therapy,* 1966, **4,** 25–37.

Zeisset, R. M. Desensitization and relaxation in the modification of psychiatric patients' interview behavior. Unpublished doctoral dissertation, University of Illinois, 1966.

Introduction to Szasz Article

Some individuals seem to have the knack of creating major problems. Thomas Szasz is one of those persons. While most of his colleagues were busily trying to identify and categorize various forms of mental illness Szasz was wondering if such a thing as mental illness existed! The title of his article (*The myth of mental illness* *) suggests which decision he will arrive at. His argument that ". . . mental illness is a myth, whose function is to disguise and thus render more palatable the bitter pill of moral conflicts in human relations . . ." will probably find many sympathetic listeners in today's younger generation.

In his paper Szasz encourages man to face his "problems in living" realistically and not to hide "behind the skirt of an all-explaining conception of mental illness." He challenges us to step forward and accept responsibility for our actions rather than blame them on mental illness. Szasz's thesis, although certainly not universally accepted in the psychological community, has been influential in recent thinking about psychopathology. It certainly alerts us to the fact that what we call psychological aberration is, in many respects, determined by prevailing sociocultural beliefs.

* The author has also written a book by the same title: Szasz, T. *The myth of mental illness: Foundations of a theory of personal conduct* (New York: Hoeber, 1961).

26

The Myth of Mental Illness

Thomas S. Szasz

My aim in this essay is to raise the question "Is there such a thing as mental illness?" and to argue that there is not. Since the notion of mental illness is extremely widely used nowadays, inquiry into the ways in which this term is employed would seem to be especially indicated. Mental illness, of course, is not literally a "thing"—or physical object—and hence it can "exist" only in the same sort of way in which other theoretical concepts exist. Yet, familiar theories are in the habit of posing, sooner or later—at least to those who come to believe in them—as "objective truth" (or "facts"). During certain historical periods, explanatory conceptions such as deities, witches, and microorganisms appeared not only as theories but as self-evident *causes* of a vast number of events. I submit that today mental illness is widely regarded in a somewhat similar fashion, that is, as the cause of innumerable diverse happenings. As an antidote to the complacent use of the notion of mental illness—whether as a self-evident phenomenon, theory, or cause—let us ask this question: What is meant when it is asserted that someone is mentally ill?

In what follows I shall describe briefly the main uses to which the concept of mental illness has been put. I shall argue that this notion has outlived whatever usefulness it might have had and that it now functions merely as a convenient myth.

MENTAL ILLNESS AS A SIGN OF BRAIN DISEASE

The notion of mental illness derives its main support from such phenomena as syphilis of the brain or delirious conditions—intoxications, for

source. *American Psychologist*, 1960, **15,** 113–118. Copyright 1960 by the American Psychological Association, and reproduced by permission.

instance—in which persons are known to manifest various peculiarites or disorders of thinking and behavior. Correctly speaking, however, these are diseases of the brain, not of the mind. According to one school of thought, *all* so-called mental illness is of this type. The assumption is made that some neurological defect, perhaps a very subtle one, will ultimately be found for all the disorders of thinking and behavior. Many contemporary psychiatrists, physicians, and other scientists hold this view. This position implies that people *cannot* have troubles—expressed in what are *now called* "mental illnesses"—because of differences in personal needs, opinions, social aspirations, values, and so on. *All problems in living* are attributed to physico-chemical processes which in due time will be discovered by medical research.

"Mental illnesses" are thus regarded as basically no different than all other diseases (that is, of the body). The only difference, in this view, between mental and bodily diseases is that the former, affecting the brain, manifest themselves by means of mental symptoms; whereas the latter, affecting other organ systems (for example, the skin, liver, etc.), manifest themselves by means of symptoms referable to those parts of the body. This view rests on and expresses what are, in my opinion, two fundamental errors.

In the first place, what central nervous system symptoms would correspond to a skin eruption or a fracture? It would *not* be some emotion or complex bit of behavior. Rather, it would be blindness or a paralysis of some part of the body. The crux of the matter is that a disease of the brain, analogous to a disease of the skin or bone, is a neurological defect, and not a problem in living. For example, a *defect* in a person's visual field may be satisfactorily explained by correlating it with certain definite lesions in the nervous system. On the other hand, a person's *belief*—whether this be a belief in Christianity, in Communism, or in the idea that his internal organs are "rotting" and that his body is, in fact, already "dead"—cannot be explained by a defect or disease of the nervous system. Explanations of this sort of occurrence—assuming that one is interested in the belief itself and does not regard it simply as a "symptom" or expression of something else that is *more interesting*—must be sought along different lines.

The second error in regarding complex psychosocial behavior, consisting of communications about ourselves and the world about us, as mere symptoms of neurological functioning is *epistemological*. In other words, it is an error pertaining not to any mistakes in observation or reasoning, as such, but rather to the way in which we organize and express our knowledge. In the present case, the error lies in making a symmetrical dualism between mental and physical (or bodily) symptoms, a dualism which is merely a habit of speech and to which no known observations can be found to correspond. Let us see if this is so. In medical practice, when we speak of physical disturbances, we mean either signs (for example, a fever) or symptoms (for example, pain). We speak of mental symptoms, on the other hand, when we refer to a patient's *communications about himself, others, and the world about him.* He might state that he is Napoleon or that he is being persecuted by the Communists. These would be considered mental symptoms *only* if the observer believed that the patient was *not* Napoleon or that he was *not* being persecuted by the Communists. This makes it apparent that the statement that *"X is a mental symptom"* involves rendering a judgment. The judgment entails, moreover, a covert comparison or matching of the patient's ideas, concepts, or beliefs with those of the observer and the society in which they live. The notion of mental symptom is therefore inextricably tied to the *social* (including *ethical*) *context* in which it is made in much the same way as the notion of bodily symptom is tied to an *anatomical* and *genetic context* (Szasz, 1957a, 1957b).

To sum up what has been said thus far: I have tried to show that for those who regard mental symptoms as signs of brain disease, the concept of mental illness is unnecessary and misleading. For what they mean is that people so labeled suffer from diseases of the brain; and, if that is what they mean, it would seem better for the sake of clarity to say that and not something else.

MENTAL ILLNESS AS A NAME FOR PROBLEMS IN LIVING

The term "mental illness" is widely used to describe something which is very different than a disease of the brain. Many people today take it for granted that living is an arduous process. Its hardship for modern man, moreover, derives not so much from a struggle for biological survival as from the stresses and strains inherent in the social intercourse of complex human personalities. In this context, the notion of mental illness is used to identify or describe some feature of an individual's so-called personality. Mental illness—as a deformity of the personality, so to speak—is then regarded as the *cause* of the human disharmony. It is implicit in this view that social intercourse between people is regarded as something *inherently harmonious,* its disturbance being due solely to the presence of "mental illness" in many people. This is obviously fallacious reasoning, for it makes the abstraction "mental illness" into a *cause,* even though this abstraction was created in the first place to serve only as a shorthand expression for certain types of human behavior. It now becomes necessary to ask: "What kinds of behavior are regarded as indicative of mental illness, and by whom?"

The concept of illness, whether bodily or mental, implies *deviation from some clearly defined norm.* In the case of physical illness, the norm is the structural and functional integrity of the human body. Thus, although the desirability of physical health, as such, is an ethical value, what health *is* can be stated in anatomical and physiological terms. What is the norm deviation from which is regarded as mental illness? This question cannot be easily answered. But whatever this norm might be, we can be certain of only one thing: namely, that it is a norm that must be stated in terms of *psychosocial, ethical,* and *legal* concepts. For example, notions such as "excessive repression" or "acting out an unconscious impulse" illustrate the use of psychological concepts for judging (so-called) mental health and illness. The idea that chronic hostility, vengefulness, or divorce are indicative of mental illness would be illustrations of the use of ethical norms (that is, the desirability of love, kindness, and a stable marriage relationship). Finally, the widespread psychiatric opinion that only a mentally ill person would commit homicide illustrates the use of a legal concept as a norm of mental health. The norm from which deviation is measured whenever one speaks of a mental illness is a *psychosocial and ethical one.* Yet, the remedy is sought in terms of *medical* measures which—it is hoped and assumed— are free from wide differences of ethical value. The definition of the disorder and the terms in which its remedy are sought are therefore at serious odds with one another. The practical significance of this covert conflict between the alleged nature of the defect and the remedy can hardly be exaggerated.

Having identified the norms used to measure deviations in cases of mental illness, we will now turn to the question: "Who defines the norms and hence the deviation?" Two basic answers may be offered: (*a*) It may be the person himself (that is, the patient) who decides that he deviates from a norm. For example, an artist may believe that he suffers from a work inhibition; and he may implement this conclusion by seeking help *for* himself from a psychotherapist. (*b*) It may be someone other than the patient who decides that the latter is deviant (for example, relatives, physicians, legal authorities, society generally, etc.). In such a case a psychiatrist may be hired by others to do something *to* the patient in order to correct the deviation.

These considerations underscore the importance of asking the question "Whose agent is the psychiatrist?" and of giving a candid answer to it (Szasz, 1956, 1958). The psychiatrist (psychologist or nonmedical psychotherapist), it now develops, may be the agent of the patient, of the relatives, of the school, of the military services, of a business organization, of a court of law, and so forth. In speaking of the psychiatrist as the agent of these persons or organizations, it is not implied that his values concerning norms, or his ideas and aims concerning the proper nature of remedial action, need to coincide exactly with those of his employer. For example, a patient in individual psychotherapy may believe that his salvation lies in a new marriage; his psychotherapist need not share this hypothesis. As the patient's agent, however, he must abstain from bringing social or legal force to bear on the patient which would prevent him from putting his beliefs into action. If his *contract* is with the patient, the psychiatrist (psychotherapist) may disagree with him or stop his treatment; but he cannot engage others to obstruct the patient's aspirations. Similarly, if a psychiatrist is engaged by a court to determine the sanity of a criminal, he need not fully share the legal authorities' values and intentions in regard to the criminal and the means available for dealing with him. But the psychiatrist is expressly barred from stating, for example, that it is not the criminal who is "insane" but the men who wrote the law on the basis of which the very actions that are being judged are regarded as "criminal." Such an opinion could be voiced, of course, but not in a courtroom, and not by a psychiatrist who makes it his practice to assist the court in performing its daily work.

To recapitulate: In actual contemporary social usage, the finding of a mental illness is made by establishing a deviance in behavior from certain psychosocial, ethical, or legal norms. The judgment may be made, as in medicine, by the patient, the physician (psychiatrist), or others. Remedial action, finally, tends to be sought in a therapeutic—or covertly medical—framework, thus creating a situation in which *psychosocial, ethical,* and/or *legal deviations* are claimed to be correctible by (so-called) *medical action.* Since medical action is designed to correct only medical deviations, it seems logically absurd to expect that it will help solve problems whose very existence had been defined and established on nonmedical grounds. I think that these considerations may be fruitfully applied to the present use of tranquilizers and, more generally, to what might be expected of drugs of whatever type in regard to the amelioration or solution of problems in human living.

THE ROLE OF ETHICS IN PSYCHIATRY

Anything that people *do*—in contrast to things that *happen* to them (Peters, 1958)—takes place in a context of value. In this broad sense, no human activity is devoid of ethical implications. When the values underlying certain activities are widely shared, those who participate in their pursuit may lose sight of them altogether. The discipline of medicine, both as a pure science (for example, research) and as a technology (for example, therapy), contains many ethical considerations and judgments. Unfortunately, these are often denied, minimized, or merely kept out of focus; for the ideal of the medical profession as well as of the people whom it serves seems to be having a system of medicine (allegedly) free of ethical value. This sentimental notion is expressed by such things as the doctor's willingness to treat and help patients irrespective of their religious or political beliefs, whether they are rich or poor, etc. While there may be some grounds for this belief—albeit it is a view that is not impressively true even in these regards—the fact remains that ethical considerations encompass a vast range of human affairs. By making the practice of medicine neutral in regard to some specific issues of value need not, and cannot, mean that it can be kept free from all such values. The practice of medicine is intimately tied to ethics; and the first thing that we must do, it seems to me, is to try to make this clear and explicit. I shall let this matter rest here, for it does not concern us specifically in this essay. Lest there be any vagueness, however, about how or where ethics and medicine meet, let me remind the reader of such issues as birth control, abortion, suicide, and euthanasia as only a few of the major areas of current ethicomedical controversy.

Psychiatry, I submit, is very much more intimately tied to probems of ethics than is medicine. I use the word "psychiatry" here to refer to that contemporary discipline which is concerned with *problems in living* (and not with diseases of the brain, which are problems for neurology). Problems in human relations can be analyzed, interpreted, and given meaning only within given social and ethical contexts. Accordingly, it *does* make a difference—arguments to the contrary notwithstanding—what the psychiatrist's socioethical orientations happen to be; for these will influence his ideas on what is wrong with the patient, what deserves comment or interpretation, in what possible directions change might be desirable, and so forth. Even in medicine proper, these factors play a role, as for instance, in the divergent orientations which physicians, depending on their religious affiliations, have toward such things as birth control and therapeutic abortion. Can anyone really believe that a psychotherapist's ideas concerning religious belief, slavery, or other similar issues play no role in his practical work? If they do make a difference, what are we to infer from it? Does it not seem reasonable that we ought to have different psychiatric therapies—each expressly recognized for the ethical positions which they embody—for, say, Catholics and Jews, religious persons and agnostics, democrats and communists, white supremacists and Negroes, and so on? Indeed, if we look at how psychiatry is actually practiced today (especially in the United States), we find that people do seek psychiatric help in accordance with their social status and ethical beliefs (Hollingshead & Redlich, 1958). This should really not surprise us more than being told that practicing Catholics rarely frequent birth control clinics.

The foregoing position which holds that contemporary psychotherapists deal with problems in living, rather than with mental illnesses and their cures, stands in opposition to a currently prevalent claim, according to which mental illness is just as "real" and "objective" as bodily illness. This is a confusing claim since it is never known exactly what is meant by such words as "real" and "objective." I suspect, however, that what is intended by the proponents of this view is to create the idea in the popular mind that mental illness is some sort of disease entity, like an infection or a malignancy. If this were true, one could *catch* or *get* a "mental illness," one might *have* or *harbor* it, one might *transmit* it to others, and finally one could get *rid* of it. In my opinion, there is not a shred of evidence to support this idea. To the contrary, all the evidence is the other way and supports the view that what people now call mental illnesses are for the most part *communications* expressing unacceptable ideas, often framed, moreover, in an unusual idiom. The scope of this essay allows me to do no more than mention this alternative theoretical approach to this problem (Szasz, 1957c).

This is not the place to consider in detail the similarities and differences between bodily and mental illnesses. It shall suffice for us here to emphasize only one important difference between them: namely, that whereas bodily disease refers to public, physicochemical occurrences, the notion of mental illness is used to codify relatively more private, sociopsychological happenings of which the observer (diagnostician) forms a part. In other words, the psychiatrist does not stand *apart* from what he observes, but is, in Harry Stack Sullivan's apt words, a "participant observer." This means that he is *committed* to some picture of what he considers reality—and to what he thinks society considers reality—and he observes and judges the patient's behavior in the light of these considerations. This touches on our earlier observation that the notion of mental symptom itself implies a comparison between observer and observed, psychiatrist and patient. This is so obvious that I may be charged with belaboring trivialities. Let me therefore say once more that my aim in presenting this argument was expressly to criticize and counter a prevailing contemporary tendency to deny the moral aspects of psychiatry (and psychotherapy) and to substitute for them allegedly value-free medical considerations. Psychotherapy, for example, is being widely practiced as though it entailed nothing other than restoring the patient from a state of mental sickness to one of mental health. While it is generally accepted that mental illness has something to do with man's social (or interpersonal) relations, it is paradoxically maintained that problems of values (that is, of ethics) do not arise in this process.[1] Yet, in one sense, much of psychotherapy may revolve around nothing other than the elucidation and weighing of goals and values—many of which may be mutually contradictory—and the means whereby they might best be harmonized, realized, or relinquished.

The diversity of human values and the methods by means of which

---

[1] Freud went so far as to say that: "I consider ethics to be taken for granted. Actually I have never done a mean thing" (Jones, 1957, p. 247). This surely is a strange thing to say for someone who has studied man as a social being as closely as did Freud. I mention it here to show how the notion of "illness" (in the case of psychoanalysis, "psychopathology," or "mental illness") was used by Freud—and by most of his followers—as a means for classifying certain forms of human behavior as falling within the scope of medicine, and hence (by *fiat*) outside that of ethics!

they may be realized is so vast, and many of them remain so unacknowledged, that they cannot fail but lead to conflicts in human relations. Indeed, to say that human relations at all levels—from mother to child, through husband and wife, to nation and nation—are fraught with stress, strain, and disharmony is, once again, making the obvious explicit. Yet, what may be obvious may be also poorly understood. This I think is the case here. For it seems to me that—at least in our scientific theories of behavior—we have failed to *accept* the simple fact that human relations are inherently fraught with difficulties and that to make them even relatively harmonious requires much patience and hard work. I submit that the idea of mental illness is now being put to work to obscure certain difficulties which at present may be inherent—not that they need be unmodifiable—in the social intercourse of persons. If this is true, the concept functions as a disguise; for instead of calling attention to conflicting human needs, aspirations, and values, the notion of mental illness provides an amoral and impersonal "thing" (an "illness") as an explanation for *problems in living* (Szasz, 1959). We may recall in this connection that not so long ago it was devils and witches who were held responsible for men's problems in social living. The belief in mental illness, as something other than man's trouble in getting along with his fellow man, is the proper heir to the belief in demonology and witchcraft. Mental illness exists or is "real" in exactly the same sense in which witches existed or were "real."

CHOICE, RESPONSIBILITY AND PSYCHIATRY

While I have argued that mental illnesses do not exist, I obviously did not imply that the social and psychological occurrences to which this label is currently being attached also do not exist. Like the personal and social troubles which people had in the Middle Ages, they are real enough. It is the labels we give them that concerns us and, having labelled them, what we do about them. While I cannot go into the ramified implications of this problem here, it is worth noting that a demonologic conception of problems in living gave rise to therapy along theological lines. Today, a belief in mental illness implies—nay, requires—therapy along medical or psychotherapeutic lines.

What is implied in the line of thought set forth here is something quite different. I do not intend to offer a new conception of "psychiatric illness" nor a new form of "therapy." My aim is more modest and yet also more ambitious. It is to suggest that the phenomena now called mental illnesses be looked at afresh and more simply, that they be removed from the category of illnesses, and that they be regarded as the expressions of man's struggle with the problem of *how* he should live. The last mentioned problem is obviously a vast one, its enormity reflecting not only man's inability to cope with his environment, but even more his increasing self-reflectiveness.

By problems in living, then, I refer to that truly explosive chain reaction which began with man's fall from divine grace by partaking of the fruit of the tree of knowledge. Man's awareness of himself and of the world about him seems to be a steadily expanding one, bringing in its wake an ever larger *burden of understanding* (an expression borrowed from Susanne Langer, 1953). *This burden,* then, *is to be expected and must not be misinterpreted.* Our only *rational* means for lightening it is *more understanding,* and appropriate *action* based on such understanding. The main alternative lies in acting as though the burden were not what in fact we perceive it to be and taking refuge in an outmoded theological view of man. In the latter view, man does not fashion his life and much of his world about him, but merely lives out his fate in a world created by superior beings. This may logically lead to pleading nonresponsibility in the face of seemingly unfathomable problems and difficulties. Yet, if man fails to take increasing responsibility for his actions, individually as well as collectively, it seems unlikely that some higher power or being would assume this task and carry this burden for him. Moreover, this seems hardly the proper time in human history for obscuring the issue of man's responsibility for his actions by hiding it behind the skirt of an all-explaining conception of mental illness.

CONCLUSIONS

I have tried to show that the notion of mental illness has outlived whatever usefulness it might have had and that it now functions merely as a convenient myth. As such, it is a true heir to religious myths in general, and to the belief in witchcraft in particular; the role of all these belief-systems was to act as *social tranquilizers,* thus encouraging the hope that mastery of certain specific problems may be achieved by means of substitutive (symbolic-magical) operations. The notion of mental illness thus serves mainly to obscure the everyday fact that life for most people is a continuous struggle, not for biological survival, but for a "place in the sun," "peace of mind," or some other human value. For man aware of himself and of the world about him, once the needs for preserving the body (and perhaps the race) are more or less satisfied, the problem arises as to what he should do with himself. Sustained adherence to the myth of mental illness allows people to avoid facing this problem, believing that mental health, conceived as the absence of mental illness, automatically insures the making of right and safe choices in one's conduct of life. But the facts are all the other way. It is the making of good choices in life that others regard, retrospectively, as good mental health!

The myth of mental illness encourages us, moreover, to believe in its logical corollary: that social intercourse would be harmonious, satisfying, and the secure basis of a "good life" were it not for the disrupting influences of mental illness or "psychopathology." The potentiality for universal human happiness, in this form at least, seems to me but another example of the I-wish-it-were-true type of fantasy. I do believe that human happiness or well-being on a hitherto unimaginably large scale, and not just for a select few, is possible. This goal could be achieved, however, only at the cost of many men, and not just a few being willing and able to tackle their personal, social, and ethical conflicts. This means having the courage and integrity to forego waging battles on false fronts, finding solutions for substitute problems—for instance, fighting the battle of stomach acid and chronic fatigue instead of facing up to a marital conflict.

Our adversaries are not demons, witches, fate, or mental illness. We have no enemy whom we can fight, exorcise, or dispel by "cure." What we do have are *problems in living*—whether these be biologic, economic, political, or sociopsychological. In this essay I was concerned only with problems belonging in the last mentioned category, and within this group mainly with those pertaining to moral values. The field to which modern psychiatry addresses itself is vast, and I made no effort to encompass it all. My argument was limited to the proposition that mental illness is a myth, whose function it is to disguise and thus render more palatable the bitter pill of moral conflicts in human relations.

REFERENCES

Hollingshead, A. B., & Redlich, F. C. *Social class and mental illness.* New York: Wiley, 1958.

Jones, E. *The life and work of Sigmund Freud.* Vol. III. New York: Basic Books, 1957.

Langer, S. K. *Philosophy in a new key.* New York: Mentor Books, 1953.

Peters, R. S. *The concept of motivation.* London: Routledge & Kegan Paul, 1958.

Szasz, T. S. Malingering: "Diagnosis" or social condemnation? *AMA Arch. Neurol. Psychiat.,* 1956, **76,** 432–443.

Szasz, T. S. *Pain and pleasure: A study of bodily feelings.* New York: Basic Books, 1957. (a)

Szasz, T. S. The problem of psychiatric nosology: A contribution to a situational analysis of psychiatric operations. *Amer. J. Psychiat.,* 1957, **114,** 405–413. (b)

Szasz, T. S. On the theory of psychoanalytic treatment. *Int. J. Psycho-Anal.,* 1957, **38,** 166–182. (c)

Szasz, T. S. Psychiatry, ethics and the criminal law. *Columbia law Rev.,* 1958, **58,** 183–198.

Szasz, T. S. Moral conflict and psychiatry, *Yale Rev.,* 1959, in press.

Introduction to Seiden Article

The discussion of psychopathology is not often a pleasant topic—particularly when it centers on a subject highly relevant to the discussants, such as, in this instance, student suicide. Yet, often the best way to combat a problem like suicide is to come to grips with it—examining it in an attempt to understand and, eventually, overcome it. In one study devoted to this end Robert Seiden investigated student suicides at the University of California (Berkeley).

Besides aiding us in our understanding of student suicides the Seiden findings also illustrate how popular conceptions of this psychopathological problem are often found to be misconceptions when subjected to scientific scrutiny. For example, if you think that student suicides occur more frequently during final exam periods than at the beginning of the semester you hold a popular but incorrect conception about this mounting campus problem.

27

Campus Tragedy:
A Study of Student Suicide

Richard H. Seiden

Prior studies of college suicides have neglected the need for an adequate comparison or control group. To remedy this situation, student suicides were compared to their nonsuicidal classmates on selected demographic variables. Suiciding students could be significantly differentiated from their fellow students on the basis of age, class standing, major subject, nationality, emotional condition, and academic achievement. The suicidal students presented similar prodromal patterns which were precipitated by scholastic anxieties, concern over physical health, and difficult interpersonal relationships. Contrary to general belief, the greatest suicidal activity occurred during the beginning, not the final, weeks of the semester. On the basis of changes transpiring in the college population, a future increase of student suicide was predicted.

The act of self-destruction rudely challenges our supposed love for life and fear of death. It is always a puzzlement, but in no case is suicide more shocking or bewildering than it is in the college student. For here are a relatively privileged group of persons enjoying valued advantages of youth, intelligence, and educational opportunity. Why should persons, seemingly so rewarded, seek to kill themselves, and, indeed, to commit suicide at a rate significantly in excess of their noncollege peers (Bruyn & Seiden, 1965, p. 76)?

This perplexing question—"Why do students suicide?"—has motivated

SOURCE. *Journal of Abnormal Psychology*, 1966, **71**, 389–399. Copyright 1966 by the American Psychological Association, and reproduced by permission. Revision of a paper presented to Psi Chi colloquium, Western Psychological Association, Honolulu, June 1965.

This research was supported by Grant #5 T1 MH-8104 from the National Institute of Mental Health.

a great deal of concern among college health authorities leading to several studies and evaluations of the problem in American universities (Braaten & Darling, 1962; Jensen, 1955; Parrish, 1957; Raphael, Power, & Berridge, 1937; Temby, 1961). Unfortunately, these studies have all had an exclusively descriptive approach. They have drawn conclusions about certain characteristics of suicidal students but, seemingly, without appreciation for the degree to which these same characteristics are shared by the entire student body population. What has been conspicuously omitted is a baseline—a standard of comparison against which the diagnostic value of their findings might be judged. One is reminded of the gentleman who, when asked, "How is your wife?" astutely responded, "Compared to what?" This very question of relative comparison must also be asked in the study of student suicides.

The present study attempted to remedy this situation by applying a reasonable standard of comparison, namely, the great majority of fellow college students who do not commit suicide. By investigating what characteristics significantly differentiate suicidal students from their classmates plus examining those situational-temporal conditions associated with campus suicides, it was hoped to achieve a clearer diagnostic picture. Once the high-risk, suicide-prone student can be identified, a large and necessary step will have been taken toward the ultimate objective of effective prophylaxis.

METHOD

The approach used in the present study was one of analytic epidemiology, that is, comparing for particular characteristics the subset of student suicides with the total student body population from which they were drawn. This particular procedure meets the methodological criteria for selection of comparison groups, as stated by MacMahon, Pugh, and Ipsen (1960):

> A comparison group is a group of unaffected individuals believed to reflect the characteristics of the population from which the affected group was drawn. Ideally the comparison group should not differ from the affected group in any respect (other than not being affected) which might be likely to influence the frequency of the variable or variables suspected of being causally connected. This means either that both the patient and comparison groups must be representative of the same population or that if selective factors enter into the choice of the patterns, the same factors ought to enter into the selection of the comparison group [p. 235].

The method of the present study involved a comparison of the sample of 23 University of California at Berkeley (UCB) students who committed suicide during the 10-year period 1952 through 1961, with the entire UCB student body population during this same decade. The objective of this comparison was to determine what special characteristics differentiated the suicide-prone student from his classmates. Within this framework the following working definitions were employed: (*a*) *Student*—the definition of a student was established by registration on the Berkeley campus of the University of California, in either graduate or undergraduate status, during the regular college semester periods. Summer sessions were not included because of the unreliability of data for these periods and changes in the usual composition of the student body population during summer sessions. (*b*) *Suicide* —refers to a completed suicide, established by a death certificate stating suicide as the legal cause of death. In one instance, involving a jump from the Golden Gate bridge, this was not possible. Since the body was never recovered, a certificate was not issued; however, the case was well-documented in police and newspaper files. By keeping to this legalistic definition of suicide, one runs the very likely probability that the true number of suicides will be underenumerated. For example, cases of equivocal student deaths, such as by falls or drowning, were regarded as accidental, in keeping with the coroner's findings, even though these deaths, listed as accidents, could have been suicides which were covered up to avoid the social stigma related to suicide. Indeed, it has been estimated that only about 70% of successful suicides are ever recorded as such (Dublin, 1963, p. 3). The advantage in using this definition is that one can be quite certain that deaths recorded as suicide are bona-fide cases since the error is, almost always, in the direction of underreporting. (*c*) *Exposure to risk*—the period of exposure to risk comprised the 10-year span 1952–1961 inclusive, a total of 10 academic or $7\frac{1}{2}$ calendar years. This important variable, the length of exposure, was to some degree controlled since both the suicidal and nonsuicidal students were exposed to the same period of risk. (*d*) *Population at risk*—population at risk was the total student body of UCB during the 10-year period cited. Case finding procedures were extremely painstaking, requiring several months of effort to detect and verify 23 bona-fide study cases. Numerous sources of information were used, but for the suicidal students the primary source was the standard death certificate, obtained from the state health department. Secondary sources consisted of newspaper clippings, police files, and University records. The source of materials for the baseline data for the total student body population was the UCB Office of the Registrar. Their publication, *A Ten-Year Survey of Certain Demographic Characteristics of the Student Population* (Suslow, 1963), was indispensable.

In terms of research design, the procedures consisted of collecting and analyzing data regarding selected attributes of the total student population. These data were then used as a baseline to which the sample of suicidal UCB students could be compared. Since suicide may also involve a strong volitional component, further analyses were made with respect to certain situational-temporal features of the academic environment.

RESULTS AND DISCUSSION

Results are presented in tabular and graphic form and discussed in the text by order of their appearance. The various comparisons were statistically analyzed by testing the significance of the difference between two proportions (Hill, 1961, pp. 122–132), specifically, the significance of proportional differences between the suicidal sample and expected population values as based upon knowledge of the student universe. All probability statements are two-tailed probabilities.

Incidence and Prevalence

Previous research on the UCB population (Bruyn & Seiden, 1965) investigated the general question of student suicide risk. By comparing the student suicide experience with the suicide incidence among a comparable group of non-college-age cohorts, it was established that the incidence of suicide among students was significantly greater than for non-student-age peers ($p = .004$). Conversely, the general mortality experience from all causes was significantly more favorable for students when compared to their non-academic-age peers ($p < .001$). In terms of total mortality, suicides accounted for 23 of the 68 student deaths which occurred during the 10-year study period. Proportionally, it ranked as the second leading cause of death (34%), exceeded only by accidents (37%).

Age

For the United States as a whole, there is a well-documented positive correlation between age and suicide (Dublin, 1963, p. 22). This same relationship holds for the student population. If the student body is divided on the basis of those who are above and below age 25, one finds that the percentage of suicides in the older age group is approximately twice their proportional percentage in the population (see Table 1). This distinction is graphically portrayed in Figure 1 which presents the relative frequency of suicidal and nonsuicidal students by 5-year age groups. It is notable that only about 6% of all students fall in the 30 to 34-year age category while more than 26% of the suicidal students are found in this interval. In fact, the median age for the student body population is 22 years, 6 months, while the median age for the suicidal students, 26 years, 5 months, is greater by almost 4 years.

Class Standing

Directly correlated with, and, indeed, almost identical to, chronological age, is the class standing of individual students. Median class standing for

TABLE 1
Selected Demographic Characteristics of Suicidal and
Nonsuicidal Students, UCB, 1952–61

Demographic Characteristics	Suicidal Students		Total Student Body Population	
	Frequency Distribution ($n = 23$)	% Distribution	% Distribution	p
Age				
Under 25	9	39	70	.001
25 and above	14	61	30	
Class standing				
Undergraduate	12	52	72	.033
Graduate	11	48	28	
Sex				
Male	17	74	67	ns
Female	6	26	33	
Marital status[a]				
Married	3	14	23	ns
Never married	19	86	77	
Race				
White	20	87	89	ns
Nonwhite	3	13	11	
Religion				
Protestant	15	65	60	
Jewish	5	22	18	ns
Catholic	3	13	22	
Nationality				
U.S.A.	19	83	96	.002
Foreign	4	17	04	
Major subject[b]				
Mechanical-mathematic	10	50	64	ns
Aesthetic-social	10	50	36	
Grade-point average[c]				
Above average	14	67	50	ns
Below average	7	33	50	
Mental health service				
Psychiatric patient	8	34	10	<.001
Nonpatient	15	66	90	

[a]Excludes one divorced student.
[b]Excludes three students who had not declared majors.
[c]Excludes two students who did not complete a semester.

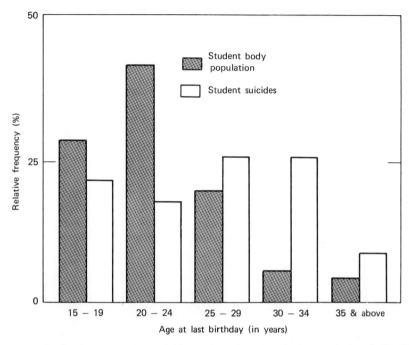

FIG. 1. Age distributions of student suicides and total student body population, UCB, 1952–61.

the entire student population was the junior year, for the suicidal subset it was the senior year. When the groups are divided on the basis of graduate or undergraduate standing, one finds that graduate students committed suicide in numbers significantly greater than could be expected from their proportions in the student body at large (see Table 1).

Sex

Of the 23 student suicides, 17 were male, 6 female, a sex ratio approximating 3:1 (see Table 1). This finding accords with those sex ratios reported in previous studies of completed suicide (Dublin, 1963, p. 23). However, an adjustment is necessary to correctly relate this information to the college population. Whereas the sexes are about equally distributed in the general United States population, they are not equally distributed on campus. For the years under study, males outnumbered females in the student body population by approximately 2:1. Accordingly, the obtained sex ratio of 3:1 must be halved to yield an adjusted student ratio of about 1.5 male suicides for each female suicide. This student sex ratio is considerably narrower than the sex ratio for the country at large. It seems to indicate a heightened risk of suicide among female students as compared to

the general female population. However, this indication must remain somewhat speculative since the female suicides were considerably older (median
age 30 years, 1 month) than were male suicides (median age 26 years, 1
month). As a consequence one cannot be entirely sure that the constricted
ratio is not an effect of confounding between age and sex. Should further
research confirm that there is, in fact, a greater risk of suicide among female students as opposed to female nonstudents, it would follow the predictions of Gibbs and Martin (1964). They proposed a rise in female suicides
due to increasing social pressures. According to their status-integration
theory, as more women enter the labor force they encounter cross-pressures
from conflicting social roles. They postulate that these stresses will lead to
increasing numbers of female suicides.

Marital Status

Of the 23 student suicides, it was possible to classify 22 persons into
the categories of "married" or "never married," which corresponded to the
available student population data. One divorced student was thereby excluded from the analysis. There was no remarkable disparity between the
suicidal and nonsuicidal students on the basis of marital status (see Table 1).
For the entire United States population, suicide is less common among
married persons (Dublin, 1963, p. 26), but this was not the case for campus
suicides. Only three of the student suicides were married, and only one of
those married had children. The remaining two cases, both females, committed suicide shortly after their marriages.

Race

Of the 23 known suicides, only three were nonwhite and all three of
these nonwhite students were Chinese. There were no suicides among Negro,
East Indian, or American Indian students who, at any event, comprised
only about 3% of the student body population. The distribution of suicides
by race corresponded closely to the racial proportions found in the student
population (see Table 1). It should be mentioned, however, that there is
good reason to question the adequacy of these racial data. Since University
records do not ask for nor indicate students' race, these breakdowns, fur-
nished by the University Dean of Students Office, were presumably obtained
from simple headcounts with all the imprecision that this method implies.

Religion

Religion was not a significant factor in differentiating suicidal students
from the general campus population (see Table 1). As was the case with

racial statistics, the religious data, likewise, must be regarded with great skepticism. The University does not conduct a religious census of its students. Consequently, the religious population figures were estimated from student residence information cards on which "religious affiliation" is an optional item. Very frequently it is left unanswered.

Nationality

Only 4 of the 23 student suicides were foreign students. Nonetheless, their representation in the student body was so negligible (only 4%) that they appear among the suicides in approximately four times the magnitude one would expect from their proportions in the student population (see Table 1). As a group, these four "international student" suicides were characterized by some striking similarities. As youngsters, all of the four had known and suffered from the ravages of war, and three of them were forced to flee from their childhood homes. Two of the students, natives of mainland China, had been dispossessed by the Communist revolution; another student, born in Austria, lost his family in the horrors of the Nazi concentration camps and subsequently migrated to Israel. The fourth student, a native Israeli, had grown up amidst the Arab-Jewish war over the Palestine partition.

Moreover, they shared a similar pattern of conflicts, centering to a large degree around strong feelings of shame. These feelings were reflected in a deep dread that they would not meet expectations that others had set for them. There was some reality to these fears, in that other persons had sent them abroad, were paying their expenses, and probably did expect from them some measure of academic achievement. Still, their excessive concern about "what others would think" was unduly frenetic. All four of them were known to the Student Mental Health Service where they had been seen for psychiatric treatment. These findings, however, must be interpreted with some caution since the median age of foreign students (26 years, 1 month), exceeded the median age of American students (24 years), raising the possibility that the differences were due in some degree to age rather than nationality.

Major Subject

For this comparison, the suicidal subjects were divided into two categories, corresponding somewhat to William James' distinction between the "tough" and "tender minded." Of the 20 suicidal students who had declared majors, the breakdown was 10 students in the "tough-minded" or mechanical-mathematics group (Engineering, Professional, Physical Sciences, Biological Sciences, Agricultural majors) and 10 students in the "tender-minded" or esthetic-social group (Arts, Social Sciences, Language and Literature majors).

Relative to their population proportions, there was a greater incidence of suicides in the tender-minded group, but not a large enough imbalance to achieve statistical significance. Further analysis, by individual subject groups, revealed that suicides were significantly more frequent among students majoring in languages and literature (five cases), especially English majors, who comprised three of the five cases (see Table 2).

Grade-Point Average

Grade-point analysis required some basic adjustments since graduate and undergraduate grading systems are not directly comparable. In practice, an undergraduate "C" is approximately equivalent to a graduate "B." For the student population, the grade-point average (GPA) for undergraduates was 2.50, while for graduates it was 3.35 (calculated to the scale: $A = 4$, $B = 3$, $C = 2$, $D = 1$, $F = 0$). Given this discrepancy, it is obviously necessary to separately compare undergraduate and graduate students with reference to their respective grade-point distributions. When the suicidal students (excluding two who did not complete a full semester at UCB) are ranked by means of achievement above or below their population GPA, we find that two-thirds of them were above average while, by definition, only half of the general student body achieved this mark. Although suggestive of a tendency toward higher grades among suicidal students, the difference, in fact, did not achieve statistical significance. However, further analysis, distributing GPA by class standing, revealed a marked discrepancy between graduate and undergraduate students. This breakdown is detailed in Table 3 and reveals that of the 11 undergraduate students who committed suicide (after one complete semester at the University), 10 of them had surpassed the undergraduate GPA. For graduate student suicides, only 4 of the 10 who had completed a semester exceeded the graduate GPA. Despite the differential grading system that rewards the graduate student with more grade

TABLE 2
Suicides Among Language and Literature
Majors vs. All Other Subject Majors

Major Subject Group	Suicidal Students		Total Student Body Population	
	n	%	%	p
Language and literature	5	25	9	.012
All other majors	15	75	91	

Note: Excludes three students who had not declared major subjects.

TABLE 3
Grade-Point Averages for Graduate and Undergraduate Student Suicides

GPA	Suicidal Students		Student Population	p
	n	%	%	
Class standing				
Undergraduate				
Above mean	10	91	50	.006
Below mean	1	09	50	
Graduate				
Above mean	4	40	50	ns
Below mean	6	60	50	

Note: Excludes two students; one graduate, one undergraduate, who suicided during their first semester.

points for a similar level of work, the suicidal undergraduate students received a higher overall GPA than the graduate student suicides (see Table 4).

This finding seems to indicate that undergraduate and graduate suicides differ markedly from one another in terms of academic achievement. The undergraduate suicides performed on a level well above their fellow classmates and performed considerably better than did graduate suicides. Looking at the personal histories of these undergraduate students one discovers an interesting paradox. To an external observer, say someone viewing their transcripts, these students achieved splendidly in their academic pursuits. They had all been A or B students in high school since a B or better average is required for undergraduate admission, a policy which is estimated to limit entrance to the top 10–12% of graduating high school seniors. Reports from family and friends, however, reveal that self-satisfaction was not the case with these students. Rather, they seemed filled with doubts of their adequacy, dissatisfied with their grades, and despondent over their general academic aptitude. This exacerbated fear of failure was tempered somewhat by the fact that in every case of undergraduate suicide the final semester's GPA was lower ($\bar{x} = 2.53$) than the previous cumulative GPA ($\bar{x} = 3.34$). An-

TABLE 4
Observed and Expected GPA of Student Suicides by Class Standing

Class Standing	GPA	
	Observed	Expected
Undergraduate	3.18	2.50
Graduate	2.90	3.35

other consideration is whether these students aspired to graduate school which requires a higher than average GPA (2.5–3.0 at UCB). Unfortunately, these exact data are not available; however, a check of those students in major subjects which definitely indicated future graduate work, for example, premedicine, revealed academic achievement in excess of grade requirements. Nevertheless, on balance, they were still achieving loftily above the average of their classmates. How can one explain their deep self-dissatisfaction despite contrary and objective indications of their competence? Two possible explanations suggest themselves: (a) The internal standards these students applied to themselves were so Olympian, the demands they imposed upon themselves so exacting, that they were destined to suffer frustration and disappointment no matter how well they fared; and/or (b) Whereas they had previously been crackerjack students in high school or junior college, excelling without much difficulty, the precipitous drop in grade points over the final semester threatened their feelings of self-esteem. Thus, faced by a sudden loss of status, they may have suicided as a response to this egoistic conflict. In any case, the discrepancy between perceived self-concept and objective reality indicates that a purely objective approach often obscures more than it reveals. What one needs to try and understand is the phenomenological response of the individual student. What is necessary to know is what inner standards, what idealized fantasy he uses to judge himself and his own personal worth. For the graduate student suicides as a group, there was no discrepancy between their academic achievements and what might be expected on the basis of the general population of graduate students. While they produced slightly below their population mean, the variation in this instance was primarily due to two students who were in considerable scholastic straits. Contrary to the undergraduates, graduate suicides showed no pattern of decline in their terminal semester GPA. Confirmation of the scholastic disparity between graduate and undergraduate suicides is further revealed by the irregular distribution of academic awards. Inspection of Table 5 indicates that undergraduate students garnered

TABLE 5
Scholastic Awards by Class Standing

Class Standing	Suicidal Students		Student Population	
	n	%	%	p
Undergraduate				
Scholarship	7	58	05	<.001
Nonscholarship	5	42	95	
Graduate				
Scholarship	1	10	23	ns
Nonscholarship	10	90	77	

scholarship honors at a rate well beyond the general undergraduate population, while the graduate student suicides did not differ significantly from their classmates in earning academic awards. Even though graduate student awards were far more plentiful, the great majority of awards (10 of 11) were held by undergraduate student suicides.

Mental Health

Of the 23 student suicides, 8 had been referred to the student mental health service for psychiatric treatment (of the 8 students, apparently only 2 were diagnosed as psychotic reactions). These 8 cases comprised better than one-third of the student suicides, significantly exceeding the approximately 10% of the total student body population seen at the mental health facilities (see Table 1). Besides the 8 students known to the student psychiatric service, an additional 3 students were in private psychiatric treatment, making a total of almost 50% of the suicidal group who gave this particular indication of prior mental disturbance.

Temporal-Situational Relationships

Among all causes of death, suicide allows for the greatest degree of volition. The suicidal person is in a position to choose the date, place, and method of his death, and it has long been speculated that there may be a special psychological significance to these choices. Through tracing the time, place, and method of student suicides, the following particular patterns were observed:

Time

When student suicides were charted by calendar months they formed a bimodal curve with peaks occurring during February and October. A more meaningful comparison obtained when the academic semester was used as the time interval. This distribution, as illustrated in Figure 2, challenges a frequently held belief about campus suicides. Academic folklore often explains student suicides as a response to the anxieties and stresses of final examinations. Yet, surprisingly, the data showed that almost the reverse relationship held. Only 1 of the 23 student suicides was committed during finals. (Even that single instance may be dubiously related to final exams since this student was doing well in school and had expressed satisfaction with his "finals" performance.) Most of the suicides occurred at the beginning of the semester. When the semester is divided into three equivalent parts, the vast majority of cases, 16 out of 23, are found to occur during the first 6-week segment. (Actually, the period is only 5 weeks from when in-

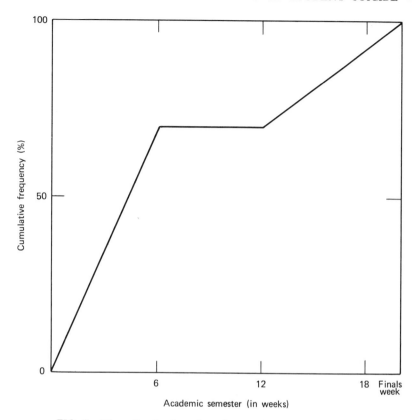

FIG. 2. Time distribution of student suicides, UCB, 1952–61.

struction begins; the first week is confined to registration procedures.) No cases were found during the second 6-week period which includes the midterm examinations. Over the remaining third of the semester there were seven cases, just one of which occurred during finals week itself (always the last week of the semester). This irregular time distribution of student suicides departed significantly from uniform expectations ($x^2_2 = 16.8$, $p < .001$). Clearly, the old saw about suicides and finals was not supported. Instead, the danger period for student suicide was found to be the start, not the finish, of the school semester. Incidentally, the day of the week departed significantly from the null hypothesis of uniformity ($x^2_1 = 4.18$, $p < .05$) with almost one-half the cases occurring on Monday or Friday, terminals of the school week. Unfortunately, the data were none too precise since some cases were based on coroner's estimates as to the date of death.

The unexpectedly low correspondence between final examinations and the commission of student suicide bears some resemblance to a parallel phenomenon involving student mental health during the recent free speech activities on the UCB campus. In the course of these supposedly stressful times, there was a striking drop in admissions to the student mental health service (20% below average) and no recorded student suicides during the 1965 academic year. (Such behavior corresponds to the drop in suicides, psychosomatic illness, and neurotic conditions observed during both World Wars.) Why, in the midst of all the controversy, turmoil, and tempest was student mental health apparently enhanced? One possibility is that some students who had previously been grappling with internal problems now had the opportunity to act out, to ventilate their inner conflicts, and to displace their intrapunitive anger and hostility by redirecting it toward an external symbol, namely, the University. Perhaps it was the galvanized and heightened sense of community that facilitated mental well-being. Certainly many students felt involved in a common cause; probably, for some it imparted meaning to their lives where previously they had felt alienated and purposeless. If so, it was also a perfect antidote to the kinds of feelings that often drive people to self-destruction.

Place

Most of the students, 12 of 23, committed suicide at their residences. The next most frequent location was the University itself, upon whose grounds 4 students ended their lives. Three students were found dead in parked autos on isolated suburban roads. Another 3 suicided in out-of-town hotel rooms, and 1 student leaped from the San Francisco Golden Gate bridge. It is difficult to determine any significance to the site of these suicides, except for the 4 cases who killed themselves on the university grounds. Of these, the most symbolic suicide was the 1 student who jumped from the Campanile, an architectural landmark of the Berkeley campus.

Method

The most frequent agent of choice was firearms, followed by ingestions and asphyxiations. A comparison with the methods used by Yale student suicides (see Table 6) revealed considerable similarity in the methods employed by the two groups of students. The relatively larger number of poisonings among UCB students is most likely due to the more recent availability of tranquilizers and barbiturates.

For only two of the Berkeley cases was there the least equivocation about assigning suicide as the cause of death. These two cases, both involving ingestions of poisonous substances, were qualified as "probably suicide" but routinely coded as "deaths due to suicide." In at least 10 instances, suicide notes were left by the decedents. These notes ranged from simple instructions

TABLE 6

Methods of Suicide Used by UCB and Yale Students

Method	UCB (1952–1961)		Yale (1920–1955)[a]	
	n	%	n	%
Firearms	8	35	10	40
Poisonings	6	26	3	12
Asphyxiation	4	17	5	20
Hanging	2	09	6	24
Jumping from high place	2	09	1	04
Cutting instruments	1	04	—	—
Total	23	100	25	100

[a]Source: Parrish, 1957, p. 589.

concerning the disposal of personal belongings to lengthy, literary dissertations, one of which finished by tersely quoting Camus: "Life as a human being is absurd."

Psychological Factors

A statistical approach, per se, can go just so far in describing the suicide-prone student. The additional use of case history materials provides a fuller, more clinically oriented dimension to the portrayal. As such, the following inferences were derived from anecdotal reports of friends and acquaintances of the students, along with those members of the University community whose lives they touched. From a preventive standpoint, the most pertinent questions which might be asked are, "What prodromal signs, what clues to suicide could be discerned from the personal lives of these students? Specifically, were there any indications or harbingers of their ultimate destinies?" Lastly, "Was there a characteristic conflict which precipitated their self-destructive actions?" The question of prodromal indications can be flatly answered "yes." There were numerous warnings in almost every case. At least five of the students had made past suicide attempts. Warnings of a more subtle nature could be discovered in the histories of the remaining students. For example, the pupil who went out of his way to modify an item on the medical history form. Where it had requested, "Whom shall we notify in case of emergency?" he crossed out the word "emergency" and substituted "death." Or the student who confided that he sometimes takes 10 or so nembutals because "I am an adventurer." Other students evidenced a long-standing infatuation with death, often initiating "bull sessions" about the futility of life, or making wry jokes about killing themselves. Prior to their suicides a disproportionately large number of these students were involved in psychiatric treatment. As a group, they presented similar symptomatic patterns featuring symptoms of insomnia, anorexia, and extreme moodiness, especially moods of despondency; in all, it was a psychological picture compatible with the general diagnosis of agitated depression.

Although their prodromal response to stress was very similar, the particular crisis that precipitated their suicides were not. Bearing in mind that each individual case was unique, for purposes of description, the main prodromal conflicts could be classified into the following three categories:

1. *Concern over studies*—In many cases acquaintances of the students made such judgments as "he pushed himself too hard," "worried over grades," "felt his grades were not as good as he thought they should be," or similar scholastic anxieties which, they felt, triggered the suicidal crisis. It is difficult to evaluate these inferences since "worry over grades" is often seen by informants as a most likely explanation. At any event, if true, their exaggerated concern over studies contrasted vividly with generally excellent academic grades.

2. *Unusual physical complaints*—A number of the students complained of inability to eat or sleep, one student warranting a diagnosis of "avitaminosis." Others worried about possible deterioration such as the student who feared that his "failing sight" might ruin a prospective medical career. A few pupils, however, presented physical complaints of a bizarre semidelusional quality, for instance, the young man whose stomach literally persecuted him. From childhood on he had suffered from anorexia and "stomach ache." Although an exploratory laparotomy did not disclose anything, by the time he entered the University he was at least 50 pounds underweight, still wracked by chronic stomach pains. He then moved from his fraternity house, in the hope of gaining weight by selecting his own food. This plan proved to no avail, nor did extensive medical testing at the student health service, all of which proved negative. He finally ended his torment, perhaps symbolically, by ingesting cyanide.

3. *Difficulties with interpersonal relationships*—Combined under this heading were two different types of conflicts, both reflecting problems in personal relationships. First were the students involved in stormy love affairs. Here the critical stresses were feelings of rejection which had been engendered by broken romances. In the one recorded instance of double suicide, the precipitating event was parental opposition to the youngsters' marriage. Much more typical, however, was the essentially asocial, withdrawn student. These particular students were uniformly described as terriby shy, virtually friendless individuals, alienated from all but the most minimal social interactions. Frequently they had compensated for their personal solitude by increased study and almost total absorption in schoolwork. The most calamitous example of such human isolation was the student, dead for 18 days

before he was found in his lonely room. It is a tragic commentary to his existence, and perhaps a cause for his suicide, that there were no friends, no people involved enough in his life to know, or to care, that he had been missing for well over 2 weeks.

Interpretation

Reviewing the results of the present study, one can reasonably conclude that significant associations between student suicide and numerous variables, both personal and environmental, have been demonstrated. Nonetheless, one cannot, with certitude, infer that these relationships are causal ones. This type of inference would require procedures more exacting than the limited epidemiological methods herein employed. For instance, the total student body population, used as a matched control or comparison group, included a number of students who had unsuccessfully attempted suicide. Quite possibly their inclusion diluted the significance of the obtained differences between suicidal and presumably nonsuicidal students. This is a relatively minor concern, compared to other more cautionary limitations. A primary concern is to what degree the observed relationships were spuriously increased by a common variable. For example, the correlation between student suicide and declining terminal GPA may very well be due to a third factor—emotional disturbance—which both depressed scholastic grades and led to self-destruction. As a corollary, it should be recognized that not all of the selected variables were independent of one another. It is known for one that age and class standing are highly dependent, and it was observed, also, that the variable of age probably confounded to some degree the comparisons by sex and by nationality. Another area of uncertainty concerns the time-order sequence of student suicide. One is unable to state, with certainty, which comes first, the disturbed student or the stresses of student life. Are the suicides due to selection into colleges of mentally unstable individuals or are they due to competitive pressures of the academic environment? The fullest answer to these questions will only come from further research. Toward this goal some salient lines of inquiry could include: the investigation of student suicide attempters and student accident cases, postcollegiate follow-up studies, and the use of "psychological autopsy" procedures, as described by Shneidman and Farberow (1961).

Within the expressed limits of the study design, what predictions about the future suicide problem are warranted? Extrapolating from results of the present study, it appears that a future increase of student suicides may be expected. This increase should occur as a function of two variables, that is, age and academic competition, both of which are directly correlated to student suicides, and both of which are slated to increase in future student body populations. Average student age is already rising as a result of ever increasing proportions of graduate students in the American University system. For example, architects of the UCB educational master plan are considering an ultimate 50:50 graduate-undergraduate ratio. The second variable, academic competition, will likely increase as a result of mounting public demands for quasi-universal college education. As a case in point, the enrollment demands at UCB have already exceeded the available academic supply. Consequently, it has been necessary to restrict enrollment to the uppermost fraction of high school graduating classes. If accepted, the pressure on the student to achieve and maintain very high GPAs gives no indication of abatement. In fact, the situation ominously resembles a suicidal problem which prevails among the youth of Japan. In the Japanese case there are tremendous pressures to attend college, and those students who fail to gain entrance frequently turn to suicide as a solution to their dilemmas. Such conflicts, in addition to a more accepting cultural attitude, have probably helped to make Japan "a country of youthful suicides where suicide has become the number one cause of death in individuals under 30 [DeVos, 1964, p. 6]."

SUMMARY

The purpose of this study was to identify distinctive attributes of the suicidal student, and to determine those environmental conditions which heighten his susceptibility to suicide.

Using an epidemiological approach, demographic comparisons were made between the sample of 23 UCB students who committed suicide during the years 1952–1961 inclusive, and the total student body population for those years. As an additional procedure, the temporal-situational characteristics of student suicides were described and analyzed.

The main findings of the research were:

1. Suicidal students could be significantly differentiated from their classmates on the variables of age, class standing, major subject, nationality, emotional condition, and academic achievement. Compared to the student population at large, the suicidal group was older, contained greater proportions of graduates, language majors, and foreign students, and gave more indications of emotional disturbance. In addition, the undergraduate suicides fared much better than their fellow students in matters of academic achievement.

2. Contrary to the popular belief that suicides frequently occur during final examinations week, time relationships indicated that the peak danger period for student suicides was the beginning (first 6 weeks), not the midterm, nor end of the semester.

3. Most of the students gave recurrent warnings of their suicidal intent. Many of them presented a similar prodromal pattern marked by anorexia, insomnia, and periods of despondency.

4. Major precipitating factors were: Worry over schoolwork, chronic concerns about physical health (sometimes of a decidedly bizarre nature), and difficulties with interpersonal relationships. This last category contained some students who had reacted to romantic rejections but, for the most part, comprised the emotionally withdrawn and socially isolated student.

5. A future increase of student suicides was predicted on the basis of changes taking place in the age structure of college populations and in the competitive pressures of student life.

REFERENCES

Braaten, J., & Darling, C. Suicidal tendencies among college students. *Psychiatric Quarterly*, 1962, **36**, 665–692.

Bruyn, H. B., & Seiden, R. H. Student suicide: Fact or fancy? *Journal of the American College Health Association*, 1965, 14, 69–77.

De Vos, G. Role narcissism and the etiology of Japanese suicide. Berkeley, Calif.: Institute of International Studies, University of California, 1964. (Mimeo)

Dublin, L. I. *Suicide: A sociological and statistical study*. New York: Ronald, 1963.

Gibbs, J. P., & Martin, W. T. *Status integration and suicide*. Eugene: Oregon University Press, 1964.

Hill, A. B. *Principles of medical statistics*. New York: Oxford University Press, 1961.

Jensen, V. W. Evaluating the suicidal impulse in the university setting. *Journal Lancet*, 1955, **75**, 441–444.

MacMahon, B., Pugh, T. F., & Ipsen, J. *Epidemiological methods*. Boston: Little, Brown, 1960.

Parrish, H. M. Epidemiology of suicide among college students. *Yale Journal of Biology and Medicine*, 1957, **29**, 585–595.

Raphael, T., Power, S. H., & Berridge, W. L. The question of suicide as a problem in college mental hygiene. *American Journal of Orthopsychiatry*, 1937, **7**, 1–14.

Shneidman, E. S., & Farberow, N. L. Sample investigations of equivocal deaths. In N. L. Farberow & E. S. Shneidman (Eds.), *The cry for help*. New York: McGraw-Hill, 1961. Pp. 118–128.

Suslow, S. *A ten-year survey of certain demographic characteristics of the student population*. Berkeley: Office of the Registrar, University of California, 1963. (Mimeo)

Temby, W. D. Suicide. In G. B. Blaine & C. G. McArthur (Eds.), *Emotional problems of the student*. New York: Appleton-Century-Crofts, 1961. Pp. 133–152.

More than ever before, psychologists are searching for ways to help contemporary man meet his contemporary problems. (HIROG KUBOTA | MAGNUM)

Section VIII
Psychology in the
Service of Man

With all this talk of a gulf between American youth and adults I find it reassuring to teach a course in introductory psychology where the generation gap does not seem so formidable. Indeed, judging from the classroom comments of my students, it seems that the psychologist and the undergraduate share many common interests and concerns. Take, for example, the current state of man. Today's student is caught up in a quest to improve the human condition; to guide mankind toward a meaningful destiny. In my introductory psychology course this effort is reflected in the question students ask most often: "What can psychology do to aid man?" This same question is being asked—and answered—by today's psychologists. There is a unity of purpose between generations here: never before have students been so concerned with psychology in the service of man; and, likewise, never have psychologists devoted as much attention to this topic (a case in point—the theme of the 1969 American Psychological Association convention was "Psychology and the Problems of Society").

Due to his training the psychologist is uniquely prepared to aid man in his quest for a brighter future. Trained in the methods of science and the dimensions of human behavior the psychologist occupies an important vantage point affording access to scientific *and* human understanding. He possesses the skills that allow him to know what science is *doing* and what man is *needing*. He is capable of translating scientific progress into human terms: to assess the impact of a scientific discovery on human action; to apply scientific knowledge in a way beneficial to man. Scientific inquiries, if properly directed, and scientific discoveries, if properly utilized, can greatly aid mankind. Today's psychologist is doing his part to see that such benefits are realized.

Of the four selections that follow, two are concerned with how the psychologist can become active in the service of man, and two present examples of how the behavioral investigator has already begun such efforts.

415

Introduction to King Article

One thing is certain: in today's hectic, mixed up, unstable, polluted, warring, starving, anxiety-ridden world, the psychologist need not search far for human problems that need solving! And of all the human dilemmas crying out for attention, are there any more urgent or deserving of psychological concern than the plight of the American black man? Many behavioral scientists think not.

How might the science of psychology be utilized in the service of black Americans? One answer is provided by the late Martin Luther King, Jr. in his 1967 address to the Society for the Psychological Study of Social Issues. It is an eloquent, moving presentation that reminds us again how much our nation lost with the passing of this great American.

In calling on psychologists to study: (1) patterns of black leadership; (2) the impact of black political actions; and (3) psychological and ideological changes in blacks, Dr. King has suggested some areas where the behavioral investigator can help the black American achieve civil rights and human dignity. Such help is urgently needed.

28

The Role of the Behavioral Scientist in the Civil Rights Movement

Martin Luther King, Jr.

It is always a very rich and rewarding experience when I can take a brief break from the day-to-day demands of our struggle for freedom and human dignity and discuss the issues involved in that struggle with concerned friends of good will all over this nation. It is particularly a great privilege to discuss these issues with members of the academic community, who are constantly writing about and dealing with the problems that we face and who have the tremendous responsibility of moulding the minds of young men and women all over our country.

In the preface to their book, *Applied Sociology*, S. M. Miller and Alvin Gouldner (1965) state: "It is the historic mission of the social sciences to enable mankind to take possession of society." It follows that for Negroes who substantially are excluded from society this science is needed even more desperately than for any other group in the population.

For social scientists, the opportunity to serve in a life-giving purpose is a humanist challenge of rare distinction. Negroes too are eager for a rendezvous with truth and discovery. We are aware that social scientists, unlike some of their colleagues in the physical sciences, have been spared the grim feelings of guilt that attended the invention of nuclear weapons of destruction. Social scientists, in the main, are fortunate to be able to extirpate evil, not to invent it.

If the Negro needs social science for direction and for self-understanding, the white society is in even more urgent need. White America needs

SOURCE. *American Psychologist*, 1968, **23**, 180–186. Copyright 1968 by the American Psychological Association, and reproduced by permission. Invited Distinguished Address presented to the meeting of the Society for the Psychological Study of Social Issues, American Psychological Association, Washington, D. C., September 1967.

to understand that it is poisoned to its soul by racism and the understanding needs to be carefully documented and consequently more difficult to reject. The present crisis arises because, although it is historically imperative that our society take the next step to equality, we find ourselves psychologically and socially imprisoned. All too many white Americans are horrified not with conditions of Negro life but with the product of these conditions—the Negro himself.

White America is seeking to keep the walls of segregration substantially intact while the evolution of society and the Negro's desperation is causing them to crumble. The white majority, unprepared and unwilling to accept radical structural change, is resisting and producing chaos while complaining that if there were no chaos orderly change would come.

Negroes want the social scientist to address the white community and "tell it like it is." White America has an appalling lack of knowledge concerning the reality of Negro life. One reason some advances were made in the South during the past decade was the discovery by northern whites of the brutal facts of southern segregated life. It was the Negro who educated the nation by dramatizing the evils through nonviolent protest. The social scientist played little or no role in disclosing truth. The Negro action movement with raw courage did it virtually alone. When the majority of the country could not live with the extremes of brutality they witnessed, political remedies were enacted and customs were altered.

These partial advances were, however, limited principally to the South and progress did not automatically spread throughout the nation. There was also little depth to the changes. White America stopped murder, but that is not the same thing as ordaining brotherhood; nor is the ending of lynch rule the same thing as inaugurating justice.

After some years of Negro-white unity and partial successes, white America shifted gears and went into reverse. Negroes, alive with hope and enthusiasm, ran into sharply stiffened white resistance at all levels and bitter tensions broke out in sporadic episodes of violence. New lines of hostility were drawn and the era of good feeling disappeared.

The decade of 1955 to 1965, with its constructive elements, misled us. Everyone, activists and social scientists, underestimated the amount of violence and rage Negroes were suppressing and the amount of bigotry the white majority was disguising.

Science should have been employed more fully to warn us that the Negro, after 350 years of handicaps, mired in an intricate network of contemporary barriers, could not be ushered into equality by tentative and superficial changes.

Mass nonviolent protests, a social invention of Negroes, were effective in Montgomery, Birmingham, and Selma in forcing national legislation which served to change Negro life sufficiently to curb explosions. But when changes were confined to the South alone, the North, in the absence of change, began to seethe.

The freedom movement did not adapt its tactics to the different and unique northern urban conditions. It failed to see that nonviolent marches in the South were forms of rebellion. When Negroes took over the streets and shops, southern society shook to its roots. Negroes could contain their rage when they found the means to force relatively radical changes in their environment.

In the North, on the other hand, street demonstrations were not even a mild expression of militancy. The turmoil of cities absorbs demonstrations as merely transitory drama which is ordinary in city life. Without a more effective tactic for upsetting the status quo, the power structure could maintain its intransigence and hostility. Into the vacuum of inaction, violence and riots flowed and a new period opened.

Urban riots must now be recognized as durable social phenomena. They may be deplored, but they are there and should be understood. Urban riots are a special form of violence. They are not insurrections. The rioters are not seeking to seize territory or to attain control of institutions. They are mainly intended to shock the white community. They are a distorted form of social protest. The looting which is their principal feature serves many functions. It enables the most enraged and deprived Negro to take hold of consumer goods with the ease the white man does by using his purse. Often the Negro does not even want what he takes; he wants the experience of taking. But most of all, alienated from society and knowing that this society cherishes property above people, he is shocking it by abusing property rights. There are thus elements of emotional catharsis in the violent act. This may explain why most cities in which riots have occurred have not had a repetition, even though the causative conditions remain. It is also noteworthy that the amount of physical harm done to white people other than police is infinitesimal and in Detroit whites and Negroes looted in unity.

A profound judgment of today's riots was expressed by Victor Hugo a century ago. He said, "If a soul is left in darkness, sins will be committed. The guilty one is not he who commits the sin, but he who causes the darkness."

The policy makers of the white society have caused the darkness; they created discrimination; they structured slums; and they perpetuate unemployment, ignorance, and poverty. It is incontestable and deplorable that Negroes have committed crimes; but they are derivative crimes. They are born of the greater crimes of the white society. When we ask Negroes to abide by the law, let us also demand that the white man abide by law in the ghettos. Day-in and day-out he violates welfare laws to deprive the poor of their meager allotments; he flagrantly violates building codes and regulations; his police make a mockery of law; and he violates laws on equal employment and education and the provisions for civic services. The slums are the handiwork of a vicious system of the white society; Negroes live in them but do not make them any more than a prisoner makes a prison. Let us say boldly that if the total violations of law by the white man in the slums over the years were calculated and compared with the law breaking of a few days of riots, the hardened criminal would be the white man. These are often difficult things to say but I have come to see more and more that it is necessary to utter the truth in order to deal with the great problems that we face in our society.

There is another cause of riots that is too important to mention casually —the war in Vietnam. Here again, we are dealing with a controversial issue. But I am convinced that the war in Vietnam has played havoc with our domestic destinies. The bombs that fall in Vietnam explode at home. It does not take much to see what great damage this war has done to the image of our nation. It has left our country politically and morally isolated in the world, where our only friends happen to be puppet nations like Taiwan, Thailand, and South Korea. The major allies in the world that have been with us in war and peace are not with us in this war. As a result we find ourselves socially and politically isolated.

The war in Vietnam has torn up the Geneva Accord. It has seriously impaired the United Nations. It has exacerbated the hatreds between continents, and worse still, between races. It has frustrated our development at home by telling our underprivileged citizens that we place insatiable military demands above their most critical needs. It has greatly contributed to the forces of reaction in America, and strengthened the military-industrial complex, against which even President Eisenhower solemnly warned us. It has practically destroyed Vietnam, and left thousands of American and Vietnamese youth maimed and mutilated. And it has exposed the whole world to the risk of nuclear warfare.

As I looked at what this war was doing to our nation, and to the domestic situation and to the Civil Rights movement, I found it necessary to speak vigorously out against it. My speaking out against the war has not gone without criticisms. There are those who tell me that I should stick with Civil Rights, and stay in my place. I can only respond that I have fought too hard and long to end segregated public accommodations to segregate my own moral concerns. It is my deep conviction that justice is indivisible, that injustice anywhere is a threat to justice everywhere. For those who tell me I am hurting the Civil Rights movement, and ask, "Don't you think that in order to be respected, and in order to regain support, you must stop talking against the war?" I can only say that I am not a consensus leader. I do not seek to determine what is right and wrong by taking a Gallup Poll to determine majority opinion. And it is again my deep conviction that ultimately a genuine leader is not a searcher for consensus, but a molder of consensus.

On some positions cowardice asks the question, "Is it safe?"! Expediency asks the question, "Is it politic?" Vanity asks the question, "Is it popular?" But conscience must ask the question, "Is it right?" And there comes a time when one must take a stand that is neither safe, nor politic, nor popular. But one must take it because it is right. And that is where I find myself today.

Moreover, I am convinced, even if war continues, that a genuine massive act of concern will do more to quell riots than the most massive deployment of troops.

The unemployment of Negro youth ranges up to 40% in some slums. The riots are almost entirely youth events—the age range of participants is from 13 to 25. What hypocrisy it is to talk of saving the new generation—to make it the generation of hope—while consigning it to unemployment and provoking it to violent alternatives.

When our nation was bankrupt in the '30s we created an agency to provide jobs to all at their existing level of skill. In our overwhelming affluence today what excuse is there for not setting up a national agency for full employment immediately?

The other program which would give reality to hope and opportunity would be the demolition of the slums to be replaced by decent housing built by residents of the ghettoes.

These programs are not only eminently sound and vitally needed, but they have the support of an overwhelming majority of the nation—white and Negro. The Harris Poll on August 21, 1967, disclosed that an astounding 69% of the country support a works program to provide employment to all and an equally astonishing 65% approve a program to tear down the slums.

There is a program and there is heavy majority support for it. Yet, the administration and Congress tinker with trivial proposals to limit costs in an extravagant gamble with disaster.

The President has lamented that he cannot persuade Congress. He can, if the will is there, go to the people, mobilize the people's support, and thereby substantially increase his power to persuade Congress. Our most urgent task is to find the tactics that will move the Government no matter how determined it is to resist.

I believe we will have to find the militant middle between riots on the one hand and weak and timid supplication for justice on the other hand. That middle ground, I believe, is civil disobedience. It can be aggressive but nonviolent; it can dislocate but not destroy. The specific planning will take some study and analysis to avoid mistakes of the past when it was employed on too small a scale and sustained too briefly.

Civil disobedience can restore Negro-white unity. There have been some very important sane white voices even during the most desperate moments of the riots. One reason is that the urban crisis intersects the Negro crisis in the city. Many white decision makers may care little about saving Negroes, but they must care about saving their cities. The vast majority of production is created in cities; most white Americans live in them. The suburbs to which they flee cannot exist detached from cities. Hence powerful white elements have goals that merge with ours.

Now there are many roles for social scientists in meeting these problems. Kenneth Clark has said that Negroes are moved by a suicide instinct in riots and Negroes know there is a tragic truth in this observation. Social scientists should also disclose the suicide instinct that governs the administration and Congress in their total failure to respond constructively.

What other areas are there for social scientists to assist the Civil Rights movement? There are many, but I would like to suggest three because they have an urgent quality.

Social science may be able to search out some answers to the problem of Negro leadership. E. Franklin Frazier (1957), in his profound work, *Black Bourgeoisie,* laid painfully bare the tendency of the upwardly mobile Negro to separate from his community, divorce himself from responsibility to it, while failing to gain acceptance into the white community. There has been significant improvement from the days Frazier researched, but anyone knowledgeable about Negro life knows its middle class is not yet bearing its weight. Every riot has carried strong overtone of hostility of lower class Negroes toward the affluent Negro and vice versa. No contemporary study of scientific depth has totally studied this problem. Social science should be able to suggest mechanisms to create a wholesome black unity and a sense of peoplehood while the process of integration proceeds.

As one example of this gap in research, there are no studies, to my knowledge, to explain adequately the absence of Negro trade union leadership. Eighty-five percent of Negroes are working people. Some 2,000,000 are in trade unions, but in 50 years we have produced only one national leader— A. Philip Randolph.

Discrimination explains a great deal, but not everything. The picture is so dark even a few rays of light may signal a useful direction.

The second area for scientific examination is political action. In the past 2 decades, Negroes have expended more effort in quest of the franchise than they have in all other campaigns combined. Demonstrations, sit-ins, and marches, though more spectacular, are dwarfed by the enormous number of man-hours expended to register millions, particularly in the South. Negro organizations from extreme militant to conservative persuasion, Negro leaders who would not even talk to each other, all have been agreed on the key importance of voting. Stokely Carmichael said black power means the vote and Roy Wilkins, while saying black power means black death, also energetically sought the power of the ballot.

A recent major work by social scientists Matthews and Prothro (1966) concludes that "The concrete benefits to be derived from the franchise—under conditions that prevail in the South—have often been exaggerated," . . .

that voting is not the key that will unlock the door to racial equality because "the concrete measurable payoffs from Negro voting in the South will not be revolutionary."

James A. Wilson (1965) supports this view, arguing, "Because of the structure of American politics as well as the nature of the Negro community, Negro politics will accomplish only limited objectives."

If their conclusion can be supported, then the major effort Negroes have invested in the past 20 years has been in the wrong direction and the major pillar of their hope is a pillar of sand. My own instinct is that these views are essentially erroneous, but they must be seriously examined.

The need for a penetrating massive scientific study of this subject cannot be overstated. Lipsit (1959) in 1957 asserted that a limitation in focus in political sociology has resulted in a failure of much contemporary research to consider a number of significant theoretical questions. The time is short for social science to illuminate this critically important area. If the main thrust of Negro effort has been, and remains, substantially irrelevant, we may be facing an agonizing crisis of tactical theory.

The third area for study concerns psychological and ideological changes in Negroes. It is fashionable now to be pessimistic. Undeniably, the freedom movement has encountered setbacks. Yet I still believe there are significant aspects of progress.

Negroes today are experiencing an inner transformation that is liberating them from ideological dependence on the white majority. What has penetrated substantially all strata of Negro life is the revolutionary idea that the philosophy and morals of the dominant white society are not holy or sacred but in all to many respects are degenerate and profane.

Negroes have been oppressed for centuries not merely by bonds of economic and political servitude. The worst aspect of their oppression was their inability to question and defy the fundamental percepts of the larger society. Negroes have been loath in the past to hurl any fundamental challenges because they were coerced and conditioned into thinking within the context of the dominant white ideology. This is changing and new radical trends are appearing in Negro thought. I use radical in its broad sense to refer to reading into roots.

Ten years of struggle have sensitized and opened the Negro's eyes to reaching. For the first time in their history, Negroes have become aware of the deeper causes for the crudity and cruelty that governed white society's responses to their needs. They discovered that their plight was not a consequence of superficial prejudice but was systemic.

The slashing blows of backlash and frontlash have hurt the Negro, but they have also awakened him and revealed the nature of the oppressor. To lose illusions is to gain truth. Negroes have grown wiser and more mature and they are hearing more clearly those who are raising fundamental questions about our society whether the critics be Negro or white. When this process of awareness and independence crystallizes, every rebuke, every evasion, become hammer blows on the wedge that splits the Negro from the larger society.

Social science is needed to explain where this development is going to take us. Are we moving away, not from integration, but from the society which made it a problem in the first place? How deep and at what rate of speed is this process occurring? These are some vital questions to be answered if we are to have a clear sense of our direction.

We know we have not found the answers to all forms of social change. We know, however, that we did find some answers. We have achieved and we are confident. We also know we are confronted now with far greater complexities and we have not yet discovered all the theory we need.

And may I say together, we must solve the problems right here in America. As I have said time and time again, Negroes still have faith in America. Black people still have faith in a dream that we will all live together as brothers in this country of plenty one day.

But I was distressed when I read in the *New York Times* of August 31, 1967, that a sociologist from Michigan State University, the outgoing President of the American Sociological Society, stated in San Francisco that Negroes should be given a chance to find an all Negro community in South America: "that the valleys of the Andes Mountains would be an ideal place for American Negroes to build a second Israel." He further declared that "The United States Government should negotiate for a remote but fertile land in Equador, Peru, or Bolivia for this relocation." I feel that it is rather absurd and appalling that a leading social scientist today would suggest to black people, that after all these years of suffering and exploitation as well as investment in the American dream, that we should turn around and run at this point in history. I say that we will not run! Loomis even compared the relocation task of the Negro to the relocation task of the Jews in Israel. The Jews were made exiles. They did not choose to abandon Europe, they were driven out. Furthermore, Israel has a deep tradition, and Biblical roots for Jews. The Wailing Wall is a good example of these roots. They also had significant financial aid from the United States for the relocation and rebuilding effort. What tradition do the Andes, especially the valley of the Andes mountains have for Negroes?

And I assert at this time that once again we must reaffirm our belief in building a democratic society, in which blacks and whites can live together as brothers, where we will all come to see that integration is not a problem, but an opportunity to participate in the beauty of diversity.

The problem is deep. It is gigantic in extent, and chaotic in detail. And I do not believe that it will be solved until there is a kind of cosmic discontent enlarging in the bosoms of people of good will all over this nation.

There are certain technical words in every academic discipline which soon become stereotypes and even clichés. Every academic discipline has its technical nomenclature. You who are in the field of psychology have given us a great word. It is the word maladjusted. This word is probably used more than any other word in psychology. It is a good word; certainly it is good that in dealing with what the word implies you are declaring that destructive maladjustment should be destroyed. You are saying that all must seek the well-adjusted life in order to avoid neurotic and schizophrenic personalities.

But on the other hand, I am sure that we all recognize that there are some things in our society, some things in our world, to which we should never be adjusted. There are some things concerning which we must always be maladjusted if we are to be people of good will. We must never adjust ourselves to racial discrimination and racial segregation. We must never adjust ourselves to religious bigotry. We must never adjust ourselves to economic conditions that take necessities from the many to give luxuries to the few. We must never adjust ourselves to the madness of militarism, and the self-defeating effects of physical violence.

In a day when Sputniks, Explorers, and Geminies are dashing through outer space, when guided ballistic missiles are carving highways of death through the stratosphere, no nation can finally win a war. It is no longer a choice between violence and nonviolence, it is either nonviolence or non-existence. As President Kennedy declared, "Mankind must put an end to war, or war will put an end to mankind." And so the alternative to disar-mament, the alternative to a suspension in the development and use of nuclear weapons, the alternative to strengthening the United Nations and eventually disarming the whole world, may well be a civilization plunged into the abyss of annihilation. Our earthly habitat will be transformed into an inferno that even Dante could not envision.

Thus, it may well be that our world is in dire need of a new organiza-tion, the International Association for the Advancement of Creative Malad-justment. Men and women should be as maladjusted as the prophet Amos, who in the midst of the injustices of his day, could cry out in words that echo across the centuries, "Let justice roll down like waters and righteous-ness like a mighty stream"; or as maladjusted as Abraham Lincoln, who in the midst of his vacillations finally came to see that this nation could not survive half slave and half free; or as maladjusted as Thomas Jefferson, who in the midst of an age amazingly adjusted to slavery, could scratch across the pages of history, words lifted to cosmic proportions, "We hold these truths to be self evident, that all men are created equal. That they are endowed by their creator with certain inalienable rights. And that among these are life, liberty, and the pursuit of happiness." And through such creative malad-justment, we may be able to emerge from the bleak and desolate midnight of man's inhumanity to man, into the bright and glittering daybreak of freedom and justice.

I have not lost hope. I must confess that these have been very difficult days for me personally. And these have been difficult days for every Civil Rights leader, for every lover of justice and peace. They have been days of frustration—days when we could not quite see where we were going, and when we often felt that our words were in vain, days when we were tempted to end up in the valley of despair. But in spite of this, I still have faith in the future, and my politics will continue to be a politic of hope. Our goal is freedom. And I somehow still believe that in spite of the so-called white backlash, we are going to get there, because however untrue it is to its destiny, the goal of America is freedom.

Abused and scorned though we may be, our destiny as a people is tied up with the destiny of America. Before the Pilgrim fathers landed at Plymouth, we were here. Before Jefferson scratched across the pages of history the great words that I just quoted, we were here. Before the beautiful words of the "Star Spangled Banner" were written, we were here. For more than 2 centuries, our forebears labored here without wages. They made Cotton King. They built the home of their masters in the midst of the most humiliating and oppressive conditions.

And yet out of a bottomless vitality, they continued to grow and develop. If the inexpressible cruelties of slavery could not stop us, the opposition that we now face will surely fail. We shall win our freedom because both the sacred heritage of our nation, and the eternal will of the almighty God, are embodied in our echoing demands.

And so I can still sing, although many have stopped singing it, "We shall overcome." We shall overcome because the arch of the moral universe is long, but it bends toward justice. We shall overcome because Carlysle is right, "No lie can live forever." We shall overcome because William Cullen Bryant is right, "Truth crushed to earth will rise again." We shall overcome because James Russell Lowell is right, "Truth forever on the scaffold, wrong forever on the throne, yet that scaffold sways a future." And so with this faith, we will be able to hew out of the mountain of despair a stone of hope. We will be able to transform the jangling discords of our nation into a beautiful symphony of brotherhood. This will be a great day. This will not be the day of the white man, it will not be the day of the black man, it will be the day of man as man.

REFERENCES

Frazier, E. F. *Black bourgeoisie.* Glencoe, Ill.: Free Press, 1956.

Lipsit, M. Political sociology. In *Sociology today.* New York: Basic Books, 1959.

Matthews & Prothro. *Negroes and the new southern politics.* New York: Harcourt & Brace, 1966.

Miller, S. M., & Gouldner, A. *Applied sociology.* New York: Free Press, 1965.

Wilson, J. A. The Negro in politics. *Daedalus,* 1965, Fall.

Introduction to Skinner Article

One word that aptly describes the eminent psychologist B. F. Skinner is "persistence." In 1948 he published a Utopian novel (*Walden Two*) about a society designed and governed by psychologists; and today (see below) he is still writing on the same topic! In the following article Skinner uses the concept of *reinforcement* in two major ways: to suggest why contemporary societal problems like excessive eating, excessive procreation, and excessive pugnacity exist; and to provide a means of overcoming these problems. His notion that "contingencies of reinforcement" can be utilized to design a culture might sound a bit grandiose—but remember that much of Skinner's beliefs about the power of reinforcement in controlling behavior comes directly from laboratory studies documenting such control in humans and lower animals.

To Skinner, the psychological scientist has the potential and the responsibility to use his knowledge in the service of man. He believes that the scientific control of behavior is not sinister or evil—quite the contrary, it is possibly the best way to insure a happier, self-actualized individual in a harmonious, smoothly functioning society (Rogers & Skinner, 1956).

REFERENCES

Rogers, C., & Skinner, B. Some issues concerning the control of human behavior: A symposium. *Science*, 1956, **124**, 1057–1066.

Skinner, B. *Walden Two*. New York: MacMillan, 1948.

29

Contingencies of Reinforcement in the Design of a Culture

B. F. Skinner

The world in which man lives has been changing much faster than man himself. In a few hundred generations, highly beneficial characteristics of the human body have become troublesome. One of these is the extent to which human behavior is strengthened by certain kinds of reinforcing consequences.

It was once important, for example, that men should learn to identify nutritious food and remember where they found it, that they should learn and remember how to catch fish and kill game and cultivate plants, and that they should eat as much as possible whenever food was available. Those who were most powerfully reinforced by certain kinds of oral stimulation were most likely to do all this and to survive—hence man's extraordinary susceptibility to reinforcement by sugar and other foodstuffs, a sensitivity which, under modern conditions of agriculture and food storage, leads to dangerous overeating.

A similar process of selection presumably explains the reinforcing power of sexual contact. At a time when the human race was periodically decimated by pestilence, famine, and war and steadily attenuated by endemic ills and an unsanitary and dangerous environment, it was important that procreative behavior should be maximized. Those for whom sexual reinforcement was most powerful should have most quickly achieved copulation and should have continued to copulate most frequently. The breeders selected by sexual competition must have been not only the most powerful and skill-

SOURCE. *Behavioral Science,* 1966, 11, 159–166. Lecture given at the Walter Reed Army Medical Center under the auspices of the Washington School of Psychiatry, March 26, 1965. Preparation of the manuscript has been supported by Grant K6-MH-21,775 of the National Institute of Mental Health of the U. S. Public Health Service, and by the Human Ecology Fund.

ful members of the species but those for whom sexual contact was most reinforcing. In a safer environment the same susceptibility leads to serious overpopulation with its attendant ills.

The principle also holds for aggressive behavior. At a time when men were often plundered and killed, by animals and other men, it was important that any behavior which harmed or frightened predators should be quickly learned and long sustained. Those who were most strongly reinforced by evidences of damage to others should have been most likely to survive. Now, under better forms of government, supported by ethical and moral practices which protect person and property, the reinforcing power of successful aggression leads to personal illness, neurotic and otherwise, and to war—if not total destruction.

Such discrepancies between man's sensitivity to reinforcement and the contribution which the reinforced behaviors make to his current welfare raise an important problem in the design of a culture. How are we to keep from overeating, from overpopulating the world, and from destroying each other? How can we make sure that these properties of the human organism, once necessary for survival, shall not now prove lethal?

THREE TRADITIONAL SOLUTIONS

One solution to the problem might be called the voluptuary or sybaritic. Reinforcement is maximized while the unfortunate consequences are either disregarded—on the principle of eat, drink, and be merry for tomorrow we die—or prevented. Romans avoided some of the consequences of overeating, as an occasional neurotic may do today, by using the vomitorium. A modern solution is nonnutritious food. Artificial sweeteners have an effect on the tongue similar to that of ripe fruit, and we can now be reinforced for eating things which have fewer harmful effects. The sybaritic solution to the problem of sexual reinforcement is either irresponsible intercourse or the prevention of consequences through contraception or nonprocreative forms of sex. Aggressive behavior is enjoyed without respect to the consequences in the donnybrook. Some consequences are avoided by being aggressive towards animals, as in bearbaiting and other blood sports, or vicariously aggressive toward both men and animals, as in the Roman circus or in modern body sports and games. (Broadcasters of professional football and prize fights often use special microphones to pick up the thud of body against body.)

It is not difficult to promote the sybaritic solution. Men readily subscribe to a way of life in which primary reinforcers are abundant, for the simple reason that subscribing is a form of behavior susceptible to reinforcement. In such a world one may most effectively pursue happiness (or, to use a less frivolous expression, fulfill one's nature), and the pursuit is easily rationalized: "Nothing but the best, the richest and fullest experience possible, is good enough for man." In these forms, however, the pursuit of happiness is either dangerously irresponsible or deliberately nonproductive and wasteful. Satiation may release a man for productive behavior, but in a relatively unproductive condition.

A second solution might be called, with strict attention to etymology, the puritanical. Reinforcement is offset by punishment. Gluttony, lust, and violence are classified as bad or wrong (and punished by the ethical group), as illegal (and punished by the government), as sinful (and punished by religious authorities), or as maladjusted (and punished by those therapists who use punishment). The puritanical solution is never easy to "sell," and it is not always successful. Punishment does not merely cancel reinforcement; it leads to a struggle for self-control which is often violent and time consuming. Whether one is wrestling with the devil or a cruel superego, there are neurotic by-products. It is possible that punishment sometimes successfully "represses" behavior and the human energies can then be redirected into science, art, and literature, but the metaphor of redirection of energy raises a question to which we must return. In any event the puritanical solution has many unwanted by-products, and we may well explore other ways of generating the acceptable behaviors attributed to it.

A third solution is to bring the body up to date. Reinforcing effects could conceivably be made commensurate with current requirements for survival. Genetic changes could be accelerated through selective breeding or possibly through direct action on the germ plasm, but certain chemical or surgical measures are at the moment more feasible. The appetite-suppressing drugs now available often have undesirable side effects, but a drug which would make food less reinforcing and therefore weaken food-reinforced behavior would be widely used. The possibility is not being overlooked by drug manufacturers. Drugs to reduce the effects of sexual reinforcement—such as those said to be used, whether effectively or not, by penal institutions and the armed services—may not be in great demand, but they would have their uses and might prove surprisingly popular. The semistarvation recommended in some religious regimens as a means of weakening sexual behavior presumably acts through chemical changes. The chemical control of aggressive behavior—by tranquilizers—is already well advanced.

A physiological reduction in sensitivity to reinforcement is not likely to be acceptable to the sybarite. Curiously enough, the puritan would also find it objectionable because certain admirable forms of self-control would not be exhibited. Paraphrasing La Rochefoucauld, we might say that we should not give a man credit for being tranquil if his aggressive inclinations have been suppressed by a tranquilizer. A practical difficulty at the moment is that measures of this sort are not specific and probably undercut desirable reinforcing effects.

A FOURTH SOLUTION

A more direct solution is suggested by the experimental analysis of behavior. One may deal with problems generated by a powerful reinforcer simply by changing the contingencies of reinforcement. An environment may be designed in which reinforcers which ordinarily generate unwanted behavior simply do not do so. The solution seems reasonable enough when the reinforcers are of no special significance. A student once defended the use of punishment with the following story. A young mother had come to call on his family, bringing her five-year-old son. The boy immediately climbed onto the piano bench and began to pound the keys. Conversation was almost impossible and the visit a failure. The student argued for the puritanical solution: he would have punished the child—rather violently, he implied. He was overlooking the nature of pianos. For more than two hundred years talented and skillful men have worked to create a device which will powerfully reinforce the behavior of pressing keys. (The piano, is, indeed, an "eighty-eight lever box." It exists solely to reinforce the pressing of levers—or the encouraging of others to press them.) The child's behavior simply testified to the success of the piano industry. It is bad design to bring child and piano together and then punish the behavior which naturally follows.

A comparable solution is not so obvious when the reinforcers have strong biological significance because the problem is misunderstood. We do not say that a child possesses a basic need to play the piano. It is obvious that the behavior has arisen from a history of reinforcement. In the case of food, sex, and violence, however, traditional formulations have emphasized supposed internal needs or drives. A man who cannot keep from overeating suffers from strong internal stimulation which he easily mistakes for the cause (rather than a collateral effect) of his uncontrollable behavior, and which he tries to reduce in order to solve his problem. He cannot go directly to the inner stimulation, but only to some of the conditions responsible for it—conditions which, as he puts it, "make him feel hungry." These happen also to be conditions which "make him eat." The easiest way to reduce both the internal stimulation and the strength of the behavior is simply to eat, but that does not solve the problem. In concentrating on other ways of changing needs or drives, we overlook a solution to the behavioral problem.

What a man must control to avoid the troublesome consequences of oral reinforcement is the behavior reinforced. He must stop buying and eating candy bars, ordering and eating extra pieces of cake, eating at odd times of the day, and so on. It is not some inner state called hunger but overeating which presents a problem. The behavior can be weakened by making sure that it is not reinforced. In an environment in which only simple foods have been available a man eats sensibly—not because he must, but because no other behavior has ever been strengthened. The normal environment is of a very different sort. In an affluent society most people are prodigiously reinforced with food. Susceptibility to reinforcement leads men to specialize in raising particularly delicious foods and to process and cook them in ways which make them as reinforcing as possible. Overanxious parents offer especially delicious food to encourage children to eat. Powerful reinforcers (called "candy") are used to obtain favors, to allay emotional disturbances, and to strengthen personal relations. It is as if the environment had been designed to build the very behaviors which later prove troublesome. The child it produces has no greater "need for food" than one for whom food has never been particularly reinforcing.

Similarly, it is not some "sexuality" or "sex drive" which has troublesome consequences but sexual behavior itself, much of which can be traced to contingencies of reinforcement. The conditions under which a young person is first sexually reinforced determine the extent as well as the form of later sexual activity. Nor is the problem of aggression raised by a "death instinct" or "a fundamental drive in human beings to hurt one another" (Menninger, 1964), but rather by an environment in which human beings are reinforced when they hurt one another. To say that there is "something suicidal in man that makes him enjoy war" is to reverse the causal order; man's capacity to enjoy war leads to a form of suicide. In a world in which a child seldom if ever successfully attacks others, aggressive behavior is not strong. But the world is usually quite different. Either through simple neglect or in the belief that innate needs must be expressed, children are allowed and even encouraged to attack each other in various ways. Aggressive behavior is condoned in activities proposed as "a moral equivalent of war." It may be that wars have been won on the playing fields of Eton, but they have also been started there, for a playing field is an arena for the reinforcement of aggressive action, and the behaviors there reinforced will sooner or later cause trouble.

The distinction between need and reinforcement is clarified by a current problem. Many of those who are trying to stop smoking cigarettes will testify to a basic drive or need as powerful as those of hunger, sex, and aggression. (For those who have a genuine drug addiction, smoking is reinforced in part by the alleviation of withdrawal symptoms, but most smokers can shift to nicotine-free cigarettes without too much trouble. They are still unable to control the powerful repertoire of responses which compose smoking.) It is clear that the troublesome pattern of behavior—"the cigarette habit"—can be traced, not to a need, but to a history of reinforcement because there was no problem before the discovery of tobacco or before the invention of the cigarette as an especially reinforcing form in which tobacco may be smoked. Whatever their other needs may have been, our ancestors had no need to smoke cigarettes, and no one has the need today if, like them, he has never been reinforced for smoking.

The problem of cigarette smoking has been approached in the other ways we have examined. Some advertising appeals to the irresponsible sybarite: buy the cigarette that tastes good and inhale like a man. Other sybaritic smokers try to avoid the consequences; the filter is the contraceptive of the tobacco industry. The puritanical solution has also been tried. Cigarettes may be treated so that the smoker is automatically punished by nausea. Natural aversive consequences—a rough throat, a hoarse voice, a cigarette cough, or serious illness—may be made more punishing. The American Cancer Society has tried to condition aversive consequences with a film, in color, showing the removal of a cancerous lung. As is often the case with the puritanical solution, aversive stimuli are indeed conditioned—they are felt as "guilt"—but smoking is not greatly reduced. A true nicotine addiction might be controlled by taking nicotine or a similar drug in other ways, but a drug which would be closer to the chemical solution promised by anti-appetite, anti-sex, and anti-aggression drugs would specifically reduce the effect of other reinforcers in smoking. All these measures are much more difficult than controlling the contingencies of reinforcement.

(That there is no need to smoke cigarettes may be denied by those who argue that it is actually composed of several other kinds of needs, all of them present in nonsmokers. But this is simply to say that cigarette smoking is reinforced by several distinguishable effects—by odor, taste, oral stimulation, vasoconstriction in the lungs, "something to do with the hands," appearing to resemble admired figures, and so on. A nonsmoker has not come under the control of a particular combination of these reinforcers. If any one should cause trouble on its own or in some other combination, it could be analyzed in the same way.)

MAKING CONTINGENCIES LESS EFFECTIVE

The problems raised by man's extraordinary sensitivity to reinforcement by food, sexual contact, and aggressive damage cannot be solved, as the example of cigarette smoking might suggest, simply by removing these things from the environment. It would be impossible to change the world that much, and in any case the reinforcers serve useful functions. (One important function is simply to encourage support for a culture. A way of life in which food, sex, and aggression were kept to a bare minimum would not strongly reinforce those who adopted it nor discourage defections from it.) The problem is not to eliminate reinforcers but to moderate their effects. Several possible methods are suggested by recent work in the experimental analysis of behavior. The mere frequency with which a reinforcer occurs is much less important than the contingencies of which it is a part.

We can minimize some unwanted consequences by preventing the discovery of reinforcing effects. The first step in "hooking" a potential heroin addict is to give him heroin. The reinforcer is not at first contingent on any particular form of behavior; but when its effect has been felt (and, particularly, when withdrawal symptoms have developed), it can be made contingent on paying for the drug. Addiction is prevented simply by making sure that the effect is never felt. The reinforcing effects of alcohol, caffeine, and nicotine must be discovered in a similar way, and methods of preventing addiction take the same form. The process underlies the practice of giving free samples in food markets; customers are induced to eat small quantities of a new food so that larger quantities may be made contingent on surrendering money. Similar practices are to be found in sexual seduction and in teaching the pleasures of violence.

Reinforcers are made effective in other ways. Stimuli are conditioned so that they become reinforcing; aversive properties are weakened through adaptation so that reinforcing properties emerge with greater power (a "taste" is thus acquired); and so on. Processes of this sort have played their part in man's slow discovery of reinforcing things. It has been, perhaps, a history of the discovery of human potentialities, but among these we must recognize the potentiality for getting into trouble. In any case, the processes which make things reinforcing need to be closely scrutinized.

The excessive consummation which leads to overweight, overpopulation, and war is only one result of man's sensitivity to reinforcement. Another, often equally troublesome, is an exhausting preoccupation with behavior which is only infrequently consummated. A single reinforcement may generate and maintain a great deal of behavior when it comes at the end of a sequence or chain of responses. Chains of indefinite length are constructed in the laboratory by conditioning intermediate reinforcers. Teachers and others use the same method for many practical purposes. We may assume that something of the sort has occurred whenever we observe long chains. The dedicated horticulturalist is ultimately reinforced, say, by a final perfect bloom, but all the behavior leading up to it is not thereby explained; intermediate stages in progressing toward a final bloom must in some way have become reinforcing. In order for early man to have discovered agriculture, certain early stages of cultivation must first have been reinforced by accident or at least under conditions irrelevant to the eventual achievement.

The reinforcers we are considering generate many sequences of this sort with troublesome results. Ultimate reinforcement is often ridiculously out of proportion to the activity it sustains. Many hours of careful labor on the part of a cook lead at last to brief stimulation from a delicious food. A good wine reinforces months or years of dedicated care. Brief sexual reinforcement follows a protracted campaign of seduction (see, for example,

Choderlos de Laclos's *Les liaisons dangereuses* or Kierkegaard's *The Seducer*.) The campaign of the dedicated aggressor, domestic or international, is often similarly protracted and suggests a long history in which a chain has been built up. Problems of this sort can be solved simply by breaking up the conditions under which long chains are formed.

Another kind of exhausting preoccupation is due to intermittent reinforcement. A single form of response is repeated again and again, often at a very high rate, even though only infrequently reinforced. Activities such as reading magazines and books, going to the theatre, and watching television are reinforced on so-called "interval" schedules. So-called "ratio" schedules are exemplified by piece-rate pay in industry and by gambling systems and devices. (Ratio schedules are so powerful that their use is often restricted or controlled by law.) Large quantities of behavior are generated by such schedules only when they have been carefully programmed. Reinforcement is at first relatively frequent, but the behavior remains strong as the frequency is reduced. Thus, a television program grows less and less reinforcing as the writer runs out of themes or as the viewer no longer finds the same themes interesting, but one who has followed a program from the beginning may continue to watch it long after reinforcements have become quite rare. The dishonest gambler prepares his victim by steadily "stretching" the mean ratio in a variable ratio schedule. Eventually the victim continues to play during a very long period without reinforcement.

There are many natural systems which "stretch" ratios. As addiction develops, the addict must take more and more of a drug (and presumably work harder and harder to get it) to achieve a given effect. To the extent that novelty is important, all reinforcers grow less effective with time. The gourmet is less often reinforced as familiar foods begin to cloy. The ratio schedule of sexual reinforcement is automatically stretched by satiation. The enormities suffered by the unfortunate Justine in de Sade's story suggest that her many persecutors were being reinforced on ratio schedules severely strained by both aging and sexual exhaustion. Frank Harris has suggested, in his biography of Oscar Wilde (1916), that the word "lead" in "lead us not into temptation" is an unconscious recognition of the progression through which more and more troublesome forms of behavior are approached. Unwanted consequences are averted in all such cases by breaking up the programs through which infrequent reinforcement comes to sustain large quantities of behavior.

ARRANGING USEFUL CONTINGENCIES

We are usually interested—for example, in education—in getting the greatest possible effect from weak reinforcers in short supply. The problem here is just the reverse—we are to minimize the effect of reinforcers which are all too abundant and powerful. Hence, instead of systematically building up long chains of responses, we prevent their formation, and instead of constructing programs which make strained schedules effective we break them up. We can use the same procedures in the more familiar direction, however, in another solution to our problem. Reinforcers can be made contingent on productive behavior to which they were not originally related. Soldiers have often been induced to fight skillfully and energetically by arranging that victory will be followed by the opportunity to plunder, rape, and slaughter. It has always been particularly easy for the barbarian to mount an attack on a more advanced civilization which emphasizes the delectations of food and sex. It has been said, for example, that the wines of Italy (and presumably her well-groomed and beautiful women) made Rome particularly vulnerable. All governments make aggressive damage to an enemy especially reinforcing to their soldiers with stories of atrocities. Religious visions of another world have been made reinforcing in the same modes. Many of the offerings to the gods portrayed in Egyptian temples are edible, and Greek and Roman gods were distinguished by their taste for ambrosia and nectar, although less advanced civilizations have looked forward only to a happy hunting ground. Sex has its place in the Muslem heaven where men may expect to enjoy the attention of beautiful virgin Huris, and some theologians have argued that one of the attractions of the Christian heaven is the spectacle of sinners being tormented in hell—a spectacle which, as portrayed for example in the *Inferno,* competes successfully with the Roman circus at its most violent.

Marriage is often described as a system in which unlimited sexual contact with a selected partner is contingent on nonsexual behavior useful to the culture—such as supporting and managing a household and family and, following St. Paul's famous principle, forsaking sexual activity elsewhere. Women have often raised moral standards with practices which were merely carried to an extreme by Lysistrata. Educators use the basic reinforcers rather timidly. Erasmus (1529) advocated cherries and cakes in place of the cane in teaching children Greek and Latin, but he was the exception rather than the rule. Homosexual reinforcement was explicit in Greek education, however, and a sadistic or masochistic violence has supported corporal punishment and competitive arrangements among students down to modern times. Economic transactions characteristically involve food, sex, and aggression since money as a generalized reinforcer derives much of its power when exchanged for them. In the nineteenth century it was expected that wages would be exchanged primarily for food, and charity was opposed on the grounds that the industrial system needed a hungry labor force. Better working conditions have made other reinforcers effective, but many of them are still related to sex and aggression.

Our reinforcers have, of course, a special place in art, music, and literature. Their place in science is not always obvious. Max Weber has argued, indeed, that the scientist is a product of the puritanical solution—profiting, for example, from the scrupulous or meticulous concern for exact detail generated by aversive consequences (the etymologies of *scrupulous* and *meticulous* show punitive origins). Feuer (1963) has recently shown, however, that almost all outstanding men in science have followed a "hedonist ethic."

A solution to our problem in which food, sex, and aggression are made contingent on useful forms of behavior to which they are not naturally related has much to recommend it. It should be acceptable to the sybarite because he will not lack reinforcement. It should also assuage the puritan, not only because objectionable consequences which seem to call for punishment have been attenuated but because a man must work for the reinforcers he receives. It should not require any change in human behavior through chemical, surgical, or even genetic means, since a natural sensitivity to reinforcement is now useful rather than troublesome.

The solution has not yet been satisfactorily worked out, however. The contingencies of positive reinforcement arranged by governmental and religious agencies are primitive, and the agencies continue to lean heavily on the puritanical solution. Economic reinforcement is badly programmed. Wage systems only rarely make effective use of positive reinforcement. In practice, wages simply establish a standard from which the worker can be cut off by being discharged. The control is aversive and the results unsatisfactory for both the employer (since not much is done) and the employee (since work is still work). Education is still largely aversive; most students study mainly in order to avoid the consequences of not studying. In short, some of the most powerful forces in human behavior are not being effectively used.

And for good reason. We are only beginning to understand how reinforcement works. The important things in life seem to be food, sex, and many other pleasant, enjoyable, and satisfying stimuli. These are the things which define happiness. They are the "good" things which contribute to the greatest good of the greatest number. They characterize human purpose, for they are among the things men live *for*. When we design a better world, either utopian or theological, we make sure that there will be an abundant supply of them. We thus go directly to the reinforcers and are no doubt reinforced for doing so. We overlook a much more important consideration—the ways in which these wonderful things are contingent on behavior.

The concept of drive or need is particularly at fault here. We neglect contingencies of reinforcement because we seek solutions to all our problems in the satisfaction of needs. "To each according to his need" is the avowed goal of both an affluent society and a welfare state. (The principle is scriptural. St. Augustine discussed it long before St. Karl.) If those whom seem to have everything are still not happy, we are forced to conclude that there must be less obvious needs which are unsatisfied. Men must have spiritual as well as material needs—they must need someone or something beyond themselves to believe in, and so on—and it is because these needs are unfulfilled that life seems so often empty and man so often rootless. This desperate move to preserve the concept of need is unnecessary because a much more interesting and fruitful design is possible.

Men are happy in an environment in which active, productive, and creative behavior is reinforced in effective ways. The trouble with both affluent and welfare societies is that reinforcers are not contingent on particular forms of behavior. Men are not reinforced for doing anything and hence they do nothing. This is the "contentment" of the Arcadian idyll and of the retired businessman. It may represent a satisfaction of needs, but it raises other problems. Those who have nothing important to do fall prey to trivial reinforcers. When effectively scheduled, even weak reinforcers generate strong, compulsive, repetitive behavior which ultimately proves aversive. Only when we stop using reinforcers to allay needs can we begin to use them to "fulfill man's nature" in a much more important sense.

Contingencies of reinforcement are far more important than the reinforcers they incorporate, but they are much less obvious. Only very recently, and then only under rigorous experimental conditions, have the extraordinary effects of contingencies been observed. Perhaps this explains why it has not been possible to design effective contingencies simply with the help of common sense or of practical skill in handling people or even with the help of principles derived from scientific field observations of behavior. The experimental analysis of behavior thus has a very special relevance to the design of cultures. Only through the active prosecution of such an analysis, and the courageous application of its results to daily life, will it be possible to design those contingencies of reinforcement which will generate and maintain the most subtle and complex behavior of which men are capable.

REFERENCES

Erasmus. *The liberal education of children.* 1529. Cited by Curtis, S. J., & Boultwood, M. E. A. *A short history of educational ideas.* London: University Tutorial Press, 1953, p. 129.

Feuer, Lewis S. *The scientific intellectual.* New York: Basic Books, 1963.

Harris, Frank. *Oscar Wilde, his life and confessions.* New York, 1916.

Menninger, Karl. Quoted in *Boston Globe,* December 13, 1964.

Introduction to
Latané and Darley Article

Sometimes the psychologist can serve man as effectively by understanding his behavior as by controlling it. See, for example, the research on bystander "apathy" reported below—research that won its authors one of the coveted American Association for the Advancement of Science awards in 1968. If we assume, as most people do, that a group of bystanders fail to come to the aid of a stranger in distress because they are "apathetic" or "indifferent," then we would try to solve the problem (change the behavior of bystanders) in a manner prescribed by our rather negative appraisal of human conduct. But what if such uncooperative behavior is not a function of "uncaring" observers but rather a product of the social situation in which the emergency occurs? In other words, what if the bystander fails to aid a person in distress not because he is "apathetic" but because he is in a social situation that discourages such involvement? If this was the case we would attack the problem of bystander noncooperation in quite a different manner!

In their article, Latané and Darley describe the experimental program that they undertook to uncover the factors underlying bystander willingness or unwillingness to aid a stranger in distress. Besides strengthening our faith in mankind, the study should demonstrate how scientific research is employed to systematically answer questions about, and gain insights into, human behavior.

30

Bystander "Apathy"

Bibb Latané and John M. Darley

> Do the work that's nearest
> Though it's dull at whiles,
> Helping, when you meet them,
> Lame dogs over stiles.

In the century since it was written, this minor bit of exhortatory doggerel has become sheer camp. We have become too sophisticated to appreciate the style—many believe that we have become too cynical to appreciate the moral. Working at dull tasks is now taken as a sign of dullness, and helping lame dogs is no longer much in vogue. At least, that is the impression we get from the newspapers.

On a March night in 1964, Kitty Genovese was set upon by a maniac as she came home from work at 3 A.M. Thirty-eight of her Kew Gardens neighbors came to their windows when she cried out in terror—none came to her assistance. Even though her assailant took over half an hour to murder her, no one even so much as called the police.

This story became the journalistic sensation of the decade. "Apathy," cried the newspapers. "Indifference," said the columnists and commentators. "Moral callousness," "dehumanization," "loss of concern for our fellow man," added preachers, professors, and other serminizers. Movies, television

SOURCE. *American Scientist*, 1969, **57**, 244–268. The experiments reported in this paper were supported by National Science Foundation grants GS1238 and GS1239 and were conducted while the authors were at Columbia University and New York University, respectively. Their forthcoming book on this research (Latané and Darley, *The Unresponsive Bystander*, Appleton-Century-Crofts, in press) won the 1968 Socio-Psychological Prize awarded by the American Association for the Advancement of Science and the Century Psychology Prize for 1968.

specials, plays, and books explored this incident and many more like it. Americans became concerned about their lack of concern.

But can these epithets be correct? We think not. Although it is unquestionably true that witnesses in such emergencies have often done nothing to save the victims, "apathy," "indifference," and "unconcern" are not entirely accurate descriptions of their reactions. The 38 witnesses to Kitty Genovese's murder did not merely look at the scene once and then ignore it. Instead they continued to stare out their windows at what was going on. Caught, fascinated, distressed, unwilling to act but unable to turn away, their behavior was neither helpful nor heroic; but it was not indifferent or apathetic either.

Actually, it was like crowd behavior in many other emergency situations; car accidents, drownings, fires, and attempted suicides all attract substantial numbers of people who watch the drama in helpless fascination without getting directly involved in the action. Are these people alienated and indifferent? Are the rest of us? Obviously not. It seems only yesterday we were being called overconforming. But why, then, don't we act?

There are certainly strong forces leading us to act. Empathy or sympathy, innate or learned, may cause us to share, at least in part, a victim's distress. If intervention were easy, most of us would be willing to relieve our own discomfort by alleviating another's suffering. As Charles Darwin put it some years ago, "As man is a social animal it is almost certain that . . . he would, from an inherited tendency, be willing to defend, in concert with others, his fellow men; and be ready to aid them in any way, which did not interfere too greatly with his own welfare or his own strong desires."

Even if empathy or sympathy were not strong enough to lead us to help in emergencies, there are a variety of social norms which suggest that each of us has a responsibility to each other, and that help is the proper thing to do. "Do unto others as you would have them do unto you," we hear from our earliest years. Although norms such as these may not have much influence on our behavior in specific situations, they may imbue us with a general predisposition to try to help others.

Indeed, in many non-emergency situations, people seem surprisingly willing to share their time and money with others. According to the Internal Revenue Service, Americans contribute staggering sums to a great variety of charitable organizations each year. Even when tax deductions don't fan the urge to help, people still help others. When Columbia students asked 2500 people on the streets of New York for 10¢ or 20¢, over half of these people gave it.

If people are so willing to help in non-emergency situations, they should be even more willing to help in emergencies when the need is so much greater. Or should they? Emergencies differ in many ways from other types of situations in which people need help, and these differences may be important. The very nature of an emergency implies certain psychological consequences.

CHARACTERISTICS OF EMERGENCIES

Perhaps the most distinctive characteristic of an emergency is that it involves threat or harm. Life, well-being, or property is in danger. Even if an emergency is successfully dealt with, nobody is better off afterwards than before. Except in rare circumstances, the best that can be hoped for if an emergency occurs is a return to the status quo. Consequently, there are few positive rewards for successful action in an emergency. At worst, an emergency can claim the lives not only of those people who were initially involved in it, but also of anybody who intervenes in the situation. This fact puts pressures on individuals to ignore a potential emergency, to distort their perceptions of it, or to underestimate their responsibility for coping with it.

The second important feature of an emergency is that it is an unusual and rare event. Fortunately, although he may read about them in newspapers, or watch fictionalized accounts on television, the average person probably will encounter fewer than half a dozen serious emergencies in his lifetime. Unfortunately when he does encounter one, he will have had little direct personal experience in handling such a situation. Unlike the stereotyped patterns of his everyday behavior, an individual facing an emergency is untrained and unrehearsed.

In addition to being rare, emergencies differ widely, one from another. There are few common requirements for action between a drowning, a fire, or an automobile accident. Each emergency presents a different problem, and each requires a different type of action. Consequently, unlike other rare events, our culture provides us with little secondhand wisdom about how to deal with emergencies. An individual may cope with the rare event of a formal dinner party by using manners gleaned from late night Fred Astaire movies, but the stereotypes that the late movies provide for dealing with emergencies are much less accurate. "Charge!" "Women and children first!" "Quick, get lots of hot water and towels." This is about the extent of the advice offered for dealing with emergencies and it is singularly inappropriate in most specific real emergency situations.

The fourth basic characteristic of emergencies is that they are unforeseen. They "emerge," suddenly and without warning. Being unexpected, emergencies must be handled without the benefit of forethought and planning and an individual does not have the opportunity to think through in advance what course of action he should take when faced with an emergency. He must do his thinking in the immediacy of the situation, and has no opportunity to consult others as to the best course of action or to alert others who are especially equipped to deal with emergencies. The individual confronted with an emergency is thrown on his own resources. We have already seen that he does not have much in the way of practiced responses or cultural stereotypes to fall back upon.

A final characteristic of an emergency is that it requires instant action. It represents a pressing necessity. If the emergency is not dealt with immediately, the situation will deteriorate. The threat will transform itself into damage; the harm will continue or spread. There are urgent pressures to deal with the situation at once. The requirement for immediate action prevents the individual confronted with an emergency from leisurely considering the possible courses of action open to him. It forces him to come to a decision before he has had time to consider his alternatives. It places him in a condition of stress.

The picture we have drawn is a rather grim one. Faced with a situation in which there is no benefit to be gained for himself, unable to rely on past experience, on the experience of others, or on forethought and planning, denied the opportunity to consider carefully his course of action, the bystander to an emergency is in an unenviable position. It is perhaps surprising that anyone should intervene at all.

A MODEL OF THE INTERVENTION PROCESS

If an individual is to intervene in an emergency, he must make, not just one, but a *series* of decisions. Only one particular set of choices will lead him to take action in the situation. Let us now consider the behavioral and cognitive processes that go on in an individual who is in the vicinity of an emergency. What must he do and decide before he actually intervenes? These may have important implications for predicting whether an individual will act.

Let us suppose that an emergency is actually taking place. A middle-aged man, walking down the street, has a heart attack. He stops short, clutches his chest, and staggers to the nearest building wall, where he slowly slumps to the sidewalk in a sitting position. What is the likelihood with which a passerby will come to his assistance? First, the bystander has to *notice* that something is happening. The external event has to break into his thinking and intrude itself on his conscious mind. He must tear himself away from his private thoughts or from the legs of the pretty girl walking down the street ahead of him and pay attention to this unusual event.

Once the person is aware of the event as something to be explained, it is necessary that he *interpret* the event. Specifically, he must decide that there is something wrong, that this ambiguous event is an emergency. It may be that the man slumped on the sidewalk is only a drunk, beyond any assistance that the passerby can give him. If the bystander decided that something is indeed wrong, he must next decide that he has a *responsibility* to act. Perhaps help is on the way or perhaps someone else might be better qualified to help. Even in an emergency, it is not clear that everybody should immediately intrude himself into the situation.

If the person does decide that he should help, he must decide what *form of assistance* he can give. Should he rush in directly and try to help the victim or should he detour by calling a doctor or the police? Finally, of course, he must decide how to *implement* his choice and form of intervention. Where is the nearest telephone? Is there a hospital nearby? At this point, the person may finally begin to act in the situation. The socially responsible act is the end point of a series of decisions that the person makes.

Obviously, this model is too rational. It seems unlikely that a bystander will run through the series of choice points in a strictly logical and sequential order. Instead, he may consider two or three of them simultaneously and "try on" various decisions and their consequences before he finally arrives at his overall assessment of the situation. Since he has no commitment to any intermediary decision until he has taken final action, he may cycle back and forth through the decision series until he comes up with a set which serves both his needs and the needs of "reality."

Second, the bystander in an emergency is not a detached and objective observer. His decisions have consequences for himself just as much as for the victim. Unfortunately, however, the rewards and penalties for action and inaction are biased in favor of inaction. All the bystander has to gain from intervention is a feeling of pride and the chance to be a hero. On the other hand, he can be made to appear a fool, sued, or even attacked and wounded. By leaving the situation, he has little to lose but his self-respect. There are strong pressures against deciding that an event is an emergency.

Intervention, then, requires choosing a single course of action through a rather complex matrix of possible actions. The failure to intervene may result from failing to notice an event, failing to realize that the event is an emergency, failing to feel personally responsible for dealing with the emergency, or failing to have sufficient skill to intervene.

SOCIAL DETERMINANTS OF BYSTANDER INTERVENTION, I

Most emergencies are, or at least begin as, ambiguous events. A quarrel in the street may erupt into violence, but it may be simply a family argument. A man staggering about may be suffering a coronary or an onset of diabetes; he may simply be drunk. Smoke pouring from a building may signal a fire; on the other hand, it may be simply steam or airconditioner vapor. Before a bystander is likely to take action in such ambiguous situations, he must first define the event as an emergency and decide that intervention is the proper course of action.

In the course of making these decisions, it is likely that an individual bystander will be considerably influenced by the decisions he perceives other bystanders to be taking. If everyone else in a group of onlookers seems to regard an event as nonserious and the proper course of action as non-intervention, this consensus may strongly affect the perceptions of any single individual and inhibit his potential intervention.

The definitions that other people hold may be discovered by discussing the situation with them, but they may also be inferred from their facial expressions or their behavior. A whistling man with his hands in his pockets obviously does not believe he is in the midst of a crisis. A bystander who does not respond to smoke obviously does not attribute it to fire. An individual, seeing the inaction of others, will judge the situation as less serious than he would if alone.

But why should the others be inactive? Unless there were some force inhibiting responses on the part of others, the kind of social influence process described would, by itself, only lead to a convergence of attitudes within a group. If each individual expressed his true feelings, then, even if each member of the group were entirely guided by the reactions of the others, the group should still respond with a likelihood equal to the average of the individuals.

An additional factor is involved, however. Each member of a group may watch the others, but he is also aware that others are watching him. They are an audience to his own reactions. Among American males, it is considered desirable to appear poised and collected in times of stress. Being exposed to the public view may constrain the actions and expressions of emotion of any individual as he tries to avoid possible ridicule and embarrassment. Even though he may be truly concerned and upset about the plight of a victim, until he decides what to do, he may maintain a calm demeanor.

The constraints involved with being in public might in themselves tend to inhibit action by individuals in a group, but in conjunction with the social influence process described above, they may be expected to have even more powerful effects. If each member of a group is, at the same time, trying to appear calm and also looking around at the other members to gauge their reactions, all members may be led (or misled) by each other to define the situation as less critical than they would if alone. Until someone acts, each person sees only other non-responding bystanders, and is likely to be influenced not to act himself. A state of "pluralistic ignorance" may develop.

It has often been recognized (Brown, 1954, 1965) that a crowd can cause contagion of panic, leading each person in the crowd to over-react to an emergency to the detriment of everyone's welfare. What we suggest here is that a crowd can also force inaction on its members. It can suggest, implicitly but strongly, by its passive behavior that an event is not to be reacted to as an emergency, and it can make any individual uncomfortably aware of what a fool he will look for behaving as if it is.

This line of thought suggests that individuals may be less likely to intervene in an emergency if they witness it in the presence of other people than if they see it alone. It suggests that the presence of other people may lead each person to interpret the situation as less serious, and less demanding of action than he would if alone. The presence of other people may alter each bystander's perceptions and interpretations of the situation. We suspect that the presence of other people may also affect each individual's assessment of the rewards and costs involved in taking action, and indeed we will discuss this possibility in some detail later. First, however, let us look at evidence relevant to this initial process. The experiments reported below were designed to test the line of thought presented above.

EXPERIMENT 1. WHERE THERE'S SMOKE, THERE'S (SOMETIMES) FIRE [1]

In this experiment we presented an emergency to individuals either alone, in the presence of two passive others (confederates of the experimenter who were instructed to notice the emergency but remain indifferent to it), or in groups of three. It was our expectation that individuals faced with the passive reactions of the confederates would be influenced by them and thus less likely to take action than single subjects. We also predicted that the constraints on behavior in public combined with social influence processes would lessen the likelihood that members of three-person groups would act to cope with the emergency.

Male Columbia students living in campus residences were invited to an interview to discuss "some of the problems involved in life at an urban university." As they sat in a small room waiting to be called for the interview and filling out a preliminary questionnaire, they faced an ambiguous but potentially dangerous situation as a stream of smoke began to puff into the room through a wall vent. Some subjects filled out the questionnaire and were exposed to this potentially critical situation while alone. Others were part of three-person groups consisting of one subject and two confederates acting the part of naive subjects. The confederates attempted to avoid conversation as much as possible. Once the smoke had been introduced, they stared at it briefly, made no comment, but simply shrugged their shoulders,

[1] A more detailed report of this experiment is given in: Latané, B. and Darley, J. M. Group inhibition of bystander intervention in emergencies. *Journal of Personality and Social Psychology,* 1968, **10,** 215–221.

returned to the questionnaires and continued to fill them out, occasionally waving away the smoke to do so. If addressed, they attempted to be as uncommunicative as possible and to show apparent indifference to the smoke. "I dunno," they said, and no subject persisted in talking. In a final condition, three naive subjects were tested together. In general, these subjects did not know each other, although in two groups, subjects reported a nodding acquaintance with another subject. Since subjects arrived at slightly different times and since they each had individual questionnaires to work on, they did not introduce themselves to each other, or attempt anything but the most rudimentary conversation.

As soon as the subjects had completed two pages of their questionnaires, the experimenter began to introduce the smoke through a small vent in the wall. The "smoke" was finely divided titanium dioxide produced in a stoppered bottle and delivered under slight air pressure through the vent. It formed a moderately fine-textured but clearly visible stream of whitish smoke. For the entire experimental period, the smoke continued to jet into the room in irregular puffs. By the end of the experimental period, vision was obscured in the room by the amount of smoke present.

All behavior and conversation was observed and coded from behind a one-way window (largely disguised on the subject's side by a large sign giving preliminary instructions). When and if the subject left the experimental room and reported the smoke, he was told that the situation "would be taken care of." If the subject had not reported the smoke within six minutes of the time he first noticed it, the experiment was terminated.

The typical subject, when tested alone, behaved very reasonably. Usually, shortly after the smoke appeared, he would glance up from his questionnaire, notice the smoke, show a slight but distinct startle reaction, and then undergo a brief period of indecision, and perhaps return briefly to his questionnaire before again staring at the smoke. Soon, most subjects would get up from their chairs, walk over to the vent, and investigate it closely, sniffing the smoke, waving their hands in it, feeling its temperature, etc. The usual Alone subject would hesitate again, but finally walk out of the room, look around outside, and, finding somebody there, calmly report the presence of the smoke. No subject showed any sign of panic; most simply said, "There's something strange going on in there, there seems to be some sort of smoke coming through the wall. . . ." The median subject in the Alone condition had reported the smoke within two minutes of first noticing it. Three-quarters of the 24 people run in this condition reported the smoke before the experimental period was terminated.

The behavior of subjects run with two passive confederates was dramatically different; of ten people run in this condition, only one reported the smoke. The other nine stayed in the waiting room as it filled up with smoke, doggedly working on their questionnaires and waving the fumes away from their faces. They coughed, rubbed their eyes, and opened the window—but they did not report the smoke. The difference between the response rate of 75% in the Alone condition and 10% in the Two Passive Confederates condition is highly significant ($p < .002$ by Fisher's Exact test, two-tailed).

Because there are three subjects present and available to report the smoke in the Three Naive Bystander condition as compared to only one subject at a time in the Alone condition, a simple comparison between the two conditions is not appropriate. On the one hand, we cannot compare speeds in the Alone condition with the average speed of the three subjects in a group, since, once one subject in a group had reported the smoke, the pressures of the other two disappeared. They legitimately could feel that the emergency had been handled, and that any action on their part would be redundant and potentially confusing. Therefore, we used the speed of the *first* subject in a group to report the smoke as our dependent variable. However, since there were three times as many people available to respond in this condition as in the Alone condition, we would expect an increased likelihood that at least one person would report the smoke by chance alone. Therefore, we mathematically created "groups" of three scores from the Alone condition to serve as a baseline.[2]

In contrast to the complexity of this procedure, the results were quite simple. Subjects in the Three Naive Bystander condition were markedly inhibited from reporting the smoke. Since 75% of the Alone subjects reported the smoke, we would expect over 98% of the three-person groups to include at least one reporter. In fact, in only 38% of the eight groups in this condition did even one person report ($p < .01$). Of the twenty-four people run in these eight groups, only one person reported the smoke within the first four minutes before the room got noticeably unpleasant. Only three people reported the smoke within the entire experimental period. Social inhibition of reporting was so strong that the smoke was reported quicker when only one person saw it than when groups of three were present ($p < .01$).

Subjects who had reported the smoke were relatively consistent in later describing their reactions to it. They thought the smoke looked somewhat "strange," they were not sure exactly what it was or whether it was dangerous, but they felt it was unusual enough to justify some examination. "I wasn't sure whether it was a fire, but it looked like something was wrong." "I thought it might be steam, but it seemed like a good idea to check it out."

Subjects who had not reported the smoke also were unsure about exactly what it was, but they uniformly said that they had rejected the idea that it

---

[2] The formula for calculating the expected proportion of groups in which at least one person will have acted by a given time is $1-(1-p)^n$ where p is the proportion of single individuals who act by that time and n is the number of persons in the group.

was a fire. Instead, they hit upon an astonishing variety of alternative explanations, all sharing the common characteristic of interpreting the smoke as a nondangerous event. Many thought the smoke was either steam or air-conditioning vapors, several thought it was smog, purposely introduced to simulate an urban environment, and two (from different groups) actually suggested that the smoke was a "truth gas" filtered into the room to induce them to answer the questionnaire accurately (surprisingly, they were not disturbed by this conviction). Predictably, some decided that "it must be some sort of experiment" and stoically endured the discomfort of the room rather than overreact.

Despite the obvious and powerful report-inhibiting effect of other bystanders, subjects almost invariably claimed that they had paid little or no attention to the reactions of the other people in the room. Although the presence of other people actually had a strong and pervasive effect on the subjects' reactions, they were either unaware of this or unwilling to admit it.

The results of this study clearly support the predictions. Individuals exposed to a room filling with smoke in the presence of passive others themselves remained passive, and groups of three naive subjects were less likely to report the smoke than solitary bystanders. Our predictions were confirmed— but this does not necessarily mean that our explanation for these results is the correct one. As a matter of fact several alternatives are available.

Two alternative explanations stem from the fact that the smoke represented a possible danger to the subject himself as well as to others in the building. Subjects' behavior might have reflected their fear of fire, with subjects in groups feeling less threatened by the fire than single subjects and thus less concerned to act. It has been demonstrated in studies with humans (Schachter, 1959) and with rats (Latané, 1969; Latané and Glass, 1968) that togetherness reduces fear, even in situations where it does not reduce danger. In addition, subjects may have felt that the presence of others increased their ability to cope with fire. For both these reasons, subjects in groups may have been less afaid of fire and thus less likely to report the smoke than solitary subjects.

A similar explanation might emphasize, not fearfulness, but the desire to hide fear. To the extent that bravery or stoicism in the face of danger or discomfort is a socially desirable trait (as it appears to be for American male undergraduates), we might expect individuals to attempt to appear more brave or more stoic when others are watching than when they are alone. It is possible that subjects in the Group condition saw themselves as engaged in a game of "Chicken," and thus did not react.

Although both of these explanations are plausible, we do not think that they provide an accurate account of subjects' thinking. In the postexperimental interviews, subjects claimed, *not* that they were unworried by the fire or that they were unwilling to endure the danger; but rather that they had decided that there was no fire at all and the smoke was caused by something else. They failed to act because they thought there was no reason to act. Their "apathetic" behavior was reasonable—given their interpretation of the circumstances.

EXPERIMENT 2. A LADY IN DISTRESS [3]

Although it seems unlikely that the group inhibition of bystander intervention observed in Experiment 1 can be attributed entirely to the fact that smoke represents a danger to the individual bystander, it is certainly possible that this is so. Experiment 2 was designed to see whether similar group inhibition effects could be observed in situations where there is no danger to the individual himself for not acting. In addition, a new variable was included: whether the bystanders knew each other.

Male Columbia undergraduates waited either alone, with a friend, or with a stranger to participate in a market research study. As they waited, they heard someone fall and apparently injure herself in the room next door. Whether they tried to help, and how long they took to do so were the main dependent variables of the study. Subjects were telephoned and offered $2 to participate in a survey of game and puzzle preferences conducted at Columbia by the Consumer Testing Bureau (CTB), a market research organization. Each person contacted was asked to find a friend who would also be interested in participating. Only those students who recommended friends, and the friends they suggested, were used as subjects.

Subjects were met at the door by the market research representative, an attractive young woman, and taken to the testing room. On the way, they passed the CTB office and through its open door they were able to see a desk and bookcases piled high with papers and filing cabinets. They entered the adjacent testing room which contained a table and chairs and a variety of games, and they were given a preliminary background information and game preference questionnaire to fill out. The representative told subjects that she would be working next door in her office for about 10 minutes while they completed the questionnaires, and left by opening the collapsible curtain which divided the two rooms. She made sure that subjects were aware that the curtain was unlocked and easily opened and that it provided a means of entry to her office. The representative stayed in her office, shuffling papers, opening drawers, and making enough noise to remind the subjects of her presence. Four minutes after leaving the testing area, she turned on a high fidelity stereophonic tape recorder.

[3] A more detailed description of this experiment is given in: Latané, B. and Rodin, J. A lady in distress: Inhibiting effects of friends and strangers on bystander intervention, *Journal of Experimental Social Psychology*, in press.

The Emergency

If the subject listened carefully, he heard the representative climb up on a chair to reach for a stack of papers on the bookcase. Even if he were not listening carefully, he heard a loud crash and a scream as the chair collapsed and she fell to the floor. "Oh, my God, my foot . . . I . . . can't move . . . it. Oh . . . my ankle," the representative moaned. "I . . . can't get this . . . thing . . . off me." She cried and moaned for about a minute longer, but the cries gradually got more subdued and controlled. Finally, she muttered something about getting outside, knocked over the chair as she pulled herself up, and thumped to the door, closing it behind her as she left. The entire incident took 130 seconds.

The main dependent variable of the study, of course, was whether the subjects took action to help the victim and how long it took him to do so. They were actually several modes of intervention possible: a subject could open the screen dividing the two rooms, leave the testing room and enter the CTB office by the door, find someone else, or, most simply, call out to see if the representative needed help. Four experimental conditions were run. In one condition (Alone, $n = 26$) each subject was by himself in the testing room while he filled out the questionnaire and heard the fall. In a second condition (Stooge, $n = 14$), a stranger, actually a confederate of the experimenter, was also present. The confederate had instructions to be as passive as possible and to answer questions put to him by the subjects with a brief gesture or remark. During the emergency, he looked up, shrugged his shoulders, and continued working on his questionnaire. Subjects in the third condition (Strangers, $n = 20$ pairs) were placed in the testing room in pairs. Each subject in the pair was unacquainted with the other before entering the room and they were not introduced. Only one subject in this condition spontaneously introduced himself to the other. In a final condition (Friends, $n = 20$ pairs), pairs of friends overheard the incident together.

Mode of Intervention

Across all experimental groups, the majority of subjects who intervened did so by pulling back the room divider and coming into the CTB office (61%). Few subjects came the round-about way through the door to offer their assistance (14%), and a surprisingly small number (24%) chose the easy solution of calling out to offer help. No one tried to find someone else to whom to report the accident. Since experimental conditions did not differ in the proportions choosing various modes of intervention, the comparisons below will deal only with the total proportions of subjects offering help.

Alone vs. Stooge Conditions

Seventy per cent of all subjects who heard the accident while alone in the waiting room offered to help the victim before she left the room. By contrast the presence of a non-responsive bystander markedly inhibited helping. Only 7% of subjects in the Stooge condition intervened. These subjects seemed upset and confused during the emergency and frequently glanced at the passive confederate who continued working on his questionnaire. The difference between the Alone and Stooge response rates is, of course, highly significant ($p < .001$).

Alone vs. Two Strangers

Since 70% of Alone subjects intervened, we should expect that at least one person in 91% of all two-person groups would offer help if members of a pair had no influence upon each other. In fact, members did influence each other. In only 40% of the groups did even one person offer help to the injured woman. Only 8 subjects of the 40 who were run in this condition intervened. This response rate is significantly below the hypothetical baseline ($p < .001$). Social inhibition of helping was so strong, that the victim was actually aided more quickly when only one person heard her distress than when two did ($p < .01$).

Strangers vs. Stooge

The response rate in the Two Strangers condition appears to be somewhat higher than the 7% rate in the Stooge condition. Making a correction similar to that used for the Alone scores, the expected response rate based on the Stooge condition is 13%. This is significantly lower than the response rate in the Strangers condition ($p < .05$).

Alone vs. Two Friends

Pairs of friends often talked about the questionnaire before the accident, and sometimes discussed a course of action after the fall. Even so, in only 70% of the pairs did even one person intervene. While, superficially, this appears as high as the Alone condition, there must again be a correction for the fact that twice as many people are free to act. When compared to the 91% hypothetical base rate, friends do inhibit each other from intervening ($p < .10$). They were also slower to intervene than would be expected from the Alone condition ($p < .05$).

Friends vs. Strangers

Although pairs of friends were inhibited from helping when compared to the Alone condition, they were significantly faster to intervene than were pairs of strangers ($p < .01$). The median latency of the first response from pairs of friends was 36 seconds; the median pair of strangers did not respond at all within the arbitrary 130-second duration of the emergency.

Subjects who intervened usually claimed that they did so either because the fall sounded very serious or because they were uncertain what had occurred and felt they should investigate. Many talked about intervention as the "right thing to do" and asserted they would help again in any situation.

Many of the non-interveners also claimed that they were unsure what had happened (59%), but had decided that it was not too serious (46%). A number of subjects reported that they thought other people would or could help (25%), and three said they refrained out of concern for the victim—they did not want to embarrass her. Whether to accept these explanations as reasons or rationalizations is moot—they certainly do not explain the differences among conditions. The important thing to note is that non-interveners did not seem to feel that they had behaved callously or immorally. Their behavior was generally consistent with their interpretation of the situation. Subjects almost uniformly claimed that, in a "real" emergency, they would be among the first to help the victim.

Interestingly, when subjects were asked whether they had been influenced by the presence of action of their coworkers, they were either unwilling or unable to report that they had. Subjects in the passive confederate condition reported, on the average, that they were "very little" influenced by the stooge. Subjects in the Two Strangers condition claimed to have been only "a little bit" influenced by each other, and friends admitted to "moderate" influence. Put another way, only 14%, 30%, and 70% of the subjects in these three conditions admitted to at least a "moderate" degree of influence. These claims, of course, run directly counter to the experimental results, in which friends were the least inhibited and subjects in the Stooge condition most inhibited by the other's actions.

These results strongly replicate the findings of the Smoke study. In both experiments, subjects were less likely to take action if they were in the presence of passive confederates than if they were alone, and in both studies, this effect showed up even when groups of naive subjects were tested together. This congruence of findings from different experimental settings supports the validity and generality of the phenomenon: it also helps rule out a variety of alternative explanations suitable to either situation alone. For example, the possibility that smoke may have represented a threat to the subject's personal safety and that subjects in groups may have had a greater concern to appear "brave" than single subjects does not apply to the present experiment. In the present experiment, non-intervention cannot signify bravery. Comparison of the two experiments also suggests that the absolute number of non-responsive bystanders may not be a critical factor in producing social inhibition of intervention. One passive confederate in the present experiment was as effective as two in the smoke study; pairs of strangers in the present study inhibited each other as much as did trios in the former study.

How can we account for the differential social inhibition caused by friends and strangers? It may be that people are less likely to fear possible embarrassment in front of friends than before strangers, and that friends are less likely to misinterpret each other's inaction than are strangers. If so, social influence should be less likely to lead friends to decide there is no emergency than strangers. When strangers overheard the accident, they seemed noticeably concerned but confused. Attempting to interpret what they had heard and to decide upon a course of action, they often glanced furtively at one another, apparently anxious to discover the other's reaction yet unwilling to meet eyes and betray their own concern. Friends, on the other hand, seemed better able to convey their concern nonverbally, and often discussed the incident and arrived at a mutual plan of action. Although these observations are admittedly impressionistic, they are consistent with other data. During the emergency, a record was kept of whether the bystanders engaged in conversation. Unfortunately, no attempt was made to code the amount or content of what was said, but it is possible to determine if there was any talking at all. Only 29% of subjects attempted any conversation with the stooge; while 60% of the pairs of strangers engaged in some conversation, it was mostly desultory and often unrelated to the accident. Although the latter rate seems higher than the former, it really is not, since there are two people free to initiate a conversation rather than just one. Friends, on the other hand, were somewhat more likely to talk than strangers—85% of the pairs did so. Friends, then, may show less mutual inhibition than strangers because they are less likely to develop a state of "pluralistic ignorance."

These first experiments show that in two, widely different types of emergency settings, the presence of other people inhibits intervention. Subjects were less likely to report a possible fire when together than alone, and they were less likely to go to the aid of the victim of an accident when others were present. Is this a general effect? Will it apply to all types of emergency? Are there situations in which the presence of other people might actually facilitate bystander intervention? One possible set of circumstances in which we might expect social facilitation of intervention is when an emergency is caused by a villain. People who fail to intervene in real emergencies sometimes claim they were afraid of the consequences of intervention—afraid of direct attack, afraid of later retribution, afraid of having to go to court. In situations involving a villain, even if one person is afraid to take action, the presence of other people as potential risk-sharing allies might embolden him to intervene. Under these circumstances, there might actually be a group facilitation of intervention. To test this possibility, two Columbia undergraduates, Paul Bonnarigo and Malcolm Ross, turned to a life of crime.

EXPERIMENT 3. THE CASE OF THE STOLEN BEER

The Nu-Way Beverage Center in Suffern, New York, is a discount beer store. It sells beer and soda by the case, often to New Jerseyans who cross the state line to find both lowered prices and a lowered legal drinking age. During the spring of 1968 it was the scene of a minor crime wave—within one two-week period, it was robbed 96 times. The robbers followed much the same modus operandi on each occasion. Singly or in a pair, they would enter the store and ask the cashier at the checkout counter, "What is the most expensive imported beer that you carry?" The cashier, in cahoots with the robbers, would reply "Lowenbrau. I'll go back and check how much we have." Leaving the robbers in the front of the store, the cashier would disappear into the rear to look for the Lowenbrau. After waiting for a minute, the robbers would pick up a case of beer near the front of the store, remark to nobody in particular, "They'll never miss this," walk out of the front door, put the beer in their car, and drive off. On 46 occasions, one robber carried off the theft; on 46 occasions, two robbers were present.

The robberies were always staged when there were either one or two people in the store, and the timing was arranged so that the one or both customers would be at the checkout counter at the time when the robbers entered. On 46 occasions, one customer was at the checkout counter during the theft; on 46 occasions, two customers were present. Although occasionally the two customers had come in together, more usually they were strangers to each other. Sixty-one per cent of the customers were male, 39% female. Since the checkout counter was about 20 feet from the front door, since the theft itself took less than a minute, and since the robbers were both husky young men, nobody tried directly to prevent the theft. There were, however, other courses of intervention available.

When the cashier returned from the rear of the store, he went to the checkout counter and resumed waiting on the customers there. After a minute, if nobody had spontaneously mentioned the theft, he casually inquired, "Hey, what happened to that man (those men) who was (were) in here? Did you see him (them) leave?" At this point the customer could either report the theft, say merely that he had seen the man or men leave, or disclaim any knowldge of the event whatsoever. Overall, 20% of the subjects reported the theft spontaneously, and 51% of the remainder reported it upon prompting. Since the results from each criterion followed an identical pattern, we shall indicate only the total proportion of subjects in each condition who reported the theft, whether spontaneously or not.

Results

Whether there were one or two robbers present made little difference. Customers were somewhat but not significantly more likely to report the theft if there were two robbers (69%) than if there was only one (52%). Sex also made no difference; females were as likely to report as males. The number of customers, on the other hand, made a big difference. Thirty-one of the 48 single customers, or 65%, mentioned the theft. From this, we would expect that 87% of the two-person groups would include at least one reporter. In fact, in only 56% of the two-person groups did even one person report the theft ($p < .01$). Social inhibition of reporting was so strong that the theft was actually somewhat (though not significantly) less likely to be reported when two people saw it than when only one did.

In three widely differing situations the same effect has been observed. People are less likely to take a socially responsible action if other people are present than if they are alone. This effect has occurred in a situation involving general danger, in a situation where someone has been the victim of an accident, and in a situation involving one or more villains. The effect holds in real life as well as in the laboratory, and for members of the general population as well as college students. The results of each of these three experiments clearly support the line of theoretical argument advanced earlier. When bystanders to an emergency can see the reactions of other people, and when other people can see their own reactions, each individual may, through a process of social influence, be led to interpret the situation as less serious than he would if he were alone, and consequently be less likely to take action.

SOCIAL DETERMINANTS OF BYSTANDER INTERVENTION, II

So far we have devoted our attention exclusively to one stage of our hypothesized model of the intervention process: noticing the situation and interpreting it. Once an individual has noticed an emergency and interpreted it as being serious, he still has to decide what, if anything, he will do about it. He must decide that he has a responsibility to help, and that there is some form of assistance that he is in a position to give. He is faced with the choice of whether he himself will intervene. His decision will presumably be made in terms of the rewards and costs of the various alternative courses of action open to him.

In addition to affecting the interpretations that he places on a situation, the presence of other people can also alter the rewards and costs facing an individual bystander. Perhaps most importantly, the presence of other people can alter the cost of not acting. If only one bystander is present at an emergency, he carries all of the responsibility for dealing with it; he will feel all of the guilt for not acting; he will bear all of any blame others may level for non-intervention. If others are present, the onus of responsibility is diffused, and the individual may be more likely to resolve his conflict between intervening and not intervening in favor of the latter alternative.

When only one bystander is present at an emergency, if help is to come it must be from him. Although he may choose to ignore them (out of concern for his personal safety, or desire "not to get involved"), any pressures to intervene focus uniquely on him. When there are several observers present, however, the pressures to intervene do not focus on any one of the observers; instead the responsibility for intervention is shared among all the onlookers and is not unique to any one. As a result, each may be less likely to help.

Potential blame may also be diffused. However much we wish to think that an individual's moral behavior is divorced from considerations of personal punishment or reward, there is both theory and evidence to the contrary. It is perfectly reasonable to assume that, under circumstances of group responsibility for a punishable act, the punishment or blame that accrues to any one individual is often slight or nonexistent.

Finally, if others are known to be present, but their behavior cannot be closely observed, any one bystander may assume that one of the other observers is already taking action to end the emergency. If so, his own intervention would only be redundant—perhaps harmfully or confusingly so. Thus, given the presence of other onlookers whose behavior cannot be observed, any given bystander can rationalize his own inaction by convincing himself that "somebody else must be doing something."

These considerations suggest that, even when bystanders to an emergency cannot see or be influenced by each other, the more bystanders who are present, the less likely any one bystander would be to intervene and provide aid. To test this suggestion, it would be necessary to create an emergency situation in which each subject is blocked from communicating with others to prevent his getting information about their behavior during the emergency. Experiment 4 attempted to fulfill this requirement.

EXPERIMENT 4. A FIT TO BE TRIED [4]

Procedure

Thirteen male and 104 female students in introductory psychology courses at New York University were recruited to take part in an unspecified

[4] Portions of these results have been reported in Darley, J. M. and Latané, B. Bystander intervention in emergencies: Diffusion of responsibility. *Journal of Personality and Social Psychology*, 1968, **8**, 377–383.

experiment as part of their class requirement. When a subject arrived in the laboratory, he was ushered into an individual room from which a communication system would enable him to talk to the other participants (who were actually figments of the tape recorder). Over the intercom, the subject was told that the experimenter was concerned with the kinds of personal problems faced by normal college students in a high-pressure, urban environment, and that he would be asked to participate in a discussion about these problems. To avoid possible embarrassment about discussing personal problems with strangers, the experimenter said, several precautions would be taken. First, subjects would remain anonymous, which was why they had been placed in individual rooms rather than face-to-face. Second, the experimenter would not listen to the initial discussion himself, but would only get the subjects' reactions later by questionnaire.

The plan for the discussion was that each person would talk in turn for two minutes, presenting his problems to the group. Next, each person in turn would comment on what others had said, and finally there would be a free discussion. A mechanical switching device regulated the discussion, switching on only one microphone at a time.

The Emergency

The discussion started with the future victim speaking first. He said he found it difficult to get adjusted to New York and to his studies. Very hesitantly and with obvious embarrassment, he mentioned that he was prone to seizures, particularly when studying hard or taking exams. The other people, including the one real subject, took their turns and discussed similar problems (minus the proneness to seizures). The naive subject talked last in the series, after the last prerecorded voice.

When it was again the victim's turn to talk, he made a few relatively calm comments, and then, growing increasingly loud and incoherent, he continued:

> I er um I think I I need er if if could er er somebody er er er er er er er give me a little er give me a little help here because er I er I'm er er h-h-having a a a a real problem er right now and I er if somebody could help me out it would it would er er s-s-sure be sure be good . . . because er there er er a cause I er I uh I've got a a one of the er sie-er er things coming on and and and I could really er use some help so if somebody would er give me a little h-help uh er-er-er-er-er c-could somebody er er help er uh uh uh (choking sounds) . . . I'm gonna die er er I'm . . . gonna die er help er er seizure er (chokes, then quiet).

The major independent variable of the study was the number of people the subject believed also heard the fit. The subject was led to believe that the discussion group was one of three sizes: a two-person group consisting of himself and the victim; a three-person group consisting of himself, the victim and one other person; or a six-person group consisting of himself, the victim, and four other persons.

Varying the kind of bystanders present at an emergency as well as the number of bystanders should also vary the amount of responsibility felt by any single bystander. To test this, several variations of the three-person group were run. In one three-person condition, the other bystander was a female; in another, a male; and in a third, a male who said that he was a premedical student who occasionally worked in the emergency wards at Bellevue Hospital.

Subjects in the above conditions were female college students. To test whether there are sex differences in the likelihood of helping, males drawn from the same subject pool were tested in the three-person, female bystander condition.

Two final experimental variations concerned acquaintanceship relationships between the subject and other bystanders and between the subject and the victim. In one of these conditions, female subjects were tested in the three-person condition, but were tested with a friend that they had been asked to bring with them to the laboratory. In another, subjects were given prior contact with the victim before being run in the six-person group. Subjects underwent a very brief "accidental" encounter with an experimental confederate posing as the future victim. The two met for about a minute in the hall before the experiment began. During this time, they chatted about topics having nothing to do with the experiment.

The major dependent variable of the experiment was the time elapsed from the start of the victim's seizure until the subject left her experimental cubicle. When the subject left her room, she saw the experiment's assistant seated at the end of the hall, and invariably went to the assistant to report the seizure. If six minutes elapsed without the subject's having emerged from her room, the experiment was terminated.

Ninety-five per cent of all the subjects who ever responded did so within the first half of the time available to them. No subject who had not reported within three minutes after the fit ever did so. This suggests that even had the experiment been allowed to run for a considerably longer period of time, few additional subjects would have responded.

Eighty-five per cent of the subjects who thought they alone knew of the victim's plight reported the seizure before the victim was cut off; only 31% of those who thought four other bystanders were present did so. Every one of the subjects in the two-person condition, but only 62% of the subjects in the six-person condition ever reported the emergency. To do a more detailed analysis of the results, each subject's time score was transformed into a "speed" score by taking the reciprocal of the response time in seconds and multiplying by 100. Analysis of variance of these speed scores indicates that the effect of group size was highly significant ($p < .01$), and all three groups differed significantly one from another ($p < .05$).

Effect of Group Composition and Sex of the Subject

Several variations of the three-person group were run. In one pair of variations, the female subject thought the other bystander was either male or female, in another, she thought the other bystander was a premedical student who worked in the emergency ward at Bellevue Hospital. These variations in the sex and medical competence of the other bystanders had no important or detectable effect on speed of response. Subjects responded equally frequently and fast whether the other bystander was female, male, or medically experienced.

Coping with emergencies is often thought to be the duty of males, especially when there are females present, but there was no evidence that this is the case in this study. Male subjects responded to the emergency with almost exactly the same speed as did females.

Effects of Friendship and Prior Acquaintance

Friends responded considerably differently from strangers in the three-person condition. When two friends were each aware of the victim's distress, even though they could not see or be seen by each other, they responded significantly faster than subjects in the other three-person groups. In fact, the average speed of response by subjects who thought their friend was also present was not noticeably different from the average speed of response in the two-person condition, where subjects believed that they alone were aware of the emergency. This suggests that responsibility does not diffuse across friends.

The effects of prior acquaintance with the victim were also strong. Subjects who had met the victim, even though only for less than a minute, were significantly faster to report his distress than other subjects in the six-person condition. Subjects in this condition later discussed their reactions to the situation. Unlike subjects in any other group, some of those who had accidentally met the victim-to-be later reported that they had actually *pictured* him in the grip of a seizure. Apparently, the ability to *visualize* a specific, concrete, distressed individual increases the likelihood of helping that person.

Subjects, whether or not they intervened, believed the fit to be genuine and serious. "My God, he's having a fit," many subjects said to themselves (and we overheard via their microphones). Others gasped or simply said, "Oh." Several of the male subjects swore. One subject said to herself, "It's just my kind of luck, something has to happen to me!" Several subjects spoke aloud of their confusion about what course of action to take: "Oh, God, what should I do?"

When those subjects who intervened stepped out of their rooms, they found the experiment's assistant down the hall. With some uncertainty but without panic, they reported the situation. "Hey, I think Number 1 is very sick. He's having a fit or something." After ostensibly checking on the situation, the experimenter returned to report that "everything is under control." The subjects accepted these assurances with obvious relief.

Subjects who failed to report the emergency showed few signs of the apathy and indifference thought to characterize "unresponsive bystanders." When the experimenter entered her room to terminate the situation, the subject often asked if the victim were all right. "Is he being taken care of?" "He's all right, isn't he?" Many of these subjects showed physical signs of nervousness; they often had trembling hands and sweating palms. If anything, they seemed more emotionally aroused than did the subjects who reported the emergency.

Why, then, didn't they respond? It is not our impression that they had decided *not* to respond. Rather, they were still in a state of indecision and conflict concerning whether to respond or not. The emotional behavior of these non-responding subjects was a sign of their continuing conflict; a conflict that other subjects resolved by responding.

The fit created a conflict situation of the avoidance-avoidance type. On the one hand, subjects worried about the guilt and shame they would feel if they did not help the person in distress. On the other hand, they were concerned not to make fools of themselves by overreacting, not to ruin the ongoing experiment by leaving their intercoms and not to destroy the anonymous nature of the situation, which the experimenter had earlier stressed as important. For subjects in the two-person condition, the obvious distress of the victim and his need for help were so important that their conflict was easily resolved. For the subjects who knew that there were other bystanders present, the cost of not helping was reduced and the conflict they were in was more acute. Caught between the two negative alternatives of letting the victim continue to suffer, or the costs of rushing in to help, the non-responding bystanders vacillated between them rather than choosing not to respond. This distinction may be academic for the victim, since he got no help in either case, but it is an extremely important one for understanding the causes of bystander's failures to help.

Although the subjects experienced stress and conflict during the emergency, their general reactions to it were highly positive. On a questionnaire administered after the experimenter had discussed the nature and purpose of the experiment, every single subject found the experiment either "interesting" or "very interesting" and was willing to participate in similar experiments in the future. All subjects felt they understood what the experiment was all about and indicated they thought the deceptions were necessary and justified. All but one felt they were better informed about the nature of psychological research in general.

We asked all subjects whether the presence or absence of other bystanders had entered their minds during the time that they were hearing the seizure. We asked the question every way we knew how: subtly, directly, tactfully, bluntly, and the answer was always the same. Subjects had been aware of the presence of other bystanders in the appropriate conditions, but they did not feel that they had been influenced in any way by their presence. As in our previous experiments, this denial occurred in the face of results showing that the presence of others did affect helping.

SOCIAL DETERMINANTS OF BYSTANDER INTERVENTION, III

We have suggested two distinct processes which might lead people to be less likely to intervene in an emergency if there are other people present than if they are alone. On the one hand, we have suggested that the presence of other people may affect the interpretations each bystander puts on an ambiguous emergency situation. If other people are present at an emergency, each bystander will be guided by their apparent reactions in formulating his own impressions. Unfortunately, their apparent reactions may not be a good indication of their true feelings. It is possible for a state of "pluralistic ignorance" to develop, in which each bystander is led by the *apparent* lack of concern of the others to interpret the situation as being less serious than he would if alone. To the extent that he does not feel the situation is an emergency, of course, he will be unlikely to take any helpful action.

Even if an individual does decide that an emergency is actually in process and that something ought to be done, he still is faced with the choice of whether he himself will intervene. Here again, the presence of other people may influence him—by reducing the costs associated with non-intervention. If a number of people witness the same event, the responsibility for action is diffused, and each may feel less necessity to help.

Both the "social influence" and the "diffusion of responsibility" explanations seem valid, and there is no reason why both should not be jointly operative. Neither alone can account for all the data. For example, the diffusion explanation cannot account for the significant difference in response rate between the Strangers and Stooge conditions in Experiment 2. There should be equal diffusion in either case. This difference can more plausibly be attributed to the fact that strangers typically did not show such complete indifference to the accident as did the stooge. The diffusion process also does not seem applicable to the results of Experiment 1. Responsibility for protecting oneself from fire should not diffuse. On the other hand, "social influence" processes cannot account for results in Experiment 4. Subjects in that experiment could not communicate with each other and thus could not be influenced by each other's reactions.

Although both processes probably operate, they may not do so at the same time. To the extent that social influence leads an individual to define the situation as non-serious and not requiring action, his responsibility is eliminated, making diffusion unnecessary. Only if social influence is unavailable or unsuccessful in leading subjects to misinterpret a situation, should diffusion play a role. Indirect evidence supporting this analysis comes from observation of non-intervening subjects in the various emergency settings. In settings involving face-to-face contact, as in Experiments 1 and 2, non-interveners typically redefined the situation and did not see it as a serious emergency. Consequently, they avoided the moral choice of whether or not to take action. During the post-experimental interviews, subjects in these experiments seemed relaxed and assured. They felt they had behaved reasonably and properly. In Experiment 4, on the other hand, face-to-face contact was prevented, social influence could not help subjects define the situation as non-serious, and they were faced with the moral dilemma of whether to intervene. Although the imagined presence of other people led many subjects to delay intervention, their conflict was exhibited in the post-experimental interviews. If anything, subjects who did not intervene seemed more emotionally aroused than did subjects who reported the emergency.

The results of these experiments suggest that social inhibition effects may be rather general over a wide variety of emergency situations. In four different experiments, bystanders have been less likely to intervene if other bystanders are present. The nature of the other bystander seems to be important: a non-reactive confederate provides the most inhibition, a stranger provides a moderate amount, and a friend, the least. Overall, the results are consistent with a multiprocess model of intervention; the effect of other people seems to be mediated both through the interpretations that bystanders place on the situation, and through the decisions they make once they have come up with an interpretation.

"There's safety in numbers," according to an old adage, and modern city dwellers seem to believe it. They shun deserted streets, empty subway cars, and lonely walks in dark parks, preferring instead to go where others are or to stay at home. When faced with stress, most individuals seem less afraid when they are in the presence of others than when they are alone. Dogs are less likely to yelp when they face a strange situation with other dogs; even rats are less likely to defecate and freeze when they are placed in a frightening open field with other rats.

A feeling so widely shared should have some basis in reality. Is there safety in numbers? If so, why? Two reasons are often suggested: Individuals are less likely to find themselves in trouble if there are others about, and even if they do find themselves in trouble, others are likely to help them deal with it. While it is certainly true that a victim is unlikely to receive help if nobody knows of his plight, the experiments above cast doubt on the suggestion that he will be more likely to receive help if more people are present. In fact, the opposite seems to be true. A victim may be more likely to get help, or an emergency be reported, the fewer people who are available to take action.

Although the results of these studies may shake our faith in "safety in numbers," they also may help us begin to understand a number of frightening incidents where crowds have listened to, but not answered, a call for help. Newspapers have tagged these incidents with the label "apathy." We have become indifferent, they say, callous to the fate of suffering others. Our society has become "dehumanized" as it has become urbanized. These glib phrases may contain some truth, since startling cases such as the Genovese murder often seem to occur in our large cities, but such terms may also be misleading. Our studies suggest a different conclusion. They suggest that situational factors, specifically factors involving the immediate social environment, may be of greater importance in determining an individual's reaction to an emergency than such vague cultural or personality concepts as "apathy" or "alienation due to urbanization." They suggest that the failure to intervene may be better understood by knowing the relationship among bystanders rather than that between a bystander and the victim.

. Our results may explain why the failure to intervene seems to be more characteristic of large cities than rural areas. Bystanders to urban emergencies are more likely to be, or at least to think they are, in the presence of other bystanders than witnesses of non-urban emergencies. Bystanders to urban emergencies are less likely to know each other or to know the victim than are witnesses of non-urban emergencies. When an emergency occurs in a large city, a crowd is likely to gather; the crowd members are likely to be strangers; and it is likely that no one will be acquainted with the victim. These are exactly the conditions that made the helping response least likely in our experiments.

In a less sophisticated era, Rudyard Kipling prayed "That we, with Thee, may walk uncowed by fear or favor of the crowd; that, under Thee, we may possess man's strength to comfort man's distress." It appears that the latter hope may depend to a surprising extent upon the former.

REFERENCES

Brown, R. W. Mass Phenomena. In Lindzey, G. (ed.) *Handbook of Social Psychology*, Vol. 2, Cambridge, Addison-Wesley, 1954.

Brown, R. W. *Social Psychology*, New York, Free Press, 1965.

Darley, J. M. and Latané, B. Bystander intervention in emergencies: Diffusion of responsibility. *Journal of Personality and Social Psychology*, 1968, **8**, 377–383.

Latané, B. Gregariousness and fear in laboratory rats. *Journal of Experimental Social Psychology*, 1969, **5**, 61–69.

Latané, B. and Darley, J. M. Group inhibition of bystander intervention in emergencies. *Journal of Personality and Social Psychology*, 1968, **10**, 215–221.

Latané, B. and Glass, D. C. Social and non-social attraction in rats. *Journal of Personality and Social Psychology*, 1968, **9**, 142–146.

Latané, B. and Rodin, J. A lady in distress: Inhibiting effects of friends and strangers on bystander intervention. *Journal of Experimental Social Psychology*, in press.

Schachter, S. *The Psychology of Affiliation,* Stanford: Stanford University Press, 1959.

Introduction to
Hamblin et al. Article

Reinforcement can be used as a powerful tool to shape human behavior as we saw in the articles by Calvin, Davison, Goorney, and Skinner. In the selection below we present an example of psychologically determined schedules of reinforcement utilized in the service of man. The research in question, conducted by a team of investigators at Washington University, demonstrates the efficacy of reinforcement therapy in correcting certain unwanted behaviors in problem children.

31

Changing the Game from "Get the Teacher" to "Learn"

New reinforcement techniques have made good students of the "too aggressive," "too young," and the autistic.

Robert L. Hamblin, David Buckholdt, Donald Bushell, Desmond Ellis, and Daniel Ferritor

Almost any educator of experience will assure you that it is next to impossible—and often actually impossible—to teach normal classroom subjects to children who have extreme behavior problems, or who are "too young." Yet at four experimental classrooms of the Central Midwestern Regional Educational Laboratories (CEMREL), we have been bringing about striking changes in the behavior and learning progress of just such children.

In the 18 months of using new exchange systems and working with different types of problem children, we have seen these results:

• Extraordinarily aggressive boys, who had not previously responded to therapy, have been tamed.
• Two-year-olds have learned to read about as fast and as well as their 5-year-old classmates.
• Four ghetto children, too shy, too withdrawn to talk, have become better than average talkers.
• Several autistic children, who were either mute or could only parrot sounds, have developed functional speech, have lost their bizarre and disruptive behavior patterns, and their relationships with parents and other children have improved. All of these children are on the road to normality.

Our system is deceptively simple. Superficially, in fact, it may not even seem new—though, in detail, it has never been tried in precisely this form in the classroom before. In essence, we simply reinforce "good" behavior

SOURCE. *TRANS-Action*, January, 1969, **6**, 2–31. Copyright by TRANS-Action Magazine, New Brunswick, New Jersey.

and nonpunitively discourage "bad" behavior. We structure a social exchange so that as the child progresses, we reinforce this behavior—give him something that he values, something that shows our approval. Therefore, he becomes strongly motivated to continue his progress. To terminate bizarre, disruptive or explosive patterns, we stop whatever has been reinforcing that undesirable behavior—actions or attention that teachers or parents have unwittingly been giving him in exchange, often in the belief that they were punishing and thus discouraging him. Study after study has shown that whenever a child persists in behaving badly, some adult has, perhaps inadvertently, been rewarding him for it.

"Socialization" is the term that sociologists use to describe the process of transforming babies—who can do little but cry, eat, and sleep—into adults who can communicate and function rather effectively in their society. Socialization varies from culture to culture, and, while it is going on all around us, we are seldom aware of it. But when normal socialization breaks down, "problems" occur—autism, nonverbal or hyperaggressive behavior, retardation, delinquency, crime, and so on.

The authors, after years of often interesting but by and large frustrating research, realized that the more common theories of child development (Freudian, neo-Freudian, the developmental theories of Gesell and Piaget, and a number of others) simply do not satisfactorily explain the socialization process in children. Consequently in desperation we began to move toward the learning theories and then toward the related exchange theories of social structure. Since then, working with problem children, our view has gradually been amplified and refined. Each experimental classroom has given us a different looking glass. In each we can see the child in different conditions, and can alter the conditions which hinder his socialization into a civilized, productive adult capable of happiness.

By the time they become students, most children love to play with one another, to do art work, to cut and paste, to play with Playdoh, to climb and swing on the playground, and so on. Most pre-schools also serve juice and cookie snacks, and some have television sets or movies. There is, consequently, no dearth of prizes for us to reward the children for good behavior. The problem is not in finding reinforcers, but in managing them.

THE BASIC SYSTEM: TOKEN EXCHANGE

One of the simpler and most effective ways, we found, was to develop a token-exchange system. The tokens we use are plastic discs that children can earn. A child who completes his arithmetic or reading may earn a dozen tokens, given one by one as he proceeds through the lessons. And at the end of the lesson period comes the reward.

Often it is a movie. The price varies. For four tokens, a student can watch while sitting on the floor; for eight, he gets a chair; for 12, he can watch while sitting on the table. Perhaps the view is better from the table—anyway, the children almost always buy it if they have enough tokens. But if they dawdled so much that they earned fewer than four, they are "timed out" into the hall while the others see the movie. Throughout the morning, therefore, the children earn, then spend, then earn, then spend.

This token-exchange system is very powerful. It can create beneficial changes in a child's behavior, his emotional reactions, and ultimately even his approach to life. But it is not easy to set up, nor simple to maintain.

At the beginning the tokens are meaningless to the children; so to make them meaningful, we pair them with M&M candies, or something similar. As the child engages in the desired behavior (or a reasonable facsimile), the teacher gives him a "Thank you," an M&M, and a token. At first the children are motivated by the M&Ms and have to be urged to hold on to the tokens; but then they find that the tokens can be used to buy admission to the movie, Playdoh, or other good things. The teacher tells them the price and asks them to count out the tokens. Increasingly, the teacher "forgets" the M&Ms. In two or three days the children get no candy, just the approval and the tokens. By then, they have learned.

There are problems in maintaining a token exchange. Children become disinterested in certain reinforcers if they are used too frequently, and therefore in the tokens that buy them. For instance, young children will work very hard to save up tokens to play with Playdoh once a week; if they are offered Playdoh every day, the charm quickly fades. Some activities—snacks, movies, walks outdoors—are powerful enough to be used every day.

As noted, the children we worked with had different behavior problems, reflecting various kinds of breakdowns in the socialization process. Each experiment we conducted concentrated on a particular type of maladjustment or a particular group of maladjusted children to see how a properly structured exchange system might help them. Let us look at each experiment, to see how each problem was affected.

AGGRESSION

Unfortunately, our world reinforces and rewards aggressive behavior. Some cultures and some families are open and brazen about it—they systematically and consciously teach their young that it is desirable, and even virtuous, to attack certain other individuals or groups. The child who can beat up the other kids on the playground is sometimes respected by his peers, and perhaps by his parents; the soldier achieves glory in combat. The status, the booty, or the bargaining advantages that come to the aggressor can become reinforcement to continue and escalate his aggressions.

In more civilized cultures the young are taught not to use aggression, and we try to substitute less harmful patterns. But even so, aggression is sometimes reinforced unintentionally—and the consequences, predictably, are the same as if the teaching was deliberate.

In the long run civilized cultures are not kind to hyperaggressive children. A recent survey in England, for instance, found that the great majority of teachers felt that aggressive behavior by students disturbed more classrooms than anything else and caused the most anxiety among teachers. At least partly as a result, the dropout rates for the hyperaggressives was 2½ times as great as for "normals," and disproportionate numbers of hyperaggressives turned up in mental clinics.

The traditional treatment for aggressive juveniles is punishment—often harsh punishment. This is not only of dubious moral value, but generally it does not work.

We took seriously—perhaps for the first time—the theory that aggression is a type of exchange behavior. Boys become aggressive because they get something for it; they continue to be aggressive because the rewards are continuing. To change an aggressive pattern in our experimental class at Washington University, therefore, we had to restructure appropriately the exchange system in which the boys were involved.

As subjects we (Ellis and Hamblin) found five extraordinarily aggressive 4-year-old boys, all referred to us by local psychiatrists and social workers who had been able to do very little with them. Next, we hired a trained teacher. We told her about the boys and the general nature of the experiment—then gave her her head. That is, she was allowed to use her previous training during the first period—and this would provide a baseline comparison with what followed after. We hoped she would act like the "typical teacher." We suspect that she did.

LET'S PLAY "GET THE TEACHER"

The teacher was, variously, a strict disciplinarian, wise counselor, clever arbitrator, and sweet peacemaker. Each role failed miserably. After the eighth day, the average of the children was 150 sequences of aggression per day! Here is what a mere four minutes of those sequences were like:

> Mike, John, and Dan are seated together playing with pieces of Playdoh. Barry, some distance from the others, is seated and also is playing with Playdoh. The children, except Barry, are talking about what they are making. Time is 9:10 A.M. Miss Sally, the teacher, turns toward the children and says, "It's time for a lesson. Put your Playdoh away." Mike says, "Not me." John says, "Not me." Dan says, "Not me." Miss Sally moves toward Mike. Mike throws some Playdoh in Miss Sally's face. Miss Sally jerks back, then moves forward rapidly and snatches Playdoh from Mike. Puts Playdoh in her pocket. Mike screams

for Playdoh, says he wants to play with it. Mike moves toward Miss Sally and attempts to snatch the Playdoh from Miss Sally's pocket. Miss Sally pushes him away. Mike kicks Miss Sally on the leg. Kicks her again, and demands the return of his Playdoh. Kicks Miss Sally again. Picks up a small steel chair and throws it at Miss Sally. Miss Sally jumps out of the way. Mike picks up another chair and throws it more violently. Miss Sally cannot move in time. Chair strikes her foot. Miss Sally pushes Mike down on the floor. Mikes starts up. Pulls over one chair. Now another, another. Stops a moment. Miss Sally is picking up chairs, Mike looks at Miss Sally. Miss Sally moves toward Mike. Mike runs away.

John wants his Playdoh. Miss Sally says "No." He joins Mike in pulling over chairs and attempts to grab Playdoh from Miss Sally's pocket. Miss Sally pushes him away roughly. John is screaming that he wants to play with his Playdoh. Moves toward phonograph. Pulls it off the table; lets it crash onto the floor. Mike has his coat on. Says he is going home. Miss Sally asks Dan to bolt the door. Dan gets to the door at the same time as Mike. Mike hits Dan in the face. Dan's nose is bleeding. Miss Sally walks over to Dan, turns to the others, and says that she is taking Dan to the washroom and that while she is away, they may play with the Playdoh. Returns Playdoh from pocket to Mike and John. Time: 9:14 A.M.

Wild? Very. These were barbarous little boys who enjoyed battle. Miss Sally did her best but they were just more clever than she, and they *always* won. Whether Miss Sally wanted to or not, they could always drag her into the fray, and just go at it harder and harder until she capitulated. She was finally driven to their level, trading a kick for a kick and a spit in the face for a spit in the face.

What Miss Sally did not realize is that she had inadvertently structured an exchange where she consistently reinforced aggression. First, as noted, whenever she fought with them, she *always lost*. Second, more subtly, she reinforced their aggressive pattern by giving it serious attention—by looking, talking, scolding, cajoling, becoming angry, even striking back. These boys were playing a teasing game called "Get the Teacher." The more she showed that she was bothered by their behavior, the better they liked it, and the further they went.

These interpretations may seem far-fetched, but they are borne out dramatically by what happened later. On the twelfth day we changed the conditions, beginning with B1 (see Figure 1). First, we set up the usual token exchange to reinforce cooperative behavior. This was to develop or strengthen behavior that would replace aggression. Any strong pattern of behavior serves some function for the individual, so the first step in getting rid of a strong, disruptive pattern is substituting another one that is more useful and causes fewer problems. Not only therapy, but simple humanity dictates this.

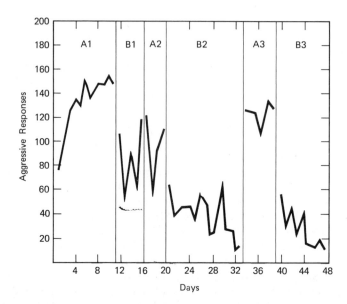

FIG. 1. Frequency of aggressive sequences by days for five 4-year-old boys. In A1, A2 and A3 the teacher attempted to punish aggression but inadvertently reinforced it. In B1, B2 and B3 she turned her back or otherwise ignored aggression and thus did not reinforce it.

First, the teacher had to be instructed in how *not to reinforce* aggression. Contrary to all her experience, she was asked to turn her back on the aggressor, and at the same time to reinforce others' cooperation with tokens. Once we were able to coach her and give her immediate feedback over a wireless-communication system, she structured the exchanges almost perfectly. The data in Figures 1 and 2 show the crucial changes: a gradual increase in cooperation—from about 56 to about 115 sequences per day, and a corresponding decrease in aggression from 150 to about 60 sequences!

These results should have been satisfactory, but we were new at this kind of experimentation, and nervous. We wanted to reduce the frequency of aggression to a "normal" level, to about 15 sequences a day. So we restructured the exchange system and thus launched A2.

In A2, we simply made sure that aggression would always be punished. The teacher was told to *charge* tokens for any aggression.

To our surprise, the frequency of cooperation remained stable, about 115 sequences per day; but aggression *increased* to about 110 sequences per day! Evidently the boys were still playing "Get the Teacher," and the fines were enough reinforcement to increase aggression.

So, instead of fining the children, the teacher was again told to ignore aggression by turning her back and giving attention and tokens only for cooperation. The frequency of aggression went down to a near "normal" level, about 16 sequences per day (B2), and cooperation increased to about 140 sequences.

Then, as originally planned, the conditions were again reversed. The boys were given enough tokens at the beginning of the morning to buy their usual supply of movies, toys, and snacks, and these were not used as reinforcers. The teacher was told to do the best she could. She was not instructed to return to her old pattern, but without the tokens and without our coaching she did—and with the same results. Note A3 in Figures 1 and 2. Aggression increased to about 120 sequences per day, and cooperation decreased to about 90. While this was an improvement over A1, before the boys had ever been exposed to the token exchange, it was not good. The mixture of aggression and cooperation was strange, even weird, to watch.

When the token exchange was restructured (B3) and the aggression no longer reinforced, the expected changes recurred—with a bang. Aggression decreased to seven sequences on the last day, and cooperation rose to about 181 sequences. In "normal" nursery schools, our observations have shown that five boys can be expected to have 15 aggression sequences and 60 cooperation sequences per day. Thus, from extremely aggressive and uncooperative, our boys had become less aggressive and far more cooperative than "normal" boys.

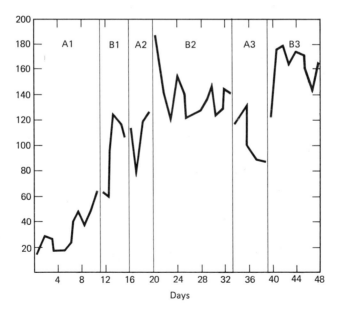

FIG. 2. Frequency of cooperative sequences. In A1, A2 and A3 the teacher structured a weak approval exchange for cooperation and a disapproval exchange for noncooperation. In B1, A2, B2 and B3, she structured a token exchange for cooperation.

Here is an example of their new behavior patterns, taken from a rest period—precisely the time when the most aggressive acts had occurred in the past:

> All of the children are sitting around the table drinking their milk; John, as usual, has finished first. Takes his plastic mug and returns it to the table. Miss Martha, the assistant teacher, gives him a token. John goes to cupboard, takes out his mat, spreads it out by the blackboard, and lies down. Miss Martha gives him a token. Meanwhile, Mike, Barry, and Jack have spread their mats on the carpet. Dan is lying on the carpet itself since he hasn't a mat. Each of them gets a token. Mike asks if he can sleep by the wall. Miss Sally says "Yes." John asks if he can put out the light. Miss Sally says to wait until Barry has his mat spread properly. Dan asks Mike if he can share his mat with him. Mike says "No." Dan then asks Jack. Jack says, "Yes," but before he can move over, Mike says "Yes." Dan joins Mike. Both Jack and Mike get tokens. Mike and Jack get up to put their tokens in their cans. Return to their mats. Miss Sally asks John to put out the light. John does so. Miss Martha gives him a token. All quiet now. Four minutes later—all quiet. Quiet still, three minutes later. Time: 10:23 A.M. Rest period ends.

The hyperaggressive boys actually had, and were, double problems; they were not only extremely disruptive, but they were also washouts as students. Before the token system (A1), they paid attention to their teacher only about 8 percent of the lesson time (see Figure 3). The teacher's system of scolding the youngsters for inattention and taking their attention for granted with faint approval, if any, did not work at all. To the pupils, the "Get the Teacher" game was much more satisfying.

After the token exchange was started, in B1, B2, B3, and B4, it took a long, long time before there was any appreciable effect. The teacher was being trained from scratch, and our methods were, then, not very good. However, after we set up a wireless-communication system that allowed us to coach the teacher from behind a one-way mirror and to give her immediate feedback, the children's attention began to increase. Toward the end of B3, it leveled off at about 75 percent—from 8 percent! After the token exchange was taken out during A2, attention went down to level off at 23 percent; put back in at B4, it shot back up to a plateau of about 93 percent. Like a roller coaster: 8 percent without, to 75 with, to 23 without, to 93 with.

NORMAL CHILDREN

These results occurred with chronic, apparently hopeless hyperaggressive boys. Would token exchange also help "normal," relatively bright

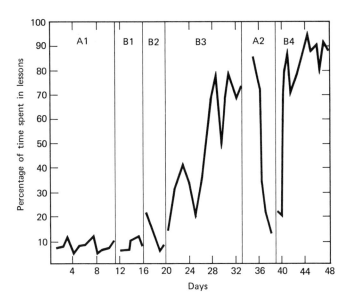

FIG. 3. Percentage of scheduled time spent in lessons by days for five hyperaggressive boys. In A1 and A2, teacher structured approval exchange for attendance, disapproval for non-attendance. In B1 and B2, a token exchange for attendance was structured, but not effectively until B2 and B4.

upper-middle-class children? Sixteen youngsters of that description—nine boys and seven girls, ranging from 2 years 9 months to 4 years 9 months—were put through an experimental series by Bushell, Hamblin, and Denis Stoddard in an experimental pre-school at Webster College. All had about a month's earlier experience with the token-exchange system. The results are shown in Figure 4.

STUDY IN 15-MINUTE PERIODS

At first, the study hour was broken up into 15-minute periods, alternating between the work that received tokens, and the play or reward that the tokens could be used for. Probably because the children were already familiar with token exchange, no great increase in learning took place. On the 22nd day, we decided to try to increase the learning period, perhaps for the whole hour. In A2 (Figure 4), note that the time spent in studying went up rapidly and dramatically—almost doubling—from 27 to level off at 42 minutes.

During B, the token exchange was taken out completely. The teachers still gave encouragement and prepared interesting lessons as before. The rewards—the nature walks, snacks, movies, and so on—were retained. But, as in a usual classroom, they were given to the children free instead of being

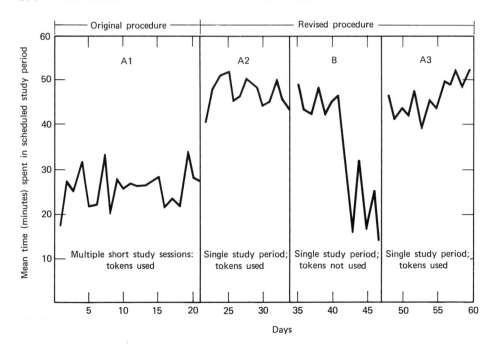

FIG. 4. Sixteen upper-middleclass pre-schoolers. In A1, A2 and A3 the token exchange was used; in B, only approval.

sold. The children continued at about the same rate as before for a few days. But after a week, attention dropped off slowly, then sharply. On the last day it was down to about 15 minutes—one-third the level of the end of the token period.

In A3, the token exchange was reinstituted. In only there days, attention snapped back from an average of 15 minutes to 45 minutes. However, by the end of A3, the students paid attention an average of 50 of the available 60 minutes.

A comparison of the record of these normals with the record of the hyperaggressive boys is interesting. The increase in attention brought by the token exchange, from about 15 minutes to 50, is approximately threefold for the normal children; but for the hyperaggressive boys—who are disobedient and easily distracted—it is about eleven-fold, from 8 percent to 93 percent of the time. The increase was not only greater, but the absolute level achieved was higher. This indicates strongly, therefore, that the more problematic the child, the greater may be the effect of token exchange on his behavior.

The high rates of attention were not due to the fact that each teacher

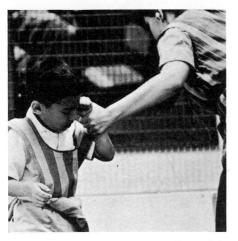

At first he thinks the whole procedure a joke.

She becomes more insistent.

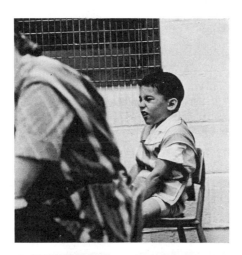

He discovers it is no joke.

Teacher "timing out" a child by seating him away from the others for a while.

The "token-exchange" system of learning reinforcement calls, in essence, for the quick and frequent reward and encouragement of desirable behavior, and non-punitive "timing-out"— usually by removing the child—to discourage undesirable behavior. By this means two-year-old children have learned to read, violent ones to sit calmly and study, and the autistic to speak and to have hope. (*Photographed by Daniel T. Magdison*)

"Say 'Nose,' Jimmy."

"Good boy, Jimmy!"

" 'Nose,' Jimmy, *'nose.'* "

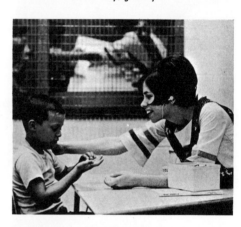

"*Good* boy!"

Jimmy says "nose."

Triumph and reward.

Jimmy, an almost mute autistic child, is rewarded with a corn chip for learning to say "nose."

had fewer children to work with. Individualized lessons were not enough. Without the token exchange, even three teachers could not hold the interest of 16 children 2 to 4 years old—at least not in reading, writing, and arithmetic.

Praise and approval were not enough as rewards. The teachers, throughout the experiment, used praise and approval to encourage attention; they patted heads and said things like "Good," "You're doing fine," and "Keep it up"; yet, in B, when the token exchange was removed, this attention nevertheless ultimately declined by two-thirds. Social approval is important, but not nearly so powerful as material reinforcers.

Finally, it is obvious that if the reinforcers (movies, snacks, toys, or whatever) do not seem directly connected to the work, they will not sustain a high level of study. To be effective with young children, rewards must occur in a structured exchange in which they are given promptly as recompense and thus are directly connected to the work performed.

THE VERY YOUNG CHILD

According to accepted educational theory, a child must be about six and a half before he can comfortably learn to read. But is this really true, or is it merely a convenience for the traditional educational system? After all, by the time a normal child is two and a half he has learned a foreign language—the one spoken by his parents and family; and he has learned it without special instruction or coaching. He has even developed a feel for the rules of grammar, which, by and large, he uses correctly. It is a rare college student who becomes fluent in a foreign language with only two and a half years of formal training—and our college students are supposed to be the brightest of our breed. Paul Goodman has suggested that if children learn to *speak* by the same methods that they learn to *read,* there might well be as many non-speakers now as illiterates.

What if the problem is really one of motivation? If we structured an exchange that rewarded them, in ways they could appreciate, for learning to read, couldn't they learn as readily as 5-year-olds?

We decided that for beginners, the number of words a child can read is the best test of reading ability. In an experiment designed by Hamblin, Carol Pfeiffer, Dennis Shea, and June Hamblin, and administered at our Washington University pre-school, the token-exchange system was used to reward children for the number of words each learned. The results are given in Figure 5. Note that the 2-year-olds did about as well as the 5-year-olds; their sight vocabularies were almost as large.

There was an interesting side effect: at the end of the school year, all but one of these children tested at the "genius" level. On Stanford-Binet individual tests, their I.Q. scores increased as much as 36 points. It was

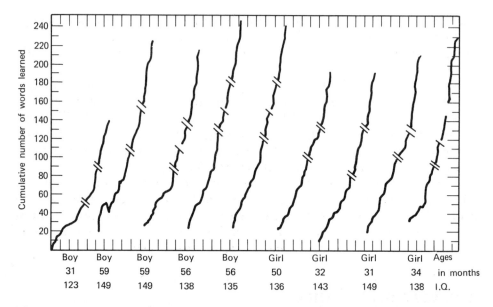

	Boy	Boy	Boy	Boy	Boy	Girl	Girl	Girl	Girl	Ages
	31	59	59	56	56	50	32	31	34	in months
	123	149	149	138	135	136	143	149	138	I.Q.

FIG. 5. Number of sight-words learned through time by five 4- and 5-year-olds, and four 2- and 3-year-olds. Note that the younger children did about as well as the older ones—except for one boy whose IQ was somewhat lower than the others in the group. (Gaps indicate absences.)

impossible to compute an average gain only because three of the children "topped out"—made something in excess of 149, the maximum score possible.

In general, the lower the measured I.Q. at the start, the greater the gain—apparently as a result of the educational experience.

THE NON-VERBAL CHILD

What happens when ghetto children are introduced into a token-exchange system? At our Mullanphy Street preschool, 22 Afro-American children—age 3 to 5—attend regularly. All live in or near the notorious Pruitt-Igoe Housing Project, and most come from broken homes. When the school began, the teachers were unenthusiastic about a token exchange, so we let them proceed as they wished. The result was pandemonium. About half of the children chased one another around the room, engaged in violent arguments, and fought. The others withdrew; some would not even communicate.

After the third day, the teachers asked for help. As in the other experimental schools, we (Buchholdt and Hamblin) instructed them to ignore aggressive-disruptive behavior and to reward attention and cooperation with social approval and the plastic tokens, later to be exchanged for such things as milk, cookies, admission to the movies, and toys. The children quickly caught on, the disruptions diminished, and cooperation increased. Within three weeks of such consistent treatment, most of the children took part in the lessons, and disruptive behavior had become only an occasional problem. All of this, remember, without punishment.

Our attention was then focused upon the children with verbal problems. These children seldom started conversations with teachers or other students, but they would sometimes answer questions with a word or perhaps two. This pattern may be unusual in the middle classes, but is quite common among ghetto children. Our research has shown that children so afflicted are usually uneducable.

As we investigated, we became convinced that their problem was not that they were unable to talk as much as that they were too shy to talk to strangers—that is, to non-family. In their homes we overheard most of them talking brokenly, but in sentences. Consequently, we set up a token exchange for them designed specifically to develop a pattern of talking with outsiders, especially teachers and school children.

As it happened, we were able to complete the experiment with only four children (see Figure 6). During A1, the baseline period (before the

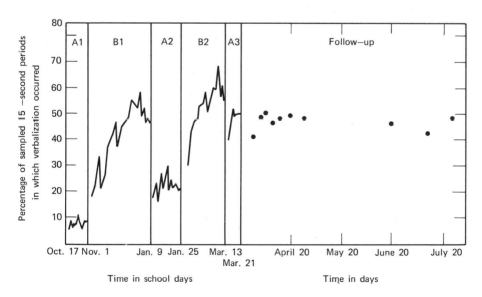

FIG. 6. Percentage of sampled periods in which talking occurred through time for four non-verbal "culturally deprived" children, and through five experimental conditions. In each of the A conditions a new teacher was introduced, and she structured a token exchange for participation in lessons. In the B conditions, the teacher then structured a token exchange for talking. The follow-up was similar to the A conditions.

tokens were used), the four children spoke only in about 8 percent of the 15-second sampling periods. In B1, the teachers gave social approval and tokens *only* for speaking; non-verbalisms, like pointing or headshaking, would not be recognized or reinforced. Note the increase in verbalization, leveling out at approximately 48 percent.

In A2 we reversed the conditions by using a teacher new to the school. The rate of talking dropped off immediately, then increased unevenly until it occurred in about 23 percent of the sample periods.

In B2 the new teacher reintroduced the token exchange for talking, and once more there was a dramatic rise: The speaking increased much more rapidly than the first time, ending up at about 60 percent. (This more rapid increase is known as the Contrast Effect. It occurs in part, perhaps, because the children value the token exchange more after it has been taken away.)

In the final test, we again took out the token exchange, and introduced yet another new teacher. This time the drop was small, to 47 percent.

We followed the children for three months after the end of the experiment. Their speech level remained at 48 percent, with little dropoff. This compares with the 40 percent talking rate for our other ghetto children, and the 42 percent rate for upper-middle-class children at the Washington University pre-school.

Frequency of speech, however, was not the only important finding. At the end of B1, the children spoke more often but still in a hesitant and broken way. By the end of B2, they spoke in sentences, used better syntax, and frequently started conversations.

Mothers, teachers, and neighbors all reported that the children were much more friendly and assertive. But some claimed that the children now talked too much! This could reflect individual bias; but there was little doubt that at least one child, Ben, had become an almost compulsive talker. He was given to saying hello to everyone he met and shaking their hands. So we terminated the experiment—what would have happened to Ben had we started *another* exchange?

This experiment shows that token exchange can bring on permanent behavior change, but that the culture must reinforce the new behavior. Talking is important in our culture, and so is reading; therefore they are reinforced. But other subjects—such as mathematics beyond simple arithmetic—are not for most people. For behavior to change permanently it must be reinforced at least intermittently.

AUTISM

The problems of autistic children usually dwarf those of all other children. To the casual observer, autistic children never sustain eye contact with others but appear to be self-contained—sealed off in a world of their own. The most severe cases never learn how to talk, though they sometimes echo or parrot. They remain dependent upon Mother and become more and more demanding. They develop increasingly destructive and bizarre behavior problems. Finally, between 5 and 10 years old, autistic children ordinarily become unbearable to their families and at that point they are almost invariably institutionalized. Until recently, at least, this meant a rear ward to vegetate in until they died.

The breakthrough in therapy from autism came in 1964 when Dr. Ivar Lovaas and Dr. Montrose Wolfe and a graduate student, now Dr. Todd Risley, simultaneously developed therapy systems using well-established principles of operant conditioning. They were particularly successful with those children who randomly echoed or imitated words or sentences (this is called echolalia).

The therapy systems we have designed, developed, and tested, though similar in some ways to those developed by Lovaas, Wolfe and Risley, are quite different in others. First, we do not use punishment, or other negative stimuli. We simply terminate exchanges that reinforce the autistic patterns, and set up exchanges that reinforce normal patterns. Second, our children are not institutionalized; they live at home, and are brought to the laboratory for twenty minutes to three hours of therapy per day. Third, as soon as possible—usually within months—we get the children into classrooms where a therapist works with four or five at a time. Fourth, we train the mother to be an assistant therapist—mostly in the home, but also in the laboratory. These changes were introduced for several reasons, but primarily in the hope of getting a better, more permanent cure for autism.

THE ETIOLOGY OF AUTISM

Is autism hereditary, as many believe? Our studies indicate that this is not the important question. Many mental faculties, including I.Q., have some physiological base. But the real issue is how much physiologically based potential is socially realized, for good or bad. As far as we can tell, the exchanges that intensify autism get structured inadvertently, often by accident; but once started, a vicious cycle develops that relentlessly drives the child further into autism.

When autism starts, the mother often reacts by babying the child, trying to anticipate his every need before he signals. Thus normal communication is not reinforced, and the child never learns to work his environment properly. But even if he doesn't know how to get what he wants through talking, he does learn, through association, that his oversolicitous and anxious mother will always respond if he acts up violently or bizarrely enough. And she must, if only to punish. He thus learns to play "Get mother's attention"; and this soon develops into "Get mother exasperated, but stop just short of the point where she punishes and really hurts." Here is an example (observed by Ferritor in the first of a series of experiments by the Laboratory's staff, not reported here):

> Larry is allowed to pick out his favorite book. His mother then attempts to read it to him, but he keeps turning the pages so she can't. He gets up and walks away from the table. The mother then yells at him to come back. He *smiles* (a sign of pleasure usually but not always accompanies reinforcement). Mother continues to talk to the child to try to get him back for the story. Finally, he comes over to the table and takes the book away from her. She lets him and goes back to the bookcase for another book. He then sits down and she begins to read. He tries to get up, but his mother pulls him back. Again. Again. She holds him there. He gets away and starts walking around the room. Goes to the toy cabinet. Mother gets up to go over and take a toy away from him. He sits on the floor. The mother comes over and sits down by him. He gets up and goes over by the door and opens it and tries to run out. She tells him he has to stay. He *smiles*. She resumes reading. He gets up and starts walking around the table. She grabs him as he comes by. He *smiles*.

A clinical psychologist who had tested Larry did not diagnose him as autistic, but as an educable mental retardate with an I.Q. of perhaps 30. Yet he had gaze aversion and we suspected that Larry, like other autistics, was feigning inability as a way of getting what he wanted from his mother, and then from other adults. He began to respond to the attractive exchanges that we structured for him, and as we did, he began to tip his hand. For example, at one point when his mother was being trained to be an assistant therapist, the following incident occurred:

> Mrs. C. told Larry that as soon as he strung some beads he could have gum from the gum machine that was across the room. For about 10 minutes he fumbled, he whined, all the time crying, saying "I can't." Finally, he threw the beads at his mother. Eventually, the mother had the good sense to leave the room, saying, "As soon as you string those beads, you can have your gum." With his mother out of the room, according to our observers he sat right down and, in less than 30 seconds, filled a string with beads with no apparent trouble.

Just two weeks later, after the mother had been through our 10-day training program, they again had a "story time."

> The mother begins by immediately asking Larry questions about this book (the same book used a few weeks before). He responds to every question. She gives approval for every correct answer. Then she tries

to get him to say, "That is a duck." He will not say it intelligibly, but wants to turn the page. Mother says, "As soon as you say 'duck,' you may turn the page. Larry says "Duck" and turns the page. He *smiles*.

After seven minutes, Larry is still sitting down. They have finished one book and are beginning a second.

Most autistic children play the game "Look at me, I'm stupid," or "Look at me, I'm bizarre." These are simply attention-getting games that most adults repeatedly reinforce. Man is not a simple machine; he learns, and as he develops his abilities, he develops stronger and stronger habits. Thus, once these inadvertent exchanges get established, the child becomes more and more dependent, more and more disruptive, more and more bizarre, more and more alienated from the positive exchanges that are structured in his environment. What is sad is that the parents and the others in the child's life sense that something is terribly wrong, but the more they do, the worse the situation becomes.

It seems to those of us who have been involved in these experiments from the beginning that the exchange techniques and theories we have used have without question demonstrated their effectiveness in treating and educating problem children. Watching these children as they go peacefully and productively about their lessons toward the end of each experimental series is both an exhilarating and humbling experience. It is almost impossible to believe that so many had been written off as "uneducable" by professionals, that without this therapy and training—or something similar —most would have had dark and hopeless futures.

But it is not inevitable that so many hyperaggressive or environmentally retarded ghetto children become dropouts or delinquents; it is not inevitable that so many autistic children, saddest of all, must vegetate and die mutely in the back wards of mental hospitals.

FURTHER READING SUGGESTED BY THE AUTHORS
The Analysis of Human Operant Behavior by Ellen P. Reese (Dubuque, Iowa: William C. Brown Company, 1966).
The Emotionally Disturbed Child in the Classroom by Frank Hewett (Boston: Allyn and Bacon, Inc., 1968).
Early Childhood Autism edited by J. K. Wing (London: Pergamon Press, Ltd., 1966).
Case Studies in Behavior Modification by Leonard P. Ullman and Leonard Krasner (New York: Holt, Rinehart and Winston, Inc., 1965).

The student of psychology: studying today to face the challenges of tomorrow.

Section IX
Epilogue:
Your Future in Psychology

"If I decide to major in psychology what kind of career opportunities can I expect?" "What kind of jobs are performed by psychologists?" "Do I need graduate school training to get a good job in psychology?" These are three frequently asked questions in any introductory psychology course.

Many students who find the subject matter of psychology interesting and contemplate a major in the field want to know "early in the game" what type of future they can expect. There are, in fact, a wide variety of career opportunities open to the psychologist; opportunities which vary as a function of his training and job preferences. The two following articles outline some of these opportunities.

In the first selection, written by members of the City College of the City University of New York psychology faculty, the various fields of psychology, and the job opportunities in them, are succinctly described. In the second article Gardner Murphy does a little prognosticating in his *Psychology in the year 2000*. Considered in combination, the two articles should give the student a feeling for what psychology is and what it might be; what it offers now and what it might offer later.

Introduction to
City College Article

The article that follows was originally prepared for the benefit of City College undergraduates contemplating psychology as a career. It is valuable in two respects.

(1) It describes some of the major fields in our discipline, defining and discussing the functions of individuals working in the following areas: clinical, developmental, industrial, physiological, mathematical, school, and social psychology.

(2) It reviews the career opportunities available in these various areas of psychology (listing the qualifications required for specified jobs).

32

Psychology: Training and Vocational Opportunities

Edited by Joseph L. Woodruff

PSYCHOLOGY AS A CAREER

(by Joseph E. Barmack)

Few people realize the enormous diversity of careers pursued by trained psychologists. The popular notion is that a psychologist is a therapist for the emotionally disturbed, or that he tests students for educational and vocational guidance. The fact is that although there are many who are engaged in these activities and their numbers are increasing, they still constitute a minority of the entire discipline. One way of obtaining an idea of the diversity within psychology is to examine the 1966 Directory of the American Psychological Association. This is the last directory in which the members were classified by professional interests.

As a guide, it should be kept in mind that there are over 25,000 members and that a member may be classified in more than one division of interest.

For example, there is a *Clinical* division (with 3567 members as of 1966) but some of the same members may also be members of the *Counseling* division (1562). They may be members of the divisions of *Psychotherapy* and the *Community Psychology* division, both of which were formed since 1966. Some of them are also members of the *Consulting* division (585). Many clinical psychologists are working in mental hospitals, VA hospitals, and with the Armed Services. They assess psychotic status and are engaged in individual and group psychotherapy. A large segment engage in diag-

SOURCE. Woodruff, J., Ed. "Psychology: Training and vocational opportunities." Used with the permission of the authors.

nostic and therapeutic activities with the emotionally troubled but un-hospitalized patients. The community psychologists are interested in pre-venting emotional disturbance. They may be involved in training police, community workers, and other subprofessionals in dealing with family crisis situations, drug addiction, school adjustment problems. A heavy re-search effort is being supported by the National Institute for Mental Health.

Specialization in clinical psychology is common. There are specialists in problems of infancy, of the child, of the adult, or of the aged. There are specialists by the nature of pathology e.g., schizophrenics, the brain dam-aged, and for almost each of the major neurological disorders. There were 882 members in the division of the *Psychological Aspects of Disability.* Here the concern is more with consequences of physical disability.

There were 1024 members of the *School Psychologists'* division. They work in the elementary and high school setting. They assess abilities, diag-nose problems of adjustment to the school, do little therapy but provide guidance to teachers in working with these children and placing them in remedial and other classes.

The largest single division is *Personality and Social* with 3567 mem-bers. Most of its members are interested in research on how the personality develops and the social factors and institutions that help shape it. Many are interested in effecting social change and the more actively interested are also members of the *SPSSI* division (1401). SPSSI stands for the *"Society for the Psychological Study of Social Issues."* Some members are in govern-ment and are also members of the division of *Public Service* (616). In gov-ernment, they may be members of the research and administrative Corps of Congress, of the Peace Corps, Departments of Labor, Justice, Commerce, and State. They may study voter behavior for a variety of contingencies, thereby helping the statesman (or politician) make better decisions on public acceptance of issues and candidates; they assist congressmen in ob-taining data for issues that bear on legislation and budgeting; they develop training, retraining and placement programs for the jobless; they study the causes of poverty and the factors which may alleviate it; they predict fluc-tuations in consumer buying interest; they are developing noneconomic indicators of stability and progress both here and in underdeveloped coun-tries; they study the effectiveness of legal and punitive systems as deterrents to crime.

There are 979 members in the division of *Industrial Psychology. En-gineering Psychology* with a membership of 362 represents a related interest.

Industrial psychologists are active in personnel selection, executive evaluation and promotion, sensitivity training of management personnel, morale studies within large plants, and training programs for groups of workers. Engineering psychologists are concerned with equipment design to simplify operation and maintenance of computers and other complex equipment; they are constantly working on the improvement of telephone communications to reduce error; they study the impact value of advertising layouts; program the selection of media; analyze in depth, product acceptance; enhance the protection of consumer interests; etc.

Industrial psychologists, engineering psychologists, and in some instances social and physiological psychologists have been contributing to standards of heat comfort and ventilation; they suggest minimum light requirements for various types of tasks; they suggest design modifications to reduce the incidence of escalator accidents; they suggest optimal arrangements for kitchen and bathroom layouts; they have designed truck loading layouts in large refineries based on studies of customer and truck driver requirements; they have studied driver behavior on access roads, intersections, and curves in order to make design recommendations for highways; they have recommended design modifications to improve the acoustical properties of concert halls; they have made essential contributions to the design of airports and control towers.

There are 464 members in the division of *Physiological and Comparative Psychology* and there is a new division of Psychopharmacology. Its members are providing strong research support to almost every branch of medicine, including neuroanatomy, epidemiology, cancer research, etc. They are developing better tests for the diagnosis and assessment of brain damage; they are designing better layouts for hospitals to reduce the requirement for paramedical services; they trace brain pathways using behavioral indices; they study the effects of drugs on animals and people; they study the causes and prevention of accidents; they study the psychological complications accompanying cancer, heart disease, defective births among others; they evaluate ways of getting underprivileged groups to adopt good health practices, or practice birth control or avoid drug addiction; they are playing a prominent role in developing better ways of treating the feebleminded, etc.

There are 364 members of the *Military* division but the Department of Defense employs far more psychologists than are represented by this number. They of course are involved, among other things, in designing tests for selection and training. Many of the members of the division of *Evaluation and Measurement* (798) are employed by the Department of Defense.

Psychologists are extensively involved in military equipment design. No weapon system can be produced without the approval of human factors scientists who evaluate the effectiveness of the equipment for ease of operation, training, and maintenance. In space, psychologists are heavily involved in finding out what the human can do *before* military systems are designed for outer space. On the ground they are challenging time encrusted reconnaissance procedures. Also under scrutiny are lie detection techniques and their validity. Psychologists have been in the forefront of recommending procedures for deescalating conflicts, exploring the meaning of the effectiveness of deterrence, and studying the consequences of a termination of the cold war.

I have made no reference to the divisions of *Teaching* (1935), *General* (1190), *Experimental* (1020), *Developmental* (829), *Educational* (2244), and *Consumer* (267) among others.

The foregoing is only a very partial and condensed list. The prime focus of the psychologist is on the behavior of living things and particularly of people. He gets involved in any field in which people play an important role. He brings to people's problems a variety of scientific methods, a body of theory and a growing body of experimentally verified statements of fact. With these resources he can and does move into almost all areas of human concern and is making significant contributions.

CLINICAL PSYCHOLOGY

(by Jerome L. Singer)

Clinical psychology is an applied branch of psychology primarily oriented toward promotion of the welfare of the individual human being through diagnostic assessment, psychotherapy, consultation, or research. Clinical psychologists carry on some or all of these functions in federal, state, or private hospitals, community clinics, social agencies, industry, military, and in private practice. A certain percentage of clinical psychologists also work in schools and universities.

Clinical psychologists work with children and adults in various settings depending on their specific training. In general those who wish to specialize in some specific form of psychotherapy go on for postdoctoral training in this area.

Graduate training in clinical psychology is available at most reasonably large universities in the country. The American Psychological Association evaluates clinical psychology training programs at the various universities and approves a limited number—approximately 60—as meeting its high standards. It is not essential, however, that a student attend an APA approved school to be able to function professionally.

Generally, clinical programs involve four to five years of full-time graduate work of which one year is usually an internship at a hospital or clinic. Because of the continuing demand on a national basis for clinical psychologists with a Ph.D. degree competition for admission to doctoral programs is high.

Clinical psychology is an exciting field that involves a variety of interesting functions and a constant involvement with human beings ranging from the most severely disturbed in hospitals to relatively normal individuals with minor adjustment problems. The field calls for a combination of scientific understanding with considerable personal sensitivity and a genuine interest in people.

INDUSTRIAL PSYCHOLOGY

(by Joseph L. Woodruff)

The aim of the industrial psychologist is to utilize the findings and methods of psychology in coping with a wide variety of industrial problems.

Division 14 of the American Psychological Association is known as the division of *Industrial Psychology*. In 1959 it issued a report entitled *The Psychologist in Industry*. The report listed the following major areas or fields of industrial psychology: (a) selection and testing, (b) management development, (c) counseling, (d) employee motivation, (e) human engineering, (f) marketing research, (g) public relations research. This list gives some indication of the numerous activities of industrial psychologists. Obviously not every industrial psychologist performs all of these functions.

In recent years the employment opportunities have been excellent in industrial psychology. Two of the more rapidly expanding areas of industrial psychology have been human engineering and management development. Human engineering is also known as human factors research. The basic idea here is the development of military and industrial "hardware," which takes into account the capabilities and limitations of the human user. Management development is an especially provocative area because the complexity of management activity requires the measurement and development of qualities which have not, up to this time, been very successfully measured by psychologists.

Those trained in industrial psychology are employed by many of the large and medium-sized corporations in this country. In addition, there are a number of consulting organizations who employ industrial psychologists and make their services available to industry on a contract basis.

For the undergraduate student interested in industrial psychology, a solid preparation in mathematics, statistics, laboratory sciences including experimental psychology, as well as social science subjects, is indicated.

Recently, Mr. David Schnarch, a psychology major, completed a study that has yielded some interesting and valuable information. He found that the use of staff psychologists by his sample of industrial organizations was increasing. His data show an increase of 300 percent over a period of 18 years, the use of consulting psychologists increased 15 percent over a period of 9 years.

He also investigated the job level attained by psychologists in his group of organizations and obtained the following information.

Percent of Psychologists Reaching this Title Level	Title
12	Related to "psychologist" as a staff function
20	Related to a "presidential" title (ex: V.P.)
29	Related to "manager"
37.5	Related to "director"

Psychologists appear to have only modest organizational influence in the selection of high-level company officials. On a five-point scale the mean influence score was 2.5.

Another interesting finding was that, contrary to popular opinion, the acceptability of the Master's degree as the highest degree offered by the prospective industrial psychologist has shown some increase with time.

PHYSIOLOGICAL PSYCHOLOGY

(by Philip Zeigler)

Physiological psychology is that specialization which deals with the analysis of physiological mechanisms underlying the behavior of organisms. The focus may be on neural, hormonal, or chemical factors and the physiological psychologist may use a variety of procedures drawn from physiology, anatomy, or biochemistry. However, his primary interest is always in the behavior itself and his primary contribution is the development of methods for the experimental or conceptual analysis of its underlying mechanisms.

Teaching and research constitute the two main vocational areas within which the physiological psychologist works, most frequently in a university setting. However, there are many opportunities for research in clinical settings on such problems as mental illness, psychosomatic disorders, physiological correlates of personality characteristics, etc. Opportunities for applied research are also available in the aerospace program and in psychopharmacology.

An undergraduate major should include some courses in biology (e.g., endocrinology, genetics) and at least introductory courses in chemistry. A Ph.D. degree is a prerequisite for either teaching or research, and many students find it useful to take further specialized training at the postdoctoral level. An excellent introduction to the field may be obtained by reading the relevant papers in *Psychobiology: The biological bases of behavior,* ed. by

J. L. McGaugh, N. M. Weinberger, and R. Whalen. The volume contains reprints from *Scientific American* covering a rather wide range of topics in both comparative and physiological psychology.

CHILD AND DEVELOPMENTAL PSYCHOLOGY

(by Francis P. Hardesty)

In recent years the phase of psychology focusing on growth and development has undergone a series of differentiations. Affected have been the range and scope of professional opportunities as well as the corresponding structure of graduate school offerings. Individuals today obtaining doctorates in child and developmental psychology find an increasing array of opportunities open to them. Apart from research and instruction in academic and other institutional settings, shortages exist for qualified persons in diagnostics, therapeutic procedures, consultation and guidance not only with problems aligned with the child in familial, school, and community contexts, but with almost every other facet of the life span. Classical roles continue to be reserved for the developmentally oriented professional in child, family and foster-care clinics and functions related to planning and guidance in educative settings. Pressing needs have more recently evolved, however, for qualified personnel to consult, design, and to implement experimental and innovative programs related to problems associated with adolescence, varied adult roles, and the challenges faced by the aged in our society. Training in child and developmental psychology becomes an asset relevant to a wide variety of societal demands for specialized knowledge and skills dealing with questions ranging from "What should I do for my child?" to "How can I design a program and physical facilities to meet the needs of people with whom I am to deal at their particular level of development?"

With respect to graduate programs, the designations developmental psychology and child psychology formerly covered the specializations. Although developmental psychology continues to retain features consistent with its tradition, child psychology—concentrating on the application of psychological principles to child behavior—is being replaced by other programs. Four subspecializations at present are clear, each of which is worthy of consideration by psychology majors making application for graduate school and advanced training. These four subareas may be briefly sketched as follows.

1. *Developmental Psychology.* More often than not, this designation is associated with the traditions of psychology as a science concerned with

the genesis and development of psychological processes and behavior. Consistent with tradition, current programs in developmental psychology frequently are combined with comparative psychology and sometimes with physiological psychology. The focus of this subspecialty tends to be on the scientific study of the nature of processes underlying behavioral stabilities, change, and on principles associated with the regulation and control in the phylogeny and ontogeny of human and infrahuman organisms.

2. *Child Development.* This subspecialization has always provided a basic footing for what has been called child psychology. Although origins can be traced to earlier points in time, child development as a graduate area of study came into its own during the 1920s and 1930s when special institutes were established interrelating applied psychology, education, pediatrics, psychiatry, social work, and other concerns with child welfare. At that time the field was typically associated with service. Today the specialization and associated graduate programs emphasize inquiry into processes underlying normative development as a function of child growth and invariants paralleling child rearing, familial patterning, school, and peer-group interactions.

3. *Clinical Child Psychology.* Of recent vintage, these programs represent an effort to articulate in formal graduate school offerings that which earlier generations could only put together through individualized experience and less related training. Typical is the focus on childhood behavior disorders, psychopathology, and treatment procedures. Students matriculating in these programs generally are exposed to principles underlying normative development and the effects of socialization processes. The emphasis of the subspecialization, however, is on therapeutic procedures applied to the child, family, and other contexts up to puberty and frequently including adolescence.

4. *Human Development.* This subspecialization is the most recently established and, consequently, the less easily discerned of graduate school offerings. Most salient is its concern with developmental tasks, behavioral regularities and change over the life span. Some graduate programs focus on cross-societal analyses and thus place human development within an inter- and intra-national context. Most programs offer concentration on some aspect of the life cycle—infancy, childhood, adolescence, adulthood, or the later years. Interrelationships between theoretical and applied phases of the area are emphasized as well as the interplay among biological, psychological, sociological, anthropological, educational, and other perspectives. In addition to the study of the aged, the infant, and the early child, it is anticipated that a prime concern of this subspecialization in the future will be the intensive study of the effects the age group 25–55 registers on the fabric and patterning of societal values with respect to other age groups.

PSYCHOLOGY AND MATHEMATICS

(by John Antrobus)

Psychology seems to fall somewhere between physics and history with respect to its use of the mathematical rather than verbal medium to present its findings and state its propositions. Even within the field, psychologists differ among one another in their preference for words rather than symbols and numbers to describe their work.

The uses of mathematics in psychology fall into 2 classes: (1) mathematical models and theories and (2) mathematical statistics. Mathematical models are simply symbolic ways of abstracting psychological or behavioral relationship. They have great precision in contrast to ambiguous verbal statements. Verbal statements tend to be fairly simple—the greater the depression, the greater the anxiety. A mathematical model is concerned with the precise form of the relationship: linear log, power, U or inverted-U functions, etc. This kind of precision will never reach psychological theories stated in verbal form. Mathematical models are used primarily in learning and sensory psychology and in other areas which study judgments, discrimination or decision making. Mathematical models are often taught in the content courses, e.g., learning, short-term memory. Psychology departments vary widely in their emphasis on math. A student who wishes to apply his mathematical aptitude to this area should ask for special guidance in planning his program. Among academic and research psychologists, those studying mathematical models are a small but very influential and expanding group.

The use of mathematical statistics, by contrast, is a skill in which every psychologist must acquire some proficiency. Mathematical statistics is concerned with the process of inferring something about everybody from measurements based on just a few. Regardless of whether his mathematical model is simple or complex, a psychologist may still have to learn the inference process associated with his model. Accordingly applied courses in this area are taught in the early part of every undergraduaute psychology program. Theory courses in the area are taught in the math department.

As theorists and model builders most psychologists work in universities or research organizations on the central problems of psychology: psychophysics or signal detection, perception, learning and memory, and, of course, teaching the trade to the next generation of psychologists. The work of a psychologist, however, touches on everything associated with living animal and human sytsems including those areas traditionally covered by economics, sociology and social work education, man-machine problems in engineering, the structure of groups, organizations, cities, law, and medicine. As measurement and knowledge in these areas becomes more precise, there is a tendency to express the knowledge in a mathematical rather than verbal form.

As an applied statistician, the psychologist has even greater vocational freedom. Since every research design is concerned with statistical inference, the psychological statistician is actively involved in just about every possible kind of research on human and animal behavior. In a university or research setting he acts as a teacher to his students and as a consultant to other faculty when unusual statistical problems arise. He is actively sought out as a consultant to government, industry and social agencies to participate in the planning and analysis stages of research. Large research organizations, hospitals, advertising agencies and government agencies employ their own statistician. For example, most medical students are now taught statistics by a psychologist. In summary, then, a psychological statistician is usually actively engaged in many research problems simultaneously and is, therefore, constantly involved with the advancing edge of knowledge in his field.

SCHOOL PSYCHOLOGY

(by Herbert Nechin)

School psychology is that branch of psychology which concerns itself with the application of psychological knowledge to the problems of the schools, with special attention to the student in the school setting. The school psychologist works with the individual and with groups of pupils, parents, teachers and administrators.

In working with individual children the school psychologist analyzes the educational and psychological strengths and needs of the child. He may do this by examining records, talking with the teacher, observing the child in the classroom or other school settings, and using clinical diagnostic procedures such as intelligence, personality, achievement and other tests. After determining the nature of the difficulty and the strengths and needs of the child the psychologist writes a report and makes recommendations for a program of action to meet the student's needs. These recommendations may involve the school—class placement, remediation, social needs, etc.; they may also involve community agencies. The psychologist is the agent for implementation of recommendations by the teacher, guidance counselor, administrator, and specialists in other agencies. While referrals to the psychologist come from teachers, administrators and guidance personnel, there are certain mandated activities, particularly in large school systems such as in New York State. For example, before a child may be placed in a class for children with retarded mental development (CRMD), or before a child who has been institutionalized in a mental hospital may be returned to a regular class in school, it is mandated by law that such children be evaluated by a certified school psychologist. In many school systems psychologists are evaluating children not only by referral but for special placements—Head Start, Classes for Emotionally Disturbed, Special Reading Programs, etc. Besides evaluation some school psychologists are helping the child in the solution of his problem through counseling.

In working with parents the school psychologist generally interprets his finds to them and helps them to get a better picture of the education and psychological needs of the child. He attempts to elicit the understanding, cooperation and involvement of the parent should referrals to another agency be necessary. He may offer suggestions as to how the parent and school can work cooperatively in helping the child. In many schools the school psychologist has the responsibility for developing and implementing parent education programs.

As mentioned before, the school psychologist interprets his findings and makes recommendations to the teacher. Together they try to enable the teacher to work with the strengths of the child and to meet his needs. In addition, he may meet with groups of teachers to study a specific common problem, i.e., the classroom management of the disruptive child, or the motivation of children, or the recognition of the troubled child. He may give an in-service course to teachers. He may, through staff meetings, share ideas and provide information concerning the application of psychological research to the classroom.

Work with administrators involves many varied functions such as aiding in the selection of teachers in some school systems, assisting in the design and planning of research, or assisting in writing grant requests for funds from various governmental agencies.

The kinds of services the school psychologist renders will vary from school system to school system and will depend upon the special needs of the school and community, the psychologist's skills and training and the size of the school system.

SOCIAL PSYCHOLOGY

(by Barbara Dohrenwend)

Examples of the kinds of problems that social psychologists investigate are: What kinds of social pressures make an individual change his attitudes? What social situations produce individual or group conflict? What conditions promote or hinder interpersonal communication and cooperation?

What social settings are most likely to promote or damage the individual's mental health? These questions are studied both in the laboratory, where social situations are experimentally manipulated, and in natural settings, where strategic comparisons are made to determine the effects of on-going social processes.

Because of the wide range of problems and procedures included in social psychology, the specialist in this area is expected not only to have a knowledge of the basic theories and laboratory experimental methods of psychology, but also to have some training in at least one related discipline, usually sociology. For this reason, the undergraduate psychology major who is interested in social psychology is urged to take at least one course in sociology. Advanced courses in sociological theory and methods, or courses in fields such as anthropology and political science are also recommended.

Social psychologists engage in both teaching and research. A prerequisite for teaching in this field is ordinarily the Ph.D. Research, however, is done by persons with varied types of training. Most experimental laboratory work, probably because it is usually related to theoretical issues, is carried out by persons with the Ph.D. Research in natural or field settings is also often directed by a Ph.D., but the complexity of the skills required for this type of work provides opportunities for participation by persons with various specialized skills. Thus, individuals with a background in psychology who have acquired skills in statistical sampling techniques, in survey interviewing techniques, or in data analysis often participate in social psychological research projects at a professional level. These special skills are at present usually acquired after the B.A. through work experience as a junior member of a research team.

Social psychological research is conducted both in university psychology departments and in a variety of other settings. Research on group conflict and on interpersonal communication and cooperation has, for example, been supported by both military and industrial organizations. Investigations of factors affecting mental health are carried out in a variety of clinical and educational settings, as well as in community studies. Persons who have acquired research skills but do not have the Ph.D. are most likely to be given the opportunity to direct research when it is carried out in nonacademic settings.

GRADUATE PROGRAMS IN PSYCHOLOGY

(by Joseph L. Woodruff)

The previous sections of this article show the diversity of vocational opportunity that exists in psychology. A study of graduate school curricula will reveal a similar diversity. This relationship exists because the expansion of professional opportunities is usually quickly followed by an expansion of training opportunities.

For example, one well-known university, the University of Michigan, offers doctoral programs in the following fields of psychology: general, experimental, physiological, comparative and sensory, learning, perception engineering, personality, developmental, rehabilitation, clinical and counseling, mathematical, industrial and organizational, psychopharmacology, social, and psycholinguistics.

Although this list of doctoral programs is more extensive than exists in many universities, it well illustrates the broad spectrum of vocational choice in psychology.

Even the Michigan curriculum does not encompass all of the possibilities. Other graduate psychology programs include the following: mental retardation, psychobiology, differential, human information processing, guidance, school, psychometrics, organizational, child-clinical, animal behavior, human factors, family relations, adulthood and aging, consumer behavior, systems and communication sciences, architectural, decision processes.

Even though some of this apparent variety is a product of semantic confusion, these programs also reflect the numerous applications of Psychology today and provide an excellent indication of career opportunities in the field.

Introduction to
Murphy Article

Predicting the course of scientific progress is never easy and is often unsuccessful. It seems that the ultimate accuracy of such undertakings hinge on the intuitive skills of the forecaster and his understandings of contemporary movements in his discipline. By such criteria, Gardner Murphy's projections should be more accurate than most. An astute observer of (and contributor to) psychology, he has utilized his excellent understanding of present trends in the field to arrive at his predictions concerning its future. His comments on extrasensory perception are of particular interest and should be considered in conjunction with the observations made by R. A. McConnell earlier in this volume.

33

Psychology in the Year 2000

Gardner Murphy

Our profound ambivalence about human futures, and our hopes and fears regarding the possibility of intelligent planning for the future, appears in a charming phrase of Sir George Thomson. Regarding the role of science in planning for new potentialities within the human germ cell, he says that the likelihood of genetic improvements is about like the probability of improving a statue by spraying it with machine gun bullets. Instantly, however, he catches himself up in the remark that with the electron microscope, the localization of individual genes is already very close. One dares not be overbold for fear the critics will laugh, while actually the science fiction, and the casual predictions of scientists for the last hundred years or so, have been much too modest—in fact, much too myopic—as to what actually can be achieved. The best guide here is a systematic and reasonable extrapolation from identifiable trends and, at the same time, a cautious but systematic utilization of the principle of emergence in which new realities constantly come into being, not through the extrapolation of separate curves, but through specific interaction processes. Many of these new emergents are known in metallurgy, in embryology, and in the field of psychology. Some of them have to do with new perceptual and conceptual wholes as shown in countless studies of music and of painting; some of them have to do with dyadic or group patterns that come into existence when new relationships are achieved, for the first time, as shown in the dynamic leadership patterns of Lewin, White, and Lippitt. In a symposium like the present one, an ultra-cautious note may indeed *sound* like science, but only like the plodding

SOURCE. *American Psychologist,* 1969, **24,** 523–530. Copyright 1969 by the American Psychological Association, and reproduced by permission. Presented to the Wayne State University Centennial Symposium, Detroit, Michigan, May 10, 1968.

science of Sir Francis Bacon's *Novum Organum,* not the creative science that indeed has remade the world, and is remaking the world through the extravagant inventiveness of a Planck and an Einstein. In this spirit, I shall attempt some predictions that, I believe, are just as likely to prove shallow and banal as to prove ultimately extravagant and exotic.

The 10 topics which I shall attempt to survey are extrapolations based upon (*a*) the current extraordinary development of *psychophysiology;* (*b*) together with such psychophysiology, the new possibilities of *internal scanning,* in the discovery of the inner human world; the renewed capacity to *observe, with full objectivity, a great deal that has long been regarded as hopelessly subjective;* (*c*) herewith, the direct *confrontation of the unconscious world* that merges into, and is isomorphic with, the world of physiology; (*d*) following these discoveries, the development of *voluntary control over the inner world,* such as scientists previously never dared to dream; (*e*) a new definition of a wide variety of nameless states, *psychological states for which there are no good names,* including feeling states, cognitive states, and volitional states, upon which human destiny almost literally may depend, with resulting understanding of those profound alterations in states of consciousness, well known to the East, regarding which Western man usually has expressed doubt or scorn; (*f*) together with these, the objective exploration of the vast sphere of *parapsychology,* at the edges of which science is nibbling, but so far has failed massively to invade; (*g*) a fresh *reconsideration of the relations of psychology to the biological sciences,* especially genetics; (*h*) a renewed *consideration of psychology in relation to the social sciences,* notably in the new science of social ecology, entailing cross-cultural collaboration of cross-cultural realities; (*i*) a note on the way in which changes in research *methods* alter all these basic concepts; (*j*) finally, a consideration, in all these terms, of the nature of the *human predicament* to which expanding science, which I am describing, may make a serious and indeed a crucial contribution.

PSYCHOPHYSIOLOGY

First, then, as to psychophysiology. Partly as a result of new concepts of the wholeness, the integrity, of the living system, as voiced for example by Sir Charles Sherrington in the *Integrative Action of the Nervous System,* and partly as a result of the sheer power of the research tools that have been developed, psychophysiology has become a dramatically new science in recent decades. Problems of specialization and subspecialization of tissues, as within the mammalian cerebral cortex, have assumed astonishing forms with Penfield's discovery of specific memory localization, with various techniques for studying the electronic functional realities inside the individual nerve cell, with X-ray studies of lattices, and with fine localization of sensory and motor function through implanted electrodes. Both the cruder spot localizations, earlier used in the study of the aphasias, and also the extreme equipotentiality concepts, based largely on extirpation studies, have yielded to a dialectical reconsideration of both local and general aspects of functioning, and with an extraordinary directness of application to the world of immediate experience. Donald Hebb's brilliant breakthrough in the study of sensory deprivation has helped scientists to think of the amazing possibilities of sensory enrichment. One can no longer speak of sensory deprivation or sensory enrichment without thinking, in the manner of David Krech, about the biochemistry and physiology of the mammalian cortex, as profoundly affected by very early postnatal experience. One begins to see, quite literally, the likelihood, in the next few decades, of a thoroughgoing isomorphism of physiological process and psychological process right across the board. Biochemical and neurophysiological progress has been so astonishing in the last few years that psychologists may look quite confidently for a rapidly advancing series of discoveries related specifically to the different kinds of human experience, essentially the sensory, the imaginal, the conceptual, the affective, and indeed certain types of experience that have never been analyzed finely enough to name. Psychopharmacology, long considered to be limited to the specific effects of toxins, is rapidly taking on the form of a powerful organist having at his command banks upon banks of keys, and hundreds of stops, calling into existence an incredible gamut of new experiences.

INTERNAL SCANNING

Following from, or upon, this concurrent study of psychophysiology and biochemistry on the one hand, and the phenomenal world of immediate experience and function on the other hand, psychologists will be drawn, as in a vortex, into the rich field of the study of internal scanning. By this I mean, first, the process by which delicate messages from the striped musculature can be identified more accurately as our subjects carry out reflex or skilled movements. Like a tea taster or a wine sampler, the subject, in several laboratories today, recognizes quickly the kinesthetic messages in different magnitude from different muscles. Specific muscular activities are experienced kinesthetically at the same time he sees on the panel the electronic evidence of what is occurring in specific muscle groups, so that he learns to identify and name them. He is learning, in the same way, to recognize on the panel many other messages that come from organs that are under autonomic control. One may think of the studies by the U.S.S.R. scientists, Bykov and Lisina, relating to proprioceptive and interoceptive conditioning.

But the work will soon move further along. Giving the subject feedback on a panel that shows him what specific internal activities are going on, he can be taught to make more and more refined differentiation within the inner world. His searching, his sweeping, his scanning, and his identifying of the different components from the proprioceptive world, as identical or isomorphic with the same messages from the exteroceptive world on the panel or conveyed to him through tones, give him more and more information as to the rich system of internal messages that have previously been nearly a blur, so precise that he can begin to play the instrument himself. The ancient prejudice that exteroceptive information has a kind of place in the reality world, which is lacking for the other sensory functions, has begun to collapse. A rich variety of internal messages has exactly the same possibility of cross-checking, consensual validation, as has held for sight, hearing, and touch. It is hard to set any limits. Something is known about discriminability when working with teas and wines, or even two-point thresholds on the finger tip, but these studies have never been pushed to their true physiological limits. Nor is it known how they are affected by a variety of parameters, anatomical distribution of receptors and afferent fibers, which in the past have never been sufficiently important to investigate; but today they are being seen in terms of individuality—an individuality based upon heredity, growth, and the learning process. A whole internal world is awaiting discovery.

CONFRONTATION OF THE UNCONSCIOUS WORLD

Third, this internal world, as Gregory Razran has pointed out, would include the entire world of the "observable unconscious," the world of psychologically meaningful, but hitherto not directly observable, processes discovered by Freud and his followers. More and more it appears to be the same world as that which anthropologists, playwrights, poets, and prophets have often enjoined without knowing, in any scientific sense, what they were doing.

But it is one thing to observe the separate components, of course, and another thing to study creatively how they can be put together into new and emergent wholes. Both Arnheim, in *Art and Visual Perception,* and Freud, in *The Interpretation of Dreams,* have applied some of the first informative steps regarding the synthesis, the creative reorganization, of a world that offers vast possibilities. Literally there are hundreds of experiences waiting patiently to be discovered through experimentation. It will not be just the clinicians and the "encounter" groups that will discover them; such discoveries will soon yield rich new harvests to general experimental psychology. I might remind you that while Chaucer, 600 years ago, had only a few words for colors, there are today some thousands of color terms, mostly representing *new* colors that have evolved in the last century as a result of industrial chemistry—colors that do not appear in any rainbow, natural sunset, or natural color schema. There are not only the stock experiences that human beings have by virtue of their anatomical equipment and their physiological capacity as human beings, but thousands of newly created colors. There also are many new kinds of inner experiences, ranging from the effects of new foods, drugs, smogs, exercise, fatigue, strain, anxiety, and ecstasy—scores upon scores of new kinds and shades of inner experience. Of course, many of the new methods may involve risks, and many of them will come under some sort of social control. Whether it will be control by a wise and humane Federal agency, or by public opinion, no present reliable clues are extant.

Inner responses include those called affective and impulsive states, and the vast range of expressions of mood and temperament used in the aesthetic world and in the personal world generally. There are new worlds just waiting; and they will not have to wait very long. Experimental methods for the study of differentiation are developing; for example, experiments in the Soviet Union proved that two-point thresholds within the body, say from the gastric mucosa, can be measured. It is believable that as such differentiations are carried out by classical psychophysical methods, experimenters may first identify a very large range of internal messages and, second, may learn how to integrate them in thousands of new ways.

VOLUNTARY CONTROL

Fourth, insofar as these new messages can be differentiated, tagged, and named, they apparently can be brought under voluntary control. A wide array of new possibilities exists, for example, in Hefferline's study of rapid acquisition of operant control over slight movements that are effective in cutting out a disagreeable hum spoiling music at the time. That is, individuals who could differentiate at all, could also learn, even though unwittingly, to bring in or shut out particular messages. Other laboratories are now continuing what Hefferline started. It appears to be a very refined, delicate, and far-below-threshold type of activity that can bring in an astonishing range of experimentally prepared visual and auditory material. Soviet work on voluntary control of cardiovascular processes appears to concur with what Robert Malmo has reported in Montreal. There are studies of bladder and of capillary control, using panel feedback techniques, strongly suggesting that the autonomically controlled organs are capable of being brought rapidly into the same sphere of voluntary control as that which obtains for the striped muscle responses. Within the next decade or two certainly a very significant control of cardiovascular and gastrointestinal responses may be anticipated, not only with immediate clinical values in bringing in or shutting out various classes of bodily information, but with the deeper scientific value of giving a much wider view of what the human potentialities for such inner experience and such inner control may be. Wenger and Bagchi studied adepts in yoga in various ashrams in India, while Anand and his collaborators pushed their studies further. The keen interest of Indian investigators in putting to experimental tests the classical yoga sutras of Patanjali means not only cross-national research collaboration but, what is more important, the serious awakening of Western psychologists to the fact that experiences treasured and cultivated on the other side of the globe may be as worthy of investigation as those encountered in Detroit, Cambridge, or Topeka.

Last, but by no means least, the process of directly observing one's own electroencephalogram, notably one's own alpha, was developed by Joe Kamiya at Langley Porter and independently by Barbara Brown at the Sepulveda Veterans Administration Hospital. With Kamiya, a 400-cycle tone is activated by the individual's own alpha rhythm, so the subject given the task of increasing the amount of alpha he is exhibiting can rapidly learn, through the feedback that this tone gives him, to bring this under his control. Soon he is turning on or turning off his own alpha. Apparently alpha is not the only rhythm that he can control. There are staggering possibilities both for the understanding of the nature of central nervous system control by the organized central nervous system itself in the form that is called voluntary, but likewise a vast area of further implications for the understanding of the isomorphic relation between a variety of subjective states that accompany the alpha and the exteroceptive patterns that are seen when observing the visual tracing or hearing an appropriate tone. While the clinical applications are important, it is this larger vision of learning to control the brain rhythms themselves that is likely to mean most to the scientist oriented to the year 2000.

NAMELESS STATES

Fifth, while neither Kamiya, nor anyone else, so far as I know, has published the implications that these new methods have for the study of whole new areas of experience only dimly describable today, it is highly probable that before the year 2000 there will be both identification of many kinds of phenomenological states that are anchored upon particular types of EEGs, and the invention of appropriate *names,* appropriate language to describe the newly identified and newly integrated components. I am thinking particularly of cognitive states, conceptualizing states, creative states that may, while retaining all their charm and all their majesty, become far more describable, controllable, and achievable.

PARAPSYCHOLOGY

Sixth, it is characteristic of science at any given period to cultivate the belief that it has a rather well-integrated system into which new observations can fit. While it is at many points open-ended, with really fuzzy edges, there would be chaos indeed if scientists relinquished their passion for a unified field of science. Suppose science was an archipelago of little, spotty, factual details, with no possibility of an implied closed system, an ocean bed unifying all the little islands that appear at the surface level. There is very good psychological reason why science, as it grows, takes on the conservative, the resistive character that is apparent. Under these conditions it is hardly surprising that there is some restlessness, or even resistance, when talking about the discovery of kinds of experience about which nothing has been known. Of course, there are many good reasons, in polite society, why people do not know too much about their insides. These have to do with delicate and complex systems of human expression, some related very broadly to love, some related very broadly to destructiveness, but a great many others that almost every human individual encounters, but does not really want at this time to communicate on a massive basis. I do not anticipate very much actual interference with science on this count, but I do think one must be honest in admitting that this quest of the inside will entail not only triumphs but occasional acrimonious encounters.

While saying this I must add that the resistance toward types of human communication, which presently are not understood, has shown the same attributes. One can understand very clearly the natural fear of scientists that their whole tough labor would be disturbed if they should admit perceptual, memoric, affective, or volitional processes that now are not explainable in terms of the basic biochemical and biophysical realities of human conduct. Even the thought elements that the Würzburg School brought into Wundt's psychological system led to much hostility. Today more serious difficulties are being dealt with as the study of *parapsychology* moves into more systematic experimental form. Most of the data, when closely observed, are like the perceptual and affective data already known, but appear to occur under conditions in which the time and space parameters are unfamiliar. For example, in several recent studies, the telepathic phenomena occur when sender and receiver are separated by very long distances; and while the data can be described psychologically without any mystery, a physical difficulty is encountered because how to conceptualize energies that could carry over these long distances is not known. In other words, the difficulty is at the level of physics, not at the level of psychology. Psychologists may be a little bewildered when they encounter modern physicists who take these phenomena in stride; in fact, take them very much more seriously than psychologists do, saying, as physicists, that they are no longer bound by the types of Newtonian energy distribution, inverse square laws, etc., with which scientists used to regard themselves as tightly bound. In the same way, new physical conceptions regarding the nature of time seem to remove a large part of the trouble that appears in precognition experiments, in which a randomly determined target order of stimulus materials can be foreseen by certain subjects. I think that with the computer methods that are now coming into use, and with the progressive rigidity in experimental controls, psychologists probably will witness a period of slow, but definite, erosion of the blandly exclusive attitude that has offered itself as the only appropriate scientific attitude in this field. The data from parapsychology will be almost certainly in harmony with general psychological principles, and will be assimilated rather easily within the systematic framework of psychology as a science when once the imagined appropriateness of Newtonian physics is put aside, and modern physics replaces it.

PSYCHOLOGY AND BIOLOGY

As I turn to genetics, I would venture to predict a period of massive reorientation of psychology to the biological roots of which it used to boast. The very substance of growth, of motivation, of the learning process, and indeed of most of the basic realities with which the modern evolutionary psychology will have to cope, are provided by the DNA-RNA system; the elements of field physics as they are known in the embryology of Spemann and Weiss; the intricacies of polygenic determination of structure and function; and the broad recognition that individuality in tissue systems, as described by Roger Williams, rewrites the psychology of individual differences in astonishing terms. These genetic terms, of course, will be held by some to be fatalistic, as indicating the genetically given limitations upon all human endeavor. But in two respects these discoveries will be most encouraging: (a) It will be realized that individuality always applies to the growth *potential,* which can be utterly different when a new environmental situation is supplied. An example is the discovery of the Mendelian basis of the phenylpyruvic type of mental defect that has nevertheless yielded, to a large degree, to a carefully prepared diet. In other words, that which was genetically determined was controllable. Through respect for the genetics of human individuality, how to become better environmentalists will be understood. (b) As Sir George Thomson's statement, quoted earlier, implied, scientific insight is moving rapidly to a point such that the electron microscope can greatly aid in studies of the internal organization of individual cells. This, together with some control of mutations and a great deal of control of selective breeding and the application of the principles of population genetics, makes it likely that, within a few generations, to a considerable degree, some of the most abhorrent threats to human development may be eliminated. In anticipating the year 2100 or 2500, biologists could talk quite rationally about not only the prevention of deterioration, but plans for the actual long-range improvement of genetic potentials.

PSYCHOLOGY AND SOCIAL SCIENCE

But the biological sciences do not have the whole exigent message. There is equal need for big gains in the social sciences, especially in the development of a social ecology. Ecology has been the most neglected aspect, I think, of the entire behavior field. The experimental psychologist may control, say, a $10 \times 10 \times 10$ foot area, and, with enormous and devoted attention to detail, think of everything that is in that space at a given time. Organisms, however, have life histories in segments of space time about which a fair amount is known if they are hatched or born in the laboratory. But if not, the higher they are in the phylogenetic tree, the more likely they are to bring more from their past into the laboratory. Mark May used to say that the American sophomore, from whom are derived findings from humanity at large, was expected to "park his culture outside." Only the regions of time and space that are involved in the experiment are observed, ignoring the whole vast area from which the individual organism comes.

The needed studies of ecological organization are vastly more complex than anybody has imagined so far. The maps that Roger Barker has drawn of a Kansas town, and the lists of situational pressures that Saul Sells has devised as a preparation for space travel, will be only a tiny sampling of that vast conception of past and present environmental totalities that Egon Brunswik asked scientists to imagine. It will be a genetics that is oriented to a systematic and scientific science of ecology that will really give new field clues to human behavior. By field clues I hope to suggest the modalities of interaction between the edge of the organism and the edge of the environment, such that a complete and real fusion is created. I mean the kind of thing that is involved in interaction between the visual centers in the brain, the retina, the external light source, the laboratory conditions, personalities of the experimenters, the laboratory tradition, and laboratory culture, all of which must be considered when a person sees an inkblot or a social scene enacted before him. There must be whole organisms and whole environments to be studied for the sake of the modalities of reciprocity that develop between them. Psychologists began to learn from Lewin, as earlier they began to learn from Clerk-Maxwell, how to think in field terms; but they really have not done much of the sort on a scale demanded by present knowledge. The subspecialization has driven them more and more from organs to tissues, from tissues to cells, from cells to molecules, from molecules to atoms, from atoms to microparticles. All this specialization is, of course, absolutely necessary. The job of seeing psychological function, however, in combined biological and cultural terms is mostly a promissory note with as yet very little backing.

Because of its rarity, I shall mention the example of audiogenic seizures in mice, which Benson Ginzburg showed to have a not too complex Mendelian basis. But some of the mice that were expected to have convulsions and die had no convulsions, or had convulsions but did not die. He then attacked the problem from the pharmacological viewpoint and, in terms of biochemistry, found a way to buffer the lethal effects of the genes. Allow me a free analogy in the field of human ecology: What will happen when one finds a human environment of space-time-sensory enrichment, maternal warmth, generous and skillful experimental reinforcement that will allow a poorly endowed, frightened, aggressive ghetto child to develop into full humanness? This is exactly the type of experiment now being launched at several outposts of research on disadvantaged children. Before long thought in terms of biology versus the social sciences will cease; an ecological science will be developed so rich and so concrete that it will articulate closely with the new biology of individual growth.

And if psychologists mean quite seriously that man, as man, is richly intertwined with his ecology, it follows that the psychology of the next two decades will depend enormously upon the discovery of new forms of cross-cultural, cross-national communication. Indeed, it follows that unless there is very broad cross-national communication and action, there will be no human race to investigate. It will not do for American psychology, now having about 92% of the world's psychological personnel and about 92% of its published communications, to undertake a bland and supposedly disinterested study of the rest of the world in order that the wise and productive science, which they represent, can convey appropriate knowledge to those struggling along in less enlightened paths of endeavor. The study of the human predicament can come from a human race familiar with the method of science, but a human race speaking many tongues, regarding many values, and holding different convictions about the meaning of life sooner or later will have to consult all that is human. There are a few living today who will still be alive in the year 2000, if there is a year 2000; and I hope they will still be battling the problem of developing a sufficiently coherent, human enough point of view to speak for all kinds of human beings. This will mean that the genetic and ecological progress that I am describing will have actually helped toward a psychology that is common human, that entails not only a study of all human beings, but a study by trained and devoted individuals within all human groups. Following the American habit of delivering "State of the Union" messages, the Secretary-General of the United Nations has been asked to report on the "state of the human race." I personally do not understand why governments, and indeed professional psychologists, as well, are almost wholly ignoring the challenge to study directly the possibilities of achieving an international and inter-cultural plan for world order. Aiming at this goal, it is conceivable that there will be world-wide human modalities of investigation like those already existing in astronomy and in medicine, but oriented to the behavioral sciences. And it is even possible that they will be oriented not only to the behaviors as such, but toward the deep inner humanness that I have tried to describe as an object of study. This, in relation to the dyadic and group problems of the behavior sciences, may give both insight and control over the more destructive tendencies, and may utilize the common human aspiration to live not only more safely and a little more comfortably, but also a little more creatively and a great deal more humanly.

THE ROLE OF METHOD

You have noted that new discoveries in the field of psychology, and, I believe, in all scientific fields, are largely the children of new *methods*. Consider what the compound microscope did to histology, what X-rays did for diagnostic procedure, and what the puzzle box, the maze, the Skinner box have done in the development and documentation of seminal scientific theories. I am raising these issues not simply to welcome the computer to our side, as a new brother, but to ask one final question. Psychologists can, as A. H. Maslow has pointed out, strip down the study of man to those methods common to the other sciences that do not deal with man; they can assume that the human sciences can best do their job by leaving humanness out. There is, however, another possibility. They might conceivably find that science can become big enough to develop fully human methods oriented to the complete panoply of human problems, that empathy, "tlc," rich dyadic methods of communication between subjects and experimenters, through patience, discipline, and imagination, might give them in the year 2000 a science more competent to deal with all the discoverable aspects of human nature.

But a still more basic problem of method relates to the way in which they try to hook together the data from laboratory, from clinic, from field observation, from home, from neighborhood, and from observation of human gatherings in schools, churches, juries, parliamentary bodies. On the one hand, they have neglected the use of laboratories, and today they are beginning to discover a more suitable laboratory approach to a wide variety of spontaneous human situations. They are discovering that inventive experimentalists can do even better work in free human situations than they can in the classical, highly planned, settings. But now I am referring mainly to the manner in which the experimental method does its work. Long ago, psychologists established for themselves the impossible task of creating a psychology through intensive observation of those phenomena that occur under controlled laboratory conditions, and then systematizing a psychology based solely on such findings. They tried to set up physics and chemistry, sometimes the biological sciences of genetics, embryology, and physiology, as models. Belatedly they have discovered that beautiful scientific structures, such as that of modern geology, with only slight use of experimental method, can be developed through the integration of many types of observations, short-term and long-term, outdoors and indoors, pinpointed or extravagantly blown up to cosmic proportions. The geologists uses experimental methods, but he uses them in the total context of his work. It is mother earth, not her fingernails, that interests him. Psychology, which attempted to pinpoint its existence in the nineteenth-century terms of Weber and Fechner, is now beginning a great awakening, a sort of Rip Van Winkle awakening; for we are discovering, and will discover more fully in the next few decades, the vast dimensions in which a mature psychology can be conceived. It will make even more use of experimental method than it does at present. But the experiments will be suggested, and the techniques controlled, rather largely by the broad perception of the nature of the human animal in his whole ecological setting. The observational systems that will develop cannot be categorized by any one word that is now known. The word *experimental* is a fine word, but it will have to be replaced by something much more systematic. Even the developmental approach will mean something quite new when conceived in the kind of general systems terms, the kind of life science terms, that I am trying to suggest. Mathematical models certainly will both benefit and be benefited by the transitions that I am suggesting; and, of course, the engineering skills, already so important in psychophysiology, will become even more important.

I think psychologists will have to admit that many of this era will be unable to see the promised land that begins to be sketched out. Psychologists who will be extant in the year 2000 will have to be smarter than the psychologists today, as well as enormously better trained—I might add, enormously more *broadly* trained—than the subspecialized people turned out today. The blade of the modern mind is sharpened until it breaks, and we damn the blade instead of asking the metallurgist to develop tools from which sharp weapons can be prepared that, while still unscathed, can cut through the hard inscrutable rock of man's basic resistance to discovering his own nature.

THE HUMAN PREDICAMENT

The year 2000 can come, and the twenty-first century can offer less terror and more joy, but only if psychologists have learned both *how to look inside* and *how to look outside;* how to recognize the reciprocities of inner and outer, through methods that are as far ranging and as deeply human as is the human stuff that is being studied.

The author received his M. A. and Ph. D. degrees from Princeton University and is currently an Associate Professor of Psychology at the City College of the City University of New York. His other books include *Persuasion* (with Herbert Abelson), *Requiem for Democracy?* (with Lewis Andrews) and a novel, *The Last Man is Out*.